UNDERSTANDING DIVERSITY

Ethnicity and Race in the Canadian Context

Dedication

To the memory of my mother, Yaroslava Isajiw (nee Konrad), who knew well what it means to be a refugee and immigrant; who knew how to overcome, persevere and succeed with the dedication that she had to life.

For Up-To-Date Data on Ethnicity and Race in Canada

The statistical data in this book are those that were publically available as of the publication date. New data is released frequently from Statistics Canada and links will be posted on the website for this book as the data is released. Please consult: www.thompsonbooks.com/isajiw.html

~ ~ ~

UNDERSTANDING DIVERSITY

Ethnicity and Race in the Canadian Context

Wsevolod W. Isajiw

Robert F. Harney Professor of Ethnic, Immigration and Pluralism Studies, University of Toronto

THOMPSON EDUCATIONAL PUBLISHING, INC.

Toronto

Requests for permission to make copies of any part of the work should be directed to the publisher. Website: www.thompsonbooks.com / Email: publisher@thompsonbooks.com
Tel: (416) 766-2763 / Fax: (416) 766-0398
Copies of the book may be ordered from General Distribution Services.

Canadian Cataloguing in Publication Data

Isajiw, Wsevolod W., 1933-
Understanding diversity : ethnicity and race in the Canadian context

Includes bibliographical references and index.
ISBN 1-55077-102-7

1. Multiculturalism - Canada. 2. Canada - Ethnic relations. 3. Canada-
Race relations. 4. Ethnic groups - Canada. I. Title.

FC104.I775 1999 305.8'00971 C99-930428-3
F1035.A1I82 1999

Copyediting: Elizabeth Phinney
Cover design: Elan Designs
Cover painting: "No two tipis are ever pitched the same..." Work by Gerald McMaster, McMichael Canadian Art Collection. Courtesy of Gerald McMaster.

Image credits: Dick Hemingway, 10, 16, 27, 36, 41, 62, 76, 84, 102, 106, 118, 140, 142, 159, 168, 170, 178, 184, 186, 206, 227, 235; TV Ontario, 102; Susan Dewar, 20; National Archives of Canada, 32, 67, 80, 99; National Film Board, Ottawa, 61; Thompson Educational Archives, 104, 114, 182, 228; Ontario Multicultural History Society, 108; Canadian National Railways, 138; Vancouver City Archives, 150, 151; Toronto Star Syndicate, 243; Denis Pritchard, 249; ISTC, 252.
Every reasonable effort has been made to acquire permission for copyright material used in this text and to acknowledge all such indebtedness accurately. Any errors or omissions called to the publisher's attention will be corrected in future printings.

We acknowledge the support of the Government of Canada through the Book Publishing Industry Development Program for our publishing activities.
Printed in Canada.
1 2 3 4 5 06 05 04 03 02 01 00 99

TABLE OF CONTENTS

CHAPTER 4
IMMIGRATION TO CANADA, 77

CHAPTER 5
THE INCORPORATION OF ETHNIC GROUPS, 109

CHAPTER 6
PREJUDICE AND RACISM, 143

CHAPTER 7
CULTURAL AND IDENTITY INCORPORATION, 169

CHAPTER 8
ETHNIC IDENTITY RETENTION, 187

CHAPTER 9
INTERETHNIC RELATIONS, 207

CHAPTER 10
ETHNIC DIVERSITY AND SOCIETAL INTEGRATION, 241

LIST OF TABLES

ACKNOWLEDGMENTS

Many people have contributed to make this book possible. Some did it indirectly, as for example the students whom I have taught throughout the years and my colleagues with whom I have had many discussions on sociology in general and the sociology of ethnic groups, in particular. Among those who have given me direct help, I would like to thank Monica Boyd for her generous and upbeat assistance with statistical data. Vic Satzewich reviewed my manuscript and offered very helpful comments. Appreciation is also expressed to those anonymous reviewers who have provided me with useful comments. Marianne Minaker and Gord Muschett exerted gentle prodding that was helpful in maintaining momentum while the manuscript was in its beginning stages. Tanuja Perera was helpful with construction of a number of tables in the book.

In particular, I thank Christina Isajiw for her constant encouragement in writing the manuscript, for her editorial assistance and for her supportive patience. My daughter, Sophia, provided me with editorial suggestions and my son, Christopher, was a helpful sounding board for a number of my ideas.

Last but not least, I would like to thank Keith Thompson for his friendly manner of approaching the publication of the book, for his valuable suggestions in the final shaping of the book and for his amazingly efficient way of bringing the manuscript to print.

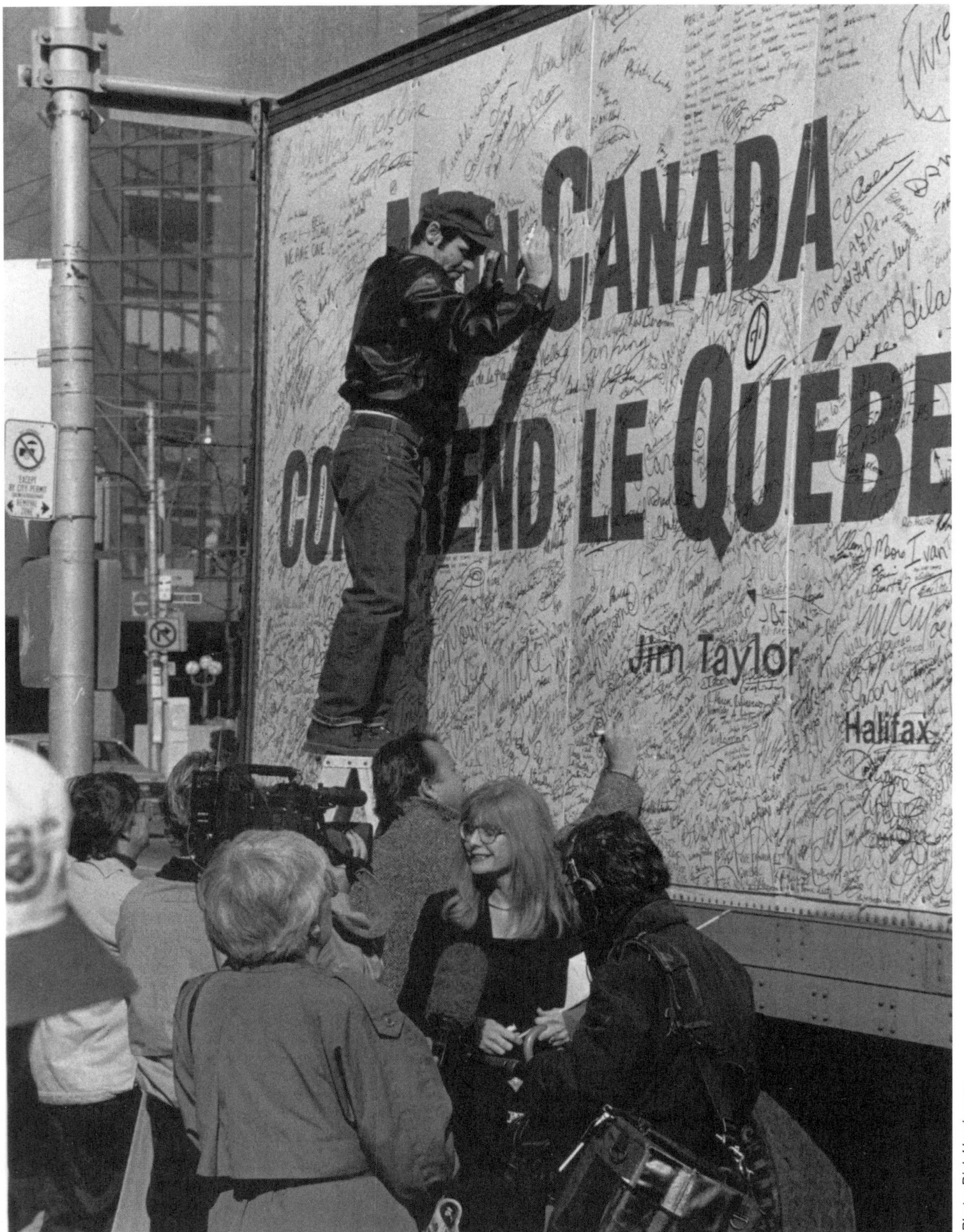

Photo: Dick Hemingway

Federalist campaign in Quebec. Wall poster reads: “Mon Canada comprend le Québec.”

INTRODUCTION

ETHNIC DIVERSITY IN THE GLOBAL SOCIETY

Towards an Understanding

Virtually all nation-states in the world are, in terms of the make-up of their population, multiethnic–meaning, generally, that their populations are made up of groups of citizens with quite different cultural ancestries. Out of a total of 189 nation-states listed in official sources, 150 such states have four or more ethnic groups within their boundaries, 29 list three ethnic groups, 8 list two ethnic groups and only 2 nation-states list only one group (*World Factbook*, 1993). In Canada, the census lists 113 ethnicities in the population (Statistics Canada, 1993), making it rather unique even among modern multiethnic nations.

In addition, statistics show that in many societies there is no one ethnic group that is numerically the largest of all. Table 1 gives percentages of total populations within a country that represent one, usually the dominant, ethnic group. The total of 255 countries includes both nation-states and various territories that are units in themselves but belong to a nation-state. The data show that there are only 61 countries (24% of all countries in the world) in which the largest ethnic group makes up 90 percent or more of the entire population. In 99 countries (39%), the largest ethnic group makes up between 75 and 89 percent of the population. In 51 countries (20%), it makes up only between 50 and 74 percent of the population, and in 44 countries (17%), it constitutes less than 50 percent of the total population in society.

Furthermore, the last quarter of the twentieth century has witnessed an emergence of interethnic conflicts and a reassertion of ethnicity around the world. In many societies, ethnic minority groups who previously appeared to have accommodated themselves to their minority position have become politicized and have begun to place demands on the larger society. In a survey of such groups, Ted Gurr (1993) singled out 233 minority ethnic groups who are "at risk." By this he meant groups that, in the post-World War II period, have either taken political action on behalf of their collective interests or have experienced economic or political discrimination or both. Hence they are actually or potentially engaged in interethnic conflict. Each of these groups is at risk of collective adversity. Of these 233 groups, only 27, or about 12 percent, have no record of political organization, protest, rebellion or other form of intercommunal conflict since 1945. He also pointed out that, out of 127 countries in the world that he examined, 75 percent had at least one, and many had more, highly politicized minorities. Gurr admitted that these were conservative figures and gave reference to other researchers. Two such researchers had identified 575 ethnic groups as being actual or potential nation-states, and one had estimated that there are as

Table 1: Largest Ethnic Group as a Percentage of Total Population

% of Population	No. of Countries
Over 90%	61
75-89%	99
50-74%	51
25-49%	29
0-24%	15
Total	295

Source: *The World Factbook* 1993-94. Washington, D.C.: Brassey's, 1993.

many as three thousand to five thousand "nations" in the world (Nielsson, 1985; Nietschmann, 1987; Gurr, 5; Minority Rights Group, 1990).

Gurr (1993: 326-339) also tried to assess the viability of the 233 groups he studied. He developed a 1-5, weak to very strong, scale of group coherence and identity. Of the total sample, 60 percent of groups were classified as being either 4 or 5 on this scale, i.e., strong or very strong in their identity.

Another way of gauging the political significance of ethnicity is to look at main events taking place over a period of time. Thus, out of 295 events that took place around the world in the year 1993, 127 or 43 percent were directly related to interethnic issues (*Statesman's Yearbook*, 1993). Included here are both events taking place among ethnic minority groups and events taking place among ethnic majority groups that bear on the question of identity, for example, a nation's decision to join the European Community, excluding purely economic European Community agreements. If one were to include events that were related to ethnic issues indirectly, the percentage would be well over 50.

A number of cases of interethnic relations have been given high global visibility by the media. They represent long-standing intergroup conflicts that have defied resolution. Among these are the conflict between Catholics and Protestants in Northern Ireland (which also shows how religion and ethnicity come to be intertwined), the conflict between Arabs and Jews in Israel, between Basques and the Spanish in Spain, and others. One long-standing conflict of high visibility, between the Black peoples and the Afrikaners in South Africa, reached the stage of resolution in the 1990s.

There are more recent interethnic conflicts with high global visibility that also had defied resolution, such as that in Rwanda, Burundi, former Zaire (the Republic of Congo), Somalia, Bosnia-Herzegovina, Fiji, Indonesia and others. New states have emerged in Eastern Europe and new awareness of ethnicity has appeared in such "old" countries as the United Kingdom in relation to the Scottish and the Welsh.

In Canada, the day-to-day chronicle of the 1990s contains no fewer events related to ethnic groups than it did one hundred years ago. The issues related to ethnicity are brought to our attention almost daily: the question of Quebec, the political movement among the Canadian Aboriginal peoples, racial discrimination and racism, the continuing stream of immigration, the changing character of immigration, the bilingualism and multiculturalism policies of the government, the persistence of the ethnic vote and others.

The globalization process itself has increased the awareness of cultural diversity, both among the nations of the world and within society. The global society has been in the process of development for the past 30 or so years. Its chief protagonists have been commerce and finance, particularly multinational corporations. At its base lies the idea of removing all trade barriers among nations in order to allow a free exchange of goods and services and enable private enterprises to have access to cheaper labour (Greider, 1997: 11-38). One example of such an international arrangement is the European Common Market, which by 1996 had also developed a political structure, the European Union (EU). Another example is the North American Free Trade Agreement (NAFTA) and the Asia Pacific Economic Cooperation (APEC) and Council (APECC). These arrangements make it possible to manufacture different parts of a product in different countries unencumbered by tariff and other former restrictions. The distinctive feature of the global society is the leadership and power exercised by the multinational finance and commercial concerns in directing national governments in financial and other economic policies, by which governments are under pressure to give up some aspects of their sovereignty (Reid, 1996: 225-267).

The global society's relation to cultural and ethnic diversity is somewhat paradoxical. On the one hand, cultural identity as the element of defining the boundaries of society is acknowledged but seen as an antiquated reality that is to be subordinated to global economic considerations. On the other hand, the leaders of the global society constantly deal with multicultural diversity and recognize it as an economic resource (Cross and White, 1996). The global society involves ethnicity in at least three ways. Firstly, in order to establish or maintain their concerns in different parts of the world, multinational corporations must constantly deal with different societies and their different laws, political systems, languages and cultures. This fact alone requires recognition of and work with identity differences. Commenting on the expansion of the Motorola Company in Malaysia, William Greider (1997: 84) observed that

> it represented one of the ripe anomalies of global economic revolution: while conservative ideologues in America fiercely contested the threat of multiculturalism, conservative American corporations were out around the world doing it. In the global context, the preoccupation of American politics with race and cultural superiority seemed ludicrous, out of touch and perhaps also dangerous.

Secondly, in order to insure efficiency of their operations, multinational corporations stimulate at least some degree of change of traditional ethnic identities and cultural patterns. In the manufacturing plants established by the multinationals in Third World countries, Muslim women, used to wearing the veil, have learned to take it off on the job. Their pattern of delivering their pay to their parents has been modified, as has their manner of speaking and not speaking out (Greider, 1997: 83). The problem, however, is that while changing the traditional ways of life, the global market economy does not necessarily raise the standard of living of all people equally. For one thing, in the poorer countries in which new enterprises are established to capitalize on cheap labour, the newly gained wealth does not necessarily benefit those in the population who do not hold jobs with the multinational corporations or have no investments in them. The global market may thus create greater gaps between the "globalized" sectors of population and the traditional sectors that remain within the old communities and in this manner stimulate further ethnic differentiation. Furthermore, while establishing industrial enterprises in the poorer countries, some corporations stimulate a global job competition not only among the poor countries, but also between the wealthy and the poor countries, including the corporations' home countries. They may remove their enterprises from their home countries and move them to the poorer ones (Greider, 1997: 82-83). For the corporations this competition may economically unite the world, but for the job seekers, it creates intercultural competition and potential hostilities.

Thirdly, the global economy has stimulated and maintained high levels of international migration into the highly industrialized countries. Statistics for the past decade present a picture of international migration. In Canada and the United States, from 1980 to 1990, the total number of immigrants arriving in one year has about tripled (Richmond, 1994: 257-258; 262). The chapter in this book that deals with international migration gives further statistics on this. Both Canada and the United States are countries to which immigration has been continuous. However, the nature and character of immigration in the 1990s is completely different from that of the 1900s, the 1920s or even the 1960s. Not only are the sources of immigration different, but the economy of the 1990s requires that immigrants have more education and skills than ever before. A place for the unskilled and uneducated still exists in the global society, but it remains in those countries to which the multinational enterprises go for their cheap labour. In the highly industrialized and computerized countries, there is less and less room for the unskilled and uneducated immigrant. But in the developed societies, the better-educated and skilled immigrants, and particularly their children, can be expected to be more aware of their identity and their place in both their host and in the global society.

A distinguishing feature of the global society is the system of communication and access to information by electronic means. Persons of different cultural backgrounds can communicate relatively easily across vast distances, engage in common conversation and undertake joint projects more easily than ever before. In this regard, the global society stimulates interethnic, intercultural networks of contact. This may lead to further culture change and a possible assimilation into a future global culture.

In search of commercial agreements, however, the global society is predisposed to accept the idea of cultural relativity, i.e., the idea that all cultures, ways and styles of life, philosophical and moral perspectives are valid in their own right but are negotiable. The consequence of this is that the global society has no cultural and fixed philosophical or moral centre of its own. In this sense, it has developed a "post-modern" orientation. Post-modern perspective holds that all social reality exists in concrete, particular, historically unique groups and persons. Accordingly, any claim to "universal" reality, i.e., any presumption of sameness of plurality, is unrealistic and futile. While this perspective may be debatable, the effect of this philosophy is a reinforcement of the validity and significance of cultural, ethnic diversity.

Looking at ethnic diversity both internationally and within society, we can now ask the basic questions which this book will try to answer.

BASIC QUESTIONS AND APPROACH

The first basic question that must be asked about ethnic diversity is: what place do ethnic groups have and how do they relate to each other in a society made up of diverse ethnicities? A second question that logically follows from the first is: how do the diverse groups incorporate into the larger society and how does the larger society become integrated, if at all?

In answering these questions, the case in point will be the Canadian society. From time to time other societies, particularly the United States, will be referred to for the sake of comparison. The aim of this book, however, is not to exhaustively describe or analyze ethnicity in Canadian society, but to use such description and analysis as an illustration of basic conceptual issues and problems related to ethnic groups, their relations and incorporation in society.

A premise accepted in this book is that, to understand any specific instance in which a phenomenon occurs, it is necessary to understand the nature of the phenomenon first. That is, to understand ethnicity and interethnic relations in Canada or in any other country, it is necessary to analyze and understand first the nature of ethnic groups, ethnic identity, the nature of social incorporation, interethnic relations and integration of society. This does not mean that the specific instance of the phenomenon, i.e., ethnicity in Canada, is not to be approached in terms of its specific and unique features. On the contrary, the book indicates many such features. However, the specific features themselves cannot be fully understood unless the nature of the phenomenon itself is understood first. For example, Canadian ethnic minority groups have been said to retain their identity more than the American groups because of Canadian pluralist ideology as against American melting-pot ideology. Yet, if one understands the nature of the process of social incorporation, it becomes clear that the process of assimilation is not necessarily antithetic to identity retention. This will indicate that in both Canada and the United States, one has to look at and examine both aspects of assimilation and aspects of identity retention. The ideological explanation then becomes problematic and one has to look for more unique features of both societies to explain the differences.

To understand the nature of the ethnic phenomenon, we will first analyze what is meant by the concept of ethnic group. This conceptualization is considered to be essential to all other derivative conceptualizations related to ethnicity, such as that of interethnic relations, ethnic identity, social incorporation and others. It provides the principles for developing an analytical conceptual scheme for the understanding of the ethnic phenomenon. Second, we will describe the structural and historical contexts within which ethnic group relations take place. We will focus on Canada as a modern society that creates an economic and social context for immigrants and on those features of Canadian history that have given Canadian society its own unique context for interethnic relations. Third, immigration will be placed within a larger context of other types of migration. We will review the history of immigration in Canada and will discuss the problems of adjustment that immigrants face after arrival.

Fourth, we will discuss the question of incorporation of diverse ethnic groups into a larger society. Three aspects of social incorporation will be considered: structural, cultural and identity. Structural incorporation will be studied as ethnic stratification, in which different ethnic groups take or are made to take different status positions in relation to each other, which they may or may not be able to change in the process of social mobility. The determinants of ethnic stratification will be singled out. Special attention is given to the study of prejudice and racism as a source of discrimination and a negative determinant of a group's ethnic status. Cultural incorporation will be examined as a process of inculturation or assimilation into the dominant societal culture. Identity incorporation will be approached as a social-psychological phenomenon related to the other aspects of incorporation but also as a process with its own nature. Fifth, ethnic identity will be seen as a phenomenon that is not necessarily contradicted by assimilation, but one that is often retained through the process of deconstruction and reconstruction, even as assimilation proceeds. Sixth, ethnic identity provides the basis for interethnic relations and we will study the determining factors of these relations. We will focus first on two main cases of interethnic relations in Canada, those involving Quebec and those involving the Aboriginal peoples. Finally, we will end with a discussion of the problem of integration of a diverse society. In this context, we will study the third main case of interethnic relations in Canada, those involving the "Other" ethnic groups. We will take up the issue of legislation and implementation of human rights and the importance of public policies of integration, such as the policy of multiculturalism. We will consider the symbolic aspects of societal integration and will propose key principles of interethnic cooperation and conflict resolution.

This text intentionally does not employ any one broad theoretical orientation as the main perspective on ethnicity. It does not use exclusively either a Marxist, functionalist, conflict, post-modern or other approach. The basic position of the author is that while each one of these approaches does contribute to our understanding of ethnicity, an exclusive use of any one such broad theoretical orientation simplifies reality to the point that, instead of enlightening a phenomenon, it obfuscates it. Ethnicity is a rather complex phenomenon, and the aim of this book is to communicate to the student a sense of this complexity and provide a systematic way of examining it. The book's main aim is to teach the student to think analytically about ethnicity. To this effect, the book tries to present a systematic conceptual scheme to serve as a framework for analyzing ethnicity and interethnic relations in Canada or in other societies. This conceptual scheme allows an understanding of the phenomenon in terms of its many aspects and components. It is based on the old sociological assumption that, although there are large differences between the experiences and cultures of specific ethnic groups and the periods of time in which they interact, there are nevertheless deeper aspects of these experiences that they share in common, and the differences among them are diverse ways in which these deeper aspects are actualized in everyday life.

The basic methodological aim of the book is therefore two-fold: to analyze ethnicity as a social phenomenon systematically and to understand it in all its ramifications as objectively as possible.

However, while the book eschews an exclusive reliance on any one broad theoretical perspective, it draws on several of them in discussions of specific subjects for which elements of these perspectives may throw an insightful light. It draws on the social conflict approach inasmuch as it views interethnic relations in terms of ethnic groups pursuing their values and interests and negotiating them in the context of differential power relations. It draws on the functional approach by emphasizing that interethnic relations have to be also seen in light of how they bear on incorporation of ethnic groups into a larger society and how they bear on the integration of society as a whole. Further, the book draws on history, holding that the structure of society within which interethnic relations take place must be understood in light of historical processes that have their roots in the events of the past. Finally, the book draws on the subjectivist, social-psychological approaches. It views ethnic identity as a subjective phenomenon that goes through a process of deconstruction and creative reconstruction. It studies ethnic boundaries as social-psychological phenomena of self-inclusion and other-exclusion in which such things as prejudice, racism and discrimination are factors. But this does not mean that prejudice, racism and discrimination cannot be reduced or eliminated. They are also social constructions that create ethnic boundaries and hence are also subject to deconstruction. In its underlying assumptions, the book relies most perhaps on the social constructionist approach.

Furthermore, the book develops and uses specific middle-range theories dealing with various aspects of ethnicity as these aspects are discussed. To name a few, a theory of social incorporation of ethnic groups and a theory of generational ethnic identity retention are presented. Also employed are Lieberson's theory of initial contact, Bonacich's theory of the split labour market and middle-man minorities, Breton's theory of institutional completeness and of symbolic resources, Porter's theory of intermeshed elites and ethnic identity as a social mobility drawback, Isajiw's theory of generational conflict and ethnic rediscovery and many others. It is these middle-range theories that throw light on the various aspects of ethnicity and provide an understanding of its complexity.

To illustrate theoretical points, references are made throughout the book to various empirical studies, particularly studies relating to Canadian society. This includes both the recent empirical works and a number of older, relevant works. The author believes that the sociology of ethnicity in Canada has in the past 30 years or so developed a body of knowledge that makes it a subdiscipline of its own. While the theoretical and methodological approaches in all these studies have varied and scholars have debated and disagreed on a number of issues, they nevertheless have shown much common concern and an agreement on the importance of employing both quantitative and qualitative empirical methods. Empirical research of ethnicity in Canada has firmly established its own tradition and has produced a number of classical studies. The studies cited or referred to in the book from the 1970s or so are considered to be of classical or defining value and are an important part of the discipline's heritage.

While in the past 20 years the ethnic composition of the Canadian population has been changing, systematic empirical research has not caught up with it as yet. Research has begun on the economic adjustment of South and East Asian immigrants, but research that is more than anecdotal, that deals with most other aspects of their social incorporation, particularly their organizational development and impact and their consecutive generations, is still to be done.

Finally, no single work should be seen as the final word on any subject. The aim of this book is to stimulate the student of ethnicity to think about it in a systematic, analytical manner that will lead to his or her further discovery of knowledge of its place and role in the Canadian and the global society.

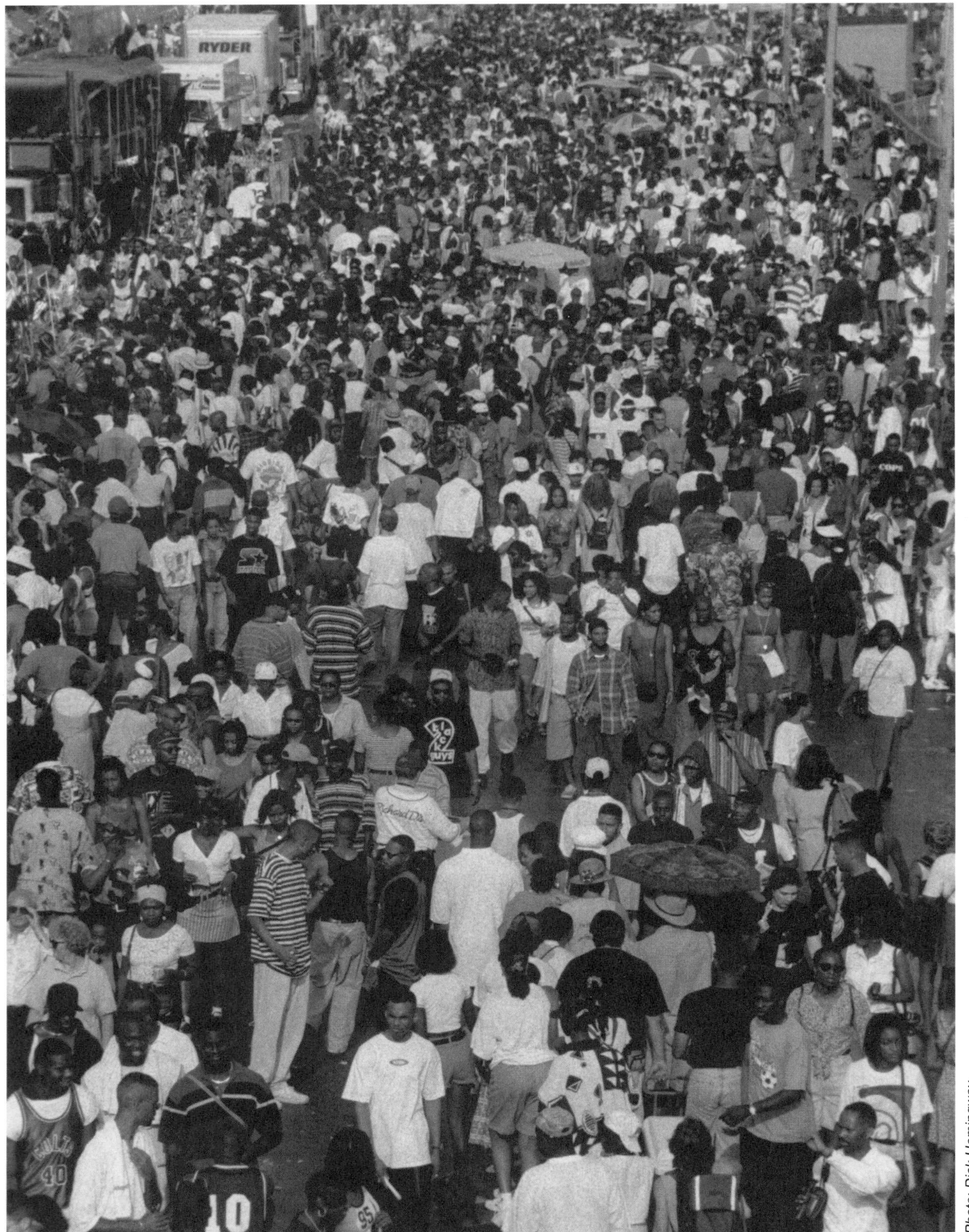

Photo: Dick Hemingway

Caribana celebration, Toronto.

CHAPTER 1

THE MEANING OF ETHNICITY AND ETHNIC RELATIONS

Understanding Diversity

This chapter defines what is meant by the concept of "ethnic group" and how it is distinguished from other concepts, in particular the concept of "race." It distinguishes different types of ethnic groups and considers the different approaches through which social scientists have tried to understand what ethnic groups are all about. It also provides the conceptual framework by means of which interethnic relations can be studied.

According to the Oxford Dictionary, the word *ethnic* derives from the two Greek words *ethnos* and *ethnikos.* In ancient Greek, ethnos meant a number of people living together, a company, a body of men or a band of comrades. In Homeric and later Christian literature, the word referred to a people or a nation, in contrast to kings, or as one nation against another, or every nation of mankind. The word *ethnikos* was closely connected with the word *ethnos* and probably derived from it. However, it referred to the people who were "not like us," who were not Christian or Jewish but Gentile, pagan or heathen. In early English, the word *heathen* came from the word *hethnic* or *heathenic,* which originally derived from the Greek *ethnikos.*

The popular usage of the word *ethnic* is closer to the second sense, referring to the "other" groups–often meaning minority groups "different from us." Unfortunately, the popular usage of the word often communicates a pejorative meaning, a put-down, and hence a bias. It is thus not a scientific usage of the term. A scientific, scholarly, meaning is closer to the first sense of the Greek word and signifies a community of people. But even among scholars the term *ethnic group* is often used interchangeably with the word *race* or with the term *minority group.* Often it is applied only to "immigrant groups," but not to their consecutive generations. All these terms relate to various types and aspects of ethnic groups, but their meanings are distinct and should not be confused. These distinctions should become clear after the term *ethnic group* is systematically defined.

The term *ethnicity* is the one most frequently found in the scholarly literature in this area. Ethnicity is an abstract term and refers to any or collectively all aspects of the phenomenon related to the ethnic group. It can refer to the ethnic culture and any of its aspects, to ethnic identity, to the ethnic community and its institutions or the ethnic group itself. The central concept in any discourse on ethnicity, however, has to be that of the ethnic group. Ethnic culture, institutions, identity and so on derive from the objective existence of real ethnic groups. Hence, to understand the phenomenon of ethnicity, one must begin by endeavouring to understand what an ethnic group is.

TOWARDS A DEFINITION OF ETHNIC GROUP

One could describe ethnic groups by various features. Some writers (Gordon, 1964) have referred to ethnic groups as people of common national or geographic origin, of common ancestry, who have the same culture or customs, same religion, language, who share common values, possess their own separate institutions, who have a consciousness of kind, a "we feeling," a sense of peoplehood and a sense of loyalty, people who are in *gemeinschaft* type relations with one another. All these features describe the meaning of ethnic group in some measure. However, a good definition is definition by means of genus and specific difference. This type of definition can have explanatory rather than simply descriptive usefulness. The aim of an ideally good definition is not to identify as many properties of the phenomenon studied as possible, but to identify the minimum number of properties which are sufficient to identify the phenomenon and distinguish it from all other phenomena. Such definition is known as denotative in contrast to merely connotative definitions, which descriptively enumerate as many properties of a phenomenon as can be found.

An ethnic group is first of all a type of group. Social groups can be classified according to the kinds of aims pursued by the members, according to the number of aims, according to the degree of organization within the group, according to size of the group, according to the quality of social relations predominant within the group, according to position in relation to other groups, according to the degree of consciousness of aims in the group and so on. Any classification is as good as the knowledge that it makes possible. In regard to ethnic groups, a fruitful way to understand them is to see them as a type of groups distinguished according to the predominant way in which members are recruited. According to this criterion two types of groups can be distinguished: involuntary and voluntary. Involuntary groups are those whose membership is recruited mostly at birth, without choice. Voluntary groups are those which a person may join at will. Involuntary groups are community-type groups; voluntary groups are organizations and associations.

Ethnic groups are involuntary groups, as most members are recruited at birth. It is, however, not birth as such that, sociologically, is the important distinguishing feature of involuntary groups. It is rather the basic process of socialization which persons undergo and which makes them members of an ethnic or other involuntary group. By the basic process of socialization we mean the formation which a child receives from its infancy through its parents and the community around him. This does not mean that persons cannot change the ethnic groups into which they are socialized. They can and do. But when a person who has undergone the basic process of socialization into the culture of one ethnic group then comes to be assimilated into another culture, he or she has to go through a process of re-socialization. This is usually a deep, psychological, sometimes a traumatic, type of experience. The product of the socialization process is development of identity. Being socialized into a group means acquiring an identity, and dropping out of it means a change of identity. Persons, however, may develop multiple identities by being socialized into two or more groups. As will be discussed later, this is usually the case with the second generation of immigrants.

An ethnic group, therefore, can be understood as a group that recruits its members primarily by the process of basic socialization. There are, however, involuntary groupings other than ethnic groups. These include castes or relatively closed social classes. Examples include the Brahman caste in India; the aristocracy in many European societies of the eighteenth and nineteenth centuries; religious denominations, such as the Protestants, Catholics and Muslims; regional groups, such as the Maritimes or Prairie regions in Canada; and categorical groupings, particularly racial categories and sex and age categories. Social categories are included here, not because of the biological characteristics themselves, but inasmuch as the biological fact becomes a criterion of membership inclusion or membership exclusion. As will be discussed below, social categories are in essence different from involuntary groups since they do not represent real social groups but only classifications of physical characteristics. Still, social categories possess some characteristics of involuntary groups. Involuntary groups develop a degree of community relations, an identity, a degree of loyalty or commitment and a way of life at least partially different from other ethnic groups, castes, classes, religions, regions or aspects of social categories. To the extent that they possess a different way of life yet exist together within a larger society, they can be called subcultural groups. What is characteristic of a subculture is that it is never a complete culture. A complete culture exists only when an involuntary group possesses all institutions to itself. Subcultural groups possess some of their own institutions, but depend upon a larger society for others. The notion of subcultural groups does not include artistic societies, cultural associations, or even newly established communes or the like, because such groups do not recruit their members at birth. The different patterns of behaviour that members of these groups exhibit have been called group cultures (Gordon, 1954: 39).

What, however, distinguishes ethnic groups from the other involuntary groups is that ethnic groups have a historical link to distinct total cultures. This is their specific difference. The concept of culture is used here in the anthropological sense of the word. This means a totality of cultural patterns of behaviour and presence of all the major institutions that would allow a population of people to survive on its own, without dependence on other populations. It also means behaviour which is meaningful only in terms of some shared, even if implicit, cognitive and value assumptions that are derived from the unique historical community experience. These assumptions serve as a base for the members of the group in understanding one another and one another's behaviour and in knowing what to expect and what not to expect from one another (Geertz, 1973). As we shall explain later, many misunderstandings that result when members of different ethnic groups come into contact with one another, even after much assimilation has taken place, may be derived from the differences in their implicit expectations and assumptions.

Religious groups, castes, classes, regions and racial, gender and age categories, as such, do not imply a totality of cultural patterns or institutions. None of these groups transmit exclusively all the cultural patterns for their members. By themselves, they do not offer total cultures. However, there are cases where members of the same ethnic group make up one religious denomination, such as the Doukhobors, the Hutterites or the Mennonites. In these cases ethnicity and religious groups become coterminous; their boundaries become the same. In other cases, there may be a bigger or smaller degree of overlap between ethnicity and religion, as is the case with the Jewish group, the Irish (excluding the Northern Irish), the Italians and others. Similar situations can exist for castes, regions and the social categories. It should be understood that this is not an either-or question, but is rather a question of degree, i.e., to the extent that a religious group, a class, a regional group, or a gender or age category is linked exclusively to a total and distinct way of life, to that extent its boundaries overlap with those of ethnicity.

Cultural patterns of behaviour are not necessarily learned as a complete and unchanging package. Rather, persons are taught cultural patterns selectively, and they are learned selectively. As time goes on, one may discard some and accept others. This is particularly the case in societies like Canada in which there is more than one prevalent culture and many subcultural groups. In such societies, members of subcultural groups tend to assimilate or "inculturate" into the prevalent cultures. This takes place especially from one generation to another. As a result, persons whose parents or grandparents have shared one distinct culture may themselves show few or no similar behavioural patterns. This, however, does not necessarily mean that they are no longer members of the ethnic group. The few behavioural patterns which they have learned may be of significance to them, and even when they have not retained any patterns, they still may identify with their ancestors, the culture or the community to which their ancestors belonged. In this case, the membership in the group depends not so much on the process of socialization as on the social-psychological link provided by identity. The nature of ethnic identity will be discussed in later chapters. At present suffice it to say that, in addition to socialization, ethnic identity, even if it is not produced by the basic socialization process, can provide a membership link to an ethnic group. The question of ethnic identity of consecutive generations will also be further discussed in later chapters.

ETHNIC GROUP DEFINED

We can now define ethnic group as referring to an involuntary, community-type group of persons who share the same distinct culture or who are descendants of those who have shared a distinct culture and who identify with their ancestors, or their culture or group (Isajiw, 1974). This is a general definition. It embraces such groups as the Aborigines of Canada, the French in France, Germans in Germany, as well as the French and Germans in Canada. These groups represent two different types of ethnic groups. There are important differences between these types that will be discussed below. But, before we can discuss the different types of ethnic groups, it is important to analyze another aspect of their nature.

• Ethnic Boundaries

The involuntary nature of ethnic groups articulates with feelings of self-inclusion in the group, feelings of sympathy and loyalty towards members of the same ethnic group and feelings of excluding oneself from membership in other ethnic groups. These feelings are reflected in the propensity to participate in informal relations with persons of the same ethnicity and in the support given to the establishment and maintenance of ethnic institutions and organizations. These form the basis for ethnic boundaries from within the ethnic group. The nature of these boundaries is social-psychological; they are a way in which individuals identify themselves with the group, include themselves in the group and exclude themselves from other groups.

When members of two or more ethnic groups interact and compete with one another, the existence of ethnic boundaries from within gives rise to ethnic

Courtesy of Susan Dewar

boundaries from without. These are also social-psychological boundaries. They refer to the fact that persons are identified by others as belonging to one or another ethnic group (Barth, 1969). This identification by others takes place when there are signs of difference, such as language and culture. But it also takes place when the persons no longer actively share any cultural patterns with that of a different ethnic group as long as a link to their different ethnic ancestors can be made. Identification by others as belonging to a different group than their own also means some degree of exclusion from that group. Identification by others, in turn, reinforces self-identification. Hence, ethnicity is a matter of a double boundary, a boundary from within, established by the socialization process and maintained by ethnic institutions, and a boundary from without, established by the process of intergroup relations. Although the two boundaries may reinforce each other, they are distinct and do not necessarily coincide. The perception of an ethnic group by outsiders quite often differs from the perceptions that members of the group have of themselves. Many misunderstandings between ethnic groups derive from the fact that these perceptions do not coincide.

The two boundaries can be said to contain two basic aspects, subjective and objective. The subjective aspects of the internal boundary involve self-perception as a member of one's group and, as stated above, feelings of sympathy, attachment and commitment to one's group. The objective aspects of the internal boundary refer to the way these subjective elements come to be expressed in the ethnic group's community institutions and organizations, the functions which these institutions and organizations sponsor, the informal groups of the same ethnicity that persons form and the group's visible customs and lore, including its recorded history, language and other parts of culture.

The subjective aspects of the external boundary refer to the feelings among the population outside any specific ethnic group that members of that group are not, as it were, "part of us," and are or are to be excluded from their own group. These feelings may or may not be accompanied by feelings that one's own group is superior to other groups and perceptions of other groups as inferior. The objective aspects of the external boundary include the institutions and organizational structures that exclude other groups from one's own. This can be a system of structural discrimination against other groups or a pattern of segregation. It also may include a lore or an ideology that functions to justify exclusion. These may become forms or degrees of racism.

The double boundary that every ethnic group possesses indicates that no ethnic group can be completely understood without its relationship to other ethnic groups. Interethnic relations are the relationships between the two boundaries. It is also in terms of the relationship between these two boundaries that the differences between ethnic minorities in different countries can be fruitfully compared. The difference may lie in either of the boundaries, but often not so much in the difference between what happens in the internal boundaries as in the different external boundaries. For example, the difference between what happens to ethnic groups in Canada and the United States is not so much a matter of faster or slower assimilation or non-assimilation (Reitz and Breton, 1994). More significantly, it is a matter of how the various ethnic groups are perceived and identified by others in the two societies, and especially how they are perceived and identified by the power-holding, policy-making and the influence-exerting bodies of the two societies. The external ethnic boundaries would be reflected in the reasons and rationales behind specific immigration, cultural and social integration policies.

RACE

The external ethnic boundaries are also the source of racial distinctions and of race as a social grouping phenomenon. Race is a category of physical characteristics possessed by people. Unlike culture, these characteristics are not possessed in common. They are possessed individually. Hence, as a unit, race is a category devised by outsiders, including scholars, that places persons with similar biological characteristics into a group.

In the past, anthropologists have tried to classify different physical characteristics possessed by people around the world into distinct racial groups. In the first part of the eighteenth century, botanist Carolus Linnaeus developed a method of classifying all living things, including human beings, into genera and species. Since then, biologists and physical anthropologists have devised racial categories of human beings, based on a set of visible biological characteristics. The most common division was into three main racial categories: Caucasoid ("white"), Mongoloid ("yellow") and Negroid ("black") (Hooten, 1946). Each race was seen as possessing distinct traits, such as skin colour, eye colour, nose shape, hair type, lip shape, cheek bone, body hair and the like (Biddiss, 1979). Other scholars (Coon, 1962; Baker, 1974) developed classifications of races based on geographical distributions of populations. This avoids a direct classification based on physical traits, but indirectly it assumes different trait categories. Stanley Garn (1971: 153-166) distinguished nine "geographical races" as large population categories. The term *geographical race* refers to the largest taxonomic unit below the Linnean category of species. These geographical races correspond to the major continents and geographical areas populated by human beings. The nine geographical races classified by Garn are:

1. The Amerindian race, including the local populations originally occupying the territories from Alaska to the southern tip of South America;
2. The Polynesian race, occupying the territory in the Pacific ranging from New Zealand to Hawaii and Easter Island;
3. The Micronesian race, referring to the populations of small islands, known as the Territory of the Pacific Islands, located east of Indonesia and the Philippines and north of Papua and New Guinea;
4. The Melanesian-Papuan race, comprising Melanesians, Papuans and New Guineans;
5. The Australian race, referring to the Aborigines of Australia;
6. The Asiatic race, occupying continental Asia and extending to Japan, Taiwan, the Philippines and Indonesia, including Sumatra, Borneo and Java;
7. The Indian race, occupying the territory from the Himalayas to the Indian Ocean;
8. The European race, including Europe and the Middle East and North Americans of European origin;
9. The African race, from sub-Saharan to South Africa and all persons of African origin taken as slaves or otherwise.

The geographical criterion of race classification has pointed to the great variation of physical characteristics among different populations. This fact has raised the question of whether it is of any value at all to categorize human beings according to physical characteristics and whether those who use such categories do it for ideological reasons (Miles, 1982). Skin colour, for example, ranges among all the racial categories between a light and a dark shade of brown, and nobody is purely white or purely black. Similarly, the size and shapes of the head, nose and other body parts vary largely within any of the broader racial categories.

Today, instead of categorizing, physical anthropologists prefer to refer to race in genetic terms, meaning a high frequency distribution of any gene or combination of genes within a larger population. This approach moves away from imposing a predetermined set of generalized categories on groups of people and thus artificially separating them.

There is no scientific evidence that any of the physical features among the different racial categories either by themselves or in combination make one racial category superior to another. Physical characteristics indicated in each racial category have evolved in relation to the geographical environment in which the people lived for long periods of time, and they have had value in adapting them to this environment. In the history of the study of racial characteristics, there have been many attempts to test the idea of superiority of one "race" over another (Benedict, 1983: 63-95; Henwood and Phoenix, 1996). Early anthropologists, in the first half of the twentieth century, measured average brain sizes under the assumption that those with a larger average brain size are superior to those with a smaller one. Some variation in the average brain sizes was found, but the overlap between the geographical races was so great that practically any individual brain size may belong to any of the three racial categories. In addition, no link could be established between the size of the brain and congenital mental advantage or disadvantage.

Since World War I there have been attempts to test differences in intelligence between different racial categories of people. Various I.Q. tests have been performed showing some differences. Yet when the regional, educational, economic, political and cultural differences are taken into account, all the intelligence differences disappear (Benedict, 1983: 69-78; Henwood and Phoenix, 1996: 843-847). Notoriously, I.Q. tests do not control for all cultural and social psychological differences, including the variables deriving from the processes of cultural assimilation, identity retention and the socio-historical and psychological variables. Most researchers whose surveys show cognitive ability differences between racial categories do not control for all these variables, and to make a claim that there are inherent differences, logic requires that the researcher show that all other explanations of the differences–social, economic, political, cultural, historical and others–have been disproved. Studies that fail to do so remain logically flawed. Furthermore, there is no evidence that can show a necessary link between any specific biological characteristic, such as skin colour or shape of head, and any particular social, economic or political or cultural system.

An assessment of the studies dealing with ethnic or racial differences in intelligence, published from the 1970s to the 1990s, concluded that, while there are differences between ethnic groups and racial categories in the intelligence test scores, no study up to now has been able to show that these differences are due to inborn genetic factors. Rather, studies have shown that, while genes may play a part in cognitive achievement, there is a closer connection between cognitive achievement and socio-economic and political factors (Herrnstein and Murray, 1994: 269-315).

What is referred to as race is thus a constructed social phenomenon. It is an external categorization and exclusion of people with one type of biological characteristics by members of a group who possess different biological characteristics. In themselves, biological characteristics are not an internal identity-generating force. Persons identify with their racial characteristics only as a response to being categorized and excluded by outsiders, especially if the outsiders are in a dominant position. It is thus the dominant outsiders that provide a social reality to race. What is defined as real by the dominant group becomes real in its consequences for the subordinate group (Omi and Winant, 1986). It is in this manner that an external boundary becomes real for a group.

External boundaries, however, are an important source of political mobilization and the unity which this brings about to the excluded group. But this unity should not be confused with the unity generated by the internal boundaries. Internal boundaries are the forces of ethnicity formation. For example, people with black skin identify with all people with black skin only when someone raises black skin as a social issue. This usually is done by those who are not black. When this is not the case, people who happen to possess black skin identify more readily with specific groups rather than categories, for example, other Jamaicans, Trinidadians, Somalians, South Africans, African Americans, Canadian Blacks and so on. The internal boundaries form only when at least some cultural construction takes place or has taken place in the past. The history of the African Americans shows that their internal identity was long maintained by the Black churches and religion in the American South. As the American Black movement formed in response to racial discrimination and progressed through its history in the past half a century, a new internal ethnic boundary among the American Blacks began to form. The group developed a consciousness of itself in historical-cultural terms. It developed its own literature, reached for the roots of American Black culture in Africa, identified itself as African Americans rather than simply "Blacks," and found its own cultural patterns and values in a new interpretation of American history. By now, African Americans are an ethnic group, different from African Caribbeans or other African groups.

Thus, the group and its intellectual issues, which to the outsiders appear to be purely racial, in effect are much more than that. They are issues of an ethnic group that has a much more rigid external boundary than do many other ethnic groups (Wallman, 1986; Wade, 1993). It is in this sense that race will be approached in this book. Race will be referred to as a categorical classification and the term *racial groups* will be used in the sense of racial categories. Racial categorization, however, has real social consequences. It becomes a social construction of reality with everyday life and legal implications (Walker, 1997). Racial categorization has usually carried assumptions of superiority of one race over another. As will be discussed later, this implies an ideology of racism. In a society, this ideology may be explicit and open or subtle and hidden. A current term referring to race that is often used is *visible minorities.* The term will not be used in this book, because it implicitly contains racist assumptions. "Visible" minorities usually means people visible to the whites. Whites are also visible to the non-whites, but they are not included among the "visible minorities." This makes the term non-symmetrical, implying that the non-whites are somehow a problem for the whites. Many who use this term do not intend any racism, but it is important that the sociology of ethnicity not include even unintended racist assumptions.

TYPES OF ETHNIC GROUPS

Typologies are important as a method of studying a phenomenon because they can identify characteristics that can be considered as independent variables, i.e., they can explain sets of other characteristics of the phenomenon under study, called dependent variables. It is important, however, to make sure that no typology is reified, i.e., mistaken for the real, concrete phenomenon itself. Typologies are only a means to understanding concrete phenomena. Hence, when using the typology given here, the following should be kept in mind. (1) None of the characteristics of groups used in the typology are biologically inherent; rather they are acquired through historical experience. (2) All of the categories produced by this classification are of the ideal-type nature. This means that no group subsumed under any of the categories is a pure type; rather, groups included in the classifications possess the specific characteristics in higher or lesser degrees. (3) All classifications are dichotomous, i.e., they involve extremes by which one extreme is one ideal type and the other extreme is the opposite ideal type. The types are thus relative to each other and should be understood as such. For example, if an ethnic group is typed as small, it should be understood that it is so in relation to some other ethnic group that is considered large, or if we say that an ethnic group is young, it should be understood in relation to others which can be considered old. (4) The same concrete group may be placed into more than one set of types. An ethnic group may be classified according to size as small and according to territoriality as segregated. This is the result of the analytical method employed here in comparing group characteristics. But no single type in any of these classifications is a subtype of any of the other classifications. The criteria of classification remain logically independent of each other. (5) Finally, while the typology may be somewhat extensive, its main purpose is to sensitize the reader to the differences between ethnic groups. The value of analytical distinctions lies in the fact that they alert the systematic student of the phenomenon to the features of reality that have real-life consequences. As will be readily seen, the characteristics of one type of groups as against another place the ethnic group studied into a different relation to other ethnic groups. This has implications for its collective action, if any, vis-à-vis other groups.

• Primary and Secondary Ethnic Groups

The distinction refers to the place where the group's culture emerged as a distinct entity. Primary ethnic groups are those existing in the same place in which historically they have been formed. Germans formed themselves culturally in Germany, Italians in Italy, Chinese in China, Indians in India, English in England and so on. All these can be said to be primary ethnic groups. Germans, Italians, Chinese or English in Canada are secondary ethnic groups. A secondary ethnic group is one which has its origin in a different society from the one in which it currently exists. It is, as it were, a transplanted group, a group which shares its culture and history with the society from which it emigrated, but which does not depend anymore on the original society for its existence.

At some time in history a primary ethnic group might have itself been a secondary ethnic group in relation to its own ancestors. However, the shift from the secondary to primary ethnic groups has been rather infrequent. Great migrations of people took place only in certain periods of history. For example, migrations of people who provided the bases for the European primary ethnic groups took place in pre-historic times and formation of most European ethnicities was a long historical process following the original migrations. Often it is forgotten that contemporary ethnic groups have important features that originated in pre-historic times and are still quite viable.

In the modern Western world, the Canadian, American, Australian and Latin American ethnicities can be said to be in the process of formation as primary ethnicities. In the United States, this process seems to be faster and has moved further ahead than in Canada, so that it is easier to speak about "American" culture than it is to characterize "Canadian" culture. Development of secondary ethnic groups has been a much more common phenomenon in modern times, especially in the context of migration to the New World and to

"Race" in Psychology

Karen Henwood and Ann Phoenix

The area of "race" and IQ highlights one important way in which the discipline, despite claims to neutrality and objectivity by many of its practitioners, is political in its constructions and effects.

Claims that black people are innately intellectually limited have been used to argue for differential treatment of black people and white people in social policy areas such as education and immigration. Although hereditarians generally claim to be apolitical, their work is not politically neutral. For example, Jensen's (1969) extended treatment of black-white differences in IQ in his 117-page paper was explicitly directed to halting the USA Head Start preschool intervention programme (which President Nixon did stop). Eysenck (1971) has also argued that black-white differences in IQ need to be taken into account in "sensible" policies on immigration. Thus, potentially, the heritability and IQ position has directly negative effects on the ways in which black people are positioned within society and policies aimed at black people. In addition, extreme right-wing groups have seized upon Jensen's and Eysenck's work as proof of black inferiority (Billig 1979). It is not possible therefore, as Eysenck (1971) has claimed, to keep "scientific facts" about "race" distinct from racist attitudes. Instead, the social and political context within which such research is reported underlines the interlinkages between scientific and popular discourses on "race" and racism. Much ink has been expended on examining whether or not the proponents of hereditarian views are intentionally racist. This, arguably, is not entirely relevant to a consideration of the "race" and IQ debate and hence the context in which "race" is taught in psychology, since hereditarian work as discursive production has material effects regardless of the intentions of the authors.

The political nature of IQ testing is exemplified by the fact that intelligence test scores have been used to argue for social policies which have negative consequences for a particular minority ethnic group, regardless of whether that group scores well or badly. Thus, the higher Porteus test scores of Chinese and Japanese people in comparison with white people were used to argue against their being allowed to immigrate into Hawaii in the 1920s.

The recursive nature of the arguments in this debate has resulted in this being an area of stagnation within psychology (although it can help to advance metatheoretical understandings of the discipline).

> How little seems to have changed, and how little advance has been made since the days of Galton and Binet, in spite of a century of accumulating biological knowledge, the advent of quantitative genetics, and the potency of modern molecular biology. Why is this? Why can't we do better?
>
> Leaving aside the willful and pernicious misinterpretations of data, there appear to be two principal sources of confusion. The first is a widespread failure to understand what biology cannot yet tell us. The second is an equally widespread failure to understand what it can (Odling-Smee 1990).

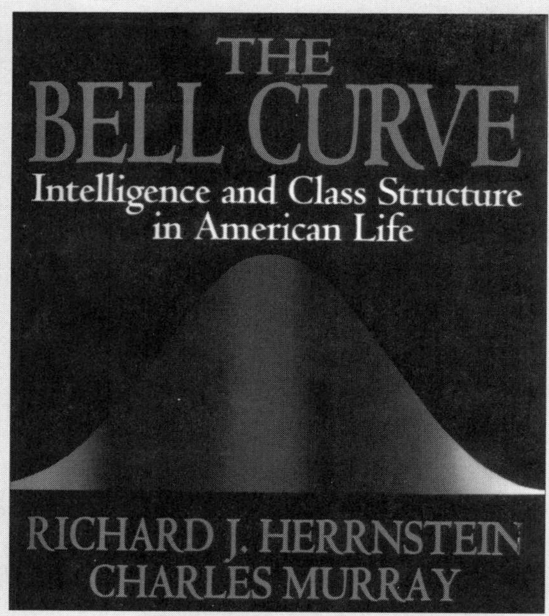

Cover of *The Bell Curve* (1994, Free Press) the latest in a long line of "hereditarian" research seeking to "prove" racial inferiority and superiority.

The only possible moves are either further to elaborate black-white differences in IQ, or continually to counter these arguments with detailed examinations of the shortcomings of the "evidence" on which the hereditarian edifice is built while highlighting the contribution of environmental factors to test scores. The debates are informed not only by psychology, but by irreconcilable ideological commitments (although these are consistently denied by hereditarians). Questions of whether or not IQ differences are hereditarily transmitted are, arguably, so archaic that the debate is akin to flogging an already dead horse. Yet, failure to counter hereditarian arguments would be seen by many to confirm their truth.

Finally, the popularization of these ideas beyond psychology has an impact, not only in stereotyping psychology outside the discipline as stuck-in-the-mud, but in perpetuating racism.

Source: Taken from Karen Henwood and Ann Phoenix, " 'Race' in Psychology: Teaching the Subject," *Ethnic and Racial Studies*, Vol. 19 (1996): 4:841-863. Reprinted with permission of the publisher.

Australia. It can be argued that formation of secondary ethnic groups will be even more prevalent in the future as international migration increases.

• Majority and Minority Ethnic Groups

According to the power-dominance criterion we can distinguish between the majority ethnic groups and the minority ethnic groups. In Canada this is the distinction between the British groups–English, Scottish, Welsh, and the Protestant Irish–and all the other ethnic groups. Majority ethnic groups are those who determine the character of the society's basic institutions, especially the political and economic institutions. Except for Quebec, British culture has historically formed the character of Canadian major social institutions. For example, the British parliamentary system has been the model for the Canadian government and the Anglo values of individualism have formed the basis for the Canadian economic style.

Majority ethnic groups also determine the norms of society as a whole, including the legal system, and thus, their culture becomes the culture of the total society into which the minority ethnic groups inculturate or assimilate. The minority groups may preserve their institutions and culture in larger or smaller degrees, or they may influence the character of the dominant institutions in larger or smaller degrees. In either case the outcome of the intergroup processes is much more the result of the minorities adjusting and adapting themselves to the majority group's institutions rather than the reverse.

Furthermore, the majority group in society is the one whose members have the decisive voice in the major institutions of society. They are the makers of decisions that will affect the life of all in society. Minority group members may have an influence on the process of decision making, but they themselves are not the makers of the important decisions.

Finally, the majority groups, because of their position of power, are at the top of the ethnic stratification system. Their members form the societal elite and the status of the other ethnic groups is measured in relation to them.

Some minority ethnic groups, however, come to occupy a middle position between the majority groups and other minority groups. These are known as middleman minority groups (Blalock, 1967; Lieberson, 1970; Bonacich, 1973; Turner and Bonacich, 1980). Many of these groups' members are engaged in occupations such as shop ownership, independent business ownership, trading, moneylending, or in professions such as medicine, law and consulting. They provide services to both the majority group and other minority groups. As a result, while having no decisive power in the major institutions of the broader society, they may have a degree of influence on the decision making processes of the majority group. Because of this intermediate position, however, these groups are vulnerable to hostilities coming from both the majority group and other minority groups and often become scapegoats for both sides. Examples of the middlemen minorities are the Jews in Europe, the Chinese in Southeast Asian societies, particularly Malaysia and the Philippines, and the South Asians, especially the Indians in Africa, the Caribbean, and parts of Oceania, particularly Fiji.

• Folk Community and Nationality Community

This distinction takes into account the degree of structural differentiation of the community, the character of culture that the group possesses and the degree of group self-consciousness or group self-awareness shared by the members of the group (Zielyk, 1975). An ethnic group that is a folk community is one whose members are little differentiated in social status. Predominantly, they are of peasant background. In Robert Redfield's (1956) words, its culture is a "little tradition" embodied in custom, song and proverb and transmitted by word of mouth. It is a culture created by the unknown many. It centres around a religious institution.

An ethnic group that is predominantly a nationality is one whose members have had urban experience and show a higher degree of occupational and status differentiation. In particular, a nationality community contains a larger percentage of more highly educated people. The culture of the nationality community, in Redfield's terms, is part of a "great tradition," including literary, artistic and intellectual achievements. It is a culture created by the known few. Unlike the folk community, it contains secular organizations; political, cultural and educational.

At some point in their history, all ethnic communities were folk communities. As occupational differentiation proceeded and as group self-awareness increased, folk communities would become nationalities, i.e., groups with a developed sense of their history and of a distinct culture. When, in addition, such groups develop a claim to their own jurisdiction over the territory in which they live, they can be said to become nations. A nation may or may not obtain this jurisdiction. It is a nation even if it does not have such jurisdiction, as long as it has what it considers to be a legitimate claim to such jurisdiction. If a nation does obtain jurisdiction over the territory in which it lives, it then becomes a nation-state. Nationalities, i.e., self-aware groups, may have no legitimate claim to any territory, as for example most immigrant groups in Canada. Yet, as a result of their group self-awareness, they may develop political claims for rights which they may see as being denied them. In the past half-century, many groups in Canada, the United States and other countries have come to recognize that they were being discriminated against and have demanded legislation to remove it.

A dynamic force in ethnic groups whose members become self-aware are ideologies that refer to human rights, freedom from oppression or exploitation, equality, or ideologies of nationalism. Unlike the folk community in which tradition is of central importance, for the nationality community, ideology constitutes an important source of motivation for community activities and political organization. Nationalism is an ideology and a social-political movement that has moved nationalities towards defining themselves as a nation and towards claiming sovereignty as a nation-state. Ideologies can range from a moderate, liberal type to an extreme radical or reactionary type (Isajiw, 1985a). Minority groups who have tried to gain independence from dominance of the majority groups have often split themselves between liberal nationalistic wings and radical nationalistic wings. The former have tended to emphasize a gradual process towards independence, a "lawful" manner of increasing the group's autonomy by means of gaining more rights for the group, often placing the strongest emphasis on language and cultural rights. Radical nationalism of minority groups has tended to be strongly political, pushing for immediate independence and sovereignty at all costs, even by use of violence. It also has tended to be a totalistic type of ideology, demanding a subordination of all values to that of national independence and an unquestioned commitment of its followers to the movement's organization and leadership.

Nationalism of majority groups, i.e., those in charge of their own nation-states, is the ideological or political movement by these groups to assert their identity or power in relation to other nations or in relation to the minority groups within their own society. It has also often split itself between liberal and reactionary types. The liberal type of this ideology has tended to be tolerant of minorities and propose "fair" methods of incorporating them into the larger society, according to the precepts of human rights legislation, compromise and the like. The reactionary type of this ideology has tended to be little tolerant or non-tolerant of minorities and differences within society, pushing for policies of exclusion and enforced assimilation. Both the radical and the reactionary extremes of the nationalist ideology have tended to align themselves with racist ideologies.

Some scholars distinguish between "civic nationalism" and "ethnic nationalism." The former is meant to refer to an ideology of support for the national legal institutions in the sense of "patriotism." The latter is meant to indicate an ideology that emphasizes superiority of one's own ethnic group and culture. The problem with this distinction is that it confuses the concept of nationalism with those of majority and minority and with the ideology of racism. My argument is that all nationalisms are ethnic and what is referred to by the concepts of civic and ethnic nationalism is better understood as nationalism of the majority and nationalism of the minority ethnic groups, in the sociological sense of the terms explained above. If a group is a minority group in respect to a more powerful group and, at the same time, the majority group in respect to other, diverse, less powerful groups, as is the case with Quebec, it then may exhibit both types of nationalism, one in relation to its more powerful group, for example, English Canada, and the other in relation to the minority groups within its boundaries, for example, the Aboriginal peoples and the Allophones in Quebec. This will be discussed in more detail in Chapter 9.

An example of predominantly folk-community ethnic groups in Canada in the 1970s and 1980s were the Portuguese, who migrated to Canada mainly from rural areas of Portugal. This was also true of the Italians, Ukrainians, Polish, Mennonites and many others at the turn of the century and, after World War II, peoples who moved to Canada from rural areas in the home country.

In Canada, a number of ethnic groups have moved from being a folk community at one time to become a nationality community at another. Most Slavic ethnic groups in Canada, for example, had been folk communities prior to World War I. Between the wars and especially after World War II, the educational level among them increased, as they received an influx of more educated immigrants who brought with them the issues of oppression in the home country. This had a decisive influence on the character of the groups' institutions in Canada. By the 1990s the process of movement away from the folk-community character of all ethnic groups in Canada and other countries was well advanced.

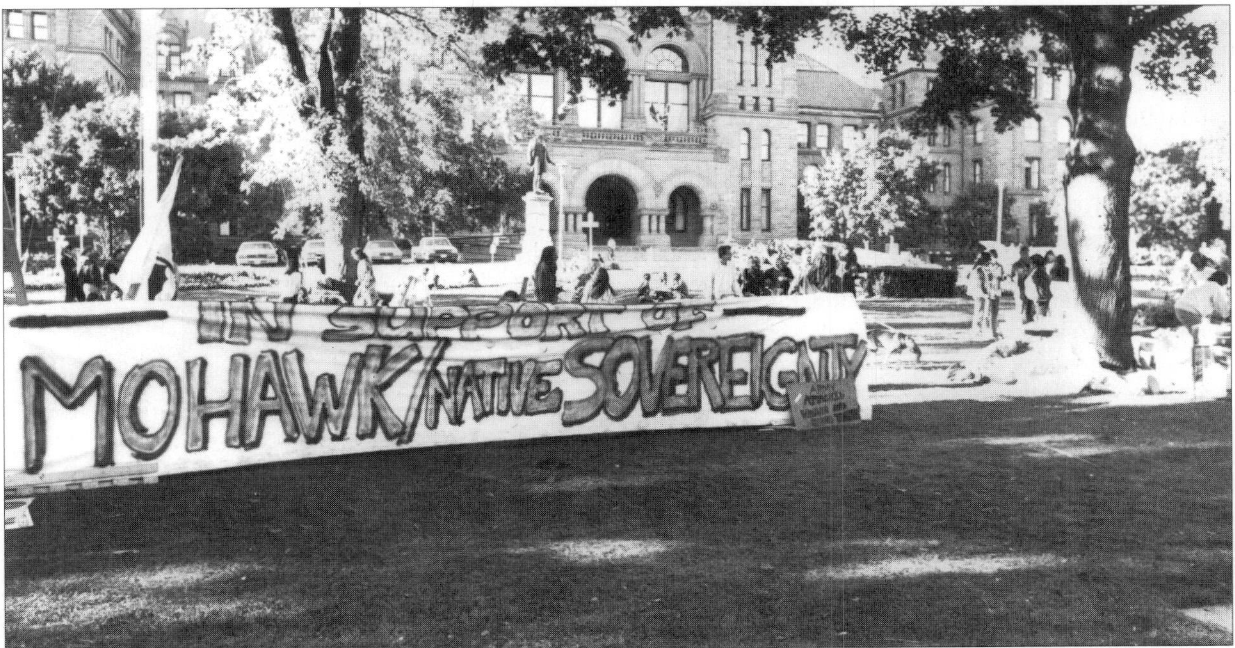

Photo: Dick Hemingway

Part of a support rally during the "Oka crisis" in 1990. Banner reads: "In Support of Mohawk/Native Sovereignty."

The Blacks in the United States who for long have been a folk community, have developed an educated elite who, since the 1950s, through their civil rights movement have changed the character of the community to a more self-aware, "nationality" type of group.

The same process can be observed among the Native peoples in Canada, who have developed an educated elite that has organized new, politically oriented organizations, such as the Assembly of First Nations. In the 1980s and 1990s, they successfully exerted pressure on the Canadian government to change the Indian Act, to honour land claims and to accept the idea of the Native peoples as self-governed nations. It is interesting to note that, in this process, the groups themselves insisted on changing what they are called. First, the claim was made to change their designation from "Indians" to "Native people." With time, as political demands were made, the designation was changed to "Native peoples" or "Aboriginal peoples" and, with the invigorated development of the land claims movement, to "First Nations."

• "Old" and "Young" Ethnic Groups

Using the criterion of generational composition, we can distinguish between "young" ethnic groups and "old" ethnic groups. This distinction has nothing to do with the age composition of the ethnic population. It refers to the length of time the group, as a group, has been in the country, as measured by the number of generations. The "young" groups are predominantly made up of the first generation, i.e., persons who were born outside of the host country. Their proportion of the second generation is either small or young in age and there may be no third generation as yet at all. If the third generation is present, it has not yet reached adulthood. The "old" ethnic groups are those already established in the larger society, i.e., they have at least a predominant proportion of adult second generation or adult third or successive generations. Whether a group is young or old is not to be determined by the date of arrival in the host society of the very first person or persons of the specific ethnic origin, but by the date of arrival of a larger group of people who can be said to have made up an ethnic community.

By this distinction it is incorrect to speak of all ethnic groups as if they were immigrants. Members of the old, established ethnic groups usually do not like to be confused with immigrants. The problems that these two types of ethnic groups pose are different. The problems of the young groups can be characterized as essentially the problems of adjustment to a new society; those of the old group, as problems of persistence in the society.

Further discussion of these problems will be presented later in several chapters.

Among the old ethnic groups in Canada, one can include the British, French, Germans, Scandinavians, Dutch, Ukrainians, Russian, Polish, Jewish, Doukhobors, Mennonites, Native Indians and Inuit, Blacks (except for those from the Caribbean region), Chinese, Japanese and others. Among the relatively young groups, one can include the Greeks, Portuguese, various Latin American groups, East Indians (except for Sikhs), Caribbeans and others.

In classifying ethnic groups as young and old, one should take regionalism into account. Groups that are old may be old in one region of the country, but young in another. The Chinese, for example, are an old group in Western Canada. In the Toronto area, they are a young group.

Old ethnic groups can be subdivided further into those groups that add significantly to their population by means of a continuous stream of new immigrants and those who have no significant numbers of new immigrants and hence can increase their population only by natural growth. Such groups as the French, Native Indians and Inuit, Doukhobors and others are an example of the latter. Groups with a continuous stream of new immigration face special problems of interrelationship between the old and the new sectors of the ethnic community. Among such problems are the questions as to what extent the ethnic institutions and organizations established by the old community are able to serve the needs of the new immigrants, to what extent status or class differences between the old community and the new immigrants create tensions or conflict between them, to what extent the cultural patterns, including the language accent and style, brought by the new immigrants differ from those of the old community, and to what extent the demands exerted on society by the new immigrants differ from or contradict the demands placed on it by the old community. The groups without significant numbers of new immigrants may define their persistence in the broader society in a different, perhaps sharper, manner than the groups with a continuous streams of new immigrants. For them, for example, the question of the ethnic language retention may be a more significant issue than for the new immigrants. For the latter, the question of learning English may be more important.

• Territorially Segregated and Territorially Intermixed Ethnic Groups

Territorially segregated groups refers to those who live primarily in one area or region of the country. This distinction refers to regional and not to residential segregation in urban areas. Territorially segregated groups can be further subdivided into two types: those with legal, *de jure*, definition of their boundaries, and those without such definition, i.e., territorially segregated *de facto*. French Québecers, the Native peoples on reserves, the Germans, French, Italian and the Romanch of Switzerland, the Dutch, French and German of Belgium, all are examples of ethnic groups territorially segregated with legal definition of their boundaries.

The legal definition of boundaries plays a very important role in the group's relationship to the society at large. It provides grounds for demands that the group may exert on society. At the same time it gives a legitimized support to and perpetuates ethnic identity of the group. It also gives special legitimate grounds for the group's establishment and maintenance of separate ethnic institutions. The groups with legally defined territorial boundaries usually claim special status in society as a whole. This means that their demands on society usually have priority over the demands of groups that are unable to claim special status.

Many ethnic groups, however, have no legal designation of territorial boundaries, yet they may historically concentrate in one or a few regions of the country, or even in an area within a region. Examples are the Doukhobors, Mennonites and Hutterites who are concentrated in the Canadian Prairie and Western regions. In the period before World War II, a number of others were examples, such as the Chinese and Japanese in British Columbia, the Ukrainians in the Prairies and the Blacks in the Southern Ontario and Nova Scotia regions.

Territorially intermixed ethnic groups are those who cannot be described as segregated either *de jure* or *de facto* in any specific region of the country, but who are more or less spread out in several or all regions and are residentially intermixed with other ethnic groups. One can of course have groups that are regionally segregated but intraregionally intermixed, as, for example, the Métis in the Prairie region.

Paradoxically, in Canada and other countries, we have recently been witnessing both trends towards less territorial segregation of some previously more segregated ethnic groups, and trends towards legislation of more autonomous *de jure* boundaries for already territorially segregated groups. The case in point is

Quebec, Native Indians and the Inuit. More will be said about these movements later.

One could talk about urban residential segregation in terms analogous to the regional territorial segregation. Sociologically, however, the two are not the same. Urban residential segregation does not derive from different territorially based economies. Urban ethnic groups tend to depend on the same economic institutions for their employment. In urban areas, members of the same ethnic group may tend to concentrate in certain industries, but just as often they work in ethnically intermixed settings.

THEORETICAL APPROACHES TO THE STUDY OF ETHNICITY

The study of ethnicity often takes its general orientation from broader theoretical approaches concerned with the nature of the social phenomenon in general. In the second half of the twentieth century, the general sociological theory, sometimes called "grand" theory, has branched out into a variety of theoretical directions. Among them have been at least four major theoretical paradigms: the structural-functional paradigm, the conflict paradigm, the social-psychological paradigm and the post-modern paradigm. This is not the place to expound on these approaches. They will be only briefly explained, since in many cases they have been at the logical roots of more specific theoretical approaches dealing with ethnicity.

Structural-functionalism, identified with Talcott Parsons (1951) and Robert K. Merton (1968), considers social reality to be a whole, i.e., a system made up of interdependent parts, in which each part contributes in one way or another to the integration or alternatively to disintegration of society as a unity. The parts contribute to integration of the social whole when there is sharing or consensus on some basic values and norms. The "contributions" of the parts to the whole are the "functions" that the social phenomena, such as different social roles, institutions, behaviour patterns, groups and organizations, perform for society as a whole. They function either towards the maintenance of the system's boundary, or else towards its dissolution. These functions can be intended and recognized ("manifest") or they can be unintended and unrecognized ("latent"). In other words, some social patterns of relations may have positive, harmonious intentions, yet have negative, unintended consequences on the social order. This state of affairs may or may not be recognized by those interacting or by others in society. In accord with this approach, ethnic groups and their relations are to be studied in terms of how they contribute to the integration of society as a whole in their intentions and in their consequences.

The conflict approaches conceive of society as being composed of distinct social groups who enter into conflict with one another over various types of scarce resources. Social order, if it exists, is simply a result of either domination of one group over others, or a balance of power between feuding groups. The conflict conception of society has produced a succession of approaches. Among the oldest approaches is the Marxist view of society in which the historical struggle of humanity is between two social classes, between those who own the means of production and those who do not. In modern times these are the capitalists and the proletarians. Everything else–values, norms, institutions and so on–rather than being the unifying element in society, is a means used in the conflict, especially by the capitalist class.

A more recent conflict approach is found in the work of Ralf Dahrendorf (1959) and Randall Collins (1975). In this approach, the conflict between the distinct groups in society is not so much over the means of production as over power. According to this approach, power is at the core of all social relationships. Power is the scarce resource over which different groups conflict. Conflict is necessitated by a group's becoming conscious of its interests and acquiring the technical and political means of organization in order to fulfil those interests. Since power is essentially coercive, any organization with a view to acquiring power for one group will be resented and opposed by another group whose interests are different. Hence, conflict is inevitable. In accord with this approach, ethnic groups are seen as actual or potential interest groups and actual or potential partners in the social conflict.

The social-psychological approaches see social reality as the interaction of individuals. All groups are made up of interactions of individuals and, in the final analysis, intergroup behaviour is the interaction of individuals acting on behalf of their groups. Among the variety of social psychological approaches have been symbolic interactionism (Blumer, 1969; Goffman, 1959), and the phenomenological approaches (Garfinkel, 1967; Berger and Luckmann, 1966). These approaches owe much to George Herbert Mead (1934), who placed an emphasis on the concept of "self" as an active principle, rather than as a passive recipient of social forces. He formulated the concept of actively taking on the attitudes of others in formation of one's self, called "the me." The social-psychological approaches hold that the meaning that things have to human beings arises out of social interaction. In the construction of meaning and in social interaction, symbols play a central role, and it is through symbols that subjective meanings come to be objectified in everyday life and social reality comes to be externalized and "constructed." In accord with this approach, ethnicity is to be examined as an aspect of one's system of meanings, as defining one's identity, and how in a society that predominantly shares a set of symbols different from those of minority groups, every day life of minority-group members changes their meanings and their identity.

Finally, the post-modernist approach holds a completely different view of social reality. In one sense, it is an extreme extension of the phenomenological approach yet it critiques all the other approaches. According to Seidman (1994), there is no substance to any general social theory of society. Generalization is futile because it posits that all societies are in some respects the same or that they are becoming the same. The latter is a great myth of modernity, which posits a model of society in which all diversity disappears. The facts, however, show that even in modern times diversity is the reality of everyday life. Hence, social reality can be understood only through understanding the meaning–reading the narrative–of everyday life and the history of each particular group of people in its own terms. In accord with this approach, no generalizations are to be made about ethnic groups or racial categories. Rather, as detailed a description as possible should be prepared of the life of each group in terms of what it means to its members. In other words, understanding of ethnicity can be achieved only through subjective ethnography.

Each of these general theoretical approaches offers an informative perspective on an aspect of social reality, but no single approach by itself is adequate for a full study of social reality. In fact, by itself, each approach can be misleading. In this text, no one single approach will be followed. Rather, we will draw on as many of these approaches as may be useful in helping to explain one or another aspect of ethnicity and interethnic relations.

GENERAL THEORIES OF ETHNICITY

While the four approaches to general sociological theory provide a basis for a perspective on ethnic groups, they themselves do not constitute any theory of ethnicity as such. One, however, can find in contemporary literature more specific theories of the nature of ethnicity. We can again single out four approaches that offer different explanations of how ethnicity emerges. Each of these approaches has its roots in a different type of general sociological theory. But whereas the general theory tries to explain the nature of society as a whole, these approaches focus on ethnicity as a phenomenon in its own right, related to society as a whole and influenced by its structure but not completely determined by it. The four approaches are: (1) ethnicity conceived as a primordial phenomenon, (2) ethnicity conceived as an epiphenomenon, (3) ethnicity conceived as a situational phenomenon and (4) ethnicity conceived as a subjective phenomenon.

• Primordialist Approach

The primordialist approach, also known as the "essentialist" approach, is among the oldest in sociological and anthropological literature. It argues that ethnicity is something given, ascribed at birth, deriving from the kin-and-clan structure of human society and hence something more or less fixed and permanent (Geertz, 1963; Isaacs, 1989; Stack, 1986). According to H. Isaacs (1975: 30-33), ethnicity is composed of "primordial affinities and attachments" that a person is born with or acquires at birth. It involves "the ready-made set of endowments and identifications which every individual shares with others from the moment of birth by the chance of the family into which he is born at that given time in that given place." This includes the shared physical characteristics of the group, the history and origins of the group into which the person is born, the group's nationality, language, religion and value system, and even the attributes that come out of the geography or topography of the person's birthplace itself. These all shape the person's outlook, way of life and identity from his or her very first day. This identity also includes the political and the economic condition of the group into which the person is born, be it dominant over other groups or dominated by other groups; rich or poor.

• Epiphenomenon Approach

The other three approaches emerged in confutation of the primordialist approach. The epiphenomenon approach was derived originally from Marxist theory. An extreme statement of it was given by Oliver Cox (1948: 321-352). According to him, ethnic or race relations are merely one aspect of exploitation of labour by the capitalist class. Ethnicity and race are a by-product of class relations. What are considered to be attributes of ethnicity are, in effect, attributes of the exploited class. In essence, according to Cox, ethnic and race relations are relations of class conflict.

In contemporary sociological literature, the epiphenomenon approach to ethnicity is represented in a different form by Michael Hechter's theory of internal colonialism and cultural division of labour and, to a lesser extent, by Edna Bonacich (1972). Hechter (1978) divides the economic structure of society into two sectors, centre and periphery. The periphery consists of marginal jobs, such as agricultural work, which turn out products that are important to society but offer little in the form of compensation, as compared with the jobs in the centre. This fact creates the structure of societal periphery, and it is this sector of the social structure that gives birth to ethnicity. It is the people who concentrate in this peripheral labour sector that become ethnic groups. They develop their own solidarity and a culture different from that of the centre. Ethnicity thus refers to minority groups only. It is something created and maintained by an uneven economy, a product of economic exploitation.

E. Bonacich's somewhat similar theory of the split labour market as a determining factor of ethnicity will be discussed in the context of ethnic stratification. In Canada, a variant of the epiphenomenal approach has been propounded by Peter Li (1990b; Bolaria and Li, 1988). According to Li, ethnicity and race are the consequence of unequal relationships, produced and maintained by differential power between a dominant and a subordinate group. Distinct cultural and racial differences are developed and used as convenient grounds for justifying the exploitation of the subordinate groups by the superordinate groups.

• Situational Approach

The situational approach is based on rational choice theory. In contrast to the epiphenomenal approach, the situational approach assumes that ethnic identity is something that can be chosen by a member of a minority group. According to this approach, ethnicity is something which may be relevant in some situations but not in others. Individuals may choose to be regarded as members of an ethnic group if they find it to their advantage. Perhaps the best explanation of this approach is the work of Michael Banton, Daniel Bell and Jeffrey Ross. Banton (1983) sees it as a rational choice option of an individual in any circumstance. Bell and Ross emphasize the political advantage of ethnic membership choice. Thus, ethnicity is "a group option in which resources are mobilized for the purpose of pressuring the political system to allocate public goods for the benefit of the members of a self-differentiating collectivity" (Ross, 1982). According to Bell (1975: 171), "ethnicity is best understood not as a primordial phenomenon in which deeply held identities have to reemerge, but as a strategic choice by individuals who in other circumstances would choose other group memberships as a means of gaining some power and privilege." While any upsurge of ethnicity may allow individuals to assert a sense of pride in what they regard as their own, it also serves as a means for disadvantaged groups to claim a set of rights and privileges that the existing power structures have denied them (Bell, 1975: 174).

In general terms, ethnicity, according to this approach, refers to an individual's pliant ascription of ethnic identity to organize the meaning of his social relationships within the requirements of variously structured social situations. This approach was popular from the mid-1970s to mid-1980s.

• Subjectivist Approach

Perhaps the most interesting of the four approaches is the subjectivist approach, which sees ethnicity as basically a social-psychological reality or a matter of perception of "us" and "them." This is in contradistinction to seeing it as something given, which exists objectively, as it were, "out there." This does not mean that all subjectivists reject all objective aspects of ethnicity. Some give them significant attention. However, they see ethnicity as dependent on the socio-psychological experience.

Two factors stimulated the emergence of this approach in the study of ethnicity in the past 20 years. First, Fredrik Barth's seminal work on ethnic group boundaries had a strong influence on both anthropologists and sociologists. Second, in American and Canadian scholarship, the approach has been spurred by empirical studies of ethnic generations, particularly the third generation.

KEY ISSUES IN CANADIAN ETHNIC RELATIONS

For Whom Does "Race" Matter, Anyway?

Is the concept of "race" a useful concept for either our understanding of human differences or for any efforts to reduce or eliminate prejudice and discrimination?

Race refers to people placing other people into categories on account of some physical characteristics possessed by them that are perceived to be different from those possessed by people whom they consider to be their own group. Racism begins when those placing people into such categories see themselves as being superior and the others as inferior.

"Race" is thus a social category, a construction forged by some people and accepted by others, but as a collective phenomenon it has no reality in itself. Some scholars, as for example anthropologist Ashley Montague, have argued that, since race is a social construction, the concept and the term "race" should be dropped from both scholarly and popular usage. The argument is further reinforced by the belief that to use of the term perpetuates racism in society.

Other scholars, however, argue in the opposite direction. They point to the observed fact that there are inequalities between people of different racial characteristics and that racial prejudices, including racism, are also an objective fact. Hence, race matters to people out there. They argue that removing the concept of race from our thinking and the term "race" from our vocabulary would take our attention away from, or even make us ignore, racial inequalities and prejudices.

The question is made more complicated by recurring attempts by some scholars to measure differences in intelligence among populations with different racial characteristics, arguing that some racial populations have genetically lower intelligence levels than others. Ruth Benedict in her book *Race and Racism*, republished in 1983, reviewed many of the early writings that tried to show this. In 1994, R. J. Herrnstein and C. Murray published a book *The Bell Curve* in which they argued that intelligence is genetically inherited and that the well-to-do white population in the United States has higher intelligence levels, as measured by the IQ Test, than the disadvantaged African-American population.

Yet every time a research like this appears, there are other scholars who point out that such conclusions are simply deductions from faulty assumptions and inadequate research methodology. In his book *The Mismeasure of Man*, Stephen. J. Gould shows that the science underlying the hereditarian approach to intelligence is flawed: the research and conclusions result from a priori convictions of the researchers rather than empirical evidence.

The Ku Klux Klan enjoyed brief popularity in parts of Canada in the 1920s. Above, Kingston, Ontario, 1947.

Photo: National Archives of Canada, PA-87848

The problem with arguing the influence of heredity on human behavior is that to do it in a scientifically correct manner would require that the researcher first examine all social, cultural and psychological factors that may account for differences in the behavior between populations of people, so as to show by empirical evidence that such factors cannot explain the differences and only then proceed to genetic-biological research. None of those who have argued hereditary intelligence levels have ever done this.

Furthermore, many scholars doubt the ability of the IQ Test to measure intelligence universally. In the Winter 1998 issue of the journal *Scientific American*, it is argued that the IQ Test does not measure intelligence universally, that it is biased in favor of the white, middle-class and the Western definition of intelligence and that it ignores other types of intelligence prevalent in other cultures that can also be found among the people in Western societies. According to these authors, one can distinguish at least eight different types of intelligence and the standard IQ Test measures only one of them.

Why then do some scholars try to find evidence that one type of racial population has inherently a superior or inferior intelligence level than does another? In particular, why do they insist on the genetic inheritance of differences in intelligence levels when they do not first attempt to discard all social and cultural factors that may explain these differences?

Barth (1969) himself took a rather extreme position. For practical purposes, he jettisoned culture from the concept of ethnicity. For him, ethnic boundaries were psychological boundaries; ethnic culture and its content was irrelevant. Ethnic group is hence a result of group relations in which the boundaries are established through mutual perceptions and not by means of any objectively distinct culture.

A less extreme position has been that of the symbolic ethnicity approach as formulated by H. Gans (1979). His idea is that ethnicity is no longer what it used to be. In modern times, ethnicity has lost its practical everyday value. It remains purely on a symbolic level on which it works to identify people who are otherwise acculturated and assimilated into a different, predominantly urban, culture and society.

Another type of subjectivist approach to the study of ethnicity–one that appears to be connected with the post-modernist movement in contemporary thought–is constructionism. It is represented by the work of W. Yancey (1976), M. Moerman (1965), Susan Smith (1984), Hanna Herzog (1984), Anderson (1991) and, to some extent, J.Y. Okamura (1981), E. Roosens (1989) and W.W. Isajiw (1975, 1990). Theoretically, this approach lies somewhere between Michel Foucault's (1967) emphasis on construction of the metaphor and Pierre Bourdieu's (1977) notions of practice and habitus as the basic factors shaping the structure of all social phenomena. The basic notion in this approach is that ethnicity is something that is being negotiated and constructed in everyday living. As Nagel (1994:162) put it:

> It is important that we discard the notion that culture is simply an historical legacy; culture is not a shopping cart that comes to us already loaded with a set of historical cultural goods. Rather we construct culture by picking and choosing items from the shelves of the past and the present.

For Bennett (1975: 1) ethnicity is not something from the past and therefore irrelevant to the present; rather it is "something new in the world ... the proclivity of people to seize on traditional cultural symbols as a definition of their own identity."

According to Isajiw (1975), each generation constructs its own form of ethnicity so that the ethnic identity of the second generation is different from that of the first, and that of the third is different from that of the second. The persistence of ethnicity over generations depends not so much on the maintenance of the form of identity constructed by the first generation, as on the emergence of new forms constructed by each succeeding generation. Ethnicity is a process that continues to unfold. It has much to do with the exigencies of everyday survival. It is constructed in the process of feeding, clothing, sending children to school and conversing with children and others, but it can also be deconstructed into selected parts or reconstructed as social and historical conditions change or as generations succeed one another. Some implications of this approach will be discussed later.

INTERGROUP RELATIONS: CONCEPTUAL FRAMEWORK

Intergroup relations refer to relations among community-type groups. Intergroup relations deal with group interaction rather than the interaction of individuals. This, of course, does not mean that we are not concerned with the actions of individuals as ultimately all group action consists of the actions of individuals. But by studying intergroup relations, we look at how individuals act on behalf of their groups and how their actions influence the state of relations between the members of the various groups.

Intergroup relations can be perceived from two points of view, from the point of view of society as a whole within which the various groups interrelate, and from the point of view of the groups themselves as subjects of the relations. From the point of view of society, intergroup relations are a process of interaction by which community-type groups either adjust to each other so as to effect a degree of social integration or, by failing to adjust to each other, effect divisiveness in society as a whole. Intergroup relations, therefore, are inherently tied to the problem of integration of society.

From the point of view of the groups themselves, the process of intergroup relations is the way in which the groups' values and goals–or interests–come to be fulfilled or fail to be fulfilled. This does not mean that, if values and interests of any one group are fulfilled, social integration follows automatically. The process is much more complex. Fulfilment of interests and values of one group may mean lack of fulfilment of interests and values of another and vice versa. Integration of society as a whole is a continuing process. It may never be fully reached. This means that some values and interests of some groups may go unfulfilled. As will be discussed later, in the North American context the process of intergroup relations necessitates a mutual articulation of interests and values of many groups.

Values and interests of a group within a larger society can be fulfilled only if there are opportunities to do so and if there are social rewards for pursuing these opportunities for both the individuals in the group and the group itself. Thus, in relating the societal and the subgroup points of view together, the process of intergroup relations involves two broad aspects. The first aspect is the problem of allocating opportunities and rewards among the different community-type groups, in particular between the minority groups. This is the question of the fulfilment of civil and human rights, of availability of opportunities for minority groups and the use that can be made of these opportunities. The entire gamut of opportunities is involved here, ranging from economic and occupational to educational and cultural. The second aspect of intergroup relations is the problem of developing and maintaining solidarity of the various groups with one another and with society as a whole. This is the question of commitment or loyalty to society as a whole, a consciousness of community that binds members of different groups together and gives them a common identity.

• Allocation of Opportunities and Rewards

In terms of interethnic relations, the problem of allocation of opportunities and rewards creates what is called ethnic status and ethnic stratification.

The opportunities that allow ethnic groups to fulfil their values and interests are economic, educational, political and cultural. Economic opportunities refers to the kinds of jobs that members of an ethnic group can acquire or create for themselves as compared with members of other groups, particularly the majority group. This also involves the question of how easy or difficult it is for members of one group, as compared with other groups, to advance to better types of jobs. Educational opportunities refers to the possibility of acquiring the highest education possible in those areas of choice that are socially most rewarding. Political opportunities refers to the acquisition of a group's members of powerful positions or of having influence on those in powerful positions. Cultural opportunities refers to both the possibility of retaining and developing the group's own culture and influencing the culture of the broader society in a creative way.

The rewards that an ethnic group receives in society are not only the economic benefits of the work of their members, but also the prestige that a group can collectively possess among other groups and the recognition by the broader society of the issues that are important to the group.

Opportunities for any one group are, on the one hand, created by other groups in pursuit of their own values and interests, as, for example, has been the case with labour immigration. That is, in opening the doors to economic immigrants, the group or groups in power, in pursuit of their own economic development, need the labour of others. On the other hand, members of a minority group may create their own enterprises and institutions and with them opportunities for other members of the group and those outside the group.

An important corollary of this is making use of the existing opportunities. Not all ethnic groups take equal advantage of the existing opportunities. Some are more adept at it than others. Likewise, some ethnic groups are more able than others to create opportunities for members of their own group or for those outside of their own group. There are various reasons for this. Some of these reasons will be discussed in a later chapter.

Opportunities, however, may be blocked for some groups while open to others. This is the situation of discrimination, and it often involves exclusion from not only one kind of opportunities, but from many or all types of opportunities, occupational, educational, political or cultural. Discrimination will be discussed in more detail in the chapter on ethnic status and ethnic stratification. Here it is important to point out that, when a group is discriminated against and the issue is not raised as a human or civil rights issue, the result is the acquiescence to and legitimization of discrimination and of the subordinate place of the group being discriminated against. Such acquiescence comes to be supported by stereotypes, public images and biases that work to maintain the limitation of opportunities for the group and perpetuate its subordinate status.

For most immigrants and minority groups, the historical pattern has been that of accepting those opportunities most readily available to them, without raising the question of why other opportunities were not available. This has perpetuated ethnic status differences. However, it should be kept in mind that, even if the problem of equity is not raised by any group, the objective situation of inequality of opportunities always remains a potential issue and a threat to social integration.

In industrialized, or post-industrialized, urbanized societies, which value progress rather than tradition and encourage social mobility and change, inequalities sooner or later come to be questioned. Hence, not only the availability of opportunities but also the utilization of available opportunities is important for social integration. If one ethnic group or racial category is blocked from availing itself of the existing opportunities, this is an objective source of potential social tensions. Yet, if a group, for whatever reason, fails to take advantage of the opportunities that are realistically open to it, then this in itself also becomes a potential source of societal tensions in the future.

• Legitimacy of Claims and Societal Solidarity

If any degree of social integration is to be the product of the intergroup relations process, equity issues raised by any group must be recognized as legitimate by other groups, in particular the majority groups in society. If these issues are not accorded legitimacy, then the group that raises them will define the relations of the majority or other groups to itself as coercive or exploitative. Although the majority groups are most important in this respect, recognition of legitimacy received from minority groups also contributes significantly to social integration. If other minority groups are unable or unwilling to recognize the legitimacy of equity issues of any other group but their own, they indirectly undermine the basis for legitimacy of their own actual or potential equity claims.

Often, however, legitimacy is given to some issues but not to others. For example, voting rights may be granted to a group but educational or occupational opportunities denied; or educational opportunities may be available, but claims to cultural retention may be disapproved.

The question of legitimacy of claims relates to the second aspect of the intergroup relations process, i.e., the problem of development and maintenance of social solidarity among the constituent groups in society. Denial of legitimacy of equity claims means exclusion from full membership in society. Recognition of legitimacy of equity claims means inclusion in the broader society and, to the extent that the problems of any one group are seen as common and shared, to that extent the population of a society becomes one community.

It is the legal system that is enacted to protect the rights of any and all claimants. But the legal system by itself is not sufficient to maintain societal solidarity over a long period of time. What is necessary is some minimum degree of sharing of common existential values. In sociology, this issue was raised by Emile Durkheim. He argued that, to make any agreement or contract effective, there must be a tacit pre-contractual agreement on the basic value of agreements themselves. In the context of intergroup relations this can be translated as meaning that, if any specific case of intergroup interaction is to be effective in bringing about social integration, there must first be a tacit agreement on the value of social integration. Without this, power becomes the only principle of intergroup relations. Although competition for opportunities is a necessary feature of contemporary societies, if guided by sheer power principle alone, it contains its own seeds of societal disintegration. Integration that is derived simply from balance of power–from compromises of different self-interests resulting from pressures of countervailing power–can persist only insofar as there is a more or less equal distribution of power among the competing groups. As soon as one competing party gains more advantages or power than another, an inequity situation is produced, and unless the competing groups have some commitment to society as a whole, the groups who gain more opportunities and more power or influence in society will tend to either ignore or disregard the equity claims of those who have less. This kind of commitment to society, however, is not derived simply from an intellectualized or purely ideological consensus on what society should be, but from the concrete social and cultural milieu in which people are born, reared, live and act. It presumes a common identity.

MECHANISMS OF INTERETHNIC RELATIONS

We may now summarize the meaning of interethnic relations as the process by which ethnic groups fulfil or fail to fulfil their goals, interests and values inasmuch as they, in the process of interaction with one another, develop or fail to develop a community of common identity.

The process of interethnic relations involves mechanisms through which it proceeds. There are at least three type of such mechanisms: (1) voluntary organizations, associations and agencies that act on behalf of ethnic groups and on behalf of society as a whole, (2) the law as a means of actual or potential conflict resolution and as a means of articulation of values into normative precepts and (3) governmental policies and activities regarding ethnic groups.

The chapters in the latter part of the book will explore the way in which the use of these mechanisms achieves or fails to achieve social incorporation and integration of ethnic groups into the broader society.

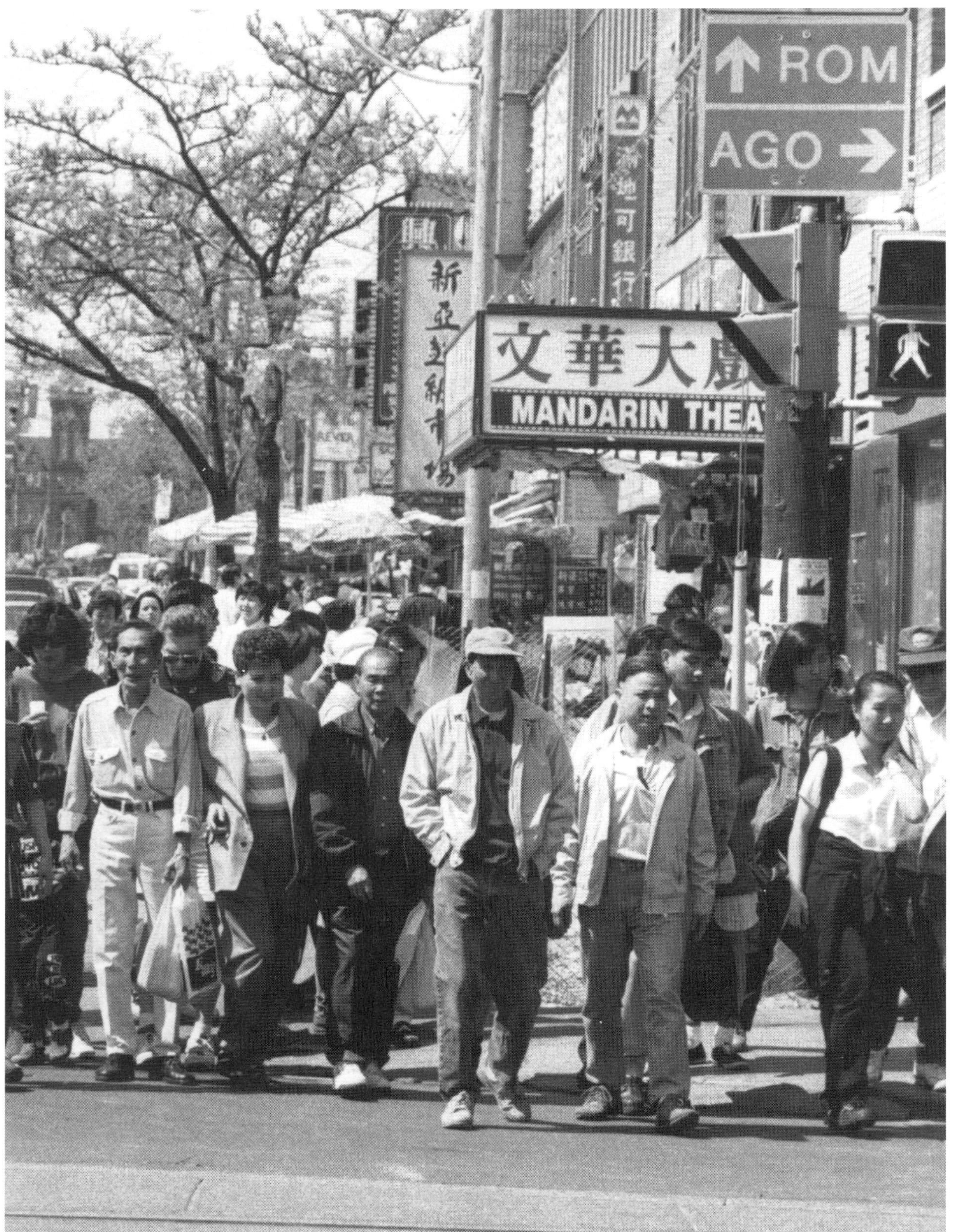

Photo: Dick Hemingway

Part of Old Chinatown in downtown Toronto.

CHAPTER 2

CONTEMPORARY ETHNIC RELATIONS

The Societal Context

To understand how ethnic groups become part of a larger society, it is necessary to know what the basic features of this society are. The basic features of a society are its socio-economic system and the social structure created by the particular society's history. This chapter discusses both of these aspects of Canadian society. It then presents a picture of Canadian ethnic diversity using Canadian census statistics.

Ethnic relations take place within a broader societal context. Much of what happens among different ethnic groups depends on this context. It is therefore essential to understand at least some aspects of this broader societal context if we are to understand the dynamics of ethnic relations.

The most important context to be understood is the structure of society. The two aspects of the social structure of Canadian society that are most relevant to ethnic group relations are those characteristics that make Canada a modern society and those that have their roots in the history of intergroup relations in Canada.

CANADA AS A MODERN POST-INDUSTRIAL SOCIETY

Modern societies have emerged as a result of the process of industrialization and urbanization. This process has produced a number of consequences that have become permanent features of modern societies. These features include occupational differentiation and its consequences, popular education and the development of the democratic process. Our interest in these characteristics is not for their own sake but in how these characteristics influence the nature of ethnic group relations.

Occupational Differentiation. Since the last century, many new types of work have developed. Most of this differentiation has been in the manufacturing, service, administrative and professional fields. Indeed, today occupational differentiation has become the key to the understanding of the social structure of modern societies.

One significant consequence of occupational differentiation has been a shift in the occupational structure of society towards occupations requiring higher skills. Thus, in Canada in 1901, only about 6 percent of the labour force was engaged in tertiary ("white collar") occupations (proprietary, managerial, financial, professional, clerical, commercial), about 50 percent in secondary ("blue collar") occupations (manufacturing, mechanical, construction, labourers) and 44 percent in primary occupations (agricultural, fishing, hunting, trapping, logging, mining and quarrying). By 1921, the percentages had changed to 19 for the tertiary occupations, 40 percent for the secondary occupations and 37 for the primary occupations. In 1951, the distribution was 42, 37 and 20 respectively. By 1971, the tertiary occupations increased to about 54 percent, the secondary occupations decreased to about 28 percent and primary occupations decreased in proportion to about 8 percent. By 1991, the tertiary occupations increased again in a substantial way to 70 percent, the secondary occupations remained more or less the same at 20 percent, and the primary occupations dropped to 7 percent (McVey and Kalbach, 1995: 313-316). The vast majority of the labour force is by now in the tertiary occupations. This development reflects the transition that has taken place in Canada and other highly developed modern societies from being industrial to becoming post-industrial or post-modern societies.

The biggest shifts have been in the primary and the tertiary occupations. These have been shifting in opposite directions. The shift in the primary occupations represents a rapid movement out of agriculture. In 1901, about 40 percent of the total labour force was engaged in farming; by 1971, only about 6. Since 1951 the fastest growing of all occupational groups have been the professional and the clerical workers. The former have increased from about 7 percent of the total labour force in 1951 to about 13 percent in 1971 and 36 percent in 1991; the latter from about 11 to 16 and to 39 in the same years. In the secondary category, the labouring occupations showed an interesting shift at the turn of the century. Between 1901 and 1911, the unskilled were by far the fastest growing occupational group in Canada. This reflected the great wave of immigration from Southern, Central and Eastern Europe. From 1921 on, however, the secondary labour force was gradually decreasing and has stabilized itself around the 20 percent mark since 1971.

Occupational shifts create and establish the structure of opportunities for ethnic groups, which, in the long run, determine the *ethnic status* of any one group vis-à-vis others, i.e., the place that one or another ethnic group comes to occupy in the societal structure. This place becomes the starting point for each group's process of social mobility. Change of ethnic status becomes one of the fundamental issues in the process of interethnic relations. This will be discussed later in the chapter on ethnic stratification.

Progressive Development of the Economy. Occupational differentiation producing upward shifts in the occupational structure of society has meant a progressive development of the economy. In social terms, this means a progressive creation of more jobs for more people. From the point of view of ethnic group relations, changes in the occupational structure of a society indicate influxes of immigrant labour into society. That is, the greater the occupational differentiation, the greater the need to fill the newly opened job positions. If, however, there are not enough people born in the country to fill all positions, the only way the economy can progress is by inviting immigrants into the country to provide the necessary labour force. In Canada, over the years, the birth rate in the general population has been gradually decreasing and reached its lowest point in Canadian history in the 1980s. Thus the population cannot significantly increase by natural reproduction. The only way that Canada can significantly increase its population is by means of immigration. Immigration becomes necessary for the progressive development of the economy (McVey and Kalbach, 1995: 315). Since 1978, the Canadian parliament has mandated that the number of immigrants to be admitted into the country must be based primarily on economic need. On this basis it determines annually the number of immigrants to be admitted. In the 1990s, this number has been set for 250,000 immigrants per year, although the actual annual intake of immigrants has been somewhat less.

Impersonal Labour Markets and Work Structures. Because of differentiation, most occupations have come to be imbedded in impersonal structures of hiring and in impersonal bureaucratic systems of management of employees. This is not to say that personal relationships have no place in modern societies. On the contrary, they develop their own type of systems, and have a way of infiltrating the bureaucratic institutions. Impersonality, however, has important implications for ethnic group relations. Some of these implications will be discussed later. At this point it is sufficient to say that one important implication is the existence of impersonal labour markets. These give freedom to hire, assign and dismiss employees solely on the principle of productive efficiency. According to this principle, employers can disregard any demands of the employees deriving from their personal or community considerations, and have none other than purely contractual obligations to them. Employees, on the other hand, have no personal or social guarantee of employment and must compete with one another on the basis of their qualifications for potential productivity. They become, as it were, interchangeable units. As a result, in principle, no one ethnic group has an entitlement to any type of employment. In actuality, however, ethnicity often does become a source of consideration in employment and competition often is reduced by various forms of discrimination. But the impersonal principle of the need to possess the necessary qualifications for a job regardless of any community membership can and often is invoked as the rule either by the employers or the prospective employees. From the 1960s on, Canada has established human rights commissions and, in 1981, it imbedded a charter of rights in its constitution that makes it possible for any members of a minority group to appeal in cases of unfair competition.

Increased Labour Force Participation of Women. An important change in modern societies has been the gradual increase of participation of women in the labour force. In particular, this includes a significant increase of participation of married women and women with children. In Canada, in 1941, the ratio of the female to male labour force participation in the age bracket of 15 to 24 was only about 50. In 1991, it was about 94. In the 25 to 64 age bracket, the ratio in 1941 was about 22, but by 1991 it moved up to over 76. Likewise, in 1991, the participation rate of women with children under 6 years was over 80 percent, higher than that of women without children (McVey and Kalbach, 1995: 313-314). These changes show that women's traditional role in society as only a homemaker has dramatically declined. More and more, women have been developing their potential beyond the marriage role. Some of these changes have been driven by economic pressures to supplement the family income or by becoming the main breadwinner of the household, but others by women's increasing interest in becoming economically independent and in pursuing their own career goals.

Changes in the labour force participation of married women have a significant bearing on both the family structure of many ethnic groups and their ethnic status. As will be discussed later, at the stage of their immigration to Canada, many ethnic groups would retain traditional family structures in which the role of women is highly dependent on that of men and involves little power in relation to men. With pressures and inducements to join the labour force, the change of this traditional family structure is often an early step in the process of assimilation. It also can be a factor in the change of an ethnic community's status in the society's system of ethnic stratification.

Mass Consumption and Credit Economy. A feature of mature modern societies that is closely related to the progressive development of the economy is the economies' mass-consumption and credit character. It has been said that Canada had reached the stage of mass consumption by 1959. In the period after 1950, the leading sectors of the economy in Canada shifted towards durable consumer goods and services and Canadians started to enjoy, on a larger scale, the fruits of industrial progress manifested in the benefits of higher standards of living. By 1966 more than 50 percent of all consumer expenditures by Canadians were for non-essential goods and services (Firestone, 1969). A large part of all consumption has been by means of credit so that consumption by credit has now been established as a normal part of the Canadian economy (*Canada Year Book*, 1943, 1965, 1972, 1982). An important consequence of the mass consumption economy is that it standardizes the cultural symbols that make people acceptable or respectable in the eyes of the general societal community. These symbols include such items as dress, foodstuffs, household furnishing and decor, vehicles and the like. For members of ethnic groups coming from diverse cultures, particularly immigrants, this makes possible a rapid assimilation of the cultural externals of their host society. The credit economy makes it possible for people to avail themselves of such symbols, including the symbols of higher social status, even if at any specific time they are financially unable to afford to do so.

Globalization of the Economy. Since the 1970s, Canada's economy has been going through the process of globalization. This has meant that fewer products are made exclusively in Canada, and more products are made up of components manufactured in other countries, often two, three or more countries. Many manufacturing and other business enterprises have become globally organized. This has meant the dispersal of their activities, such as research and development, sourcing, production and marketing, among many different countries. Globalization has also meant a rapid rate of increase of foreign direct investment in Canada, which reached $137 billion in 1992. It has also meant the rapid increase of investment by Canadians in enterprises outside of Canada so that, by 1992, 41 percent of the country's assets, or $99 billion, were invested abroad (*Canada Year Book*, 1994: 598-99).

A number of international trade agreements have created supra-national bodies that make binding decisions regarding many Canadian economic processes. For example, the General Agreement on Tariffs and Trade and the North American Free Trade Agreement (NAFTA) mean that Canada now has to meet the needs, not only of its own citizens, but also many needs of citizens of other countries (*Canada Year Book*, 1994: 423). As a result of NAFTA, many Canadian enterprises have moved south of the border to the United States and Mexico and now Canadian labourers have to compete directly with American and Mexican labourers.

Globalization means also an increased frequency and ease of communication, not only within a country, but also between different countries anywhere in the world. The Internet and electronic mail allows individuals to communicate readily, not only with other individuals within or outside one's country, but also with various societal institutions and vice versa. In this way, some of the difficulties created by the growth of bureaucracy, particularly the so-called "red tape," can, to an extent, be surmounted.

Inasmuch as globalization means greater communication and interaction between citizens of different countries, the implications of globalization for ethnic relations are many and not all of them can be yet foreseen. Globalization has also created greater interdependence between people of different cultures. This requires a recognition of differences among people and a need to accommodate diverse values. There are also implications for international migration. Migration flows within Canada must now be viewed in relation to the migration flows to the United States, to Western Europe and to other countries. Globalization is thus another structural feature that, in addition to its being a modern society, makes Canada a post-modern nation.

Geographical Mobility. A very important feature of modern societies, made possible by the combination of the processes of occupational differentiation, the presence of impersonal labour markets and the progressive development of the economy, are the patterns of geographical mobility of large sectors of populations. Physical shifts of large percentages of a population from one area to another in search of employment have produced both international and national patterns of migration. In modern societies, the availability of jobs attracts people from less developed countries, who have limited and sometimes non-existent occupational opportunities. In addition, highly developed countries, such as North America and Western Europe, have been able to absorb people, who, due to various non-economic, political circumstances, have been forced to leave their homelands.

The physical movements of population within countries have been movements into cities with ever-increasing population concentrations. Thus, while in 1871 only about 18 percent of the Canadian population was considered urban, in 1991 the percentage rose to over 77. Most of those who by 1991 lived in rural areas, however, were a rural non-farm population. Only about 3 percent of the total population in 1991 was actually farm population (McVey and Kalbach, 1995: 146-155). In 1991, about half of all urban Canadians lived in three metropolitan areas, Toronto, Montreal and Vancouver (McVey and Kalbach, 1995: 163). An effect of this process of urbanization has been a high concentration of population with diverse social and cultural backgrounds. This concentration of population, however, has not necessarily meant the integration of all people into one community. To a large extent, it has meant living side by side rather than living together. The usual pattern has been one of segregation of people by residence and personal ties. Closer ties within residential neighbourhoods have tended to segregate along ethnic and class lines. Recently, however, friendship ties have been developing less along residential lines and more within the context of jobs and membership in special interest groups.

A paradox of this diversity is the fact that people in industrialized and urbanized societies share the same external cultural patterns and there is strong social pressure to conform to them. As a result, modern society comes to be characterized by internal heterogeneity, yet external homogeneity. The latter is the fruit of technology, manifested in highly standardized patterns. It is not only the consumer products of industry, such as dress, furniture, automobiles, houses, foodstuffs and so on, that are standardized, but also many patterns of behaviour, such as patterns of work, recreation and even reading habits. Various ethnic groups bring into society and maintain for a period of time diverse customs and patterns of behaviour. This, to an extent, balances the pressures towards uniformity. Still, even though diverse patterns and unique ways of behaviour do exist in highly urbanized societies, they seem to emerge or be maintained in spite of, or sometimes in opposition to, the pressure to conform to the impersonal culture.

Social Mobility. A significant consequence of occupational differentiation has been a development of a diversified *status hierarchy*. In the traditional agricultural society of, say, the eighteenth century, occupational diversity was relatively small, and social class corresponded to such statuses as landowner, farmer, merchant, craftsman, labourer. In Europe, the differences were even more rigid, with peasants as a large class in their own right. Today, however, there is quite a gradation of statuses within each class, corresponding to a diversity of occupations. Indeed, in North American societies today, class boundaries cannot be sharply defined.

Occupational differentiation and progressive development of the economy, in combination, however, make possible another very important modern process in society, namely, social mobility. All stratified societies have had some degree of social mobility, but it is only in modern societies that we can speak of social mobility as taking place on a larger scale. Social mobility has been assessed by sociologists primarily by means of the shifts in the occupational, educational and income composition of society. Of the three indices, occupation is the most important variable. We can speak of vertical and horizontal occupational mobility. *Vertical mobility*, i.e., mobility on a hierarchical status

Photo: Dick Hemingway

Daycare workers taking children to school. Changes in the labour force participation of women have a significant bearing on both the family structure of many ethnic groups and their ethnic status.

ladder, can be either upwards or downwards, i.e. from lower status to higher status occupations and vice versa. *Horizontal mobility* refers to shifts from one type of jobs to another, but on more or less the same status level. Furthermore, we can speak of *generational mobility* and *career mobility*, i.e., shifts in type of occupations from parents to children, and shifts of occupations within one's lifetime.

Although there are variations in the degree of mobility between various specific modern societies, twentieth-century Western societies have shown considerable and roughly comparable rates of social mobility (Lipset, 1959). In Canada, prior to World War II, the process of social mobility was slower than in the United States and in most other Western societies. But the development of the economy and occupational differentiation after the war increased the rate of mobility in Canada very rapidly and made it comparable to that of the United States and other Western societies (Clark, 1976).

In regard to ethnic groups, upward generational mobility is of special interest. The incorporation of ethnic groups into society depends to a great extent on the possibility of the younger members of ethnic communities moving up the status ladder in comparison to their parents. Latent or open interethnic conflict may often be generated when opportunities for either generational or career mobility are either diminished or blocked. It can be stated that, to the extent the opportunities for generational and career mobility exist in society, to that extent the incorporation of minority ethnic groups into said society can proceed. More will be said about this later.

Popular Education. A significant trait of modern societies is the extension of formal education to large proportions of the population. In its less developed stages, it means the elimination of illiteracy and the teaching of elementary knowledge of the sciences and humanities under the requirement of compulsory school attendance up to the age of 16 or so. In its more developed stages, it means the extension of opportunities for post-secondary and higher, university level, education to large portions of the population or to all interested and eligible people in society.

Education in modern societies is seen as a right rather than a privilege. Everyone has a right to it. Hence the responsibility for education is assumed by the government, and education tends to become a public good. Furthermore, education is seen as a social duty. Laws are established requiring children and adolescents to attend school.

Very few contemporary societies outside of selected Western societies have reached the stage where all persons in the population have equal opportunity for higher education. In Canada, the percentage of population attending university has been gradually, but significantly, increasing. In 1951, for example, about 60 percent of all Canadians 15 years of age and over had less than grade 9 education, and only about 2 percent had university education. By 1991, only 14 percent of the population aged 15 and over had less than grade 9 education, 32 percent had at least some post-secondary education including university and over 11 percent had university degrees (*Statistics Canada,* 1992b).

A significant social change is also indicated by a rapid increase in the proportion of women with higher education. In 1971, 6.6 percent of men and 3 percent of women in Canada had a university degree. In 1996, 16.2 percent of all men and 15 percent of all women in Canada had a university degree. But in 1996, for the first time in Canadian history, more than half, 51 percent, of all women in their twenties had some post-secondary degree or diploma, as compared with 42 percent of all men in their twenties. Likewise, in the 1990s more women than men in their twenties would hold university degrees: 20.7 to 16.2 percent in 1996 (*Statistics Canada,* 1998a).

The character of education in modern societies tends to be utilitarian. That is, the educational system functions as a service institution, especially to the economy. The curriculum places a priority on technical competence and emphasizes skills useful for industrial and administrative types of employment. On the other hand, indirectly, secondary and higher education function to ease the pressure on the society's labour market by keeping young people in school for longer periods of time. Finally, education functions as the most important channel of social mobility in society by being an indirect employment channel and by giving children of parents of lower occupational status qualifications for higher status occupations. In 1996, according to the Canadian census, the unemployment rate of Canadians between 25 and 34 years of age who had not graduated from high school was 18 percent. In contrast, the unemployment rate of those in the same age bracket who had completed university was only 4.6 percent. This is of particular importance to ethnic group relations, since education, particularly higher education, has been the main means of ethnic generational mobility.

The Democratic Process. Modern societies have been generally democratic societies. Three factors establish and maintain a well-developed democratic society: (1) representatives of the people, elected at regular intervals; (2) a presence of voluntary associations, representing as many sectors of the population as are able to maintain them, that act as lobbying power groups; and (3) popular media that presents and freely discusses important issues concerning all the sectors of the society's population.

There are many countries in the world where democracy has existed in a very tenuous way. Elections may take place at one time but the incumbent may refuse to hold elections again, or may be removed by a military dictator. This, for example, has for long been the case in many countries, such as, until recently, Chile, Argentina, Haiti, Philippines, many African countries, East European countries and others. In Canada, as in the United States and most Western European countries, regular elections are by now a well-established, taken-for-granted institution. In relation to ethnic groups, at election time, politicians who campaign to be elected cater to what has been known as the "ethnic vote." Many ethnic groups make up electoral constituencies and favour certain political candidates and policies that may meet the groups' interests. Some ethnic groups, through membership in political parties, may champion and promote their own political candidates.

In addition to elections, the democratic process involves other forms of citizen participation. In a well-developed democratic process, citizens may organize voluntary associations to serve as lobbying groups and exert an influence on the government and on society as a whole. As lobbying groups, voluntary associations act on behalf of larger communities whose interests they represent. For example, the labour unions represent the interests of the workers, manufacturers' associations represent the interests of the manufacturing business, medical associations represent the interests of physicians and so on. In a similar manner, ethnic communities organize associations to influence the government and to promote their interests in the broader society. Examples of these are the National Congress of Italian Canadians, the Assembly of First Nations, the National Association of Japanese Canadians, the Canadian Jewish Congress, the Canadian Ukrainian Congress and so on.

This does not mean that all the associations have an equal influence on the government or in society. Some are able to muster more influence than others. The important thing is that the democratic process and the structure of society allow voluntary groups to exert pressure on the government and to influence public opinion. The government itself becomes responsive to the pressure groups to the extent the issues raised by them become the issues on the governmental agenda. For example, if an ethnic organization raises a civil rights issue, is able to involve the public media in its discussion and at the same time consistently exert demands on the government for action, the government is pressed to deal with the issue. In exerting its demands, the group may use a variety of tactics, including such shock tactics as demonstrations and sit-ins and the like. This will be discussed later in further detail. The most successful pressure groups in modern societies have been those representing the interests of occupational class groups, such as the manufacturers' associations and the labour unions. In short, in modern societies, voluntary groups become successful pressure groups when, acting on behalf of larger involuntary groups, they are able to raise issues that come to be seen as relevant for society as a whole.

Closely related to the possibility of organizing pressure groups is the possibility of expressing diverse views in public. In its minimum degree, this means that public institutions, particularly the government, allow without sanction the expression of diverse and disagreeing views on social issues. In its higher degrees, it means that societal groups have access to the influential communications media. In the democratic society, the media is an important resource for whose attention various groups compete. Access to the media is a necessary means used by pressure groups, including ethnic groups, in the pursuit of their goals.

Since the goals and interests of various groups exerting pressure on the government and society often do not coincide, conflicts are inevitable. Conflict of group goals and group interests is a characteristic of modern societies. What provides safeguards against a breakdown of social structure resulting from such conflicts is a system of law responsive to group pressures. In modern societies it is possible to interpret or change the law to accommodate the interests of various groups. In this manner the law is flexible. Those who have more power can move the law farther. There is of course a problem as to how far the law can be moved to accommodate the goals and interests of specific groups and still safeguard the common good. This, however, is beyond the scope of our discussion. The main point here is that, in modern societies, the system of law comes to reflect a variety of group interests. It is precisely on this account that it is an important means of management of intergroup tensions and of resolution of intergroup conflicts.

SALIENT HISTORICAL FEATURES OF THE CANADIAN SOCIAL STRUCTURE

Social structures develop in the process of history. They also change in the same process. Yet some features of social structures tend to remain long after many other features have come to be modified. In Canada, a number of characteristics of the old social structure dating back to the eighteenth century remain and continue to influence the process of ethnic relations. They can be said to provide, as it were, a frame for this process, ensuring its continuity. In what follows, only selected historical features of the Canadian social structure are discussed. They are the features most salient to our understanding of contemporary ethnic group relations. Statistical data about ethnic groups, which will be introduced later, combined with general theoretical propositions, are one important way of understanding the structure and processes of ethnic group relations. Historical backgrounds, however, make it possible to understand the phenomenon, not only as explicable by means of general theoretical propositions, but also as a result of past series of specific events, arrangements, attitudes and policies. Full understanding of the social phenomena is a consequence of the combination of both approaches, the theoretical-statistical and the historical.

• Historical Background: Britain, the Supervised Frontier and Intermeshed Elites

Historically, Canadian social structure depended upon its colonial tie with Britain. The Canadian Anglophone elite, for a long time, was made up and continuously replenished by British-born persons. From the conquest of New France in 1759 until the twentieth century, there was a constant traffic of British governors, colonial officials, soldiers, clergy and teachers, as visitors or as immigrants. This established a strong orientation towards Britain in the political, moral and social life of Canadian society. The elite regarded British institutions as the standard in the development of Canadian institutions. This included not only the political institutions, such as the parliamentary system and the criminal law, but also an intellectual orientation towards English culture. Throughout the nineteenth and a part of the twentieth century, the Canadian British elite identified itself with the British Empire (Underhill, 1964).

The French elite, on the other hand, from the time of the conquest, had been considerably constrained by the English elite. The conquest and the legal acts that followed it, notably the Quebec Act of 1774, induced the French elite to orient themselves almost totally to a "survival" ideology to preserve the French language, culture and the Catholic religion. Until the post-World War II period, the French elite was relatively ineffective in exerting any pace-setting influence on creating new institutions for Canadian society as a whole.

The United States cut itself off from Britain early in the colonial game. As a result, a social structure evolved whose elite was oriented towards its own society and its own indigenous cultural development. The effect of the American Revolution was not simply to intensify the already developing differences between the British and the colonial social structures. The revolution gave an impetus towards development of a social order and culture based on principles essentially different from those imbedded in the British society.

In Canada that impetus never came. Throughout the past two hundred years, the ideals of an individualistic and entrepreneurial democracy influenced Canada only slowly, and in a degree, due to the mingling of the American and Canadian peoples (Hansen, 1970).

The social structure of the Canadian frontier, as compared with the American frontier, likewise did not favour indigenous cultural development. It has been said that one of the most important factors in the formation of the American character and culture was the American expansion to the West. Those who went West in the United States were people who relied entirely on their own individual abilities to survive, upon their physical strength, their cleverness and their gun. There was no law or governmental institutions to rely upon. It was only with time, after the Westward-bound population settled, that the law caught up with them, as it were, that local governments were established, marshals appointed and other institutions like schools and churches developed.

In Canada the frontier developed in a different manner. From the start, it was carefully supervised by the representatives of the established institutions, in particular the government and the church. The military and the clergy went along with the settlers and often they were there even before the settlers arrived. The areas of frontier in Canada were not merely new areas of opportunity for individuals; they were also, and perhaps more important, outposts of the British Empire (Clark, 1962).

In the United States the frontier was a great leveler of political and social loyalties. The breakdown of former attachments and values, disruptive and conflict ridden as the process was, made possible the development of new ones, deriving, to a large extent, from the exigencies of the frontier's physical and social environment. In Canada, the "protective custody" in which the frontier developed tended to check any revolutionary tendencies. It made the frontier settlements more peaceful and organized, but, at the same time, it ensured the continuity and supremacy of the traditional cultural institutions and constrained the development of new ones.

Throughout the nineteenth century until our own day, the Canadian elites have been to a high degree intermeshed. The elites referred to here are primarily persons in the top echelons of politics, economics, governmental bureaucracy, the military, the mass media, education and the church. They have linked together informally through friendship and marriage, i.e., members of one institutional elite would cultivate friendship with, or marry into, another institutional elite. On the formal level, members of different institutional elites have tended to participate together in the same governmental commissions, advisory bodies, councils, directorships and boards (Porter, 1965).

These interrelationships of the elites have their roots in the first 50 years of the nineteenth century in what is known in Canadian history as the *Family Compacts*. These were oligarchies who literally ran the colonial government, and included in close interrelationship the heads of departments in the colonial administration, judges, most barristers, and the bishop or the ranking churchman of the Church of England. Closely associated with them were the leaders of the commercial and banking community (Careless, 1963: 168-175; Mills, 1988).

Although the power of these oligarchies was substantially reduced by the second half of the nineteenth century, the tendency towards elite intermeshing still remains. John Porter (1965), in his 1951 study of the Canadian elite, found a high degree of such intermeshing. Wallace Clement (1975, 1985) confirmed Porter's findings, but discovered that by 1972 the degree of such intermeshing was even higher, both within the corporate business elite itself and between the corporate and state elites. According to him, among 113 dominant corporations in Canada, there were 1,848 interlocked positions on the directorial boards. Of the executives in dominant corporations, 60.3 percent held an outside directorship in at least one of the other 113 top corporations. In addition, 41 percent of the uppermost positions of senior management in the next 175 largest corporations were held by the members of the same elite. A total of 946 individuals resident in Canada held 1,456 of corporate directorships.

Furthermore, 46 percent of all the financiers in the study, and 35 percent of the bankers, had family connections to the corporate elite. Those who switched from one elite to another in their careers were of smaller proportions, yet, according to Clement, this proportion had more than doubled from 1951. About 6 percent of the corporate elite in 1971 were "switchers" from other types of elites, primarily political. What does such elite intermeshing mean for interethnic relations? By means of interlocks, the elite has maintained ethnic homogeneity in its own composition. Historically, there has been little intermeshing between the Anglo-Celtic and the French elites. Clement's data showed that only 8.4 percent of the total corporate elite in 1971 was French and 4.1 was Jewish. Other ethnic groups had virtually no membership at all in the corporate elite. Since W. Clement's research, other researchers have found that the elite system has been changing and more members of other ethnic groups have been joining the ranks of the corporate elites (Ogmundson, 1990; Rich, 1991; Herberg, 1990; Lautard and Guppy, 1990).

Intermeshing of homogeneous ethnic majority-group elites functions to maintain the continuity and dominance of the traditional culture in society. It also has a bearing on the process of incorporation of minority ethnic groups into society. It allows social mobility into non-elite positions, but slows down social mobility into elite positions.

• The Place of Ethnic Groups in Early Canadian Social Structure: Canadian Pluralism

Ethnic groups are constituent of the social structure of both North American societies, Canada and the United States. This means, first of all, that the Canadian or American system of social stratification cannot be fully understood without ethnic stratification. The higher the social status level, the less mixed has been its ethnic composition, with the highest elite levels occupied predominantly by the British groups, and the lowest levels, although historically variable, almost continuously occupied by Native peoples and Blacks. Social mobility in North America has meant a modification of the ethnic stratification system, but largely in the lower to middle to upper-middle strata of society.

This ethnic stratification shift is not unique to North American societies, but in no society in the world has there been such a great variety of ethnic groups intricately interpenetrating the social status and class fabric of society as in Canada and the United States. Consequences of this for the institutional structure and culture of society will be discussed later. The significance of these consequences should not be underestimated since immigration into Canada has been a constant feature of its history and can be expected to continue to be such.

In Canada, however, unlike in the United States, the French-English dualism has formed a basis for all intergroup relations. It has imprinted a stamp on Canada's entire history, so that the relationship of other ethnic groups to Canadian society, with the exception perhaps of Native peoples, has to be understood in relation to this dualism. The root of this dualism was, of course, the conquest of New France. Ever since the conquest, French Canadians have struggled to preserve their own identity and to gain a measure of equality vis-à-vis the British. This struggle, however, has had implications beyond the French-English relationship. The Canadian government's policies in relation to other ethnic groups have been affected by this struggle.

After the conquest, the British attempted to incorporate the French into the new colonial society with as little conflict as possible. To this effect, the British passed the Quebec Act in 1774. The Act did two things. It provided public recognition of the French as a group with community rights, and it legitimized the processes of maintaining ethnic identity. Thus, matters of religion, education, language and culture were recognized as legitimately belonging to the French themselves and outside of the purview of the British colonial government (Neatby, 1972). It should be remembered that, for a period of more than two hundred years, continental Europe in its intergroup relations used the principle of *cujus regio eius religio* (whose rule, his religion) to impose the religion of the ruling parties upon the territories they ruled. The policies of the Quebec Act did not follow this principle.

The Quebec Act represented a form of pluralism. Whatever the long-term intentions of governor Carleton (who introduced the Act in Quebec) were, in its consequences the Act gave official recognition to the principle of ethnic pluralism in Canada. The same type of pluralism was reflected in the British North America Act of 1867, in which control of civil rights and especially education, jealously guarded by the French, remained in the hands of French Quebec, and by the same principle, in the hands of all the other provinces.

It can be argued that the pluralism by which an ethnic group dominated by another ethnic group retains and is legally guaranteed the right to maintain its culture was a rational outcome of a confrontation of two different ways of life. As Arthur Lower (1946) described it, the French peasantry duplicated in North America the pre-Reformation peasant society of the old world. To the rural Catholic, life was more than livelihood. It was "a series of ritual acts such as being born, becoming of age, marrying, begetting children, dying, each of which properly performed, brought its satisfactions and its reward." To the English merchants who came into Quebec with the conquest, life was a busy striving to gain individual ends motivated by a passion of greed. This type of greed, however, was not an ordinary human quality, but was something "erected into a way of life and fortified both with the majesty of law and the sanction of a religion." The early British governors of Canada, James Murray and Guy Carleton, both followed a policy of pluralism in regard to the French. They assumed that, although under the British rule, Canada would continue to be French, and its language and institutions would remain French.

This variety of pluralism, however, can also be seen as a case of the British pattern of "indirect rule" over colonies, a pattern followed in the British African and Asian colonies (Ossenberg, 1967; Crowder, 1978; Guindon, 1988: 40-42). According to this pattern, a policy of non-assimilation makes possible a more rational yet more effective control over potential tensions arising from cultural differences by containing the demands of the differing cultural groups within the bounds of pre-established autonomies. Thus, preservation of Native cultures or preservation of the indigenous social structure, e.g., the indigenous elite, ensures that the same rights as those possessed by the people of the colonizing country will not be extended to the indigenous people and that the two social orders, that of the dominant group and that of the subordinate group, will remain apart.

The reserve structure established for the Native peoples, first by the French in the seventeenth century and later maintained by the British and by the Canadian government since the beginning of Confederation, manifested the specific character of the pluralism. The right to possession and use of Native peoples' land on their reserves was until recently defined by the Crown as an "unsufructory right." That is, the possession and use of the land was always subject to surrender to and extinguishment by the Crown. Notwithstanding the fact that Native peoples were the original occupants of the lands, the Crown has always held the underlying title to them and therefore has been entitled to extinguish the Native right to them even without the Native peoples' consent. In other words, the Native peoples' relation to their land has always been dependent upon the good will of the Crown (Macklem, 1993). This has given Canadian pluralism a temporal quality, implying that differences are tolerated until the different groups assimilate, and hence the ultimate aim of pluralism is assimilation.

The character of Canadian pluralism was also influenced by the group-settlement of the Prairies. From the last quarter of the nineteenth century until the beginning of World War I, many immigrants settled Western Canada not individually but as communities, thus forming bloc settlements. Since the overwhelming majority of immigrants to the Prairies were of rural origin, settling in blocs in an uninhabited rural environment was a rational course of action. But this was also a process of community transplantation that could ensure longer retention of the community's language and culture. The groups who settled in the Prairies thus were the Doukhobors, Hutterites, Mennonites, Mormons, German Catholics, French Canadians, Scottish, Scandinavians, Icelanders, Ukrainians, Polish and Russians (Dawson, 1936).

The group settlement of the Prairies was a result of both the wishes of the ethnic groups themselves and of government policies. Such groups as the Mennonites, Doukhobors and Mormons already had a tradition of living as an agricultural minority community within a larger society, and hence their group settlement was a continuation of this tradition. For the others, kinship, community, cultural ties and pragmatic considerations conditioned preferences to settle in physical proximity. In the last quarter of the nineteenth century and the first decade of the twentieth century, the Canadian government favoured a policy of ethnic group settlement of the Prairies. But the idea of group settlement already existed in the colonial times. In the late 1840s, Canadian colonial government considered agricultural group settlements of the Irish and might have carried it out had it not been uneconomical and impractical at that time (Elliott, 1988).

After 1874, ethnic diversity began to play a significant role in Prairie settlement. In that year, reservations were made for French Canadians repatriated from the New England states, and in the following 10 years, they formed 10 settlements in the West. From 1875 to 1876, an Icelandic colony was formed on the west shore of Lake Winnipeg. There were also many "nominal reservations" made, i.e., reservations without exclusive right to entry to allocated territory, for groups from England, Scotland, the Scandinavian countries, Germany, Belgium and others. The government had definite preconceptions as to what type of settlers the East Europeans would make. The government wanted stability of population in the Prairies, and the East Europeans were seen as and defined as farmers, whose forefathers had been farmers, who themselves would be farmers and whose children would remain on farms (Yuzyk, 1953: 40).

This recognition of "functional" ethnic pluralism was also related to the English-French relations factor. In parliament, the group-settlement immigration policy was attacked by the French Canadians as an attempt to preclude the French from settling in the West, in order to swing the population balance against the French. Unlike in the United States, in Canada the government has always played a very direct and active role in bringing over immigrants. Until near the end of the nineteenth century, the main focus of Canadian immigration policies was population development.

ETHNIC COMPOSITION OF CANADIAN POPULATION

Prior to and including 1971, the Canadian census data on the ethnic origin of the population was based on the question: "To what ethnic or cultural group did you or your ancestor (on the male side) belong on coming to this continent?" The question asked for ethnic ancestry only on one's father's side. After 1971, this measure of ascertaining ethnic origin was criticized for including a bias in favour of males. Critics argued that if the question asked for ethnic origin on the female side of the family, the statistical results would be different. Furthermore, the measure was criticized for failing to give any picture at all of the ethnically mixed origins of the Canadian population. The critics attested that, after so many years of continuous immigration to Canada, the Canadian population was significantly ethnically intermarried and the census should be able to show the population's mixed origin. Finally, some critics pointed out that ethnic origin is not really a biological question of one's ancestry, but rather a question of subjective identity, and many respondents may choose to identify with either the group on their father's or their mother's side or they may choose not to identify with any ethnic group at all. The census hence should measure, not so much the objective fact of one's ancestry, as the subjective fact of one's identity.

In response to this criticism, Statistics Canada changed the ethnic-origin question in the 1981 census and modified it further for both the 1991 and the 1996 censuses. In 1991 and 1996 the question read simply: "To which ethnic or cultural group(s) did this person's [your] ancestors belong?" Phrased this way, the question allows the respondents to choose either their father's or mother's side, depending on how strongly they subjectively identify with each. The question also allows the respondents to list multiple responses, i.e., their ethnic origin on both their father's and mother's side. Likewise, the question allows the respondents to record the ethnic group with which they subjectively identify, without reference to the real ancestry on either side of their parents, but with reference to the symbolic ancestors of the ethnic group. The question thus measures either or both the subjective and the objective aspects of a person's ethnicity.

The assessment of ethnic origin was further complicated in the 1996 census by a new question format, different examples of the answer to be given, different instructions to respondents and a different method of data processing. The 1991 census included 15 mark-in categories and two write-in spaces for the ethnic origin question. In 1996, respondents were required to write in their ethnic origin or origins in four write-in spaces. Twenty four examples, including "Canadian," were provided. In 1991, "Canadian" was not one of the mark-in categories. The respondents who reported this ethnicity wrote it in the two spaces provided.

As a result, the tables that summarize these responses cannot be interpreted in a simple way. It is particularly difficult to compare the results of the ethnic origin question from the 1981, 1991 and 1996 censuses with the results from all previous censuses. Likewise, it can be problematic to compare the results from the 1991 and 1996 censuses. Comparisons can still be made in terms of the broader ethnic categories, but this difficulty should be kept in mind. We will present both sets of results here from the 1991 and the 1996 censuses. Most of our analysis in the succeeding chapters will be made in terms of the 1991 census.

Table 2 presents the answers to the ethnic-origin question for the 1996 census, and Table 3 and 4, to the 1991 census.

Ethnic Origin. Tables 2 and 3 show that in 1991 almost one-third (28.9 percent) and in 1996 a little more than one-third (35.8 percent) of the Canadian population reported multiple ethnic origins, evidence that a substantial number of Canadians identify with more than one ethnic group. In 1991, among those who reported single

Table 2: Canadian Population by Ethnic Origin: Single and Combined Single and Multiple Origin Responses, Canada 1996

Ethnic Origin Groups and Categories	Single Origin Responses (Descending Order)	Percent Single Origin in Total Population	Combined Single and Multiple Origin Responses	Percent of Combined Origin
Canadian	5,326,995	18.7	8,806,275	22.0
French	2,665,250	9.3	5,597,845	14.0
English	2,048,275	7.2	6,832,095	17.1
Chinese	800,470	2.8	921,585	2.3
Italian	729,455	2.6	1,207,475	3.0
German	726,145	2.5	2,757,140	6.9
Scottish	642,970	2.3	4,260,840	10.6
South Asian	590,145	2.0	723,345	1.8
Irish	504,030	1.8	3,767,610	9.4
Aboriginal	477,630	1.7	1,101,955	2.8
Ukrainian	331,680	1.2	1,026,475	2.6
Dutch	313,880	1.1	916,215	2.3
Polish	265,930	0.9	786,735	2.0
Portuguese	252,640	0.9	335,110	0.8
Philippine	198,420	0.7	242,880	0.6
Jewish	195,810	0.7	351,705	0.9
Greek	144,940	0.5	203,345	0.5
Jamaican	128,570	0.5	188,770	0.5
Hungarian	94,185	0.3	250,525	0.6
Spanish	72,470	0.3	204,360	0.5
Norwegian	47,805	0.2	346,310	0.9
Russian	46,885	0.2	272,335	0.7
Swedish	31,200	0.1	278,975	0.7
Welsh	27,915	0.1	338,905	0.8
American	22,085	0.1	211,790	0.5
Other	1,617,845	5.6	N/A	
Total Single Origin Responses	18,303,625	64.4		
Multiple Origin Responses	10,224,500	35.8		
Total Combined Origin Response			39,999,750*	100.0
Total Population	28,528,125	100.0		

* Since the number of other ethnic groups in the combined category is not available (fall 1998), this may not be an accurate figure. Since this column includes multiple origin responses, the total number does not correspond to the total Canadian population.
Source: Statistics Canada. 1998. *Census 1996*, Internet Catalogue No. 93F0026XDB96002

Table 3: Canadian Population by Ethnic Origin: Single and Combined Single and Multiple Origin Responses, Canada 1991

Ethnic Origin Categories*	Single Origin Responses (Descending Order)	Percent Single Origin in Total Population	Combined Single and Multiple Origin Responses	Percent of Combined Origins
French	6,146,600	22.8	8,389,180	24.5
British	5,611,050	20.8	12,047,920	35.3
Southern European	1,379,030	5.1	1,981,905	5.8
Western European	1,355,485	5.0	3,751,685	11.0
East & South East Asian	961,225	3.6	1,067,065	3.1
Eastern European	946,810	3.5	2,177,410	6.4
Canadian	765,095	2.8	1,033,030	3.0
Aboriginal	470,615	1.7	1,002,675	2.9
South Asian	420,290	1.6	488,370	1.4
Other European	251,140	0.9	381,405	1.1
Black	224,620	0.8	351,665	1.0
Northern European	213,605	0.8	805,555	2.4
Arab	144,050	0.5	194,880	0.6
Caribbean	94,395	0.4	166,620	0.5
Latin, Central & South	85,535	0.3	119,980	0.4
West Asian	81,660	0.3	97,975	0.3
African	26,430	0.1	39,610	0.1
Pacific Islands	7,210	0.02	11,815	0.03
Other Origins	14,945	0.06	64,140	0.2
Total Single Origin Responses	19,199,790	71.1		
Multiple Origin Responses	7,794,255	28.9		
Total Combined Origin Responses			34,172,885**	100.0
Total Population	26,994,045	100.0		

Note: The single and multiple origins totals for the various ethnic groups in Tables 3 and 7 may not correspond exactly because of selective inclusions and deletions within categories by Statistics Canada in each table and because of computer rounding-off. For details, please refer to the original tables published by Statistics Canada and to the explanatory notes included with the original tables.

* To locate specific ethnic groups within the categories of groups refer to Table 4.
** Note that since this column includes multiple origin response the total number does not correspond to the total Canadian population.
Source: Statistics Canada. 1993. *Census 91–Ethnic Origin: The Nation.* Catalogue No. 93-315, Table 2A. Ottawa: Minister of Industry, Science and Technology.

Table 4: Ethnic Categories and Groups, Canadian Census, 1991

	Single Responses	Multiple Responses
BRITISH ORIGINS		
English	3,958,405	4,646,720
Irish	725,660	3,057,695
Scottish	893,125	3,355,240
Welsh	28,190	169,665
Other British	5,670	14,105
WESTERN EUROPEAN ORIGINS		
Austrian	27,135	66,780
Belgian	31,475	59,435
Dutch (Netherlands)	358,180	603,415
Flemish	3,010	7,825
German	911,560	1,882,220
Luxembourg	520	1,465
Swiss	23,610	52,700
NORTHERN EUROPEAN ORIGINS		
Finnish	39,230	59,865
Danish	40,640	94,880
Icelandic	14,555	48,785
Norwegian	63,035	223,200
Swedish	43,350	193,310
Scandinavian	12,800	29,380
FRENCH ORIGINS		
French	6,129,680	2,239,535
Acadian	10,345	12,825
Québécois	6,575	4,985
SOUTHERN EUROPEAN ORIGINS		
Albanian	1,550	1,015
Bulgarian	4,750	3,840
Croatian	41,550	11,045
Macedonian	14,030	7,005
Serbian	13,085	3,820
Slovenian	8,050	3,465
Yugoslav	48,420	40,905
Cypriot	1,300	500
Greek	151,150	40,330
Italian	750,055	397,720
Maltese	15,520	10,045
Portuguese	246,890	45,295
Spanish	82,675	76,235
OTHER EUROPEAN ORIGINS		
Basque	495	1,340
Jewish	245,840	123,725
Other European	4,805	5,595
ABORIGINAL ORIGINS		
Inuit	30,090	19,165
Métis	75,150	137,500
North American Indian	365,375	418,605
CANADIAN ORIGIN	765,095	267,935
EASTERN EUROPEAN ORIGINS		
Estonian	12,940	8,315
Latvian	11,495	8,950
Lithuanian	15,180	17,335
Byelorussian	1,015	1,815
Czech	21,190	25,985
Czechoslovakian	21,990	32,040
Slovak	15,945	13,405
Hungarian	100,725	112,975
Polish	272,805	467,905
Romanian	28,655	45,405
Russian	38,220	120,630
Ukrainian	406,645	647,650
ARAB ORIGINS		
Egyptian	18,950	6,475
Iraqi	3,525	1,265
Lebanese	74,250	27,440
Moroccan	5,005	2,315
Maghrebi	3,920	1,665
Palestinian	4,050	1,680
Syrian	7,080	5,955
Arab	27,270	11,640
WEST ASIAN ORIGINS		
Afghan	5,875	455
Armenian	26,005	7,280
Iranian	38,915	4,295
Israeli	755	1,095
Kurdish	1,175	255
Turk	8,525	3,525
West Asian	410	355

	Single Responses	Multiple Responses
CARIBBEAN ORIGINS		
Barbadian	1,600	2,545
Cuban	660	1,080
Guyanese	16,760	9,675
Haitian	22,885	21,095
Jamaican	20,910	15,595
Trinidadian & Tobagonian	8,935	6,340
West Indian	18,820	12,710
Other Caribbean	3,825	5,885
PACIFIC ISLANDS ORIGINS		
Fijian	6,670	2,175
Polynesian	545	2,490
LATIN, CENTRAL & SOUTH CENTRAL AMERICAN ORIGINS		
Argentinian	3,090	2,025
Brazilian	2,520	2,325
Chilean	12,800	3,650
Colombian	3,105	1,255
Ecuadorian	2,700	660
Guatemalan	3,855	1,035
Hispanic	5,655	1,465
Mexican	8,015	8,445
Nicaraguan	3,210	875
Peruvian	4,925	2,210
Salvadorean	12,440	2,345
Uruguayan	1,470	505
Other Latin/Central South American	21,740	11,075
EAST & SOUTH EAST ASIAN ORIGINS		
Chinese	586,645	66,000
Filipino	157,250	17,725
Burmese	585	635
Cambodian	16,940	1,675
Laotian	13,365	1,475
Thai	1,645	1,125
Vietnamese	84,010	10,245
Indonesian	2,215	3,295
Japanese	48,595	17,085
Korean	44,100	1,790
Malay	1,720	2,000
Other Asian	4,175	1,755

	Single Responses	Multiple Responses
SOUTH ASIAN ORIGINS		
Bengali	1,200	320
Punjabi	20,960	6,340
Sinhalese	980	475
Tamil	8,690	7,005
Bangladeshi	4,790	380
East Indian	324,845	54,435
Pakistani	35,685	7,465
Sri Lankan	23,150	8,285
AFRICAN ORIGINS		
Ethiopian	6,955	1,805
Somali	7,080	1,990
Other African	12,400	9,850
BLACK ORIGINS		
Black	214,270	124,020
African Black	6,715	8,490
Ghanaian	3,630	1,545
OTHER ORIGINS		
American	11,000	38,390
Australian/New Zealander	3,195	10,495
Other	745	310

Source: Statistics Canada. *Ethnic Origin: The Nation.* Table 2A 1991 Census. Ottawa: Industry, Science & Technology Canada 1993. 1991. Census of Canada. Catalogue No. 93-315.

Table 5: Selected Ethnic Origins of the Canadian Population by Census Years, 1961, 1971, 1981, 1991

Ethnic Group	1901	1921	1951	1971	1991†
	%	%	%	%	%
TOTAL PERCENT**	100.0	100.0	100.0	100.0	100.0
BRITISH	57.0	55.4	47.9	44.6	28.7
English	23.5	29.0	25.9	29.0	20.3
Irish	18.4	12.6	10.3	7.3	3.7
Scottish	14.9	13.3	11.0	8.0	4.5
Other	0.2	0.5	0.7	0.4	0.2
FRENCH	30.7	27.9	30.8	28.7	31.4
OTHER EUROPEAN	8.5	14.2	18.3	22.9	21.2
Austrian[a]	0.2	1.2	0.2	0.2	0.1
Belgian	*	0.2	0.2	0.2	0.2
Czech & Slovak	-	0.1	0.5	0.4	0.3
Danish	-	0.2	0.3	0.3	0.2
Finnish[b]	*	0.2	0.3	0.3	0.2
German	5.8	3.3	4.4	6.1	0.6
Greek	*	*	0.1	0.6	0.7
Hungarian[c]	*	0.1	0.4	0.6	0.5
Icelandic	-	0.2	0.2	0.1	0.1
Italian	0.2	0.8	1.1	3.4	3.8
Jewish	-.3	1.4	1.3	1.4	1.2
Lithuanian	-	-	0.1	0.1	0.1
Netherlander	0.6	1.3	1.9	2.0	-
Norwegian	-	0.8	0.8	0.8	0.3
Polish	0.1	0.6	1.6	1.5	1.4
Romanian[d]	*	0.1	0.2	0.1	0.1
Russian	0.4	1.1	0.6	0.3	0.2
Scandinavian[e]	0.6	-	-	-	0.1
Swedish	-	0.7	0.7	0.5	0.2
Ukrainian	0.1	1.2	2.8	2.7	2.1
Yugoslavic	-	*	0.1	0.5	0.2
Other	0.1	0.2	0.2	0.9	4.3
ASIAN	0.4	0.7	0.5	1.3	9.2
Chinese	0.3	0.4	0.2	0.6	3.0
Japanese	*	0.2	0.1	0.2	2.5
Other	*	0.1	0.1	0.6	3.7
OTHER ORIGINS	3.3	1.7	2.5	2.4	9.4
Aboriginal & Inuit	2.4	1.3	1.2	1.5	2.4
Black	0.3	0.2	0.1	0.2	1.5
Other, not stated	0.6	0.2	1.2	0.8	5.8
TOTAL N	5,371,315	8,787,949	14,009,429	21,568,310	19,536,495

Sources: Statistics Canada, *Census of Canada 1971, Vol. 1 Part 3, Bulletin 1.3-2,* October 1973—Tables 1 and 2; D. Kubat and D. Thorton, *Statistical Profile of Canadian Society.* Toronto: McGraw-Hill Ryerson Ltd., 1974, pp.25-27; Statistics Canada. *Census of Canada 1991, The Nation: Ethnic Origin*, Table 1A, Catalogue No. 93-315.

† Note: All data based on "Single Responses" for all Census dates reported. "Total" category for 1991 does not indicate the total population for that year due to exclusion of category "Multiple Responses." 1991 Census data may not be exactly comparable to the data in previous censuses due to revision of the Ethnic Origin question in that census.

[a] Not otherwise specified; for 1901, includes Bohemian, Bukovinian and Slavic.
[b] Includes Estonian prior to 1951.
[c] Includes Lithuanian and Moravian for 1901.
[d] Includes Hungarian for 1901.
[e] Since 1921 listed under Danish, Finnish, Icelandic, Swedish.
*Less than one-tenth of 1 percent.

** Percentages may not add up to 100 (or to total percentages) because of computer rounding.

origins only, the largest groups were the French, at 22.8 percent of the total Canadian population, and the British, at 20.8 percent of the total Canadian population. This is followed by Southern Europeans, at 5.1 percent, Western Europeans, at 5.0 percent, East and Southeast Asians, at 3.6 percent, and then others in smaller proportions. Aboriginal peoples giving single responses, including the Inuit, Métis and Canadian Indian, make up 1.7 percent of the total population.

If, however, we look, not at the total Canadian population, but at the total number of responses identifying different origins, and keeping in mind the fact that many people report more than one ethnic origin (columns 3 and 4 in Table 2 and columns 3 and 4 in Table 3), then the percentages divide differently. The largest proportion of all ethnic origin responses in Canada in 1991 was given by the British, at 35.3 percent, followed by the French, at 24.5 percent, followed by Western Europeans (excluding the British and French), at 11 percent, Eastern Europeans, at 6.4 percent, and Southern Europeans, at 5.8 percent. All other categories of groups make up the remaining 17 percent with no single category making up more than 3.1 percent of the total ethnic origin responses.

The 1996 census, however, presents a different picture. The publicly released data (Table 2) identifies a number of specific ethnic groups but it intermixes them with several categories of ethnic groups (South Asian, Aboriginal). Of those who in 1996 reported single ethnic origin only, the largest group is "Canadian," at 18.7 percent. It is followed by the British, at 11.4 percent, if we add up all four groups of the British Isles, of which English are the largest group, at 7.2 percent, French, at 9.3 percent, Chinese, at 2.8 percent, Italian, at 2.6 percent, German, at 2.5 percent, South Asian, at 2 percent and the Aboriginal at 1.7 percent.

Again, if we look at the combined single and multiple ethnic origin responses for 1996, the picture looks different. As in 1991, the single largest category are the British, at 37.9 percent, but this time they are followed by the "Canadian" group, at 22.0 percent, and then the French, at 14.0 percent, German, at 6.9 percent, Italian, at 3.0 percent, Aboriginal, at 2.8 percent, Ukrainian, at 2.6 percent, and then the other.

What the two tables show is that the number of the multiple origin responses increased from 1991 to 1996. This is partly a function of the new format of the ethnic origin question in the census questionnaire. It does show, however, that a rather large proportion of the Canadian population, about 36 percent, is made up of people of mixed ethnic backgrounds.

The census data also show that the British make up the largest proportion of all origins, but no single ethnic group has a numerical majority in the Canadian population. In this regard Canada is not alone. As was pointed out in the introductory chapter, 13 percent of the world's nation-states have populations in which no one ethnic group encompasses more than 50 percent of the country's population (Table 1).

The "Canadian" ethnicity became quite prominent in the 1996 census. The large increase in the number of "Canadian" origin responses since 1991, however, is puzzling. Partly, again, this increase is a function of the new format of the ethnic origin question in the census questionnaire. Statistics Canada (1998b) cautions about the interpretation of the "Canadian response." According to them, the increase in the reporting of "Canadian" ethnic origin has impacted on the reporting of single ethnic origin of many groups, but particularly that of the British and the French. This raises the question as to what the designation "Canadian" meant to different respondents of the census questionnaire. It is possible that to some respondents of British origin, the name is synonymous with that of "British." Further, since the French respondents, especially those in Quebec, probably used the French version of the census questionnaire, the word "Canadien" might not have meant the same thing to them as to the other groups. We know that historically for many people in Quebec the word has conveyed the meaning of the "original Canadians," i.e., the French. Finally, since the respondents had at least four blank spaces to write in their ethnicity, many might have put down "Canadian" not as an ethnic designation, but as a political designation, referring to being part of the Canadian state. This does not exclude any other ethnicity. All this makes it difficult to interpret the census statistics. The shifts in the way the census questions are asked from one census to another indicates also that the census is subject, not only to methodological rules of scientific accuracy, but also to political influences.

Changes over time. Table 5 presents selected ethnic origins of the Canadian population as reported in five Canadian censuses from 1901 to 1991. One can compare the data over this period of time for changes in the proportions of any one ethnic group in relation to any other ethnic group or a category of groups in relation to other categories. Note that for 1991 the data is based on single origin responses only. The data exclude multiple ethnic origin responses altogether. This does not make the data comparable with previous censuses, but it gives some indication of proportional differences.

Table 6: Ethnic Group Distribution by Province, Canada, 1991

Ethnic Origin	Total for Canada	Nfld	PEI	NS	NB	Que	Ont	Man	Sask	Alb	BC	Yukon	NWT
Percent	100.0	%	%	%	%	%	%	%	%	%	%	%	%
Total Population	**26,994,045**	**2.1**	**0.5**	**3.3**	**2.6**	**25.2**	**36.9**	**3.9**	**3.6**	**9.3**	**12.0**	**0.1**	**0.2**
Single Origins													
British	5,611,050	7.8	1.0	6.9	4.2	5.0	45.2	3.2	2.8	8.7	14.4	0.1	0.1
French	6,146,600	0.2	0.2	0.8	3.8	82.6	8.5	0.8	0.4	1.2	1.1	-	-
Canadian	765,095	0.2	0.1	1.2	1.2	2.6	68.7	2.0	3.8	12.1	7.9	0.1	0.1
Western European	1,355,485	0.1	0.1	2.5	0.5	4.0	37.0	9.2	10.1	18.3	17.5	0.1	0.1
Northern European	213,600	0.2	0.1	0.7	0.7	1.8	24.2	6.9	11.4	22.6	30.5	0.2	0.1
Eastern European	946,810	0.1	-	0.5	0.1	6.4	41.3	11.2	8.9	17.8	13.2	0.1	0.1
Southern European	1,379,030	0.1	-	0.4	0.2	21.0	65.4	1.6	0.4	3.7	7.1	-	-
Other European	251,140	-	-	0.6	0.2	31.2	53.4	4.9	0.5	2.3	5.5	-	-
Arab	144,050	0.2	0.2	1.8	0.5	43.8	40.9	0.6	0.4	8.8	2.6	-	-
West Asian	81,660	0.1	-	0.4	0.3	28.6	53.6	1.2	0.5	3.7	11.1	-	-
South Asian	420,295	0.2	-	0.5	0.2	6.9	55.2	2.1	0.7	9.5	24.6	-	-
East and South East Asian	961,225	0.1	-	0.3	0.2	8.8	46.6	4.2	1.2	11.9	26.4	-	0.1
African	26,430	0.1	0.1	0.7	0.1	10.2	69.6	2.4	2.1	7.1	7.2	-	-
Pacific Islands	7,215	-	-	0.3	-	0.3	6.2	0.3	-	19.3	73.2	0.2	-
Latin, Central & South American	85,535	-	0.1	0.4	0.1	33.0	43.6	3.4	1.3	8.3	9.4	-	-
Caribbean	94,395	0.1	-	0.2	0.1	28.3	63.4	1.8	0.3	3.8	1.8	-	-
Black	224,620	-	-	4.8	0.5	18.3	67.1	2.0	0.5	4.1	2.6	-	-
Aboriginal	470,615	1.1	0.1	1.6	0.9	13.9	15.1	15.8	14.1	15.4	15.8	0.8	6.3
Other	14,940	0.2	0.1	0.6	0.5	7.4	41.9	2.1	4.2	18.6	23.7	0.3	0.2
Multiple Responses	7,794,250	1.3	0.7	4.6	2.7	7.3	42.0	5.3	5.4	13.7	16.6	0.2	0.2

Source: Statistics Canada, Census 1991, *The Nation: Ethnic Origin,* Table 1A, Catalogue No. 93-315.
Note: "-" indicates small numbers not listed in the 1991 census.

Table 7: Selected Ethnic Origins Showing Single and Multiple Responses by Age Groups, Canada, 1991

Ethnic Group	Total		Total	Less than 15 years		15-24 years		25-44 years		45-64 years		65 years and over	
	Single	Multiple	% *	Single	Multiple	Single	Multiple	Single	Multiple	Single	Multiple	Single	Multiple
British	5,605,380	11,229,320	100	15.7	30.4	12.3	16.4	31.8	32.4	22.7	14.1	17.2	6.6
French	6,140,030	2,252,355	100	19.1	34.2	13.2	17.7	35.3	32.4	21.8	11.4	10.6	4.2
Canadian	765,095	267,935	100	25.6	26.6	15.4	15.2	34.8	33.8	17.1	16.8	6.9	7.1
Western European	1,351,955	2,664,550	100	11.6	36.5	11.3	17.8	33.7	30.4	28.0	11.1	15.3	4.1
Northern European	213,595	649,425	100	6.1	36.0	8.1	17.8	30.0	32.0	32.0	11.4	24.0	2.0
Eastern European	945,800	1,500,615	100	9.2	37.8	8.9	17.8	33.3	32.6	26.7	8.6	21.6	2.9
Southern European	1,363,360	632,405	100	14.7	43.5	16.5	18.4	33.4	27.8	25.8	7.9	9.4	2.1
Other European	245,840	123,725	100	19.1	30.8	11.6	14.8	29.4	32.9	20.1	14.5	19.6	6.8
Arab	120,470	45,555	100	24.2	41.4	15.6	17.5	37.2	29.0	17.2	9.6	5.7	2.3
West Asian	64,925	11,575	100	20.0	42.2	12.5	16.3	40.0	27.4	18.0	10.8	8.0	3.1
South Asian	404,640	76,515	100	25.4	34.9	15.4	18.5	36.4	30.8	18.3	12.4	4.5	3.4
East and South East Asian	950,895	116,005	100	21.0	45.0	15.0	19.9	39.7	24.6	16.6	8.2	7.2	2.1
African	12,400	9,850	100	21.1	31.8	16.7	18.1	41.4	32.3	17.3	13.8	3.1	4.0
Latin, Central and South America	46,980	17,065	100	27.7	43.4	18.2	14.6	39.9	31.4	11.7	8.3	2.5	2.3
Caribbean	79,375	59,085	100	24.5	31.5	17.4	17.8	36.9	32.6	16.8	14.1	4.4	4.0
Black	214,265	124,020	100	26.5	34.4	18.8	18.2	34.3	31.3	16.4	12.8	4.0	3.2
Aboriginal	470,610	575,275	100	34.5	37.5	18.3	18.3	30.2	33.1	12.0	9.0	4.0	2.0
Other Origins	11,000	38,395	100	9.5	27.8	9.7	14.0	36.9	32.5	25.3	17.2	18.6	8.5

Note: The single and multiple origins totals for the various ethnic groups in Tables 3 and 7 may not correspond exactly because of selective inclusions and deletions within categories by Statistics Canada in each table and because of computer rounding-off. For details, please refer to the original tables published by Statistics Canada and to the explanatory notes included with the original tables.

Source: Statistics Canada, Census 1991, *The Nation: Ethnic Origin*, Table 3—Selected Ethnic Origins and Sex, Showing Single and Multiple Responses by Age Groups for Canada, Provinces and Territories, Catalogue No. 93-315.
* Note: percentages do not add up to 100% due to rounding.

Several significant features of the shifts in the ethnic composition of the population in the past almost one hundred years stand out. The proportion of the British in the total population has been gradually declining, while the proportion of the French has kept more or less the same level. Europeans other than English and French have shown a gradual but steady increase in proportion. In 1901, they made up only 8.5 percent of the total population. By 1921 the proportion increased to 14.2, due mainly to the large immigration numbers from Central, Southern and Eastern Europe in the first decade of the century. The proportion gradually climbed to 18.3 in 1951 and 22.9 in 1971 and leveled off in the 1980s. This was due mainly to the emergence of a new factor in Canadian immigration, an increased rate of immigration from Asia. In 1991, the other Europeans made up more or less 21.2 percent of the population. The most significant increase, particularly in the last 40 years, was in the Asian category. Although small in comparison with the other categories, the proportion of Asians more than doubled from 1951 (0.4 percent) to 1971 (1.3 percent) and between 1971 and 1991, it appears to have increased seven times to 9.2 percent.

Another significant shift can be seen in the British category itself. Although the proportion of the total British category has been declining, the significant decline has taken place among the Scottish and the Irish rather than the English. In 1971, the English reached an all-time high of 29 percent, comparable only to the year of 1921. For the Irish, the decline has been quite pronounced, from 18.4 percent in 1901 to 7.3 percent in 1971 and an all-time low of 3.7 percent in 1991. For the Scottish, the decline has been more moderate, but still quite definite, from 14.9 percent in 1901 to 8.0 in 1971 and also an all-time low of 4.5 percent in 1991.

The sociological implications of these shifts do not indicate a dramatically different numerical position of the English group itself in Canada. They do, however, indicate the increasingly greater role of the non-British and non-French ethnic groups in Canadian society. This especially appears to be true of the Asian groups.

Regional concentrations. Table 6 shows how ethnic groups were distributed geographically by provinces in Canadian society in 1991. Only small percentages of any one ethnic group reside in either the Maritimes or the Yukon and Northwest Territories. All other groups are spread throughout mainly six provinces. To most ethnic groups, the most attractive provinces are Ontario, Quebec, British Columbia, Alberta, Manitoba and Saskatchewan, in that order. By far the most attractive province to the different ethnic groups is Ontario. With the exception of 4 categories of ethnic groups (Northern Europeans, Arabs, Pacific Islanders and Aboriginal) all other 15 categories of ethnic groups reported by the census have the highest percentages of population in Ontario.

It is job opportunities that attract populations to specific regions. But a high concentration of population in a specific region itself works to attract more population. Many members of ethnic groups like to be in a region where there are already many members of that group. In highly concentrated areas, there are usually more institutions that cater to specific ethnic groups. Immigrants, in particular, prefer to move into areas where their ethnic communities are already established. Often their relatives are already there and they can help in the immigrants' adjustment process.

The high degree of ethnic concentration in Ontario is a post-World War II phenomenon, deriving from the vigorous industrial and general economic development of the province after the war. At the turn of the century, the Prairie region and British Columbia were more important centres of ethnic concentration. This was due primarily to the government policy in the last quarter of the nineteenth century of linking the Canadian continent from east to west by building the transcanadian railroad and the policy of settling the Prairies. Immigrant labour was required to work on the railroad, especially in the Rocky Mountains, and immigrant farmers were needed to cultivate the Prairie land. This established a historical pattern of migrating to the West coast for such groups as the Asians, particularly the Chinese who performed the early labour for the railroad in that area, and the Ukrainians, Polish, Dutch, Germans, Mennonites, Icelanders and others who migrated to settle the Prairies.

After World War I, the Prairies became less attractive; the minetowns and milltowns of Ontario and the developing industry in the Toronto and Montreal area became immigrant-attracting centres. World War II intensified the need for industrial development. After the war, industry in Ontario and Quebec shifted to consumer production. For the next 20 years, the pattern of migration was to the Toronto and Montreal areas by both immigrants to Canada and by persons from other provinces searching for better jobs. The continuous flow to the Montreal area was somewhat broken at the end of the 1970s with Quebec's attempts to separate from the rest of Canada, and the flow to Ontario was somewhat slowed by the economic recession in the 1980s, but the pattern of migration to the Toronto metropolitan area remained into the 1990s.

Age and Ethnicity. Table 7 illustrates the differences in age distribution between the different categories of ethnic groups for both, those identifying with single and those identifying with multiple ethnic origins. The table shows clearly that younger people of all ethnic groups tend to have substantially more multiple identities than older people. This, as can be expected, reflects higher rates of intermarriage among the younger generations. Furthermore, the table shows that the groups with the highest proportions of young people are Canadian Aboriginal groups, Asian groups, Arab groups, Southern European groups and Caribbean and Black. The highest percentages of persons in the age categories of less than 15 years of age and persons between 15 and 24 years of age are among these groups. This applies equally to those who have single and multiple ethnic identities. Still in these groups, the percentage of young people who have multiple identities is higher than among those with single identities.

In contrast, the groups with the highest percentages of older people, those 65 years of age and over, are Northern Europeans, Eastern Europeans, Western and Other Europeans and the British. The French are between those groups with the highest percentages of young persons and those with the highest percentages of old persons.

In general, all other things being equal, it can be said that the younger the members of an ethnic group are, the greater is the physical reproduction potential of the group, and the greater the pressures the group will exert on the labour market. Furthermore, all other things being equal, the younger the members of a group are, the more one can expect the group to be self assertive. This means that one can expect more of either generational rebellion or ethnic "rediscovery" in the group. On another level, one may expect from the younger groups increased pressures on the government, the media and other institutions of society. Inversely, the older the members of an ethnic group are, the more conservative or traditional it will tend to be. These are hypotheses, and their predictability depends upon the assumption that all other conditions between ethnic groups remain the same. This, of course, is not always so. Some of the conditions that account for variations will be considered later in the discussion of the determinants of ethnic status and change of ethnic status, and as factors of assimilation and ethnic identity retention.

Generations. The study of successive generations is one of the most important aspects of our full understanding of ethnicity. Sociologically, the first generation is defined as the foreign born, i.e. persons born outside Canada who have immigrated to Canada. The second generation are those born in Canada whose parents were born outside of Canada. The third generation are those born in Canada whose parents were also born in Canada, but whose grandparents were foreign born. Any successive generation removes the foreign-born ancestry by one more generation.

The demographic definition of generations does not fully correspond to a more strictly sociological definition of the differences between generations. Sociological definition places the emphasis on socialization. The significant difference between the first and the second generation depends on within which society or community a person has gone through the basic process of socialization. Persons may be born outside of Canada, but because they immigrated to Canada as small children, they might have gone through the process of socialization in the host society through the general societal agencies of socialization. They may thus, in their social character and behaviour, be more like those born in Canada than those who have immigrated to Canada during their adult life. The young, pre-school age, childhood immigrants may thus be included in the second generation for the purposes of sociological analysis. They may also be considered separately as the first-and-a-half generation. More will be said about generational differences later.

The generational composition of an ethnic group indicates whether the group, as a whole, is "old" or "young" in Canada. As explained in the previous chapter, an "old" group is one that has at least three adult generations in Canada and whose first generation constitutes less than 50 percent of the group's population. A "young" group is one who has not yet had three adult generations in the country and whose first generation makes up 50 or more percent of the group's total population.

It is difficult to assess statistically the ethnic generational composition of the total Canadian population. The only Canadian census that included a question on parental place of birth, enabling the measurement of ethnic generations, was in 1971. The results of this census give us insight into how different ethnic generations made up the Canadian population at that time (Richmond and Kalbach, 1980). From these we can project (with some hesitation) to the present. In 1971, of the ethnic groups presented in the census, only the Italian and the East Asian (represented by the Chinese and Japanese) groups could be considered as "young" groups. In both of these groups, the first generation

KEY ISSUES IN CANADIAN ETHNIC RELATIONS

Canada vs. the U.S.—Multiculturalism or Melting Pot?

How much different are ethnic relations in Canada from those in the United States? Is the difference significant? A long-standing popular answer to this question has been that the US follows the "melting pot" model whereas Canada follows a pluralistic "multicultural" model. Popularly, the melting pot idea has been understood to mean a mixture or a mish-mesh of different cultures producing an eclectic American culture. Multiculturalism, on the other hand, has been understood to refer to the preservation of different cultures, resulting in a "cultural mosaic." Accordingly, it has been assumed that Americans discourage preservation of ethnic cultures, whereas Canadians encourage it.

Sociologists Jeffrey Reitz and Raymond Breton, in their book *The Illusion of Difference*, examined as much empirical evidence as they could find to ascertain how different are the social processes among the immigrants and ethnic groups in the two countries. They examined public opinion surveys regarding cultural retention, surveys of racial attitudes, statistics on changes in occupational, educational and income distributions of ethnic groups in Canada and the US and other variables. Not all data was exactly comparable. The authors concluded that the differences between the two countries are not as evident as the two models would have it. In fact, while there are differences, there are many similarities.

Nevertheless, the structure of ethnic relationships in Canada and the United States possesses basic differences. In the US the largest groups setting priorities for ethnic issues are Blacks, now called Afro-Americans, and the Hispanics, mainly immigrants from Latin America, particularly Mexico. In Canada, the two main groups that set issue priority are, above all, the French of Quebec and the Native Peoples. In the US, Native Peoples also present important issue demands and these are very similar to the issues raised by the Native Peoples in Canada. Still, in Canada the Native People's issues are more in the forefront.

The issues of the largest groups in Canada and the United States are different. The Blacks in the US are predominantly the descendants of the slaves brought over by force from Africa. Their issues have been solidly human rights issues—a struggle to eliminate discrimination and gain political and economic equality with the white population. In Canada, Quebec's claims derive historically from the conquest of previously settled population and they have a territorial claim that is absent in the case of the American Blacks. In view of this claim, the demands for territorial rights among the Canadian Native Peoples gain a much higher profile than they do in the United States. In the US, however, the claims of the Hispanics are for equality, but also significantly for language and cultural rights. This is much more similar to the demands of the French and the "other" ethnic groups in Canada. The latter have gained public recognition in Canada through the federal policy of multiculturalism. In the US, the "other" ethnic groups also show efforts to retain their identity but there is no general public policy giving recognition to these diverse identities.

It is also worth noting that the popular meaning of the melting pot and multiculturalism is not the same as the originators intended. The author of the term "melting pot," Israel Zangwill, a writer of plays, never meant by it a mish-mesh of cultures. For him, the American melting pot was a crucible in which different cultures would rid themselves of their bad ways, but would retain and fuse together their good patterns of life into what would become a superior culture, based on daily work and future-looking ideas. It was an idealistic vision, but not one of a hodge-podge America. Likewise, multiculturalism, as the originally formulated policy in Canada, was never intended to mean the isolation of diverse ethnic groups from one another. Rather, as pointed out in Chapter 10, its aim was the opposite, i.e., integration of ethnic groups into Canadian society. The recognition of diverse identities had as its purpose acceptance of diversity by all Canadians, i.e., the vision of all as being "one of us." It also intended to instill a feeling of a secure self among culturally different minority individuals so that, as a result, they can contribute their best to the Canadian society. It is perhaps interesting to ask why these ideas or ideals later come to be interpreted in ways completely different from their original meaning.

This debate raises a number of interesting questions for researchers and laypersons alike. Most importantly, how much do governmental policies influence ethnic identity retention among minority groups and how much do they influence the process of their incorporation into the broader society? In view of the Reitz and Breton survey, moreover, is there something in the structure of both societies that leads to acceptance of similar ideas in practice if not in ideology? Still further, will the persistent fact of a completely different historical past, a different political system and a different economy, among many other things different, insure that a level of cultural differences between the two countries will remain in the future?

made up more than 50 percent of the groups' populations and their third and consecutive ("third generation+") generations were rather small, involving less than 15 percent of their populations. On the other hand, the "oldest" groups reported in the census were the Native peoples and the French. Both of these groups have had none or very little immigration over the years, as reflected in their very small first and second generations. Their third and consecutive generations, however, encompassed about 95 percent of their populations. All the other ethnic groups could be considered as "old." All of them had both a substantial third and consecutive generations and a first generation with less than 50 percent of their total populations. There were, however, variations between the different groups in the size of their generations, showing different degrees of the group's age. The British, historically an old and established set of groups in Canada, still showed in 1971 a significant first and second generations, reflecting the immigration influx of the British in Canada in the post-World War II period. Their third and consecutive generations made up 67.2 percent of their total population, substantially more than in all the other ethnic groups, except for the Native peoples and the French.

The 1971 census showed another important characteristic of Canadian population that, at the end of the nineties, has probably become even more pronounced. The total Canadian population in 1971 was made up of 15.4 percent first generation, i.e., immigrants, 18.5 percent second generation, i.e., children of immigrants, and 65 percent of third and consecutive generations. The percentages were even higher if Quebec is excluded: 18.3 immigrants, 22.9 children of immigrants, and 58.7 the third and consecutive generations (Richmond and Kalbach, 1980). We can infer that at the end of the 1990s these percentages are much higher. An important significance of this is cultural. The immigrants who arrive as adults or even as older children have usually gone through the process of their basic socialization in the original culture of their ethnic group. On the other hand, the children of immigrants born in the host society, i.e., the second generation, usually go through the process of simultaneous double socialization. That is, they are taught their ethnic culture at home and at various ethnic community institutions, and the culture of the host society at the general school, through their other-ethnic peers and the media. The data indicates that at least one-third of the total Canadian population and more than 40 percent of the Canadian population outside Quebec are people who have gone through the basic process of socialization in a culture different from the dominant culture in Canada. For them, cultural pluralism is something very real, including the problems that it poses and the opportunities that it offers.

Differences in the generational composition of ethnic groups also indicate differences in the kind of relationship that an ethnic group has in relation to the rest of society. Likewise, each ethnic generation stands in a different relation to its own ethnic group. A number of concerns an ethnic group has are derived from the presence or absence of a large proportion of one or another generation in its population. A large percentage of the first, immigrant, generation poses the problems of adjustment for the group–economic, cultural, psychological and so on–to a new society. On the other hand, an ethnic group that is predominantly second generation in its population has to deal with the problem of cultural or identity duality, including "rebellion" of sectors of the second generation. At this point, the group may also raise the issues of its acceptance and place in the total society, including the question of discrimination and civil rights. Predominance of the third or consecutive generation may raise the issue of one's "roots." Later chapters will discuss the rebelling syndrome of the second generation and the rediscovery syndrome of the third generation. Not enough research has been done as yet to assess thoroughly the differences in the relationship of each ethnic generation to its own group and to society at large. These sociological differences, however, go beyond the question of native born versus foreign born.

RELIGIOUS DIVERSITY OF THE CANADIAN POPULATION

Ethnic identity is usually intertwined with religious identity. Hence, to understand ethnic diversity fully one also has to take into account religious diversity. As was pointed out in Chapter 1, in some cases religious and ethnic boundaries overlap. What is important is the extent to which religion becomes a way of life for a group. All cultures have important religious aspects. Thus, for example, many ethnic customs, calendar observances, art and values have their roots in religious beliefs and practices. Furthermore, much of the community and organizational life of the early immigrants in North America centred around the church, synagogue, temple or other religious institution. Religious institutions

Table 8: Population by Religion, 1981 and 1991 Censuses

	1981		1991	
	Number	**%**	**Number**	**%**
Total population[1]	**24,083,495**	**100.0**	**26,994,045**	**100.0**
Catholic	**11,402,605**	**47.3**	**12,335,255**	**45.7**
Roman Catholic	11,210,385	46.5	12,203,620	45.2
Ukrainian Catholic	190,585	0.8	128,390	0.5
Other Catholic	1,630	—	3,235	—
Protestant	**9,914,575**	**41.2**	**9,780,715**	**36.2**
United Church	3,758,015	15.6	3,093,120	11.5
Anglican	2,436,375	10.1	2,188,110	8.1
Presbyterian	812,105	3.4	636,295	2.4
Lutheran	702,900	2.9	636,205	2.4
Baptist	696,845	2.9	663,360	2.5
Pentecostal	338,790	1.4	436,435	1.6
Other Protestant	1,169,545	4.9	2,127,190	7.9
Islam	**98,165**	**0.4**	**253,260**	**0.9**
Buddhist	**51,955**	**0.2**	**163,415**	**0.6**
Hindu	**69,505**	**0.3**	**157,010**	**0.6**
Sikh	**67,715**	**0.3**	**147,440**	**0.5**
Eastern Orthodox	**361,565**	**1.5**	**387,395**	**1.4**
Jewish	**296,425**	**1.2**	**318,065**	**1.2**
Para-religious groups	**13,450**	**0.1**	**28,155**	**0.1**
No religious affiliation	**1,783,530**	**7.4**	**3,386,365**	**12.5**
Other religions	**24,015**	**0.1**	**36,970**	**0.1**

— amount too small to be expressed.
[1] Based on sample data, which exclude institutional residents.
Source: Statistics Canada, Catalogue No. 93-319-XPB.

Photo: Courtesy of National Film Board, Ottawa

Ethnic identity is often intertwined with religious identity. Roman Catholic Church, Normandin, Quebec, 1965.

continue to play an important role in the preservation of ethnic communities and the retention of ethnic identity. The exact interrelationship between religion and ethnicity has not yet been sufficiently researched, but it is obvious that religious diversity and ethnic diversity are interconnected.

Table 8 gives the breakdown of the Canadian population by religion for 1981 and 1991. In both years, the two largest categories of religious denominations were Catholic and Protestant. In 1991 they made up 45.7 and 36.2 percent of the total Canadian population. The next largest percentage was made up of persons without any religious affiliation (12.5). Among the smaller percentages, the largest was for the Eastern Orthodox (1.4), followed by the Jewish (1.2), Islamic (0.9), Buddhist and Hindu (0.6 each), Sikh (0.5), para-religious and other religious groups (0.1 each).

Table 8 also shows the changes in religious affiliation from 1981 to 1991. The denominations that gained membership in the 10-year period were the Roman Catholic, which gained almost one million new members, and other Catholic, non-Roman, denominations, except for the Ukrainian Catholic. Only the Pentecostal and other non-establishment denominations gained significant membership among the Protestants. The membership of all the largest Protestant denominations declined over the period. The Muslims, Buddhists, Hindu and Sikhs made significant gains in membership. Each more than doubled, and some tripled, their membership. This reflects the increased immigration of people from the countries in which these religions predominate. The Eastern Orthodox and the Jewish religions made small gains in membership. Para-religious groups and the group with no religious affiliation, however, made substantial gains. This may reflect a search for alternatives to those offered by established religions or a falling out with the ways of the established churches. It may also indicate an increased number of immigrants with secular traditions.

CONCLUSION

Chapter 2 has presented the social-structural context for ethnic group relations in Canada. This included an analysis of those features of Canadian society as a modern society that are relevant to ethnic relations. Further, the chapter focused on those patterns in the history of Canada, beginning with the conquest of New France, that established the basis and have provided the principles for ethnic diversity and its integration in Canada. Finally, the chapter presented a picture of ethnic diversity in Canada by means of statistics, using mainly those provided by the census. In this, we have tried to point out the sociological implications of the many aspects of the ethnic composition of the Canadian population.

Before we can move on to analyze further sociological implications of ethnic diversity in Canada, it is important to look first at the phenomenon of immigration itself, as, with the exception of the Native peoples, ethnicity in North America begins with immigration. We need to understand the different types of immigration and immigrants, to understand the Canadian history of immigration, and to understand the process of immigrant adaptation and adjustment after arrival in a new country. This is what we will explore in the next two chapters.

Photo: Dick Hemingway

A place to call home. It has been estimated that in the early 1990s there were as many as 80 million migrants in the world searching for a new home.

CHAPTER 3

INTERNATIONAL MIGRATION

Its Sociological Significance

The ethnic diversity of any society results from the migration of groups at one time or another in the society's history. Yet not all migrations are alike. This chapter presents a typology of international migration and discusses the sociological implications of migration. It also examines the kind of relationships that develop between the established and the migrant groups.

Migration takes place when groups of persons move to another place and stay there for a significant period of time or go to another place at significant intervals of time. By significant period or significant intervals is meant a period or periods of time that makes an important difference in the life or history of the migrating group of peoples or the society in which the migration takes place. It is difficult to specify the period of stay exactly; depending upon the type of migration, it may range from a lifetime, as in the case of permanent immigration, to a few weeks or even days, provided it is repeated regularly, as in the case of seasonal workers or tourists who migrate back and forth every season. Sociologically, important migrations take place, not when isolated individuals move to another place, but when socio-economically and/or demographically significant populations do so.

This means that the migrating populations are of such size that they either make a difference in any aspect of the economic institutions, for example, they provide a labour force that otherwise could not be found, or they are such that they at least potentially allow for development of some ethnic institutions or for development of a significant network of ethnic contact, or they are of such size and composition as to allow for endogamy.

TYPES OF INTERNATIONAL MIGRATION

Migration can be classified as international or within a nation and as either permanent, temporary or periodic. Here we will deal only with international migration. The typology of migration that follows is based on the motivation for going to another country. Its value derives from the difference that motivation for going to another country can have on the adjustment process of the migrants and upon the way they integrate or come to be incorporated into the host society. It should be kept in mind, however, that these are ideal types, and in reality the motivations for coming to another country may overlap. Thus the distinctions between the types may in many concrete cases be blurred. Still, ideal types are helpful in our understanding of such complex phenomena as human actions. The types and their subtypes can be outlined as follows (see Chart 1 on next page).

PERMANENT MIGRATION

• Settlement

Settlement takes place when people move to an area that is not occupied by any other society. They do not enter the structure of an existing society, but establish one of their own. This new structure may or may not be connected with that from which the migrants came. Often, in the early stages of settlement, there is a closer connection with the home society, but as time goes on the settlements develop their own social structure.

Among the Canadian Native peoples, most tribal groups settled uninhabited territories at one time or another, beginning with prehistoric times. They were the original settlers, creating their own social structures of the band and tribal type. The early English settlements of North America were, in the beginning, dependent in large degree on the old society. Yet, from the start they

Chart 1: Types of International Migration

I. PERMANENT MIGRATION
  A. Settlement
  B. Colonization
  C. Immigration/Emigration
    1. Economic
      (a) "push"
      (b) "pull"
    2. Political
      (a) refugees
      (b) exiles
      (c) forced labour
    3. Family-related
  D. Return migration

II. TEMPORARY-STAY MIGRATION
  A. Occupation-related
  B. Education-related
  C. Re-migration
  D. Nomads

III. PERIODIC MIGRATION
  A. Seasonal workers
  B. Visitors
    1. Tourists
    2. Businesspersons
    3. Friends and relatives
    4. Pilgrims
    5. Health, weather-related

began to develop their own structures. As some historians have pointed out, by the time of the American Revolution, the social structure of the 13 colonies was already indigenous and for practical purposes independent of the British society; hence, severing of political ties with Britain was only a logical step (Morrison, 1965: 69-89; Erickson, 1974).

A similar situation existed in the settlement of French Canada up until the conquest. The governorial system with its seigneurial structure was intent on extending the structure of the old French society into its colony. Yet because only a few seigneurs could be noblemen and because of the fur trade and the need of the seigneurs to work the land closely with their tenant farmers, an indigenous structure began to develop from the very beginning. With the conquest of New France, the society lost all dependence upon Old France (Clark, 1962: 20-40).

It took most of the nineteenth century for British Canada to develop an indigenous social structure. Perhaps this was due to the loyalist experience. As was pointed out previously, in the face of the American Revolution, the loyalists consciously tried to maintain a close link with Britain for as long as possible.

The settlement of the West in Canada and in the United States is another example of the two types of settlements. As was explained previously, the Canadian West was much more closely tied to the structure of British Canada, whereas the American West grew by and large unsupervised and began to develop its own indigenous structure practically with the very first settlements.

• Colonization

Colonizers are people who migrate not to uninhabited lands but to places where there is already a society. Colonizers, however, do not enter the structure of the existing society. Rather they modify the structure of the existing society in such a way as to ensure the dominance of their home society. They thus build a superstructure over the existing society. The typical examples of colonizers have been Europeans in the African and Asian societies. It should be remembered that colonizers have also been those who have gone together with the settlers and, from the start, built into the structure of the settler society a superstructure to serve as a link between the old and new societies.

As pointed out in the previous chapter, colonizers are typically the administrators, the military, the businessmen, the educators, clergy and others who come to be linked with the political and/or the business administration of the colonies. They are people who generally have been trained in the old society and who migrate either because of a definite career advantage or in the line of duty or both. The superstructure that they establish offers them privilege over the indigenous society (Memmi, 1965). This in itself serves as a motivation for migrants to come and stay, and lays the foundation for the development of exclusive institutions that will maintain a boundary between themselves and the rest of the population.

• Immigration

Immigrants, unlike settlers and colonizers, are those migrants who move into another society and become part of its existing structure. They may enter the society at any of its structural levels depending upon their socio-economic and ethnic backgrounds and upon the state of the society's economy at any given time. Thus some immigrants become part of the majority ethnic group, others, part of the minority groups.

Emigration refers to migrants moving out of their society. In terms of motivation, emigration and immigration are two sides of the same process. In terms of the impact on society, however, the two are different. What is one society's gain may be the other society's loss, although this is not necessarily so. The discussion here will focus on immigration.

Four main types of immigrants can be distinguished: economic immigrants, political immigrants, family-related immigrants and return migrants.

Economic immigrants are people who migrate in search of livelihood opportunities. They can be further subdivided into "push" and "pull" immigrants. The *push* economic immigrants are those who leave their country because its economic conditions are such that their very subsistence is threatened or there is no gainful work for them available. Economic disasters or catastrophes often provide the push factor for immigration.

The potato crop failure in Ireland and the resulting famine around the middle of the nineteenth century, for example, induced about 1.6 million survivors to migrate to Great Britain, the United States and Canada in search of the basic means of subsistence (Percival, 1995; Kane, 1993). The Eastern European immigration to Canada at the turn of the century was made up almost entirely of peasants who had nothing to do on the land of their fathers and grandfathers because there was practically no land available for them to till. Fathers would subdivide their land and will parts of it to their children until each child's inheritance was so small that it offered little chance of livelihood from its harvests. New land could not be purchased as few peasants had enough money to do so (Yuzyk, 1953: 27-28; Olsson, 1996). Hence emigration was practically an imperative. The fact that Canada had an abundance of land and was ready for a new stage in its economic development was a timely opportunity for Eastern European peasants.

Similar push factors have been operating to induce many recent Portuguese and Italian immigrants to migrate to Canada. The industrial growth of both Portugal and Italy, although different in nature, has not been fast enough to offer occupations to the rural population for whom opportunities on the land or in other primary jobs have been vanishing (Anderson, G., 1974: 19-20).

The push type of immigration may, to some extent, overlap with the pull type. The *pull* economic immigrants are those who go to another country, not because they are impelled by the complete lack of opportunity for livelihood in their home country, but because the country to which they immigrate offers better opportunities. That is, the immigrants could survive without moving to a new society, but they do so because the new society holds the promise of economic betterment and social mobility. For many immigrants this promise may never be fulfilled, but its attraction is an important motivational factor. Probably the majority of economic immigrants to Canada in recent years have been of this type. Admittedly, the distribution between the push and pull type of immigrants is not often clear in reality, but analytically it is a clear and useful distinction.

Statistics for the past decade present a large picture of international migration. In Canada, between 1981 and 1991, about 1,238,455 persons entered the country as permanent residents. This is 4.6 percent of the total population of the country at the end of this decade. In the United States, between 1980 and 1990, about 7,868,600 persons entered the country, 3.2 percent of the total population of the country at the end of the decade. In the United Kingdom, between 1982 and 1991, about 513,470 persons migrated into the country, 1 percent of the total population in 1991. Germany, whose in-migration, on the average, exceeds that of all other Western European countries combined, in the period of 1980 to 1989 brought in about 4,112,900 persons as permanent residents, i.e., 5.2 percent of the total German population in 1989. Finally, Australia, between 1981 and 1991, admitted 1,152,316 immigrants or 6.7 percent of its population at the end of the decade (United Nations, 1994a, Table 5; Richmond

1994: 261-70; Statistisches Bundesamt, 1994, Tables 3.21, 3.22).

Political immigrants are those who are compelled to move outside of their society by, or on account of, the power structure or change of power structure in their society. A number of types of political immigrants can be distinguished depending upon the kind of compulsion involved in the removal of people. *Refugees* are those immigrants who leave their country because of the probability that, if they stay, the political regime or the conflict between political powers and groups would threaten their lives, their freedom or their property. *Exiles* are those who are ordered by the political regime to leave the country. Usually the order is accompanied by a threat. The basis for the threat in the case of both refugees and exiles is usually either the political activities of the persons involved, which are contrary to the political orientation of those in power, or their different views and beliefs, or their social status in society, which the regime decides to replace, or their being of an ethnic ancestry, religion or class that is disliked and considered suspect by those in power. Finally, the basis for the threat may be simply the unsettled situation and physical danger that is produced by war, revolutions or other political conflicts.

The twentieth century has produced more refugees and exiles than any other preceding period since the fall of the Roman Empire. It has been estimated that, since World War II, there have been more than 40 million refugees and exiles of various types worldwide. Even though most of them have either returned home or were resettled, the number of refugees in the world increases every year. It has been estimated that an average of 10,000 people a day become refugees. When the Office of the United Nations High Commissioner for Refugees was created in 1951, it was supposed to operate for only three years. It was assumed that the roughly one million refugees of the time would be integrated into one or another society. Yet, in 1960, 1.4 million persons throughout the world were refugees; by 1970, 2.5 million; by 1980, 8.2 million; by 1990, 17.2 million; and by 1995, close to 19 million (UNHCR, 1993: 1-3). By the middle of the 1990s, not only did the work of the Office of the U.N. High Commissioner for Refugees continue, but its resources were stretched to the limit.

Each political and military upheaval produces a wave of refugees. The Russian Revolution of 1917 and its aftermath produced 1,500,000 refugees and exiles, who later scattered throughout Western Europe and parts of the Far East. Between 1915 and 1923, more than a million Armenians were deported or fled from Turkish Asia Minor to surrounding countries and to the Americas. In the wake of the 1936-1939 civil war in Spain, about half a million Spanish Loyalists fled to France, North Africa, Mexico and South America.

During World War II, in 1944, there were approximately 7,414,650 Europeans who moved outside their own countries because of the war or who escaped from German- and Soviet-controlled territory. At the end of the war, in 1945, in the areas of Europe occupied by the Western Allies and in those occupied by the Soviet forces, there were approximately 13,661,660 persons displaced by the war. This included persons who were brought over to Germany by the Nazi government as forced labour (Proudfoot, 1957; Vernant, 1953).

Following the unsuccessful Hungarian Revolution in 1956, some 203,000 Hungarians fled to the West. Between 1945 and 1969, after the communist regime in East Germany erected the Berlin Wall, over 3,800,000 refugees from East Germany crossed the border to West Germany. After 1960, following Fidel Castro's take-over in Cuba, some 750,000 Cubans–9 percent of Cuba's population–left Cuba, mostly for the United States.

When the People's Republic of China was established in 1949, some two million Chinese escaped to Taiwan. Others went to other countries in South Asia, but the majority went to Hong Kong where, together with earlier refugees, their numbers amounted to an additional two million. In 1959, when the People's Republic of China took over Tibet, some 76,000 Tibetan refugees fled to India, Bhutan, Sikkim, Nepal and Macau.

Between 1947 and 1960, about 205,000 Jewish refugees were brought over or fled, mostly to Israel, from Yemen, Aden, Iraq and Syria. Some of them went to the United States and Latin America. The establishment of Israel produced about 750,000 Palestinian refugees in 1948, who fled to the neighbouring Arab States where most of them remained in separate camps. In 30 years as refugees outside of their homeland, their number increased by natural increase to almost three million.

The partition of the Indian subcontinent in 1947 resulted in a two-way flight of 18,000,000 Hindus from Pakistan and Muslims from India. Between 1962 and 1971 this was followed up by the eviction of 1,032,000 Hindus from Pakistan and flight or eviction of 260,000 Muslims from India and Kashmir. In 1971, the creation of Bangladesh created, temporarily, eight to ten million refugees.

The war in Vietnam, Laos and Cambodia in the 1960s and 1970s produced at least 365,000 refugees, most of them Vietnamese. The bulk of them resettled in the United States and the rest in France, Canada, Malaysia and Australia (Hein, 1995).

In the early 1990s, ethnic groups in what was formerly Yugoslavia embarked on "ethnic cleansing." Besides the great numbers of people killed, close to four million people became refugees (UNHCR, 1993).

In Africa the number of refugees has been rapidly increasing. The causes have been remnants of colonialism, the power struggle between new states, tribal animosities, tensions created by involvement of the great powers and so on. As a result, and while in 1968 there were 860,000 refugees in Africa, by 1971 the number had increased to 1,858,000. In 1991, over 500,000 Liberians had to move outside the country's borders to escape killings by fighting political factions and, between 1993 and 1996, in two different outbursts of interethnic conflict between the Hutus and the Tutsies in Rwanda and Burundi, about two million refugees fled to neighbouring countries before genocidal killings.

Sociologically, refugees are people caught in the process of sudden change or disruption of the social structure of a society or set of societies. This change may range from a lesser to a considerable extent. It may involve a change only of personnel of the political institutions, in which a new set of people take over the existing political institutions, or it may involve change of the political institutions themselves or changes in other social institutions accompanying the change in the political institution. Finally, the change may mean a breakdown of the total social structure, as is the case of many African tribal societies. Difficulty in establishing new institutions after the change or breakdown of the old ones is in itself another factor that often produces additional refugees.

Photo: Courtesy of National Archives of Canada, C-30620

Immigration posters, such as the one above, inspired hundreds of thousands of settlers to move to the prairies from 1896 to the mid-1940s.

Another type of political immigrants is *forced labour.* The classical example of forced labour is the slave trade. Often the slave trade is defined as an economic rather than a political phenomenon. From the point of view of those who import slaves, this indeed may be an economic matter. Our classification, however, is based on the principle of motivation for migrating from the point of view of the migrant. For the slave, migration is not a matter of economics, but a matter of being overpowered by a physically superior party. Similar to the refugee or the exile, the slave is forced to migrate under threat, except that instead of moving into a social structure that frees him from the threat, he moves into one that maintains it.

Although a slave trade existed in many ancient societies, the most notable example of it is the movement of Black peoples from Africa to the Americas in the seventeenth, eighteenth and nineteenth centuries.

It is estimated that between 1510 and 1870, when the last slaves were brought into the Americas, about 9.6 million Africans were introduced into the New World and Europe. About 43 percent of them were brought over to the Caribbean islands, 38 percent to Brazil and about 4.5 percent to North America (Curtin, 1969).

The slave trade created a structure of racial relations often described as the caste system. The change of this caste system in the United States has been at the heart of the American interracial relations in this century that have reflected themselves also in the interethnic relationships of other groups.

Before it was outlawed in the British Empire in 1834, slavery was technically legal in what is now Canada, but was practiced only by a few and the total number of slaves was never high. Before the first Europeans settled in Canada, a number of Indian tribes practiced slavery, particularly those on the Northwest Coast. Portuguese explorers brought a small number of slaves with them to what is now Newfoundland, and Black slaves were introduced by the French in 1608. New France had a legal provision for slavery and began to bring over Black slaves directly from Africa in 1629. By 1759, there were 3,604 recorded slaves, of whom 1,132 were Black. After the American Revolution, the American Loyalists brought their slaves with them, but after 1793, John G. Simcoe, lieutenant-governor of Upper Canada, challenged the legality of slavery, and the institution declined. The slaves usually worked as personal servants and as workers on the wharves, but only a few settlers would own as many as 20 slaves (Winks, 1988).

In the twentieth century a new form of forced labour emerged, i.e., large groups of people forcibly moved by governments outside the structure of their society in order to serve as labour in the planned development of an industry or an area.

The Soviet government under Stalin introduced the system of concentration camps in the frontier areas of the Soviet Union, such as Siberia and Kazakhstan, to serve both as penal colonies and forced labour camps. It is estimated that, during Stalin's regime and for a period thereafter, there were approximately two million people in these camps at any given time. Their labour had been the main factor in the economic development of the frontier areas (AFL, 1949; ICFTU, 1951; United Nations, 1953). In 1942, the Nazi regime forcibly deported over eight and a half million persons to Germany from occupied countries, mostly Eastern Europe and France. They were placed in camps and required to work as labourers in industry, on farms or as domestics (Proudfoot, 1957: 78-93).

Family-related, or family-class, immigrants are persons who migrate to other countries to join their families. These may include immediate and lineal relatives, such as spouses, children, parents and grandparents or lateral and more distant relatives, such as brothers, sisters, uncles in-laws and so on. A significant pattern among many immigrants from Eastern Europe at the turn of the century was for the husbands to immigrate first alone and, after finding a job and a place to live, to bring over their wives and children. Today, the pattern is for the immediate family to immigrate together, but there is a significant tendency towards bringing over, by means of sponsorship, one's relatives. Since the early 1970s, the percentage of family-related immigrants to Canada has hovered around 50. In 1994, 42 percent of all immigrants to Canada were family-related (CIC, 1996: 4).

The type of immigrants who are sponsored by somewhat distant relatives merges into the economic, and to a lesser extent, political type of immigrants. In the past, many immigrants who migrated to join their families have, in effect, been economic immigrants, migrating under a pretext. In Canada, the category of "nominated" relatives, introduced in 1967 but retracted later on, allowed lateral relatives to be brought into the country. Many who were nominated as "uncles," "cousins" and so on were more economic than family class immigrants. Since 1978, the family-related immigrants are essentially of linear and only immediate lateral kinship with those who sponsor them.

• Return Migration

The concept of return migration refers to persons who have come to another country for permanent stay, but, after a period of time, for whatever reason, become dissatisfied with their stay and decide to return to their original country. The concept of return migration is different from that of temporary-stay re-migration. The latter involves the initial intention to stay in another country for only a limited period of time, while return migrants are those who initially intended to stay permanently but have later changed their mind. Admittedly, in practice, there may be an overlap between these two phenomena, since migrants may not always be exactly certain of their intentions. The exact extent of return migration is difficult to determine. Most statistics on emigration do not identify the numbers of persons emigrating to their original home country. Between 1851 and 1948, about as many persons emigrated out of Canada as immigrated into Canada. Traditionally, emigration from Canada has been mainly to the United States, and during several time periods, it was indistinguishable from re-migration. In the decade between 1983 and 1993, it is estimated that close to 500,000 persons emigrated out of Canada, including return migrants (Kubat, 1984).

TEMPORARY-STAY MIGRATION

Temporary-stay migration refers to people who move to another country with the intention of staying there for only a limited period of time and then either returning to their previous country of residence or going on to another country for another temporary or permanent stay. The most common reason why persons move for temporary stay is their occupation. Many *multinational businesses* send their executives and experts to different countries to work with the branches of their corporations or with their subsidiaries. They may stay there for a period of a year or longer and then move to another country to work at another branch or subsidiary. Anthony Richmond (1969) named the highly qualified persons, employed by various companies for a limited period of stay in different countries, "transilients." In addition to business, the temporary-stay migrants also include *government functionaries* and persons working for various *international organizations.* Among these are members of official delegations, such as embassies and consulates; international political bodies, such as the United Nations, the International Labour Organization, UNESCO and the like; the military garrisoned in foreign countries; and emissaries of various private organizations, such as Oxfam, the Red Cross, the Salvation Army and other religious bodies, who are stationed often for three or so years in any one foreign country.

Temporary-stay migration includes also persons of labouring occupations, skilled and unskilled. These are often confused with seasonal workers, and many statistics do not distinguish between the two types. In general, there is a tendency among European scholars to use the term *migrant worker* to refer to temporary-stay labour, meaning persons of foreign nationalities who stay in the host country for at least a year or more. North American terminology tends to include under the term *migrant workers* essentially seasonal workers, who come into the country to labour for only one season, summer or fall, usually in relation to agricultural work. Here the latter workers will be considered as periodic migrants.

In Canada, logging, mining, railway and road construction and the like attracted hundreds of thousands of migrant workers in the first half of this century. Although many were internal migrants rather than persons crossing the border, many of them were recent immigrants in the country, who intended to return to their home country after earning enough money. In this case the categories of immigrant and temporary-stay migrant overlapped. It is estimated that in some years during the first two decades of this century there were as many as three thousand migrant workers' camps, employing about 200,000 men annually, more than 5 percent of the total male labour force (Bradwin, 1972).

Since the 1980s, domestic workers have been arriving in Canada for temporary work under a special employment authorization program. Many of them have experienced exploitation by the families they have served. Of special concern is the discipline of nannies from different cultures, who have used or abused young children. More will be said about domestic workers in Canada in the next chapter.

Today, the migration of workers from one country to another has become one of the central characteristic features of the global economic system. It has been estimated that, in the 1980s, about 20 million workers were employed outside their countries. About 12 million of these were persons who migrated from economically underdeveloped countries to the highly developed countries of the West and the high-income oil exporting countries of the Middle East (*UN Chronicle*, 1985, 2: 12). In Western Europe, particularly Germany, France and Switzerland, during the 1960s and 1970s, migrant workers, largely from the Middle East and Yugoslavia, were invited to come for three years to work in the expanding industry and then were expected to return home. They were called "Guestworkers." In the early 1970s, their numbers in Western Europe reached about six million. The idea of going home after three years, however, proved to be impractical and most of the migrant workers stayed. They have not been given the status of immigrant or citizen; the term guestworkers has been dropped, but they are still accorded the status of foreigners and are refused citizenship. The only change that has begun to be introduced in this regard has been in France.

In the oil-producing countries of the Middle East, particularly United Arab Emirates, Quatar, Kuwait and Oman, the migrant workers from other Middle Eastern countries and from Asia actually outnumber the local populations. In the United States in the 1980s, there were about 2.5 million migrant workers, many of them from Mexico and other Latin American countries (*UN Chronicle*, 1985, 2: 12). These numbers, however, overlap with those of the seasonal workers.

Another type of temporary-stay migrants are persons who go to another country to obtain education, i.e., *foreign students.* The tradition of going abroad to obtain a higher education is as old as universities themselves. In the Middle Ages, when the first universities were established, a few, because of the excellence of their teaching, became famous and attracted students from all over Europe. In the twelfth century, the number of students travelling to and from the known universities increased to the point where, to travel in security, they were given special protection by the king against arbitrary arrest and extortion in financial matters. In contemporary times, seeking education abroad has become quite widespread. A new trend emerged whereby students from underdeveloped countries, such as those in Africa, Middle East and parts of Asia, would travel to the universities in the more developed countries to obtain an education and knowledge that they could later apply in their own country to help bring about its greater development. In 1993, there were close to one million foreign students enrolled in universities and other institutions of higher learning throughout the world (UNESCO, 1995: 3-395-428). The countries that hosted the largest numbers of foreign university students in the 1990s have been the United States (about 450,000 in 1993), France (140,000), the United Kingdom (95,500 in 1992), the Russian Federation (83,000), Australia (43,000) and Canada (35,500). The countries from which most foreign students come are Africa, Asia, the Middle East, South America, United States, Canada, Japan and Korea. These statistics do not include elementary and secondary school students. In Canada from 1992 to 1993, elementary and secondary level foreign students numbered an additional 51,500 (Chui, 1996).

In Canada, the number of occupation-related and education-related temporary-stay migrants rapidly increased in the 1980s. In 1981 the number of nonpermanent residents, staying in Canada for one year or more, was about 143,000, but by 1990, it had more than doubled to 369,100. By 1990s, the annual number of temporary-stay residents coming to Canada was much larger than the annual intake of landed immigrants (McKie, 1994).

Re-migration occurs when migrants move to one country as a way station to still another country. They intend to stay only long enough to enable them to immigrate into another country. The first country of migration is used as a stepping stone for immigration into a second country. From the middle of the nineteenth century until the end of World War II, Canada was a way station for immigrants travelling from Europe to the United States. In the 1980s and 1990s, many refugees from Vietnam, Cambodia, Laos, Yugoslavia and other countries would move to a Western European country first, especially Germany, and then from there would apply for immigration to Canada, the United States or other countries. Many migrants, including refugees, from the Soviet Union, and after 1990 from the countries of the former Soviet Union, would migrate to Israel first with the intention of moving permanently to North America.

Lastly, *nomads* represent another kind of temporary migrants. Nomads are groups or tribes of people who move from one location to another as a way of life. In prehistoric times, much of humanity was nomadic, moving from place to place collecting food. In contemporary times there are still two types of nomads, pastoral and trader nomads. Pastoral nomads, as, for example, various tribes in Siberia, Central Asia and Africa, depend on domesticated livestock for their livelihood and migrate in order to find pasture for the animals. Today, however, they rarely move out of the areas of their country. The trading nomads, however, move across borders more often. The main example in contemporary times are the Gypsies or *Roma*. It is estimated that in the late twentieth century, there are between two and three million Gypsies in the world, most of them in Europe, although there are also some in North America. Typically, Gypsies have moved in kin groups and along tribal links that have ignored national boundaries. For this reason many nation-states have forced the Gypsies of their territories to become sedentary. By the end of the twentieth century, most Gypsies appear now to have settled, yet their self-consciousness and identity appears to have been in large measure retained by formation of their own religious, political and cultural associations and by their own pressure groups created to defend their minority rights–for example, the "Central Council of German Sinti and Roma," the "Romani International Union," the World Romany Congresses, and others (Fraser, 1992; Salo and Salo, 1977).

The sociological significance of the temporary-stay migrants is derived from the fact that their stay in a foreign country generates intercultural interaction. The impact of this interaction proceeds in several directions. For one, it makes both those who come for a temporary stay and the people of the host country more conscious of cultural differences. This may effect greater intercultural understanding, but it may also evoke hostilities. Frequently, there is a tendency for both the persons on temporary stay and the larger population to develop a degree of insulation from each other. The newcomers often develop their own organizations or community institutions, even if these are temporary. In turn, the people of the host society tend

KEY ISSUES IN CANADIAN ETHNIC RELATIONS

The World Refugee Problem: Who is to Care?

It is estimated that in the early 1990s there were as many as 80 million migrants in the world searching for a new home. Among these, special attention has to be given to the plight of refugees. The United Nations High Commissioner for Refugees' *World Refugee Survey* of 1993 has shown that in one decade the number of refugees on the global level increased by 80 percent, sometimes at a rate of one million per year. In the 1990s alone there have been large new waves of refugees created by political conflict and violence in Bosnia-Herzegovina, Serbia, Croatia, Somalia, Rwanda, Burundi, Republic of Congo, Angola, Sri Lanka, Haiti, Chechnya, Afghanistan, Indonesia, and other countries. Smaller numbers have continued to come from the countries that produced large waves of refugees in the previous three decades, such as Southeastern Asia and some of the African countries.

Although there are different types of refugees, in general, refugees are people who have to leave a country because they are denied a human existence and are accepted by another country on account of this country's humane or humanitarian considerations. This raises a number of questions. One is: do the developed nations of the world have a responsibility to give a haven to the refugees of the world, or for that matter, the starving people of the earth? Some argue that the responsibility for the welfare of people ends at the state borders. That is, it is the function of the state to protect and care for the welfare of its own citizens and not those of other nations. If other states are either in flux or are unable to care for their citizens, then another state may help if it chooses, but it has no mandate or responsibility to do so.

Yet, over the last five decades many developed nations have given a haven to hundreds of thousands of refugees. Very important in this regard has been the creation in 1950 of the Office of United Nations High Commissioner for Refugees (UNHCR). This agency has not only coordinated many refugee resettlement efforts, but it has acted to exert social and moral pressure on the well-developed countries to open their doors to refugees. Would these countries, including Canada and the United States, readily accept refugees if it were not for such pressure? Is social and moral pressure sufficient? In the rapidly developing global society in which many states are inadvertently relinquishing some of their economic sovereignty, does the old presumption hold that the responsibility for the life and welfare of citizens of a country is that country's business only?

Traditionally, the United Nations has accepted three basic solutions to the refugee problem. These are local settlement, resettlement and voluntary repatriation. Local settlement refers to having the refugees settle in the country that has given them the initial asylum. In most cases, this is the country that is geographically contiguous to the one from which the refugees came. This, however, may not be a durable solution since many countries, especially those that are economically poor, cannot absorb large influxes of new populations. Resettlement has been an effective way of solving the refugee problem, but it depends on two important conditions, the willingness of a country to accept the refugees and an economic level in the country that will insure adequate integration of the refugees.

There have been pressures to use the third solution, i.e., repatriation. Some countries have engaged in forced repatriation, but this solution is contrary to the principles of the United Nations which favours voluntary repatriation only. The prospects for voluntary repatriation of refugees, however, are limited by the fact that one has to wait for a change in the political and economic conditions that has produced the refugees in the first place. Often, such change is long in coming and even if it does come, not all refugees want to go back.

A fourth solution has also been suggested; the "early warning" solution. It consists of scientifically predicting the potential conflicts that would produce refugee movements and then using internationally respected agencies to negotiate their prevention. Sociologist Michael Lanphier has tried to specify the measures that would be necessary to make this solution effective. Among them are information gathering, verification and interpretation of information, timing, early intervention and others. But even he sees problems with this approach.

Many questions remain regarding the solutions to the global refugee problem. For example, is intervention in the country in which a conflict occurs a legitimate course of action? If the receiving countries are to care for another country's refugees, does this not give them a right to make some demands on the country whose conflicts induce their citizens to become refugees? Would this involve also a right to settle the internal conflicts in a sovereign country? The answers to the world refugee problem are complicated for all these reasons. Meanwhile, throughout the world millions of people are on the move and simply looking for a place to call home.

to associate with the "guests" mainly in the context of the society's formal institutions that relate to the work of the "guests" or in the context of the impersonal market. In spite of this, a mutual impact on consciousness is made as a result of the dealings between the newcomers and the local population.

In another way, the ideas, values, attitudes and styles of the cultures that the temporary groups represent are often diffused into the host population, especially if those who come for temporary stay represent powerful nations. After World War II, many Americans have stayed in Europe and other parts of the world as members of the military forces, as representatives and workers of international organizations or as business persons. They were instrumental in spreading American culture in these societies, particularly among the younger generations. Some observers have identified this process as "Americanization of the world."

Furthermore, some societies may come to depend economically on the foreign populations that are on temporary stay. This is particularly the case in less-developed societies. The presence of American military bases in the Philippines and some islands in Japan and other parts of the world had often created jobs for the local populations and brought money into local economies. The presence of foreign or multinational businesses in a country usually has the same effect. It creates jobs in societies where jobs are not readily available and pours money into the economy. Yet, at the same time, it may have the effect of undermining the traditional local cultures and even the existing social order of the society.

Many foreign students from underdeveloped countries, after obtaining education in Western universities, return home and obtain leading positions in the government, the economy and in the local universities. They become members of the elite of their societies and often apply Western ideas to bring about development and change in their society and their traditional cultures.

Lastly, today international organizations and multinational corporations are creating institutions that link major economic and political institutions of many societies and cultures into a global structure. These institutions are directed and managed by persons of diverse cultural backgrounds on temporary stays in different countries. The global structure created in this manner may, in the future, impact on diverse societies more powerfully than their own national governments or economic institutions. An example of this is the European Union and the free trade agreements between many nations of the world.

Some forms of periodic migration may make similar impacts on the society in which they take place.

PERIODIC MIGRATION

Periodic migration refers to the groups of people who, at more or less regular intervals, migrate to the same places for a short period of time and then return to their former place. The groups of people who migrate in this way may not be necessarily the same individuals every time, although they often are. What is important is that there are large categories of people who periodically move back and forth to and from certain places. There are three main types of such periodic migrants: seasonal workers, visitors, and health and weather-related migrants.

• Seasonal Workers

Seasonal workers are people who travel to another country to do temporary labour related to the calendar seasons or to special projects. The main types of such work involve agricultural seasonal work, such as tomato, grape or fruit picking.

Since the 1970s, tens of thousands of seasonal workers have been coming to Canada every year. It is estimated that this constitutes about 1 percent of the total male labour force (Michalowski, 1996). Most of them come from the Caribbean and others from Latin America. Their seasonal jobs include mainly vegetable and fruit picking (Satzewich, 1991).

It is estimated that in the United States there are about 200,000 seasonal workers annually. Most of them come from Mexico. California's and Florida's fruit and vegetable industry, during the picking season, depend on seasonal workers. These include men, women and children (Martin, 1988).

From the point of view of ethnic group relations, the significance of seasonal workers consists of the fact that most of them have been of an ethnic or racial background other than that of the permanent population, their wages have been low and their working conditions have persistently been poor (Friedland and Nelkin, 1971). Seasonal work has meant interethnic contact not only at the cultural borders of society but also at the bottom of class and ethnic stratification scales.

• Visitors

Intercultural contact is also an important aspect of the second major type of periodic migration, i.e., visitors in a country, particularly tourists. International *visitors* are defined as persons who go to another country for the purpose of recreation, sightseeing, taking care of business or call of courtesy or religious homage, for a limited period of time and with the intention to return. For statistical purposes a distinction is often made between overnight and same-day visitors. As a phenomenon of migration, the first type is more meaningful. The concept of visitor thus is meant here to apply to persons who travel abroad for the purposes indicated and stay at least overnight or longer (Theobald, 1994a).

Visitors include five large categories of travellers: tourists, businesspersons, persons who travel to visit their friends or relatives, persons who travel for health or weather-related reasons and pilgrims. Tourists are persons who travel to places other than those in which they usually live and work for the purpose of recreation or sightseeing, usually in appropriate seasons of the year, for example, summer or winter holiday seasons. Tourism may overlap with other types of visiting, i.e., business trips, periodically visiting relatives or friends, periodically making religious pilgrimages or periodically going to warmer climates for health reasons. In Canada, persons in the last group are often called "snowbirds," i.e., people who in winter months travel to Florida or other warm regions to stay there for a period of time away from cold weather. Often people who travel combine several purposes.

Visitors represent one of the greatest mobility of people in the world. In 1995, there were about 19,806,000 visits made to Canada from other countries. Of these, 59 percent were visits by tourists, 19 percent were visits by friends or relatives, 14 percent were visits for business purposes, and 8 percent, other visits (Statistics Canada, 1996: 39, 47). Tourism represents the largest part of periodic migration. In 1992, there were about 481,563,000 tourist visits made to points all over the world. The country that receives the greatest number of tourist visits is the United States. In 1992, 44,647,000 tourist visits were made to the United States, 39,638,000 to Spain, 31,326,000 to the Caribbean, 25,878,000 to Italy and 14,741,000 to Canada. Tourism represents one of the biggest international businesses. In 1992, international tourist expenditures amounted to about 276 billion U.S. dollars (United Nations, 1994b: 891-925)

Many national and local economies depend on the tourist trade. The social and economic structures of many countries in the world and many cities and areas within these countries have adjusted themselves so as to receive large numbers of tourists. The cultural impact of tourism has been considerable, although more research is needed to assess it with precision (Theobald, 1994b). Similar to the impact of temporary-stay migration and that of seasonal workers, the typical situation appears to be that of contact between people of different cultural backgrounds and between those who are poor and those who are rich. Seasonal workers and, in most cases, those who cater to tourists are derived from those aspects of social structure that produce poverty; tourism is derived from those aspects of social structure that produce affluence in society. Thus, it is important to study both temporary migration and periodic migration in order to understand the intercultural, interethnic processes in the global society. Here, however, we will focus on immigration as an important phenomenon and process in Canadian society.

STRUCTURE OF RELATIONSHIP BETWEEN MIGRANT AND ESTABLISHED GROUPS

Each type of migrants discussed above implies a different relationship of the migrating group to the structure of the society to which they migrate and that from which they migrate. The structure of the relationship between a minority ethnic group and the broader society in which it exists is established by the initial contact between the group and the majority, dominant, group in the society. The initial contact usually involves at least one migrating group and, with the exception of settlers, another already established group. Once, as a result of this contact, a structure is established, it tends to persist and does not change easily. It gives direction to the processes of intergroup relations for some time to come. Many issues of interethnic relations throughout the history of a society have their roots in the initial contact between the established and the migrant groups. Thus, one type of initial contact may produce an early conflict between the groups; another type, a delayed conflict, often delayed for a few generations. Likewise, a successful resolution of an early conflict may become a precedent for resolutions of later successive conflictual issues. Inversely, the lack of an early successful resolution may make finding a successful resolution to interethnic conflicts more difficult later on.

Stanley Lieberson (1961) has developed a theory of interethnic initial contact in which he explains how the relationship established as a result of the initial contact influences interethnic conflict and assimilation. The rest of this section will briefly summarize Lieberson's theory inasmuch as it is relevant to our discussion here. It will also creatively develop some aspects of the theory beyond Lieberson's own original statement.

Lieberson postulates two basic types of initial interethnic group contact, migrant superordination and indigenous superordination. By the word *indigenous* he does not mean necessarily only the aborigines, but also any other population sufficiently established in an area so as to possess the institutions and the demographic capacity to maintain some social order through generations. Thus, what at one time had been a migrating group, for example, the British in Canada, becomes at another time an indigenous group in relation to other immigrating groups.

• Migrant Superordination

Migrant superordination takes place when the migrating population imposes its own political and economic institutions on the indigenous population by means of superior technology, particularly weapons, and by means of a tighter social organization. Lieberson refers here to a typical colonial situation. We can add that an additional important factor in establishing migrant superordination is the colonizers' attitudes or ideology of superiority over the people on whose society a new institutional structure is imposed. This ideology may take different forms, as for example the idea of "civilizing the savages" or the idea of superiority of the white race. Whatever its specific content or form, it becomes an ideology of racism.

This type of initial contact is usually accompanied by early conflict or warfare, since the migrants begin to interfere with the indigenous established order. A number of changes in the indigenous social structure take place. There is often a numerical decline of the indigenous population, caused either by warfare or the introduction of various diseases or the disruption of established sustenance activities or the like. Furthermore, the superordinate migrants frequently create political entities that have no relation to the political boundaries or structures existing in the indigenous society prior to contact. Examples are the British and Boers in South Africa, who created political states that included areas that previously belonged to separate, warring groups, or the states created by the colonial powers in much of the rest of Africa that had little relation to the distinct ethnic identities of the indigenous people. A current example is the states of Rwanda and Burundi, whose boundaries cut across the same ethnic groups in both states. We can add that the migrant group either destroys the elite of the indigenous society and substitutes a new one made up of their own members, or they become a super-elite over the old indigenous elite.

Furthermore, the migrant group restructures the economy of the area. The subordinate, indigenous population often fails or is unable, at first, to participate in the new economic or political order. Hence, the superordinate migrants frequently introduce new immigrant groups to fill the niches created in the revised economy. With time, the immigrant groups themselves become indigenous by establishing themselves through generations.

This kind of development of the social structure is often related to a sequence of processes. Although Lieberson does not develop this in detail, his ideas suggest the following sequence. Several concepts may be added to make these sequences complete. As was already mentioned, the initial contact in which migrant superordination occurs is often accompanied by early conflict or warfare. This tends to be of relatively short duration and is followed by a period, often long, of accommodation. With consecutive generations, a degree of incorporation develops, both culturally and structurally. Conflict, however, does not necessarily disappear but often becomes latent and emerges later in the form of nationalism and may involve violence and rebellion.

The reason for this emergence of conflict is the creation or development of ethnic or racial consciousness. A number of factors condition this creation. The most important among them are the categorical subordination to the migrant population, the dissolution and decay of previous ethnic or tribal forms of social organization and the fact that, as the indigenous group becomes increasingly incorporated within the larger system, the saliency and the symbolic significance of its subordinate position increases. Hence, for the bulk of the indigenous population, the only alternative appears to be change or destruction of the institutions of political, economic and social subordination.

Furthermore, the conflict that emerges is often exacerbated and complicated by the fact that parts of the migrant population have become indigenous through generations. Thus the racial conflict has been more severe in those colonial countries such as South Africa and Algeria in which the percentages of whites born in the country has been high. The reason for this is that, when the migrant population becomes firmly established, it is more difficult for the indigenous subordinate group to change the social order. The conflict becomes even more complicated when among the established migrant population are middle-men minority groups that are also subordinate to the colonial group, yet superordinate, at least in some respects, to the original indigenous population. When change does occur and the colonial superordinate group is removed from its dominant position, the position of the other ethnic groups tends to shift to being subordinate to that of the original subordinate and now superordinate indigenous group. Lieberson gives as an example the Chinese in Indonesia, who were encouraged to immigrate under the Dutch domain but were faced with a series of restrictive laws and measures designed to limit their activities after the government representing the indigenous population took over. Another example is the South Asians in Africa, as in Uganda. In some cases, as for example the South Asians in Fiji, after the removal of the colonial power, the middle-man minority group may itself become the superordinate group over the indigenous population.

• Indigenous Superordination

According to Lieberson, indigenous superordination takes place when a population migrates into a subordinate position in another society. His model here is, with some exceptions, North America and Australia. The initial contact is not accompanied by conflict. The experience of those migrating into a subordinate position is typically different from that generated by colonial indigenous subordination. Thus, many immigrants fare better economically in the host society than they did in their mother country. Furthermore, the option of returning to the homeland often exists for the immigrants. Immigrant dissatisfaction with subordination or other condition of contact can often be resolved by withdrawal from the society. Likewise, threats of demographic or institutional imbalance are often reduced by the superordinate group limiting the number of immigrants and the types of groups immigrating by means of quotas. Immigrant restriction thus provides a mechanism whereby some potential conflict is prevented.

Similarly, when other ethnic groups are admitted in great numbers by the indigenous group, the introduction of a variety of groups serves to ensure that no single different ethnic or racial group is sufficiently large in number to challenge the supremacy of the indigenous group. Lieberson gives the example of Hawaii, in which a succession of immigrant groups shifts–from Chinese, to Japanese, Portuguese, Puerto Ricans, Koreans, Spanish, Russians and Filipinos–was a conscious attempt to prevent any single group from gaining too much power.

The processes that accompany migrant subordination are, according to Lieberson, not so much conflict as assimilation. The indigenous superordinate population places great emphasis on the assimilation of immigrants, and the issue is usually phrased in terms of the immigrants' capacity and willingness to become part of the existing social order. Conflicts that do arise are limited and sporadic, and occasional flurries of violence are generally initiated by the dominant, indigenous group itself as a consequence of fears of competition for labour, nativist fears of foreign political domination and the like. The conflicts between the subordinate migrants and the superordinate indigenous population, however, tend to be resolved by some form of accommodation within the context of a consensual form of government.

Lieberson's theory is important because it makes possible an understanding of a great variety of ethnic processes and phenomena in terms of a single distinction between two types of initial interethnic contact. The latter is seen as cause, the former as effect. This may involve some over-simplification, but, in this manner, the theory inherently links the processes of interethnic relations with the process of migration. In applying the theory to concrete societies, however, both concepts of initial contact may be useful in explaining interethnic processes within the same society, rather than reserving one for such colonial societies as Africa and the other for North America. The theory of migrant superordination and subordination will be useful in explaining the structural base for Canadian interethnic relations in Canadian history. The next chapter will apply this theory in a discussion of the historical stages of migration in Canada.

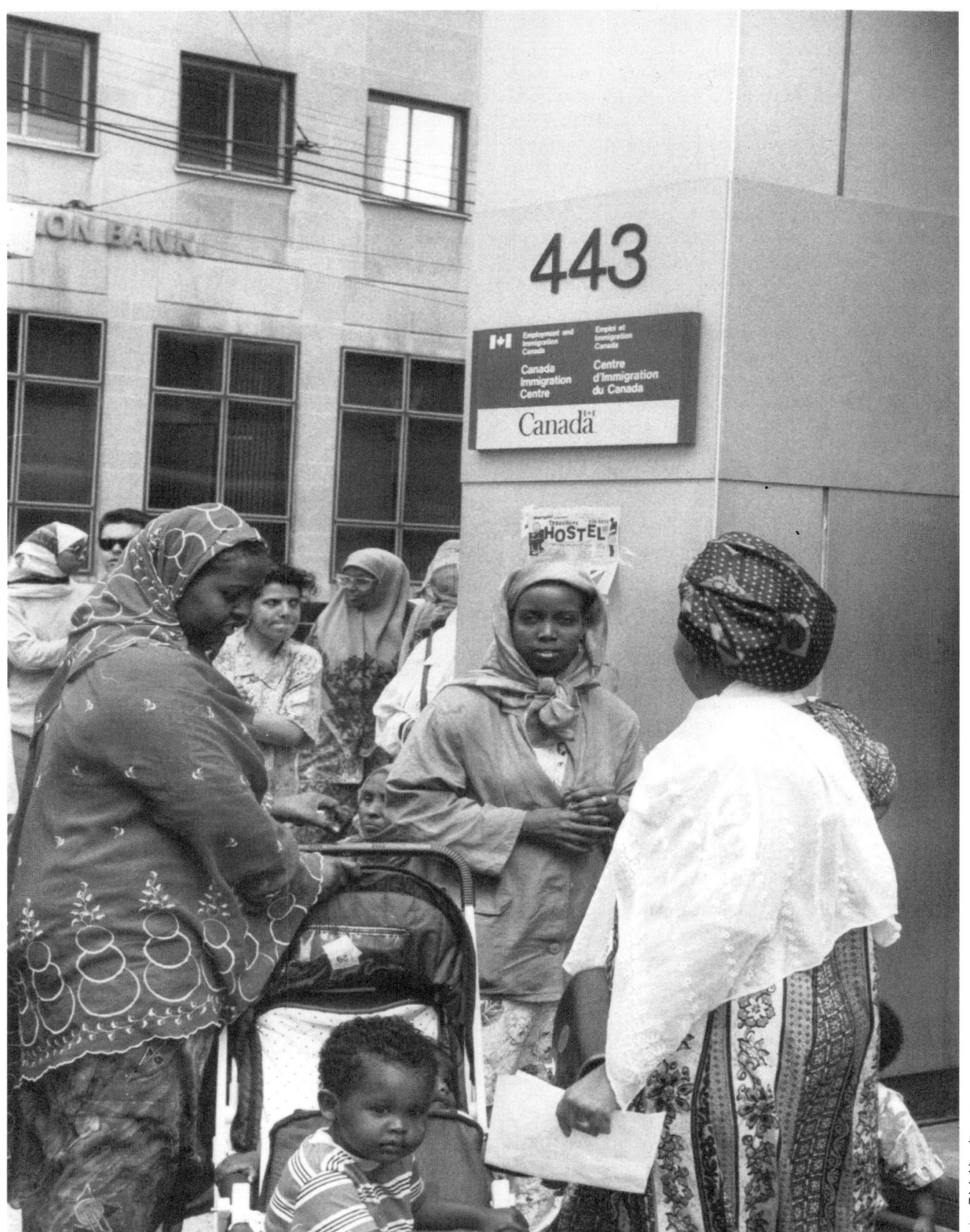

Photo: Dick Hemingway

Immigration policy now allows for family reunification. In 1992, for the first time in Canadian immigration history, more women than men migrated to Canada.

CHAPTER 4

IMMIGRATION TO CANADA

New Faces in the Crowd

Like other immigrant-receiving nations, Canada is highly dependent on immigration for population and economic growth. This chapter outlines various stages in the history of Canadian immigration and describes the important changes that have taken place in recent years. The chapter goes on to describe and examine the many difficulties immigrants and their families face in the course of settling in Canada.

To get a concrete picture of how migration engages ethnic groups in patterns of contact and establishes a structure of relationship between them, it will be useful to examine and characterize the stages of settlement and immigration in Canada. The distinction between the stages is based on the assumption that migration in each period studied is sufficiently different in character. The criteria for distinguishing periods of migration were chosen in answer to the following questions: Have there been different types of migrants at different points in time? Have there been large waves of migrants of one type as against another? Have there been changes in policy or legislation relating to migration into the country that made a difference as to the type of migrants coming, their source or their numbers? What has been the role that one or another wave of migrants has played in the establishment of viable ethnic communities? What has been the role one or another wave of migration into Canada has played in the socio-economic and political development of the country? The periods described below are based on a combination of these criteria.

The description of the earlier periods will be brief. The most recent periods, however, will be examined in more detail. The purpose of distinguishing these periods is not to give a thorough description of migration in each period, but rather to characterize them in such a way as to show how the structure of interethnic relations in Canada was historically established and developed.

STAGES OF SETTLEMENT AND IMMIGRATION IN CANADA

The history of settlement, colonization and immigration in Canada can thus be divided into the following stages. The last two stages will be further subdivided into substages:

1. Pre-European Settlement
2. 1600 to the Conquest of New France
3. 1760 to the War of 1812
4. 1815 to the "Opening of the West"
5. 1880 to World War I
6. Between the Wars
7. End of World War II to 1967
8. Since 1968: The "Merit Point System"

• Pre-European Settlement

The original settlers in Canada, in the sociological sense of the word, were the Indians and Inuit, today called the Native peoples or the First Nations or Aboriginal peoples. The ancestors of the Indians came to Canada probably around 40,000 B.C. and those of the Inuit around 8,000 B.C. At the time of the European arrival, there were approximately 220,000 Indians and Inuit living in Canada. They comprised something like 80 to 100 different ethnic groups. A number of the groups were continuously migrant. The best known of these were the Indians of the Plains and the seasonally migrant Inuit (Denevan, 1976: 235-288; Valentine assisted by Taylor, 1980b).

Since the groups lived in separate geographical areas, and since they all depended on a primary economy, i.e., hunting, fishing and agriculture, the stratification system between the groups was rather loose. To be sure, there were richer groups and poorer groups, those with more prestige and those with less prestige, but there does not appear to have been any definite system of superordination and subordination of one group in relation to another (Quimby, 1960:84).

• 1600 to the Conquest of New France

The general feature that characterizes this period is that settlement and immigration were by and large aspects of the process of colonization, i.e., the colonization of Canada by the French, until the defeat of New France by the British in 1759. The period involves primarily two types of migrants, settlers and colonizers, and involves the establishment of the first structure of migrant superordination.

The settlement of New France was a slow process at first. Samuel de Champlain brought over less than 100 settlers. By 1660 there were only 2,000 settlers in New France. It was only through the efforts of the able intendant Jean Talon that vigorous migration was undertaken. As a migration policy-maker, Talon can be compared to Clifford Sifton. Both can take credit for establishing viable permanent settlements in new and unpopulated or little populated areas. Thus, by 1672 the population of New France had risen to 6,000. In 1700 there were about 15,000 settlers, but by 1760 the figure had increased to 60,000 or 70,000. We don't know, however, how much of this increase can be accounted for by migration and how much by a high birth rate.

The French, like the English later on, were a peculiar mixture of both settlers and colonizers. On the one hand, the migrants settled in unpopulated areas and developed their own society. On the other hand, their contact with the Indians ultimately led to an imposition of a superstructure on the Indian society. The French established reservations for the Indians. Overtly, the reservations were established for the benefit of both the French and the Indians, but the ultimate purpose was to assimilate them into the French culture (Jaenen, 1973: 159-184). The effect, however, was the establishment of a superstructure over the ancient Canadian Indian societies that would remain in place for centuries to come. It is only in recent decades that this superstructure for the First Nations has begun to change.

• 1760 to the War of 1812

The distinct feature of this period is the establishment of the second structure of migrant superordination. By this time, the French were established as an indigenous population. The British now became the second colonizers of Canada.

The period also features an influx of immigrants from the United States. Two types of these immigrants have been distinguished, early and late. The early ones were the Loyalist refugees and exiles from the American Revolution. This was the first large political immigration to Canada. About 30,000 refugees migrated to Nova Scotia, and about 10,000 to Quebec. Most of the latter occupied the farmlands west of what was New France, in what soon came to be called Upper Canada. The socio-economic background of the refugees was mixed. They included farmers, soldiers, government employees, teachers, lawyers and clergymen.

The second type of immigrants from the United States were, as some called them, the "Late Loyalists." To a great extent, these were farmers, attracted purposefully by Lord Simcoe in order to build up the population of British Canada. They were, thus, primarily economic immigrants. In 1791 the population of Upper Canada was only about 14,000, but 20 years later, due primarily to these immigrants, it had increased to 90,000. Almost all of them were of English ethnicity, and settled north of Lake Ontario, between what is today Niagara-on-the-Lake and Kingston. However, in the 1790s there were already German and French immigrants from the United States settling in the Markham and Waterloo regions, and Scottish settlers establishing themselves in the Lake St. Clair area (Cook, et al., 1963: 19-25).

Immigration in this period was an important part of the process of establishing migrant superordination over the French. For the first governor of Upper Canada, John Simcoe, this was a conscious and planned process. Among all his plans for the development of the colony, developing the population was of prime necessity if Canada were to become the "bulwark of the British Empire in North America" (Cook, et al., 1963: 21). This became an important principle in Canadian immigration policies for years to come.

• 1812 to the "Opening of the West"

The successful conclusion of the War of 1812 created a new confidence in British North America and brightened the prospects for its expansion and growth. The war, however, gave a new and definite direction to the trade routes of the British, Montreal-based merchants–west, rather than south. The trading companies, in particular the Hudson's Bay Company, played a significant role in opening up the route and stimulating the settlement of the Canadian West. Thus, as early as 1812, Lord Selkirk planted a colony of Scottish settlers in the Red River Valley, near the current site of Winnipeg. This settlement was to develop a population in order to provide support and a base for trading operations in the West. The basic assumption that came to be shared by both the merchants and the government and that provided a basis for immigration policies throughout this period was that commercial and economic development depended upon a large population. Immigration thus served the immediate aim of population development. This assumption was the basis for Canadian immigration policies almost into the twentieth century. Later, particularly after World War II, Canadian immigration policies were directed towards economic development.

A variety of means were used to attract immigrants. These included offers of free or cheap land, the establishment of immigration agencies and the commissioning of immigration agents, intensive and often exaggerated advertising (pamphlets, posters, articles in newspapers, letters from successful settlers and so on), assisted passages, colonization companies, group settlements, delegations of influential people, exhibitions and other means (Macdonald, 1966: 30-48).

The need for more immigrants was constant, due to the large numbers of immigrants migrating on from Canada to the United States, where land was often better and general social and economic development was further advanced. There was, however, a strong push factor for British immigration to Canada. Economic snags, unemployment and crop failures caused hundreds of thousands of the British to look for a better life elsewhere. Examples of this are the heavy unemployment following the conclusion of the Napoleonic Wars in 1815 and the famine in Ireland in 1846. In 1847 alone, 110,000 Irish emigrated to Canada. Indeed, Britain used emigration to the colonies as one means of solving its domestic economic problems.

In 1812 Upper Canada had a population of 90,000; by 1838, it had increased to 400,000. From 1815 to 1880, 1,623,984 emigrants left Britain for Canada. Thousands, however, would die on the way. By 1881, the population of Canada, according to the census, was 4,324,810. Of these, 59 percent were of British origin, 30 percent of French origin, 2.5 percent Indians and Inuit and 8.6 percent other and not stated origins.

Of the non-British, non-French and non-Indian and Inuit people in Canada at the time, the largest group were the Germans. Small numbers of Germans had settled in New France in the seventeenth century, and in the middle of the eighteenth century several thousand German Protestants went to Nova Scotia. After 1780, small numbers of German sectarians–Mennonites, Moravians, Tunkers–came to Upper Canada from the United States. However, larger numbers of German immigrants, particularly the Mennonites, begun to settle in Canada between the 1830s and 1870s. They settled in Waterloo County of what is now Ontario, in the Maritimes and, after 1870, in the Prairies and British Columbia. Thus, between 1874 and 1880, about 6,000 Mennonites settled in Manitoba.

There were also smaller numbers of other ethnic groups. A Danish settlement was established in New Brunswick in the 1870s. In 1875-1876 about 1,000 Icelanders established communities on the west shore of Lake Winnipeg at Gimli. Around the same time, Norwegians, mostly from the United States, settled near Brown in Manitoba, near Calgary in Alberta and in British Columbia. Finns settled in the 1870s in the Port Arthur area. There were also colonies of the Dutch with roots going back to the Loyalist migration (B & B Report, 1970: 17-21).

There were other small first settlements. In the 1850s, with the advent of the Gold Rush in the Fraser Valley in British Columbia, the first Chinese migrated to Canada from the United States. In 1858, the first small group settlement of Polish families was established in the Renfrew, Ontario, area, which by 1864 increased to about 500 (Radecki and Hydenkorn, 1976).

A significant form of migration into Canada in this period was the use of the Underground Railroad. Between 1820 and 1860, the American Blacks, as fugitive slaves and as freedmen, formed sizable settlements, particularly in southwestern Ontario and the Maritimes. A census taken in 1860 in Upper Canada showed a total of about 50,000 Blacks, but the 1871 census, the first census after the Confederation of Canada, gave a total of 21,500 Blacks in Canada. It is probable that the 1860 number was inflated. Historians, however, have thought that many Blacks may have returned to the United States after the Emancipation Proclamation in the United States in 1863, since consecutive Canadian censuses reported a further decline in their number (Winks, 1971).

Another group of refugees who migrated to Canada during this period were the Sioux Indians. Both in 1862 and 1876-1877, groups of Sioux Indians escaped

Photo: Public Archives of Canada, Ottawa

"Only farmers need apply" was the slogan of immigration policy under Clifford Sifton, Canadian Minister of the Interior at the turn of the century. But already a new wave of "urban" worker immigrants from Europe were arriving in large numbers. Immigrants on board the S.S. Empress of Britain, 1910.

to Canada after defeat by the American army. In 1876-1877, about 4,000 Dakota Sioux, headed by Chief Sitting Bull, were given asylum in Canada after the American forces struck back following George Custer's defeat (Patterson II, 1972: 100-102).

It was thus in this period that the basic immigration pattern to Canada was established. The periods that followed gave this pattern different sources of immigration and modified it with various restrictions on immigration, but the pattern of continuous, annual immigration was set. This period involved both economic pull and push immigrants, many of whom settled in unpopulated areas. It also included refugees. The basic pattern of migration strengthened and developed the previously established migrant superordination of the British over the French and the Native peoples. A new pattern, however, was also being established, that of migrant subordination of other ethnic and racial groups who were beginning to immigrate to Canada. This pattern was enormously reinforced in the next period of Canadian history.

• 1880 to World War I

The immigrants of diverse ethnicities, who were only a trickle before 1880, became a torrent in the period between 1880 and World War I. Sociologically this period is especially important, because it was during this time that the basic structure of ethnic stratification in Canada, outside of the French-English and Native relationship, was established. The period provides a good example of the process of migrant subordination of ethnic groups new to Canada.

In one sense, the period after 1880 is a continuation of Canadian societal expansion westward. However, soon after 1880 a number of events converged to make it the most unique period in Canadian immigration history. The most distinguishing feature of this period was the new ethnicities of immigrants. For the first time in Canadian history, large numbers of people from Eastern Europe and from Asia began to arrive.

A set of factors conditioned the immigration of new ethnic groups. First, completion of the transcanadian railroad opened up the West for settlement. It became more and more difficult to attract enough immigrants from Britain and the United States to establish solid permanent blocks of population in the Prairies. At the same time, Canada was shifting into a new export economy based on wheat, which could be produced mainly in the Prairies. The National Policy was an important instrument in the development of this economy, but little could be done without more people in the Prairies. The old immigration policy of preferring Anglo-Saxon immigrants was thus inadequate for the new pattern of economic development. New sources of immigration had to be tapped. Ethnic origin, hence, came to be considered by the government of less importance than the immigrants' fitness as permanent rural settlers (Macdonald, 1966: 148). This is where Clifford Sifton came in. As Minister of the Interior from 1896 to 1906, he applied this new principle with vigour and created one of the biggest movement of people in modern history. The date 1896 is thus significant because the trend towards the new ethnicities of immigrants, already in progress since the 1880s, became a major event in Canadian history due to Sifton's policies until World War I.

The need for settler-farmers, however, was not the only factor inducing immigration. The period after 1880 was also a period of gradual industrial growth, brought about in large measure by the railroad. The building of the railroad itself required large numbers of workers who could not be easily obtained from among the older, previously settled population. Thus it was in this period that the need for large-scale industrial labour was created. For the first time in Canadian immigration history, there were large numbers of immigrants who did not settle on the land as farmers, but went directly into industrial work. Formally, the immigration policies were aimed at attracting the land settlers. Informally, however, the government cooperated with the railroad and industrial developers in allowing them to induce immigrants into industrial labour. Thus, the character of the immigrants in this period was determined. They were mostly of two types: settlers-farmers and industrial, unskilled labourers. As in all other periods, however, there were also refugees.

Between 1881 and 1884, 15,700 Chinese were brought over from China as contract labourers to work on the Canadian Pacific Railway. By 1901, the number of Asians rose to 23,700, including 4,700 Japanese and 1,700 East Indians. Most of them settled in British Colombia. It has been estimated that in 1907, 25 percent of the labour force in British Columbia was of Asian origin (B & B Report, 1970: 21).

In the 1880s, thousands of Jewish refugees fleeing from pogroms in Russia arrived in Canada. By 1901, they numbered about 16,000, and in 1911, about 46,000. In 1886, Hungarians began to settle in what later became Saskatchewan. In 1887, Mormons immigrated from the United States to Alberta. In 1891, the first Ukrainians began to arrive in Manitoba followed in 1896 by larger groups in response to Sifton's invitations. In 1899, more than 7,000 Doukhobors arrived from Russia and settled in Saskatchewan and later in British Columbia. Between 1905 and 1908, 5,000 East Indians, mostly Sikhs, came to British Columbia, and in 1907, over 8,000 Japanese arrived. Italians began arriving in Canada in the 1880s as workers for the CPR; by 1901 they numbered about 11,000; by 1911, about 46,000 (B & B Report, 1970: 18-25).

At the same time British and American immigrants continued to arrive. Between 1880 and 1914, 1,250,000 persons from the United Kingdom and 1,000,000 persons from the United States immigrated to Canada. Yet, whereas in 1880 persons of ethnic origins other than the British and French made up a negligible percentage of the total population, by the conclusion of World War I, in 1921, they made up abut 17 percent of Canada's population. By the end of World War I, Canadian society was not the same. Levels of social structure had been created that were based on ethnicities other than those of the charter groups. These ethnicities did not represent isolated communities like the Indians and the Inuit at the time, but were communities that became an essential part of the economy.

This new level of social structure gave the problem of integration of Canadian society a new dimension. It introduced a new source of potential tensions into society, thus complicating the already existing English-French conflicts. Yet it also formed a basis for a new principle of potential societal integration–one emerging from the new groups themselves–which much later, in the 1960s, came to be defined as multiculturalism. At the end of World War I, however, to many members of the majority group, this level of social structure appeared as a threat.

• Between the Wars

The period between the wars was a period of immigration restriction and immigration reduction. By the end of World War I most of the immigrants to Canada were concentrated in the cities and were working in rapidly growing industry. Yet, many were continuously looking for work. The most significant city in this regard was Winnipeg. The war ended in a period of economic recession, which resulted in wage cuts and increased unemployment. Many immigrants joined labour unions; between 1914 and 1918, their membership doubled. With the end of the war, union leadership attempted to gain the right of collective bargaining. All this resulted in a series of labour strikes culminating in 1919 in the Winnipeg General Strike. The business and professional community reacted by charging that the strikes were an attempt to overturn British institutions. East European immigrants served as an easy scapegoat and were accused of Bolshevik-style subversion. This only added to the already existing prejudices against East Europeans (Avery, 1977).

There were also anti-German sentiments, including pressure to stop German immigration. There were feelings that immigrants were taking up scarce jobs, and there were movements to fire immigrants and give their jobs to the returning soldiers.

The consequence of these feelings and pressures was the Immigration Act of 1919, which considerably reduced the number of non-British European immigrants, temporarily stopped Mennonites, Doukhobors and Hutterites from immigrating, developed measures for deporting immigrants and produced a list of prohibited immigrants. The latter included illiterates, the sick, the physically defective, revolutionaries and anarchists, enemy aliens and anyone who might become a public charge. Instructions were issued to immigration officers overseas to discourage immigration of Ukrainians, Russians and Finns on the avowed grounds that they were not readily assimilable. The minister was given broad powers to admit or exclude any immigrants as he might see fit without being subject to the provisions of the Act.

This Act was followed in 1923 by the Chinese Immigration Act, which admitted to Canada only certain specified classes of Chinese and almost stopped Chinese immigration completely. This was another step in the trend to restrict Asian immigration, which had already begun in the preceding period. The "Head Tax" on Chinese immigrants had been used since 1885. The "Gentlemen's Agreement" that restricted the immigration of Japanese to 400 persons a year had been in effect since 1908. In 1928 it was revised to allow only 150 persons a year. In 1910, the Canadian government passed an order in-council, aimed at stopping immigration from India, which came to be known as the "Continuous Journey (Passage)" rule. According to this rule, persons from India were free to come but only on direct, non-stop ships travelling from India to Canada. However, there were no direct, non-stop ships. The *Komagata Maru* affair was a result of this legislation. When in 1914 the ship with 376 Punjabis, intending to immigrate to Canada as British subjects, arrived at Vancouver, the passengers were not allowed to disembark–the ship had sailed out of Hong Kong. The passengers were detained on the ship by Canadian authorities for two months and then ordered to sail back to India (Ferguson, 1975; Johnston, 1989; Andracki, 1978; Avery, 1995: 43-59).

The entry of Blacks was also restricted when, in 1923, the government decided that only citizens of Commonwealth countries with predominantly white populations would be considered British subjects.

The Depression of the 1930s further reduced immigration and virtually cut off immigration of ethnic groups other than the British. In 1931, an order-in-council restricted immigration to only British subjects and American citizens. Thus, whereas between 1922 and 1931 there were still a total of about 1,166,000 immigrants arriving in Canada, between 1932 and 1941 the figure fell to 140,000. Emigration out of Canada in that period amounted to about 100,000.

The entire period of immigration between the wars was a period in which those in charge of immigration policies showed intense concern with the question of the ethnic composition of the Canadian population. This was nothing new in Canadian immigration policies. As was mentioned above, this had also been an important question for Governor Simcoe. In the early nineteenth century, however, since the British population in Canada was small, the solution to this question was to encourage immigration so as to build up a large British population base in relation to the French. In contrast, in the 1920s and 1930s the solution was thought to lie in restricting the immigration of people whose ethnicity was considered to be "non-preferred." Sociologically, this renewed concern can be interpreted as reflecting feelings of threat to indigenous superordination on the part of the majority group. Immigration restriction in this period was a preventive measure to ensure indigenous superordination in the face of the changing balance of the ethnic mix.

Nevertheless, in the entire period between the wars, but mostly between 1920 and 1930, and besides the British immigrants, about 67,000 Ukrainians, 20,200 Jews, 20,000 Swedes, 19,500 Norwegians, 17,000 Danes, 20,000 Mennonites and others arrived in the country. Yet, there were ethnic groups who lost substantial numbers of their population in that period. A number of groups were subject to deportation. Thus, between 1931 and 1941 the number of Germans in Canada fell by almost 9,000, Russians, by 4,500 and Asians by 10,500. Other groups, in particular the Italians, stopped arriving because of emigration restrictions at home. In 1941 in Montreal and Toronto, there were about 38,000 Italians.

Most immigrants arriving in Canada in this period went to cities and industrial areas. This included those who had stated that farming was their intended occupation in Canada. Montreal, Toronto, Winnipeg, Vancouver, Sudbury, Timmins, Port Arthur and Sault St. Marie became the main immigrant reception areas, but many settled also in the mine towns and mill towns of Northern Ontario and British Columbia.

On the eve of World War II, in 1938-1939, about 8,000 Jewish refugees from Nazi Germany were admitted to Canada. This foreshadowed a new immigration period that would immediately follow the war. (Most of the statistical information for this period is derived from B & B Report, 1970: 25-28 and Manpower and Immigration, 1974b: 11-17).

• End of World War II to 1967

Since World War II, immigration into Canada has gone through a number of phases. Immediately after the war, Canada joined other Western countries in resettling refugees. Yet in the 1950s and early 1960s, it still retained racial biases inherited from the previous periods. A movement emerged to develop a completely racism-free immigration policy. With the post-war economic boom, Canada aligned its immigration policies to economic needs and admitted large numbers of immigrants of the greatest ethnic diversity ever. By the end of this period Canada had developed a new approach to immigrant admission: a merit-point system of immigrant eligibility. This removed formal racial discrimination from the immigration procedures but it did not prevent the emergence of new pressures for immigration restriction that became more pronounced in the next period.

We can distinguish three substages of this period:

A. 1946 to 1952
B. 1953 to 1961
C. 1962 to 1967

All statistics for these periods, unless otherwise indicated, are derived from the yearly reports of the Canadian Department of Employment and Immigration, formerly called Department of Manpower and Immigration.

1946 to 1952. With the war, the economic depression was over. After the war, immigration increased again. Between 1946 and 1952, 789,278 immigrants arrived in Canada. The old restrictions regarding Asian immigrants still applied and concern with the ethnic composition of the population was still quite strong. Thus, in 1947 Prime Minister MacKenzie King was stating that he was sure that people of Canada did not wish to make a fundamental change in the character of their population. Since large-scale immigration from the Orient would change the "fundamental composition" of the Canadian population, the government had no intention of removing the restrictions on Asian immigration (King, 1947). Preference was given to British immigrants. Of the total immigration in this period, 46 percent were of British ethnic origin (Richmond, 1967: 7-11).

However, a new, distinguishing feature of the period, the larger scale admission of political immigrants, emerged. In 1946, admission was granted to 4,527 Polish ex-servicemen who had fought in the war on the side of the Allies. There were strong international pressures on Canada to take in some of the large number of post-war refugees, known as the Displaced Persons, who were primarily in Western Europe. As a result, between 1946 and 1952, Canada admitted around 166,000 refugees (Walmsley, 1954). From 1946 to 1955, these refugees included about 55,000 Polish, over 33,000 Ukrainians, close to 8,000 Russians, close to 14,000 Hungarians, about 8,000 Jews and close to 35,000 other Eastern Europeans, in particular, Latvians, Lithuanians, Estonians, Czechs, Slovaks, Rumanians, Slovenes, Serbs, Croats and others (Kalbach, 1970:367).

In addition to the policy allowing resettlement of the Displaced Persons, in 1949 the same criteria as those used for immigration from Britain were made available to France. However, immigration from France remained small after the war; the French made up less than 3 percent of total immigrants in that period. Furthermore, special arrangement was made to allow 15,000 farmers from the Netherlands into Canada, quotas for immigrants from the East Indies were slightly increased and the sponsoring of immigrants from previously enemy countries, especially Italy, was made possible.

1953 to 1961. In 1952 a new Immigration Act was passed. It reflected a renewed concern with ethnicity. It gave rather large powers to the Minister of Immigration to admit or deny admission to immigrants on the basis of ethnicity, citizenship, peculiarity of customs, suitability as judged by the immigration officials, probable inability to become assimilated and the like. Although this was invalidated in 1956, nevertheless a strong preference for British immigrants was expressed. Between 1953 and 1961 more than one-third of the 1,287,641 immigrants were of British origin. Yet, percentages of other ethnic groups were increasing. The proportion of Italian immigrants between the same years increased to 17 percent of total immigration. In 1956, following the Hungarian Revolution, about 38,000 Hungarian refugees arrived in Canada, and the Suez Crisis induced more immigration from the United Kingdom. In 1959-1960, as a gesture of observance of the World Refugee Year, 3,500 additional refugees were admitted to Canada. These included handicapped and chronically sick persons who otherwise would not have qualified for entry.

1962 to 1967. In 1962 new immigration regulations were issued that, in principle, abolished almost all restrictions based on ethnicity. This was an important step in Canadian immigration history. Instead of ethnicity,

Photo: Dick Hemingway

Immigration regulations of 1960s established education, training and skill as the main criteria in the selection of new immigrants, opening the door to a great many skilled workers from southern Europe.

the regulations addressed the economic needs of the country and established education, training and skill as the main criteria in the selection of unsponsored immigrants (Hawkins, 1972: 125). In practice, Britain was still favoured, because there were more professional and higher skilled workers in Britain who could or were willing to emigrate and because emphasis on professional qualifications resulted in an intensification of the promotional campaign in Britain (Richmond, 1967: 18). Thus, between 1962 and 1967, 844,720 immigrants arrived in Canada. In 1961, the proportion of the British was 17 percent of the total immigration; in 1966, it rose to 37 percent, more than the general average for British immigration since the war. From after the war until 1963, two-thirds of all professional workers immigrating to Canada had come from Britain and the United States, with Britain accounting for over half of the total. Now the percentage increased even more.

Of the other ethnic groups, the largest single group of immigrants were Italians, about 20 percent of the total immigration. Other groups included Germans (8 percent), Asians (more than 6 percent), French (3.5 percent), Polish (3 percent), Jewish (2.5 percent), Dutch (2.5 percent), Blacks (2.5 percent) and Portuguese, Greeks and other Europeans (total of more than 21 percent). What is interesting is that, in this period, between 80 to over 90 percent of Italian, Portuguese and Greek immigrants were family-sponsored immigrants. Furthermore, because ethnicity was no longer a barrier to immigration, the percentages of Asians and Blacks increased rather rapidly and continued to increase in the next period. Thus, in the five-year span from 1956 to 1960, the percentage of Asian immigrants was 2.21 of the total, and of the Blacks, only .56; in the 1961-1965 time span it rose to 6.25 for the Asians and to 2.37 for the Blacks (Richmond, 1967: 5,18).

In 1966 the *White Paper on Immigration* was published. It reaffirmed the non-discriminatory principles already contained in the 1962 regulations but suggested their further rationalization. It did, however, propose some restrictions on the sponsored immigrants. This latter proposal produced a negative reaction from the Canadian immigrant communities themselves. This indicated that, now, more than ever before, immigrants were gradually becoming a political factor to be reckoned with. The *White Paper* was a prelude to the new Immigration Regulations of 1967.

SINCE 1968: THE "MERIT POINT SYSTEM"

From one point of view, the period after 1967 was a continuation of the previous one. It shows a further attempt to rationalize immigration and to relate it to economic development. However, the Immigration Regulations of 1967 gave a new structure to Canadian immigration. They created a system of admissions to Canada based on merit points. The new regulations provided that the independent and sponsored applicants be assessed by immigration officials according to their possession of a set of characteristics, and each characteristic was assigned a range of merit points. Nine characteristics were singled out: education and training (0-20 merit points, one point for each year of education or training); personal qualities, such as adaptability, motivation, initiative and so on (0-15 points); occupational demand for the occupation the applicant would follow (0-15 points); occupational skill, from unskilled to professional (1-10 points); age (0-10 points); arranged employment (0 or 10 points); knowledge of English and/or French (0-10 points); relatives in Canada (0 or 3 or 5 points); and employment opportunities in the area of destination (0-5 points). The same assessment of characteristics was provided for the sponsored applicants, except that the last four were to be substituted by arrangements provided by the relative in Canada (15, 20, 25 or 30 points). In each case, the original regulations stipulated that the applicant, to be admitted, must receive at least 50 points (*Canada Gazette*, 1967).

In the periods that followed, some modifications to the numbers of points were introduced, but new legislation provided for new types of designated classes of immigrants. Two new immigration acts reflected the new concern, expressed in the media, with the question of absorption and type of immigrants coming into the country. This period can be divided into the following substages:

A. 1968 to Immigration Act of 1976
B. 1978 to 1993 amendments to Immigration Act
C. 1993 to present

• 1968 to Immigration Act of 1976

In 1974 a further requirement to the merit point system was added. In addition to the 50 points, the applicant had to receive at least one point for occupational demand or have arranged or designated employment, and if either of the latter two were missing, the applicant must have at least 60 points to enter the country. Applicants sponsored by those relatives in Canada who were willing to take responsibility for their sustenance were not required to be assessed on any of the characteristics.

Thus, under the point system, from 1968 to 1977, 1,592,013 immigrants entered the country. What is interesting is that after 1968 the percentage of sponsored immigrants doubled, whereas that of independent immigrants fell almost to half. In 1968, of all immigrants, 21 percent were sponsored and over 60 percent independent, whereas in 1976, almost 42 percent were sponsored and only about 33 percent were independent.

The most significant change in this period, a consequence of the new non-racist merit point system, was a change in the structure of the ethnic composition of immigration. In 1968, the British and Americans were the largest groups of immigrants arriving in the country (about 51,000). They were followed in size by the Italians (about 21,000), other southern European groups (about 23,500) and Asians (over 19,000). In 1978, the numbers of British and American immigrants substantially decreased (to about 33,500) and they were followed predominantly by Asian groups (about 32,000). Italians and other Southern European groups dropped to rather small numbers (about 4,000 for the Italians). The Caribbean groups also increased substantially in number (from less than 9,000 in 1968 to almost 17,000 in 1976). This period thus represented the reversal of the proportion of the white to non-white immigrants to Canada. In the periods of immigration that followed, this structure of immigration became even more defined with the non-white immigrants, particularly Asians, constituting the largest groups of immigrants arriving annually in Canada in the 1990s.

Traditionally, the government has dealt with refugees outside of the provisions of the regular immigration regulations. By 1970, Canada had submitted to the United Nations Convention on Refugees and accepted the obligation to take in a certain number of refugees as needed. Among the refugees admitted in this period were the following: since 1968, 12,500 Czechoslovakians; in 1970, 228 Tibetans; in 1972, 7,000 Ugandan Asians; in 1973, 5,000 Chileans; in 1975-1976, 6,700 Vietnamese and Cambodians. Altogether, between 1968 and 1976, more than 35,000 refugees were admitted to Canada (Manpower and Immigration, 1974b: 46; Bonavia, 1977: 43-45).

The 1967 immigration regulations, however, retained a feature that soon became the source of a serious problem. The regulations allowed visitors to

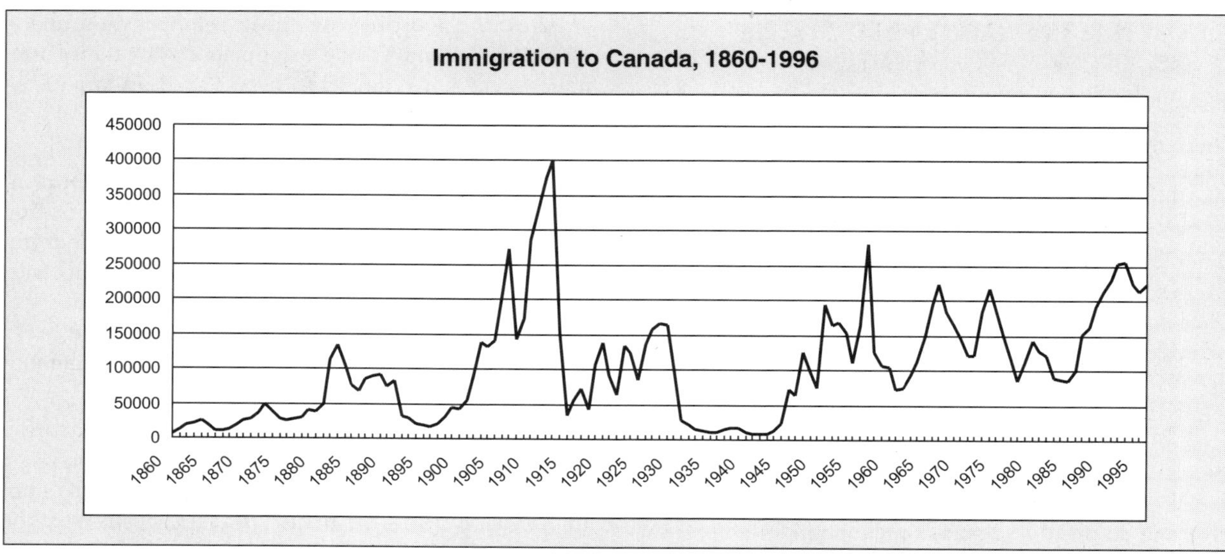

Chart 2: Selection Criteria for Independent Immigrants, 1998 (Business Immigrants, Skilled Workers and Assisted Relatives)

Factor	Units of Assessment	Notes
Education	16 maximum	
Specific vocational preparation	18 maximum	
Experience	8 maximum	0 units is an automatic refusal, except for persons with arranged employment or designated occupation
Occupation	10 maximum	0 units is an automatic refusal, unless arranged employment, designated occupation or self-employed. N/A for entrepreneurs and investors
Arranged employment or designated occupation	10 maximum	N/A for entrepreneurs, investors and self-employed
Demographic factor	8 maximum	Established by the Minister
Age	10 maximum	10 units if 21 to 44; 2 units deducted for each year under 21 or over 44
Knowledge of English or French	15 maximum	
Personal suitability	10 maximum	
Bonus for assisted relatives	5	
Bonus for self-employed immigrants	30	

Minimum Selection Units Required Per Category *

Entrepreneur	25	
Self-employed	25	
Assisted relative	70 (includes 30 bonus points)	

* The Province of Quebec has some variations of these.
Source: Citizenship and Immigration Canada. 1998 (April). *Canada's Immigration Law.* Internet: http://cicnet.ci.gc.ca

Canada to apply for landed immigrant status after arrival in Canada. Within five years, one-third of all landed immigrant applicants were persons who originally came to Canada as visitors. Consequently, in 1972, the government changed this regulation.

Furthermore, the number of illegal immigrants entering the country increased substantially. To manage the problem, in 1972 the government issued a proclamation, "The Immigration Adjustment of Status Program," allowing all illegal immigrants in the country to register within a period of 60 days and apply for permanent residence. By the end of the period, a total of 31,947 persons had come forward to register and virtually all of them were approved for legal residency (Bonavia, 1977: 56-57).

The year 1974 witnessed a new peak in the number of immigrants arriving in Canada. A total of 218,465 persons arrived. Since the war, this number had been exceeded only in 1957, when 282,164 persons arrived, and in 1967, when 222,876 persons arrived. A new concern over the entire issue of immigration began to develop. In December, the Minister of Manpower and Immigration stated that over half of all immigrants coming to Canada took up residence in Toronto, Vancouver and Montreal. As a result these cities had been growing too rapidly, whereas many regions of Canada were losing population and showing workpower shortages. At the same time, the Canadian economy was showing recessional tendencies. A few years before, a new study of immigration had been commissioned. This study was published and came to be known as the *Green Paper on Immigration.* It reviewed the existing knowledge of Canadian immigration and stated four main options that a future immigration policy could take. The Paper itself did not take a position on any of the options (Manpower and Immigration, 1974a).

Public response to the *Green Paper* was mixed, but many interpreted it as an attempt to provide a rationale for the restriction of immigration. Representatives of the Asian ethnic groups in particular expressed fears that the impact of the Paper would be to curtail Asian immigration, especially in view of the high proportion which the Asian immigrants were already making up in the total numbers of immigrants (Palmer, 1975). In 1975 the Gallup poll of public opinion showed that the percentage of people favouring a decrease of immigration had increased significantly. In 1978, as the birth rate of the general population in Canada declined and the ethnic composition of immigration shifted, the old concern with the ethnic composition of Canadian population was re-emerging and there were signs of a resurgence of racism. A statement by the head of Ontario Royal Commission on Declining School Enrolment talked about "racial suicide," resulting from the decline of the birth rate in the Canadian population and concomitant immigration to Canada from nations of "uncontrolled fertility" (*Toronto Star*, 1978: May 15).

• 1978 to 1993 Amendments to Immigration Act

The *Green Paper on Immigration* was tabled in the House of Commons on February 3, 1975. This was followed by public hearings on immigration across the country. The result was the Immigration Act of 1976, which went into effect in the spring of 1978.

Under this Act there was an explicit commitment to link immigration flow to economic conditions and to demographic needs even more. The point system was revised. The same categories were retained but were given different point values. The revisions included the requirement that an independent immigration applicant have a job offer or obtain at least 2 points for experience in the occupation to be undertaken and 1 point for job demand. Furthermore, a location factor was introduced. Thus, applicants could obtain up to 5 points if they were willing to locate in areas that needed workers, but would lose up to 5 points if they intended to go to areas without such need.

Furthermore, the Act defined the family class of immigrants more specifically. To eliminate the loose definition of the family relatives, which in the early 1970s permitted laterally related relatives to be admitted into the country and allowed for abuse of this category, it limited, with some exceptions, the definition of family reunification to linear relatives.

In an innovative fashion, the Act included the categories of refugees and "people in refugee situations" as admissible, "designated" classes of immigrants. Since 1969, Canada has been a signatory to the United Nations Convention Relating to the Status of Refugees and hence has been obligated to take in a certain number of refugees as needed. However, prior to 1976 refugees were admitted on an *ad hoc* basis, by specific decisions of the cabinet or parliament. After 1976, refugees were given statutory status among the other immigrants to Canada (Dirks, 1995: 19-29). In 1979, following the Tokyo summit, Canada decided to take in 50,000 Indochinese refugees, the so-called "Boat People." The government brought over 8,000 of these refugees. It then introduced a matching formula: it would bring over one refugee for every one sponsored privately. The public response was overwhelming and easily surpassed the goal of 21,000 privately sponsored refugees envisioned in the matching formula. Nevertheless, the government later refused to maintain the matching formula, and a number of refugees sponsored by private organizations became illegal (Matas with Simon, 1989).

By the end of this period, in 1992, as the main areas and arenas of interethnic conflict shifted, the greatest number of refugees were coming from different sources: from Sri Lanka (7,972), Poland (4,872), Somalia (4,701), Iran (4,323), El Salvador (4,009), Vietnam (2,266), Lebanon (1,830), Ethiopia (1,588), Iraq (1,518) and Ghana (1,263) (CIC, 1992).

In addition, the Act required that the Minister of Employment and Immigration report every year to parliament on the immigration levels and that the Ministry set these levels from year to year after consultation with the provinces. In the setting of levels, the Act required that relevant demographic considerations be taken into account.

Right after the Act went into effect the levels were set for 1978 and the following years at 100,000 immigrants per year. For 1980, the level was set at 120,000 immigrants, but towards the end of the period, in the early 1990s, the level was increased to 250,000. The targets, however, have not often been reached. Thus in 1978, only 85,000 immigrants arrived. From 1982 to 1986, less than 90,000 per year arrived, in spite of target levels of more than 100,000. In 1985, 84,302 immigrants arrived. After 1987, however, this number began to increase. In 1989 it went up to 192,001; in 1990, 214,230; in 1991, 230,781; and in 1992, 252,842 (CIC, 1992). The target had been set at 250,000, but by the mid-1990s, the actual number of arrivals began to fall short of this level.

By the mid-1980s, the sources of immigration had reversed completely from the 1960s. The trend set in the 1970s continued; the largest groups of immigrants continued to be Asian (Badets, 1993). Furthermore, in 1992, for the first time in the history of Canadian immigration, more women than men migrated to Canada: 127,800 (50.5 percent) women versus 125,042 (49.5 percent) men. This has also been the case internationally in the 1990s (Lim and Oishi, 1966). What emerges is a new picture of the immigrant: a pioneering female rather than the traditional pioneering male.

In addition to its now well-established merit point system and in order to encourage migrants who would fill certain types of jobs for which there appeared to be a demand, in the early 1980s, the government introduced an *employment authorization program.* This program invited persons from outside of Canada to come to Canada to do designated types of work, particularly domestic work (Boyd, Taylor and Delaney, 1986). The program was aimed at persons who would come to Canada, not as landed immigrants, but as temporary workers, but it allowed them the option of applying for landed immigrant status later. The program was aimed particularly at women, and the largest groups who arrived were Filipino and Jamaican women. What is interesting is that, of those Filipino women who came to Canada to work as domestics, close to 50 percent had some post-secondary education, and about 15 percent of these had either some university education or a bachelor's degree (Chen, 1998; Bakan, 1987; Barber, 1991).

Another special immigration program introduced by the government in this period was an attempt to attract "business immigrants," that is, persons who would come to invest money in Canadian business. In 1978 new immigration regulations allowed the admission of entrepreneurs without the assessment for occupational demand or arranged employment that the merit point system required. In 1985, the new immigration legislation amended these regulations by expanding the class of business immigrants to include self-employed persons, investors and other entrepreneurs. The program allowed persons who had at least half a million dollars and promised to invest them in Canada to enter Canada without assessment on the merit point system (Bagambiire, 1996: 35-54). In 1990, 18,445 "business immigrants" came to Canada, most of them from Hong Kong, and others from South Korea, Taiwan and the United States (Li, 1993). There were, however, some abuses of this program by persons who obtained entry into Canada but then failed to fulfill their investment obligations (Malarek, 1987).

Towards the end of the 1980s and into the 1990s, new criticisms of immigration appeared in the media. They centred, first, around the refugees. Since the beginning of the 1980s, an increasing number of persons seeking asylum had arrived in Canada, claiming refugee status after arrival. By the end of that decade the determination boards charged with ascertaining the status of these arrivals were backlogged and unable to handle such caseloads. In addition, a number of refugee status claimants who had been in Canada for several years and were then refused entry went "underground" and became illegal immigrants. Over 1,100 arrest warrants were issued. Then cases of refugee smuggling into Canada came to light. The media reported that criminals were making refugee claims and that a convicted terrorist had obtained refugee status (Lam and Richmond, 1995). The media demanded a re-vamping of the refugee program.

Furthermore, with the recession of the early 1990s and the level of immigrants in the two hundred thousand categories, some popular voices clamoured for cut-backs, not only on the number of immigrants, but on all multicultural programs sponsored by the federal and provincial governments. The stage was set for new government regulations or legislation.

• 1993 to Present

In 1993, a new amendment to the 1976 Immigration Act went into effect (Bill C-86). It further revised the amendment introduced in 1989 (Bill C-55 and C-84). It gave the government the authority to set limits on the number of immigrants accepted in each specific category, including refugees and business immigrants. It also gave power, previously held by the determination boards, to the senior immigration officers at the point of entry to determine the credibility of refugee claims and it authorized the government to use various preventive measures to unearth potential illegal immigrants before they arrived in Canada (Lam and Richmond, 1995). In summary, the new revisions of the Act linked immigration more closely to the population and labour market needs; provided for an annual announcement of the number of immigrants Canada could absorb following mandatory consultation with provincial and territorial governments and optional consultation with groups or individuals in the private and voluntary sectors; allowed Canadian citizens and permanent residents in Canada to sponsor close relatives; confirmed Canada's commitment and responsibilities to refugees under the United Nations Convention; required immigrants and visitors to obtain visas or authorization abroad; introduced security measures to protect Canada from international terrorism and organized crime and measures to safeguard the civil rights of immigrants and visitors through a quasi-judicial inquiry; provided short-term alternatives to permanent deportation for cases involving less serious violations of immigration law; and spelled out in specific terms the powers granted to government officials (CIC, 1998: 3).

In administering immigration acts, Citizenship and Immigration Canada issues specific regulations to immigration officers. These have included regulations that specify the assessment process of immigration applicants, regulations requiring medical examination for specific diseases, terms and conditions that may be imposed on prospective immigrants, regulations regarding prospective immigrants' arrival at the point of entry, regulations specifying valid reasons for refusal of entry and removal of prospective immigrants and others. The purpose of these regulations is to reduce the arbitrary elements in the admission of immigrants, but special emphasis was now placed on assessment of the prospective immigrant's ability to become economically successful once established in Canada (CIC, 1997a; Bagambiire, 1996).

By the mid-1990s, the merit point system challenged prospective immigrants much more than when it was first instituted. New definitions of the classes of immigrants emerged. Thus, the 1993 amended Immigration Act identified three classes of immigrants: family class, refugees and independent immigrants (CIC, 1998). The *family class* category stipulated that Canadian citizens and permanent residents, aged 19 and over and living in Canada, have the right to sponsor the applications of close relatives who wish to immigrate to Canada. The relatives eligible for sponsorship included wife or husband, fiancé(e), dependent son or daughter, parents and grandparents, brothers, sisters, nephews, nieces, grandchildren who were orphans, unmarried and under 19, children under 19 whom the sponsor plans to adopt, and any other relative if the sponsor has no family members in Canada. Dependent children were defined as being either under 19 years of age and unmarried, or full-time students at a college, university or other educational institution and supported financially by their parents from age 19 or from the date of their marriage, or children with a disability who were unable to support themselves and were supported mainly by their parents.

Family-class applicants were not assessed under the point system, but they had to meet Canadian standards of good health and character. The sponsor had to commit to supporting and housing them for up to 10 years.

Refugees, called convention refugees, were those persons who fell under the United Nations Convention and Protocol Relating to the Status of Refugees and were members of a designated class of persons. The latter were persons displaced by emergency situations in any country of the world whom the government of Canada had recognized as a special class for humanitarian reasons. Canadian citizens or permanent residents 19 years of age or older or legally incorporated organizations could sponsor refugees and their families, but they had to agree to provide settlement assistance for them for a period of one year.

KEY ISSUES IN CANADIAN ETHNIC RELATIONS

"Visible Minorities" in 2016

Of all the issues associated with recent immigration, possibly none is more widely discussed, if not hotly debated, than the sociological impact of increasing numbers of "visible minorites."* In a period of economic instability, if not decline, the concern of course is that racial prejudice and scapegoating will gain a greater foothold and that Canadian society will become a less hospitable place to live. Paradoxically, the sheer numbers of visible minorities, and the critical role immigrants play in economic and population growth, may help to ameliorate any widespread racial backlash.

The number of Canadians in "visible minority"* groups is expected to increase to 7.1 million by 2026 from 2.7 million in 1991, according to Statistics Canada's projections. As a proportion of the overall population, this represents a doubling to 20 percent in 2016 from 10 percent in 1991. The largest visible minority group in 1991 (as in 1996) was the Chinese (about 666,000 people), and this group will continue to be the largest over the projection period (nearly 2 million by 2016). The proportion of Canadians who are of Chinese ancestry will grow to 5 percent in 2016. Blacks were the third largest visible minority group in 1991 (540,000) but are expected to become the second largest group by 2016 (almost 1.3 million). South Asians will drop from second largest to the third largest group, moving from 543,000 in 1991 to a projected 1.2 million in 2016. West Asians and Arabs will continue to rank as the fourth largest visible minority over this period. However, this group is expected to increase at the fastest rate (217 percent) to approximately 1 million in 2016 from 315,000 in 1991.

The vast majority of visible minority adults live in the large urban areas and large proportions of the populations in each of these CMAs are now visible minorities. In 1991, for example, the adult visible minority population accounted for 24 percent of the adult population in Toronto, 23 percent in Vancouver and 10 percent in Montreal.

Visible minority adults are much more likely to have a university degree and less likely not to have completed high school than are other adults. In 1991, the most recent year for which socio-economic data are available at this time, 18 percent of the visible minority population aged 15 and over had a university degree, compared with 11 percent of other adults. Also 33 percent of visible minorities had less than a high school level education, while this was the case for 39 percent of other adults.

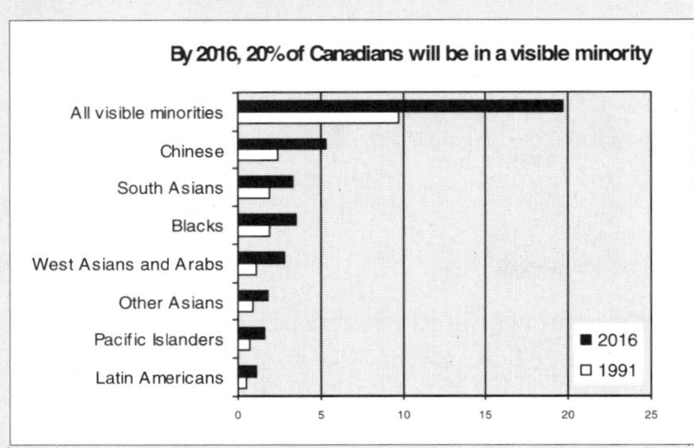

Visible Minority Population, 1996 (20% sample data)

Total Population	28,528,125
Total visible minority population	3,197,480
Chinese	860,150
South Asian	670,590
Black	573,860
Arab/West Asian	244,665
Filipino	234,195
Southeast Asian	172,765
Latin American	176,970
Japanese	68,135
Korean	64,835
Visible minorities (not included above)	69,745
Multiple visible minorities	61,575
All others	25,330,645

Source: Statistics Canada, Catalogue Numbers 93F0026XDB96004, 93F0026XDB96005, 93F0026XDB96006, Nation Series.

The 1996 census was the first census to ask a direct question on visible minorities. The table above provides counts of the visible minority population as defined for employment equity purposes in the 1996 census.

The impact of this demographic change is still uncertain, but the substantial increase in the visible minority population in recent years is an issue that has already dramatically affected public policy (e.g., multiculturalism and anti-racism policy) and it seems likely to continue to do so in the future.

**Note:* Statistics Canada uses the term "visible minorities" rather than the term racially different groups. As was pointed out in Chapter 1, this term implies a bias. Statistics Canada does not present a clear rationale for singling out such groups instead of analyzing their socio-economic characteristics alongside other ethnic groups. This may be a subject for classroom discussion.

Source: The above information draws heavily on Karen Kelly, "Projections of Visible Minority Groups, 1991 to 2016," *Canadian Social Trends*, Summer 1995, pp.3-8 (Catalogue 11-008E).

Independent immigrants were defined as either *business immigrants, skilled workers,* or *assisted relatives.* Business immigrants were persons applying under the business programs mentioned above. They could include "entrepreneurs," "investors," and "self-employed." Immigrants coming as entrepreneurs had to show their intention and financial ability to establish and manage a business that could create at least one job for a non-relative. Those coming as investors had to have a proven track record in business and have accumulated a personal net worth of half a million dollars or more. They had to be willing to invest a minimum of $250,000 in the Canadian economy and contribute to the creation or continuation of employment opportunities for Canadian citizens or permanent residents. Those coming as self-employed had to show their intention and ability to establish or purchase a business in Canada that would create employment opportunity for them and would make a significant contribution to the economy or the cultural or artistic life of Canada.

Skilled worker category refers to applicants who wished to immigrate on the basis of their education, training, experience or other skills and the *assisted relative* category refers to those applicants who applied as independent immigrants but who had a relative in Canada who was able and willing to help them become established. The applicants' relation to their relative in Canada could be similar to that indicated under the family class except that they did not qualify in the family class, and in addition this category included uncles and aunts of the Canadian relative.

The merit point system was modified in such a way as to fit the prospective immigrants as closely as possible to the Canadian demographic and labour market needs. Chart 2 summarizes the selection criteria and the numbers of required merit points.

In the 1990s, the largest number of immigrants admitted to Canada in a single year was 255,819 persons, in 1993. Since then, the numbers have somewhat decreased. In 1994, 223,875 immigrants were admitted. Of these, 19,089 were refugees, with most coming from Bosnia-Herzegovina, Sri Lanka, Iraq, Vietnam, Somalia, Iran and Ethiopia. This represents a decrease from 1991, when 53,401 refugees were admitted. Of all those admitted, 24,629 were entrepreneurs and investors and their families, with most coming from Hong Kong, Taiwan, South Korea and the Middle East. In 1995, 212,491, and in 1996, 224,050, immigrants were admitted to Canada.

In regard to the intended occupation, entrepreneurship and investment represented about 6 percent of all the non-family-related immigrants of working age. The largest single category of intended occupations, however, were professional and constituted 23 percent of all intended occupations. The other categories of intended occupations were substantially smaller: about 9 percent clerical and sales occupations, 7 percent service occupations and only 5.5 percent manufacturing or product fabrication occupations. About 50 percent of non-family-related immigrants of working age gave unspecified occupational intentions and more than 50 percent of all immigrants admitted were family related immigrants (CIC, 1997b). This statistical description is typical of yearly immigration to Canada in the 1990s.

Table 9 shows how, by the second half of the 1990s, the composition of immigration to Canada has changed. Using the census data, it compares the place of birth of immigrants in two periods of immigration, the period before 1961 and the period between 1991 and 1996. The table shows that in the 1990s the origin of most immigrants is substantially different from those of about forty years ago. Before 1961, over 90 percent of all immigrants were coming from Europe, and over half of these, from Northern and Western continental Europe and the United Kingdom. Immigrants from Asia constituted only a small percentage (3.1 percent) of all immigrants arriving in the country. In the 1990s the picture differs significantly. Europeans make up only about one-fifth of all the immigrants, and the largest number, close to 60 percent, come from Asia. The largest proportion of Asian immigrants arrive from Eastern Asia, mainly China, but Southern Asia, mainly India and Sri Lanka, is also an important source of Canada's newcomers. The remaining proportion–almost one fifth (16.6 percent)–come from Central and South America, from the Caribbean and Bermuda and from the United States. Among the European immigrants in the 1990s, the largest proportion is not from the United Kingdom or Northern and Western continental Europe, but from Eastern Europe.

Globally, in the 1990s, the need for countries to open their doors to immigrants has increased. In 1994, it was estimated that there were as many as 100 million migrants in the world, 20 million of whom were genuine refugees (Dirks, 1997; Weiner, 1995). Hence, it can be projected that in the twenty-first century the pressure on Canada to open its doors to immigrants even more widely will increase.

Table 9: Immigrant Population by Place of Birth, Showing Period of Immigration before 1961 and between 1991 and 1996

Place of Birth	Period of Immigration*			
	Before 1961	%	1991-1996**	%
United States	**45,050**	**4.3**	**29,025**	**2.8**
Central and South America	**6,370**	**0.6**	**76,335**	**7.3**
Caribbean and Bermuda	**8,390**	**0.8**	**57,315**	**5.5**
Europe	**953,360**	**90.4**	**197,480**	**19.0**
United Kingdom	265,580	25.2	25,420	2.4
North & West Europe without UK	284,285	26.9	31,705	3.1
Eastern Europe	175,430	16.6	87,900	8.5
Southern Europe	228,145	21.6	52,455	5.0
Africa	**4,945**	**0.5**	**76,260**	**7.3**
Asia	**32,580**	**3.1**	**592,710**	**57.1**
West Central Asia & Middle East	4,975	0.5	82,050	7.9
Eastern Asia	20,555	1.9	252,340	24.3
South-east Asia	2,485	0.2	118,265	11.4
Southern Asia	4,565	0.4	140,055	13.5
Oceania & Other	4,250	0.4	9,875	1.0
Total Place of Birth	**1,054,930**	**100.0**	**1,038,992**	**100.0**

Sources of the Canadian Immigrant Population: Europe vs. Asia

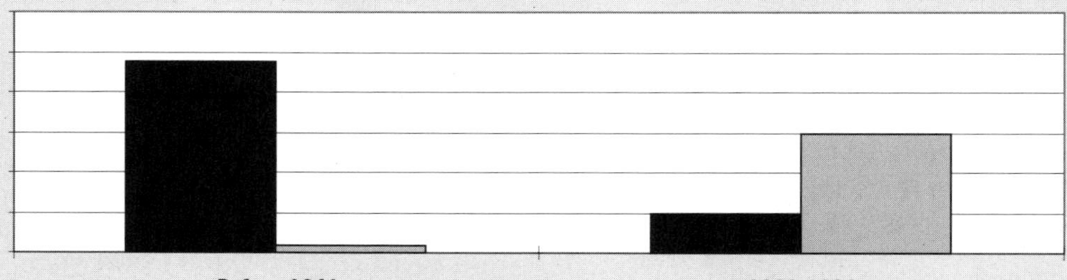

*Non-permanent residents are not included.
**Includes only the first four months of 1996.
Source: Statistics Canada. 1998. *Census 1996*. "Population by Selected Age Groups and Sex for Canada, Provinces and Territories," Internet Catalogue No. 93F0023XDB96005, the Nation Series.

CONCLUSION: AN "HONOURABLE HOST-NEWCOMER AGREEMENT"

Settlement and immigration have been a continuous fact and a constitutive part of the history of Canadian society. But the history of immigration to Canada has shown periodic fluctuations between widely opened and relatively closed doors. By and large, those periods of admitting large numbers of immigrants have been followed by attempts to limit the numbers of all immigrants or to limit the number of some categories of immigrants. For racial groups, the Asians and the Blacks, the history began with a long period of restriction to their numbers. This period was followed, after the 1960s, with the removal of all formal restrictions.

The story of immigrants, however, should not be seen only through their migration alone. The history of immigrants is much more than the history of immigration. As soon as they arrive in the host country, immigrants enter a process of adaptation, adjustment and assimilation. But they also form or become part of existing ethnic communities, they form or join existing ethnic neighbourhoods, organizations and institutions, such as churches and schools, and they participate in the programs and functions sponsored by them. While immigrants send their children to publicly accredited schools, they often also send them to their ethnic Saturday or Sunday schools or classes so that they can retain their ethnic language or learn the history and culture of their ethnic group (Burnet with Palmer, 1988). The significance of this and how it interrelates with the process of assimilation will be discussed in later chapters.

The entire history of immigration, however, has been based on the presupposition that immigrants, after entering the host country, will accept the position of migrant subordination in a form that will be beneficial to both the majority group in society and the immigrants themselves. That is, immigrants who have been needed for the growth and economic development of the country have been given the opportunity to come in, to work and to live in the country in relative freedom. Conversely, those immigrating into the country have looked for just such opportunities. There has been only one implicit proviso in this mutual formula, i.e., that the country would retain a relative political and cultural stability at all times. This has never meant the absence of change, but rather change only within the bounds of the existing political and cultural structure. Immigrants have been expected to adapt and adjust and thus subordinate to this structure and present no threat to it. It has been understood that immigrants would undergo a willing assimilation in the final step of their incorporation into a unified society. This has constituted the essence of what can be called the "North American honourable host-newcomer agreement."

Any potential dissension from this "agreement" by new immigrant groups or already established groups or categories of persons within these groups has always been viewed with suspicion. At times this suspicion has taken the form of racism, involving an unsubstantiated fear that different races may upset the "traditional racial composition" of the population. The recurring attempts to limit the number of immigrants from Asia and the Caribbean is an example of this. At other times, this suspicion has produced an unsubstantiated fear of "alien subversion," as in the case of the internment of immigrants labeled as "enemy aliens" in World War I or of the Japanese and Germans in World War II. Another example is the opposition to publicly supported expressions of diverse ethnic identities as revealed in the political pressures of the 1980s and 1990s to reduce or eliminate the policy of multiculturalism. Nevertheless, fears of this type usually come to be seen as unfounded, since throughout Canadian history ethnic and racial groups have pretty much kept "the agreement."

Canada continues to be a country with a constant stream of immigrants. The number of immigrants arriving yearly has substantially increased since the 1980s. Yet, the mood in the country appears to be an uneasy balance between an understanding and acceptance of the immigrants and feelings of suspicion or even moderate hostility towards them and towards minority ethnic groups in general. A factor in this mood is a degree of racist feeling against the predominantly non-white immigrants. Another factor is the economic uncertainty of the 1990s, produced by the downsizing of most institutions in society and the accompanying loss of jobs. Under the conditions of social change, immigrants and minorities often become objects of scapegoating.

Before they can become established and incorporated into their new society, immigrants have to go through the process of adaptation and adjustment. It is to this process and the problems involved that we will turn our attention now.

PROBLEMS OF IMMIGRANT ADJUSTMENT

Immigration means uprooting oneself, disrupting established relationships, detaching from a social structure of society and a consequent process of "growing roots" in a new society, establishing new relationships and becoming part of the structure of a new society. Sociologically, the process of becoming part of a new society is a lengthy one. It may take an entire lifetime, and it may involve several generations. Two phases of this process can be distinguished: that of immediate adjustment and that of long-range incorporation into society, involving structural integration and cultural assimilation. Each phase presents a different set of problems that immigrants have to overcome. Subsequent chapters will deal with the long-range phase. In the remainder of this chapter we will analyze some of the main problems of adjustment faced by immigrants immediately after their arrival in the new society.

Adjustment after arrival involves two types of adjustment: *practical adjustment*, sometimes called adaptation, and *social-psychological adjustment.* Each type of adjustment presents a set of difficulties and problems that immigrants must overcome and resolve. Practical adjustment involves, above all, the problems of finding employment, earning an adequate income and finding appropriate housing. Social-psychological adjustment involves the problem of "culture shock," problems in child-parent relationships and problems in husband-wife relationships. Each of these will be discussed separately.

• The Problem of Finding Work

There are substantial variations among different types, ages and ethnicities of immigrants in the length of time it takes them to find work after arrival and the degree of their participation in the labour force in their new society. One can also observe that, since the 1960s and 1970s, the differences between the immigrant and the Canadian-born population in regard to work and occupations have decreased.

In the early 1970s, the Canadian government, as part of the research for the *Green Paper on Immigration*, commissioned a longitudinal study of immigrants who entered Canada between 1969 and 1971 to ascertain how well they adjust after arrival (Manpower and Immigration, 1974c). The selected group of immigrants was observed over a three-year period from the date of their arrival in Canada. At the same time, a control group of non-immigrant persons was selected and observed in order to make comparisons possible with the Canadian-born population. No other longitudinal study of immigrants has been undertaken since.

The study found that the average length of time required to find a job was slightly over four weeks. Fifty percent of the immigrants sampled by the survey began working after one and one-half weeks, and another 25 percent who had pre-arranged jobs began working approximately two weeks after arrival in Canada. The study noted that independent immigrants were generally able to find work faster than were refugees or sponsored immigrants.

Younger immigrants, especially those in the age range from 20 to 34 years, found work the most quickly. The survey also found a correspondence between the country of origin and time taken to find work. In general, British immigrants were working two and one-half weeks after arrival in Canada, German and Portuguese immigrants, three weeks after arrival, Italian, Filipino and West Indian immigrants, four and one-half weeks after arrival, immigrants from Greece and India, approximately five and one-half weeks after arrival, and Chinese and Yugoslavian immigrants were often not working until six and one-half weeks after arrival in Canada (Manpower and Immigration, 1974c: 19).

The longitudinal survey also found that, during the first year of residence, the unemployment rate for immigrants was two to three times higher that the unemployment rate for the control group of Canadians. The immigrants' unemployment rate, which was 10 percent after approximately six months in Canada, did drop off over the following two years, and by the third year of residence, it was approximately the same as for the general population, at 5 percent.

Job demand for particular skills was the factor found to most affect the length of unemployment experienced. While individuals with pre-arranged jobs were usually employed within three months of arriving in Canada, immigrants whose skills were not in demand suffered much longer periods of unemployment. Twenty percent were without jobs for longer than three of their first six months, and about 17 percent were unemployed beyond six months.

Sponsored immigrants had more problems than independent immigrants with respect to unemployment. This fact reflected the generally lower skill and educational levels of sponsored immigrants as compared to those persons who had applied as independent immigrants and thus had to fulfil more stringent occupational and educational criteria. This difference between the independent and family-sponsored immigrants has also been observed in the United States (Jasso and Rosenzweig, 1995).

The greatest amount of unemployment was experienced by immigrants who had less than a high school education, although more highly educated immigrants suffered from greater status dislocation. Older immigrants also tended to experience longer periods of unemployment. Among immigrants with a higher education, problems with acceptance and recognition of qualifications meant that they suffered a good deal more unemployment during their first year or two of residence in Canada than a comparable group of native Canadians.

Later studies support the conclusion of the longitudinal study that family-class immigrants, but especially refugees, have greater difficulty in finding jobs after arrival than do independent immigrants. The findings of the study by the Economic Council of Canada (Canada, 1991b:84) showed that, between 1980 and 1982, independent immigrants, on the average, were unemployed for 4.4 weeks, whereas the family-class immigrants were unemployed for 6.2 weeks and the refugees, for 11.3 weeks. Furthermore, in 1982, the immigrants who took the least time to find a job were from Hong Kong (2.8 weeks), South Africa (4.0 weeks), Britain and Ireland (4.4 weeks), and Northern and Western Europe (4.6 weeks). The immigrants who took the longest time to find a job were from the Caribbean (8.8 weeks), Eastern Europe (9.2 weeks), Vietnam (11.2 weeks) and Laos (11.9 weeks).

By the 1990s the ethnic composition of immigrants had substantially changed, but as yet we have no comparable longitudinal data on the time it takes different ethnic and racial groups to find employment or on the length of their unemployment. Comparisons over decades, however, can be made when labour participation rates for immigrants and non-immigrants are examined.

In the 1960s and early 1970s, the immigrant labour participation rates tended to be higher than for the Canadian-born population. In 1961 and 1971, for example, the immigrant labour participation rate was 65.2 percent and 68.5 percent respectively, but the Canadian-born population's rate was 53.7 percent and 56.6 percent respectively (Richmond and Kalbach, 1980: 101-105). In the 1980s, this tendency changed, and the immigrant labour participation rate tended to be somewhat lower than the non-immigrant participation rate. In 1986, for example, the rate for the immigrant population was 64.9 percent, and for the non-immigrant population, 67.1 percent (Badets, 1989). This shift may reflect a change in the economic structure of society, indicating that, since the 1980s, it has been more difficult for immigrants to find jobs. The shift also reflects the somewhat older immigrant population of this period. On the whole, the younger adult immigrants, particularly in the 25 to 44 age range, have tended to have a slightly higher labour participation rate than the non-immigrant population in the same age range. Females' labour participation rate has always been lower than the male rate for both the immigrant and the non-immigrant populations. However, on the whole, the immigrant female participation rate in the 25 to 44 age category has tended to be higher than that of the non-immigrants in the same age category (Badets, 1989). This indicates that immigrants have tended to work more than the Canadian-born population. Still, the labour participation rate for newly arrived immigrants has tended to be lower than their participation rate after some stay in the country. In 1986, for example, of the immigrant men aged 25 to 44 who had been in the country for three years or less, 87.1 percent were in the labour force, but of those in the same age category who had been in the country for twenty years or more, 96.3 percent were in the labour force. Female immigrants in the same age category showed a similar trend (Badets, 1989). This is a substantial difference, indicating that there are difficulties in finding work after arrival and showing that labour force participation of immigrants increases with the length of residence in Canada.

There are, however, significant differences in labour force participation between different ethnic groups. South Asians have adjusted better economically than a number of other groups. By far the majority of South Asians, about 94 percent of all South Asian immigrants, have immigrated to Canada since 1967. Within 20 years they have shown a labour force participation substantially higher than the general population, by about 10 percent, and earned incomes almost the same as the general population (White and Nanda, 1989). The Indochinese immigrants, however, most of whom were refugees, have experienced serious difficulties in their economic adjustment process. Most of them, 92 percent, arrived in Canada since 1976, with two-thirds of them coming from Vietnam. In 1986, their male labour force participation in the 15 to 64 age range was 10 percent below that of the general population (67 to 77 percent). This discrepancy prevailed in all age categories and between the Indochinese women and the women in the general population. While only about 25 percent of the South Asian male immigrants held jobs in product fabricating or processing occupations, 42 percent of the Indochinese male immigrants were employed in these occupations. The percentage for women was about the same, while the percentage for the total population was only 18 for men and 7 for women. Finally, the annual employment income of Indochinese immigrants was substantially lower than that of the general population: $20,200 for men and $14,500 for women, as compared with $30,500 for men and $20,000 for women in the general population (White, 1990; Neuwirth and Clark, 1981).

• The Channels of Finding Work

An important aspect of the problem of finding work is the channels through which immigrants search for work. The most commonly used channels are informal ethnic contacts. A number of studies have shown that, in searching for work, immigrants tend to rely on their own ethnic groups and their friends or acquaintances in the group more than on public or any other institutional employment-search facilities. Grace Anderson (1974), in her study of the Portuguese immigrants, found that, to obtain information regarding employment opportunities, the newcomers frequented such places as the ethnic pool halls, club rooms of ethnic soccer clubs, boarding houses, restaurants, taverns, street corners, ethnic church services, church festivals or picnics and the like. It was rare that the newly arrived Portuguese immigrant tried to locate a job through impersonal networks. This preference of relying on their own ethnic resources in finding work was also found by Grygier (1975: 162) in his study of German, Hungarian and Italian immigrants.

Employment obtained through these channels may ease the search of the immigrant. Often, however, it has negative long-term consequences. The job opportunities available within the network of one ethnic minority group are often limited. Hence a new immigrant using only these channels to find a job may become locked into a low-status job with no chance of advancement and few contacts that will lead to a better paying, higher status job. Furthermore, as will be explained in the next chapter, the exclusive immigrant occupational networks are an important factor in the creation and maintenance of a double labour market in society in which the newly arrived immigrants are often exploited by members of their own group. They are often paid less than what they should be. Likewise, such jobs may offer the immigrant little chance to learn the language of the broader society, since everyone on the job may use the ethnic language as the main language of communication. Immigrants may also be slowed down in learning about opportunities in the society at large. This in turn may reduce the feeling of belonging to the larger society (Montgomery, 1996).

Immediately upon arrival, however, immigrants are not as much concerned with the long-range aspects of a job as they are with the problem of getting a job, often any job, in order to support themselves and their families. They are also concerned with establishing themselves as soon as possible among the people of their own ethnic background. This may not necessarily increase their job satisfaction, but it does provide a more amenable social and psychological environment, one in which they do not feel alienated and in which they can interact with people whose values, concerns, lifestyles and language they can readily understand and on whom they feel that they can count in case of need.

Two other important factors limit the immigrants' opportunities for better employment. These are a lack of knowledge of the language of the host society and discrimination. Lack of knowledge of the dominant language works against the immigrants in two ways. It cuts them off from those channels of finding a job that require the language to obtain job contacts and job leads, and it closes the doors to those jobs that require the use of the dominant language as part of the job itself.

Discrimination also limits the employment opportunities of newly arrived immigrants; discrimination based on their ethnicity or race and on differences in their professional and technical qualifications. Discrimination and prejudice as factors of exclusion will be discussed in following chapters. In regard to qualifications, in many cases employers do not give full recognition to training acquired in countries other than Canada. The problem is most severe in the medical and health professions, architecture, teaching, social work and a number of technical trades. Qualifications obtained in the United States and Great Britain are generally more acceptable in Canada than those obtained elsewhere (Richmond, 1974a: 13). Furthermore, some jobs require Canadian experience, a requisite that newly arrived immigrants obviously cannot fill.

• The Problem of Status Dislocation

Many immigrants experience a drop in social status when they begin their first jobs in Canada, i.e., their new jobs in Canada are of lower status than their previous jobs or they do not require the qualifications that they obtained in their previous country. According to

Richmond's (1967) early survey of post-war immigrants in Canada, one-half of non-United Kingdom immigrants, and one-fifth of United Kingdom immigrants suffered a fall in status with their first job in Canada. While British immigrants were generally able to "catch up" within a few years, immigrants from other countries (with the exception of those having a higher educational level) were far less likely to make a full recovery. Richmond observed that British immigrants were "markedly" under-represented in lower social classes and over-represented in the upper social classes. He also noted that, while British immigrants tended rapidly to improve their positions relative to their fathers, immigrants from other countries did not show such rapid improvement.

The longitudinal study *Three Years in Canada* found that by the end of the three-year residence in Canada, at least one-third of the immigrants sampled had not found or begun jobs in the fields in which they had intended to enter upon arrival in Canada. After the immigrants had spent one year in Canada, they were asked to give reasons for why they had not obtained jobs in their intended occupations. The reasons given were as follows: 20 percent could not obtain acceptance or recognition of their qualifications, 20 percent lacked requisite Canadian experience, 21 percent simply could not find a job in their intended area, 16 percent found that lack of knowledge of the language was a barrier and 10 percent simply chose different jobs.

By the end of their third year, some of the difficulties had fallen away. Language problems still hampered one-third of those who had originally experienced them. The number of people deemed unacceptable because of a lack of qualifications dropped by 40 per cent. By this time, however, 22 percent of the group had chosen a different occupation.

K. Victor Ujimoto's study of post-World War II Japanese immigrants in British Columbia also clearly illustrates the problem of status dislocation. According to his study (Ujimoto, 1979), of those immigrants in his sample who arrived with professional qualifications, only 24 percent were able to obtain employment in the same occupational category after arrival. After four years in Canada, a few more were able to obtain jobs appropriate to their professional qualifications, yet this still represented only 52 percent of the original professional sample. Similarly, among those immigrants whose occupations before arrival were proprietorial, managerial and lesser professional, only 40 percent obtained appropriate employment immediately after arrival. After four years, 73 percent did so, but few of them remained in these occupations later on. Most of them had to change to another type of employment. In the clerical occupational category, made up mostly of women, 42 percent secured only semi-skilled jobs. The most successful in obtaining the same occupations as before arrival were the skilled, semi-skilled and agricultural workers, many of whom also substantially improved their status after a few years.

The occupational status drops are often quite substantial, from professional or skilled workers to manual, unskilled types of jobs; for example, from professors, teachers, lawyers or bank clerks to dishwashers or hotel housemen, or from draughtsmen, tool and die makers or top electricians to menial helpers (Slinger, 1971). Since 1967, the merit point system has worked to reduce the extent of the status dislocation experienced by immigrants, but significant variations between ethnic groups have remained. By the end of the 1980s, South Asian and Chinese immigrants were experiencing much less status dislocation than Indochinese immigrants, especially when measured in terms of their educational and skill backgrounds and their involvement in professional occupations in Canada (White and Nanda, 1989; White, 1990; Li, 1990a; McDade, 1988). Analysis of a sample taken from the 1986 census tried to assess the match between the education of immigrant women and their occupations in Canada. The study concluded that, in the 1980s, immigrant women were less disadvantaged by mismatch between their education and occupation than were Canadian-born women. This, however, did not apply in the same way to immigrant men (Sorensen, 1995).

The effect of status drop or dislocation on the psychological well-being of immigrants can be substantial. For some immigrants, especially those more highly educated, this experience can cause feelings of bitterness or hostility to develop, which they may then turn towards society at large. It can also work to keep them removed from the society at large and induce them to live, as it were, in the utopian world of the past. That is, rather than attempting to move into society at large, they may orient themselves primarily in their ethnic community, where they can still enjoy the prestige they derived from their positions or their titles back in the old country. This often stimulates the motivation to work to preserve and maintain ethnic cultures and ethnic institutions as long as possible. More will be said about this in the section on social mobility.

Free Adventurers and Good Canadian Women: German Immigrant Maids in Postwar Vancouver

Alexander Freund, University of Bremen

In 1993, I interviewed ten German women who had immigrated to Canada in 1951, 1953, and 1957, respectively, via the route of domestic service. Based mainly on the narratives of these ten women, I will in the following offer an interpretation of how and within which conditions the migrants' identity changed during the process of migration. In which situations did they construct, abandon, shift, or alter their self-concepts? How did they reconstruct their identities within new cultural and socio-economic structures as well as individually encountered work and life conditions? How did they use notions of gender, class, and ethnicity to negotiate the uncertainties and conflicts in the processes of migration and adjustment?

They had experienced "uprooting" and migration during and after the war. Six were refugees from Eastern Europe while two had fled from their work places in East Germany. On the flight, they had lost not only their belongings and perhaps their social status, but often relatives and friends. Spatial and social displacement as much as violent physical and mental disruptions had become everyday-life experiences. The feeling of "uprootedness" played a major part in the women's decision to emigrate.

Beneath the ruins of forced migration and uprooting, physical and psychic violence, shortages of food, shelter, and marriageable men, high unemployment, family break-downs, and society's denial of alternatives to marriage lay buried many incentives to leave West Germany — and if it was only for one or two years. In one way or another, all of these incentives appeared in the narratives of the women I interviewed. But are they sufficient to explain why the women were motivated to emigrate? Who, after all, was not affected by those postwar conditions? How, then, can we come to understand why some people perceived migration as a strategy to deal with social, familial, and personal conditions and others did not? Perhaps, we should take a closer look at how those who eventually emigrated perceived themselves and the world around them. And ask: Was this self-perception linked to their decision? It is in the same sentences that Margot Buchwald tells us about her image of immigration. To be an immigrant meant to her to finally start her own family ("to be married") and to succeed economically ("have my own house") as well as emotionally ("I didn't want to be alone"). For the young woman, immigration promised the fulfillment of her dreams, her fantasies, her wishes. In other words, she expected that once she had become an immigrant she would succeed. This image of the immigrant who could not fail to succeed shaped her self-image, which consequently provided the framework within which she decided to leave Germany. In other words, she had come to perceive of herself as an immigrant, before she even entered the gangway onto the *M.S. Neptunia* in Bremerhaven. She had construed her self as the imagined immigrant.

The women's self-images were fuelled by notions of adventure, independence, and freedom. "I always liked adventure. I always wanted to be on a boat. I didn't care of the consequences of my not speaking English," Margot Buchwald said.

At the core of migrants' decisions then are perhaps not so much socio-economic, familial, or personal conditions and constrictions, but rather identities that are constructed around specific images of migration.

Thus, in the process of deciding to migrate, the women had constructed a new self. A self that was stable and provided security. A self that could contain, numb, or even forget the feelings of insecurity, uprootedness, and loss which had come to shape the women's lives as children in Nazi and war-torn Europe and as adolescents in postwar Germany. The new identity promised closure of the old life and the beginning of a new one.

Instead of adventures, tedious housework and babysitting shaped the everyday life. ... How did they negotiate this clash between their self-concepts and the almost diametrically opposed conditions of their lived experiences? How did they "overcome these expectations" and "get used to" their new lives? Domestic service needed to be inserted into the image of successful immigration without having to abandon this image. The women did so by ascribing specific meanings to their experiences as maids. Slowly, they began to reconstruct their identities.

Domestic service, they argued, really was a bridge into the new world, a "stepping stone" on their path to successful immigration. Domestic service limited their personal freedom and independence and was not exactly an adventure, but, as Heidi Schute said, "It was the best way. I don't know what I would have done." Susanne Unterleitner felt similarly: "It was a really really good way to get into the Canadian way of life."

The construction of domestic service as a "stepping stone" and a necessary "learning experience" on the path to successful immigration did not emerge from an observation of a transparent, self-evident fact. The women could have just as well interpreted their experiences as maids as a reason to return to Germany as soon as they had saved up enough money. But the specific interpretation of domestic service as a "really good way to get into the Canadian way of life" allowed the women to save their identity or alter it as little as possible. How did the women arrive at just that interpretation?

Contemporary gendered discourses about work, family, and women informed the women's perception of themselves and the world around them. Women, it was generally claimed and believed, are "by nature" destined

Photo: Courtesy of Provincial Archives of Alberta

Many women who immigrated to Canada as domestic service workers ended up in dead-end factory jobs. Above, seamstresses at work in the Great West Garment Company, Edmonton, earlier in the century.

to be homemakers, wives, and mothers. "Labour for love" and not for money was expected from them (except for the times of shortages in the paid labor force). At the same time, the theory and policy of assimilation had become dominant. Most of the German immigrants accepted Canada's demand for assimilation. The necessary corollary to this interpretation of domestic service as a strategy specifically for young, single immigrant females to become a "real woman" and a "good Canadian" was the redefinition of their identities. Successful immigration no longer meant adventure, freedom, and independence, but fast and thorough assimilation. They had consented to the demands of Canadian postwar society.

On the other hand, from a limited variety of interpretations, the women had chosen the one which they felt best aided them in the maintenance of their identities. The women could reconstruct an identity that still resembled the one they had constructed in Germany. Their identities had been shifted and altered but ultimately rebalanced after the first shock, disappointment, and feeling of betrayal. To be a successful immigrant no longer meant to be an independent and free adventurer, but to be a "natural woman" and "good Canadian." This allowed the women both to persist in the alienation of unfulfilled dreams and to sustain their choice to immigrate.

Source: Alexander Freund, "Immigrants' Identities: The Narratives of a German-Canadian Migration" in *A Chorus of Different Voices: German-Canadian Identities*, ed. by A.E. Sauer and M. Zimmer (New York: Peter Lang, 1998), pp.187-208.

• The Problem of Poverty and Housing

Poverty is often a serious problem for newly arrived immigrants. The longitudinal survey found that, in the first six months of residence, 22 percent of the immigrants studied had incomes below the poverty line. This appeared to be due mainly to very low starting wages. By the third year of residence, only 4 percent of the sample group still had incomes below the poverty line, and most of these low incomes appeared to be due to the effects of unemployment. Yet, by the third year, the income level of the immigrant group was still only 83 percent of the non-immigrant control group mean level. In the 1990s, much of the poverty among immigrants has been reduced or even eliminated. However, it remains among the Indochinese immigrants and particularly among women immigrants (Badets, 1989; White, 1990; Ptolemy, 1989).

Housing for most immigrants during their first year in Canada is a real problem, as incomes are at their lowest level. During the first six months of residence, the average immigrant family in the longitudinal survey spent approximately 37 percent of their income on housing. By the third year of residence, the proportion of income spent on housing fell to a more suitable 23 percent. Home ownership was problematic for the immigrant group. After three years, the proportion of immigrants owning a home was found by the longitudinal survey to be only one-half that of the Canadian control group. Discrimination in housing was also found to be a serious problem, particularly for non-white immigrants.

Analysis of the 1986 data on home ownership has shown that home ownership varies substantially by ethnicity, even when income is held constant. Ownership rates are higher among such groups as Italians and Chinese and lower among Blacks. Although cultural differences may be a factor, discrimination in the housing market is a significant cause (Balakrishnan and Wu, 1992). In the process of residential relocation, as in the case of finding a job, members of ethnic groups tend to rely on their own community networks, particularly on real estate agents who come from the same ethnic background as themselves (Teixeira and Murdie, 1997).

• Idealistic Expectations

We now will look at some of the social-psychological problems of immigrant adjustment. Immigrants coming to North America often have an idealistic conception of the society and the conditions of life. They have a tendency to see Canada or the United States as a country in which life is bound to be better than what it has been before immigration. They often have a perception that it will be easy to find a job, that there is a demand for people like them and that they will be treated with justice and consideration and without prejudice and discrimination.

The reasons for such idealistic expectations are derived, on the one hand, from the nature of being an economic or political immigrant. A person moving away from a condition of poverty, lack of opportunity or lack of political and social freedom is bound to see his or her place of destination as something better, as a place where the old problem will be no more. On the other hand, idealistic expectations among immigrants are stimulated by the international image of Canada and the Unites States as countries that are rich and free. This image is propounded by North American products, by American power politics, by tourists and by the immigration authorities themselves (Luong and Luong, 1972).

Unfortunately, reality often does not measure up to the preconceptions of the immigrants and disappointments ensue. The greatest disappointment after arrival appears to be with employment opportunities, income and cost of living, and discrimination. The *Three Years in Canada* study found that, on average, 23 percent of all the immigrants studied were "very satisfied" with employment opportunities in Canada, 39 percent were "satisfied," 25 percent were "dissatisfied" and 13 percent were "very dissatisfied." The sponsored immigrants were more dissatisfied with employment opportunities than were the independent immigrants. Although since 1967 better educated persons have a higher chance of being admitted into Canada, the immigrants with a university education and professional qualifications are those who are quite likely to be more disappointed after arrival. The following autobiographical stories are illustrative of the idealistic expectations of immigrants and the disappointment that later followed:

> There were times during my first months in Toronto, when I had homicidal thoughts about the Canadian Immigration Officer who interviewed me in Sao Paulo. When this man learned I had a university degree he said "You won't have any trouble finding employment in Canada. In fact my advice is: choose very carefully. Don't take the first job that's offered." He made it sound that Canada was crying for young skilled workers and money was no object. Instead, it took me three months to become a shoe salesman in a Toronto department store (*Toronto Star*, 1972: June 10).

> Ubale remembers that the immigration officer warned him that it might take up to six months to land the job he wanted.... But with a Ph.D. in economics from the University of Bradford (England) the Officer reasoned, Ubale should have no difficulty in finding a position.... Today, well over a year later, Ubale works as a $100.00 a week clerk... (*Toronto Star*, 1977: March 2).

In the longitudinal study, high percentages of dissatisfaction were expressed in regard to the cost of living in Canada. Ten percent of the immigrants reported that they were "very dissatisfied" with the cost of living, and 30 percent, that they were "dissatisfied." Only 12 percent were "very satisfied," and 48 per cent, "satisfied."

Many immigrants come to Canada because they see it as a peaceful, multicultural country where all races can live and work in peace and dignity. Yet after arrival, instances of discrimination often do take place. Problems with finding employment and housing are often a result of discrimination or come to be attributed to discrimination by the immigrants. The attribution, even if without a completely objective basis, is logical, because of the immigrants' perception of the country as a land of opportunities. Alternatively, these problems, even in objective situations of discrimination, may be attributed by immigrants to their own lack of ability or to "chance" in an equal competition with others and as a transitional stage in the process of becoming part of a better society.

• Culture Shock

Many immigrants experience what has come to be known as culture shock. This is a phenomenon that often has several phases: an immediate phase, usually taking place at the time of the immigrant's initial exposure to a different society, and a later phase, resulting from the immigrant's deeper awareness of the society's relationship to him or her. However, not all immigrants necessarily experience culture shock and not all who experience it do so in the same degree.

The *immediate phase* of culture shock for the immigrant is bewilderment with a new and different way of life and customs and an accompanying realization that, not only is one different from others, but that one is a "foreigner" and not readily accepted by members of the host society. This bewilderment may be accompanied by feeling conspicuous, by feeling like a stranger and by uncertainty about what behaviour is expected. Feelings of embarrassment, shame and guilt are often present, side by side with feelings of injustice about the situation (Barer-Stein, 1988; Cohon, 1981). Lack of knowledge of the language of the host society is an important contributing factor to culture shock, but it is not the primary cause. Biographical statements from interviews with newly arrived immigrants can illustrate this phase well. A housewife talked thus about her experience:

> There have been many times when I have been sure I was going crazy. And many times when my husband and my children thought it too. I feel in myself, you know, a kind of dignity. Do you understand me? I feel I am a good person with much to offer especially to those close to me. But it has been destroying for me the past five years to see the look in the eyes of people in the street, in stores, in buses, when I have met the teacher of my children at school. It is a cold look which tells me I am different. It supposes I am not so good, not so equal. After a long time of this, there are days when I start inside myself to believe those eyes and what their cold looks say. Then sometimes I start to do crazy things (Montero, 1977: 90).

Another person reported that, in order to get to a fish store, she followed the streetcar tracks on foot for miles downtown and back rather than ride the streetcar. She did this because she was afraid that, if she got into the streetcar, the driver might say something to her that she would not understand (Montero, 1977:111). A keypunch operator reported:

> At coffee breaks or lunchtime in the cafeteria, the immigrants always group together. We make friends among ourselves with the English we have all learned at English classes. There might be a Chinese, a Korean, a Pole, a Yugoslav, a Japanese, a Spaniard–but you seldom see even one Canadian. They sit together in another group apart. They keep quite separate from us. This hurts, and we are inclined to feel resentful. The immigrant from Northern Europe seems to have it easier. Perhaps it is because physically she looks more like a Canadian whereas immigrants from the South of Europe, from the Caribbean, from Asia or Latin America often look very different (Montero, 1977: 42).

The *later phase* of culture shock is akin to the phenomenon of social change in which there is a shift or disruption of the group support for values or norms that have been traditionally accepted and deemed to be correct. Unlike the initial phase, this phase takes place within the context of one's personal, informal, interaction with both persons from outside of the ethnic groups and those close to the immigrant, especially the immigrant's own growing children. It is a realization that those close to oneself do not necessarily support or share the same values and norms that one has accepted as normal and universal. The consequence may be self-doubt, disorientation and heightened feelings of alienation from both the society at large and the immi-

Photo: Courtesy of TV Ontario

Changes in family structure—one set of problems that immigrants face derive from changes in husband-wife and parent-children relationships, particularly as children adapt to the new lifestyles more quickly than their parents.

grant's ethnic group. The consequence may also be a tendency to keep to a small circle of friends in the same ethnic group for support, especially the informal groups and organizations of the first generation, and a heightened criticism of, or hostility towards, the host society. A biographical statement made from within the context of a mixed marriage can illustrate this phenomenon:

> We came to Windsor right after we were married. Culture differences didn't matter too much in the first few months. I was pregnant, living in a suburb, trying to cope with shopping in a plaza and being able to speak to my neighbours. I became Canadianized very quickly but when the baby was born I suffered a kind of reaction. I wanted her to have a Polish name. I wanted to meet people who spoke Polish. I wanted to speak to her in Polish. I was suffering from a delayed culture shock.
>
> My husband was very resentful. He seemed to feel it was a rejection of him. There was no way he would agree to the baby having a "foreign" name. No way he felt I should talk Polish with anyone in front of him, as he did not understand it. In fact, he made it very clear that he did not want a "foreign" wife. I was alone in the enemy camp and I very quickly surrendered (Montero, 1977: 183).

Much of the later phase of culture shock takes place within the context of the parent-children relationship and within the context of changing family structure. A study of the problems of adjustment among the Vietnamese reported:

> The new habits and customs challenge Vietnamese traditions in painful ways, beginning at the basis of Vietnamese life, the family. The Vietnamese took it for granted that the elderly would be venerated, that youth would know its place, and that the entire extended family would live (and multiply) under one roof. All that is different here. The old people have the most confused position now. They have become more of a burden, relegated to being baby sitters, completely isolated during the long winter, and without the comfort of their families or their contemporaries. Their wisdom is no longer applicable... (Bong, 1980: 253).

• The Problem of the Parent-Child Relationship and Changes in Family Structure

Since children usually learn the language of the host society much faster than their parents, immigrant parents who come over with school-age or even pre-school-age children often tend to rely on their children for everyday use of the new language. For example, instead of going themselves, they may send their children to the English-speaking stores or they may use their children as translators. Initially, this may stimulate child and parent cooperation. But in the long run, this dependency of the parents on their children works to produce social-psychological gaps between them. When translating for their parents in front of others, children tend to develop feelings of embarrassment or shame about their parents. They may also develop feelings of being inferior because of their parents. In addition, immigrant mothers often react to being in a foreign country by over-protecting their children and indirectly create problems or conflicts for them outside of the home (Nagata et al., 1970; Danziger, 1971).

The school to which the child is sent often increases the gap between them and their parents. Indeed, the school that teaches all subjects in the language of the host society and gives no positive significance to the child's ethnic group is a significant factor in bringing about a gap between the immigrant generations. Such a school creates the impression that ethnic minority language is undesirable or bad. As a consequence, ethnic language and the child's ethnicity become symbolic of backwardness, and the child comes to define his or her parents, and everything they stand for, as in some way inferior. Children may be embarrassed to bring their parents to school or to bring their school friends home. Children may become ashamed of their parents and blame them for their problems at school or for problems with their friends. As the child grows into adolescence, this may develop into severe parent-child conflicts.

In order to reduce the problems that result from throwing newly arrived immigrant children into a completely English school environment, the Toronto Board of Education, following the successful experiments with immigrants in Boston, at one time experimented with a transitional program for immigrant children. This was a two-year kindergarten program, conducted in the same manner as a regular kindergarten program, except that the language used was Italian and English was only gradually introduced into the classroom. Various methods of observation, testing and comparison with control groups were used to assess the program's success (Purbhao and Shapson, 1974, 1975). An important finding of the experiment was that parents of the children in the experimental program developed a greater number of contacts with the school than did parents whose children were in the regular classes. They attended more school open houses and interviews and helped with classroom events more often. The study concluded that acknowledgment of the child's linguistic and cultural background was an important factor in integrating both the child and the child's parents into the English school system. This was also an important factor in reducing the incipient gap between the immigrant parents and their children.

An important aspect of immigrant parent-adolescent relationship, which is indicative of changes in the family structure, is conflict over dating patterns. Most immigrant ethnic groups are accustomed to adolescents going out in groups rather than on individual dates. There is pressure on adolescents for individual dating from the Canadian teen-age sector of society, and immigrant parents are often confronted with norms and values that differ from their own (Naidoo, 1986). Ensuing family conflicts only reinforce the developing cultural gap between generations. An interesting aspect of the generational conflict is the way in which parents handle it. As in the case of finding employment, most non-British immigrants tend to rely on their ethnic connections in finding help with the problems of their children. Grygier, in his study of two hundred immigrant families, asked where the immigrants would seek advice if they had great difficulty with their children's behaviour. The Italians reported that they would seek help from their relatives. The Germans chose their doctor as their source of advice. The Hungarians chose first the clergy and, secondly, private Catholic agencies. The wives had a tendency to choose the doctor as well as the clergy. The most frequent choice of the British was a public or government agency, including school services (Grygier, 1975: 167).

Another set of family problems that immigrants face are derived from the changing husband-wife relationship. Many immigrant wives have to find employment to supplement their husbands' income. Yet for many of them, working independently outside of the home is a new experience to which neither they, nor their husbands, have been accustomed. In the past, many European, especially Southern and Eastern European, and Oriental traditions have maintained a clear distinction between the man's role as the family's breadwinner and the woman's role as exclusively housewife and

KEY ISSUES IN CANADIAN ETHNIC RELATIONS

Are There Limits to Immigration and Diversity?

The chapter on immigration to Canada shows that immigration to Canada continues at more than 220,000 persons per year. It also shows that since the end of the 1970s the diversity of ethnicities has increased. While before that time Asian groups comprised small percentages of all immigrants, since then they have been making up the largest percentages of immigrants. The numbers of immigrants from the Middle East has also been increasing and there is reason to believe that in the future immigration from Eastern Europe, particularly from the countries of the former Soviet Union, will increase substantially. It is also estimated that the pressure on all highly developed countries of the world to accept more refugees will increase to the extent that interethnic conflicts persist or new ones develop around the world.

Canada, the United States, Australia, Germany and a number of other European countries have welcomed waves of immigrants to the extent that their economies have called for more labour than the indigenous population could supply. Since the end of the 1970s, for example, Canada linked its immigration flow to the economic needs of the country. Every year now, the Parliament sets the total number of immigrants to be admitted into the country on the basis of economic need and every year in the 1990s the quota set is at least 220,000. From 1981 to 1991, 1,238,455 immigrants entered Canada and from 1991 to 1998 Canada has admitted 1,559,985 immigrants. Still, an acute demand for highly skilled workers, especially in the field of electronics and computers, has remained and throughout the 1990s the immigration authorities have not been able to bring to Canada the required number of people with these skills. Furthermore, Canada needs more immigrants if it is to maintain its current population growth. There are definite indications that without more immigrants Canada's population will decline in the 21st century and with it will decline Canada's economic growth.

In spite of the economic and demographic need for more immigration, there have been voices raised expressing fears of immigration. Some of these voices of apprehension claim that immigrants take jobs away from Canadians, that they cost the Canadian government too much in welfare payments, that they create pockets of poverty and the like. All these are of course unproven assumptions. Yet, the conservative political parties in Canada and even the government have at various times expressed a concern that the cultural diversity brought about by the immigrants and their succeeding generations may threaten "the Canadian way of life." As pointed out in Chapter 10, some of these sporadically raised voices have argued that multiculturalism is divisive, that retention of minority ethnic identities should be discouraged because sooner or later it can only produce ethnic conflicts and undermine Canadian unity.

Photo: TEP Archives

A typical Canadian road sign in English and French. In many urban centers, street signs are in English and in the language of the dominant ethnic group.

Are there any grounds for such fears? Are there limits to diversity? Is there a point at which ethnic diversity produces negative effects on the larger society? Is there a point at which society begins to disintegrate due to ethnic diversity?

Perhaps the best way to answer such questions is to look at Canada's history. Canada has been the country of ethnic diversity and a country of immigrants since its very beginnings. By and large, it has encouraged integration into the dominant society, but it has allowed its diverse ethnic groups to retain their culture, religion and their institutions if they so wished. In its educational system, it has given recognition to several religions. It has gone through two world wars, through waves of different ideological thinking, some of them of almost subversive character. Yet throughout all the years of its existence, it has had relatively little interethnic violence compared with many other countries in which ethnic diversity has been much smaller. Canada's ethnic composition has never shown itself to be a source of the country's weakness. If anything, ethnic diversity has been one of the country's main sources of strength.

mother. With their wives working, the immigrant husbands are often required to do some housework and child care to which they are not accustomed. In cases of unemployed husbands and employed wives, the roles often get reversed, and husbands have to stay at home and engage in housework. All this undermines the traditional status difference between husbands and wives and may have the effect of undermining self-image and self-confidence. This may disrupt family life, prompting conflict and even wife-abuse as a form of psychological compensation.

Studies of South Asian immigrant women point to problems that result from the traditional structure of marriage and family relationships in which women have been dominated by men and have been accustomed to passively accepting men's demands. The studies find them particularly vulnerable to exploitation both at their place of work and in the home. This often means extremely long hours of work, and isolation and alienation from the community and even from their extended family (Naidoo, 1987).

In general, immigrant housewives, especially those with a low level of education, tend to be more socially isolated from the larger society than are their husbands. A study of immigrant women from Latin America found that inadequate language skills, unavailability of daycare for children and lack of ethnic community support placed serious constraints on the women's leisure, community participation and their physical and social mobility (Rublee and Shaw, 1991). Single mothers, particularly among the refugees, are subject to violence, which often goes unreported and unrecognized (Boyd, 1994).

Special problems are faced by immigrant women who work as live-in domestics in white, middle-class households. Domestic work often presents an exploitative situation, which perpetuates both gender and race discrimination. Mobilization of community resources from outside the work situation is one way in which such discrimination has been approached (Cohen, 1991).

• Special Problems of Political Refugees and Exiles

In addition to the problems of adjustment already discussed, political refugees and exiles face other problems. Here we are referring to those political immigrants who, in the face of hostile governments, have attempted to uphold or retain their values, convictions, religion, cultural or national identity or have been involved in dissident activities against these governments. The people of the host society to which these refugees come, and even the intellectual and governmental circles of the host society, quite often fail to understand the psychology of such political refugees.

A political refugee's self-conception often includes a feeling of pride that is derived from a decision not to give in to the pressure or persecution by a hostile government. It includes the choice of refusing to act externally or publicly against one's own convictions or one's own family or group as the new government in power would require or force them to do. As a consequence, political refugees, after their escape or exile, emerge from the crisis with a new sense of dignity and freedom (Adolf, 1977: 127-132, 202; Cirtautas, 1963).

This new identity, however, can be best understood and appreciated only by people who themselves have gone through the same or a similar crisis. The population of the host society not only has little appreciation of the refugee identity, but often may consider this identity to be deviant. Jacek Adolf (1977: 203-204), a researcher of the adaptation process of émigrés, i.e., political refugees, states:

> There is no institutionalized role into which ... [the émigré] could fit as an émigré. His situation is not unlike the predicament of a toreador thrown among people who don't know anything about bullfights and could not care less about them. His exile self-conception is perceived in the receiving society at large as one of those things that one finds in any immigrant's past, idiosyncratic, exotic, and completely irrelevant. An identity will be assigned to him on the basis of more general criteria commonly used in the receiving society: his income, occupation and all the other indices and determinants of socioeconomic status, including his skin colour, but not on the basis of his refusal to submit to totalitarianism.

What refugees appreciate most about Canadian life after their arrival is the experience of individual freedom. Often, in the early period after migration, the refugee has to adjust to this newly gained freedom, but it tends to remain the refugee's main source of satisfaction with life in Canada.

A biography of a refugee family from Vietnam briefly illustrates this refugee experience (Khong, 1995: 117-118):

> Pham was a graduate of Saigon National University of Art when South Vietnam fell into the hands of the North Vietnamese communist regime in 1975. The communists introduced an agricultural revolution, seizing–often violently–privately held lands and converting them to state ownership. Many resisted and faced harsh repercussions, even death.
>
> Pham decided to escape from the oppression he was suffering. He and his youngest brother, the two youngest of

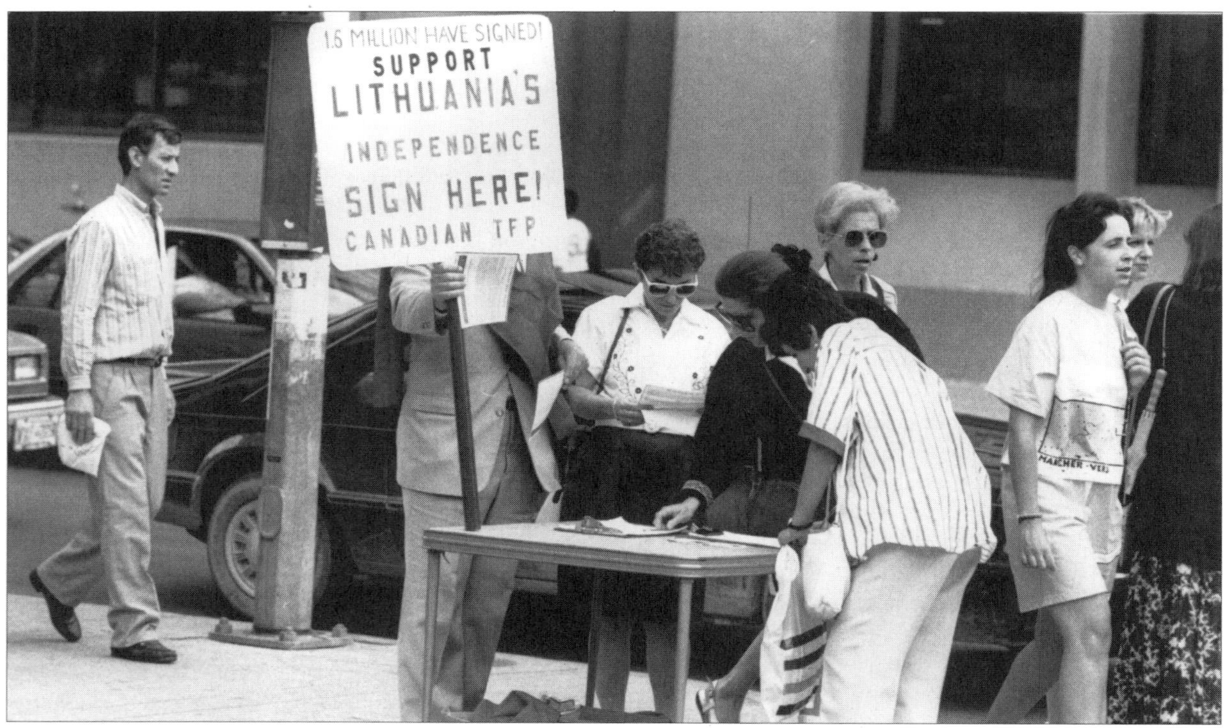

Photo: Dick Hemingway

Petitioning in support of Lithuanian independence. Forced out of their own country against their will, many political refugees champion the cause of freedom for their homeland and may have difficulty adjusting to their new home.

> seven children, left their family after the New Year's Eve family dinner to search for freedom.
>
> For Pham and his brother it was a beginning of a five month long journey to freedom.
>
> Many of [the] Vietnamese refugees, who were also known as the boat people, have since rebuilt their homes and community in Canada. Pham, The-Trung and his wife Thai, Ni Phan, are two of them.

For the refugee this experience involves both the absence of a number of things that in the old society had been a constant threat, and the presence of opportunity to do things that in the old society were forbidden by the government. This includes freedom from police surveillance and control and freedom to move around the country without governmental permission to look for a job or accommodation wherever one pleases. Above all, it includes freedom to express one's views and opinions, to practice religion, to join or found voluntary organizations, to avail oneself of many newspapers or books. Political refugees tend to perceive all these as a sensational contrast to what they were used to before they arrived in Canada.

The value of freedom in all these forms comes to be at the core of the refugees' self-conception. It affects the meaning they attach to their immigrant experience and tends to influence the decisions that shape the course of their later life. The population of the receiving society, however, tends not to appreciate the refugees' excitement and concern over freedom. People in North America tend to take their various freedoms for granted. They may suspect the refugees' stories of being exaggerated and may doubt whether the refugees' decision to leave the old country was a purely moral decision. They tend to see immigrants in economic terms and to presume that the concern over freedom by immigrants who have already settled in the country is unnecessary, fortuitous or even deviant.

To many refugees, the lack of appreciation of their experience is discouraging. They tend to draw into themselves and to form their own informal networks and organizations. These organizations not only function to support their identity, but they also champion the cause of freedom for the old country and preserve or develop those aspects of culture of the old society that are repressed or are under threat of extinction. As a result, political refugees tend to develop strong loyalty to their ethnic group and a strong sense of a legacy that they must fulfil and transmit to their children.

CONCLUSION

The practical and the social-psychological aspects of immigrant adjustment are closely interrelated. Practical problems, such as unemployment, will affect family relationships, and social-psychological factors, such as culture shock, will affect how persons go about solving their practical problems, such as looking for a job. Conditions that help one solve one type of problem will indirectly influence the possibility of solving the other type of problem. The solution of practical problems, such as employment, may be a condition of solving some social-psychological problems, such as loss of male self-image.

In studying any specific group of immigrants at any one period of time, it is very difficult to assess the total picture in which the factors that may help to solve one type of problems are weighed against the factors that may be more useful in solving another type of problems. This can be done to some extent by means of statistical analysis when the factors can be quantified, as, for example, years of education, occupational qualifications and the like (Richmond and Kalbach, 1980). It is, however, more difficult to quantify social-psychological phenomena, such as culture shock, drop in self-esteem or marital conflict. In this regard qualitative case studies are important, including life histories and in-depth interviews in which the immigrants themselves can indicate and explain how the different types of problems have been linked in their lives (Fuchs, 1991).

After a period of stay in the country, immigrants achieve a level of adjustment, as the *Three Years in Canada* study has indicated. It should be remembered that not all reach the same degree of adjustment. Some may be frustrated and return to their home country, others may remain practically but not psychologically adjusted for the rest of their lives and some may have difficulties in practical adjustment for their entire stay in the country.

Ethnic groups within a society do not all enjoy equal economic, political or prestige level. Some ethnic groups enjoy a higher status than others. Immigrants usually become part of their ethnic group within the country and share the group's status. They may or may not contribute to the increase of this status. If they do, this usually would take place over several generations. We will now turn our attention to the phenomenon of ethnic status and ethnic stratification.

Photo: Courtesy of the Ontario Multicultural History Society

Immigrant labourers.

CHAPTER 5

THE INCORPORATION OF ETHNIC GROUPS

Ethnic Stratification in Canada

This chapter tries to answer the question of how ethnic groups come to be part of a larger society. It shows that they are not incorporated equally but rather come to be incorporated into a hierarchical status system. The chapter discusses the factors that place an ethnic group into one or another status within this hierarchy. It also shows how this status can be measured and discusses the factors that perpetuate the status hierarchy itself.

Over a longer period of time ethnic groups and their members become part of the structure of the larger society, i.e., in some degree they come to be incorporated into the larger society. **Social incorporation** can be defined as a process through which a social unit is included in a larger social unit as an integral part of it. Social units can be collectivities or individuals acting in a patterned manner. Theoretically, becoming an integral part of a larger unit means that both the smaller and the larger units become in some way interdependent and come to share certain characteristics that designate them as a distinct larger unit. Thus diverse ethnic groups come to be an integral part of the larger society by becoming part of the society's structure, by assimilating or inculturating into the larger society's culture and by transforming their identity so that they subjectively identify with the larger society and other members of the society identify with them.

Hence, the process of social incorporation of ethnic groups can be said to be of at least three types: (1) structural incorporation, sometimes called integration, (2) cultural incorporation or inculturation, usually known as assimilation, and (3) identity incorporation. As we will discuss later, the three types of incorporation do not necessarily go hand in hand. Social incorporation can proceed on the individual and on the collective level. That is, members of ethnic groups may come to be incorporated as individuals, but the group itself, as a group, does not necessarily disappear. It often remains as part of the differentiated structure of society, and some of the group's institutions and organizations may also be incorporated as such. Lastly, social incorporation involves some degree of reciprocity between the host society and the minority ethnic groups. Minority groups, particularly immigrants, give up much of their own culture and identity as they incorporate into the host society. However, for incorporation to take place, the host society must also meet the minorities at least some way and give up something to accommodate them.

Cultural and identity incorporation will be discussed in a later chapter. In this chapter, we will consider structural incorporation. **Structural incorporation** is of two types: incorporation into the *secondary group structure* and incorporation into the *primary group structure* of society. The former refers to the process of inclusion in work and occupational groups, educational and political groups and other relatively formally structured groups in the mainstream sector of society. The latter refers to inclusion in the structure of informal relations, i.e., in friendship groups and marriage with members of the mainstream sector of society. In this chapter, we will discuss only the structural incorporation with an emphasis on the secondary group structure of society. The other types will be discussed in separate chapters.

ETHNIC STRATIFICATION AS DIFFERENTIAL SOCIAL INCORPORATION

Incorporation into a structure means that, at least in some important respect, the smaller units come to depend on the larger unit, and in turn, the larger unit comes to depend on the smaller units. In reality, this interdependence is never symmetrical, i.e., any single smaller unit depends much more on the larger unit than the other way around. Hence, social incorporation is a process that over time produces a persistent asymmetrical structure. In relation to ethnic groups, this structure is known as *ethnic stratification.* It implies that different ethnic groups are *differentially* incorporated into the larger society.

Differential incorporation received attention in the early works on ethnicity in terms of a variety of frameworks, colonial Asian, Caribbean, American and Canadian (Furnivall, 1956; Wiley, 1967; Williams, 1964; Gordon, 1964; Porter, 1965; Smith, 1965, 1984; Rex, 1970). In Canada, John Porter (1965: 60-103) formulated the concept of the **vertical mosaic**, by which he referred to the fact that ethnic groups in Canada form a hierarchical structure of statuses, based on their over- or under-representation in different occupational, educational and income categories. The nature of this structure, he argued, was determined by the "charter" groups, the British and the French, particularly the British, who form the top level of this structure. Porter's concept gave rise to many studies and scholarly discussions of the relationship between ethnicity and the socio-economic structure of society. Notable among them were the studies of the Canadian elite (Clement, 1975). As will be discussed in later chapters, some of these studies disagreed with Porter. Porter's work, however, was an important pioneering work on the issue of differential incorporation.

Incorporation of ethnic groups into a larger society means the inclusion of minority ethnic groups into a society whose structure and culture has been historically established by a different ethnic group than their own, i.e., by a majority ethnic group. At least initially, the majority group acts as a gate-keeper of the access to prestige, power and the wealth of society. It establishes the criteria of incorporation of minority ethnic groups and gives the process of incorporation its initial direction. With time, however, while some minority groups may remain relatively unincorporated into the larger society, other minority groups may become sufficiently incorporated to exert influence to effect change and help to bring about new criteria of incorporation. This process, however, may be accompanied by latent or open tensions or conflict.

All people in the same society are not socially equal. Some enjoy more prestige, power and wealth; others, less. Similarly, ethnic groups, as groups, possess different levels of prestige, power and wealth in relation to one another. This is the meaning of **ethnic stratification**. In purely descriptive terms, any system of social stratification can be seen as a system of differences in the distribution of various characteristics among groups of people. Thus we can describe a stratification system by saying that a certain percentage of population earns annually between $0 and $15,000 a year, another percentage earns annually between $16,000 and $24,000 a year, and still another, between $25,000 and $40,000 and so on. Or we may show that a certain percentage of people in society hold unskilled kinds of jobs, another percentage, semiskilled types of jobs, still others, skilled jobs, clerical jobs, professional jobs and so on. Similar differentiation can be shown in terms of education, value of residential areas and the like.

By itself, however, such description does not yet tell us much about the nature of intergroup relations. If we look at social stratification, not simply as a given structure, but as a result or consequence of intergroup relations, then we can see the distributions of these attributes–income, occupation, education–as combining into a more composite social phenomenon "out there," rather than as simply a system of classification. Thus we move from phenomena that can be easily statistically described to phenomena that cannot be directly statistically described. The aforementioned characteristics become only indicators of a larger, complex social whole.

The main characteristic of this social whole is its hierarchical nature. That is, people in society come to be perceived not only by the statistical investigators but by people themselves as fitting into places in relation to one another on a scale of values–higher or lower, better off or worse off, more important or less important. In other words, people are accorded *statuses* in the hierarchical system. This applies not only to individuals, but also to groups, in our case, ethnic groups, including racial groups.

Being higher or lower in this system of statuses involves subordination and superordination. This is the reality to which the concept of power refers. Following Max Weber, **power** can be defined as the possibility people have to fulfil their goals in spite of potential or actual opposition from other people. Possibility to fulfil goals may refer to the possibility of obtaining or doing what one wants or doing what one thinks is proper. Usually, in a stable society, power is derived from the positions persons have that define and legitimize the scope of their actions over other people. Opposition from others does not mean that there is always conflict between those who are subordinate and those who are superordinate. In fact, in stable societies, there is usually little actual conflict between those on top and those on the bottom or those in-between. But a degree of tension between them and the potentiality of opposition and conflict, even if remote, is always there. The concept of power is meaningless without the element of potentiality of opposition.

The concept of power is used here to apply not only to individuals but to groups, in our case, the ethnic groups. It is the power and influence that one group has in society as compared with other groups. As was previously explained, groups who possess power in a society are called, sociologically, majority groups, as against minority groups, who have little or no power. Groups, however, do not exercise power directly as groups, but indirectly, through social institutions, public and private agencies and voluntary associations. Groups who have little or no "real" power in society may nevertheless have some degree of influence. These are the groups that have been referred to as "middle-man minorities." This will be discussed in detail later. Here it is important to point out that exercise of power and influence is the essence of all intergroup relations. It is the primary feature of the system of ethnic stratification.

The idea of being "better off" usually means being wealthier than others. Sociologically, this means having better life-chances as individuals, families or groups as compared with others. Although the concept of life-chances is not very precise, it refers to the idea of being able to avail oneself of the goods and services that enhance the quality of life. When applied to a group of people, the concept of wealth means two things: (1) that individuals or families in that group are more or less able to enhance their quality of life in comparison with those in other groups and (2) that the group, as a group, in comparison with other groups, has the resources necessary to organize its own community institutions, associations, and organizations that would be effective, not only in providing services to the members of the group, but also in being influential in the group's collective action in its relations with other groups and the society at large.

There is, however, a way in which individual or family life-chances enter into intergroup relations directly. When individuals of one ethnic background come into contact with individuals of other ethnic backgrounds, they often, in an indirect, social-psychological manner, represent their ethnic group. That is, their interaction with others often contributes to the formation of images and stereotypes of their ethnic group or the confirmation of already existing, learned images and stereotypes. The standard of living and the quality of life enter significantly into this interaction and thus play an important part in intergroup relations.

The third aspect of the hierarchical order refers to prestige. That is, those at the top are perceived as being more "important" in society, more "remarkable" and more "respectable" than those at the bottom. The implication of this is that those lower in the hierarchical order accord more prestige to those who are higher. Psychologically, this means that those lower in the stratification system possess feelings of less worth in relation to those in the higher strata and are likely to show deference to them in their behaviour. Here again the reference is to the prestige accorded to individuals on the basis of their being members of the prestigious group or groups. We will later examine some of the implications of this deference.

We can now define **ethnic stratification** as a hierarchical system of ethnic groups, arranged according to the degree of power that the groups have in society, the level of the quality of life their members enjoy and the collective resources possessed, and the amount of prestige the groups and their members enjoy in relation to one another. *Ethnic status,* then, is the place that any particular group holds in this hierarchical system, i.e., the specific degree of power it has in society, the specific level of the quality of life its members share and the collective resources they possess, and the specific amount of prestige the group enjoys in relation to other ethnic and racial groups in the same society. The standard of comparison is the group at the top of the stratification system, i.e., the majority ethnic group or groups. The place in society of all other groups must be understood in relation to it.

DETERMINANTS OF ETHNIC STATUS

The status of any particular ethnic group is a result of a combination of a great many sociological factors. For purposes of understanding, it is helpful to group these factors according to their source. Three such sources may be readily identified: (1) those factors deriving from the majority ethnic group, (2) those from the economic and political state of society as a whole at any given time, and (3) those from the minority ethnic group itself.

ETHNIC STATUS DETERMINANTS DERIVING FROM THE MAJORITY ETHNIC GROUP

• Ethnocentrism

The most significant factor deriving from the majority groups is that of ethnocentrism. The phenomenon of ethnocentrism will be discussed later in the book in relation to prejudice. Here it is sufficient to define **ethnocentrism** as an attitude by which members of a group tend to consider their group to be in all or some ways better or superior to other groups. Such an attitude is especially significant in relation to the majority groups because it is conditioned by the positions of power that members of a group hold.

Ethnocentrism can be considered to be a form of prejudice, i.e., prejudice in favour of one's group. As such, it is inherently related to the other form of prejudice, i.e., prejudice against other groups. An important aspect of prejudice is stereotyping. The type of stereotyping we are interested in at the moment is one that has to do with occupations and type of work, that is, *role stereotyping.* Ethnocentrism leads to role stereotyping. This means that members of the majority group tend to feel that the more important and the more responsible work in society should be done by themselves rather than by members of minority groups. As a result, differential roles come to be ascribed to different ethnic groups. The socially more important roles are identified with majorities, the less important ones, with minorities. The British in Canada are often identified with business and finance and with high political offices, the French, with industrial work, Jews, with trading, Italians, with construction, Chinese, with small grocery stores and laundries and so on. This does not mean that, in reality, most members of ethnic groups engage in occupations with which their group is stereotypically identified. In fact, the contrary is more often true. It does mean, however, that members of ethnic groups engaged in these occupations become socially highly visible and, most importantly, it means that in recruitment to the higher status, more responsible and influential occupations, members of the majority tend to give preference to those of the same ethnic background as themselves or to groups preferred by them.

In this manner, ethnic role stereotypes lead to preferential treatment, which involves discrimination in occupational recruitment and other areas of social relationships. This contributes to the creation and persistence of differences in ethnic status.

Ethnocentrism is often supported by various ideologies that justify the superior position of the majority group. We can say that, the higher the degree of ethnocentrism, the more pronounced or articulated is the ideology. In Canada, for example, the position of the British in relation to the French has at times been supported by means of the ideology of the "right of the conqueror" or, in regard to many other ethnic minority groups, the ideology of "bearing civilization," by which the majority group is seen as possessing a higher civilization that others are to accept in time. In regard to the non-white racial groups, especially the Blacks, ideologies articulating white superiority in genetic terms have been popular in various periods of history, both in Europe and North America.

Ideologies of extreme nationalism have tried to justify the majority superior position in terms of cultural superiority. The word *racism* (although, strictly speaking, it applies to race rather than ethnic ideologies), has been generally used to indicate any expression of ideology justifying the superiority-inferiority positions of any ethnic or racial group. More will be said about this in the chapter on prejudice, stereotyping and racism.

• Discrimination

The process by which ethnocentrism determines the ethnic status of any group or groups takes place when those who have the power to decide who fills the existing opportunity vacancies develop a pattern of choosing proportionally more persons from their own ethnic group, or from their preferred groups, than from other groups. **Discrimination** results when any one group or a set of groups is continuously excluded from these vacancies. Vacancies here are meant to refer, not only to occupational vacancies, but also to opportunities of other types, residential, educational, cultural and even friendship and marital. The most important opportunities, however, are occupational, since in our society they are the main determinants of social structure.

It is difficult to study discrimination empirically, since few people will openly admit to discriminating against ethnic groups and since the manner of discrimination is often subtle. Sociologists usually gather all the more readily available data on occupational distribution and related variables among ethnic groups, and if differences in the distribution cannot be explained in terms of any other variables, in particular qualification and education, the conclusion is drawn that they are due to discrimination (Herberg, 1990).

Often sociologists undertake studies of discrimination reported by people who feel that they have been discriminated against. One early such study was Wilson A. Head's (1975) study of perceptions of discrimination against Blacks among four samples in Metropolitan Toronto: 210 Black adults, 54 Black youths, 32 Black leaders and 53 non-Blacks. Almost 60 percent of the adult respondents reported having personally experienced one or more instances of discrimination. The highest percentages of discrimination were reported in two areas: employment and housing. Of the adult sample, 36.2 percent reported great amounts of discrimination in employment, and 22.9 percent, great amounts of discrimination in housing, primarily renting. In addition, 40.1 percent reported at least some discrimination in employment, and 45.4 percent, at least some discrimination in housing. Furthermore, 8.2 percent reported great amounts and 35.4 percent some discrimination in community services, i.e., schools, social service agencies, medical services, recreational programs. Similarly, 9.9 percent reported great amounts and 36.5 some discrimination in commercial services, i.e., banks, mortgage companies, insurance companies and the like.

Slightly more "white collar" workers (62.2 percent) than "blue collar" workers (56.5 percent) indicated an experience of discrimination. Head's adult sample was fairly well educated, with 22.7 percent having completed Grade 13 or one or more years at community college, and 36.9 percent having completed between Grades 10 and 12.

When asked about the general character of discrimination, almost 90 percent of respondents indicated that discrimination in Toronto was subtle rather than overt. Head (1975: 198-199) pointed out:

> The subtle nature of much discrimination is reflected in the lack of awareness by many respondents of the actual forms this phenomenon takes. For example, few respondents reported discrimination in buying a house. However, other informants, including some real estate sales people, inform us that many mortgage companies are extremely reluctant and often refuse to lend mortgage money to Blacks. This hidden discrimination is not made known to the buyer, and is typical of the "polite racism" which many of our respondents suggest is so prevalent in Canadian society.

A survey by J. S. Friederes (1973) in Western Canada confirmed that many immigrants there also reported that they have been discriminated against. Friederes studied a sample of 984 adult immigrants who arrived in Alberta in the period between 1946 and 1970. In the survey, 20.8 percent of the immigrants reported that they had been discriminated against. Some groups however, had higher percentages. Thus, 64 percent of Jews, 58 percent of Asians, 52 percent of Yugoslavians, 52 percent of Italians, 48 percent of Austrians, 44 percent of Ukrainians, 24 percent of the English and 22 percent of the Germans reported that they had been discriminated against at one time or another since coming to Alberta.

Self-reported discrimination, however, while a valid method of measuring discrimination, involves the danger that some respondents may attribute all their failures to discrimination while there may be other reasons for them. Likewise, it is very difficult to observe and study discrimination directly. One study attempted to do this by using a unique method. Frances Henry and Effie Ginzberg (1985) employed white and Black actors to masquerade as job applicants. They created four teams of matched applicants. Each team consisted of one white and one Black applicant. The teams were matched with respect to age and sex. Thus there were two teams of men, young and old, and two teams of women, young and old. The jobs they applied for were picked from newspaper advertisements in Toronto. The applicants would call, present their qualifications and ask for interviews. Each applicant for the same type of job would give the same list of qualifications. The prospective employers who interviewed the applicants were white. The results showed that out of 37 valid job offers, 27 offers went to whites and 9 to Blacks. Since the qualifications for the jobs, the age and the sex were exactly the same for both the white and the Black applicants, the results indicated discrimination as the main cause of difference.

This study, however, was repeated in 1989, and the results were different. The number of job offers to Blacks was the same as to whites (Henry, 1994: 115). The author explains this difference as being due to a tight labour market that had emerged at that time, but also to a greater willingness of employers to hire

I'M SORRY MISS BUT - ER - THE JOB HAS BEEN FILLED
HELP WANTED

Source: TEP archives

minority applicants, indicating a change in the level of discrimination. This was also supported by the conclusions of the Economic Council of Canada's study of wage differentials between the immigrant and the native-born population (Canada, 1991b: 75-93). To what extent this actually does indicate a lessening of the degree of discrimination in Canadian society, however, is not clear and has been debated by researchers (Reitz, 1993; De Silva, Palmer and Reitz, 1994).

• Structural Discrimination

The above study measured direct discrimination where the prospective employers intentionally chose applicants of the same race as they were and excluded the Black applicants. Just as often, however, discrimination takes place not directly, but indirectly, as a consequence of established practices, procedures, rules and regulations that by themselves are not intended to discriminate against anyone, but that do so in consequence. This consequence may or may not be recognized by those who are in charge of hiring or of allocating any opportunities to others. This indirect discrimination is often called **structural discrimination**.

The subtle, indirect way in which this form of discrimination works was described by David H. Stymeist (1976) in his study of relations between Native Indians and other ethnic groups in a northwestern Ontario town. Stymeist used the anthropological method of participant observation. He lived and worked at different jobs in the town, talked to as many people as he could, observed them in different situations and recorded their own informal observations on their lives and community. Stymeist describes the manner in which discrimination against Native Indians takes place. What happens, he says, is that valuable items of information concerning various opportunities in town are not published openly, but are passed by word of mouth through various information networks. One hears about jobs and apartments, not through the newspaper or notices on bulletin boards, but through friends and acquaintances. He describes a case in which brakemen for the CNR were hired without any official announcement of the vacancies but simply as a result of the friends of a clerk obtaining the information about the vacancies from him and spreading it to their friends. As a result, all those who were hired were white, all had lived in the town for most of their lives and many had relatives working for the CNR. He described a similar situation involving the renting of a house.

Stymeist observed that, although there was much prejudice against Indians in town, none of the white people involved in these incidents acted out of a conscious desire to exclude Indian people from either jobs or rental accommodation. He says:

> During the time I lived and worked in Crow Lake these scenes were, with variations, repeated again and again. The ultimate effect was to rigidly exclude most Indians as job holders or residents: Indian people were simply not part of the "right" information networks. It was a classic vicious circle in that it was difficult if not impossible for an Indian person to become part of an information network unless he was already part of that network, to get a job unless he already had a job, or to find a place to live unless he already had a place to live. Such informal problems of exclusion operate in virtually every area of Indian-white encounter (Stymeist, 1975: 77-78).

Rex Lucas' (1971) classic study of Canadian single-industry towns presented the same conclusion regarding discrimination and ethnic stratification. Lucas drew attention to what he called pre-employment ethnic sponsorship, by which, when a job is posted formally, it has already been filled informally. In a typical rail town, after 60 years of living, the British still retained 100 percent of managerial jobs and only 15 percent of labouring jobs. The latter were largely filled by minority ethnic groups. He pointed out that the system of local hiring, including ethnic sponsorship, was typical of all one-industry towns in Canada.

The last two studies presented above have dealt with small towns. It could be argued that in larger contexts the pattern of filling vacancies is different. A study of a sample of Canadian middle-level civil servants by Christopher Beattie (1975), however, suggests that in large, urban organizational contexts the pattern has been essentially the same. Beattie interviewed a total of 296 civil servants in five departments of the federal government. Of these, 168 were Anglophones and 128, Francophones. He collected data on their early socialization, type of career and the organizational setting of their careers. He found that in each department the Francophones were concentrated in routine types of jobs and were under-represented in creative positions. Beattie pointed out that previous studies of the federal administration confirmed his findings by showing that Francophones have been virtually absent from the higher levels of the important and dynamic departments of the federal civil service (Beattie, 1975: 144).

Beattie explained his findings by using Oswald Hall's idea of the sponsorship system, by which senior personnel bring into the higher levels of the organization younger people who think and feel like they do and who can show a good deal of social compatibility. This involves extensive interaction among employees and adeptness at informal communication. Hence, Francophones, with their linguistic differences, usually find themselves outside of the informal circles of the Anglophones and are not recruited for the more prestigious creative jobs by the Anglophone bosses. The result of this is that creative work remains an Anglophone preserve (Beattie, 1975: 133, 146).

A study by Brenda Billingsley and Leon Muszynski (1985) of the employment practices of 199 public, quasi-public and private organizations in the Metropolitan Toronto area also found that informal channels within the organization were by far the most used method of hiring persons for senior and junior managerial positions. The effect of this method of hiring was discriminatory, particularly against racial groups.

The studies cited above show how ethnocentric tendencies function to produce a system of filling opportunity vacancies by giving preference to one's own or favoured ethnic groups and excluding others. In all cases, the ethnic groups excluded were subject to one type or another of negative images or stereotypes. Most respondents in Head's study felt that there are negative images of the Black community prevalent in society. They felt that the media promote a negative image of Blacks much more frequently than a positive one, by reporting such news as crime by Blacks more often than any positive community news, by distorting news and often by paternalism.

Henry and Ginsberg (1985: 36) observed that the Black job seekers faced not only discrimination in the sense that they received far fewer job offers than did whites, but they were also subjected to a considerable amount of negative and even abusive treatment while job seeking. In cases where such differential treatment took place, Blacks did not receive offers of employment.

Stymeist (1975: 75-76) listened to and recorded discussions and talk by white men about Indians. An attitude of "us against them" would develop, followed by a list of stock complaints made in a serious or half-serious tone: "Indians are dirty; they smell bad; they are lazy; they won't work; they are all drunks; they live off welfare; they are given too much" and so on. He pointed out that the statements were rarely challenged. Rather, they were repeated and elaborated.

Lucas (1971: 137-139, 309-310) found quite a number of ethnic stereotypes held by people, especially bosses and fellow workers, in small towns, and Beattie (1975: 146) indicated that the Francophones, because they were perceived by the Anglophone superiors as not fully fluent in English, were also seen by them as not being completely trustworthy in the more independent, creative occupations. In the Billingsley and Muszynski (1985: 82) study, the racial minorities were perceived as "unqualified" and "untrained" "just because they're coloured."

More will be said about stereotypes in the chapter on prejudice and racism. The point made here is that stereotypes play a significant role in the process of filling opportunities and hence in the development and perpetuation of a system of ethnic stratification.

ETHNIC STATUS DETERMINANTS DERIVING FROM THE STATE OF THE ECONOMY AND POLITY: AVAILABILITY OF OPPORTUNITIES

The second set of determinants of ethnic status and ethnic stratification are factors deriving from the state of the society's economy and its political exigencies at any given time. The state of society at any given time may open up opportunities to all ethnic groups or only to some, or it may make few opportunities available to anyone. While the Depression years in Canada closed opportunities for a large sector of the Canadian population, the period after World War II witnessed a vast opening up of opportunities in all areas of life, with a resulting pattern of social mobility of practically all ethnic groups and increases in the numbers of immigrants.

Four mechanisms can be singled out by which the economic or political state of society at any given time influences the development or perpetuation of the ethnic stratification system. They are the ethnic entrance status, a dual labour market, ethnic occupational concentrations, including enclave enterprise, and political conjuncture, including governmental policies. The term mechanism is used here not in the strict mechanical sense of the word that implies an invariant relation between cause and effect, but in the looser sense of the word, implying the processes that usually function together with other processes and factors to bring about or maintain a system of ethnic stratification. In what follows we will briefly explain each one of these mechanisms.

• Ethnic Entrance Status

The idea that the place an ethnic group holds in society is determined by the group's entrance status was developed by John Porter (1965: 68). The concept of **entrance status** refers to the type of jobs that immigrants are funneled into upon their arrival in the country. In particular, it is relevant to young ethnic groups whose first waves of immigration flow into one type or one level of jobs with which they become identified and that serve as starting points for any social mobility that may take place later on. The idea is that some groups may start with better kinds of jobs and others, with worse.

The assumption made here is that the entrance status is to a large extent determined by the type and level of economic development at any given time, which works to funnel the immigrants predominantly to one or another type of jobs.

Economists claim that there is a definitive positive association between rates of economic investment in the country and demand for foreign labour (Green, 1976; Economic Council of Canada, 1991). Thus, the period from the turn of the century to World War I was a period of rapid expansion of the Canadian West, pushing back the frontier and integrating the region with the domestic and world markets. The latter in particular was in response to the international demand for wheat. Wheat and railway created a demand for farmers and for semi- and unskilled labour. During this period, the bulk of immigrants to Canada were farmers and labourers, taking up work in the fields of the Prairies and in the jobs connected with the railroad and other types of related fledgling industry. These were the jobs that determined the entrance status of most Eastern European immigrants coming into the country in that period for the first time in large numbers, to some extent Germans and several other Northern European groups, and to some extent the Chinese.

In the interwar period, unlike the pre-war period, only a small proportion of fixed investment occurred in sectors of the economy dependent on foreign trade. Most investments were in industries dependent on domestic demand, such as housing, manufacturing and service. The demand for foreign labour also started to shift to skilled craftsman and factory operatives. Similar trends also took place in the period following World War II. Fixed investment in agriculture declined sharply, as did investment in the primary industries. Instead, big investments were made in utilities and construction–on the average, more than 21 percent from 1950 to 1970–housing, about 19 percent throughout the same period, manufacturing, about 15 percent, and government, about 13 percent.

The demand for labour in the post-war period became more diversified. There was still need for unskilled labour, but it declined with time. There were significant increases in demand for mechanics, construction workers and for white-collar and professional workers. Yet in spite of a greater diversification of the economy, job funneling of immigrants remained quite pronounced. Over 50 percent of all immigrants from the United Kingdom and from the United States went into white-collar occupations: professional, clerical, commercial. In contrast, less than 10 percent of Southern European immigrants–Italians, Greeks and Portuguese–went into white-collar occupations. The bulk of them went into blue-collar, manufacturing and labouring occupations, 68, 55 and 39 percent respectively from 1951 to 1970, with the Portuguese funneled into the labouring jobs much more than the other two groups. The Northern and Western European immigrants were in-between. In the period from 1951 to 1970, about 19 percent of the German immigrants and 26 percent of the Dutch went into white-collar occupations, and about 50 and 32 percent respectively, into blue-collar jobs (Green, 1976: 149-154)

In the 1980s and 1990s, the number of unskilled immigrants has grown considerably smaller. As explained in the previous chapter, the new immigration regulations placed a much heavier preference on attracting skilled, educated and wealthy immigrants. As a result the entrance status of many groups has increased. As of 1986, among the South Asian groups, 48 percent of immigrants were in the professional, managerial, clerical and sales occupations, and 31 percent in processing, product fabricating, construction and processing occupations (White and Nanda, 1989: 9). Their entrance status has thus been higher than the entrance status of the same groups in earlier periods. The same has been the case with the Chinese immigrants in Canada (Li, 1993).

Entrance status thus gives a place within the stratification system to new ethnic groups and, with newer waves of immigrants, either reinforces the existing ethnic status of a group or contributes to a change of ethnic status of the group. Change of a group's ethnic status derives also from the social mobility of members of a group in the host society, especially the social mobility of the group's second and consecutive generations. But the starting point of an ethnic group's social mobility is its entrance status.

• Dual Labour Market

The theory of the **dual labour market** is derived from the observation that minority groups, particularly immigrants, have often been paid lower wages than the majority population. The theory holds that there are two labour markets, one in the mainstream structure of society and the other in the minority group structure of society. The first offers relatively well-paying, stable employment, with good working conditions, chances of advancement and equitable administration of work rules, and the second offers less desirable pay, little chance of advancement, poor working conditions and is characterized by low profits and productivity and instability, i.e., a high degree of labour turnover (Beck, Horan and Tolbert, 1978). Competition is presumed to exist within, but not between, the two markets. As a result, for those in the second labour market, transition to the first labour market is difficult. Those who work in the second labour market tend to be, as it were, trapped in the inferior types of jobs for long periods of time or even throughout their lifetime.

For immigrants, getting a job, any job, as soon as possible upon arrival has usually been a matter of primary importance and urgency, but the jobs that have often been most readily available to them, especially in periods of economic slump, have been those in the second labour market. Many immigrants have taken these jobs in the hope that their very first job will not necessary be their last in the new country. Yet, by taking such jobs, they may limit their chance of switching to the mainstream labour market structure and may stay in them for longer periods of time. Thus, the dual labour market can be said to be a result of the labour situation in a specific state of the economy and, as such, functions as a determinant of ethnic status for some ethnic and racial minority groups, particularly those who have large proportions of newcomers in the country.

R.A. Helling (1965: 32-38) studied, among other groups, the position of Italians in the social structure of the city of Windsor and singled out several mechanisms by which the wages of the immigrants in construction work were kept low. According to him, construction work, especially subcontracting work, is obtained on a bid basis. By and large, the lowest bidder is awarded the contract. The subcontractor has to resort to various practices that will allow him to be a low bidder and still increase his net earnings. Three such practices were singled out: "the wage-split," "the sweetheart agreement" and the "padrone" system. In the wage-split practice, the employer pays the workers less than what is recorded in the books of the company. The employer presumes that the immigrant workers will not complain to the authorities or often will not know what their minimum wage is supposed to be. Usually his presumption is justified. A variation of this is a kickback system, which works especially in periods of high unemployment as it is better to pay kickbacks to an employer than not have a job at all.

A sweetheart agreement is a tacit agreement between a union official and an employer not to enforce the collective bargaining agreements with the company, even if only for a limited period of time. During that period, the employer can often save labour costs at the expense of the workers. Under the padrone system, an employer, usually a subcontractor, imports his workers directly from another country, usually from the country he has come from himself. The padrone may forward the passage money to his prospective workers and may run a boarding house for them when

Photo: Dick Hemingway

Some ethnic minorities are concentrated in low-paying occupations where the prospects for mobility are low and discrimination is widespread. This situation is worse for female workers, who also face sexual discrimination.

they arrive. Thus, the newly arrived workers become indebted to their employer and remain quiet about the wages offered them and the conditions of their work.

While contributing to the creation and maintenance of the second labour market, the padrone system nevertheless made immigration possible for many people who would otherwise not have been able to come to Canada. It also enabled a sector of immigrants to establish their own businesses and become self-employed (Harney, 1991a; Sturino, 1990: 93-108).

• Split Labour Market

The theory of the **split labour market** was developed by Edna Bonacich (1972) to explain the economic sources of ethnic antagonisms. It is similar to the dual labour market theory, except that it applies to the structure of the mainstream labour market rather than to the minority labour markets. Both split and dual labour market theories are variants of the labour market segmentation theory (Krahn and Gartrell, 1983). The split labour market theory is derived from the observation that, in the mainstream labour market, there are categories of jobs in which a concentration of some ethnic minority groups can be found but in which the wage is kept at a lower rate than what it would be if other ethnic groups were filling the jobs and in which other discriminatory practices take place.

Agnes Calliste (1987, 1988) applied this theory to explain the status of the Black sleeping railway car porters in Canada between the 1880s and 1950s. She showed how Canadian National Railways (CNR) and Canadian Pacific Railways (CPR) kept the wages for the Black porters low by inducing them to sign agreements that allowed employers to fire the porters at any time and by a collusion with the higher priced white railway labour who shared the same racist stereotypes. Because of discrimination in other occupations, members of minority groups, such as the Black porters, often have no choice but to take these types of jobs. This in turn contributes to the perpetuation of their lower ethnic status.

• Ethnic Occupational Concentrations and Enclave Enterprise

The dual labour market is related to ethnic occupational concentrations and ethnic enclave enterprise. This does not mean, however, that all ethnic occupational concentrations or enterprises necessarily involve a degree of worker exploitation. **Ethnic occupational concentration** refers to the extent to which members of an ethnic group work in an occupation of a specific type as compared with those not in the group. The measure of occupational concentration is the ratio of the odds that a person from an ethnic group would have to work in a specific type of occupation to the odds that persons not from this group would have to work in this same type of occupation (Reitz, 1990: 164). Thus, for example, members of the ethnic group *x* may be eight times as likely to work in the textile industry than persons in the general labour force who are not members of that group.

Reitz (1990: 165-167) found that in Toronto:

> Italian men are 16.8 times more likely than others to work as masons or tilesetters, and are concentrated in other construction work. They are also 14.4 times more likely to be barbers. Italian women work in textile products (as much as 11.5 times more likely than other women), and also in metal working, factory and other work (including in the construction industry).
>
> Jewish men...are 8.0 time more likely than other men to work in textile products. They are also 6.0 time more likely to be physicians, 7.9 time more likely to be lawyers and 3.5 times more likely to be university teachers. Jewish women are 3 or 4 times more likely than other women to work in sales (particularly real estate sales). Jewish women are also concentrated as social workers (2.7 time more likely), in commercial and fine art (2.3 times more likely), and as lawyers and social scientists.
>
> In the other established groups, there are also significant patterns of concentration, though they are less visible. German men work in tool and die making (4.2 times more likely) and other metal-working occupations, and food preparation. German women work in electrical products and as hair dressers. Ukrainian men work in railways, baking and hotel management. Ukrainian women work as cleaners, and in food preparation....
>
> Chinese men work as cooks (5.2 times more likely), and in various service occupations (3.7 times more likely; this category includes laundering but not protective services, in which Chinese are not concentrated). Other Chinese men are concentrated in medical occupations (3.2 times more likely) and science and engineering (2.7 times more likely). Chinese women have jobs that overlap with Italian women (in textiles), but that are also distinctive (electronic data processing and office-machine operators).
>
> West Indian men are concentrated in medical and health occupations (including as physicians), as welders (3.4 times more likely), clerks, guards, and taxi drivers. West Indian women also work in the medical field as nurses, in personal services, and in data processing.
>
> The Portuguese men, like Italians, are concentrated in construction. Even more often, however, they work as janitors (4.6 times more likely than other men). Portuguese women work as cleaners more often than do Ukrainian women (10.3 times more likely than other women).

Reitz cautions that not all occupational concentrations are a result of discrimination. Some groups have achieved equality, yet are among the most occupationally concentrated groups. There are other factors that produce occupational concentrations. The demand for workers in specific kinds of jobs, which often gives new immigrants their entrance status, often also influences their occupational concentration. In the 1960s, for example, the demand for construction workers and related work was high, and immigrants from Italy and Portugal came to fill it. Other examples are the demand in the 1980s for domestic workers, filled to a large extent by the Filipino women, the demand for rich entrepreneurs, filled by the Hong Kong Chinese and immigrants from Singapore at the end of the 1980s and into the 1990s.

An important factor in the formation of occupational concentrations are the ethnic community networks that motivate members to help each other find jobs. Franca Iacovetta (1992: 57-64) described the manner in which Italian immigrants in the 1960s would bring in their kinsmen and *paesani* to fill available jobs and thus create occupational concentrations.

A special form of ethnic occupational concentration is ethnic enclave enterprise. **Ethnic enclave enterprise** refers to businesses that are established in ethnic neighbourhoods and are owned and operated by self-employed persons who are members of an ethnic group. These persons employ their workers mainly from that same ethnic group and cater to customers coming mainly, but not exclusively, from that ethnic group. Examples of such an enterprise are a corner grocery store in an ethnic minority neighbourhood, a Chinese restaurant, an Italian barber shop, a small manufacturing shop and the like. Typically, such an enterprise is a family effort, where members of the family or their kin all work together to make the enterprise a success. Iacovetta (1992: 63) described such small businesses in the Italian community in Toronto as being associated with men, but which usually draw on the labour power of wives and other family members. Often one of the marriage partners will run the family store while the other will earn money outside in the wage-paying labour force. This provides the needed funds to help develop the store, funds that serve as a buffer against the insecurity of the newly established business. Self-employment provides the minority members with a sense of independence, status and prestige in their community and contributes to their dedication to community causes (Suyyagh, 1995).

The Toronto study (Reitz, 1990: 169) showed that, of the eight ethnic groups studied, the highest percentage of self-employed people were among the Jews (42 percent for males and 16 percent of females in the sample), followed by the Italians (19.2 percent for males and 5.5 for females), Germans (17.9 and 6.2 percent), Chinese (14.1 and 3.4 percent), Majority Canadians (11.6 and 3.4 percent), Ukrainians (10.6 and 0.9 percent), Portuguese (4.2 and 8.7 percent) and West Indian (5.5 and 0 percent).

Ethnic occupational concentrations may contribute to an ethnic group's low status in the ethnic stratification system. However, they may also be a resource for their social mobility and thus contribute to the change of their ethnic status. They may also contribute to the maintenance of a group's higher status if the concentrations occur on the higher occupational and self-employment levels. We will discuss this further in connection with the question of social mobility and social incorporation.

• Political Conjuncture and Governmental Policies

The final category of determinants that derives from the state of society is of a political nature. It refers to the historical-political events that involve an ethnic minority group in relation with the majority group. The significance of these events for ethnic stratification is the power and prestige relationship that they establish for an ethnic group along with its long-range consequences. The way this process works is that a certain conjuncture of historical events presents an intergroup relations problem that must be solved. The solution to the problem is usually given by the government in power, and it becomes a policy of relations between the majority and minority group. In time, the policy may be modified or a new policy may be instituted, but the original problem and the original solution remain as a basic reference point for intergroup relations.

As pointed out in the chapter on historical background, the conquest of the French in Canada established the group in a definite subordinate position to the British for a long period of time. The original policy solution allowing maintenance of the French language and culture, as exemplified in the Quebec Act of 1774, remains as a precedent for the relationship between the French and the English and for further policy development. Reservations for the Indians were an early solution to the confrontation between them and the colonizing people in 1637. The reservation became an enduring feature in the white and Native relationship, placing the latter in a definite subordinate position. Even as these treaties are now being questioned and changed, their influence on the status of the Indians is still pronounced.

Immigration policies likewise either open or close the gates to immigrants of specific ethnicities. For long periods of time, immigration policies included categories of preferred and non-preferred immigrants. Until the 1960s, Asian immigrants were not preferred immigrants. This buttressed racist attitudes towards them with negative consequences for the current prestige of the Asian ethnic groups.

Policies of internment of the Japanese in World War II lowered the prestige of this group. It was only as a result of their conscious efforts to change this ethnic status through education and achievement, and the prosperity of their mother country, that the status of the Japanese has risen to a relatively high level in the 1990s (Makabe, 1976).

Governmental policies can also function to change the ethnic status of a group. The policies of *employment equity* have been used to remove discrimination from the hiring process. *Human rights legislation* allowed the establishment of human rights commissions on the national and the provincial levels. These have served as means of dealing with individual cases of discrimination, not only in employment, but also in housing, customer relations and the like. The policy of *bilingualism* in Canada gave the French a certain recognition of equality with the British. It also gave them an opportunity to gain entry and more influence in the civil service of the federal government. The policy of *multiculturalism* has functioned to give more positive recognition to ethnic groups, other than the English and French, as being Canadian rather than "foreign" elements. Whether it has given them any political advantage is a debatable question. The policy of recognizing *Native claims* has changed the image of the Native peoples. They are no longer seen as disadvantaged and dependent, but as more independent, with their own dignity and positive cultural contributions. More will be said about government policies in the chapters on interethnic relations and societal integration.

ETHNIC STATUS DETERMINANTS DERIVING FROM THE ETHNIC MINORITY COMMUNITIES

Up to now we have discussed ethnic status determinants that derive from outside of the minority ethnic groups. The attributes of the minority ethnic groups themselves that have the most direct bearing on their ethnic status are the educational, occupational and income backgrounds of the immigrant populations of ethnic groups before their arrival in the country, the values and attitudes prevalent in the group and the organizational capacity of the group.

• The Immigrant Backgrounds

The place of the group in the ethnic stratification system is substantially influenced by the level of education of the immigrants before their arrival in the country, the kind of work the immigrants have engaged in before arrival and the financial resources they have been able to bring with them. In general, it can be said that the higher the educational and occupational level of the immigrants, and the more resources they are able to bring with them, the higher the status of the group of which they become a part will be. This presumes that, upon arrival in the host society or within a short period of time afterwards, the immigrants will be able to obtain jobs appropriate to their education, jobs that are the same or better than those they held in the old country, and that they will be able to use the resources brought over with them to establish themselves as well as or better than in the old country. As was discussed in the section on the problems of immigrant adjustment, this is not always the case.

We will use the data on education as an example. The educational level of the immigrants coming to Canada up to about the 1970s had been lower than that of the Canadian-born population. A Metropolitan Toronto survey conducted in 1970 (Richmond, 1974a: 16-19) showed that foreign-born persons had an average of 10.3 years of education, whereas the Canadian-born had 12 years. Among the foreign-born, 21 percent had some post-secondary education, as compared with 28 percent of the Canadian-born population. There were significant differences between the foreign-born groups. The highest levels of education were among the Asian and Black groups, the English and the Western Europeans. The lowest levels of education were among the immigrants from Italy, Greece and Portugal.

In the 1980s and 1990s, the educational backgrounds of immigrants coming to Canada changed substantially. In 1991, 14.4 percent of the immigrant population had a university degree, as compared with 10.5 percent of the Canadian-born population. However, the immigrant population also had a much higher percentage of persons with less than a Grade 9 education: 18.9 percent as compared with 12.7 of the Canadian-born population (CIC, 1996: 1-7). Immigrant women in particular were likely to have less than a Grade 9 education. The highest levels of education were among the Middle Eastern, South Asian and East Asian immigrants, and the lowest levels were among the Caribbean immigrants.

We do not know exactly how the higher educational levels of the immigrating population arriving since the end of the 1970s has influenced the ethnic status of the respective ethnic groups in Canada. In the 1990s there has been much evidence of more public recognition of the issues of the Asian minorities, as reflected in the greater emphasis placed on race by the Canadian government and in public life.

• Values and Attitudes

Values are general criteria of what is desirable and what is undesirable. In the social world, they refer to what general types of action are seen as desirable and what is seen as undesirable. One may value honesty, democracy, freedom, equality, community and so on. **Attitudes** are predispositions or tendencies towards a specific course of action, derived from one or another type of value or simply from the likes and dislikes established by tradition, popular custom or personal habit. One may have authoritarian or liberal tendencies, optimistic or pessimistic tendencies, industrious or inactive tendencies, biases and the like. When internalized into personalities, values and attitudes become motivating forces, which, in conjunction with other, situational, factors, determine behaviour and its consequences.

The type of values that are important in relation to ethnic stratification are those having to do with individual success, achievement, getting ahead in life, systematic work and efficiency and those values that centre on community life, family life, friendship and communication. All other things being equal, ethnic groups that internalize the primacy of individual achievement and success will have higher ethnic status than those whose members internalize the primacy of community life and expressiveness. It should be emphasized that the same person or group may internalize both sets of

Table 10: Educational Attainment of First-Generation Males and Females, Aged 25-65, of Selected Ethnic Groups in Canada, 1986

	Males		Females	
Ethnic Group	Mean Years of Education	Percent with University Degree +	Mean Years of Education	Percent with University Degree +
British	14.0	19.3	12.8	9.6
French	13.5	23.7	12.7	9.2
German	12.4	12.0	11.5	6.4
Italian	9.0	5.4	7.8	3.4
Ukrainian	11.1	14.8	10.1	11.4
Jewish	14.7	42.7	13.6	30.9
Portuguese	7.9	2.7	7.1	1.7
South Asian	14.2	33.7	12.2	20.8
Chinese	13.0	27.0	11.4	15.7
Black	13.3	17.5	12.1	7.4

Source: Boyd, Monica. 1992. "Gender, Visible Minority, and Immigrant Earnings Inequality: Reassessing an Employment Equity Premise." In *Deconstructing a Nation: Immigration, Multiculturalism and Racism in 90s Canada*. V. Satzewich, ed. Halifax and Saskatoon: Fernwood Publishing and Department of Sociology, University of Saskatchewan, pp.279-321.

values, but it is the primacy of one set over the other that makes the difference.

To what extent do the various ethnic groups in Canada both have and teach their children these different sets of values and attitudes? To what extent are there significant differences in this regard among different ethnic groups? There are no extensive data on the subject, but the available findings indicate that there are differences in achievement-success values among ethnic groups. However, there are also differences in these values within the ethnic groups themselves. A study in the United States in the 1950s (Rosen, 1959), which later became controversial and gave impetus to other studies, including Canadian, examined the differences in values and attitudes of six ethnic and racial groups in order to explain their dissimilar social mobility rates. The study showed that these groups differed in their orientation towards achievement. Achievement motivation and aspirations were more a characteristic of Greeks, Jews and white Protestants than of Italians, French-Canadians and Blacks. At the same time, Greeks, Jews and white Protestants showed a higher rate of social mobility than did the Italians, French-Canadians and Blacks.

A study (Breton and Roseborough, 1968) tested the hypothesis that French-Canadian businessmen's attitudes towards business were subordinated to familistic and kinship priorities. The investigators used a sample of over one thousand French and English employees in a large, national business organization. The results showed that there were few differences in value orientations between the French and the English employees. The French were just as willing as the English to work long hours for success, and both valued education. As a means of promotion, the French were even more willing than the English to accept jobs that required heavy overtime and constant availability for duty. Yet the French, especially the blue-collar employees, were less willing than the English to move to another province in order to increase their chances for promotion.

K. Danziger (1975), in his study of a sample of 1,173 Grade 8 children in the Italian section of Metropolitan Toronto, noted differences in educational and occupational aspirations between Canadian-born and immigrant children. In answer to two questions, "How far would you like to go in school?" and "What kind of work would you most like to do when you grow up?", the Canadian-born boys showed higher aspirations than did the immigrant boys. There were also marked differences between the Italian boys who were classified as "highly acculturated" and those classified as "little acculturated." Thus, only 7 percent of the Canadian-born, non-Italian boys indicated that they would like to finish only Grade 12 or less, as compared with 16 percent of the "highly acculturated" and 28 percent of the "little acculturated" Italian boys. Similarly, 78 percent of the non-immigrant boys stated that they would like to go to university, as compared with 54 percent of the "highly acculturated" and 49 percent of the "little acculturated" Italian boys. A similar pattern was shown in the case of occupational aspirations.

Maykovich (1975: 158-179) compared orientations towards success of three samples of about 480 persons of Japanese, Mennonite and Italian ethnicities in Toronto. Unlike the other studies, she concluded that all groups value success in one way or another, but that the definitions of success vary. For the traditional and the transitional Mennonites, success means something quite different from what it usually means for white, middle-class Canadians. Material success through educational and occupational achievement is considered not only irrelevant, but harmful to religious life. Success for the Mennonites is the kind of life that would please God. A successful life consists of the ownership of land, high productivity and transfer of land to children, but not the amount of money one makes by selling agricultural products. Conspicuous consumption for the traditional and transitional Mennonites, Maykovich states, is not an index of high social status, but an index of sinful living. Children are encouraged to go to grade school, but are discouraged from going further because higher education often teaches anti-religious doctrine and destroys the child's commitment to the land.

Progressive Mennonites, however, subscribe to the values of educational and occupational achievement as do the Italians and Japanese. Nevertheless, Japanese tend to see the successful life as one that gives their family a good reputation, and Italians understand it as one that provides much personal security. In fact, according to Maykovich, very small percentages of all three ethnic groups studied gave self-improvement or personal achievement as a reason for material success. Security, family reputation and religious considerations are for them the most important components of the success value.

A study of the Afro-Caribbean community in Toronto by Frances Henry (1994: 126) found that Caribbean parents place an inordinately high value on education. It is seen to be both important in its own right and the only avenue of social mobility for people from the lower social classes. According to the study, even poor single mothers will do their utmost to ensure that their children receive as much schooling as possible. Giving reference to other studies of the Afro-Caribbeans (Solomon, 1992), Henry (1994: 145) points out that Black Caribbean students have a belief in "making it" and a commitment to the achievement value. However, these students are able to "'work the system' to achieve their goal of educational success while creating their own culture and resisting incorporation into a white cultural identity" (Henry, 1994: 145).

A similar emphasis on both individual achievement and community commitment can be observed among the Canadian Aboriginal peoples. The report of the Royal Commission on Aboriginal Peoples (1996: 2: 797) has pointed out that persons in the Aboriginal communities have an appreciation for the need of Aboriginal people to make their way as individuals in the broader Canadian society, but this need must be balanced with the development of the community and should be compatible with and strengthen Aboriginal culture and identity rather than undermine it. According to the report, young people in the Aboriginal community place emphasis on personal health, skills and hard work, but they also want to be recognized and given a voice in the development of their community and culture. According to the report:

> Many Aboriginal youth see themselves facing an economic wasteland. They see high unemployment rates, inadequate training and a lack of meaningful jobs. Their unemployment rate is 31.8 per cent, more than double that of non-Aboriginal youth (15.1 per cent). Added to this is pressure to choose between the traditional way of life and the modern world, the implication being that there is no way to accommodate the two worlds. Many youth are beginning to reject this argument. They want employment, but they seek employment that contributes to the community, not just to the gross national product (Royal Commission on Aboriginal Peoples, 1996: 4:184).

Differences in values and attitudes thus do have a bearing on the ethnic status of groups. It is not so much that these differences prevent some groups from achieving a higher status than others, but that the status system itself has to be understood not only in an objective, statistically expressed way, but it must be understood relative to the culturally different definitions of the meaning of success and social status.

• Group Organizational Capacity

The last type of ethnic status determinants considered here is the **organizational capacity** of ethnic groups. The organizational capacity of an ethnic group refers to the ability and possibility of a group to establish and effectively use such organizations that would

Table 11: Occupational Participation of First-Generation Males and Females, Aged 25-65, of Selected Ethnic Groups in Canada, 1986 (Percentages)

	Males			Females		
Ethnic Group	White Collar Occupations*	Service Occupations	Product Fabrications**	White Collar Occupations	Service Occupations	Product Fabrications
British	42.7	7.2	15.6	32.1	11.7	3.2
French	41.7	8.5	15.6	41.2	15.7	5.9
German	28.9	5.3	20.4	26.3	17.3	5.5
Italian	15.2	9.7	20.8	11.2	20.0	28.2
Ukrainian	19.0	14.1	20.4	28.5	21.5	7.0
Jewish	56.4	2.8	8.3	46.7	4.0	4.0
Portuguese	7.7	12.4	21.6	7.5	28.4	24.9
South Asian	36.4	7.3	18.4	25.6	13.2	12.0
Chinese	34.3	24.8	12.8	21.8	19.6	17.4
Black	33.1	13.1	24.5	32.4	18.0	13.9

* Includes managerial and administrative occupations and occupations in natural sciences, engineering, mathematics, social sciences, teaching, medicine and health, and artistic, literary, recreational and related occupations.
** Refers to machining and product fabricating, repairing and assembling occupations.

Source: Boyd, Monica. 1992. "Gender, Visible Minority, and Immigrant Earnings Inequality: Reassessing an Employment Equity Premise." In *Deconstructing a Nation: Immigration, Multiculturalism and Racism in 90s Canada*. V. Satzewich, ed. Halifax and Saskatoon: Fernwood Publishing and Department of Sociology, University of Saskatchewan, pp.279-321.

have an impact on society at large in moving the group's ethnic status upwards or maintaining an already established high status.

Organizational capacity for changing or maintaining ethnic status includes the ability of an ethnic group to establish and effectively use instrumental organizations in exerting pressure on society and its public opinion. Ethnic groups may establish effective expressive organizations, i.e., those concerned with cultural and identity maintenance, but few instrumental organizations, i.e., those concerned with the group's adaptation to the broader society, usually organizations of economic or of broader political character. The latter can have a direct effect on the group's status in relation to other groups, especially in terms of influencing public opinion as to the importance of the group's issues. This will be discussed in detail in the section dealing with interethnic relations as a negotiating process.

ETHNIC COMMUNITY INTERNAL STRATIFICATION

Ethnic stratification is complicated by status stratification within ethnic communities themselves. Such **internal community stratification** follows a number of lines: class, religion, regional, immigrant versus local-born and gender.

• Internal Class and Status Systems

Even though a group, as a group, may hold one ethnic status relative to other ethnic groups, currently no ethnic group is made up of individuals and families who are all of the same social class. As Tables 12 and 13 indicate, some ethnic groups include a relatively small percentage of persons with higher education and large percentages of persons with only elementary school education. Some have the opposite. Similarly, in terms of occupation and income, some ethnic groups have a relatively large middle-class and a small labouring class, whereas others have the opposite, with a large labouring class and a smaller middle class. Class differences create inequalities among people of the same ethnic group in addition to the inequalities among the ethnic groups themselves. Yet the fact that class lines cut across different ethnic boundaries reduces the actual and potential tensions in the larger society that would result from ethnic group differences. By the same token, the fact that ethnic differences cut across class stratification in the larger society reduces the actual and potential tensions that result from class inequalities.

The status differences within ethnic groups are not necessarily based on the same criteria as those in the larger society. As was explained above, ethnic groups define success in terms of their own different values.

For some, family name may be more important than individual economic achievement, and the status differences within the group may have more to do with coming from a family that has enjoyed a high respect in the group than from achievement in the larger society outside of the group. Likewise, in many ethnic minority groups, individual prestige is derived from holding important positions in respected ethnic organizations or from coming from regions in the home country that enjoyed higher prestige than other regions.

Community studies and historical studies of structures within various ethnic groups provide a good picture of the ethnic internal differentiation and stratification. Robert F. Harney (1991b) described the different layers of the Italian community in Toronto, including a variety of competing elites and non-elites. In his social history of Indo-Canadians in Ontario, Milton Israel (1994) described the different sectors of the community, related to each other in some indefinite vertical and horizontal manner. Thus, the community includes Bengalis, Goans, Indo-Caribbeans, Wahindi and Gujaratis. It is further criss-crossed by religious identities and organizations, such as Hinduism, the Sikhs, the Jains, Islam, Parsees, Buddhists, Kerala Christians, Bene Israel, Cochin and Baghdadi Jews. Each one of these groups has its own elites and its own community activities and functions. Yet the community had a sense of being a community of communities with a number of joint institutions. Studies of other ethnic communities give similar pictures of internal diversity (Anderson, 1974; Radecki and Heydenkorn, 1976; Reid, 1976; Con, et al., 1982; Lupul, 1982; Iacovetta, 1992).

An ethnic minority group's own system of statuses often functions as an alternative to the status system of the mainstream society. That is, persons who for whatever reason are not moving up in the class system of the mainstream society may move up in the status system within their own group. Some may not be able to move up in the mainstream society, because of discrimination, lack of opportunities, insufficient knowledge of the language, inappropriate skills or lack of education and so on. Others, particularly some among the immigrant generation, may not be interested in moving up in the mainstream society because their frame of orientation is their own group or their society of origin. Whatever the reason, the ethnic minority group can offer, at least to some extent, prestige and respect within a familiar group. In general, I propose that the lower the ethnic status of a group in the societal ethnic stratification system, the greater the reliance of the members of the group on the group's own status system, and inversely, the higher the ethnic status of the group, the greater the reliance of the members of the group on the mainstream status system. That is, in the latter case, in the groups with higher ethnic status, the societal status system carries over and becomes part of the minority group's status system. The members of the minority group that enjoys a higher ethnic status tend to evaluate each other more in terms of the status criteria of the mainstream class system. Empirical studies of this phenomenon are lacking and comparative research is needed to assess its implications.

• Gender Inequality Systems

A striking system of internal stratification, typical of most ethnic groups, is the inequality between men and women. As is the case in all stratification, there are many aspects of this inequality: those that can be assessed by the objective measures of employment, type of occupation, education and income, and those that have to be assessed indirectly, such as power differential, prestige and cultural expectations.

Table 10 shows the differences in educational attainment, and Table 11, the differences in occupational participation between first-generation (i.e., foreign-born) men and women of 10 selected ethnic groups in Canada. Table 10 shows that, in all 10 ethnic groups indicated, women had less education than men. The average mean number of years of education for men in the 10 groups was 12.3, whereas that for women was 11.1, more than one year less than men. There were of course variations between the 10 ethnic groups, with the lowest mean number of years of education for women being 7.1 and the highest, 13.6. In general, however, the lower the mean was for men, the lower it also was for women.

The big difference between the first-generation men and women in regard to education is in the percentage of persons with a university degree or higher. On the average among the 10 groups, 20.0 percent of men possessed a university degree or higher, whereas only 11.6 percent of women did so. The greatest discrepancy between men and women in this respect was among the French (14.5 percentage points), followed by South Asians (12.9), Jewish (11.8), Chinese (11.3), Blacks (10.1), British (9.7), German (5.6), Ukrainian (3.4), Italian (2.0) and Portuguese (1.0). One factor that may explain these differences may be the higher value placed on the education of males rather than females, derived from cultural preconceptions or from familial situations in which choices have to be made between a son

Table 12: Occupational Distribution of Selected Ethnic Groups' Labor Force, 15 Years of Age and Over, Including Combined Single and Multiple Ethnic Origin, in Percentages and Showing Percentages of Over- and Under-Representation, Canada, 1991

Ethnic Group(s)	Managerial & Administrative	Professional	Clerical	Sales	Service	Product Fabrication & Processing	Construction Trades	Transportation	Primary	Other	Frequency Estimate for Total Ethnic Group Population, 15 and Over	Total %
British	12.2 (0.0)	18.0 (+0.6)	18.6 (+0.5)	9.8 (+0.6)	13.1 (+0.3)	8.8 (-2.3)	5.4 (-0.5)	3.7 (+0.1)	5.3 (+0.5)	5.2 (+0.4)	9,245,300	100
French	11.4 (-0.8)	17.6 (+0.2)	18.5 (+0.4)	8.9 (-0.3)	13.8 (+1.0)	11.9 (+0.8)	6.0 (+0.1)	3.6 (0.0)	3.9 (-0.9)	4.5 (-0.3)	6,436,300	100
Dutch	11.5 (-0.7)	17.5 (+0.1)	16.9 (-1.2)	9.4 (+0.2)	12.6 (-0.2)	8.8 (-2.3)	6.6 (+0.7)	3.6 (0.0)	8.3 (+3.5)	4.9 (+0.1)	622,000	100
German	11.3 (-0.9)	17.5 (+0.1)	17.8 (-0.3)	9.3 (+0.1)	13.1 (+0.3)	9.0 (-2.1)	5.9 (0.0)	3.5 (-0.1)	7.7 (+2.9)	4.9 (+0.1)	2,016,300	100
Hungarian	10.8 (-1.4)	18.3 (+0.9)	17.4 (-0.7)	9.5 (+0.3)	13.0 (+0.2)	11.0 (-0.1)	6.3 (+0.4)	2.8 (-0.8)	5.5 (+0.7)	5.3 (+0.5)	160,800	100
Polish	11.0 (-1.2)	18.8 (+1.4)	18.2 (+0.1)	9.7 (+0.5)	12.8 (0.0)	10.6 (-0.5)	5.6 (-0.3)	3.1 (-0.5)	7.0 (+2.2)	5.4 (+0.6)	525,700	100
Ukrainian	10.8 (-1.4)	17.6 (+0.2)	19.5 (+1.4)	10.5 (+1.3)	12.9 (+0.1)	8.1 (-3.0)	5.4 (-0.5)	3.6 (0.0)	5.8 (+1.0)	4.8 (0.0)	761,200	100
Greek	12.8 (+0.6)	9.9 (-7.5)	15.9 (-2.2)	9.9 (+0.7)	26.1 (+13.3)	13.8 (+2.7)	4.9 (-1.0)	2.3 (-1.3)	1.1 (-3.7)	3.3 (-1.5)	153,100	100
Italian	12.1 (-0.1)	13.7 (-3.7)	19.6 (+1.5)	10.8 (+1.6)	12.5 (-0.3)	13.2 (+2.1)	8.2 (+2.3)	2.5 (-1.1)	1.8 (-3.0)	5.4 (+0.6)	856,800	100
Portuguese	7.6 (-4.6)	7.9 (-9.5)	15.7 (-2.4)	6.4 (-2.8)	17.7 (+4.9)	18.2 (+7.1)	13.1 (+7.2)	2.3 (-1.3)	3.1 (-1.7)	8.2 (+3.4)	213,100	100
Spanish	8.9 (-3.3)	15.6 (-1.8)	17.9 (-0.2)	8.2 (-1.0)	19.1 (+6.3)	15.2 (+4.1)	5.2 (-0.7)	2.0 (-1.6)	2.3 (-2.5)	5.5 (+0.7)	107,800	100
Jewish	20.3 (+8.6)	30.2 (+12.8)	17.0 (-1.1)	15.1 (+5.9)	7.2 (-5.6)	3.5 (-7.6)	1.9 (-4.0)	1.4 (-2.2)	0.9 (-3.9)	2.5 (-2.3)	273,200	100
Canadian	12.6 (+0.4)	15.8 (-1.6)	19.8 (+1.7)	10.0 (+0.8)	12.2 (-0.6)	9.3 (-1.8)	5.7 (-0.2)	4.5 (+0.9)	3.9 (-0.9)	6.1 (+1.3)	757,200	100
Chinese	13.0 (+0.8)	18.9 (+1.5)	19.3 (+1.2)	9.8 (+0.6)	18.3 (+5.5)	12.4 (+1.3)	1.5 (-4.4)	1.3 (-2.3)	1.1 (-3.7)	4.4 (-0.4)	492,300	100
Philippine	6.1 (-6.1)	21.2 (+3.8)	19.4 (+1.3)	5.7 (-3.5)	27.4 (+14.6)	12.6 (+1.5)	1.2 (-4.7)	0.8 (-2.8)	0.6 (-4.2)	4.9 (+0.1)	131,700	100
Vietnamese	5.7 (-6.5)	13.8 (-3.6)	11.0 (-7.1)	6.2 (-3.0)	16.7 (+3.9)	32.4 (+21.3)	3.2 (-2.7)	1.0 (-2.6)	2.4 (-2.4)	7.7 (+2.9)	67,900	100
Black and Caribbean	8.1 (-4.1)	19.0 (+1.6)	21.8 (+3.7)	7.5 (-1.7)	15.7 (+2.9)	13.8 (+2.7)	3.6 (-2.3)	3.1 (-0.5)	0.9 (-3.9)	6.5 (+1.7)	340,600	100
Balkan	10.5 (-1.7)	15.1 (-2.3)	16.5 (-1.6)	8.9 (-0.3)	13.8 (+1.0)	15.7 (+4.6)	7.5 (+1.6)	2.6 (-1.0)	2.6 (-2.2)	6.8 (+2.0)	152,100	100
Arab	14.9 (+2.7)	19.1 (+1.7)	15.4 (-2.7)	12.8 (+3.6)	16.8 (+4.0)	10.4 (-0.7)	3.5 (-2.4)	2.6 (-1.0)	0.8 (-4.0)	3.7 (-1.1)	133,300	100
West Asian	12.1 (-0.1)	17.5 (+0.1)	17.2 (-0.9)	11.7 (+2.5)	13.7 (+0.9)	14.3 (+3.2)	4.5 (-1.4)	4.5 (+0.9)	0.9 (-3.9)	3.4 (-1.4)	70,100	100
South Asian	10.6 (-1.6)	14.8 (-2.6)	20.2 (+2.1)	9.3 (+0.1)	13.2 (+0.4)	16.0 (+4.9)	2.4 (-3.5)	2.9 (-0.7)	3.4 (-1.4)	7.1 (+2.3)	355,400	100
Central, South American	6.5 (-5.7)	15.0 (-2.4)	14.1 (-4.0)	7.0 (-2.2)	22.1 (+9.3)	16.0 (+4.9)	5.8 (-0.1)	2.1 (-1.5)	3.2 (-1.6)	8.2 (+3.4)	79,200	100
Aboriginal	8.5 (-3.7)	14.9 (-2.5)	16.9 (-1.2)	6.6 (-2.6)	18.7 (+5.9)	9.0 (-2.1)	8.4 (+2.5)	4.1 (+0.5)	6.6 (+1.8)	6.4 (+1.6)	638,800	100
National	**12.2**	**17.4**	**18.1**	**9.2**	**12.8**	**11.1**	**5.9**	**3.6**	**4.8**	**4.8**		**100**

Note: *Professional occupations* include occupations in natural sciences, engineering, mathematics, social sciences and related, teaching, medicine and health, artistic, literary, recreational and related occupations. *Service occupations* include protective services, food preparation, lodging accommodations, apparel and furnishing and related services. *Product fabrication and processing* includes metal, glass, stone, chemicals, petroleum, rubber, plastic, wood, textile, food, beverage and related processing and metal machining, shaping and forming, wood machining, clay, glass, stone and related machining. *Transportation* includes railway, air, motor transport and operating. *Primary occupations* include farming, horticultural and animal husbandry, fishing, trapping and related, forestry and logging and mining and quarrying.
Source: 1991 Canadian Census, special tabulations. Also: Statistics Canada. 1993. *Census 91 - Occupation: The Nation*, Catalogue No. 93-327, Table 1. Ottawa: Minister of Industry, Science and Technology.

Table 13: Highest Level of Schooling of Population, 15 years of Age and Over, of Selected Ethnic Groups, Including Combined Single and Multiple Origin, in Percentages, Canada 1991

Ethnic Group(s)	University Certificate and Degree Above Bachelor	University, Bachelor or University or Non-University 1st Professional Degree	University Without Certificate, Diploma or Degree	Post-Secondary, Non-University and Trades With Certificate or Diploma	Post-Secondary, Non-University Without Certificate	Secondary With Graduation Certificate	Secondary Without Graduation Certificate	Elementary (Less than Grade 9)	Frequency Estimate for Total Ethnic Group Population, 15 and Over	Total %
British	3.6	13.3	5.3	20.5	6.6	15.0	27.2	8.5	9,245,300	100
French	2.8	12.1	2.6	20.1	6.6	16.5	22.0	17.5	6,436,300	100
Dutch	3.3	12.2	5.5	23.5	7.6	14.6	24.5	8.8	622,000	100
German	3.7	13.2	5.5	22.5	6.8	13.5	24.8	10.0	2,016,300	100
Hungarian	4.5	14.3	5.4	24.1	7.2	13.3	20.2	11.2	160,800	100
Polish	5.2	14.7	5.9	20.5	6.4	14.5	22.6	10.3	525,700	100
Ukrainian	2.9	13.5	5.8	19.6	6.5	13.7	25.8	12.1	761,200	100
Greek	2.7	10.1	5.7	13.5	6.9	13.4	20.7	26.9	153,100	100
Italian	2.9	11.4	4.7	17.0	6.4	13.9	18.9	24.9	856,800	100
Portuguese	1.4	5.1	3.0	11.1	5.6	13.1	24.7	36.2	213,100	100
Spanish	4.5	15.9	6.6	17.7	7.1	14.8	23.3	10.3	107,800	100
Jewish	12.6	26.0	8.6	11.6	5.4	12.0	17.2	6.7	273,200	100
Canadian	2.7	11.9	5.6	20.6	7.3	16.2	29.1	6.9	757,200	100
Chinese	5.3	20.6	7.6	12.8	6.0	12.6	19.7	15.4	492,300	100
Philippine	4.0	36.5	11.6	12.2	4.7	10.6	13.3	7.1	131,700	100
Vietnamese	2.8	13.8	5.6	9.1	6.3	13.6	28.4	20.4	67,900	100
Black, Caribbean	2.9	12.6	5.0	21.5	9.8	14.1	25.8	8.2	340,600	100
Balkan	3.7	13.7	5.8	22.5	5.7	12.9	18.8	16.9	152,100	100
Arab	8.4	22.8	7.2	12.8	5.6	15.0	17.0	11.3	133,300	100
West Asian	9.2	21.5	7.0	12.5	6.2	17.3	14.4	11.9	70,100	100
South Asian	6.8	19.2	6.3	14.2	6.5	14.4	20.5	12.1	355,400	100
Central and South American	5.3	15.7	7.5	16.8	7.5	15.0	20.1	11.9	79,200	100
Aboriginal	1.3	7.6	4.1	18.1	8.1	10.7	31.7	18.3	638,800	100
National	**3.9**	**12.5**	**4.4**	**19.7**	**6.5**	**14.8**	**24.3**	**13.9**		**100**

Source: 1991 Canadian Census special tabulations. Also: Statistics Canada. 1993. Census 91: *Educational Attainment and School Attendance–The Nation*, Catalogue No. 93-328, Tables 4 &7; 93-332, Table 1. Ottawa: Minister of Industry, Science and Technology.

Table 14: Average Total Income of Selected Ethnic Groups Indicating Ethnic Stratification, Canada, 1990

Ethnic Group(s)	Average Total Income* Canadian $
Jewish	32,826
Canadian	23,607
British	22,854
Hungarian	22,637
Balkan	22,224
Polish	22,220
Ukrainian	22,082
Italian	21,996
German	21,986
National Average	**21,668**
Dutch	21,624
French	20,157
Portuguese	18,949
South Asian	18,631
Chinese	18,463
Greek	18,370
Arab	18,014
Black and Caribbean	17,613
Spanish	17,374
Philippine	17,226
West Asian	16,576
Aboriginal	15,199
Vietnamese	14,239
Central and South American	13,717

* *Total income* refers to the total money income received by individuals 15 years of age and over during the calendar year 1990 from the following sources: wages and salaries, net non-farm self-employment income, net farm self-employment income, family allowances, federal child tax credits, old age security pension and guaranteed income supplement, benefits from Canada or Quebec pension plan, benefits from unemployment insurance, other income from government sources, dividends and interests on bonds, deposit and savings certificates and other investment income, retirement pensions superannuation and annuities and other.

Source: 1991 Canadian Census special tabulations.

or a daughter when family resources for educational support are limited. Other factors may be that childraising is delegated to women in most cultures and that women may marry at an earlier age than men.

The differences between the occupational participation of first-generation men and women among ethnic groups is also significant. Table 11 shows that, while more men than women work in white-collar occupations, significantly more women than men work in service occupations. On the average among the 10 groups reported in the table, 31.5 percent of males and 27.3 percent of females work in white-collar occupations. But, on the average, only 10.5 percent of males as compared with 17.0 percent of females are employed in service occupations. This includes such occupations as various kinds of restaurant work, domestic work, laundry, custodial work and others.

The highest percentages of the first-generation women doing service work are among the Portuguese (28.4), followed by Ukrainians (21.5), Italians (20.0), Chinese (19.6), Blacks (18.0), German (17.3) and French (15.7). The lowest percentages are among the Jewish (4.0), British (11.7) and South Asians (13.2).

As in the case of education, the higher participation of the first-generation women in comparison to men in the service occupations can be, to an extent, explained by the greater availability of this work to women. This is because of the supporting role to men that the mainstream society and many other cultures appropriate to women. Other factors, however, are the greater availability of service work because of lower wages and fewer required qualifications, and the fact that many immigrant women work for relatively low pay in family-owned restaurants and similar enterprises as a way of reducing the business' expenses.

Statistics have consistently shown that, in Canada, the income of women is considerably lower than that of men. This is also typical of ethnic groups. In 1985, the mean annual income of foreign-born males categorized racially as from a "visible minority" was $24,079, whereas that of foreign-born "visible minority" females was $15,088. Similarly in that year, the mean annual income of foreign-born "not visible minority" males was $29,441, whereas that of foreign-born "not visible minority" females was $15,176. Similar discrepancies were observed among the Canadian-born "visible" and "not visible" minority males and females (Boyd, 1992: 290-294). Thus, gender stratification is inherent in the ethnic minority communities just as it is inherent in the mainstream community.

• Articulation of Ethnicity and Gender

Gender stratification derives in large measure from the historically conditioned patriarchal structure of many societies (Stasiulis and Yuval-Davis, 1995). What is sociologically significant is how, in modern times, ethnic groups articulate gender stratification with ethnicity in a subjectively meaningful way. Women who come from cultures and family structures with sharply defined gender status differences change, or manage, the patriarchy in a number of ways. The most common, basic way is for women to obtain a job independent of the marriage and the family. This has a double consequence. On the one hand, the woman supplements her husband's income and thus contributes to family security. On the other hand, by doing this she removes herself from a complete dependence on her husband. A South Asian woman who visited a women's counselling centre in Toronto indicated to her counsellor the importance of having a job for a woman-immigrant in a patriarchal family. According to her, for South Asian women (Agnew, 1990: 69-70), immigration removes the protection of the cultural norms of their home communities, leaving them more vulnerable to male oppression within the family. Other immigrant women might be more willing to go

> to an outside agency for help to which our women are not used. Our women are used to other women helping them within the extended family or within the community. If the husband beats them up there is always the mother-in-law or sister-in-law or someone whom the husband respects that might come and give him a talk. So the husbands have this built-in inhibition, or they might get a bad name or the family gets a bad name. So there are all these circumstances by which women are protected. This is totally taken away in a society such as this where everyone is on his own, where even husbands and wives are at war with each other. Practically, a woman who doesn't work is totally at the mercy of her husband and the society.

A job outside the family often provides a woman with new self-confidence and empowerment and may raise her status in relation to her husband. It also provides an opportunity to establish new friendships and networks of relationships. However, it also presents new pressures and the stress of living in two worlds, whereby women may cherish their new empowerment, yet still wish to maintain their original identity and culture.

Working for, or actively participating in, ethnic organizations and contributing to the development of ethnic community programs is also a way by which the status difference vis-à-vis men comes to be outweighed. This is a pattern particularly observed among middle-class women (Gabbacia, 1994; Tastsoglou, 1997: 234). Tastsoglou (1997) presents case histories of women who constructed their identity outside of the familial roles, within the context of their commitment and work in creating and developing programs for their ethnic community. Thus the enhancement of the status of the female role is not necessarily only a consequence of stepping outside the ethnic minority community, but also a consequence of active organizational participation within the community itself.

In her study of Italian women, Franca Iacovetta (1992) pointed out that the conception of patriarchy as simply a superordinate-subordinate relationship in which men make all final decisions and women follow them is an oversimplification. According to her, in many working-class families, Italian housewives acted as the family financial manager, making decisions and allocating money for various family needs. Men often brought the money home and gave it over to their wives (Iacovetta, 1992: 90-91). Although the idea of the primacy of men may be the prevailing ideology, in practice the decision-making roles were often informally divided between men and women in various ways.

Similarly, in her study of the Caribbean diaspora, Frances Henry (1994: 60-61) indicated that, although

Afro-Caribbean women have been socialized to accept the patriarchal ideology, in reality they have considerable power in family matters. This is derived from the women's own income-generating activities and from their main role in relation to their children. Historically, this more independent role of women has its roots in slavery and colonialism. The frequent removal of men from their families undermined their ability to be the main wage-earners in the family. This role had to be assumed by women. As a consequence, mothering and nurturing became of high value to the Afro-Caribbean women and children have become a source of women's identity and fulfilment, outweighing feelings of inequality with men. Census data from 1986 indicated that Afro-Caribbean children were more likely than white children to live in single-parent households whose income was under $20,000. Afro-Caribbean women were more often separated, divorced or never married than were white women. The Afro-Caribbean population in Canada showed an imbalanced sex ratio due to the Canadian immigration policy that has encouraged the immigration of female domestic workers (Christensen and Weinfeld, 1993).

MEASUREMENT OF ETHNIC STRATIFICATION

The study of the determinants of ethnic stratification indicates that there are two aspects involved, an objective aspect and a subjective aspect. The *objective aspect* refers to what can be directly observed and measured, things that are relatively easily quantifiable, as, for example, the distribution of persons in various occupations and income and so on. The *subjective aspect* refers to what can be observed and measured only indirectly, things that are difficult to quantify. These are attitudes, prejudices, images, feelings of closeness or remoteness and the like that make up the prestige of a group. To obtain a complete picture of ethnic stratification, both aspects have to be measured. What follows is a discussion of the basic measures of the objective and the subjective aspects of ethnic stratification.

• Measurement of the Objective Aspects of Ethnic Stratification

The simplest method of measuring occupational, educational, income or other differences between various groups is by means of the measure of **over- and under-representation**. The measure compares the percentage of members of an ethnic group in a specific occupational, educational, income or other category with the percentage of all persons of the total population in that category. If the percentages are the same, then the ethnic group in question can be said to be equally represented in that category. If the percentage for the group is lower than that for the total population, then the ethnic group is said to be under-represented in that category. If the percentage is higher than that for the total population, then the ethnic group can be said to be over-represented in that category.

For example, in 1991, 14.9 percent of the labour force of the Aboriginal peoples in Canada was engaged in professional occupations (Table 12), but 17.4 percent of the national, i.e., total Canadian, labour force was engaged in these occupations. Hence, the Aboriginal groups can be said to have been under-represented in the professional occupations by 2.5 percent (17.4 – 14.9). Of the British Canadian labour force, however, 18.0 percent were engaged in professional occupations in the same year. The British groups can thus be said to be over-represented in the professional occupations by 0.6 percent (18.0 – 17.4).

To evaluate what these percentages of over- and under-representation may mean in reality, one can figure out the number of individuals in a group to be added or taken away in order to have equal representation. Thus, the 2.5 percent of the Aboriginal labour force means 2.5 percent of 638,800 individuals (Table 12, column 12) or 15,970 individuals. In practical terms, this may mean that this number of individuals would have to be trained in professions and/or given the appropriate jobs if one were to have equal representation in the professional occupations and have no ethnic stratification on this account. This, of course, is a considerable task.

According to this logic, a more sophisticated variation of this measure is the **index of dissimilarity**. This index indicates the percentage of the ethnic group that would have to be redistributed in order to attain the same percentage distribution that exists for all persons in the population. The score is a measure of deviation from a hypothetical condition of equal representation in the categories studied. It thus refers to the differences between observed and expected numbers of persons in the respective categories as a proportion of the differences that would obtain if there were complete equality.

Here, for simplicity's sake, we will use only the measure of over- and under-representation to assess the basic character of ethnic stratification in Canada. Tables 12, 13, and 14 present the 1991 Census of Canada data

Table 15: University and Professional Education Attained by Selected Ethnic Groups, 15 Years of Age and Over, Indicating Ethnic Stratification, Canada 1991

Ethnic Group(s)	University and Professional Education Attained* Percentages of Group in Labour Force
Philippine	52.1
Jewish	47.2
Arab	38.4
West Asian	37.7
Chinese	33.5
South Asian	32.3
Central and South American	28.5
Spanish	27.0
Polish	25.8
Hungarian	24.2
Balkan	23.2
German	22.4
British, Ukrainian, Vietnamese	22.2
Dutch	21.0
National Average	**20.8**
Black and Caribbean	20.5
Canadian	20.2
Italian	19.0
Greek	18.5
French	17.5
Aboriginal	13.0
Portuguese	9.5

* Includes persons with university certificate and degree above bachelor, persons with bachelor degree, university or non-university first professional degree and persons with university education but without certificate, diploma or degree.

Source: 1991 Canadian Census special tabulations.

on the occupational, educational and income distribution among 23 ethnic groups and categories of groups in the census. Table 12, occupational distribution of ethnic groups, includes in parenthesis after each figure the over- and under-representation percentages for the occupations. To illustrate more clearly the stratified character of the distribution of these socio-economic characteristics, Tables 14, 15, 16 and 17 arrange the data in a hierarchical order, indicating the groups that are above and below the national average.

Table 15 shows the percentages of persons in the 23 groups and categories who have attained university and professional education. The national average of this attainment is 20.8 percent. There are many groups that are well above this average. As many as 52.1 percent of the Philippine population aged 15 years and over have reached this attainment. Comparatively high percentages are also true of the Jewish, Arab, West Asian, Chinese and South Asian groups. In fact, as compared with the other socio-economic characteristics presented in the other tables, more groups show above-average university and professional attainment than is the case with regard to either occupation or income. This indicates that many ethnic minority groups place a high value on university and professional education. But it also indicates that, by itself, higher education does not always translate into better jobs or higher income. It should also be remembered that there is a stratification ladder among the professions themselves for which persons are trained. The category of university and professional education includes such occupations as medicine and law, but also such less prestigious occupations as nursing and school teaching. The five groups with the lowest university and professional

Table 16: Participation in Managerial and Administrative Occupations of Selected Ethnic Groups' Labour Force, 15 Years of Age and Over, Indicating Ethnic Stratification, Canada 1991

Ethnic Group	Percent of Group's Labor Force in Managerial Occupations
Jewish	20.3
Arab	14.9
Chinese	13.0
Greek	12.8
Canadian	12.6
British, National Average	**12.2**
Italian, West Asian	12.1
Dutch	11.5
French	11.4
German	11.3
Polish	11.0
Hungarian, Ukrainian	10.8
South Asian	10.6
Balkan	10.5
Spanish	8.9
Aboriginal	8.5
Black and Caribbean	8.1
Portuguese	7.6
Central and South American	6.5
Philippine	6.1
Vietnamese	5.7

Source: 1991 Canadian census, special tabulations. Also: Statistics Canada. 1993. *Census 91–Occupations: The Nation.* Catalogue No. 93-327, Table 1. Ottawa: Minister of Industry, Science and Technology.

educational attainment are the Italian, Greek, French, Aboriginal and Portuguese.

In Table 16, we observe that, out of the 23 groups and categories of groups, only four groups and one category of groups (Arab) have percentages of persons in the managerial and administrative occupations that are above the national average. These are the Jewish, Arab, Chinese, Greek and Canadian groups. The British representation in these occupations is the same as the national average. All the other groups are in varying degrees below the national average in these occupations, with the lowest five being Black and Caribbean, Portuguese, Central and South American, Philippine and Vietnamese.

Table 17 shows the stratified participation in professional occupations. The five groups with the highest percentages above the national average are Jewish, Philippine, Arab, Black and Caribbean and Chinese. Note that here the Black and Caribbean and the Philippine groups are among the top participants, whereas in the managerial and administrative occupations, they are among the lowest participants. The least represented in the professional occupations are the Portuguese and Greek groups, followed by the Italian, Vietnamese, South Asian and Aboriginal.

In Table 14, the average total income of the same groups is presented. Total income should not be confused with employment income. As recorded by the Canadian census, employment income refers only to income from employment, reported by those employed and self-employed. While the total income includes employment income, it encompasses also all other income categories, including retired persons living on their pensions and persons below 15 years of age who are employed on an occasional basis. Hence, the average total income is lower than employment income, since it includes more persons with lower incomes (see note in Table 14).

The five groups with the highest average total income, and well above the national average, in 1990

Table 17: Participation in Professional Occupations of Selected Ethnic Groups' Labour Force, 15 Years of Age and Over, Indicating Ethnic Stratification, Canada 1991

Ethnic Group(s)	Percent of Group's Labor Force in Professional Occupations*
Jewish	30.2
Philippine	21.2
Arab	19.1
Black and Caribbean	19.0
Chinese	18.9
Polish	18.8
Hungarian	18.3
British	18.0
French, Ukrainian	17.6
Dutch, German, West Asian	17.5
National Average	**17.4**
Canadian	15.8
Spanish	15.6
Balkan	15.1
Central and South American	15.0
Aboriginal	14.9
South Asian	14.8
Vietnamese	13.8
Italian	13.7
Greek	9.9
Portuguese	7.9

* Professional occupations include occupations in natural sciences, engineering, mathematics, social sciences and related, teaching on all levels, medicine and health, including nursing, artistic, literary, recreational and related occupations.
Source: 1991 Canadian Census special tabulations.

were the Jewish, Canadian, British, Hungarian, Balkan and Polish. Those with the lowest average income were Central and South American, Vietnamese, Aboriginal, West Asian and Philippine. Note that, while the Philippine group is well above the national average in university and professional education and in participation in professional occupations, they are considerably below the national average in terms of total income. West Asian and the Black and Caribbean groups are in a somewhat similar position. This indicates that not all higher educational background and not all professions result in higher-than-average incomes.

If we look again at Table 13, we can observe that some groups have rather high percentages of their population who have attained only elementary education or some secondary education, but who have not obtained their graduation certificate. The five groups with the highest percentages of those with only elementary education who are far above the national average are the Portuguese, Greek, Italian, Vietnamese and Aboriginal. Yet, the six groups with the highest percentages of those who have only secondary education but who have not obtained their graduation certificates are the Aboriginal, Canadian, Vietnamese, British, Black and Caribbean and Ukrainian. The last two have the same percentages. It is interesting that both the younger ethnic minority groups, such as the Vietnamese and Caribbean, and the older, established majority groups, such as the British and Canadian, have similar percentages in this category. This indicates that the immigration policy that selects for higher education at the expense of those with less education and the policy that favours family-sponsored immigrants are not the only factors that may account for this.

Finally, in Table 12, service occupations, product fabrication and processing and primary occupations are considered in our society to be lower on the status scale than managerial, administrative and professional occupations. The five groups who, in 1991, were engaged in service occupations the most and were the most over-represented in these occupations were the Philippine, Greek, Central and South American, Spanish and Aboriginal. The Chinese and Portuguese closely followed them. Most other groups were closer to the national average of representation in these occupations.

The groups engaged mostly in factory work, i.e, product fabrication and processing, and the most over-represented in these occupations, were the Vietnamese, Portuguese, South Asian, Central and South American and Balkan. Finally, the groups most over-represented in the primary occupations, particularly agriculture, were the Dutch, German, Polish, Aboriginal and Ukrainian. The groups engaged mostly in product fabrication and processing are all younger groups in Canada, whereas those groups engaged mostly in primary occupations are the older, established ones.

• The Problem of Consistency of Measures and Other Objective Criteria of Ethnic Status

Although there is a general correspondence between the three measures of ethnic stratification, it is clear that in specific cases the ethnic status obtained by the use of one criterion is not necessarily the same as that obtained by the use of other criteria. As was already pointed out, Filipinos, Blacks and Caribbeans are among the most highly educated groups, yet they are also among those with the lowest income. Italians are over-represented in the higher income categories, but they are under-represented in the higher educational categories and over-represented in the lowest educational categories. Each of these inconsistencies can be explained by the specific history of each group and by the effects of Canadian immigration policies. Many Filipino women, for example, arrived in Canada in the 1980s to work as domestics, an occupation that does not offer a high income. Yet, among them was a high concentration of persons with university education, who saw their work as domestics under the special immigration program as a way of entering Canada and hoped for better opportunities later on. In the case of the Italians, the low educational level reflects the strong tendency among those Italians who have immigrated previously to sponsor their relatives, many of whom came from rural areas of Italy with only elementary education.

The measures employed above show that the British group, although it is under-represented in the lowest educational category, is not among those most highly over-represented in the highest educational categories. The British group is equally represented in the managerial-administrative occupational category and is over-represented in the highest income category. Its representation in the managerial-administrative category, however, is not as high as among the other groups mentioned.. The census indicates that the historical educational advantage of the British groups has been lost by the 1980s (Geschwender and Guppy, 1995). The question therefore arises as to the status of the British, particularly the English, as the sociological majority group in society.

None of the measures examined here so far actually directly measure a group's majority status. Since majority status indicates having the decisive voice in the major social institutions, we need to assess the place of the British in the biggest corporations in the economy and in the political institutions of society. As pointed out in the section dealing with the historical features of Canadian society, the work of Wallace Clement (1975, 1985) showed that the highest decision-makers in the large Canadian business corporations have been predominantly of British origin, with only small percentages of members of other ethnic groups. Since the time of his study, this elite group has opened up more to other ethnicities, but the British predominance has remained (Ogmundson, 1990; Ogmundson and McLaughlin, 1992; Rich, 1991; Herberg, 1990; Lautard and Guppy, 1990).

British and French predominance has also been the case in the highest political institutions. In almost one hundred years of elections to the House of Commons, the vast majority of the parliamentarians have been of British origin. Of the total number of 2,723 new members, elected between 1867 and 1964, 1,883, or 69.1 percent were of British origin, 736, or 27 percent, of French origin, and only 104, or 3.8 percent, of other ethnic origins (Manzer, 1974). Again, since then the House of Commons has opened up more to other ethnic groups, but remains predominantly British Canadian and French Canadian.

The position of the majority group in the ethnic stratification system can be also assessed through the measurement of the subjective aspects of ethnic status, to which we will now turn.

MEASUREMENT OF THE SUBJECTIVE ASPECTS OF ETHNIC STRATIFICATION

Ethnic groups who are high on the stratification scale according to the objective criteria can be relatively low on the scale according to the subjective criteria. The subjective measures refer to the prestige that ethnic groups enjoy relative to one another in the society at large. In this sense, the measure refers, to a large extent, to the biases or prejudices that people have towards various ethnic groups, i.e., the fact that some ethnic groups are valued more than others.

• Bogardus' Social Distance Scale

The measurement of the subjective aspects of ethnic stratification used most often in the past has been the Bogardus Social Distance Scale. The notion of **social distance** refers to the degree to which members of one ethnic group are willing to accept members of another ethnic group into a close relationship. Thus the degree may range from acceptance into close and intimate relationship, through indifference, to determined rejection and hostility. When asked for a number of ethnic groups, different degrees of acceptance of different groups produces a stratified scale of groups, ranging from those that are preferred most to those that are preferred least.

Emory S. Bogardus (1928: 25), who pioneered the scale, asked a sample of 1,725 Americans to answer seven questions in regard to four ethnic groups, English, Swedes, Poles and Koreans. Each question was assumed to represent a degree of acceptance or rejection. The questions were:

1. Would you allow [the group] to close kinship by marriage?
2. Would you allow [the group] to your club as personal chums?
3. Would you allow [the group] to your street as neighbours?
4. Would you allow [the group] to employment in your occupation?
5. Would you allow [the group] to citizenship in your country?
6. Would you allow [the group] as visitors only to your country?
7. Would you exclude [the group] from your country?

All seven questions were asked about each of the four groups, and when the percentages of those in the sample who answered "yes" to each question were tabulated, the order of preference on all seven counts emerged to be: English, Swedes, Poles, Koreans. Since this method produces seven scales rather than one, William J. Goode and P. K. Hatt (1952: 243-246) consequently merged them into one by assigning weights to each question. Thus, question (1) was given a weight of 1, symbolizing the smallest social distance, question (2), a weight of 2, and so on until question (5). For consistency reasons, they dropped questions (6) and (7) from the calculation altogether. The percent of respondents in Bogardus' study answering "yes" to each question was then multiplied by the question's respective weight, and the results of the five questions were added together for each ethnic group. Thus each group obtained a total number that placed it on a scale in relation to the other groups. The higher the number, the higher the group's ethnic status. The order thus produced was the same as that obtained by Bogardus, with the English at the top and Koreans at the bottom.

The Social Distance Scale has been used quite widely. In 1970, A. Richmond (1974a: 7) used the scale in his study of a sample of 3,218 respondents in Metropolitan Toronto. The results produced the following rank order of 10 selected groups: American, French Canadian, Polish, German, Italian, Canadian Indian, Jewish, Japanese, Hindu and Negro. As in Bogardus' study, the racial groups were rated at the bottom of the scale.

• Social Standing Scale

Another important measurement of the subjective aspect of ethnic stratification is the **Social Standing Scale**. To obtain a hierarchical scale of ethnic groups, Peter C. Pineo (1977) employed the same principle as that of the occupational prestige scale. He asked a national sample of 393 adult Canadians to sort cards printed with the names of 36 ethnic, racial and religious groups. Each respondent was instructed as follows:

> Canada is a country made up of many different kinds of people. Some of these groups of people have higher social standing than others do. Here is a card with the name of one such group on it. Please put that card in the box at the top of the ladder if you think that group has the highest possible social standing. Put in the box at the bottom of the ladder if you think that group has the lowest possible social standing. If it belongs in between, just put it in the box that comes the closest to representing the social standing of that particular group of people.

Table 18: Ranking of Ethnicities by English-Speaking Canadians (0-100 Scale)

Ethnic Groups in Origin Categories	Mean Rank	Standard Deviation
Charter Group Members and Related Groups		
British	81.2	21.4
English	82.4	20.1
English Canadians	83.1	20.5
French	60.1	24.8
French Canadians	56.1	27.8
Irish	69.5	22.8
Scots	75.2	22.1
Western and North Europeans		
Belgians	49.1	22.9
Danes	52.4	23.7
Dutch	58.7	22.6
Germans	48.7	25.2
Icelanders	45.6	24.7
Norwegians	55.3	22.8
Swedes	56.6	23.3
Swiss	55.7	21.9
Mediterranean and Central Eastern European		
Austrians	49.6	22.2
Czecho-Slovaks	41.2	22.9
Finns	47.6	22.7
Greeks	39.9	23.7
Hungarians	42.6	22.6
Italians	43.1	25.0
Jews	46.1	28.0
Lithuanians	41.4	21.9
Poles	42.0	22.4
Rumanians	42.1	23.5
Russians	35.8	26.2
Ukrainians	44.3	22.6
Non-Caucasian Groups		
Canadian Indians	28.3	28.3
Chinese	33.1	25.4
Coloureds	26.3	26.2
Japanese	34.7	25.3
Blacks	25.4	26.1
Not Ethnicities		
Catholics	70.1	25.6
Protestants	75.3	23.4
People of Foreign Ancestry	50.1	24.6
People of my Own Ethnic Background	74.4	24.9

(N = 300 cases less the number not ranking each title)
Source: Pineo, Peter C. 1977. "The Social Standing of Ethnic and Racial Groupings." *Canadian Review of Sociology and Anthropology*, 14: 147-157.

After the first card was placed, the interviewer went on to say:

> Here are a few more groups. As you did before, just put them in the boxes on the ladder which match the social standing you think these groups have. Place them the way you think people actually treat these groups, not the way you think they ought to treat them.

Table 18 presents the results on a ranking scale from 0 to 100, the latter being the highest possible social standing. The ethnic groups have been categorized into four origin categories. The highest social standing or prestige was accorded to the majority groups, the lowest to the "visible" racial groups. The Western and Northern Europeans enjoyed a higher prestige than did the Mediterranean and Eastern European groups. The ranking in the table was by 300 English-speaking Canadians. Pineo, however, asked the same question of a sub-sample of 93 French Canadians. His results showed that the latter place virtually all non-English and non-French ethnicities further down the rank. Pineo concluded that in general the ranking obtained by his Social Standing Scale was very similar to the rankings that had been obtained by the use of the Social Distance Scale.

THE PROBLEM OF A UNIFIED MEASURE OF ETHNIC STRATIFICATION

When we compare the ranking of ethnic groups obtained by the measurement of the objective aspects of ethnic status with those obtained by the subjective aspects measurement, it is evident that they do not converge for many ethnic groups. Thus, Asians and Jews in recent decades have been relatively high on the stratification scale according to the objective measures, yet relatively low according to the subjective measures. The French tend to be low on the objective scales, yet in the higher brackets on the subjective scales. Italians are more or less in the middle on the subjective scales, rather low on the educational and occupational scales, yet above average on the income scale.

The highest degree of convergence between the scales is for the English group and for the Canadian Indians and Inuit. The English are high on all the scales, although not necessarily the highest of all on the objective scales. The only exception, however, is the income scale, on which the English, although above average, are not very high above it. The Indians and Inuit, however, are consistently low on all objective and subjective measures.

Two concluding points can be made regarding the different measures of ethnic stratification. First, it is possible to work out a unified measure that would combine both the objective and the subjective approaches. Probably the simplest way of doing this would be to assign weight to each place on each objective and subjective measure and then find the rank for each ethnic group by multiplying its score on each scale by the respective weight and averaging the results. Different weights can be given to the different objective and subjective criteria. Thus, for example, participation in certain occupations can be given more weight than the average annual income. A rationale for this can be adduced, but to some extent, such assigning of weight is bound to be arbitrary.

To obtain more precise comparisons between ethnic groups, scales should be obtained for various subcategories within each ethnic group. For example, the measures of occupation, education and income should be taken for each gender, for each ethnic generation, for various age cohorts, for various waves of immigration and so on. Increased precision will make the ethnic stratification picture more meaningful.

ETHNIC STRATIFICATION: SOCIAL-PSYCHOLOGICAL MECHANISMS OF PERPETUATION

We have discussed those factors that determine the place in the stratification system of any one specific ethnic group. In this section, we want to focus on several mechanisms that contribute to its perpetuation.

These mechanisms are related to ethnocentrism, in particular to role ascription, by which the more important roles in society are reserved for the majority group, and the minorities come to be identified with less important ones.

• "Keeping One's Place"

Role ascription is often supported by a belief that it is quite proper for immigrants or any "foreign" group in society to perform what are seen as less desirable roles. Since immigrants are newcomers, it is often felt that it is justifiable to funnel them into jobs that have a need for labour, but which the native population does not want to do. Usually, this refers to manual occupations that require little skill. In this manner, the dual labour market system discussed previously comes to be sanctioned. The fact that, in the past, especially prior to

KEY ISSUES IN CANADIAN ETHNIC RELATIONS

"Making Good" in Canada—Upward Social Mobility

Much of the sociology of ethnic groups in Canada and the United States deals with ascertaining what obstacles exist to the economic mobility of minority ethnic groups in the mainstream society. In general, the theoretical arguments on this issue have ranged between two opposite positions: one argues that the obstacles are to be found in the minority ethnic communities themselves; the other, that the drawbacks are in the structure of the mainstream society that discriminates against minority groups.

Those who point to the minority communities like to focus on such factors as education, occupational skills, motivation to achieve and the ethnic community structure that may encourage or discourage achievement. They argue that ethnic minorities often have less education and lower occupational skills than the mainstream population and this retards their economic and social mobility. Some go further and argue that minority ethnic communities fail to inculcate an ethic of individual achievement and success among their members and instead foster the collectivist values of ethnic community participation and involvement as sufficient ends in themselves. Canadian sociologist John Porter, for example, held that not only is involvement in ethnic community life a drawback to social mobility, but even the retention of ethnic identity as part of the individual's personality is a distraction from and a liability for economic success.

Those at the other end of the spectrum, however, argue that ethnic identity and community involvement have little to do with social mobility of ethnic minorities. The obstacles to mobility derive from the structure of inequality that exists in the institutions of the mainstream society itself. Intentionally or unintentionally, these institutions exclude many minority ethnic groups, even if their members have the appropriate educational or skill levels. Jeffrey Reitz in his book *Warmth of the Welcome* brings together statistics on economic success of immigrant groups in Canada, the United States and Australia. He discusses such mainstream institutions as the immigration policy, educational system, the labour markets and the taxation and social welfare system. He concludes that when these institutions are structured in a highly individualistic manner—as for example in the United States—immigrants in their initial years after entry into the country, face greater obstacles to the realization of their economic potential.

It was pointed out in Chapter 5 that one has to look for the determinants of ethnic status and social mobility in at least three areas: the majority group, the economic and political state of the society, and the ethnic minority communities themselves. Only a combination of factors from these three sources will provide a full picture. It is important to determine how these factors combine together and to determine under what conditions one group of factors becomes more important than another. Perhaps some factors are obstacles to the economic success of some ethnic groups but not of others; or perhaps the obstacles faced by some groups are sources of social mobility for others?

Dutch immigrants en route to central Canada, leaving Pier 21 in Halifax, about 1950.

Photo: Courtesy of Canadian National, X-32168

As discussed in Chapter 4, not all immigrants are disadvantaged equally. In the 1980s and 1990s, some immigrant groups, for example Asians, came to Canada with educational levels higher than the average Canadian-born population. Also, some recent immigrants show lower unemployment levels than are found in the general population. Some minority ethnic groups are more socially mobile than other groups, including the general population. Some groups who may have a lower average educational level, as for example Italians, have nevertheless been able to move into higher income levels than the majority groups themselves.

It is not always wise, therefore, to make simple generalizations about all ethnic groups or new arrivals in this country. The precise circumstances of each group needs to be taken into account in order to explain the degree of success with which various waves of immigrants "make good" in Canada.

World War II, most immigrants to North America had indeed been little skilled and without much education has worked only to reinforce this preconception.

The belief justifying role ascription often involves a phenomenon that can be called **"keeping one's place."** This is an important mechanism in any institutionalized hierarchical system, be it an organizational bureaucracy, traditional family hierarchy or system of class stratification. It is derived from the organizational creed that, once there is a division of roles, the proper behaviour is to fulfil them and improper behaviour is to step outside of them. Disorganization is feared to be the result if the people filling these roles step outside of them.

Hence sanctions are developed–consciously or unconsciously, depending upon the institution–to prevent people from engaging in behaviour outside the boundaries of their roles. The same holds true of ethnic stratification, and we can say that, the more rigid the system of ethnic stratification, the stronger the sanctions to keep one's place. These sanctions may be either formal, such as laws and regulations, or informal, such as pressures of public opinion, social acceptance or non-acceptance. They can also be a combination of both.

T. Shibutani and K. Kwan (1965: 254-263) have analyzed the meaning of "place" as applicable to relatively rigid systems of ethnic stratification, such as the former white-Black system in the southern United States and the apartheid system in South Africa. According to them, men who are in an inferior position and keep their place address those in higher status with deference and wait to be addressed before speaking. They try to make the best of their status, and hence may take pride in discharging their subordinate duties well. People in privileged positions also have a "place" and are expected to behave accordingly–with dignity and elegance.

A man who knows his "place" has no aspiration beyond those regarded as appropriate for his category. If he is especially competent, he may work for people in higher positions as a special assistant. As such, he may receive higher pay and have some special privileges. However, there is no hope of moving into positions that are reserved for the dominant group without at least some negative reaction.

Often the "keeping place" complex is reinforced by those who were themselves immigrants or whose parents were immigrants but who have been socially mobile and have become successful. They may take the attitude that, since they had to work hard at poor jobs when they or their parents arrived in the country, all the new immigrants should also "work hard" and be satisfied with poorer jobs. The following is an excerpt from a letter to a newspaper editor, which typifies such an attitude:

> It is time for the silent majority of Canadians to speak up and put these demanding immigrants in their place, the place every immigrant–new or old–had to take for the first hard and tough years: Keeping your mouth shut and working hard at whatever job you can find regardless of what position you have held back home.
>
> Immigrating does not mean travelling to a foreign country and expecting to be welcomed with open arms and conveniently being put into a position that you find suitable.
>
> It more often than not means heartbreak and struggle for many years, learning and accepting differences and finally building a new life for oneself and one's family and finding one's rightful place in society (*The Toronto Star,* 1978: February 4).

• Paternalism and Inferiority Complex

Another social-psychological mechanism, closely related to that of "keeping place," that functions to support the persistence of ethnic stratification is the attitude of **paternalism**. In relation to ethnic groups, paternalism can be defined as an attitude that members of majority groups may have towards members of minority groups analogous to the attitude that parents have towards their children.

Paternalistic attitudes involve two basic elements, condescension and dependency. Condescension is an attitude that results in going out of one's way in order to interact with or assist others. Persons in superior positions usually have to interact or work together with persons in lower positions. Often, however, the feeling exists that they do not do it freely, but of necessity. This does not mean that people in the dominant position hate or dislike those in minority groups. On the contrary, they are often viewed with affection. Their folkways–dances, songs, craft–are appreciated and enjoyed, as long as they remain in their minority position, i.e., as long as they remain in their "place."

Noblesse oblige can be considered to be a form of condescension. It exists in relatively rigid systems of stratification in which the dominant groups have been well established. It refers to a tradition by which those in power in the dominant groups have a positive responsibility to protect and help the minorities. The concern with minorities becomes a matter of honour. Codes are established by which those who have power over minority group members are responsible for mistreatment. In the American South, prior to the Civil War,

Photo: Dick Hemingway

Paternalism and Superiority – racist garden ornaments near Picton, Ontario, 1993. Most Canadians nowadays find such symbols, recalling the period of slavery in the US, as demeaning and extremely offensive.

slaveholders exercised customary control on each other to limit the extent of slave exploitation. Cruel owners were often socially ostracized, whereas those who fulfilled their "honourable obligation" to give protection and help to the Black slaves were not only respected by other members of the dominant group, but were also served with loyalty by the slaves themselves (Shibutani and Kwan, 1965: 258-59; Weinstein and Gatell, 1968).

Another aspect of paternalism is the *attitude of dependency.* This implies that any changes in the position of a minority group or its members are ultimately a matter of decision or good will of the members of the dominant group. This notion has a variety of expressions. In a more rigid ethnic stratification system, it implies that members of minority groups can advance themselves by obtaining favours from the dominant majority rather than by insisting on their rights (Shibutani and Kwan, 1965: 260). In a less rigid system, it signifies an attitude by which members of a minority group are expected to, as it were, "prove themselves" worthy before they can be given higher positions, political rights or anything implying equality with the majority group. Thus they may be defined as not having the right amount or the right type of education, not being adequately organized politically, or simply as not having enough clout to be given either important strategic positions in society or given an official recognition implying equality with the majority group. By this attitude, minority ethnic groups are encouraged to concentrate on personal matters or matters internal to their groups rather than meddling in matters belonging to the majority group.

Similarly, the attitude of dependency regarding minority groups implies that any changes in the structure of society itself, if they are to be made, are to be made by the majority ethnic groups. Attempts by members of minority ethnic groups to change the structure are often defined as subversive.

Closely related to paternalism, and probably produced by it, is the phenomenon of an inferiority complex that is often shared by members of minority ethnic groups. **Inferiority complex** implies a set of attitudes about oneself in relation to others. These attitudes can be a combination of the following: (1) low self-esteem, i.e., seeing oneself as unimportant in relation to others, a feeling that what one says or does is unimportant, that what others say or do is much more important, (2) self-effacement, or submerging of one's own needs or demands, or constantly postponing dealing with them or bringing others' attention to them, (3) a feeling that one cannot win in any competition with members of the majority ethnic group, that one is doomed to lose, (4) an accompanying feeling that it is useless to try to win, that there is no sense in working hard at it, (5) deflation of one's own abilities and understanding what one can do, (6) fear of being overwhelmed or over-powered by members of the majority group, either socially, culturally or even physically; this includes a fear of being embarrassed by others, (7) a tendency to blame oneself for all failures and a tendency to take failures out on oneself by self-recrimination, (8) an attitude that institutions of one's own ethnic group are inherently inferior to those controlled by members of the majority group, (9) a de-valuing conception of other members of one's own group, including a certain mistrust of their competence in their chosen roles.

An inferiority complex as shared by members of an ethnic group of people is usually a result of long standing contact between majority and minority groups, especially if this contact has involved institutionalized paternalism. The complex comes to be internalized in the personalities of individuals through socialization, not by conscious inculcation, but as a by-product of interaction of minority and majority adults and a by-product of the inculcation of values that strongly emphasize internal minority community life. When deeply internalized, the complex holds back members of a minority group from effectively competing with members of the majority group in any area of economic, political, social or cultural life and thus reinforces their place in the ethnic stratification system.

CONCLUSION

This chapter has examined the meaning of, and the factors determining and perpetuating, ethnic stratification. Ethnic stratification is seen here as the structure within which interethnic relations take place. That is, ethnic groups, as groups, relate and interact with one another so as to change or maintain their ethnic status. This interaction may take the form of competition for jobs, for power or influence, for public recognition and the like. The ethnic groups who are at the lower end of the stratification system can be said to interact with other groups so as to move their ethnic status upwards. Those at the top, the majority groups, can be said to act so as to maintain their position, whereas those underneath them, the middle-man minorities, can be said to interact so as to both maintain their higher position and to improve it.

In this process of interethnic relations, prejudices, stereotypes and racism often play a significant role. Prejudice is expressed in various forms of interethnic conflict and is often a serious barrier to its resolution and to the incorporation of diverse groups into the broader society. We will now turn to its analysis.

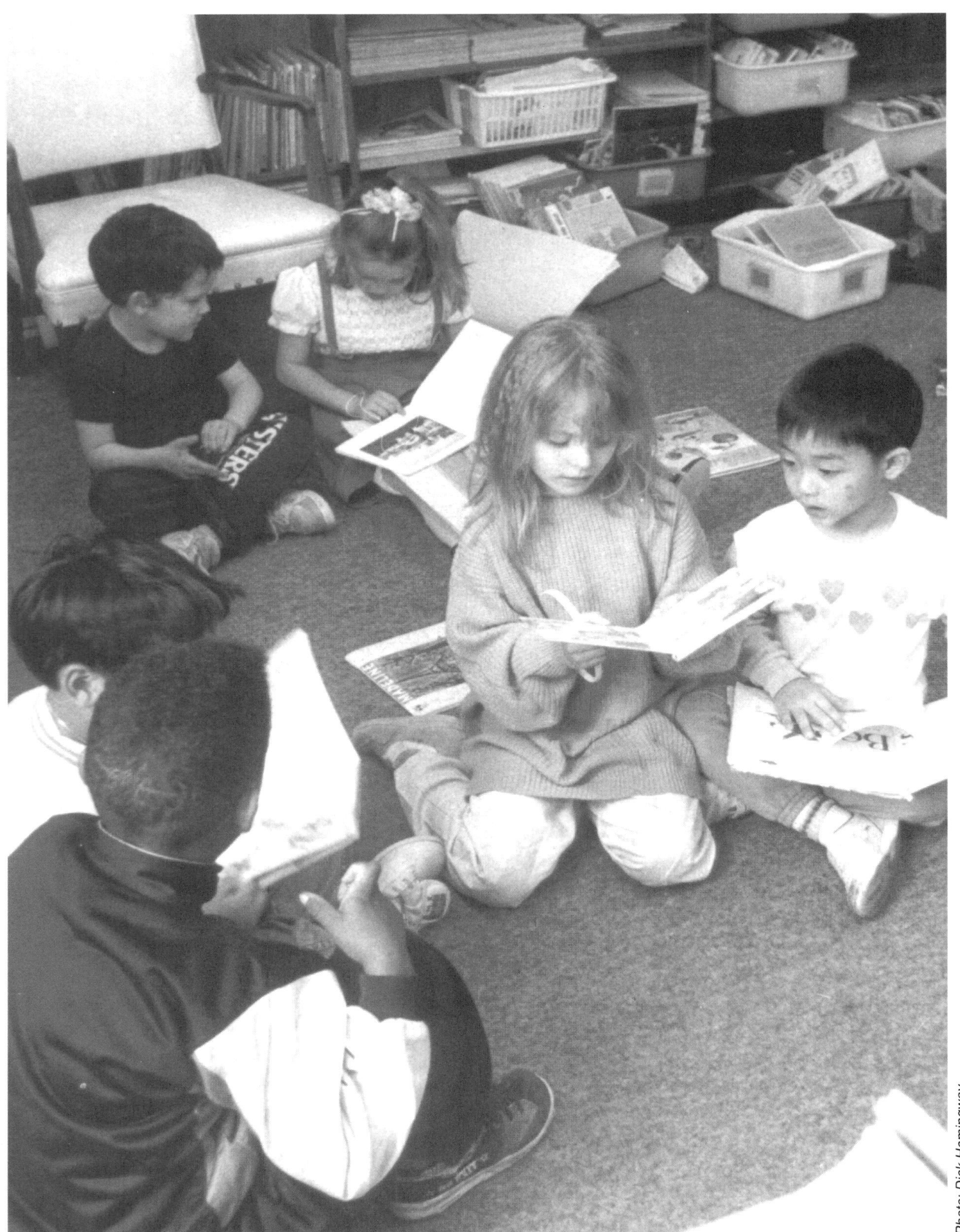

Photo: Dick Hemingway

Schools have an especially important role to play in combating all forms racial prejudice and promoting an understanding of ethnic diversity.

CHAPTER 6

PREJUDICE AND RACISM

Social Policy and Anti-Racist Practice

Members of ethnic minority groups often face prejudice and racism. Prejudice and racism are two factors that influence the place an ethnic group holds in the ethnic status hierarchy. What are the different types of prejudice? What is racism? What causes people to be prejudiced towards other groups of people? What effect does prejudice have on people and groups? Are there ways in which prejudice can be reduced or eliminated? These are the questions that this chapter tries to answer.

As pointed out in the previous chapter, prejudice is one of the strongly determining factors of ethnic stratification inasmuch as its effect is often that of discrimination. Prejudice enters significantly into intergroup and interpersonal relations. It is often a source of conflict among groups, particularly ethnic and racial groups, and a source of ill-feelings and hatred among individuals coming from different ethnic groups. It is also at the root of the predisposition to regard one's own group as superior to others.

In general terms, **prejudice** is a positive or negative orientation towards groups of people without regard to all the facts (Allport, 1954: 6). As such, it involves a "put-down" of some groups of people and an "up-put" of others. Thus a person may think that all members of another ethnic or racial group are "lazy," and this would explain why they are not highly socially mobile and have a low place in the ethnic stratification system. This person, however, would make such assertions, not because he or she has known or surveyed all members of the other group to determine if they are "lazy," but rather because he or she has accepted such ideas uncritically from someone else or has encountered one or a few persons with such characteristics and has applied them to the entire group.

Likewise, a person may see his or her own group as being "efficient" and therefore justified in holding more responsible positions in society and relate to other groups as being inferior. Again, this kind of assertion is not based on a thorough knowledge of all members of the group, but rather accepted on faith or by generalizing from those members of the group known to be in responsible positions.

Furthermore, the persons described above may dislike those whom they see as inferior and avoid associating with them, may mistrust them and avoid establishing close or durable relations or interdependency with them. Inversely, they may prefer associating with members of their own group, be readily willing to trust them and to establish close and lasting relations with them. When asked, they may provide what would appear to others to be a logical explanation and justification of this type of behaviour and even a prescription for others to follow suit.

The example above indicates that there are at least two types of prejudice and that prejudice is made up of a number of closely interrelated components. The relationship between these two types and the components determines the degree of prejudice, ranging from mild to extreme. First, we can speak of prejudice "for" and prejudice "against," i.e., prejudice in favour of one's own group and prejudice against other groups or group. At the basis of prejudice is the orientation that can be characterized as "us" and "them," by which both groups are seen as units with their own definite characteristics, but one's own group is seen as possessing a prevalence of positive characteristics, and the outside group, a prevalence of negative ones.

The deeper, social-psychological elements of this "us-them" dichotomy derive from the belief in the unique value of one's own group by which other groups are either lumped together as falling short of this value or one or a few groups are singled out as examples of people who fail to possess this value. It includes satisfaction with being a member of one's own group and with not being a member of the other groups or group. It also involves a conviction that the experience or history of the group evidences the rightness of its value, in contrast to other groups whose experience or history fails to evidence such value. For example, the dominant group in society may believe itself to be of special value because its position of dominance "proves" that other groups have fallen short of such value.

Prejudice in favour of one's own group is often called **ethnocentrism,** and prejudice against other groups, especially when it is systematic, **racism.** Some scholars use the term racism to apply only to the negative orientation towards racial categories and the term prejudice, to the negative orientation towards ethnic, cultural, groups (Henry et al., 1995). This, however, introduces conceptual confusion, since it assumes that racism is not prejudice. As will be explained below, however, while prejudice against racial categories has specific features, the basic components and dynamics of racism are in fact those of prejudice. Furthermore, in the past, the term race has often been used to apply to both racial categories and ethnic groups. While today scholars avoid this confusion, many still use the word racism to refer to the ideology that considers both racial and ethnic minority groups as inferior. Hence, while underscoring the specific features of racial prejudice we will use the term racism to refer to systematic prejudice against both of these types of minority groups.

Secondly, prejudice consists of four basic components: *stereotypes, attitudes of likes and dislikes, trust or mistrust* and *rationalized judgment.* Each of these will be discussed separately.

STEREOTYPES

Stereotypes are the cognitive components of prejudice–image-labels that we assign to a group of people that show what we believe the group is like and how we think persons in that group will behave. Stereotypes are "pictures in our heads," or images, of a group or statements about a group of people that presume to identify their characteristics (Lippman, 1936). They are, however, *categorical* statements, i.e., they assume that all people of a group are the same. Hence they are generalizations not based on the examination of individual facts, yet asserted, often emphatically, as if they were. Examples are "the Newfoundlanders are ignorant," "Blacks are lazy," "the French like easy living," "Jews are materialistic" or "Jews are smart," "East Indians are arrogant," "Germans are authoritarian," "the English are efficient" and the like.

All of these examples show the summary, categorical character of stereotypes; that is, we ignore differences among individuals in a group and view all members as being the same. The summary, categorical nature of stereotypes is represented by the tendency of the prejudiced persons to use names of groups in a twisted manner and, by doing this, make them stand for a set of stereotypes. Thus, Black persons in the United States were labeled by prejudiced persons as "Niggers," the poor East Indians in Canada, as "Pakis," the Newfoundlanders, as "Newfies," Jews, as "Kikes," Chinese, as "Chinks" and the like. Each of these labels would represent one or another set of stereotypes discussed below.

In general there is a tendency to perceive one's own group (the *in-group)* as including more individual differences than the groups with which we do not identify (the *out-group*). We tend to perceive more readily even the subtle differences among "us," but to see "them" as being all alike (Linville and Jones, 1980). Furthermore, the more definite the stereotype of an out-group in the minds of individuals, the more they think that everyone in the out-group fits the stereotype (Judd et al., 1991).

• Conventionality of Stereotypes

Stereotypes come to be shared by people in the same ethnic group, in the same society or even among different societies. They are often transmitted by word-of-mouth, from parents to children, from peer to peer or in informal adult conversations. Stereotypes may be arbitrary and incorrect, but they become part of popular cultures and become resistant to change. Discussing stereotypical categories in their influential book, T. Shibutani and K.M. Kwan (1965: 87) have pointed out:

> When such categories become conventional...they are no longer arbitrary, no matter how inaccurate they may be. They become group definitions, and they are supported by collective sanctions. An individual may disagree with them, but unless he works with conventional meanings, others will not understand him. Thus, the lines of demarcation between ethnic categories are drawn by common consent. The characteristics attributed to each category are established in popular beliefs, and the symbols of identification in terms of which individuals are located in each type are also matters of convention. The meanings of ethnic categories are learned by participating in an organized society, and they are constantly reinforced in social interaction.

Stereotypes are often maintained even if it is shown that many or most persons in the group are not what the stereotypes state they are. One reason for this is that perception is selective; people often see what they want to see. It is often possible to find some people in a group to whom a stereotype seems to apply. Some characteristics contained in stereotypes may objectively be there among some persons in a group (Mackie, 1980). These persons are then used as "proof" of the stereotype and because of this acquire high visibility. This visibility in turn serves as "evidence" for the stereotype.

Usually people hold mixed stereotypes about a specific group. That is, they intermix negative stereotypes with positive stereotypes. However, it can be said that the lower the group is on the ethnic stratification scale, the more negative stereotypes it receives. In the first empirical study of stereotypes ever undertaken, D. Katz and K.W. Braly (1933) found that Jews were described by their sample of college students as intelligent, ambitious, industrious, shrewd, mercenary and grasping. The Irish were described as quick-tempered, pugnacious, witty, honest and religious. Blacks were regarded as ignorant, superstitious, lazy, happy-go-lucky, ostentatious and musical. In Canada, M. Mackie (1980) found that in the Canadian West, Hutterites were seen as, among other things, hardworking, thrifty, healthy, sexually moral and mentally healthy, but also cliquish and shy and quiet. Ukrainians were regarded as hardworking, ambitious, thrifty, warm towards others and happy, but also cliquish and uncouth. Indians, however, were predominantly seen in negative stereotypes as unambitious, lazy, dirty, incompetent in work habits, shy and sad.

• Types of Stereotypes

As the examples above have shown, people tend to group stereotypes together and certain types of stereotypes tend to be grouped together more often than other types. It is not by accident that one type of stereotypes is directed at some ethnic groups and another type at other ethnic groups. Ethnic groups in dominant positions are subjects of different sets of stereotypes than those in subordinate positions. Ethnic groups who are in the middle-man position on the ethnic stratification scale are subjects of still different sets of stereotypes as are those groups who are in the process of reaching for more rights for themselves and changing their ethnic status. Thus people in a group can be seen as valuable objects, as inferior objects, as objects of condescension, as useful objects, irritating objects, dangerous objects or as esoteric objects. This typology of stereotypes was originally proposed by T. Shibutani and K. Kwan (1965: 94-107). We will follow this typology here with a number of modifications and will try to locate each type in the ethnic stratification system.

Valuable and superior objects. People in groups that occupy the dominant majority position in society usually perceive of themselves as valuable, admirable or superior objects and are often also seen as such by others. The predominant stereotypes in this category are self-controlled, intelligent, efficient, proud, well organized, punctual, honest, benevolent, tolerant.

Members of minority groups often relate to members of the majority groups as to their superiors and think of them in terms of the same stereotypes that the majority group applies to itself. They relate to members of the majority group with respect and deference. They often give them more personal and public attention than they give to members of the minority group. They often use their perception of the majority group as a standard of comparison of their own behaviour and the behaviour of other members of their own group.

To perceive of oneself as being valuable or admirable is an aspect of ethnocentrism. All groups, majority and minority, are ethnocentric in some degree. That is, members of a groups tend to favour their own group and hence see a value in it (Coser, 1956; Hinkle and Schopler, 1986). This ethnocentrism, however, becomes problematic when members of a group begin to perceive their group as superior to other groups (Shibutani and Kwan, 1965: 107-114). This is especially so when they develop ideologies that define and rationalize their superiority in a systematic way. This ethnocentrism then becomes a significant component of racism. More will be said about it in the section on racism later in this chapter.

Inferior objects are objects of condescension. People from ethnic groups at the bottom of the stratification ladder are often seen by those in higher ethnic statuses as inferior. The predominant stereotypes leveled at them are lazy, slow, tardy, incapable of serious responsibility, stupid, superstitious, dirty, filthy, smelly.

Persons of the Black race, the American Black and the Caribbeans, were often referred to in these terms before the influence of the civil rights movement. The label "Nigger" would be used as a symbol of inferiority (Henry, 1994: 107-108). The Native peoples in North America were seen in these terms before their movement for their rights, and in the urban areas, recently arrived immigrants from poor countries, especially those from East India, were also until recently subjects of such stereotypes and were often labeled "Paki."

Persons at the bottom of the ethnic stratification scale are not only seen in negative terms. Often the stereotypes of inferiority are intermixed with stereotypes that express, as it were, an understanding of the "inferior" people's situation and express positive characteristics about them. However, this apparent understanding usually involves an attitude of condescension. This attitude is reflected in such stereotypes as hard-trying, poor things, pitiful and naïve (don't know any better), or in positive stereotypes related to the physical make-up of the people, such as strong, virile, healthy, but these in the sense of subhuman-like attributes.

Useful objects. The groups not at the bottom of the ethnic stratification system but rather closer to the middle are often seen through more positive stereotypes. Many immigrant groups find themselves on this level of stratification, some of them with only a young second generation and others with two or three generations in the country. Still, these stereotypes often include hidden negative attitudes or other components of prejudice. Thus, for example, many ethnic groups may be seen as friendly, trustworthy, reliable, solid, hard working, thrifty, courageous, practically smart and the like. These preconceptions recognize the contribution these groups make, but they often hide the apprehension or dislike of the cultural and identity differences that the groups represent and often maintain.

Irritating objects. When ethnic groups become socially mobile, when they begin to organize and claim rights and thus begin to change their ethnic status, they often become the subjects of different stereotypes. These stereotypes reflect the fact that other groups, majority and minorities, perceive these new demands as upsets and are responding to them with irritation or anger. When people who might previously have been seen as inferior or as useful begin to place demands on society, the images of them change. They are now often labeled as pushy, greedy, aggressive, unfairly demanding, troublemakers, uncaring about others and the like.

In 1954, the American Black civil rights movement achieved a breakthrough legal success. The U.S. Supreme Court struck down the segregation laws that maintained the idea of "separate but equal" institutions. Many whites saw this as upsetting the balance of the social order and viewed it with apprehension and anger (Ringer, 1983: 424-465). In Canada, in the 1970s, there was a successful movement among the ethnic groups of Eastern and Southern European background to establish the multiculturalism policy. Many French Québecers saw this move as an attempt to take attention away from the meeting of their demands. Even several decades later, the mainstream majority and several highly visible members of a few minorities expressed an agitation about the policy and labeled the work of those behind the policy as divisive, in spite of the policy's explicit goal of social integration (Isajiw, 1997).

Dangerous objects. Somewhat like the irritating objects but in a higher degree, the ethnic groups that come to be established as middle-man minorities are subject to stereotypes that portray them as dangerous objects. Middle-man minorities are in a position in which they are used as surrogates of the majorities in the performance of jobs that are important for the majorities, but that require special skills that may not exist in sufficient numbers among the majority group. Middle-man minority groups, however, also compete with the majority group for positions of power and influence. In turn, other minority groups may compete with the middle-man minority groups. In this context, the middle-man minority groups come to be seen as dangerous objects by both the majority group and by other minority groups. The stereotypes leveled against the middle-man minorities are often abundant. They include such labels as ambitious, aggressive, intelligent, shrewd, cunning, adept, clannish, arrogant, greedy, crafty, corrupt, immoral, exploiting and the like.

Middle-man minorities, such as the Jews in Europe and North America, the Chinese in South East Asia as also in North America, and the South Asian Indians in Africa, Oceania and again to some extent in North America, have been subject to these types of stereotypes (Selzer, 1972; Wu, 1972; Ringer, 1983: 665-680; Nash, 1989: 21-60).

Exotic objects. The last type of stereotypes discussed here refer to groups who are culturally different from both the dominant group and other minority groups in society and who differ from all the others by being outside the structure of the larger society or are at most tangentially connected with it. Because of this, they neither compete with other groups in society, nor present a threat to them. Two types of groups are represented in this category. First, in many contemporary societies, there are groups of persons who reside in society only temporarily. These include temporary-stay migrants and periodic migrants, many of whom come with different cultures. Some even establish their own temporary institutions. For example, diplomatic delegations come for a temporary stay, but bring large staffs of persons who can often be seen in public in large cities, dressed in their folk or other costumes. These costumes appear unusual to the viewer to whom these groups of people are "foreign." Other examples of temporary-stay persons were given in the chapter on migration.

The second type of groups that are often subjects of stereotypes that define them as exotic objects are established ethnic groups in society, usually small in size as compared with other groups, that remain territorially segregated, usually with the goal of maintaining their distinct identity. In Canada, such groups are the Doukhobors, the Hutterites and, to some extent, the Mennonites. The Inuit and the Native peoples on their reserves, though not in the cities, were also in this group until their recent active involvement in the political process of the country.

The stereotypes used to refer to such groups are: strange, unusual, interesting, fascinating, remarkable, funny, different, quaint, weird, wild and the like. These stereotypes are neither particularly negative nor particularly positive. They express a wonder about the groups, indicating difficulty in understanding them and in mentally placing them in the prevalent stratification schemata. Writings describing territorially segregated groups, as for example the Doukhobors, are often popular reading about a people who are, as it were, "far away from us, yet so close to us" (Woodcock and Avakumovic, 1977).

If such groups, however, begin to place demands on society, or if they come to be seen as a threat by the surrounding population, the stereotypes shift to those of irritating or even dangerous objects. A study of the history of the Hutterite community in Canada (Peter, 1987: 211-224) showed how the Hutterites were first considered to be good, though unusual, settlers in Western Canada. But when the community began to buy some of the best land in the area, the Hutterites came to be defined as "invaders" into the area.

• Manifestations of Stereotypes

Prejudiced people may express stereotypes quite consciously. However, many people are often unaware of their stereotypes. In conversations with others, they may express their opinions of others and stereotype them while thinking that they are stating facts about them. In general, the less a person knows about other groups, the more one is prone to use stereotypes about them. In common conversations, stereotypes may manifest themselves in such accidental phrases as, for example, "I jewed him down," "He is mafia," "white and good" and the like. Put-downs of a group may not be intended in the conversation, yet prejudice is expressed when such phrases are used. If members of the stereotype's target group are present when such stereotypes are uttered, objectively such expressions are offensive to them, regardless of the subjective intention and regardless of whether the target person has subjectively felt the hurt produced by the stereotype.

Another manner in which stereotypes are expressed is in the form of ethnic jokes. In general, ethnic jokes put down ethnic groups either directly or indirectly. They compare two or more groups, one of which is usually the butt of the joke. The put-down stereotype represents members of a group as lacking intelligence, "stupid" or the like. For example, the widespread joke that asks "How many ____ does it take to screw in a bulb?" is answered with "Five; one to hold the bulb and four to turn him around" and is a direct put-down. In this joke, however, the specific ethnic group that is being put down is substitutable. Several Eastern European groups and the Newfoundlanders have often been the butt of this joke.

Another way in which stereotypes may be manifested is when persons who hold them show a "bend-over-backwards" pattern of behaviour; that is, when they over-state the opposite sentiment. For example, if someone begins to praise a group of people by incessantly or emphatically underscoring its positive characteristics by saying, "How good or smart or talented they are," this kind of praise may indicate that the real feelings and preconceptions are the opposite, and the positive stereotypes function to cover up the negative stereotypes hidden underneath the expressed "political correctness."

ATTITUDES OF LIKES AND DISLIKES, TRUST AND MISTRUST: SOCIAL DISTANCE

The second component of prejudice are attitudes of likes and dislikes. **Attitudes of likes and dislikes** refers to socially shared predispositions of liking some types of people and disliking other types. While stereotypes make up the cognitive aspects of prejudice, attitudes of likes and dislikes constitute prejudice's affective aspects.

As in the case of stereotypes, attitudes of likes or dislikes refer to groups of people. Thus, for example, in

Northern Ireland, the Protestant and the Catholic Irish have disliked each other for a long historical period of time. These feelings have led to violent conflicts and the inability to resolve the conflict peacefully. Similarly, dislikes or hatreds have existed in the Middle East between the Arabs and the Israelis, in Germany between the Neo-Nazi groups and the migrant Turks, in Bosnia between the Serbs and the Muslim Bosnians, in Africa between the Hutu and the Tutsi, in the United States between the whites and the African Americans, in Canada between the French and the English, the whites and the Native peoples and so on in many other parts of the world. The fact that these conflicts cannot be peacefully resolved shows that the relationship between these groups has been based more on emotion than on any other consideration.

Persons who are disliked in a prejudicial manner can be disliked in two ways. In either case, the dislikes combine with stereotypes. Thus, persons are often disliked simply because they identify or are identified by others as belonging to a group against which the prejudiced persons hold negative stereotypes. That is, they are not disliked because their individual behaviour patterns or beliefs are disliked. In fact, the prejudiced person may have little or no knowledge of the personal behaviour or characteristics of those they dislike. Also, if they come to know the person, they may have no objection to that person's behaviour or may even agree with that person's attitudes or beliefs. They dislike the person simply because he or she is a member of a group they think is inferior or "bad" or is otherwise defined by them in negative terms.

For example, persons may be disliked by prejudiced persons simply because they are Jewish or German or East Indian or Chinese and so on. The prejudiced persons have stereotypical preconceptions that all persons in these groups are alike.

Persons may also be disliked because their looks or behaviour exhibit characteristics that the prejudiced persons think are bad or improper. For example, a Black person may be disliked by a white person upon encounter, because the Black person's skin colour is assumed by the white person to be not as good as the white person's skin colour. Or a person may speak English with an accent that sounds aggressive and identifies him with the East Indian group. The accent may immediately produce negative feelings in the person spoken to, and the speaker with the accent may be seen as being "arrogant" or "pushy." Or members of an East European group may talk to each other in loud voices, and this may evoke in some persons of Western ethnicity a dislike of the East Europeans, along with the labels "rude" or "uncouth."

In all these cases, prejudice is rooted in ethnocentrism, i.e., in the often unconscious assumption by people that their own behavioural patterns, their own etiquette and culture, are better or more proper than that of others. Persons who react to people from ethnic groups other than their own in this manner often claim that they are not prejudiced against any specific group, but that they dislike anyone who is "loud," "pushy," "uncivilized" and so on. They may be quite sincere about it. Yet the fact that the dislike resulting from this is expressed in relation to specific ethnic groups whose behaviour is imbedded in different cultural patterns indicates an unconscious prejudice.

Combined with attitudes of likes and dislikes are feelings of trust and mistrust. When it comes to personal or intergroup relations, prejudiced persons usually have difficulty in trusting persons from groups other than, or much different from, their own. Rather, they tend to restrict relationships that require trust to members of their own group. Hence the trust aspect of prejudice articulates with ethnocentrism, and it is a significant factor in ethnic groups' maintenance of their community. More will be said about this in the chapter on ethnic identity retention. Feelings of likes and dislikes of other people and readiness to trust other people combine to create *social distance* between them. As was previously explained, **social distance** refers to the willingness or unwillingness to establish permanent relationships with members of a different ethnic group. This includes the willingness to accept persons from one or another ethnic group into informal or intimate relations as friends, neighbours or spouses and into more formal relations, as on the job, as trusted customers or clients and as fellow-citizens. Small social distance means a high degree of willingness to do so; large social distance means a low degree of willingness to do so on any level. Measuring this distance was discussed in Chapter 5.

Social distance includes feelings of comfort or discomfort when interacting with members of other ethnic groups. If persons feel very uncomfortable in the presence of and when interacting with persons of other ethnicities or races, this becomes an indicator of a heightened degree of social distance and the possible presence of prejudicial attitudes.

Furthermore, social distance between ethnic groups depends also on the degree of mutual understanding of what members of each group actually want. In his classic study of Black-white relations in the Southern

United States, Gunnar Myrdal (1944) pointed out that what the whites thought the African Americans wanted at that time was completely different from what the African Americans wanted. The whites thought the Blacks wanted sexual equality first and economic equality last, whereas the Blacks wanted the opposite, economic equality first. A similar lack of mutual understanding of motives has existed in Canada between the English and the French. The so-called "Quebec Problem" or the question of "What does Quebec want?" has been interpreted differently from the English Canadian and the French Quebec perspectives. From the English Canadian perspective, the problem has been seen as one of extending economic and political advantages to the population of Quebec within the national Canadian structure and modifying the constitutional structure of Federal Canada in such a way as to make it legitimate in the eyes of Québecers. From the French Quebec point of view, the problem has been one of maintaining Quebec's own identity and developing it culturally, economically and politically in the process of modernization into the structural changes that modernization necessitates (Posgate and McRoberts, 1979: 1-14).

Similar differences in perspectives exist in regard to the understanding of the relationships with the Native peoples, the diverse understandings of multiculturalism by other minority groups, and the majority group in Canada. More will be said about this in later chapters. The problem is that the lack of mutual understanding as to what each group wants produces suspicion of motives and consequent mistrust and dislikes on both intergroup and interpersonal relations levels, and this functions to maintain a larger degree of social distance.

IDEOLOGICAL PREJUDICE: RACISM

This term refers to the evaluative or judgmental aspects of prejudice. **Ideological prejudice** takes place when rationalization is provided for prejudicial attitudes and stereotypes. By rationalization is meant a rational justification of an already accepted judgment. That is, the judgment refers to already accepted stereotypes and attitudes towards other groups or towards one's own group in relation to the other groups. What it adds to these is an intellectual type of argument that makes the stereotypes and attitudes appear as a logical conclusion of a rational, common-sense or scientific consideration. Some of these apparent explanations may be very simple and others, more complicated. In either case, these explanations contain, either implicitly or explicitly, a justification for a certain course or program of action in regard to a group or groups of people. For this reason they are called ideological.

As a rule, these ideologies assume that one group, or one set of groups, is superior to another group or sets of groups and, as a result of this, certain actions by the superior group in relation to the inferior groups are warranted. For this reason such ideologies are racist. All words ending in *ism* refer to ideologies. Marxism is an ideology based on the idea of the superiority of the working class in the context of class conflict; idealism is an ideology based on the idea of the superiority of non-material reality; nationalism is an ideology based on the idea of preferability or the superiority of a nation. **Racism** is an ideology based on the idea of the superiority of one racial category or one ethnic group to other racial categories or ethnic groups.

For example, the Nazi regime in Germany in the 1930s fostered the racist ideology that held the white "Nordic" race to be inherently superior to all other races in the world. Consequently, the Nordic race, in particular the Germans as the leader of the race, were justified in subjugating all other races and ethnic groups to themselves by force or extermination if they saw fit. This was an extreme form of racism. Other racist ideologies are less extreme and as a result are more difficult to recognize as forms of prejudice. From the fourteenth century until about the middle of the twentieth century, different European powers were colonizing most regions of the world. This usually meant the subjugation of other peoples by force. In this process of colonization, the prevalent ideology employed to justify it was the idea of "civilizing the uncivilized" or "savage" peoples. It included the presupposition that the Western European cultures were superior to the what were often labeled "primitive" cultures outside of Europe, and hence Europeans had the right and the duty to "bear civilization" to these peoples. At different periods of time, additional argumentation was added to support the basic presupposition. In the nineteenth century, the theory of evolution was used to argue that, in the natural process of evolution, some peoples developed faster than others, that evolution proves the survival of the "fittest" and that, since the conflict for survival is a "natural" process, conquest gives the conqueror certain rights over the conquered and the like.

73602

DOMINION OF CANADA

IMMIGRATION BRANCH — DEPARTMENT OF THE INTERIOR

RECEIVED FROM

Photo: Courtesy of Vancouver City Archives

A part of Canadian history—certificate of head tax paid by Quan Lum, 1912.

• Racist Ideologies and Social Policies

Racist ideologies are often built into *social policies.* In Canadian history, the most obvious policies guided by a racist ideology were immigration policies legislated at different periods of time. As was pointed out in the chapter on immigration, the Chinese Immigration Act of 1885 and the Head Tax of $50 on Chinese immigrants set in 1885 that was raised to $100 in 1900 and again to $500 in 1903, the "Continuous Journey" regulations of 1910, the Immigration Act of 1910 that established "undesirable" classes of immigrants, the Chinese Exclusion Act of 1923, all intended to exclude or limit the number of Chinese and South Asian immigrants to Canada. On what grounds? As William Lyon Mackenzie King, then Deputy Minister of Labour, put it in 1907, it is "natural that Canada should remain a White man's country." In 1947, when new pressures to accept more immigrants into Canada emerged, Mackenzie King, then Prime Minister of Canada, still insisted that the immigration policy must not change the original racial and cultural character of the Canadian population (Buchignani and Indra, 1985; Bolaria and Li, 1988).

In addition to racial categories, racist ideologies can also be focused on policies towards specific ethnic groups. During and immediately after World War II, the Canadian government was reluctant to admit Jews as refugees to Canada. It undertook informal measures to restrict their immigration (Abella and Troper, 1982).

Racist ideologies, however, exist and are fostered within society outside of official policies. One of the most influential agencies in this regard are *the media.* The media–the press, periodicals, television and radio transmissions–through editorials and editorialized news items, is today the main institution that influences and forms public opinion. It can transmit stereotypes, influence the formation of attitudes and, by taking positions on social issues, it explicitly and more often implicitly propounds one or another ideology (Herman and Chomsky, 1988; Fleras, 1995). This is not necessarily a systematically presented ideology. It may be included in specific articles or broadcasts only in a partial way. It is often subtly implied rather than explicitly stated. It may also be inconsistent from one period of time to another, reflecting political winds and responding to and creating its own intellectual climates, fads or fashions, depending on the biases and interests of the various groups behind the media.

An example of the media transmission of stereotypes and racist ideology regarding specific ethnic groups is the press coverage of the population settlement process in the Prairies at the turn of the twentieth century. In the last decade of the nineteenth century, the Prairie newspapers published positive stories about the settlement of East Europeans, extolling them as good farmers. In the decade preceding World War I, however, the stories changed. The newspapers began criticizing the settlers as bad farmers, telling other prospective farmers not to buy land next to East Europeans and warning them that their land would grow weeds if they did so and so on (Dasko, 1974).

Elements of racism are also transmitted by the media in an implicit and subconscious manner. A study of Canada's national newspaper's editorial columns dealing with multiculturalism since the end of the 1970s until 1995 showed not a single editorial that was supportive of the policy of multiculturalism (Ewins, 1996; Mallet, 1997). The implicit message communicated to the reader is one of downgrading the ethnic groups for whom the policy has stood and whom it has served.

A study initiated by John Miller, a journalist and chair of the School of Journalism at Ryerson Polytechnic University in Toronto, and quoted by the journalist Cecil Foster (1996: 189), found that by reading the largest newspapers in Canada's five major cities, one can easily develop the impression of racial minorities that "half are either athletes or entertainers; if they are in the news otherwise, they are probably in trouble of some sort. And few make any contribution to business or have noteworthy life styles." Foster (1996: 188) concludes:

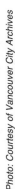

More history—fishing boats belonging to Canadians of Japanese descent were confiscated during World War II.

> One reason for the negative stereotypes is that the news media often do not see Blacks and other minorities as part of their audience.... Most of the programming is for the friends and family of the people that produce the programs. And these planners and producers are traditionally white. When they deal with Blacks and minorities it is not from a position of explaining one of them to the wider group. It is to explain a group that is either exotic, threatening or something in between–but definitely not part of the wider circles of friends and families.

Varieties of racism are often shared by people in the form of *stock answers* given as explanations of behaviour or conditions of existence of other ethnic groups. These answers often acquire a folkloric character in the sense that those sharing them expect others to agree because they are self-evident. For example, in a study of white-Indian relations in a small town in western Saskatchewan (Braroe, 1980), the local white people would often give two types of reasons for the poverty and elusive economic behaviour of the Indians. Some considered the Indians as childish and therefore irresponsible: "They can't help it, they're just kids with money. They got nothing, and whenever they do get a little money, they can't wait to spend it." Others would take the opposite approach, stating, "I can make a living off this land, why can't they? It's because we help them so much that they are so lazy." Similar "rationales" in relation to Native peoples were expressed in D. Stymeist's (1975: 75-76) study of ethnic relations in a northwestern Ontario town. In both cases, the presupposition is made that Indians are in one way or another inferior to the whites and hence such stock answers are of a racist nature.

PREJUDICE, ETHNICITY AND GENDER

Ethnic prejudices and prejudices against racial categories of people are made more complex by **gender prejudice**. A woman who is of a minority ethnic group and in the racial category against which there are prejudices is subject to a four-way prejudice. There are prejudices against her ethnicity, her race and against her as a woman coming from those outside of her own group and prejudices against her as a woman coming from her own group.

In the periods of larger influxes of immigrants of culturally different minorities, prejudices against immigrant women would often rise. During the early immigration of the Chinese to Canada, at the end of the nineteenth century, Chinese women were often viewed as prostitutes or polygamous second wives. In Vancouver, the Women's Missionary Society dedicated itself to "rescuing" Chinese women from dangerous "Chinamen" and preventing miscegenation between the whites and the Chinese (Anderson, K., 1991). Similarly, during the difficult, pioneering period of Ukrainian settlement of the Prairies in the twenty years preceding World War I, the middle-class women in the West stereotyped Ukrainian women as "child brides," "domestic drudges," "beasts of burden" and victims of male abuse (Swyripa, 1993: 34-35).

In the 1970s and 1980s, many East Indian women immigrants–many with higher education–felt put down by Canadians (Agent, 1986). They felt that Canadians thought that "Indians are dirty" and that Canadians were superior to East Indians. At the same time, they felt that Canadians stereotyped Indian women as being traditional, conservative and as having a low status in their culture. Some Indian women felt that Canadians considered Indian women as "domestic, shoplifters or prostitutes" (Mukherjee, 1885: 2-3).

In addition, many Indian women feel that their traditional Indian dress–the sari–is often disliked, especially on the job, and that they would be more acceptable to their employers and co-workers if they would abandon their traditional dress and adopt pants or the Western style of dresses (Das Gupta, 1986).

At the same time, Indian and other South Asian women face a patriarchy at home. Their fathers and husbands consider their primary role to be that of wife and mother. From childhood on, they are reared for marriage, and their value to their husbands is often measured in the kind of dowry that they bring with them. They are not expected by their fathers or husbands to be vocal or outgoing, and violence by their fathers or husbands is used as the means of ensuring their subordination (Das Gupta, 1986).

The perception that a woman's proper place is "in the kitchen and with children" has also been a long-standing, traditional ideology in Western societies and is shared by most ethnic groups coming from Europe. It has often been associated with the stereotypes of women as "the weaker sex" and as being more emotional than men. If they do succeed in business or other "man's occupations" independently of men, they do so by female enticing or the like (Burnet, 1986).

This prejudicial ideology has prevented scholars in the past from adequately seeing the input that women have made into the successful incorporation of ethnic groups, both minority and majority, into the structure of the larger society. In the 1970s, however, this ideology of women began to slowly change, as more women began to participate in the labour force alongside men, as the number of single mothers increased, as more women obtained higher education, as the feminist movement began to be heard more often and as the legal system in Canada and the United States began to be more responsive to women's issues. This does not mean that all these stereotypes of women have disappeared. On the contrary, many of them continue to persist alongside ethnic stereotypes. Yet structures have been established that can have an influence on change.

Gender prejudice does not refer only to minority women. It also extends itself to minority men. A study of how white persons in the United States react to Black males, particularly young Black males (Anderson, E., 1990: 164-168, 173-182), showed that, on the street, white persons are often afraid of Black males and view them as "predators." When young Black men appear on the street, white women may clutch their pocketbooks and edge up against their companions or begin to walk swiftly. Other pedestrians often cross the street upon spotting Black males at a distance. They see them as "dangerous" or as being "deviant" or as belonging to "wolf packs." Anderson points out that even when older Black men disavow the image of the predator in front of others, such disavowals are not seen as the norm but as the exception, as "different from the rest," thereby confirming the status of the "rest." Thus, ethnic minority men as well as women are subject to the four-way prejudice.

PREJUDICE AND DISCRIMINATION

Ethnic and racial discrimination takes place in many social institutions: occupations, schools, housing, police, courts, service-delivery agencies, the arts and so on. Discrimination and prejudice, however, are not the same. **Discrimination** refers to actions; **prejudice**, including racism, refers to preconceptions, attitudes, trust and rationalized judgments. There is, however, a relationship between the two, although not always a close relationship. In general, those who discriminate against others are prejudiced against them. Studies (Triandis, 1973) have shown that attitudes are related to behaviour, though not necessarily under all conditions. The conditions that may work against prejudice being acted out in discrimination are strong norms against discrimination, especially those governing performance of social roles that are formal, and situations that require non-discrimination. Under such conditions, people who are prejudiced against others do not necessarily discriminate against them. The inverse, however, can also be true. Triandis (1973) refers to situations in which a group possessing power may establish norms that require discrimination, even if persons engaged in discrimination are not prejudiced themselves. This had been particularly true in colonial situations.

In his classic article on prejudice and discrimination, Robert K. Merton (1949) pointed to the variable relation between the two by distinguishing four types of linkages between them. The first type is the *unprejudiced non-discriminator,* or the "All-Weather Liberal." This refers to persons who accept the idea of equal opportunity for all and practice what they believe. This type can be seen as a model citizen in a democratic society. Merton, however, qualifies this by stating that the all-weather liberal has three problematic tendencies. One is a tendency to gather in small groups of like-minded people who reinforce each other's convictions and attitudes rather than joining other groups and influencing them. The second tendency is what he calls the fallacy of unanimity, i.e., a tendency to exaggerate the extent to which other people hold the same views. The third tendency that limits the all-weather liberals' effectiveness to influence others is their preference for private solutions to social problems, i.e., a tendency to try to solve them in the context of small circles and without much clamour.

The second way in which prejudice and discrimination come to be linked, according to Merton, is in the *unprejudiced discriminator,* or the "Fair-Weather Liberal." This is the type of persons who believe in the idea of opportunities for all and hold no prejudice against any ethnic group or racial category. However, they are people of expediency who would discriminate against others when it is the socially condoned, easier or profitable way to achieve their goals. The Ontario Human Rights Commission in its early period of work in the 1960s recorded a case of tavern owners in southwestern Ontario who apparently held no prejudice against the Blacks who had lived for generations in that area. They did not allow them to enter the tavern, however, because they claimed that this would drive away their white clientele.

Type three of the linkages between prejudice and discrimination is that of the *prejudiced non-discriminator*, or the "Fair-Weather Illiberal." This type of person has definite ethnic stereotypes and may believe that opportunities are not and never can be equal, that one creates opportunities only for oneself. They, however, do not discriminate against other ethnicities or races because of expediency, especially if they need more labour or need to do business with persons of other ethnicities, out of fear of sanctions that exist in the law against discrimination. Stymeist's (1975: 59-61) study includes a description of a sector of a small-town community that can be seen as an example of this type. The community was divided between non-Native people and Native Indians. The latter were strongly prejudiced and discriminated against by the former. The non-Native people, however, were made up of at least 18 different ethnic groups, including the English, Irish, Finlanders, Norwegians, Swedish, Ukrainian, Polish, Yugoslavs, Germans, Dutch, Chinese, Japanese, Filipino, Pakistani and others. According to Stymeist, they all had very definite stereotypes, negative and neutral, of each other and would exchange them in local taverns. However, in their economic and other activities, they would draw freely on persons across ethnic lines.

The fourth type of linkage discussed by Merton was the *prejudiced discriminator*, or the "All-Weather Illiberal." This is the true bigot, who believes that certain ethnic or racial groups have no place being equal to others in society and hence ought to be discriminated against. Persons of this type will discriminate to the extent they are permitted by custom and the institutions of their community. When customs and institutions support their position, they conform. But when these do not support them, they become social deviants, possibly forming fringe groups, some of which may be prone to violence.

INSTITUTIONAL RACISM

Although it is always individuals who are prejudiced and discriminate against others or in favour of their own group, we can also speak of racism that has become part of a social institution. In the chapter on ethnic stratification, we discussed the situation when discrimination becomes part of the structure of an institution.. Here we will consider prejudice, in its racist form, becoming part of an institution, or **institutional racism**. Racism can become part of an institution in at least three ways. First, the norms, regulations and customs of an institution may be based on an ideology that holds or assumes that one ethnic group or a set of ethnic groups or one racial category is superior to others. Until the changes in the 1950s, most institutions in the Southern United States were segregated between the Southern whites and Blacks. This included jobs, neighbourhoods, schools, hospitals, government, churches, transportation and so on. The norms of these institutions explicitly required that no Black persons be accepted into the white institutions. A similar state of affairs existed until the 1980s under the apartheid system in South Africa.

Second, there may be no formal racist norms or regulations requiring discrimination, or the opposite may be the case, i.e., non-racist, anti-discriminatory norms and regulations are present, but informal, implicit racist norms may be accepted, consciously or subconsciously, by the members of an institution. Thus, members of a group in charge of an institution may have an understanding that, even if the employment opportunities in that institution are formally open to all regardless of race, ethnicity and so on, they will pick from the applicants persons from ethnic or racial groups preferred by them and exclude others. Usually those in charge of an institution do not see their informal norms as being racist. Rather, they may define the opportunities in terms of qualifications. But what is defined as good and appropriate qualifications may in effect mean persons who communicate and behave like they themselves do. Other forms of behaviour or communication may come to be seen as being indicative of a lack of appropriate qualifications.

A variant of this can be institutional racism in the institutions dealing with art and culture, such as museums, galleries and publishing houses. Those in charge of these institutions will exhibit and promote art that fits their idea of what "good" art is. This idea, however, is often derived from the kind of art or writing promoted and made acceptable by the members of the majority group, or at best middle-man minority groups, in society. It is art that reflects and is relevant to their experience. As a result, forms of art or culture created by and relevant to many minority groups may be seen as not quite being up to par or as something curious, anthropological, folk, naïve or "primitive" or otherwise "foreign." Interestingly, in cases such as Inuit art, it could become incorporated as part of "Canadian" art only after it has been "repackaged" by the members of the mainstream artistic world (Henry et al., 1995: 208-226).

Third, institutional racism may develop even if the norms and regulations of an institution are non-racist, and even if there are no informal prejudicial norms shared by the members, if it happens to attract personnel that individually have definite prejudices against minority groups. There are some social institutions to which prejudiced persons are attracted. Among these are police forces. Most evidence for this is not direct, but indirect. Social researchers and media commentators (Henry et al., 1995: 107-131) have drawn attention to the fact that the police force often uses stricter measures against some minority groups than against others. This is particularly so in regard to the Blacks and the Native peoples. In Canada, there have been many investigations by royal, provincial and city commissions into cases of alleged police brutality towards the Native peoples and the Blacks (Henry et al., 1995: 108-109). Overall, these groups experience proportionally much higher numbers of incidents with the police than does the general population. This includes unnecessary shootings, beatings, apprehension of motor vehicle drivers, unnecessary over-policing of the communities in many cases and under-policing in other cases and the like. A study of the attitudes and judgment making of 251 uniformed police officers in Canada (Ungerleider, 1992) found that 25 percent of the officers were confused or made irrationally negative judgments about people they had to deal with.

A number of factors may explain why prejudiced persons are attracted to police forces. One of the reasons may be the fact that the police force is an institution that deals decisively with social issues, and prejudiced persons tend to see people in clear categorical ways, dividing them into the "good guys" and the "bad guys" and hence are predisposed to decisively approach those whom they define as the "bad guys."

THEORIES OF PREJUDICE

How do we explain prejudice? Why do some people become prejudiced against others? Why do some people become very ethnocentric? A variety of theories that attempt to answer these questions have been proposed by sociologists and social psychologists. Here we will review and elaborate on five different types of theories. Some of these theories better explain the emergence of prejudice; others, their persistence. However, the two processes, emergence and persistence, different as they are, are nevertheless interrelated and hence for most theories it is difficult to identify them as theories of either one or the other. Furthermore, it should not be assumed that these theories are exclusive of one another. Rather, they are complementary. Each type of theory focuses on a different aspect of the issue. Under some circumstances, one type of theory may be better in explaining prejudice, but under other circumstances, another type of theory may be more useful. Yet it is often difficult to identify a priori what type of circumstances are connected with which type of theory. One of the earliest classifications of theories of prejudice was given by Gordon W. Allport (1954: 206-392). This typology has now become classical. The following typology incorporates some of Allport's types, but expands on them in a somewhat different approach.

• Socialization Theory

Socialization theory holds that prejudice is transmitted in the process of a person's socialization from childhood to adulthood. Instrumental in this process are the agencies of socialization, parents, peers, school and the media. The process of socialization is of particular importance because it is during this process that one's personality and identity are formed. When transmitted in the process of socialization, prejudice can become part of one's personality and part of one's identity to the extent that it becomes difficult to change it or eradicate it in adult life.

Parents may transmit prejudice early in their children's life by telling them not to play with children of a different skin colour or a different ethnic group. They may associate the colour black with bad things and white colour with good things and thus indirectly teach stereotypes (Horowitz and Horowitz, 1938; Ehrlich, 1973). They may also point to children of another ethnic group in the neighbourhood as examples of bad behaviour, not to be followed by their own children.

Furthermore, parents may often transmit traditional prejudice against one or another group. This is the prejudice that is shared by the community the parents are part of and is often derived from the perceived history of one's group in relation to another group or groups. This prejudice is usually transmitted in the form of a historical narrative by word of mouth. In the narrative, the other group or groups may be presented as primitive and inferior, or as exploitative or malicious and the like. In the family, at meal times or other occasions, parents may talk about their group's relation to the other group, using stereotypes, expounding an ideology and explicitly or implicitly manifesting their dislike of it with explicit or implicit warnings about trusting it. At the same time, they may talk in opposite–positive–terms about their own group, reinforcing feelings of ethnocentrism.

In modern times, however, the influence of the family on children has somewhat diminished and the other agencies of socialization have become more influential. Daycare workers and teachers have become parent surrogates and a child's or an adolescent's significant others. If the teachers themselves are prejudiced, consciously or unconsciously, they will transmit prejudice to their students. Educational research has shown that students can judge a teacher's attitude from verbal and non-verbal behaviour, even when the teacher believes that he or she is concealing an attitude (Babad, 1991; Hansen, 1993).

Teachers may transmit prejudice by treating students of a different race or ethnicity less favourably than other students, even if unwittingly. They may even transmit prejudice by trying hard to teach immigrant children English. In the process, they may insist that in school they talk with other children of their ethnicity only in English, with the idea that they will learn English faster. In either case, the indirect, even if unintended, message that the child receives is that somehow the ethnic language is less valuable, less important and possibly inferior to English.

The school environment may also transmit prejudice in other ways. The textbooks used in class may contain stereotypes or racism. A study of textbooks used in elementary schools and high schools in Ontario in the 1960s and 1970s (McDiarmid and Pratt, 1971; Pratt, 1984) found that many of them contained negative stereotypes, prejudicial pictures and text about immigrants, ethnic, racial and religious groups, with the most prejudicial treatment given to Native peoples. Another way in which prejudice may come to be transmitted to students in the school environment is when the school curriculum completely ignores the issues of ethnic and racial differences. The implicit message communicated by this is, again, that these differences are something that should not be talked about and therefore, by implication, something undesirable, bad or inferior. Realizing this, many schools in Canada since the mid-1970s have introduced some programs with a positive emphasis on racial and cultural pluralism.

In the lives of adolescents, the peer group becomes a powerful agency of socialization. This is particularly so because adolescent peers are in the process of identity formation, and prejudice against selected groups can function as an instrument in this process. Peer groups provide a sense of belonging, ostensibly by choice, which serves as an identity boundary in relation to family belonging, which for a young person symbolizes childhood and dependence. The need to distance oneself from childhood creates a momentum that pushes young persons to develop loyalty, often strong loyalty, to the peer group. But the peer group, made up of a number of persons with the same momentum, can claim loyalty from its members only if it generates its own boundary that will provide it with its own identity. The easiest way in which this boundary is established is in terms of a negative reaction to another group, to society as a whole, or in contradiction of the traditional cultural norms. That is, the peer group readily develops the "we versus them" perspective. Racial categories and ethnic groups provide a ready-made, easily visible, target for the "them" designation. For this reason, in peer group communication, racial and ethnic stereotypes may abound among other stereotypes, such as sexual, regional, religious, political and other (Brake, 1985).

An important factor in peer group cultures is the development of what the members can see as a clear, definitive perspective on life and society. For this reason youth peer groups are prone towards ideological commitment, because ideologies tend to simplify reality into dichotomous images and advocated steps of action that appear to be logical and simple. Racism is one ideology to which peer groups can easily be subject.

We have already discussed the media in relation to the transmission of racism. The media, however, has been acquiring a continuously more significant role as an agency of socialization of children and adolescents. This is particularly true of television and video (Liebert, Sprafkin and Davidson, 1989). Until the 1960s or so, some of the most popular films were "Westerns," which often portrayed victorious cowboys and usually "savage" and vanquished Indians. This in itself communicated racism against the Indians. The Westerns were later succeeded by films that had no Indians in them but instead introduced a generation of superheroes and supervillians, as for example in the stories of Batman, Star Wars, Rambo and the like. While these stories do not include racism as such, they have continued to articulate, in an even more powerful manner, the idea of the good guys and the bad guys, and with it, the idea of us and them, with us being always the superior winner. While this in itself may not be prejudice and may not necessarily stimulate prejudicial feelings against any group, it nevertheless can lay the conceptual foundations for prejudice in the mind and the psyche of young people. The iconoclastic lyrics of popular music can likewise contribute to the conditions that in cases of interethnic conflict may evoke prejudice and racism.

• Structure of Society Theories

Another approach in trying to locate the factors of emergence and maintenance of prejudice has been the **structural approach**. According to this approach, prejudice is derived from the fact that society comes to be divided between those who have power and those who do not, or between the rich and the poor. In the first case, the division is between the *elites and non-elites.* The elites will always have a conception of ethnicities other than their own as being at least somewhat inferior to their own. The fact that they themselves are at the top of society's power structure is proof to them that they are at least in some way superior to those who are not. John Porter (1965: 60-68) points out that, to the majority elite who were in charge of establishing and developing Canada, this was an obvious fact. The idea of the English and French being the "Charter groups" in Canada was a way of legitimizing the elite ethnicities' superiority in the face of other ethnicities that existed in the country or were coming to Canada as immigrants, with a concession to the French.

In a society that invites new members from the outside because it needs their labour, the majority elites also have positive conceptions of the immigrant ethnicities. However, these conceptions relate to the qualities that are useful for the work the elite wants the immigrants to do, and as was pointed out previously, it is usually work that is less important than that of the elite. The most important work, such as the top levels of the government or top levels of the economic enterprise, is reserved for itself (Porter, 1965: 66).

Further, according to this variant of the structural theory, elites will always have prejudices against other ethnicities, but especially against those outside of the elite because prejudice is an instrument for keeping non-elites in their place and out of the elite positions. Prejudice establishes the criteria of preference in society and makes persons who come from the groups prejudiced against less marketable. Likewise, prejudice creates feelings of inferiority among those who are prejudiced against, and these feelings of inferiority hold the non-elites back from aspiring to elite positions and make them less effective in any competition with them. Non-elites become a threat to the elites if they aspire to elite positions, especially if they can offer skills that are absent among the elites. For this reason, even if non-elites come to fill elite positions and make a claim for equal membership, they will still be prejudiced against by the original elites.

Another variant of the structural theory is the theory of the division of society between *the rich and the poor.* The rich are seen as always being prejudiced against the poor. In this case the poor are not perceived as a potential threat to the rich, but rather the rich are seen as having no interest in taking any responsibility for the poor. Prejudice becomes a way in which the rich dismiss their responsibility for the poor. Prejudice of the rich defines the poor as lazy, indolent, preferring to receive something for nothing (as, for example, welfare benefits), unwilling to take initiative in their own lives and the like. Prejudice is a way in which victims are blamed for their own lot. While it absolves the rich of any responsibility for this lot, it also masks the fact that the poor are poor because they are exploited by the rich. Ethnic groups are defined exclusively as minority groups and hence are seen as being in the category of the poor. Prejudice against them is part of the prejudice against the poor.

A different type of the structural theory is the theory of prejudice against the *middle-man minorities.* The structural position of the middle-man minorities is that between the majority group and other minority groups who are lower in status than the middle-man minority. In this position, the middle-man minority group serves as a broker between the majority group and the other minority groups. That is, it performs certain functions for both types of groups. It deals with members of other minority groups on behalf of the majority group, and it intervenes with the majority group on behalf of the other minority groups (Bonacich, 1973; Lieberson, 1970). The problem, however, is that the dissatisfactions of the majority group with the minorities and the dissatisfactions of the minority groups with the majority group are projected into the middle-man minority. That is, both sides, the majority group and the other minority groups, will tend to blame the middle-man minority group for their problems. Hence, the middle-man minority group becomes the subject of prejudice from both sides.

• Interethnic Competition and Conflict Theory

Somewhat related to the structural theories but different from them are the theories that focus on **competition and conflict** between different ethnic groups. In social psychology, the theory is known as Realistic Group Conflict Theory (Brown, 1995: 163-179). According to this theory, prejudices are generated in the process of competition and conflict between ethnic groups. This can be competition for jobs, for influential positions, for political office, business competition for markets, competition for media attention, cultural competition, competition for recognition and the like. Some of these forms of competition will be discussed in the chapter on interethnic relations.

The theory holds that whenever the interests of groups are incompatible in intergroup relations, i.e., when the interests of one group are met at the expense of another, then the response of one group to another will tend to be negative and prejudicial. When the interests of the groups are complementary, i.e., if one group can gain with the assistance of another, then the response of that group will be positive and show little prejudice (Brown, 1995: 163).

• Social-Psychological Theories

A number of theories explain the emergence or persistence of prejudice in terms of **social-psychological dynamics.** They hold that a social phenomenon, such as war, increased crime rate, economic depression or recession, influx of new immigrants into the country and the like, produce psychological arousal in people. In their attempts to deal with these arousals, people often resort to psychological mechanisms that evoke prejudice.

Scapegoating is one such mechanism. In critical social situations, people often look for someone to blame for their problem and prejudice develops against those who become the subjects of the blame. Immigrants are one of the most common scapegoats. In periods of economic recession in North America, immigrants are often blamed for "taking jobs away from the people." With the development of hostility towards immigrants, pressure is put on the government to curtail immigration flow. A number of studies have tested the claim that immigrants take jobs away from the native-born population and have concluded that this is not the case. The studies show that the contrary is true, that even in periods of recession, immigrants have no negative effect on the employment structure and often, in the long run, create new jobs through the businesses they establish (Simon, 1989; Economic Council of Canada, 1991). This conclusion shows that immigrants come to be blamed without any basis in fact. Rather they become an easy target for displaced blame.

Frustration-aggression hypothesis is closely related to the scapegoating theory and can be said to complement it. The hypothesis argues that frustration occurs when people are unexpectedly blocked from achieving a goal that they thought was within their grasp or was legitimately their due. The unexpected nature of frustration arouses a drive whose goal is that of harming some person or object (Berkowitz, 1993). Aggression resulting from frustration can be directed at the source of frustration, but it can also be directed at other persons or objects, unrelated to the source of frustration. The latter can particularly be the case when the source of frustration is difficult to change. If aggression is directed at other than the source of frustration, it will tend to fall on those who are the weakest and who will not readily strike back. This can explain why the groups that are most often prejudiced against are those that are the weakest in society. In Canada, the Native peoples were long seen to be the least prestigeful and most prejudiced against (Pineo, 1977). Until the 1970s, they were also a relatively powerless group. It is their own organizational and political activity that has raised their status and influence on the government and society.

The frustration-aggression hypothesis can also be useful in explaining the prejudices of members of minority groups against other minority groups or against the majority group itself. Many members of minority groups are frustrated by discrimination against them. On the job, in housing, but also politically and culturally, they often feel that they are blocked from what is their due or that they are not given the kind of rewards or recognition that they should be given for their work or as is their right in a democratic society. This produces aggressive and prejudicial feelings against the mainstream of society or against other minority groups.

"Threats to group identity" theory. This theory is related to the interethnic competition and conflict theory,

A Place Called Home: The Meaning of Being Black in Canada

by Cecil Foster

On an evening like this, with a hint of spring and a sense of renewal in the air, I was once again in love with Canada. Immigrating to this country in 1979 was one of the best decisions—if not *the* best—I had ever made. Obviously, this place can be heavenly when it wants to be, a place to raise my kids and offer them all those opportunities that I could only have dreamt about for myself. But alas, as we all know, as is so typical of Canada, one pleasant evening does not mean the end to a harsh winter. The unusual warmth can be just a delusion, a passing respite at most, something to lull us into dropping our guard.

I saw flashing lights in my rear-view mirror. The police. *Shit*, I thought, *what's up now?* At the first break in the traffic, which had been pushing me along as part of the flow, I pulled over to the side of the roadway and waited for the policeman to pull up behind me. He approached from the passenger side. I rolled down the window and waited.

"Is this *your* car?" he asked. *So that is why he stopped me*, I thought. *He is on the lookout for a stolen car.*

"Yes," I said.

"Your driver's licence!" he snapped.

Slowly, I opened the front of my overcoat and jacket to let the officer see that I was reaching for my wallet, and not for a weapon. I very deliberately took out my wallet, removed the licence in its plastic folder and handed it to him. He took a quick look at the picture and then at me, matching my face with the picture on the licence.

"Ownership and insurance," he demanded. By now he was leaning into the car, his elbows propped on the window, noisily flicking the end of the licence with his fingers, as if showing his impatience, intolerance and superiority.

Through my rear-view mirror, I watched this representative of Metro's finest get into the car, turn off the flashing lights and merge with the traffic zooming by. I still wondered why he was so angry and why he would use that tone for an alleged traffic violation. And I remembered all the stories and anecdotes by Blacks about how they were stopped by the police for driving fancy cars—not that my fairly new Chrysler Intrepid was all that fancy—-and how not so long ago police used to hand out DWBBs—Driving While Being Black violations—just for the fun of it. And I reflected on how in the past week I had tried to explain, as a guest on a talk show on CFRB, why so many black people everywhere are distrustful of the police, why they do not like the way some bad apples in the force treat Blacks and how, as I had said, we all have to start breaking down barriers, build bridges of understanding and trust, stop shouting at one another and open a dialogue in the hope of producing a better society.

And while sitting in my car, I remembered something else about February 24, 1996. That was the day the black community buried the black man in Toronto most recently killed by a police bullet—in this case three bullets and all apparently fired from close range. Tommy Barnett, a 22-year-old, was gunned down when police said they were driving by in their cruiser and stopped to deal with a man brandishing a Samurai sword in the middle of the road early one morning. Once again, the black community had questioned the killing and was calling for an independent investigation. Barnett's family had delayed the burial for 46 days so an independent pathologist could come into the city and examine the body. Ironically, the family included an elder sister who, as a respected community activist, had campaigned relentlessly for Blacks to gain a better appreciation of police work. Now, she found that justification for the shooting was lacking, and wondered how she could continue to work to raise the level of respect between the police and black youth.

I remember my first year in Canada, how four months after arriving in a new country and feeling homesick, I went to the Caribana festival in downtown Toronto and instantly felt at home. There, I found the music, the faces, the people, the accents, the food and the excitement of the Caribbean. Over the years, we would joke that Caribana is the best spiritual tonic for the social and political alienation so many of us feel in Canada, including so many of us born and raised in this country.

One of the great things about this festival is that you never know who you will meet for the first time, or which old friend or acquaintance you will rediscover in the crowd. Perhaps an actor like Lou Gossett Jr. or Billy Dee Williams will show up and mix, excited as little boys at being in such a festival. The parade with its glamorous costumes is secondary to the joyful camaraderie along the parade route. And for the participants, Caribana is not first and foremost about making money, about their festival being reduced to simple balance sheet issues. Caribana is always a renewing of the spirit—more than just dancing, something spiritual.

And over the years, I have noticed how young black and Caribbean people, especially teenagers, blossom during Caribana. So many of our children seem so lost. They do not know who they are, confused by what they are hearing at school and in their home and church, unsure of their place in a white-dominated society.

With Caribana comes a breaking out. Suddenly, these youths appear free, strong and confident. They are proud of discovering their heritage and exult in it by dancing in the streets, just like their elders. Oh, to see the young people liberated! Could this freedom come about through paying an admission fee and sitting pas-

Photo: Dick Hemingway

Caribana celebration, Toronto.

sively while watching some pageant? I don't think so; Caribana's spirituality is fed by spontaneous participation, by the celebration of a way of life.

On the Canadian cultural calendar there is simply nothing like Caribana. Nothing so authentically outside the mainstream that makes as big an impact on the cultural landscape of Canada. Nothing is so beneficial to the psyche of black and Caribbean people in this country. Nothing is so capable of causing the colourful political leaders in this community to be so divisive and so viciously attack one another as putting together one of the world's most spectacular and glamorous festivals. Nothing so epitomizes the mountain peaks and deep valleys of being black in Canada. For Caribana has become a symbol of the divergent paths facing Canadians in the area of race relations: the harmony that can arise from different ethnic groups working together with the financial help and encouragement of the wider society, or the discord and economic uncertainty that can result from too much distrust and infighting.

Caribana is a two-week festival of rhythmic Caribbean and African music, of humour and brotherly and sisterly love openly displayed, of dancing on the streets and meeting new friends, of enjoying exotic foods and, for many businesses, hearing cash registers ring. Caribana is all pageantry and glamour, when men, women and children abandon themselves to frolicking, to decking out in elaborately designed costumes and parading on a route in downtown Toronto, with the eyes of the world looking on. It is a musical cacophony of different voices and accents; of faces representing the cultures of the world and, in turn, reflecting back a peaceful multicultural Canada to the rest of humanity.

Source: From *A Place Called Home,* by Cecil Foster. Published by HarperCollins Publishers Ltd., 1996.

since in the process of competition, ethnic groups may come to feel that their identity is threatened. It differs, however, from the competition and conflict theory because it does not focus on economic or political interests that the groups may compete for, but rather on symbolic interests. A group's identity is tied up with cultural symbols. These can be many, ranging from the group's language, various forms of art, religious expression and other elements of culture. When there is a challenge to the distinctiveness or dominance of any of these symbols, it comes to be seen as a challenge to the existence or dominance of the group itself. The response to this challenge is usually defensive, with group members attempting to reinstate the group by belittling those who speak for the challenging groups and/or reinforcing the distinctiveness or dominance of the group challenged.

In the United States, for example, the large presence of the Hispanic groups, mostly Mexican Americans, Puerto Ricans and Cubans, has made use of the Spanish language quite widespread in many areas of the country, particularly in large cities. Many official government forms are printed in two languages, English and Spanish, street signs are often in two languages and public schools teach Spanish. In the United States this unofficial bilingualism is a relatively new phenomenon. It has produced a strong reaction, however, among the dominant English-speaking population. In a number of states constitutional amendments have been passed, establishing English as the state's official language. At the same time, the ranks of conservative parties have swelled, the number of extreme nativistic groups has become bigger and surveys have shown that negative attitudes towards immigration and the foreign-born in the country have substantially increased (Schmid, 1996).

In Canada, a similar reaction has developed since the end of the 1980s against the policy of multiculturalism (Canada, 1991). In both the United States and Canada, the minority groups do not represent either a political or economic threat to the majority groups. They do, however, represent a symbolic threat to their hegemony, i.e., a threat to the symbols of their group identity. In turn, this threat evokes prejudicial reactions.

The cases above illustrate prejudice by the majority group against minority groups. Threat to the group identity of minority groups likewise evokes prejudices among minority groups, either against the majority group or other minority groups, depending on which is the source of threat. An interesting experimental study among students attempted to test the negative reaction to identity threat (Bourhis and Giles, 1977). In the study, the students were confronted by an external speaker who intentionally denigrated the students' languages. In answer, tape recorders recorded the students muttering obscenities and insults directed towards the speaker.

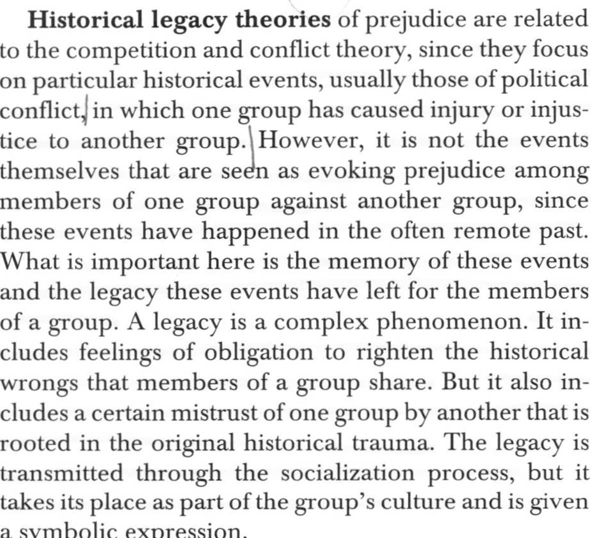

• Historical Legacy Theory

Historical legacy theories of prejudice are related to the competition and conflict theory, since they focus on particular historical events, usually those of political conflict, in which one group has caused injury or injustice to another group. However, it is not the events themselves that are seen as evoking prejudice among members of one group against another group, since these events have happened in the often remote past. What is important here is the memory of these events and the legacy these events have left for the members of a group. A legacy is a complex phenomenon. It includes feelings of obligation to righten the historical wrongs that members of a group share. But it also includes a certain mistrust of one group by another that is rooted in the original historical trauma. The legacy is transmitted through the socialization process, but it takes its place as part of the group's culture and is given a symbolic expression.

Many interethnic conflicts in the present are in some degree driven by a legacy of past events. This is true of the English-French and the Aboriginal-English relations in Canada. In the first case, the past event that evokes negative feelings of one group against the other is the conquest of New France that happened almost two and a half centuries ago. In the second case, the event is the treaties between the two that were agreed to in the past but can be determined to be still binding. Other cases abound: Catholic-Protestant relations in Northern Ireland, white-Black relations in the United States, the legacy of apartheid in Africa, the Jewish Holocaust, man-made famine in Ukraine, Spanish-Basque relations in Spain and so on and on.

EFFECTS OF PREJUDICE

Prejudice has negative effects on the person who is prejudiced, on the persons prejudiced against and on the society in which prejudices are widespread.

Effects on prejudiced persons. Prejudiced persons tend to see others in society in a dichotomous way. For them there are always the good ones and the bad ones, "those like us and those who would like to be like us." This type of thinking influences one's judgment ability. Persons predisposed to think in a dichotomous way tend to seek out only those facts about others or the world around them that confirm the goodness of those who by preconception they know to be good and ignore those facts that may disprove their preconception. This tendency is often generalized into a cognitive tendency to seek out only the information that confirms what the person already knows (Brown, 1995: 94). In effect, this impairs the person's learning ability. It also influences a person's judgment, especially when it comes to expectations of others. Experimental studies (Darley and Gross, 1983) have found that, in the absence of any clear information about the abilities of an individual child, persons with stereotypes of middle-class people, as against working-class people, expect children of the middle class to perform much better in school than the others. This has serious implications regarding judgments made by persons with responsibility for making decisions that affect the future of other persons, as, for example, school counsellors and teachers responsible for academic streaming, immigration officials responsible for admitting or rejecting prospective immigrants at the border and employers.

Furthermore, a person who is prejudiced against other ethnic groups or racial categories is one who will be increasingly unadjusted in a society that has a constant flow of immigration with different racial characteristics and from diverse ethnic origins. As societies become more and more a part of the global structure, ethnic and racial prejudice will be more and more a liability and a personal handicap in occupational, political, social and all other relations.

Effects on victims of prejudice. The effect of prejudice on persons and groups against whom prejudice exists is also quite damaging. First of all, as has been pointed out above, prejudice often results in discrimination. Discrimination has many aspects. Discrimination in employment unjustly excludes persons from jobs for which they are qualified. The persons who feel that they have been discriminated against develop, consciously or subconsciously, feelings of hurt, injustice and bitterness against society as a whole. On the job, however, persons of different race or ethnicity often experience various degrees of harassment. F. Henry's (1994: 106-108) interviewers reported that in the sample of Caribbean respondents, racial verbal harassment on the job was a common theme for most respondents regardless of class. Name calling was common, such as "Nigger," and requests, such as "Hey you," even though the foreman knew their proper names. Of particular interest were the responses of the victims of prejudice to verbal harassment. According to Henry, women most often responded with silence for fear of losing their jobs. Men's most common response was a desire to quit the job immediately. Two social-psychologically damaging patterns are indicated by this study: internalizing one's hurt and quitting. The damaging social effects of the first reaction is that of turning one's psyche away from the racially mixed social environment and that of the second, a pattern of social instability, particularly among the males.

Furthermore, prejudice produces a **self-fulfilling prophecy**. When prejudice comes to be shared by people of a community, those who are prejudiced expect their victims to behave in a certain manner and create conditions that will induce them to behave in this manner. Once they do behave in the expected manner, this becomes a "proof" to those who are prejudiced, and even to the victims of prejudice, that the expectations were correct and that the stereotypes included in these expectations accurately describe those they refer to, as they really are. For example, if persons of a minority ethnicity or race are treated arrogantly because they are assumed to be inadequate, for example, slow and disorganized, and if they respond to the arrogance by being nervous and stumbling, this response will come to be seen by those who are arrogant as proof of their inadequacy. As the arrogance persists, this response may actually become a pattern imbedded in the behaviour of the members of the minority group.

This self-fulfilling consequence of stereotyping was demonstrated in the classical, experimental social-psychological study by Carl Word and his associates (Word, Zanna and Cooper, 1974). In the study, white students were asked to interview Black and white applicants for a job. Without realizing it, the student interviewers showed a marked difference in the style of their interviews with the Black and white applicants. In the case of the white applicants, they sat closer to them and conducted longer interviews. In the case of the Black applicants, they sat farther away, conducted shorter interviews and showed a marked discomfort and lack of interest. In reviewing the videotapes, independent judges saw the white applicants as poised, effective and competent during the interview, while the Black applicants were seen as nervous, ineffective and less competent. To test whether the response of the Black applicants was affected by the behaviour of the interviewers, the experimenters set up a second experiment. They employed confederate interviewers and instructed them to act in the same way in which the student interviewers had acted towards the white and the Black applicants. This time, however, all the applicants were white. The results showed that the applicants who were interviewed in the same manner as the Black applicants had been displayed a behaviour that was seen as nervous, ineffective and less competent, even though the applicants were white. Likewise, applicants who were interviewed in the manner in which the white applicants had been responded in a manner that was seen as poised, effective and competent. The conclusion was obvious. The nervous and ineffective manner of behaviour of the Black applicants was not their inherent pattern, but a response to the type of treatment they had received by the interviewers.

Since, as was explained previously, prejudice is a significant factor in bringing about a system of ethnic stratification, many effects of prejudice overlap with the effects of ethnic stratification. A number of these effects were discussed in the previous chapter. One of these is the fact that prejudice imbeds an inferiority complex in the victimized minority groups. When members of a minority group are treated as inferior over a long period of time, they begin to feel and act inferior. The insidious aspect of the inferiority feeling is that it undermines self-confidence and self-esteem. Lack of self-confidence and low self-esteem bring about a set of negative personality characteristics that often come to be shared by a victimized minority (Allport, 1954: 142-162; Dion, Earn and Yee, 1978). Among these is fear of taking initiative. This includes taking initiative in interpersonal relations with members of the majority group or taking initiative in task performance on the job or in other interethnic contexts. A consequence of this can be a passivity in activities initiated by others or a passive acquiescence to the demands of others. This can also be accompanied by expectations of failure in all undertakings, especially collective undertakings within the minority's community.

Other effects of prejudice are over-sensitivity to potential expressions of prejudice against the group. Minority persons may continuously expect others to utter something prejudicial or to act towards them in a prejudicial manner. While this may be partially a realistic reaction to prejudice, it is also partially an exaggerated, defensive reaction and may have negative consequences for the persons' health.

Effects on society. Finally, prejudice has negative effects on society as a whole. For one thing, prejudice begets prejudice. Prejudice against one's own group can produce prejudice against other groups. A pecking order of prejudice becomes established. Victimized minority groups, in turn, often victimize other minority groups, especially those who are weaker than them and those who are most disadvantaged and have the least power in society. A society in which prejudices abound is one that limits opportunities for many people. As a result, it fails to make use of the many talents and creative work of persons to whom opportunities are denied.

Furthermore, a society in which prejudice abounds tends to be negatively segmented. All societies are to a larger or smaller extent segmented along class and occupational status lines, gender, age, regional, religious and ethnic lines. These segments develop naturally as a result of different interests and historical origins. When the different segments see themselves as complementing each other and as being equally accepted in society, we can say that the segmentation is positive and the diversity that is derived from it contributes to the functioning of society. If, however, the different segments do not see that they are equally accepted, if some feel that they are treated as inferior and blocked by others in the pursuit of their values and goals or feel that their identities are dismissed as unimportant or unnecessary for society, the tendency for self-centredness develops. Each segment acts only for itself. The cultural atmosphere of society comes to be filled with feelings of hostility and mistrust, and commitment and loyalty to the "commons" begin to disappear. A society in which prejudice reaches a high degree is on its way to disintegration.

ELIMINATING PREJUDICE

How can prejudice be eliminated from society? If prejudice has damaging effects on individuals and society, there must be ways and measures that can be employed to eliminate it or at least reduce it and prevent it from developing and spreading. Any methods undertaken to reduce prejudice must address themselves to its causes. Some methods may focus on one cause, others on another. In the social reality, however, causes are often closely intertwined and hence methods aimed at addressing one cause of prejudice may be indirectly reaching other causes.

The general approaches to the reduction of prejudice can be classified as follows:

1. Educational approaches: (a) child education; (b) adult education
2. Contact approaches
3. Image dissemination approaches: (a) informational; (b) representational
4. Discrimination elimination approach
5. Social policy approaches
6. Anti-racism activities

Educational approaches. The main goal of educational approaches is to ensure that the school, as an agency of socialization, does not transmit prejudice to young people and to use educational institutions as a means of changing stereotypes and attitudes of those who are already prejudiced. Hence, educational approaches can be used to reach two age categories, that of children and adults. Many schools today include programs that teach children about other cultures and expose them to different ethnicities and races. These programs may include lessons that give children a picture of the ethnically and racially mixed nature of their community, their city, their country. Methods may include "show and tell," by which the children themselves are called upon to make other children aware of their different identities. They may include projects or school trips focusing on appreciating diversity.

Studies have experimented with various techniques of putting the child, as it were, in the shoes of persons from groups other than their own. One of a number of such studies (Ijaz, 1984) aimed at the development of emphatic skills by asking white children to play "Let's pretend" games. In the study (Hohn, 1973), children were asked to pretend that they were "poor," "dirty," "the teacher," " the President" and the like. The group met twice a week for six weeks. The children's attitudes towards races were measured before the start and at the end of the program. A significant decline in the bias in favour of the white race was found to be the result of this program.

Another study (Weiner and Wright, 1973) asked children to alternate playing roles of members of a "superior" and then "inferior" group. The experience of being the "underdog" proved to positively influence the children's racial attitudes. A study of Ontario fifth- and sixth-graders' reactions to the explanation of symbolisms in ethnic dancing (Ijaz and Ijaz, 1981) showed that, after live dancing presentations and an explanation of the symbols and traditions involved, students themselves willingly acted out the different ethnic roles to which the dances referred. There are other educational techniques of combating prejudice that combine with contact approaches. Some of these will be discussed below.

On the adult level, educational techniques of eliminating prejudice have to do with correcting the effects of socialization and of countervailing all the other causes of prejudice. Although some correction takes place on the level of children and adolescents, educational techniques against prejudice on this level are essentially preventive. On the adult level the techniques have to deal with changing attitudes and stereotypes.

The most standard techniques on the adult level are special courses for adults and conferences that bring together persons of different ethnicities for the exchange of ideas and perspectives. Special courses usually provide information about other ethnicities and attempt to give adult students an appreciation of the issues involved in interethnic conflicts. The effectiveness of these courses depends on the extent to which they can distance adults from their emotional reactions to different ethnic groups and races and help them develop an intellectual appreciation of diversity. To be effective, however, courses of this type need to be part of required training for persons whose jobs involve relations with people of diverse ethnic and racial backgrounds. These include police officers, government officials, persons in business, social workers, nurses, teachers and so on.

Conferences or workshops that bring together persons of different ethnicities and races are more and more a common occurrence. How effective they are in reducing prejudice has not yet been determined. The success of such gatherings as an instrument of prejudice reduction depends on the extent to which they are able to motivate the participants to come to understand and appreciate the perspectives of other groups. At such conferences participants are often more interested in publicizing their own perspective and obtaining their own goals than in understanding how their own goals and perspectives fit with those of the others. Likewise, such conferences are usually attended by representatives of different agencies, governmental and private, and by representatives of various ethnic organizations, many of whom may already be committed to anti-racist ideas. Nevertheless, conferences do produce some ripple effects by which they influence some groups of people who do not attend them. With increased globalization, one can expect more conferences and workshops to be taking place around the world, bringing diverse ethnicities and races together.

An effective educational technique of reducing prejudice on the adult level is "sensitivity training." In contrast to conferences and workshops that attack the problems of prejudice mainly on an impersonal level, sensitivity training approaches the problems at an in-depth, personal level. Sensitivity training allows a small group of people to gradually reveal the deeper aspects of their feelings about others and to analyze them with the help of the group (Golembiewski and Blumberg, 1970). The technique has been widely used in therapy, but it has been also applied in business as a means of training managers to acquire sensitivity to persons subordinate to them. Its use, however, is by its nature limited to small numbers of people.

Contact approaches. Contact approaches are based on the presupposition that to reduce or eliminate prejudice between any people it is necessary that they come to know each other directly, through face-to-face communication, over a certain period of time. A further assumption of this approach is that increased contact enables people to realize that they are more alike and have more in common than they previously thought.

Contact, however, will not necessarily in itself reduce prejudice. Coming to know directly persons against whom one may be prejudiced can work only in a group context in which all are motivated to find out something positive about one another or that places them in a situation in which they learn positive things about one another. A number of studies have tried to specify the conditions under which contact reduces prejudice. The classical experiment by Muzafer Sherif and his associates (Sherif et al., 1961), known as the Robber's Cave Experiment, was one of the early attempts to do so. In the experiment, the researchers first created conditions under which contact produced prejudice and then conditions under which it reduced it. The experiment involved 22 white, 11-year old boys placed in a summer camp. First, the boys were divided into two groups, called Rattlers and Eagles. The groups were then put through a series of competitions with each other. In the process of competition the two groups developed strong feelings against each other, called each other names and even came to blows. At this point the researchers tried to reduce the prejudice that had developed among the boys by having the two groups engage in pleasant common activities, such as eating, viewing films, shooting off firecrackers. This contact, however, did not eliminate the hostility. The pleasant common experiences quickly turned into food fights and shoving matches.

The researchers then created a different set of conditions. They secretly disconnected the water supply, so that the campers awoke one morning without water. They told the boys that they could rent a movie if they pooled their funds together. The supply truck suddenly broke down in a place where, in order to fix it, the boys together had to pull a rope to move the truck. After an exhausting day of work in which the boys had had to cooperate together to fix the problems, their attitudes towards each other changed and the original tensions and name-calling disappeared. The experiment showed that contact under the condition of cooperation produced the expected result. The reason for this is that the need for cooperation subordinated both groups to higher goals requiring interdependent work. It is the condition of interdependence in the context of a response to a common need that induces people to realize each other's importance and as a result reduces or eliminates prejudice.

A number of techniques of prejudice reduction combine the contact approach with the educational approach. One such technique is the "jigsaw" technique developed by Elliot Aronson. The technique induces a class of ethnically diverse students to enter into interdependent contact with one another. Aronson (1988: 276-283) required six-person groups of elementary school students to read a six-paragraph biography of a famous person on which they would be tested. The paragraphs, however, were cut up separately and each paragraph was given to a different student in the group. As a result, to acquaint themselves with the entire biography, the students had to cooperate and each had to communicate their knowledge to the others. The students were used to competing, rather than cooperating, with one another, and many of them thought that some of the students of different ethnicity who had difficulty expressing themselves in class were simply "stupid." To know the entire biography, however, the students had to approach all the others in the group and listen to them explain their part of the biography. At the end they realized that the students of different ethnicity were actually quite intelligent in explaining their parts of the story. The interdependence thus induced the students to approach one another as equals and this changed their perception.

With adults, the contact approach is most successful in reducing ethnic and racial prejudice when persons of diverse ethnic and racial backgrounds join in a common task in which each person is considered to be equally important and necessary in his or her contribution to the common goal. A concrete example of such cooperation is neighbourhood committees, who get together to fight a common external threat such as the re-zoning of their neighbourhood, potential develop-

KEY ISSUES IN CANADIAN ETHNIC RELATIONS

Stereotypes—Can We Think of Others without Using Them?

We often think of other people—especially of groups—in terms of stereotypes. For example, we may think of Italians as being loud, using their hands to talk to others or as being short and dark-haired. Or we may think of the English as being tall, light-eyed, and sparse in their words; of South Asians, as dark-skinned with a rigid pronunciation of English words and grammar, and so on. These are examples of only a few stereotypes. Are they positive or negative stereotypes? Are they praiseworthy or blameworthy assertions? As the chapter on prejudice points out, there is a great variety of stereotypes, ranging from positive to very negative that imply racism.

On the interpersonal level, we often develop first impressions of other persons that are stereotypical and which remain in our minds for the duration of our relationship with those persons. We may think of somebody as being slow or always late, yet that person might have been late only a few times in our encounters. We may think of another person as being aggressive, rough, "having an attitude" or alternatively as being kind or considerate–all this often as a result of one or a few encounters, encounters that created in us a stereotype and an expectation of the same type of behaviour from that person in future encounters.

Stereotypes are never correct when categorically applied to an entire group of people or even to one person's entire personality or life. A special winter 1998-99 issue of *Time Magazine* reported a number of studies dealing with stereotypes of Europeans. A few examples from these studies illustrate how what we assume about other people is often incorrect in fact. Italians are often thought of as loving children and as a result procreating large families. Eurostat survey, however, showed that in the mid-1990s Italy has had one of the lowest fertility rates in Europe, with an average of 1.22 children per family. The French have been thought of as wine-loving and being the heaviest drinkers in Europe. Eurostat study showed that they are not. Others, such as Luxembourgers drink more alcohol a year than do the French. The Spanish are often thought of as addicted to bullfighting. Opinion polls revealed that between 55 and 70 percent of people in Spain are opposed to bullfighting. Germans have been thought of as being hardworking and stolid, but unimaginative. Yet, the Eurostat survey showed that of all the patent applications filed with the European Union, almost three times as many applications came from Germans as from the French, who are thought to be more creative.

Is it possible to think of other groups or persons without using any stereotypes? Is it possible not to apply to them any category of long-standing characteristics; is it possible not to label them at all?

Some social psychologists have thought that people cannot think of any objects or persons without categorizing or typing them. Since stereotypes are categories, we cannot get rid of them altogether. According to this theory, what we should do is get rid of all the negative stereotypes of people and substitute them with positive stereotypes. This way, the theory argues, we will focus on the positive aspects of groups of people and reduce or even eliminate inter-group hatreds and conflict.

Social theorist Alfred Schutz (1899-1959) suggested that the more we come to be removed from direct, personal, face-to-face relations with others, the more we are prone to see others as types. The direct, personal relations Schutz called the "we relations." He characterized them as relationships "in which partners are aware of each other and sympathetically participate in each other's lives for however short a time." The indirect impersonal relations he called "they relations." These relations were inherently subject to typification.

We can ask the question, if all people were to participate directly in each other's lives would the use of stereotypes be eliminated or at least reduced?

Obviously, such general direct participation is not practically possible. Yet, the famous sociological theorist Max Weber has pointed to one method by means of which sociologists can come to understand the people and groups whom they study. This is the so-called method of *verstehen*. This is a method of understanding others by putting ourselves in their place by means of thought and intuition. It is possible to, as it were, put ourselves into somebody else's shoes by thinking of all the circumstances and constraints that the other person or group is under and then assessing their needs and aspirations as being similar to those that we may have but existing in a different social, cultural, economic or other situation.

By using this method of understanding can we become closer to others and not think of them in terms of stereotypes? Is such a method practical? Can everybody use it? Or is the method of substituting negative stereotypes by positive ones more practical? Is there any other method?

ers, crime, natural disaster or the like. Such joint cooperation usually stimulates mutual understanding, reduces mistrust and decreases feelings of social distance between diverse identities.

Image dissemination approaches. In modern society the public images of people and groups are either continuously reinforced or changed. Many groups compete for space and place in the public view. The main instruments of public image management are the media and the public relations activities of any organization, business, special interest groups, the government or community. As pointed out above, the media or any public expression of group interests may reflect old prejudices or may introduce new ones. Hence, in a modern society, if prejudice is to be eliminated or reduced, the use of techniques of image dissemination concerning ethnic groups and racial categories is absolutely necessary. Two types of these techniques can be distinguished: informational and representational.

Informational techniques are those that disseminate news about different groups. If prejudices against minorities are to be eliminated, it is important that the public be objectively informed about these groups' communities. Two kinds of media coverage are important to reduce prejudice: coverage of both positive and negative events taking place in a community and the explanation and discussion of issues that are of concern to the respective minority community.

In general, the mainstream media regularly reports on the events and issues of the mainstream majority community and, at best, of the middle-man minority communities, but reports little on the other minority communities. When the mainstream media does report on minority communities, attention is often given to the sensational and the negative rather than the regular and the positive. It is important that the background issues of the negative be discussed and that some sense be given to the different sides of the issues. Otherwise, only the negative image is projected, and the coverage, rather than reducing prejudice, reinforces it.

Representational techniques of prejudice reduction refers to exhibitions. This would include exhibits of the arts of minority communities, film, video, and theater. It also includes festivals that publicly display aspects of the cultures of the minority communities. Since the 1960s many cities in Canada have introduced annual festivals that celebrate cultural diversity, such as the "Caravan" and "Caribana" in Toronto. More will be said later about competition among different ethnic communities for access to "public viewing space."

Discrimination elimination approach. Prejudice is closely associated with discrimination. Although the two are not the same, as prejudice is one of the causes of discrimination, the presence of discrimination justifies and legitimizes prejudice. Hence, reduction or elimination of discrimination in as many areas of social life as possible will de-legitimize prejudice and show in practice that it is not justified.

The most effective method of reducing discrimination is by legislation that criminalizes it. Such legislation must be imbedded in a constitutional code of human rights to which appeals can be made in specific cases. Most Western democratic societies have by now accepted codes of basic human rights. In Canada, the Canadian Bill of Rights was legislated in 1960, and by 1975 all provinces had some human rights codes. In 1982, the Bill of Rights was superseded by the Charter of Rights and Freedoms as part of the new Canadian constitution. The Charter provides protection against all forms of discrimination. The specific technique that was developed to make anti-discrimination legislation workable was the establishment of human rights commissions on the provincial and federal levels. Such commissions make it possible to investigate concrete complains of discrimination and to decide whether to forward them for prosecution in the courts. A study of the Canadian Human Rights Commission files, however, showed that, of all the types of complaints of human rights violations, cases based on race and ethnicity were the most difficult to investigate (Frideres, 1989). The importance of human rights legislation will be further discussed in the chapter on societal integration.

A technique of reducing discrimination that was also legitimized by the Charter of Rights and Freedoms was that of positive encouragement and the requirement of placing a certain number of members of racial, ethnic and gender minority groups in new job openings. This has come to be known in Canada as *equity legislation.* In 1986 the Federal Employment Equity Act (Bill-62) was passed with the goal of equalizing minority participation in all federally regulated establishments that hire one hundred persons or more. The Act called for efforts of "reasonable accommodation" towards equal representation of minorities in hiring, but it did not mandate any quotas of minority persons that are to be hired. It relied on the voluntary participation of private companies in applying the Act. A number of provinces have also brought forth their own equity legislation. In the 1960s the United States introduced this type of legislation, known as "Affirmative Action." It, however, differed substantially from the Canadian legislation, since it called for devising definite quotas for hiring of minority groups. It also created controversy as to whether such quotas amounted to "reverse discrimination." The US Supreme Court, in its 1978 decision in the *Bakke* case involving this controversy, ruled that, while the specific execution of the quota principle was a case of reverse discrimination, the principle of establishing quotas to remove the long-standing consequences of discrimination itself did not violate the American Bill of Rights. A number of European societies, such as the Netherlands, have introduced other versions of equity legislation (Blakemore and Drake, 1996; Agocs et al., 1992; Penninx, 1997).

Social policy approaches. The development of modern societies has been made possible by active participation of the government, not only in the economic sphere, but also in social, educational and cultural spheres. Governmental policies establish programs that can significantly stimulate future development of any activity deemed beneficial to society. The value of public policy consists precisely in its orientation of activities towards the future. When these activities prove to be successful and assist in bringing society up to a higher level of development, public policies or elements of them come to be entrenched in societal institutions. For example, social security, unemployment compensation, medical assistance, scientific research and so on have all become part of the society's accepted way of life. Social policy, therefore, is also a method that is used to reduce prejudices in society. It is, however, a method that emphasizes the positive rather than the negative. That is, rather than leading to punishment for transgression, as in the case of anti-discrimination legislation, it focuses on developing a common spirit of acceptance of ethnic and racial diversity. Recent examples of such policy are the policies of bilingualism and multiculturalism. The first one, by establishing the French language as officially equal to the English language, attempts to bring about the acceptance of the French identity as an equal partner with the English identity in Canada. The policy of multiculturalism has attempted to achieve something similar for the other ethnic and racial groups in Canada by emphasizing the common social value of identity differences (Isajiw, 1983). A number of other policies and programs that will reinforce the value of equality and respect for human dignity are also possible. More will be said about social policies in the chapter on social incorporation.

Anti-racism activities. Whereas social policy approaches to prejudice reduction call for government participation, anti-racism activities call for the participation of individuals. These activities refer to the formation and participation in voluntary pressure and protest groups that would react to all or any manifestations of prejudice, particularly those in its racist form. The activities of such groups could include monitoring the media, examining the rules and regulations of institutions, business establishments and other organizations for hidden or unconscious prejudicial demands or requirements and monitoring various practices for discrimination. Anti-racism activities should focus on dominant beliefs and values within institutions, particularly the powerful institutions, and examine their mission statements in relation to their decision-making structures and practices (Fleras and Elliott, 1996: 96-97). They could also include the development and teaching of educational strategies for prevention of harassment and discrimination (Ruemper, 1996).

Anti-racism activities can also include identifying and fighting racist hate groups. Some ethnic groups have long-standing organizations dedicated to anti-racism activities, as, for example, the Anti-Defamation League in the Jewish community. In those ethnic groups who have no standing organizations of this type, other community organizations may mobilize *ad hoc* activities when racism against the group becomes manifested. Again, this will be discussed further in the chapter on interethnic relations.

The question now arises as to how it is possible to incorporate the ever-increasing ethnic and racial diversity into a unified society when prejudice and discrimination are present in spite of attempts to eliminate them. To answer this question adequately, we need to examine the nature of social incorporation and look at the unity of Canadian society in an analytical and critical way.

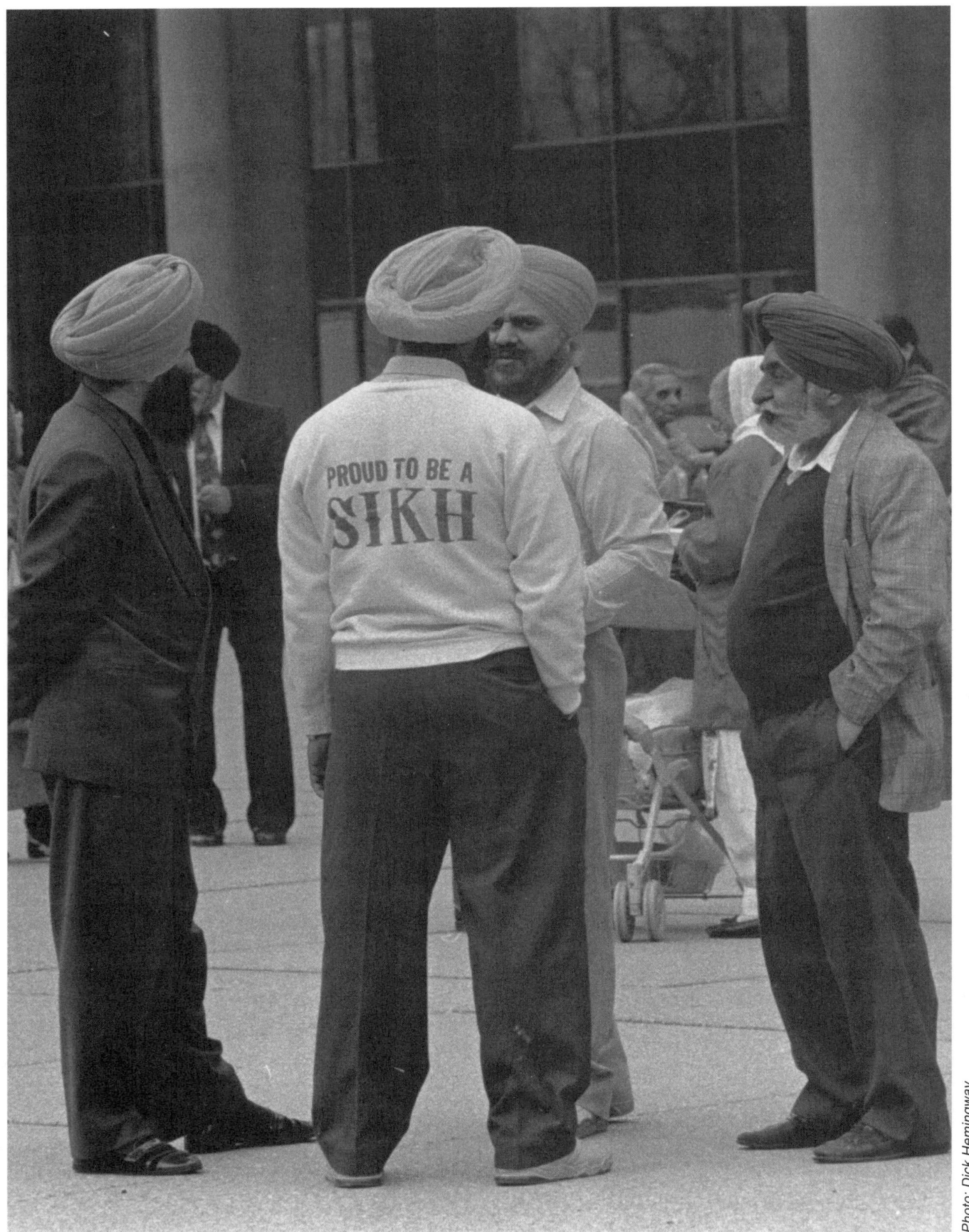

Photo: Dick Hemingway

"Proud to be a Sikh." For social incorporation to take place, the host society must be prepared to meet new arrivals at least some of the way in order to accommodate them and to learn from them.

CHAPTER 7

CULTURAL AND IDENTITY INCORPORATION

The Factors Hastening or Retarding the Process

In becoming part of the larger society, ethnic groups go through the process of assimilation or, more specifically, the process of inculturation and identity change. This chapter discusses the components that make up this process. It also analyzes the stages in the process of social incorporation and the social factors that hasten or slow it down.

The original question was: As time proceeds, how do ethnic groups become an integral part of a larger society? In Chapter 5, we saw that ethnic groups become differentially incorporated into the structure of society by becoming part of an ethnic stratification system. We have discussed prejudice as a significant factor in this process. The further question is that of how ethnic groups become incorporated into the culture and the identity of the larger society.

The process of incorporation into the dominant culture of a society has been usually called **cultural assimilation**. In sociological writings, Milton Gordon's theory of assimilation is frequently referred to. Gordon (1964: 71) distinguished between seven types of what he called assimilation: (1) cultural or behavioural, (2) structural, (3) marital, (4) identificational, (5) attitude receptional, (6) behaviour receptional, and (7) civic. He defined cultural or behavioural assimilation as the change of cultural patterns of ethnic groups to those of the larger society; structural assimilation as large-scale entrance into cliques, clubs and institutions of the larger society on a primary group level; marital assimilation as large scale intermarriage, sometimes called "amalgamation"; identificational assimilation as a development of a sense of peoplehood based exclusively on the larger society; attitude receptional assimilation as the absence of prejudice; behaviour receptional assimilation as the absence of discrimination; and civic assimilation as the absence of value and power conflict.

Gordon's typology was the first typology of assimilation ever proposed in the sociological literature, and it was quite germinal in the development of the sociology of ethnic groups. The typology, however, included several problems that necessitated its reformulation. Gordon's concept of cultural assimilation included only primary group relationships and ignored the secondary group structure of the larger society. To exclude the latter is to ignore a large part of the reality of the minority groups' everyday life, a part that to a large extent determines the other types of assimilation.

It is more logical, we would suggest, to use the concept of **social incorporation** as the broader concept and conceive of *assimilation* in a narrower sense as referring only to cultural incorporation. Thus, as previously explained, the social incorporation of ethnic groups involves three basic aspects: *structural incorporation, cultural incorporation* and *identity incorporation.* Structural incorporation itself can be subdivided into incorporation into the secondary group structure and into the primary group structure of society. Viewed this way, Gordon's concept of cultural assimilation is thus only one type of structural incorporation.

In this book, we have conceived of social incorporation into the secondary group level of society as differential incorporation and dealt with it under the heading of "ethnic stratification." Social incorporation on the primary group level will be discussed in the chapter on interethnic relations as a negotiation process, when we consider the question of social mobility and change of ethnic status. In this chapter, we will focus on cultural and identity incorporation.

Photo: Dick Hemingway

Inculturation takes time. Patterns of behaviour, thought and feeling are learned over long periods, even generations. Meanwhile, new immigrants bring with them values and beliefs that, in turn, also help to shape the new society.

INCULTURATION (CULTURAL ASSIMILATION)

Cultural incorporation of ethnic minority individuals into the majority culture has been studied under the concept of cultural assimilation. The preferred term here would be **inculturation**, since it appears to express better the nature of the process. The term assimilation derives from the idea of similitude. It means becoming similar to others, becoming like others. Inculturation refers to internalizing some or all patterns of behaviour typical of a group or society. Becoming similar to others is only the external manifestation of the process. The process itself is, in its essence, the same as the process of socialization by which new patterns of behaviour, attitudes and values are learned and accepted as one's own.

We can distinguish between inculturation of external and internal patterns of behaviour. Inculturation of *external cultural patterns* refers to three levels: (1) taking over of styles of dress, foodstuffs, manners; (2) engaging in national holiday celebrations, attendance at various functions in the broader society, rule observances; and (3) learning a new language as means of communication. Taking over of *internal cultural patterns* of the "mainstream" society also refers to two levels: (1) tastes, likings, opinions, attitudes, biases, ideologies; and (2) norms, goals and values. Note that each level here is a gradation from more external to more internal, or from more superficial to more deeply meaningful patterns. The internal aspects refer to attitudes, values and so on as learned from the broader culture. The deeper level of this inculturation involves a positive personal response to these values, as, for example, feelings of personal commitment to behave in accord with them. It carries with it the emergence of new identity, which is discussed below.

The distinction of all these levels of inculturation is important because few individuals can be said to take over all of them at once. Likewise, inculturation of one level of patterns does not automatically lead to or guarantee inculturation of any of the other levels. Usually the patterns of behaviour or thought and feeling represented by each level are learned over longer periods of time, i.e., many people take over, for example, manners typical of the mainstream society without necessarily taking over the attitudes or the values behind them. They often learn the English or French language as a useful instrument of communication without necessarily learning the subtleties of the language's idiomatic expressions or without acquiring the modes of thinking, feeling and identifying in which the language is imbedded. They may even abstractly learn the basic values of the mainstream society, as, for example, those of democracy or individualism, without necessarily being motivated to follow them in their own daily life.

• Inculturation of Social Patterns

A prerequisite to internalizing cultural patterns, especially the internal ones, is the development of patterns of interaction with persons from the larger society. Patterns of interaction lead to structural incorporation on the primary group level. Among such patterns is attendance at various functions that are also attended by persons of other ethnicities, particularly the dominant ethnicity. The functions referred to range from those at which personal interaction may be minimal, such as concerts, lectures and rallies to those that place a higher emphasis on personal interaction, such as dances, parties and other informal gatherings. Yet even such functions as concerts or lectures, at which there may be no personal interaction, serve as a means of inculturation to the extent that they expose the participants to aspects of the dominant culture. There is, however, a tendency for members of minority groups who attend the functions at which other minority groups also participate to interact much more with members of their own ethnicity rather than with those of the mainstream. Many members of minorities feel that they are socially discriminated against by the majority Canadians, especially if they are of the Black race (Montero, 1977: 42; Foster, 1996: 140-141). Many minority ethnic groups regularly hold their own functions, and this may slow down their structural and cultural incorporation, but it may also take place together with their incorporation.

In the Toronto study (Isajiw, 1990: 56-60), among the four ethnic groups with three generations, on the average 49 percent of the first generation, 70 percent of the second generation and 72 percent of the third generation attended functions specified as "Canadian" and "non-ethnic." Yet at the same time, 55 percent of the first generation, 38 percent of the second generation and 27 percent of the third generation also attended "ethnic group" functions. Thus, in terms of the patterns of attendance at various cultural and social functions in the larger Canadian society, the extent of incorporation increases with each generation. A substantial percentage of the first generation also becomes inculturated in this respect. The data also shows that many persons participate in both "Canadian" and "ethnic" functions. The two are not necessarily contradictory, but may be complementary. While this duality diminishes by the third generation, it does not completely disappear. The process of cultural incorporation is not a unilinear, zero-sum phenomenon in which, to the extent that one inculturates, to that extent one loses one's ethnic background. Rather, the process involves both taking over the mainstream patterns and retaining some ethnic patterns. This will be discussed further in the chapter on ethnic identity retention.

Friendship with members of ethnic groups other than one's own, particularly friendship with members of the majority group, is a result of patterns of interaction usually established at various functions that encourage personal interaction. It also is a measure of structural social incorporation on the primary group level of society. The Toronto study referred to above ascertained the ethnic origin of three closest friends among the five groups studied. It found that from one generation to another there was a general tendency to develop close friendships across ethnic lines. However, there were substantial variations among different ethnic groups. Thus, among the Germans in Toronto at that time, all closest friends of 34 percent of the first generation and 76 percent of the third generation came from ethnic groups other than German. Among Italians, all closest friends of 5 percent of the first generation, but 45 percent of the third generation, were other than Italian. Among Ukrainians, the percentages for the first and third generations were 13 and 62 respectively. Among the Jewish, however, the percentages went in the opposite direction, 12 for the first and 4 for the third generation. Similarly, for the English, who had only two generations in the sample, the percentages were 30 for the first and 22 for the second generation respectively.

This indicates a gradual incorporation into the general society from one generation to another. However, there are differences in this process between different ethnic groups, and while establishing close friendships with persons of other ethnicities, particularly the British, significant numbers of people retain close friendships with persons of their own ethnic background.

Likewise, for the five groups studied, the percentage of marriages outside of one's group–mainly into the majority group–increased with each generation. On the average for these groups, 20 percent of the first generation married outside of their group, 50 percent of the second generation and 68 percent of the third. Again, different ethnic groups had different percentages. Thus on the average for all three generations, 76 percent of Germans married into the majority community, 39 percent of Italians, 14 percent of Jews, and 66 percent of Ukrainians. English exogamy percentage was 53 (average of first and second generations only).

• Language Inculturation

There is no single study that has attempted to measure how all minority ethnic groups in Canada inculturate and internalize all these aspects of cultural incorporation. The partial studies that do exist, however, are quite indicative. One of the most frequently studied indicators of inculturation is the learning and use of English. Language is an important pattern because it stands somewhere in the middle between the external and the internal cultural patterns. Although it was classified above as an external pattern, language is the key to the deeper feelings, attitudes and values shared in a society. That is, to fully understand these, one has to have an ample knowledge of the language of the people. However, as pointed out above, simply knowing the language or having the ability to communicate in it does not by itself necessarily mean that the person has come to accept the internal aspects of culture that stand behind the language.

The census of Canadian population has regularly ascertained what persons report to be their mother tongue and what language they use most often at home. Mother tongue is defined by the census as "language first learned at home in childhood and still understood." In 1991 (Statistics Canada, 1992), 97 percent of the Canadian population reported having a single mother tongue. The remaining 3 percent reported two or more mother tongues. English was reported as mother tongue by 61 percent of the population (16.4 million people), French by 24 percent of the population (6.6 million people) and other, non-official, languages by 15 percent of the population (4 million people).

The vast majority of the people of Quebec, 82 percent, reported French as their mother tongue, while a similar majority of people in the rest of Canada, 80 percent, reported English as their mother tongue, confirming the well-known fact that there are two main streams of inculturation in Canada. The percentages of persons reporting their mother tongue to be a language other than English or French is the highest in large urban areas. In metropolitan Toronto, 34 percent of the population reported their mother tongue to be other than English or French. The percentage in Vancouver was 28, in Winnipeg, 22, and in Montreal, 18 (Statistics Canada, 1992). Today, large cities are places in which recent immigrants concentrate.

In regard to the language most often spoken at home, about 68 percent of all Canadians in 1991 spoke English most often, 24 percent spoke French most often, and the rest, 8 percent (2.1 million people), spoke other languages most often at home. The most frequently reported home languages other than English and French were Chinese (430,000 people), Italian (288,000), Portuguese (153,000), Spanish (145,000) and German (134,000). What is interesting is that, in the country as a whole, less than 1 percent of people who in 1991 reported English to be their mother tongue spoke another language most often at home. Yet, among those who reported French as their mother tongue, some 6 percent used another language most often at home, and among those who reported their mother tongue to be other than either English or French, as many as 44 percent used English or French most often at home. For persons of this last group living in Quebec, the tendency to use English at home was much stronger than the tendency to use French at home; 63 percent of persons living in Quebec whose mother tongue was other than English or French used English at home most often, as compared with 37 percent of this group who used French (Statistics Canada, 1992a). The census thus shows a strong tendency among the diverse groups in Canada towards the acceptance of English as the language of everyday use at home.

Language inculturation among diverse ethnic groups proceeds relatively rapidly from one generation to another. The study of three generations of ethnic groups in Metropolitan Toronto (Isajiw, 1990: 51) showed a steady and sharp increase across generations in the number of respondents with English as their mother tongue and a parallel decline in the number of respondents reporting other languages as their mother tongue. Thus, on the combined average of the four groups with three generations in the sample studied (German, Italian, Jewish, Ukrainian), in the first generation, 11 percent of respondents considered English to be their mother tongue, 70 percent held their ethnic language to be their mother tongue and 10 percent claimed a combination of mother tongues. In the second generation, the percentages shifted to 51 for the English language, 47, their ethnic language, and 2 for a combination of languages. In the third generation, however, the percentages shifted completely: 95 percent of the third generation claim English as their mother tongue, only 4 percent claim their ethnic ancestral language and less than 1 percent claim any combination of languages. There are variations between the different ethnic groups and some show different patterns, but in general by the third generation the process of lingual inculturation is almost complete.

This process, however, does not mean that by the third generation ethnic groups have completely forgotten their ancestral language or never use it. The study showed that on the average between the four groups, 60 percent of the second and 44 percent of the third generation whose mother tongue was English reported at least some knowledge of their ancestral language. This will be discussed in more detail in the chapter on ethnic identity retention.

Language inculturation is not a uniform process that works exactly the same way for all persons learning the dominant language. Not only may some persons learn the language faster than others, but different minority group members may learn different usage styles of the dominant language without fully realizing that the same style is not appropriate in all situations. John Edwards (1995: 79-80), following Martin Joos's (1967) work, distinguishes five different styles of language usage: consultative, casual, intimate, formal and frozen. Each style relates to a different social situation. Consultative style requires an explanation of the background of whatever the issue is and the participation of the listener in the conversation. Casual style does not require an explanation of the context or the participation of the listener and is often couched in slang. Intimate style takes for granted the knowledge of the context and uses words and expressions that are clearly understood only within a circle of friends or family. Formal style is the lecture style that requires planning, logical formulation and detachment, and the "frozen" style is the written word that can be referred to time and again by persons not present in any immediate situation.

Minority group members who have no knowledge of the dominant language usually learn it in their work or neighbourhood environment and/or in school or special courses. Immigrants who come into the country as adults often learn the language at work or in their neighbourhood. There, they may learn, for example, the casual style of English language usage, i.e., the slang that is predominant in the place. While this style may be adaptive to their immediate environment at work or in the neighbourhood, it may trap the immigrant in the kind of work he or she had first obtained after arrival. Unless the immigrant takes pains to study the language, this style of language usage may become a detriment to advancement to better positions or occupations. This may particularly be a problem for those immigrants who after arrival obtain work that is lower in status than the type of work they had in their country of origin or for which they were trained.

Another problematic aspect of language inculturation is the accent. Adult immigrants who learn English as a second language usually speak it with an accent. Likewise, immigrants who come from countries where English was their mother tongue, as, for example, Great Britain, South Asia and Jamaica, appear to Canadians to have a "foreign" accent. This includes the English from England (Greenhill, 1994: 33-63). While all languages contain a variety of regional, class and other accents, there are prejudices against some accents. In fact, there appears to be a hierarchy of accent prejudices among people; some enjoy prestige as being "fine" or "proper," while others suffer denigration as being "low" or "ugly." Prejudices towards different accents exist because they connote different personality characteristics to people. In effect, these are not really prejudices towards the spoken language itself, but rather prejudices towards the categories or groups of people whom the language accents are seen to stand for. Thus, one type of accent may connote to the listener a speaker from a "high class" of people, another type of accent, a speaker from a "low class" of people. Furthermore, accents may connote to people such characteristics as intelligence, industriousness, competence, friendliness, helpfulness, trustworthiness, integrity or, alternatively, lack of these (Edwards, 1995: 99). This does not mean that the people who speak with such accents actually possess these characteristics. More often, accents mislead in this regard. However, they do influence how people with different accents may perceive each other and, as a result, how they relate to each other.

In a study of how people evaluate personalities on the bases of spoken words only, Wallace Lambert and his associates (1972) tested the reactions of English and French subjects to a tape-recorded passage read by the same person in English and in French. The fact that it was the same person reading the passage first in the one and then in the other language was not revealed to the subjects. Hence the subjects thought that they were evaluating two different persons. The results showed that the English subjects evaluated the person giving the English language reading more favourably than they did the believed-to-be-different person giving the French language reading. Interestingly enough, the French subjects also evaluated the person behind the English language reading more favourably than they evaluated the person behind the French language reading. This shows that the stereotypes of themselves and others adopted by the majority group are often also shared by persons belonging to minority groups (Edwards, 1989). It also indicates that, together with language inculturation, ethnic groups internalize the prejudices prevalent in the mainstream. Yet, on account of their accent, they themselves become objects of such prejudices.

A complex language situation that may often evoke negative stereotypes towards an ethnic group can result when immigrants come to the country already knowing the English language but speaking it with an accent, as, for example, immigrants from South Asia. The immigrants may try to speak a very "proper" English and may use the more formal style of speaking, which, as pointed out above, comes through as the lecture style. In combining their accent with the lecture style, the immigrants may be seen by other Canadians as not only "foreign," but also as "arrogant." And yet, the immigrants' intention may be simply to speak properly to others.

• Value Inculturation

Turning now to the internal aspects of inculturation, the question is: what are the cultural values and attitudes that immigrants and minority groups inculturate?

To answer this question one has to consider first what the distinguishing features are of Canadian culture. Scholars often cannot easily answer this question (Lapierre et al.,1996). Since the end of World War II, scholars have tried to ascertain what Canadian culture is. Of particular preoccupation has been to discern how distinct Canadian culture–its values, its arts and so on–is from the American culture. The latter has been continuously perceived as actually or potentially influencing and threatening Canadian cultural identity (Park, 1957; Smith, 1990; Olive, 1996). While American cultural influences in Canada have been strong, they have also been continuously modified by Canadian attitudes towards them.

When looking at Canadian history, we can say that Canadian culture is made up of at least eight layers. We can discern: (1) aspects of the Anglo-Celtic culture, rooted in Protestantism and the British historical experience, which has left a basic imprint on the Canadian national institutions; (2) aspects of the French Quebec culture; (3) the legacy of the Canadian historical experience, especially its history as a British colony, the historical relations between the English and the French, between the government and the Native peoples and between Canada and the United States; (4) regional subcultures, many of them representing a modification of the Anglo-Celtic culture; (5) aspects of other ethnic minority cultures that have become part of the Canadian experience; (6) aspects of American culture; (7) popular group-cultures, i.e., the current in-patterns of relatively short duration; and (8) the technological culture, derived from the marketplace, i.e., a culture that is common to all modern, industrial societies and that places a premium on standardization and homogeneity. Combined together, these layers of culture create a set of values and attitudes.

It can be said that the minority groups of diverse cultural backgrounds inculturate most readily into the technological level of culture. This is the level that appears to be shared most widely by the communities and individuals in our society. This is the level of the marketplace. Central to this level is the value placed on access to and use of the products of technology, such as the gadgetry that makes work at home and on the job easier, furnishings produced in a standardized fashion, mass-produced clothing, easy travel to remote places and so on. This is the first level of the inculturation of external patterns of culture, but it does involve values and attitudes. In particular, central to this level of culture is the value of success. There have been variations in the meaning of this value. An historical early meaning of it was captured by Max Weber (1958) in his study of the spirit of capitalism. Weber, however, linked this value with that of early Protestantism. Today, the value of success carries with it little or no religious implication. It simply focuses on achieving the position that gives one the ability to obtain the readily available products of technology and, if possible, can bring one fame (Huber, 1971). There are variations among ethnic groups in the emphasis placed on this value, and some groups put the value into a broader cultural and even religious context (Maykovich, 1975). However, the value of success itself appears to be quite widely accepted, especially among the second and consecutive generations.

The value of success in North America is tied closely to a central cultural value, that of individualism. Individualism had been developing in the West since the fifteenth century, but it saw its greatest development in the Anglo-Celtic world, particularly in the United States. It is this primary value that ethnic groups of non-Anglo background inculturate and that to some of them can pose a problem. The North American version of individualism emphasizes the desirability of thinking, planning, deciding and working for oneself, with as little constraint from others as possible. Many ethnic groups who immigrate to North America bring with them cultures with familistic, community-oriented values. According to these values, individuals, in all their actions, should keep others in mind, particularly their family–often, extended family–and their community. Thus, young sons or daughters may hand over all the money they earn at their part-time jobs to their parents, younger sisters may have to delay their marriage until their older sisters are married, parents may feel it is their obligation to their ethnic group to teach children their ethnic language, to contribute to the group's causes and the like.

With consecutive generations, many, though not necessarily all, familistic, community-oriented values become less significant, and individualistic values acquire more significance. In the Toronto study (Isajiw, 1990: 76-82), the respondents were asked to what extent they felt obliged to support their group's causes and needs and the importance they attached to their children, actual or potential, learning their ethnic language. There were variations in answers between the four ethnic groups, but on the average, while 63 percent of the first generation felt that they had an obligation to support the causes and needs of their ethnic group, 46 percent of the second, and only 36 percent of the third generation, felt such an obligation. Similarly, 77 percent of the first and 57 percent of the second generation thought that teaching their ethnic language to children was important, but only 34 percent of the third generation attached any importance to it. These results confirm that, from one generation to another, the familistic, community-oriented values lose their meaning. However, they do not completely disappear but rather become intertwined with individualistic values. We will discuss this intertwining in the next chapter.

There are other aspects of Canadian culture that ethnic minority groups come to accept. Historically, Canadian society has always been divided into two large societies, the English and the French of Quebec, that have never integrated into one. However, for well over two hundred years, the two ethnicities have made up one political unit. As a result, a large part of Canadian political life has always had to do with balancing the political demands of the two societies. Over the years, this has developed a certain sensitivity to internal social diversity that has become part of Canadian political culture and by extension, Canadian culture in general. This has been the root of Canadian pluralism. It also developed a unique pattern of tolerance of differences. This is a pattern different from that of the United States (Morton, 1961: 85-87; Smith, 1994). The uniqueness of this pattern is that, while Canada in the twentieth century has been one of the most ethnically diverse societies, it has shown the least degree of violent interethnic conflict of any other ethnically diverse society in the world, including the United States. While social scientists may explain this in various ways, acceptance of the value of tolerance by immigrants and other minority groups is an important factor.

At the root of this pattern of tolerance is the fact that historically the Canadian government has participated relatively closely in Canadian society. While there has always been the commitment to the value of democracy, there has also always been a close cooperation, or as one social scientist called it, an "embrace," between private enterprise and the government (Park, 1957: 200-201). While in English Canada this close relationship goes back to the coming of the British merchants after the conquest of New France and to the Family Compact system of the first part of the nineteenth century, it has maintained itself, in different forms, until today. The support and protection that the government has continuously extended to the arts, publishing and scholarship is another example of the close relationship between the private and the public sphere (Smith, 1990; Schafer, 1990: 63-73). A consequence of this relationship has been a cultural pattern of respect for public authority and other forms of authority as distinct from the pattern of relationship to public authority prevalent in the United States. In the latter case, the more typical pattern has been that of a form of anti-authoritarianism.

The respect for authority and authoritative institutions articulates in Canada with the value of individualism. The Canadian version of individualism includes a regard for authoritative, but public-welfare-oriented, institutions. Again, to explain this it is useful to compare it with the American version, which appears not to include this element. A summary of American individualistic philosophy has been caught in the popular saying, "Live and let live." In Canada, the saying can be rephrased to state, "Live and keep in mind the public authority. They will help you to let others live." Admittedly these phrases over-simplify the differences between the two cultures. Yet they point to an important characteristic of the Canadian culture.

Finally, for many members of both majority and minority groups, success is perceived, not only as an accomplishment, but also as a vindication. Canadian literature, art and film often present Canadians as victims and survivors of a struggle with harsh nature, hard unrewarding work, inadvertent circumstances, historical injustices (Atwood, 1972; McGregor, 1985; Collins, 1990). Examples are pioneers clearing thick, unfriendly bush and struggling to survive a cold snowy winter, fisherman sailing out to uncertain seas to make a living, broken promises made to Natives by colonizers, immigrants beginning new life, starting from nothing and the like. As Margaret Atwood (1993) put it:

> A preoccupation with one's survival is necessarily also a preoccupation with the obstacles to that survival. In earlier writers these obstacles are external–the land, the climate, and so forth. In later writers the obstacles tend to become both harder to identify and more internal; they are no longer obstacles to physical survival but obstacles to what we may call spiritual survival, to life as anything more than a minimally human being (p.261).

For French Canada after the English took over, it became cultural survival, hanging on as a people, retaining a religion and a language under an alien government. And in English Canada, now that the Americans are perceived as taking over, success is acquiring a similar meaning.

Personal success and accomplishment in North America but particularly in Canada has often taken place in the context of the stories of survival against the odds of one's parents or ancestors, or one's ethnic group, or oneself. The accomplishment thus becomes also a vindication, a restoration of justice for oneself, one's ancestors or one's ethnic group.

• Identity Incorporation

Rather than being a process of taking over someone else's identity, identity incorporation is the process of the development of one's own new identity within a new society. Identity is a social-psychological phenomenon that is not shared in the same way as culture or group membership. It is something that is possessed individually, even though it refers to identification with the same social unit. It is something that has to be understood through subjective assessment or interpretation rather than through the study of common features. Even if the symbolic content of identity is shared, as for example the language, we really do not possess identities *in common*. The object of identity may be common, but each person has to develop this identity for himself or herself rather than take it over from others.

Identity can be defined as the manner in which persons locate themselves psychologically in relation to one or more social systems and in which they perceive others as locating them in relation to those systems (Lewin, 1948). This refers to the social-psychological process of self-inclusion or exclusion and inclusion or exclusion by others. The social systems may be one's ethnic community or the society at large, or other ethnic communities and other societies, or a combination of these. It can be said that identities always have double boundaries, those from within and those from without, self-identifying and being identified by others. The subjective process of self-inclusion or self-exclusion carries with it elements of (1) self-conception and self-knowledge, (2) emotional connectedness, (3) feelings of commitment and (4) feelings of trust and solidarity. Some social psychologists (Aboud, 1981) limit the concept of identity to cognitive self-conception. If, however, the concept of personality includes emotional and normative-moral behaviour in addition to cognition, there is no reason why the concept of identity has to be limited to cognitive aspects of one's personality. Erik Erikson (1968: 22-25) defined identity as a phenomenon of total relationship between the intellectual-psychological, the social and the historical reality. When one psychologically includes and involves oneself in a social group and perceives oneself to be its member, one does so not only intellectually, but also emotionally, morally, and by having some confidence in the group. Hence the four aspects of identity.

Self-conception. Social incorporation of one's self-conception and self-knowledge into a "host" society implies two kinds of perception: a conception of oneself as being a member of, or "being of" the broader society, and the perception that the broader society accepts oneself as "one of ours." Symbols of representation become the main means through which such perceptions are achieved. Identification with such symbols also becomes indicative of the depth of incorporation into the broader society. Thus, one may perceive of oneself as, say, "Canadian" by seeing the Canadian flag as representing oneself. Or one may see oneself as "Canadian" because one has taken part in the election of members of the Canadian parliament in which the elected members are perceived of as representing oneself. One may perceive of oneself as being represented by the history of immigration to Canada if Canada is perceived as a country of immigrants, or as being represented by the country's constitution if it includes a charter by which one's diverse identity is protected or given certain rights. Again, one may see oneself as belonging to Canada because one's ancestors, i.e., members of the same ethnic group or one's real kin ancestors, have been part of Canadian history. Or further, one may see oneself as belonging to Canada because the members of one's ethnic group were the initial "makers" of the country, the "founding fathers" of the country or, even further, on account of one's real kin ancestors having been the "founders" of the country.

Not all members of minority groups can share with the members of the majority group, i.e., the English in Canada as a whole or the French within Quebec, the same symbolic content of identity. Likewise, not all generations of the same ethnic group, minority or majority, can share the same symbolic identity content. Thus, the identity of some ethnic minority group members may never be incorporated into the "host" society to the same degree or depth as that of other minority group members or that of the majority group members.

Full identity incorporation, however, also requires identity perceptions from the "outside," particularly of the members of the mainstream society. There are two aspects of this perception. The mainstream members may or may not perceive of ethnic minority group members in the same way as the latter think they perceive of them. Minority members may see themselves as "Canadian" and may think that others also perceive of them as Canadian and equal to all Canadians, but this may not be so at all. Chances are that these perceptions rarely overlap exactly.

The second aspect of the perceptions from the "outside" by the members of the mainstream relates to the extent to which the mainstream members' perceptions of themselves allow for variations. If the mainstream self is defined in very narrow terms, incorporation of other identities into the mainstream will be slow, if not impossible. If the mainstream's conception of itself as "Canadian" includes only those who are of British ancestry, then obviously any other ancestry will remain foreign to it, and no overlap of self-conceptions with those of other ancestries will be possible. In this case, for the members of the mainstream, other identities, even if subjectively defined as Canadian, will always remain alien or, at best, Canadian only in the political-bureaucratic sense of the word rather than as part of the "true" Canadian identity.

Emotional connectedness. Self-conceptions of identity, however, combine with emotional factors, i.e., feelings of being connected to others in society. Feelings of connectedness include empathy and sympathy with persons who are perceived to be in the same group as oneself. Persons incorporated into the host society can be said to be those who feel a personal closeness to others in the society. This includes both those in the mainstream and those outside of it. Personal closeness involves feelings of willingness and desire to enter into interpersonal relations with others and feelings of freedom and acceptance in interacting with them. These feelings underlie the preferences that persons have in choosing, entering and maintaining friendships. They also engender identity with other persons.

Persons who strongly identify with others usually can "feel" themselves into the place of the others and develop sympathy towards them. This includes feelings of discomfort, pain and humiliation if those they identify with experience discomfort, pain and humiliation, and feelings of gratification, happiness and pride if those they identify with experience gratification, happiness and success.

A person incorporated into the mainstream society will develop empathy and sympathy with the mainstream society. This may be manifested by an attitude of defensiveness in the face of criticisms of the mainstream society and an attitude of seeing it, at least in some degree or some respect, as "better" than other societies.

The reciprocity of this, however, is also essential for full identity incorporation. That is, full incorporation of minority identities requires that at least significant numbers of the members of the mainstream society develop feelings of empathy and sympathy with members of ethnic minority groups. This is especially so if the latter choose to retain some degree of their minority ethnic identity.

Commitment. The above two dimensions of identity and identity incorporation (self-perception and emotional connectedness) relate to, as it were, passive aspects of identity. The last two dimensions (commitment and solidarity) are action-oriented aspects. In one sense, they are those things in one's subjective make-up that translate identity into modes of activity. Once activity takes place, identity acquires an external, objective character and is communicable to others. By the same token, these dimensions provide the link between the self, the structural and the cultural reality of the broader society, as well as the structures and the culture of the minority community to which a person belongs.

Feelings of commitment articulate obligations towards the group or groups of which one is a member. Social incorporation of one's identity into the broader society involves a development of feelings of obligations to that society in relation to feelings of obligations to oneself. These may include a wide range of obligations: to abide by the laws and regulations of the host society, learn and use the language of the host society or teach it to one's children, send children to school,

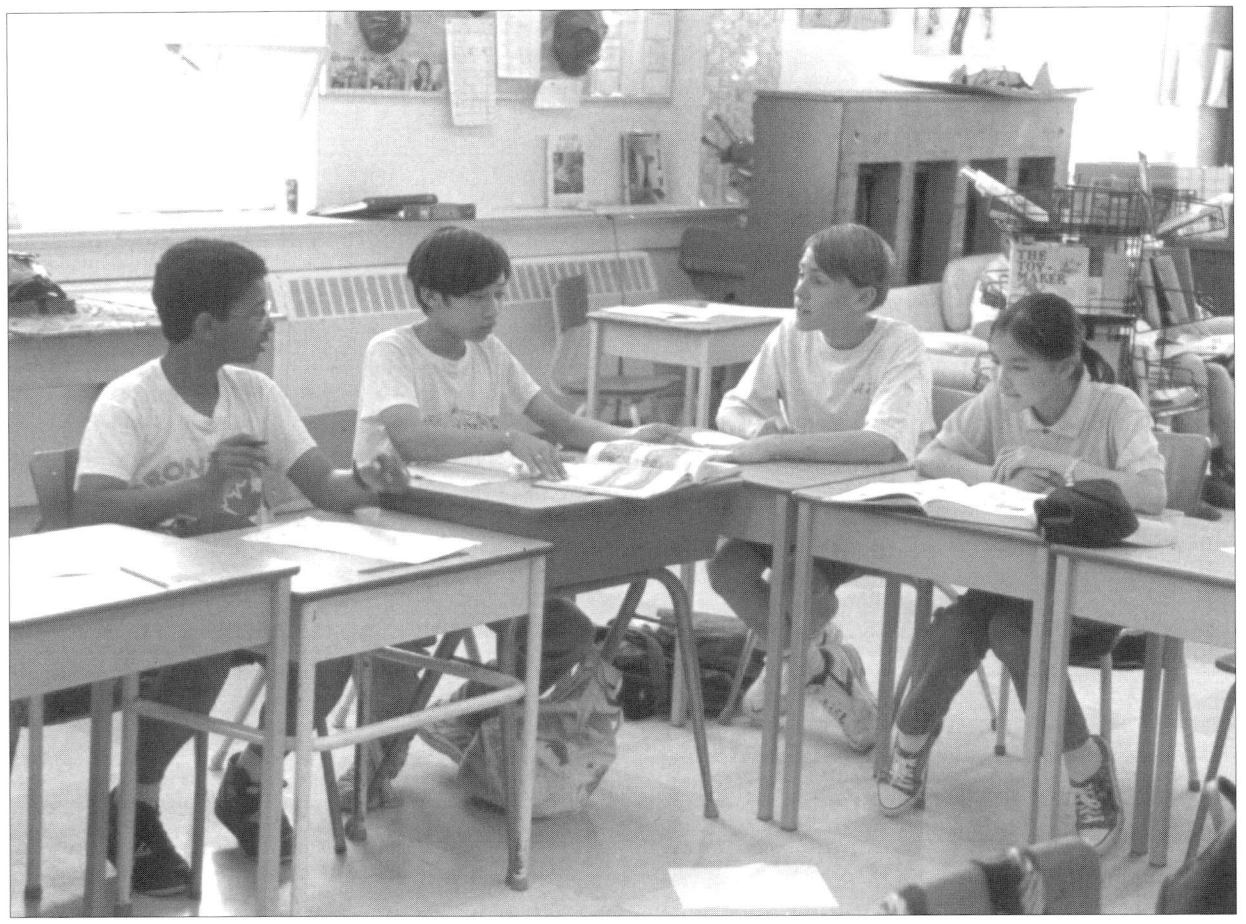

Among other things, social incorporation involves the development of a trust in the institutions of the broader society, including such things as taking for granted that the educational system will offer all children an equal chance to get a good education regardless of their particular ethnic and racial background.

work to support one's family, be on time for work or other engagements, abide by the accepted political process, belong to certain organizations, observe certain holidays and courtesies, deal with others equally and the like. The term "feelings of obligations" is used here in the sense of commitment, i.e., subjective feelings of "rightness," not simply in a purely pragmatic sense. These feelings are the subjective consequence of inculturation of the predominant values. As mentioned before, values may be learned as abstract things and may be verbalized by persons who have learned them without those persons necessarily applying them to their own behaviour. They can be known to apply "to all," but in practice mean "to others." They become part of one's identity only when they come to be applied to oneself in one's everyday life as personal commitment.

Problems arise when the values and norms of the broader society are learned but do not fully become part of personal commitment. This may be a widespread phenomenon in the process of culture and identity incorporation. It raises many questions about the integration of the broader society itself.

Another problematic and probably widespread aspect of this phenomenon is the fact that many members of ethnic groups, while developing feelings of obligation to the mainstream society, still retain some such feelings towards their original ethnic group. These two sets of obligations may complement each other, but they may also be inconsistent with each other and produce psychological identity conflicts.

The reciprocal aspect of the commitment dimension is the question of the mainstream members' feelings of obligation towards the members of the minority groups. Full social incorporation involves some feelings of obligations towards the minorities in one's society. This especially includes the obligation of tolerance towards diverse identities as part of one's personal commitment in everyday relations with others. Problems in the process of incorporation arise when intolerance, prejudice or racism among mainstream members is high. In such situations, the incorporation of minorities may be completely precluded.

Trust and solidarity. The last aspect of identity is that of trust and solidarity. It may appear to be similar to either the emotional connectedness or commitment aspect, but its character is basically different. Trust in others involves a subconscious reliance on a relationship of interdependence. It involves psychological security that one can depend on others for fulfillment of important needs and taking for granted that one can safely go about one's legitimate business in society because "when need be," one can fall back on "them" for support. One can say it is the other side of obligations, as it were, the promise of support in return for their fulfillment. Trust assumes that one belongs to, and is accepted by, a group. The following situations can serve as examples: if persons are hungry or starving, they can assume that their family or the society at large will try to help to feed them; if they are threatened by outsiders, they can assume that their group or the society will help defend them; if they have any special needs, they can assume that their group or the society will try to accommodate them and so on.

Social incorporation into a broader society implies a development of trust in the institutions and groups of the broader society. This may include such things as taking for granted that the society's protective institutions, say, the police, would come to one's assistance in the case of a serious threat, taking for granted that if one follows all the accepted rules, one would have the benefit of all the institutions of society, for example, banks will not refuse to lend money, hospitals will not refuse admittance, stores will not refuse to sell items, other persons will not refuse to associate and communicate with one or will not deny membership, residence, employment and so on.

The reciprocal side of this form of incorporation is the trust that the members of the mainstream would have in the members of minority groups, taking for granted that they will abide by the values and norms of the broader society and freely accepting them in their relationships. The obvious problems are indicated by repeated discrimination against ethnic and racial minorities and by interethnic conflict. It is probable that such complete reciprocity is a limited case.

The social-psychological consequence of a developed mutual trust is solidarity. Solidarity is a phenomenon that can be characterized in popular terms as that of "one for all and all for one." In different periods, such solidarity may be manifested by individuals' willingness to go to war to "fight for one's country," by the degree of positive support of public policies, including that of taxation, by a government's protection of individual citizens abroad, by individuals' involvement in community benefit activities and the like. A higher degree of such activities involving members of minority groups and the mainstream alike would indicate a higher degree of social incorporation of minorities. The practical question, however, remains as to the consistency of the extent of social solidarity existing in the broader society, and the extent to which, like social incorporation itself, it remains segmented.

• Some Empirical Studies of Identity Incorporation

John Berry and his associates (Berry et al., 1977: 36-37) interviewed a national sample of 1,849 individuals with the aim of ascertaining their attitudes towards multiculturalism. One of their questions ascertained the subjective identification of the respondents in relation to their objective ethnic origin. The authors analyzed the discrepancy between the objective identity and the subjective identity as stated by the respondents as an identity shift. The results showed that of those respondents who were of British origin, only 5.4 percent identified themselves as "English Canadian," most of them, 80.5 percent, shifted to "Canadian" identity, 3.3 percent shifted to French identity and 12.8 percent shifted to other identities. Of those who were of French origin, 66.1 percent retained a French identity, while 26.3 percent shifted to "Canadian" identity. Of those respondents who were of other ethnic origins, 59.2 percent shifted to "Canadian" identity, while 33.3 percent retained their different identities.

As could be expected, the study indicated that those of British origin have the least difficulty in accepting simply a "Canadian" identity. Those of origins other than the British and the French incorporate this identity more slowly. As other studies referred to below show, they often develop the so-called hyphenated identity, as, for example, Italian-Canadian, Chinese-Canadian and the like. The Berry survey also confirmed that there are two cultural and identity contexts in which ethnic groups inculturate in Canada, English and French. The survey also pointed to several important variables that hasten or slow down identity incorporation. These will be discussed below.

A survey of a representative sample of 2,433 persons 18 years and older, representing 10 ethnic groups in five major Canadian cities, attempted to ascertain the state of affairs in Canada regarding non-official languages (O'Bryan et al., 1976). The groups studied were the Chinese, Dutch, German, Greek, Hungarian, Italian, Polish, Portuguese, Scandinavian and Ukrainian. In the study, questions about ethnic identification were asked. When controlled for generation, the data for all the groups showed that, of the first generation, only 22.5 percent of respondents identified themselves as Canadian, 50.7 percent identified themselves as ethnic Canadian, and 23.6 percent, as only ethnic. In the second generation, the percentage of those who identified themselves as only Canadian rose to 58.6, those as ethnic Canadian went down to 34.6 and those of ethnic only identification, down to 5.1. In the third generation, the percentage of the Canadian only category went up to 66.9, that of ethnic Canadian category went down slightly to 29.6, and that of ethnic only category, down to only 1.6 (O'Bryan et al., 1976: 100).

The study clearly showed that identification with Canada increases with each generation. This conclusion was supported by the results of the Toronto study referred to above. In fact, the Toronto study's data indicated the shift to the hyphenated and to the purely Canadian identity even more so than the above study. In the Toronto study, for five ethnic groups with multiple generations and including the English, the percentages of the three types of identity–ethnic, ethnic Canadian, Canadian–were (excluding no answers and don't know answers): for the first generation, 17.3, 64.7, and 16.2; for the second generation, 8.8, 34.4, and 55.3; and for the third generation, 0.6, 15.3, and 84.1 (Isajiw, 1980). In both studies there were significant variations among the different ethnic groups. For a number of groups, the percentage of those who expressed a hyphenated identification was much higher than the average. Here again, the data show that incorporation into the Canadian identity does not necessarily exclude the retention of some degree of different ethnic identities. More will be said about this in the next chapter.

The quantitative studies indicating identity incorporation do not tell us much about what Canadian identity means to those who acquire it. Adele Ashby (1985) aimed to discern the common subjective features of the process of developing a sense of Canadian identity by both persons who were born in Canada and those born outside of it. The study consisted of interviews with 54 persons, one-third of whom were of the first generation and two-thirds of at least the third generation. Almost half of the respondents reported identification with another ethnic group in addition to being Canadian. The interview procedure consisted of personal narratives provided by the respondents. In her analysis of these narratives, the investigator concluded that attainment of Canadian identity is a process of accumulation for both those born outside and those born in Canada with their parents also born in Canada. Development of Canadian identity, according to Ashby, is "the assemblage of experiences and insights that eventually blends into a recognizable shape. It is...a learning process in which one becomes increasingly aware of 'things Canadian' and one increasingly pays attention to them" (p.87). The sense of Canadian identity developed in this manner, according to Ashby, is a by-product of the process of self-discovery that ends with a "sense of arrival," a feeling of "being at home." Being Canadian for the respondents also meant having the freedom to have other definitions of one's identity, for example, to be able to feel Chinese when one is with other Chinese, and to be able to feel Ontarian, Torontonian or a citizen of the world depending on the context. According to Ashby (1985: 92): "The respondents who seemed to be the most centred, the most secure in their sense of themselves as Canadians were those to whom a measure of freedom to create their own range of cultural definitions had been granted."

An example of the importance of real symbols with which persons can identify because they represent them in the general society is given in Cecil Foster's journalistic study that attempted to assess the meaning of being Black in Canada. Foster (1996: 162-164) discussed the role that Black politicians play in the Black Canadian community. He focused on Jean Augustine, first on her role as the Liberal candidate in federal elections and then on her and her constituency's attitudes following her successful election as a Member of Parliament in 1993 and her appointment as parliamentary secretary. Foster mentioned the symbolic importance that Augustine had for the Black community and the support she received from it and points to the pride that the presence of this person on the national level produces in the community. This is not only pride in being Black, but pride in the country as a whole as a place in which an immigrant can be accepted on the highest levels and, by this, offers a reassurance that there is a voice in the country not only for the Black community but for all others seeking "social justice and opportunity and pride of place in this country."

STAGES OF SOCIAL INCORPORATION PROCESS

Up to now we have discussed different aspects of the incorporation process. In Chapter 5 we discussed structural aspects and in this chapter, cultural and identity aspects. The logical question that arises is: Is there a time sequence to the various aspects of incorporation? Can we say that structural incorporation precedes cultural incorporation and the latter precedes identity incorporation, or should the sequence be in the opposite direction? A number of scholars have held that there is such a sequence of stages. Milton Gordon (1964) assumed that cultural incorporation precedes structural incorporation. Andrew Greeley (1971, 1974) also felt that there is a time sequence to this phenomenon. The question has still not been satisfactorily answered. One reason for this is that this question cannot be answered without empirical research. Only research can specify the conditions under which one stage precedes another stage.

One can, however, hypothesize that there is a sequence to the process, but the sequence should not be conceived of in purely linear terms. Theoretically, and on the basis of some empirical studies, we can say that the sequence is a process of moving back and forth between different types of social incorporation. Thus, starting with the early phases after immigration, we can hypothesize that the process begins with some structural incorporation on the secondary group level, particularly incorporation into some level of the occupational structure of society. Note that there is no assumption here that incorporation means instantly becoming part of a larger whole on equal or an equitable basis with everyone else. It may or may not be so, and for most minority group immigrants, it is not so. Typically, social incorporation is a process that takes a long period of time and usually involves several generations.

This stage is followed by a degree of inculturation on the external cultural level, such as dress, foodstuffs, some manners and language. This may be followed by some primary group level incorporation, particularly friendships. Again, first friendships with persons from the mainstream may not be deep. They may revolve around co-workers on the job or peers at school. Yet this may be sufficient to evoke a passive sense of identity with the society at large, making the person see oneself as "Canadian," "American" and so on. As a result, the person may identify with the flag and politics of the country and develop some pride in the country's achievements. Some feelings of active identity may also begin at this point, but they may not develop far until the process of incorporation on the structural level continues.

The next phase, thus, is further incorporation on the secondary group level in terms of occupation, educational participation and the like, but notably in terms of voluntary associations, such as becoming a member of school clubs, youth groups, unions, political party associations, religious associations, neighbourhood associations and so on. This in turn may lead to deeper friendship associations, including marriage, and to inculturation into the internal aspects of the mainstream culture–attitudes, preferences, ideological positions–and an acceptance of the values, goals and norms of the mainstream society.

Further stages of incorporation on the individual level involve a growth of the active aspects of identity, feelings of responsibility and trust relative to the goals, norms and values accepted and a consequent feedback of this commitment and self-confidence, into the passive aspects of identity, i.e., self-conception and feelings of connectedness. These in turn may stimulate a further incorporation into higher levels of culture and social structure.

It should be remembered that the social incorporation of minority groups is a process that takes place over several generations and not all persons will go through all the stages of social incorporation. Furthermore, since incorporation is a process, we can speak of complete incorporation only as an ideal type, i.e., as a theoretical case that may be rarely reached in reality.

FACTORS HASTENING OR RETARDING SOCIAL INCORPORATION

Whether social incorporation proceeds rapidly or slowly, or the form that incorporation may take for one group as compared with another, is a question that depends on a number of factors. The main factors derive from the structure, attitudes and policies of the society into which the minority groups incorporate. We will single out the following factors: the availability of opportunities, prejudice and discrimination, education, intermarriage and governmental policies.

• Availability of Opportunities

Availability of opportunities in society is one of the strongest factors that hasten the incorporation process. Above all, this means occupational opportunities, that

KEY ISSUES IN CANADIAN ETHNIC RELATIONS

Diversity of Values: Is Unity Ever Possible?

Immigrant-receiving societies like Canada inevitably come to be comprised of peoples with fundamentally different basic values: religious values, moral values, family values, political values and so on. Even the many different Christian denominations, for example, have radically different beliefs; and the religions of many recent immigrants – Muslim, Hindu, Buddhist and others – present very different models of the ultimate value of life. Such basic differences are often expressed in public on questions such as contraception, abortion, cloning, mercy killing, capital punishment, marriage, singlehood, homosexuality and others. The question that must sooner or later arise is how can people who do not share the same values cooperate without conflict?

This was also a question that was raised in the middle of the twentieth century when different nations of the world were asked to cooperate together in the context of the newly established United Nations. In his inaugural address to the second international conference of UNESCO in 1947, philosopher Jacques Maritain tried to address this question. He conceded that it is difficult to establish a true community if people share no deeper values. Referring to the complexity of modern, bureaucratic, specialized way of life, he stated:

> As human thought is pigeonholed into more and more specialized compartments, it becomes more difficult to bring to consciousness the implicit philosophies to which each of us, willy nilly, is committed in actual fact. Doctrines and faiths, spiritual traditions and schools of thought come into conflict without it being possible for the one even to understand the signs, which the others use to express themselves. Every man's voice is but noise to his fellow men.
>
> How then, under these circumstances, is an agreement conceivable among men assembled for the purpose of jointly accomplishing a task dealing with the future of the mind, who come from the four corners of the earth and who belong not only to different cultures and civilizations, but to different spiritual lineages and antagonistic schools of thought? Should an agency like UNESCO throw up the game, give up any assertion of common views and common principles, and be satisfied only in compiling documents, surveys, factual data and statistics? Or should it, on the contrary, endeavor to establish some artificial conformity of minds, and to define some doctrinal common denominator - which would be likely, in the course of discussion, to be reduced to the vanishing point.

Photo: TEP archives (source unknown)

Quebec separatist sentiment has deep roots in Quebec. Above, a rally in the 1960s by supporters of the Rassemblement pour l'independence nationale.

But then Maritain went on to say:

> I believe that the solution must be sought in another direction; ... agreement ... can be spontaneously achieved, not on common speculative notions, but on common practical notions; not on the affirmation of the same conception of the world, man and knowledge, but on the affirmation of the same set of convictions concerning action. This is doubtless very little; it is the last refuge of intellectual agreement among men. It is, however, enough to undertake a great work and it would mean a great deal to become aware of this body of common practical convictions (*The Range of Reason*, 1952).

Maritain was convinced that no matter how deep the differences between them, all people can cooperate and work together on specific, immediate practical problems and can come to agree on reasonable, practical solutions. Can we apply this answer to society like Canada? Has Canadian society kept together because of the people's focus on practical, everyday problems? Can working together with people with different basic values on solutions to practical problems produce, in the long run, a sharing of deeper, basic values? These and similar questions lie at the root of understanding and living with diversity in today's complex world.

is, opportunities of rewarding employment for immigrants after arrival, opportunities to obtain the employment of one's choice, particularly employment consistent with one's training and qualifications, opportunities for advancement on the job or advancement by changing jobs. The objective existence of these opportunities is the main validation of the culturally shared values of success and accomplishment prevalent in North American society. It is the promise that existing opportunities hold that has motivated millions of people to come to North America, and it is the realization of this promise that has functioned as a strong motivating factor for minorities to become part of the Canadian or American way of life. In a society that places a high premium on success, lack of job availability, loss of jobs, impossibility of advancement and difficulty in establishing self-employment are all strongly dismotivating factors that work to alienate individuals and groups from the broader society. This is particularly discouraging for members of minority groups. Under such circumstances, they tend to turn more to their own group for support with the consequence of producing the segmented labour market discussed in the chapter on ethnic stratification.

John Berry's study of ethnic attitudes in Canada (Berry et al., 1977: 192-196) showed a definite negative correlation between economic security and ethnocentrism and authoritarianism. That is, those who felt economically secure in relation to immigrant groups showed less ethnocentrism and less authoritarianism, while those who felt economically threatened by minorities showed higher ethnocentrism and higher authoritarianism. Berry and his associates concluded that economic security or lack of it is a factor strongly correlated with positive or negative attitudes towards other groups in society.

• Prejudice and Discrimination

Often the factor limiting the availability of opportunities is prejudice and discrimination. In Chapter 6, we discussed the alienating effects of prejudice. The same alienating effects are produced by discrimination. In the chapter on prejudice, we referred to Frances Henry's (1994: 106-108) study of reactions to cases of discrimination on the job by Caribbean immigrants. The most typical reaction was either not to react but withdraw emotionally from the relationship with the white persons who discriminated against them, or to quit the job. In his study of discrimination, Wilson Head (1975: 170-175) found that in his sample of respondents, very few reacted to incidents of discrimination against them by being indifferent or ignoring it. Most respondents showed either anger or became upset and some accepted the humiliation passively. As in the study by Henry, most Caribbean immigrants handled their anger or upset within their own group, by talking about it with their relatives or friends or by taking no action at all. Both studies show that in response to discrimination there is a tendency among the Caribbean Canadians to withdraw, either psychologically or into their close community. Head also reported that a significant percentage of his respondents stated that they had received disapproval from their friends and other Caribbeans for "socializing" with white persons. This again can be seen as a pattern of disengagement from the broader society in response to prejudice and discrimination.

Readiness to discriminate against minorities is in itself indicative of an unwillingness to incorporate them into the broader society. John Berry and his associates (Berry et al., 1977: 181-190) found a significant correlation between attitudes of discrimination against immigrants, ethnocentrism and negative attitudes towards minority groups. That is, the greater the discriminatory attitude shown by respondents, the more ethnocentric they are and the more negative feelings they have towards other ethnic groups. Thus, from the point of view of those who are discriminated against and from the point of view of those who discriminate, discrimination is a very significant factor in slowing down all aspects of minority group incorporation.

• Education

Education has been an important factor of modernization and is an important factor in the process of social incorporation of minority groups. In general, the higher the educational level of a minority group and the higher the educational level of the larger society, the faster will be the incorporation of the group into the larger society. Usually persons with more education obtain better jobs and receive higher incomes than persons with less education. Census statistics show a definite positive relationship between educational attainment level and labour force participation. The relationship is particularly strong in the case of women. In the 1981 Canadian census, the participation rate for women with university degrees was 195 percent greater than the participation rate for women with less than a Grade 9 education. For men, the difference was smaller, 52 percent greater than for men with less than a Grade 9 education (McVey, Jr. and Kalbach, 1995: 325). Education, particularly higher education, has

Photo: Dick Hemingway

Education for diversity. Daycare centres and schools facilitate the incorporation of new immigrants and their offspring by promoting economic mobility, social participation and tolerance.

been an important channel of social mobility for all ethnic groups and hence a factor of change of the groups' ethnic status and of their closer incorporation into the broader society.

Education, however, functions as much more than simply a channel of socio-economic mobility. Higher educational background results in better language facility. This can be a significant asset in interpersonal and occupational relations and be an important factor of incorporation into the primary level group structure. This is especially significant for minority group women (Ghosh, 1984). Further, education helps one function better in technological society and as Ghosh points out gives one, especially women, greater access to information and codes regarding matters of personal appearance that minimize social distance. Educated persons also tend to participate more in the wider community organizations, in cultural, civic and political activities (Ghosh, 1984).

Education is also related to tolerance of other ethnic groups. In general, the higher the education, the higher the tolerance of other groups. John Berry's study (Berry et al., 1977: 163-166) showed that, on all questions regarding tolerance of ethnic groups and immigrants, respondents with more education, but especially respondents with higher education, were more tolerant than those with less education. This is particularly important as a factor of minority group incorporation that is derived from the mainstream society.

Education, however, also functions in a way that can bring about special tensions and conflict over the question of incorporation. Since World War II, the history of minority group relations in North America and in other parts of the world reveals that when minority groups develop their own educated elites, they begin to exert demands on the broader society for civil rights, social justice and recognition. In other words, while education, especially higher education, works to stimulate minority social mobility into the structure of the broader society, it also functions to make members of minority groups more conscious of their backgrounds and hence may create new boundaries between them and the broader society. This may appear to be paradoxical. Exerting demands on society, however, may be seen as an indicator of a group's incorporation into the broader society inasmuch as it reflects inculturation into the socio-political values of the society. More will be said about minority group elites and their demands in the chapter on interethnic relations as a process of negotiation.

• Intermarriage

In a society like Canada or the United States, the intermarriage of persons of different ethnic identities is itself a form of incorporation into the primary group level of the broader society. Intermarriage, however, is also a factor influencing a loss of ethnic identity in consecutive generations. It affects the inculturation and the identity formation processes. Jay Goldstein and Alexander Segall (1985) conducted interviews with a sample of 524 residents of Winnipeg with the goal of ascertaining how intermarriage affects the ethnic identity of their adult children. Their results showed that ethnically mixed parentage tended to be associated with lower levels of both the external and the internal dimensions of ethnic identity. This finding was also confirmed by the findings of the Toronto study (Isajiw, 1983).

Ethnic intermarriage can thus be seen as a factor hastening the process of social incorporation by effecting a greater loss of ethnic identity. However, loss of minority ethnic identity should not be seen as a positive indicator of identity incorporation, because loss of ethnic identity may not necessarily be accompanied by an equal development of the mainstream identity or the broader societal identity. Loss of an identity may simply produce an anomic personality, a personality without a definite identity or a personality of confused identity. Empirical studies of this phenomenon are needed. More discussion of it will be presented in the next chapter.

• Rigidity or Flexibility of the System

An important general factor of incorporation is the rigidity or flexibility of the social system into which ethnic groups incorporate. By rigidity or flexibility of the system is meant the extent to which the society is willing to allow members of different ethnic groups into its own structure, culture and identity. In practice, this means the extent to which the mainstream elite is willing to accept members of other ethnic groups into its own ranks, the extent to which this elite defines its own identity and the identity of the society in more than terms of a single ethnicity and the extent to which this elite is willing to develop social policies that would give recognition to diverse ethnic groups.

In general, the Canadian society has been a relatively flexible system. On the level of popular culture, many minority customs, festivals, foodstuffs, art, music, words or expressions, etc., have become part of the "national" culture. For example, Oktoberfest, Inuit art, Native Indian art and elements of clothing, jazz, such words as "hutzpah," "pasta," "perogies" and so on are often appreciated or used by members of the mainstream as part of their daily life. This is the reciprocal aspect of the inculturation process. That is, while individual members of minority groups internalize the elements of the mainstream culture, the mainstream culture itself has changed and modified itself over the years by incorporating some elements of minority group cultures. This reciprocal cultural incorporation works in a selective fashion, by which only some elements of minority ethnic cultures are incorporated into the mainstream culture.

The incorporation of elements of other cultures into the mainstream culture of society, however, may pose a symbolic threat to the society's dominant ethnic group. This may produce defense reactions and interethnic conflicts over symbolic issues that go deeper than conflicts over practical issues. We will discuss this and the other aspects of the rigidity-flexibility issue–social mobility and social policies–in the chapter on interethnic relations as a negotiation process.

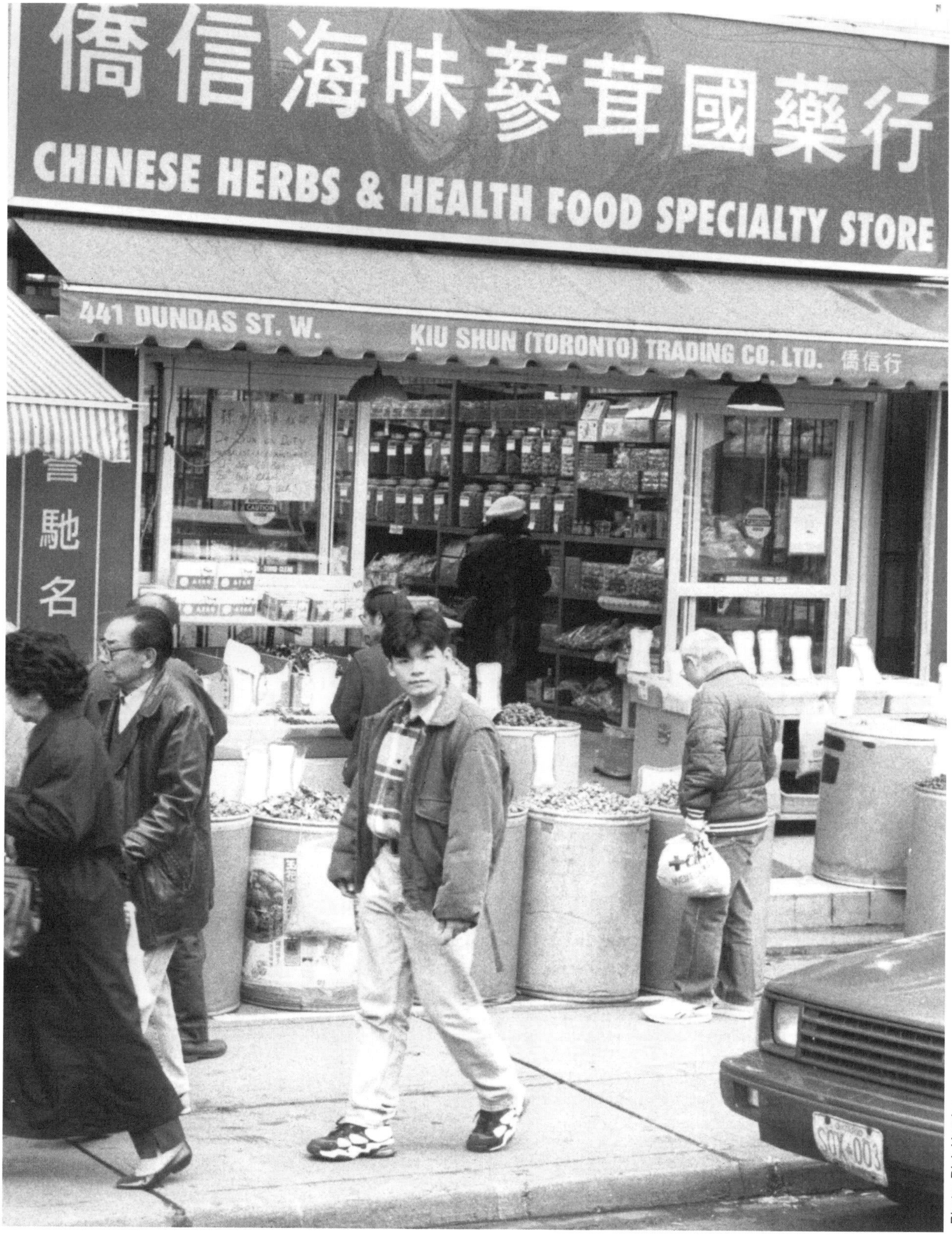

Old Chinatown in Toronto.

Photo: Dick Hemingway

CHAPTER 8

ETHNIC IDENTITY RETENTION

Communities in Transition

While members of diverse ethnic groups adapt to the dominant culture, they also select and retain some elements of their diverse identities. In this process, the younger generation often conflicts with the older generation. Different persons handle the worlds of two cultures and identities in different ways. This chapter discusses the ways in which this identity doubleness comes to be negotiated. It also examines the factors that help to maintain diverse identities and the social change that this retention stimulates.

In the previous chapter, we saw that the process of social incorporation does not necessarily mean a complete loss or rejection of one's ethnic identity. Rather, as persons become structurally and culturally incorporated, they often still retain some aspects of their ethnic identity. In varying degrees, a person may develop and retain multiple identities. In the global society, in which people often move from one place to another, multiple identities become commonplace. In regard to ethnicity, a typical pattern that has developed among minority groups is what is known as "hyphenated" identity, i.e., an identity with both the larger society and the ethnic group of one's ancestry, as, for example, Italian-Canadian, Chinese-Canadian and so on. (The trend today, however, is to write the two identities without the hyphen.) Furthermore, a person may have different minority ancestries on their father's and mother's side and as a result develop a double ethnic minority identity in addition to the identity with the larger society.

In addition to ethnic identities, people possess gender identity, age identity, regional identities, religious identities, class identities. The latter divide themselves further into various occupational identities. Further, persons often possess identities deriving from their membership in voluntary associations, such as clubs or other organizations. All these identities have to be managed one against the other, and different persons and groups develop different strategies to do so. Ethnic identity becomes one among the other identities that has to be managed in relation to them. In this chapter, we will try to explain what this "management" involves, particularly as it relates to the different ethnic generations.

In the previous chapter it was shown that the process of social incorporation does not necessarily mean complete substitution of ethnic minority identity by mainstream identity, but rather a simultaneous retention of some aspects of ethnic identity. For example, it was mentioned that persons may participate in both the functions of the mainstream society and those of the ethnic minority community. They also may fulfil their commitments as members of the society at large and feel a part of it, but also feel some obligations towards the group of their origin. The questions that will be considered here are of two kinds, empirical and theoretical. That is, how much of ethnic identity is retained from one generation to another and what aspects of ethnic identity are retained most? Further, how do we explain this retention? That is, what are the dynamics of this process and what factors contribute to the retention of ethnic identity, particularly from one generation to another?

In the previous chapter, we defined the meaning of identity and analytically distinguished its external and internal elements. Now we will apply this framework to assess retention of ethnic identity among Canadian groups, particularly ethnic identity retention from one generation to another. In other words, ethnic identity involves all the same elements as identity with any society, as singled out in the previous chapter. The difference is that the group of inclusion is not society at large, or its majority group, but a minority group that has a link with a different culture.

STUDIES OF ETHNIC IDENTITY RETENTION

A number of studies have shown that there is a considerable retention of ethnic identity among Canadian ethnic groups, but different ethnic groups retain their identity in different degrees (Weinfeld, 1994). Driedger (1975) studied a random sample of 1,560 students at the University of Manitoba to assess the differences in ethnic identity between different groups. He asked the students questions about six external aspects of identity: ethnic best friends, ethnic education, participation in ethnic organizations, ethnic language use, endogamy in the family and religious practice. His findings showed a great variation among the seven groups analyzed in the extent of retention of these patterns. Some groups, such as the French and Jews, were high retainers, others, such as the Scandinavians, were low retainers, while still others, such as the Germans, Ukrainians, Polish and British, were in the middle, involving significant percentages of retention of some of these patterns and little or no retention of others. Among the latter groups, the most highly retained external patterns were endogamy in the students' families, ethnic education and religious practice in the ethnic community. The least retained patterns were ethnic friendships (except for the British), participation in ethnic organizations and the use of ethnic language.

A study by O'Bryan, Reitz and Kuplowska (1976) focused on one element of ethnic identity, ethnic language. It tried to assess the extent of ethnic language knowledge and use and the attitudes towards language retention among members of 10 selected ethnic groups; the Chinese, Dutch, German, Greek, Hungarian, Italian, Polish, Portuguese, Scandinavian and Ukrainian. The special value of the study consisted of two of its features. First, it used a sample of 2,433 adults representative of 1,343,595 persons living in the five largest Canadian cities: Montreal, Toronto, Winnipeg, Edmonton and Vancouver. Second, the sample included three generations. The generational factor is one that had been little studied in Canadian sociology preceding this study. Even 20 years after the study, it is still only occasionally used in research samples.

The results of the sample showed that ethnic language knowledge and language use are strongly related to generation. That is, while the first generation retains both in a very high degree, the second and third generations lose both rather quickly. The authors point out that knowledge and use of a language depend to a large extent on the opportunities available for the language's use. As the younger generations come to depend less on the economic and social life of their ethnic group, these opportunities are reduced more and more to home. But while the language aspect of ethnic identity experiences a loss from generation to generation on the external, behavioural level, on the internal, attitudinal level, it shows a significant retention. In O'Bryan, Reitz and Kuplowska's (1976: 131) study, almost 50 percent of the second and more than 30 percent of the third generation would insist or encourage their children to take ethnic language courses were they available in local public primary and secondary schools.

Anthony Richmond's (1974b) study of ethnic groups in Toronto showed even higher percentages of identity retention. Richmond asked his respondents the classical question as to whether they see themselves as ethnic, hyphenated ethnic or Canadian. His results showed that, in the second generation, 68 percent, and in the third generation, as many as 56 percent, of the respondents identified themselves as either ethnic or hyphenated ethnic.

Baha Abu-Laban (1980: 4; 202-226) studied Arab Canadians in Toronto and Montreal to ascertain their social status and their identity retention. His sample consisted of 349 respondents, representative of the various sectors of the Arab community. The survey was done in 1974. The sample included generations, as measured by place of birth outside Canada and in Canada. Those born in Canada might have included both second and third generations, although apparently the majority of them were second generation. Like other studies, his findings showed a decline of ethnic identity from the non-Canadian to the Canadian-born generations, yet a retention by significant percentages of the Canadian-born generations. According to his measure of the strength of identity, the immigrant generation included 70 percent of persons whose ethnic identity strength was either "high or medium."

Of the Canadian-born generations, however, only 42 percent could be classified as "high or medium" in their identity; 58 percent were classified as "low." Similar generational differences were manifested in term of close ethnic friendship, use of ethnic language and other identity indicators. While 57 percent of foreign-born respondents spoke Arabic at home "often" and 20 percent only "sometimes," 49 percent of the Canadian-born generations spoke the language at home "sometimes" and only 21 percent "often." The percentages were similar for both the Canadian-born Christian Arabs and the Canadian-born Muslim Arabs.

• Toronto Study of Ethnic Identity Retention

The most intensive study of ethnic identity retention was part of the Toronto study of nine ethnic groups surveyed in 1979 (Breton, Isajiw, Kalbach and Reitz, 1990). The groups studied included the Chinese, Portuguese, West Indian, German, Italian, Jewish, English (first and second generations only) and "Majority Canadians," consisting of the English, Scottish, Irish and Welsh whose families have been in Canada for three or more generations. The sample was random and representative of Metropolitan Toronto, consisting of 2,338 respondents. The distinctive feature of the study was that it included a subsample of three generations of four groups–German, Italian, Jewish and Ukrainian–and two generations of the English. The four groups with three generations included 350 persons from each group, 150 representing the first generation, 100, the second, and 100, the third.

The objective of the part of the study dealing with ethnic identity was to ascertain which aspects of ethnic identity are retained most from one generation to another, how extensive is the retention and what differences there are between ethnic groups in regard to what and how much is retained from one generation to another. A basic assumption of the study was that identity has many aspects or components. Many sociological researchers of ethnic identity have tried in the past to measure ethnic identity by one or a few variables, such as knowledge of ethnic language, reported parental origin or self-inclusion in a pure or hyphenated ethnic category. It was felt that such measurement of identity was inadequate and that the phenomenon of ethnic identity was sufficiently complex to require a much greater variety of indicators. The conceptual framework employed in the study made the distinction between the external and the internal aspects of ethnic identity. A total of 16 indicators of the external aspects and 9 indicators of the internal aspects were chosen. The former included knowledge of ethnic mother tongue, knowledge of ethnic language if mother tongue is English, ability to read the ethnic language, ability to write the ethnic language, frequency of use of the ethnic language, speaking the ethnic language to parents, speaking the ethnic language to one's children, retention of ethnic friends, frequency of participation in ethnic functions, use of ethnic recreational facilities, reading ethnic newspapers, listening to ethnic radio or television programs, eating own ethnic group's food on calendar holidays, eating own ethnic group's food at other times, practising ethnic customs and possession of ethnic ornamental and artistic articles. The indicators of the internal aspects of ethnic identity included feelings regarding importance or significance of one's ethnic background, feelings of closeness of ties with the ethnic community, subjective identification as being either ethnic, ethnic-Canadian or Canadian, and six kinds of feelings of obligation–to have a job that would benefit one's group, to hire other members of one's group if one is in a position to do so, to help other members of one's group to find a job, to marry within the group, to support one's group's causes and needs, and to teach one's children one's ethnic language.

The results of the study are summarized in Table 19 (Isajiw, 1990: 83-85). They show that there is a substantial variation in ethnic identity retention between the different ethnic groups. Some groups are high retainers, other groups are low retainers. The highest overall retainers in the study were the Jewish groups, followed by Ukrainians, Italians, English, "Majority Canadians," and Germans. Germans were by far the lowest overall retainers. One has to be careful in generalizing any finding to all groups. If however, we add up and average these groups' percentages of retention in each generation, the average retention of the external aspects of ethnic identity for each generation is as follows: about 59 percent for the first generation, 44 percent for the second generation, and 30 percent for the third generation. Note that the average percentage for the first generation is not near 100. There are, however, differences in the averages between the ethnic groups studied. Thus we find that 52 percent of the Jewish, 51 percent of the Ukrainian, 47 percent of the Italian and 34 percent of both the English and the German second generation significantly retain the external aspects of ethnic identity. In the third generation, we find that on the average about 49 percent of the Jewish, 30 percent of the Ukrainian and the Italian, 25 percent of the "Majority Canadian," and only 14 percent of the German third generation retain the relevant indicators of external ethnic identity.

The internal aspects of ethnic identity are retained in a similar though somewhat lesser degree. Thus among the six groups with the generational component, about 47 percent of the first generation, 36 percent of the second generation and 27 percent of the third generation in the Toronto study answered positively on the nine (collapsed into six in the table) internal ethnic identity factors. Again, there are significant variations among the ethnic groups. In the second generation, 61 percent of the Jewish, 42 percent of the Ukrainians, 37 percent of the Italians, 21 percent of the English and 19 percent of the Germans showed a

Table 19: Ethnic Identity Retention by Ethnic Origin and Generation (Percentages)

Aspects of ethnic identity retained	Generation	Ethnic Origin					
		Majority Canadian	English	German	Italian	Jewish	Ukrainian
External Aspects							
Ethnic mother tongue	1 2 3	- - -	- - -	90 34 1	99 62 3	34 23 0	92 71 12
Knowledge of ethnic language (by those whose mother tongue is English)	1 2 3	- - -	- - -	60 41 12	- 55 46	60 86 69	- 56 48
Read ethnic language	1 2 3	- - -	- - -	89 54 17	92 38 17	58 42 46	78 53 10
Write ethnic language	1 2 3	- -	- -	85 43 17	89 27 8	49 25 25	78 50 10
Frequent use of ethnic language ("every day" and "often")	1 2 3	- - -	- - -	57 30 0	94 74 10	43 15 9	84 58 9
Occasional use of ethnic language	1 2 3	- -	- -	27 31 25	3 10 23	23 24 17	10 23 24
1-2 closest friends of own ethnicity	1 2 3	- - 39	43 35 -	51 29 23	30 47 45	36 42 41	41 46 35
3 closest friends of own ethnicity	1 2 3	- - 19	27 43 -	15 0 1	65 32 10	52 51 55	46 20 3
Participation in ethnic-group functions	1 2 3	- - 17	22 32 -	33 7 6	71 46 28	46 50 41	71 49 33
Usage of ethnic-group-sponsored vacation facilities	1 2 3	- - 5	12 13 -	5 2 4	17 4 6	19 28 37	46 13 2
Hear/watch ethnic radio/TV	1 2 3	- - 30	65 51 -	61 24 1	84 30 13	48 30 26	61 35 18
Read ethnic newspapers/ magazines, periodicals	1 2 3	- - 15	31 17 -	51 15 2	69 17 6	59 57 55	63 20 1
Practice of ethnic traditions:							
1. Eat ethnic food on holidays/special occasions	1 2 3	- - 30	52 38 -	70 58 28	96 87 74	90 95 91	92 89 86
2. Eat ethnic food at times other than holidays and special occasions	1 2 3	- - 34	67 54 -	94 77 52	97 98 92	92 91 87	91 92 82
3. Observe ethnic customs	1 2 3	- - 25	31 20 -	59 45 15	70 59 39	85 90 90	92 67 47
4. Possess ethnic articles	1 2 3	- - -	59 32 -	63 54 23	84 74 64	87 85 93	96 80 64

Internal Aspects							
Intensity of ethnic identity (Ethnic Identity Index):							
High	1	-	29	14	58	51	60
	2	-	5	9	29	46	27
	3	3	-	1	14	49	10
Medium	1	-	38	39	34	32	28
	2	-	32	24	41	34	38
	3	17	-	10	33	25	35
Group Obligations:							
				34	56	57	66
1. Help group members find jobs	1	-	26	32	45	62	54
	2	-	25	20	45	67	53
	3	26	-				
2. Marry in-group	1	-	8	7	39	73	61
	2	-	14	2	10	78	20
	3	7	-	2	4	66	5
3. Support group needs and 4 causes	1	-	24	24	65	82	79
	2	-	27	7	40	86	49
	3	11	-	7	20	80	36
4. Teach children ethnic language	1	-	-	65	94	64	83
	2	-	-	42	58	60	66
	3	-	-	15	31	54	37

Source: Breton, Isajiw, Kalbach & Reitz (1990). Table 2.13. *Ethnic Identity and Equality.* Toronto: University of Toronto Press, pp.83-85.

significant retention of the nine internal identity aspects. In the third generation, the percentages were 57 for the Jewish, 29 for Ukrainians, 25 for Italians, 13 for the "Majority Canadians" and only 9 for the Germans.

Overall, combining the external and the internal ethnic identity indicators of the six ethnic groups studied, over half of the first generation, less than half of the second generation and about one-third of the third generation retained significant elements of their ethnic identity. These are average rates of retention. Average rates, however, may be misleading, since they assume that all the indicators used are of equal importance. In fact they may not be. For example, little use of ethnic recreational facilities or low attendance at ethnic functions may reflect lack of money or time on the part of the respondent rather than loss of ethnic identity. Hence the indicators should be examined separately rather than as an aggregate. Table 19 shows some of the most highly retained single items. If we use the third generation as the measuring stick of ethnic identity retention, and if we consider the items most retained to be those whose combined percentage add up to over 100, then the following elements of identity appear as the most highly retained: ethnic food consumption, possession of ethnic objects of art, feeling of obligation to help other members of one's group to find a job if in a position to do so, some knowledge of ethnic language by those whose mother tongue is English, feeling of an obligation to support the needs and causes of one's group, the feeling of obligation to teach children the group's language, and having close friends of one's own ethnic background.

SELECTIVE ETHNIC IDENTITY CONSTRUCTION

The studies of ethnic identity retention indicate that ethnic identity is retained from one generation to another, not in its entirety, but only in selected aspects. The Toronto study in particular pointed to a number of such aspects that are most retained by the third generation. The theory that can best explain this process is Isajiw's theory of *selective generational identity construction.* According to this theory, ethnic identity is retained from one generation to another, not through reproduction of the same type of identity, but through a process by which some elements of the old identity are singled out and maintained or developed while other elements are forgotten or discarded. The elements selected from the traditional identity usually acquire a more symbolic rather than instrumental meaning and even a few elements thus selected may function to marshall strong feelings of identity (Isajiw, 1975, 1977). The elements thus selected become *foci of identity*, i.e., patterns of behaviour and attitudes around which other patterns that have to do with ethnic identity come to be organized. They are also often considered to be the most important patterns about one's ethnic identity in the sense that the group members feel that if they are lost, then the identity would be lost altogether.

As the Toronto study has shown, language as mother tongue and the daily use of the ethnic language is one of the elements that is relatively quickly dropped by consecutive generations. Yet knowledge of some ethnic language by those who do not consider it to be their mother tongue is still significant in the third generation. In terms of the theory presented here, this knowledge performs a symbolic function for the members of the third generation. That is, while they do not use the language as a regular instrument of communication, they may use a few words of it in their conversations with other members of the same group or may intersperse some words from their ethnic language with their use of the English language. But even the use of a few words may have the effect of evoking feelings of ethnic connectedness, trust or group responsibility between those communicating.

A similar function can be said to be performed by the possession of ethnic objects of art or consumption of ethnic food. These can evoke images of oneself that link one to one's ethnic group, even if there is no direct interaction with other members of that group.

Some groups may see their language as the main focus of identity and even centre their policies around language maintenance. Examples of such groups in Canada are the French and, among others, the Ukrainians. Retention of French language has been a basic issue in French-English relations, in the formation of Quebec and federal policies. In the case of Ukrainians, emphasis on language teaching in Saturday schools and pressure on the Canadian educational system to include language teaching in the public school programs often has been a central issue. This does not mean that ethnic language teaching is not important to other groups. It is, but it does not occupy a central place as an issue. For some groups endogamy is a more significant focus of their identity retention. As the data has shown, the Jewish group emphasizes this aspect of identity retention much more than the other groups and, in fact, shows much higher rates of endogamy among consecutive generations than do the other groups.

Looking at the data given by the studies of ethnic identity retention, at least five foci of identity retention can be distinguished: (1) an identity focusing on the ethnic language; (2) an identity focusing on the retention of symbolic objects, including ethnic food and ethnic artistic articles; (3) an identity focusing on having friends of the same ethnicity and marrying within the group; (4) an identity focusing on community participation and on practising some of the ethnic customs, such as holiday celebrations; and (5) an identity focusing on giving support to the group's causes and needs and helping the group's members.

These five different emphases are different routes to ethnic identity retention among the second and third generations. The same persons and groups may follow several of these forms. However, as the data presented above indicate, in specific cases one focus gains primacy over the others. Some persons and some groups appear to rely on some foci of identity more than on others.

GENERATIONS: CONFLICT AND FORMS OF IDENTITY

Underlying the different foci of identity is a distinction between a traditional and symbolic orientation to identity. That is, people act out different patterns of behaviour and attitudes, on the one hand, because their parents and grandparents did so and they have learned these patterns from them, they are used to them, and everyone else in the community in which they grew up and live shares and engages in these patterns. On the other hand, people engage in behaviour patterns and accept certain values and attitudes because they have meaning for them, they stand for something other than themselves, they represent some reality for them that goes beyond the patterns themselves. For example, persons may celebrate Christmas because everyone at home and in the community is doing so, or they may celebrate it because it signifies the birth of Christ and a number of moral imperatives are represented by it. Similarly, persons may hang a painting on their wall because it is a decoration for the room and others whom they know have similar paintings on their walls, or they may hang it because what is in the painting stands for the history or experience of their group and this is meaningful to them. In both of these cases, the first type of orientation can be called *traditional*, customary, the second type, *symbolic*, ideological. These two orientations provide the basis for two different forms of identity.

These forms of identity relate to different generational experiences. Thus in general, the identity of the second and third generations are different forms of identity than that of the first generation. The first generation, that is, those who arrived in the country of immigration as adults or, more specifically, those whose basic process of socialization took place before immigration tend to retain the traditional form of identity. If they come in larger waves of immigration, they usually try to "transplant" the culture of their homeland. They establish ethnic institutions based on the model of those of the home country. This is the process of building ethnic ghettos in the new country and establishing or re-establishing relations with people whose sympathy and acceptance can be taken for granted.

Transplanted things, however, never grow the same. Transplantation is not a continuation of old ways. Re-establishment of relations under different conditions of existence even with persons sharing the same heritage cannot result in a simple continuation of the old ways. At this point some reconstruction of identity is necessary and begins to take place. In his classical work, Oscar Handlin (1951) described how the new church built by peasant immigrants has never "felt the same" and how the old village and regional affiliations were never completely adequate for a group life full of "in-fellow feeling." The organizational life of immigrants is usually full of activities never engaged in by the villagers or urban dwellers in their former country.

Nevertheless, in the first generation, even with the modifications that immigrants have to make to their traditional patterns of life, the essential features of the home country's community life-style and identity prevail. The ethnic identity of the second generation, however, is a completely different matter. Typically, the second generation goes through a double process of socialization. That is, through their parents and ethnic institutions, on the one hand, they receive basic socialization in the culture and identity of the first generation. On the other hand, in the public school system and through all the other societal agencies of socialization, they are socialized into the culture and identity of the broader society. These two identities are built into the personalities of the second generation from their infancy. As a result, a social-psychological world of doubleness becomes an everyday reality for them.

Double socialization and its gradual imbeddedness in second-generation personalities is a significant source of conflict between the first and the second generations. The arenas of this conflict can be as many as there are elements of culture and identity. The most common disagreements between the first-generation parents and their second-generation children are over the use of ethnic language at home and with friends as against the English language, group dating patterns as against individual dating patterns, attendance at ethnic Saturday school or other after-hours courses as against playing games or going out with friends, belonging to ethnic organizations, sharing one's income with the family as against keeping it only for oneself, obligations to one's group and extended family as against obligations only to oneself (Kurian, 1991; Lan, 1993: 185-186).

For the second generation, a need is created to develop ways of handling this social-psychological doubleness. Different persons and small groups of persons may develop different strategies and techniques of approaching this doubleness. By the word "strategy" we do not refer to a carefully thought-through plan of action. Rather these are social-psychological strategies, i.e., ways of behaviour that may be engaged in with only some degree of consciousness or even subconsciously, with some rational thinking mixed with emotion or even with emotion alone. A number of such strategies can be identified:

1. Keeping the "two worlds" apart.
2. Pushing the world of the broader society aside, and engaging oneself primarily in the ethnic world.
3. Pushing the ethnic world aside and engaging oneself primarily in the world of the broader society.

4. Pushing the ethnic world and the world of the broader society away and involving oneself in alternative activities.
5. Bringing the two worlds together in creative activities.

• Keeping the "Two Worlds" Apart

To explain, the strategy of keeping one's ethnic identity and one's identity with the broader society as two separate compartments is probably the most common strategy, although there is no empirical data available to demonstrate this. The problem faced by persons who have gone through the double socialization process is one of managing the inconsistencies that the "two worlds" present. For example, persons may relate to the members of their ethnic group by speaking to them in their ethnic language, whereas to those who are "Canadian," in the English language. But in the presence of friends from both groups, it becomes socially awkward and psychologically embarrassing or taxing to keep continuously switching from one language to the other. With each switch one group of friends or the other may feel left out. It becomes easier not to bring the two sets of friends together, but to interact with each set separately.

The situation is similar with the internal aspects of identity. Young persons may never resolve for themselves the dilemma presented to them by the inconsistency of such values as, for example, what is more proper in dating. Is it proper to go out with members of the opposite sex together with larger groups of friends, as many first generation parents may insist, or is it proper to date individually, as the mainstream society seems to do? Or, is it more important to participate in and do things and share one's income with one's extended family, or is it more important to work for oneself and achieve success as an individual? Or, again, to whom does one owe one's primary trust or loyalty, to one's ethnic group or to the mainstream society or only to oneself? Often it is easier not to raise these issues for oneself and to leave the potential or actual value conflict unresolved.

• Engaging Oneself Primarily in the Ethnic World

The second strategy consists of giving precedence to one's ethnic identity and becoming amply involved in the ethnic community, friendship and organizational life. This does not mean that such persons reject their socialization into the mainstream society altogether. Rather, what it means is that they apply the benefits of this socialization to their ethnic community involvement, often helping the community to adjust better to the broader society. Still, their main concerns and identity are directed at and located in the ethnic community. This context exposes them to more interaction with the first-generation members of the community, which in turn reinforces their ethnic identity and produces at least a partial resolution of the problem of doubleness.

• Pushing the Ethnic World Aside

The third strategy is a much more complex one. The process of "pushing aside" one's ethnic identity, acquired through family or ethnic community socialization, can take place in at least two ways. As second-generation persons reach adolescence or young adulthood, they can either *distance* themselves from their ethnic community and identity or they can social-psychologically *rebel* against them. They distance themselves when they commit their time and energy to the pursuit of the values of the mainstream society, particularly working or studying for their own career and success. As a result they have little time for participation in the ethnic community's organizations and functions. They do not try to avoid ethnic community participation and may occasionally attend ethnic community functions, but their main orientation is towards the mainstream society with which they strongly identify.

Rebellion against one's ethnicity is a different phenomenon. In this pattern persons develop a negative attitude towards the patterns of behaviour that represent their ethnicity. These patterns symbolize for them inadequate or backward ways of behaviour as compared with those of the mainstream society. They become critical of their ethnic community, often over-critical. They may constantly and negatively compare the community to the mainstream society and use certain ways of acting that prevail in the community as negative models of behaviour. A form of *negative ethnocentrism* may develop. They may feel embarrassed or ashamed of their parental cultural patterns. As a result, they may consciously reject their ethnic community and their ethnic identity and claim that they are no longer "ethnic," but rather "Canadian," "American," and so on. They may even exhibit an over-identification with the mainstream society and its cultural ways as being superior to others.

Even though those following this pattern of adaptation to doubleness consciously reject their ethnicity, they do so as a result of a heightened awareness of it in the face of the dominant mainstream culture and identity. This awareness accounts for their critical evaluation. In other words, they see their background as a negative symbol. Thus, their orientation towards their ethnicity, albeit negative, becomes symbolic rather than traditional. However, even though consciously they may reject their ethnicity, they still know that it is part of their background. Hence, it still remains for them a form of ethnic identity, a negative, rebelling identity, but an ethnic identity nevertheless.

• Involving Oneself in Alternative Activities

The fourth strategy is similar to the third, except that the "pushing away" also includes the mainstream society. As in the third strategy, the process of pushing away may include either rebellion or distancing, or it can include behaviour that exhibits elements of both. In the case of rebellion, the strategy derives from the feeling that the mainstream society is not an embodiment of justice and human brotherhood, but instead comprises an oppressive structure, discrimination or racism. Hence, one is to search for an alternative and for means of bringing justice and brotherhood to society. This may mean joining and becoming active in such groups as socialist or Marxist organizations that purportedly pursue "universalistic" goals or unorthodox religious movements, such as the Hare Krishna, meditation societies, or informal groups and gatherings, which champion some universalistic causes.

This rebellion pattern does not necessarily relate only to ethnic communities. It is applicable to any generational relationships. It relates, however, very intimately to ethnic identity. The "ethnic rebels'" criticism of their ethnicity often assumes that the ethnic community, rather than pursue its traditional ways, should be engaged in the universalistic search, and they even offer an interpretation of the nature of their ethnic community as one whose destiny is to do so (Nahirny and Fishman, 1966: 349). The rebels thus present an ideology for the ethnic community to follow and this kind of identity can also be characterized as symbolic-ideological.

When the mainstream society thrusts the barrier of discrimination and racism against a group, then the problem of managing one's second-generation doubleness acquires a more acute character. This is particularly a problem when the second-generation persons are of a non-white race, especially of the black race. In such cases, second-generation persons are placed at a distance by the society's mainstream itself. The consequence can be a compound distancing, from the mainstream society and from one's own ethnic group. This may be accompanied, though not necessarily, by a rebellion and engagement in patterns of behaviour that demonstrate this rebellion. In an autobiographical statement, Vicki English-Currie (1993), a Blackfoot Indian, not an immigrant child and yet from young childhood subject to double socialization, describes how she was raised as a small child in the Indian way of life and then removed to a residential school. There she was given books in which all the pictures were of white persons, all the role models presented were of professional, white, middle-class persons and nothing they were taught had to do with the Native people. Rather, Native people were portrayed as having a savage culture and language and as being incapable of logical reasoning and scientific learning. She concludes about the consequences of this:

> Many of the adults of that era walk around with anger and resentment. These feelings inhibit their ability to venture forward in education, careers or marriage. They are carrying bitterness towards the white man; many have become alcoholic or have committed suicide. As a result of the lack of self-esteem and self-determination taken from them in residential schools, they are demonstrating self-destructive, self-deprecating behaviour.

This statement clearly illustrates that the kind of identity that emerges under these conditions is of an *anomic* type, that is, one that is caught in-between two cultures and hence is distanced from both. The frustration and the anger generated by this anomie may be channeled into a rebellious, defiant or non-conformist kind of behaviour.

An anomic pattern deriving from racism and discrimination was observed in a qualitative study of the Afro-Caribbean youths in Toronto (Gobin, 1997). In the study, the first and one-half and the second-generation high school students were interviewed in depth to ascertain their perception of their process of becoming a part of Canadian society and their own identity in the Canadian context. An inherent part of this perception is being discriminated against and being trapped in a situation in which they are unable to be what other Canadians are and what they themselves want to be. Statements by several respondents are quite revealing:

> Like I come from [Toronto] Park and I have no money and my parents have no money and my father is gone, I am not getting any money from him. My mother has hardly any money. First of all, I'm gonna be under a lot more stress because I live in that type of a situation and then I'm gonna bring that stress to school, and that's

> going to pull me down in school and plus maybe I can't stay in school all this time because I have to go somewhere else to work or do something else like that just to get money. And if I can't work or something like that, maybe I may even go into selling drugs or some business like that because I can' get money any other way ... And because of all of that it pushes the people down even more and those people now grow up and they have kids and they're in the situation. This guy has been selling weed to get money for his mother and when he grows up he is still selling weed because that's all he can do now because he has no education ... then he ends up in jail and his kids [do the same] and the same cycle ends up happening. If you grow up in Rosedale and your parents can afford to send you to this lessons and that lessons, and when you walk down the street, you're not gonna get lynched from the side and you don't have to worry about money because your parents have everything, you don't even have to worry about TTC or food, you have all the money in your pocket. All you have to concentrate on in your life is going to school and getting good marks and after that it's like ... even little things, no one is worrying you in stores, or [when] you're walking down the street, no one is looking at you in a certain way. You don't have this perception of yourself on TV when you're watching Menace to Society or something. You have this perception of yourself as a successful person. Black people have Boys in the Hood, Menace to Society and Juice, and they have frigging Tu Pac and that type of crap as [role models].

Another respondent states:

> Like I realize most Black youths when they come to Canada or North America, instead of sticking together, Black people they are all niggers we are all scattered, we don't like together as one and stick together to defend each other and I guess I find that true because if you do look at it, the home is more respected in other cultures and helping your own, you know what I mean? Black youths you see all these absent fathers and you see pregnant mothers on welfare, you see them on drugs or in a gang or something and so. There is nobody really helping them, when you look for help no one is there. And there should be a bunch of Black people saying yes we would help you out right and it's not like that.

And, a statement describing the perception of racism and a form of rebelling against the mainstream society by wilfully playing games with the whites:

> On the public transit ... on the bus ... there was one seat that was empty and this white lady was sitting there and I sat beside her and she got up and move. So as soon as she got up and move ... I was saying why she move? She got up to stand up cause there was no more seats so I went and I [stood] beside her just to see and she was moving, and we were playing. Everywhere I would go beside her she would move, move until she got off and just laughed at her. And I remember I was in the bank, going in the bank there was this old lady and she was like oh going through her bag coming out and I was going in and she saw me and she like locked her bag and put a tight wrap around it. Or in stores if I go in a store, the women would be watching me, watching me with all four eyes.... Sometimes when I realize they are watching me cause they think I am probably coming in to thief, steal or rob them or hold them up I would just play around with their nerves, walk around, look, walk around ... [just so as to occupy their time].

In the second decade of the twentieth century, in their classical study of the assimilation of the Polish peasant immigrants in the United States, W.I. Thomas and F. Znaniecki (1927) had already pointed out that, with the second generation, the ethnic family begins to be disorganized. At the basis of this disorganization is, not only the conflict of two different cultures, but also the gradual removal of the second-generation members from their ethnic community. A consequence of this is a change in their attitudes towards the old values taught by their first-generation parents, yet a failure to inculturate the new values of the mainstream society from which their changed attitudes are derived. We can add that the barriers of racism are a powerful factor in preventing a realistic inculturation of the values of the mainstream society.

• Bringing the Two Worlds Together

The last type of strategy of managing the doubleness is a creative approach. Persons who are a product of double socialization can engage in activities that bring the two worlds together in an innovative and meaningful manner. Example of this approach are the creative writers, artists and scholars who try to understand their experience of doubleness by writing about it or by expressing their understanding of it in an artistic or intellectual form. They may not consciously engage in these activities in order to resolve the doubleness of their background, but the creative process itself in which this background plays a role functions as a process of resolution and as a process of building up new identity not only for oneself but also for others. That is, the creative writers, artists and scholars whose work either indirectly implies or directly deals with their ethnicity, articulate the issues connected with it and thus the process of creating is itself a strategy of dealing with one's problem. In addition, when read, viewed or otherwise appreciated by others, the products of such work are relevant to others who have the same or similar problems and hence such work becomes relevant to the resolution of their problems. In this manner new identity forms can emerge and become established. As the Canadian novelist Robert Kroetsch (Mandel, 1977: 59) put it, "In a sense we haven't got an identity until somebody tells our story; the fiction makes us real."

Examples of this kind of writers and artists in Canada are such known figures as writers Mordecai Richler, Leonard Cohen, Irving Layton, Rudy Wiebe, Rienzi Crusz, Visanji, Cecil Foster and artists William Kurelek and Natalka Husar, just to name a few. These are, however, persons who have become widely known for their creative work and hence can serve as clear examples. There are many who do creative work that articulates their double background who are not publicly known. Creative work is done in professions, in social interaction in daily life around the home, in neighbourhood work and so on. Most of this type of everyday creativity has not been researched at all, yet it remains one of the most important aspects of ethnic identity construction.

Typical for the third generation and for consecutive generations is a form of ethnic identity called **ethnic rediscovery** (Isajiw, 1975: 133-134; 1990: 37-38). The third or consecutive generations typically go through the process of basic socialization in the culture of the mainstream society rather than in the culture of their ethnic ancestors. They may learn some of their ethnic patterns, including some language, from their parents or even from the courses some have been sent to by their parents. However, there is no longer a double basic socialization, and hence no confrontational intensity. Nevertheless, a number of persons who have been inculturated into the mainstream society do develop an interest in their ethnic background as part of their identity. They may turn to the group to find out more about it in order to fill out more completely this aspect of their identity.

In the sociological literature, this aspect of the third generation had been discussed in the context of the *Hansen hypothesis*. Marcus L. Hansen (1952) proposed that the second generation tries to forget their ethnic background, but the third generation wishes to remember it. This hypothesis has also been known as the "third generation return" hypothesis. Since then many studies have tried to test this hypothesis (Isajiw, 1990: 38-49). The problem with the hypothesis is that the third-generation phenomenon should not be seen as a "return" in any literal sense of the word, that is, picking up where forgotten grandfathers left off. Rather, it has to be seen in the sense of "rediscovering" one's ancestral past.

Ethnic rediscovery is a process of identity construction based on selected elements of tradition and selective knowledge of the ethnic group history. This process includes the selection of elements from the ancestral culture and even a few cultural symbols, such as a few words of the language, objects of ethnic art, music, foodstuffs, dancing or selected rituals. These symbols provide the identity link with an ancestral group. Part of this rediscovery process is learning the history of the group. The turn towards the past is symbolic. To find the cognitive basis for one's rediscovered identity, a recourse to the past is made. It tends to be a recourse to the more remote rather than to the immediate past. For example, for the Blacks in the Americas, it may be a turn towards Africa, rather than to the past of the slave period, with the resulting identity of "African Americans." For the Jews, the symbolic turn to the past may involve an interest in the Ancient Hebrews through their archeological discoveries. For the Ukrainians, an interest in the original village folklore or art or in the Medieval or Cossack period of history. For the Indo-Caribbeans, an interest in the original Hindu religion and art, and so on. The remote past, signifying primordial origins or "roots," functions as a better symbol of identity than the immediate past.

A study of a Hindu temple near Toronto illustrates this process well (Singh, 1997). The temple has brought together for religious services generations of those of South Asian ancestry from the Caribbean, South Africa, East Africa, Fiji, Mauritius. The uniting force has been the interest in rediscovering the ancestral Hindu religion as it presumably existed in its genuine form in ancient times. According to the study, the effect of this rediscovery is the development of a new Canadian Hindu identity.

To conclude, ethnic identity is retained by changing its form, particularly from traditional form to selective-symbolic form. The traditional form of identity is more typical of the first generation and the selective-symbolic rediscovery form, of the third generation. The second generation shares partly the traditional form and partly a symbolic-rebellious or ideological form. The second generation in particular can serve in the creative construction of new forms of ethnic identity. While these different forms may be prevalent in one generation or another, it should be understood that, under certain conditions, members of any generation may develop any of the discussed forms of identity. These conditions cannot be discussed here, especially since there have been few systematic empirical studies of this issue.

All of Baba's Children

by Myrna Kostash

> I remember walking into a barracks one time in Winnipeg. I was looking for a friend and mistakenly I walked into another barracks, and a guy asked my name and I said, "Pawliuk." And he said, "Oh, a bohunk." That's what he said, right off the bat. And I said, well, what could I say? I was just one among the whole barracks full of them. But I recall little things like that very clearly, because it did hurt me. I felt, gee, I am as much Canadian as anybody else. I spoke no other kind of language except English, I did all the things that everybody else did, and why should I be called something different?

This Canadian-born generation, rebuffed by the "outside" world of the Anglo-Canadian— "You will go this far and no further"—socially and economically, was also emotionally, psychologically, culturally, set adrift from the "inner" world of their parents. The generation gap of the ethnic. To the natural and inevitable drift between two generations separated by peculiar but overlapping experience was added the yawning alienation between two mentalities formed under utterly different circumstances. The points of contingency were so few! Formally, they were there. The two generations cohabited, they ate and worked and played and prayed together in a shared milieu; they conversed together in a common language and repeated the same proverbs and prejudices. But, in terms of personality and style, it was as though the Ukrainian-Canadian was a character built from scratch. There was no picking up where the preceding generation had left off, for the immigrants' habits and perspectives and sensibility were buried with their bones. It was up to the Canadian-born to evolve the culture and character that referred only to the given of their experience: Canadian society. Responses and values derived from the cumulative effect of centuries'-old economic and social patterns in a Ukrainian village obviously no longer applied. The parent could feed, clothe and house you, introduce you to a Byzantine God, enrich you with Slavic folk-arts and pass on homilies of peasant wisdom. Beyond that, you were on your own in the uncharted territory of the Canadians. And no amount of Ukrainian education was going to protect you from their pervasive and irresistible cultural biases. If ... the principle of the third generation interest [is true] ... it is because the grandchild, thoroughly at home in Canada and the beneficiary of the establishment's liberalism towards white middle-class arrivals at least, is free of the psychological equivocation between shame and defiance which so bedeviled the intervening generation and is free, then, to identify with information and a history that are finally unthreatening. The pursuit of ethnic information and the perusal of Ukrainian history are intellectual activities a Ukrainian-Canadian can now undertake without running the risk of confusing his or her identity with that of "bohunk" predecessors. It's not so portentous after all to be proud of one's ancestral Ukrainianness now that there is no organic Ukrainianness to haunt and scandalize the establishment.

Ukrainians are now a "legitimate" group because there are no more Ukrainians. Discrimination against us is gone because we are gone. We have accepted the premises of the majority group and once we were safely assimilated we were legitimatized.

Here are a group of people who are a quarter generation away from expressing the Ukrainian culture in their daily lives; twenty-five years later they find themselves expressing it not at all in their daily lives, they go to an ethnic festival where the culture is "staged" and doesn't resemble anything like how they used to live ...

That said, it must also be said that there is, in my generation, a resurgence of ethnicity as identity which is not romantic or mystified and which rejects the easy notion that acculturation is the same thing as assimilation.

For many of us, our Ukrainian-Canadian origins do describe our personality and life-style, however sentimentally or abstractly, and condition for us the nature of our family ties, some of our social activities, where some of our money is spent, and our reactions to the symbols of our ethnicity—an anthem, a prairie church, a flag. Like it or not, there does seem to be still an emotional significance in our continued attachment to the ethnic group. Home, as the saying goes, is the place where, when you go there, they've got to take you in. And so it is that, no matter the alienation or mistrust or crossed purposes between generations, there is one thing that makes of the ethnic group a collective: we are all related. I may be denounced by the group, insulted and ostracized, I may even leave it behind, but nobody can ever say I don't belong.

A tourist I came, a tourist I leave. Like thousands and thousands of Ukrainian-Canadians of my generation and beyond, I only travel these ethnic sideroads when I need to find a breathing space awhile, away from the fumes of the cosmopolitan metropolis and all its works. But, metropolis is what I return to when it's time to go home. It is, after all, where Baba meant to have me live, when she mortgaged her life so mine would be deflected as much from the CPR quarter as from the *kolkhoz*, near Tulova, in Galicia. When I look at the remnants of the cultural reality left from her history and finger them like curios in a Tijuana souvenir shop, it's not that I'm ungrateful or even unmoved. I can store them in a trunk, along with my high school yearbooks and my mother's wedding dress. But if I tried to use them, they would fall apart in my hands. I have other skills now and assignments to fulfil that Baba never dreamed of. Not that she wouldn't be pleased.

If there's any way at all that I carry on from where she left off, it won't be with her language, because I never knew it, nor with her habits, because they make no sense, nor with her faith, because I have lost it, nor with her satisfaction, because my needs have changed. It will be perhaps with the thing she had no choice in bequeathing: her otherness. As the alien, the bohunk, the second-class citizen, and the ethnic, she passed on to me the gift of consciousness of one who stands outside the hegemonistic centre, and sees where the real world ends and the phantasma of propaganda begins. As for the generation between us, my parents, her children, they gave me the possibility of action as one who is of this place and this time, free of the ghosts of diffidence. Seeing clearly and acting surely: the journey from Tulova ends here.

FACTORS OF ETHNIC IDENTITY RETENTION

The selective construction of identity by the second and consecutive generations is not a random process by which any element of the old identity can be dropped or retained. Some writings on identity construction (Anderson, 1983), especially those that try to emphasize the difference of the constructionist approach from the primordialist or the essentialist approach, seem to imply that ethnic identity can be constructed, as it were, at will. The process of construction and retention by different generations of new forms of ethnic identity is affected by a number of factors that are derived from both the exigencies of the existence of ethnic communities and the conditions of the larger society.

• Factors of Retention Deriving from the Ethnic Community

Typically ethnic communities exert efforts to ensure the transmission of their identity to their younger generations. The main manner in which they try to achieve this is through *ethnic socialization.* This includes socialization in the family and neighbourhood, association with ethnic peers and ethnic schooling.

Analysis of data from the Toronto study (Isajiw and Makabe, 1982) showed that ethnic socialization is a rather important factor associated with ethnic identity retention. The specific elements of ethnic socialization measured in the study were the language used by parents in speaking to their children, the language used by the children in speaking to their parents, the subjective importance of ethnic background when growing up, the ethnicity of the three closest friends during the teenage period, dating inside one's ethnic group and the parental disapproval of dating outside of it and ethnic school attendance. Thus those persons in the second and third generations who scored high on these experiences retained their ethnic identity in a higher degree.

The study also showed that ethnic socialization becomes more salient as an explanatory factor with each consecutive generation. By use of the measure of statistical variance, the study showed that, in retention of ethnic identity, ethnic socialization has more influence on the second generation than it has on the first and even substantially more influence on the third generation than on the second. That is, with each consecutive generation, retention of ethnic identity depends more on factors related to the family than to the ethnic community as a whole. The first generation's identity can to a large extent depend on participation in the organizational and general social life of the ethnic community. By the third generation, substantial participation in the organizational life of the ethnic community is uncommon. Hence, ethnic identity is to a larger extent conditioned by the parents' use of the ethnic language with their children and their willingness and the opportunity they have to enroll their children in ethnic schools or classes.

The Toronto study also showed that the most important factor of ethnic language retention was the frequency with which parents spoke the language to their children while they were growing up (Isajiw, 1985b: 226-227). Home interaction was also found to be the most significant means through which language use is retained in a Toronto-Montreal study of Arab Canadians (Abu-Laban, 1980: 206-209). In the Toronto study, respondents also considered their ethnic language to be their mother tongue if their parents were bilingual and spoke to them in their ethnic language and in English. Once there was some language socialization at home, the ethnic school was significant in supporting ethnic language retention. Those who had attended ethnic schools reported more knowledge of the language and more use of it and more considered it to be their mother tongue than did those who did not attend ethnic schools. Further, as can be expected, the school is more important than the home in learning to read and write in the ethnic language. However, not all of those who attended ethnic schools could read or write the language efficiently. The school is also more important than the home in raising the young persons' consciousness of their ethnic identity.

A factor of ethnic identity retention connected with ethnic home socialization is *endogamy*, i.e., marriage within the group. Ethnic socialization, particularly socialization within the family, depends on the degree to which the parents share the ethnic culture and identity, whatever form it may take. In the case of the intermarriage of partners of different ethnic identities, such sharing is usually absent and hence there is less chance of transmitting one ethnic identity to children. This does not mean that there is no transmission at all. However, studies of the issue show that children of ethnically mixed parents retain ethnic identity in a much lower degree than children of ethnically endogamous parents. In the previous chapter, we referred to the study by J. Goldstein and A. Segall (1985) in which the results clearly showed this difference. These results were also confirmed by the Toronto study. Thus, while ethnic intermarriage, or *exogamy*, is a factor of social incorporation into the larger society, ethnic endogamy is a factor of ethnic identity retention.

Structural factors deriving from the degree and the nature of the ethnic community's organized life are also a basic factor in ethnic identity retention. Raymond Breton has proposed a theory of ethnic *institutional completeness* to explain the functioning of ethnic organizational structure in this regard. According to this theory, "the presence of formal organizations in the ethnic community sets out forces that have the effect of keeping the social relations of the immigrants within its boundaries. It tends to minimize out-group contacts" (Breton, 1964). That is, the presence of many institutions and organizations within an ethnic community generates a social life in the community, not only among the members of these organizations themselves, but one that extends beyond them to persons in the community who are not members of any organization. Breton's data showed that, among the ethnic groups with high institutional completeness (i.e., ethnic communities that had many of their own institutions, such as churches, publications and welfare organizations), as many as 89 percent of persons in those communities conducted most of their personal relations with persons of the same community, as compared with only 21 percent of those whose ethnic communities had only a few or no formal organizations. Thus, the structural level of an ethnic group, i.e., its institutional completeness, is a factor of ethnic identity retention on the personal level.

Another factor of ethnic identity retention is the *community viability* of the ethnic group. That is, those ethnic communities who have a higher degree of viability increase the opportunity that their members will retain their identity longer. By degree of viability is meant the degree of activity and openness of the community life. A viable ethnic community is one that exhibits a will to survive as a community by developing institutions, organizations and informal structures that are able to adapt themselves to changing conditions in the larger society. Ethnic community organizations will be discussed in more detail in the next chapter. Here it will suffice to say that, over time, ethnic institutions and organizations can act in two basic directions: the *inward* or the *outward.* The inward direction takes place when ethnic structures, in order to preserve their identity, undertake activities that try to preserve the transplanted culture in as much of its entirety and detail as possible. The emphasis is on cultural activities that are repetitious or cyclic, as, for example, regular holiday celebrations, regular anniversary celebrations or marking off events important in the history of the community, regular presentations of the same forms of dancing, singing and so on and engaging in the internal ethnic politics that have little relevance to the society at large. While all viable communities engage in regular gatherings of people, a complete emphasis on the preservation of tradition tends to favour participation of the first generation at the expense of the consecutive generations. The latter, since they undergo the process of inculturation into the larger society, must negotiate their traditional cultural patterns at least to some degree. Hence, over a longer period of time the membership in the inward-directed ethnic structures reduces itself to the predominance of the first generation without a viable replacement by younger persons. The consequence of this is increased isolation of the respective organizations from the total ethnic community and the loss of their significance as factors of identity retention.

The outward direction in the activities of ethnic institutions and organizations refers to activities aimed at better incorporation of the ethnic group into the larger society. Such organizations may serve the recreational needs of the members who are inculturated into the mainstream culture, as for example, many ethnic community centres do when they provide fitness facilities or club facilities for their members. Further, such structures as ethnic business and professional organizations aim to assist members in their work in the context of the larger society. Such organizations may also function as lobbying groups with the mainstream governments. Because of their orientation outside of the ethnic group and towards the society at large, they tend to be more open to the second and consecutive generations and can accept and articulate their reconstruction of the traditional ethnic identity. The use of the English language rather than the ethnic language in the organization's transactions is one example of this reconstruction. Over a longer period of time, this type of organization may lose all of its ethnic patterns and identity and thus its significance to the community.

A viable ethnic community would be one that finds an optimum balance between the two extremes of the inward and outward directions. In this manner, some, but not all, traditions are retained, others are modified and the younger generations are included in significant numbers in the organized life of the community

• Factors of Retention Deriving from the Mainstream Society

In addition to the factors deriving from the ethnic community, there are factors that function to produce ethnic identity retention that derive from the structure and culture of the mainstream society. For one thing, exclusionary pressures coming from the mainstream society, particularly discrimination and racism, work to push the ethnic minority groups either into the inward direction or, as pointed out above, into the direction of anomie. The dynamic factors involved in ethnic identity retention of consecutive generations are located to a large extent also in the structure of the larger society. The structure of ethnic stratification and its concomitant occupational, economic and political competition, all influence one's awareness of ancestry. The rediscovery pattern may emerge when members of ethnic groups begin to realize that inculturation alone is not sufficient to achieve their economic and social aspirations. Owing to community closure or discrimination by the dominant groups, their opportunities are limited. They may have the qualifications relative to the positions or the membership to which they aspire, yet be excluded because they are identified as members of an "undesirable" ethnic group or a racial category. Or they may be excluded because preference is given to persons who are of the same ethnicity or race as those who are in charge of the respective place of work or the prospective membership group. Under such conditions a degree of ethnic community closure, i.e., turning inward towards one's group, may enable the members of the group to open the doors more widely to higher levels of the occupational, social and political structure that they, as single individuals, would be unable to attain. More will be said on this in the next chapter.

When second or consecutive-generation members of minority groups aspire to better positions in society and when they have already been mobile in the structure of society, competition with other groups, majority or other minorities, can make them more conscious of their ethnic background. Competition is a mechanism through which self-awareness is increased, especially awareness of one's ascribed background characteristics (Morse and Gergen, 1970). Competition for higher status occupations, in particular, makes ascriptive characteristics more apparent. One reason for this is that administrators often define certain ascriptive background characteristics as achievement characteristics, as, for example, the name of the school or university that a person attended. Administrators often take the prestige of a school itself as an indicator of the quality of prospective performance of the persons who have attended the school (Mayhew, 1968). Similarly, prestige that an ethnic group enjoys, or cannot enjoy, is often translated into an indicator of the quality of prospective performance of those who belong to the group or category.

Secondly, competition for higher status jobs usually focuses attention, not only on the skills required by the job, but also on the personality of the applicant and on his family and community life. Participation by the employee and the employee's spouse in various informal functions of the enterprise or the organization is often seen as an important aspect of the job. This makes the ethnic background of the prospective employee a potential asset. Social mobility, therefore, especially on higher-middle-class occupational levels, produces a higher degree of ethnic awareness and thus stimulates the process of ethnic identity retention, particularly in the form of ethnic rediscovery. This retention is also stimulated by the pervasiveness of the technological

Bill of Rights for Racially Mixed People

I have the right
- not to justify my existence in this world
- not to keep the races separate within me
- not to be responsible for people's discomfort with my physical ambiguity
- not to justify my ethnic legitimacy

I have the right
- to identify myself differently than strangers expect me to identify
- to identify myself differently than how my parents identify me
- to identify myself differently than my brothers and sisters
- to identify myself differently in different situations

I have the right
- to create a vocabulary to communicate about being multiracial
- to change my identity over my lifetime—and more than once
- to have loyalties and identify with more than one group of people
- to freely choose whom I befriend and love

Source: Maria P.P. Root, ed., *The Multiracial Experience: Racial Borders as the New Frontier.* Thousand Oaks, California: Sage Publications, 1996.

KEY ISSUES IN CANADIAN ETHNIC RELATIONS

Diversity is Us: Finding an Identity in the Global Society

As the twenty-first century begins, a realization is emerging that no identity is pure and fixed and that "home" is not necessarily the place of our origin. At some time in the new millennium there will be nobody who has not encountered or who has never established a relationship with persons of different cultural identities. Already in some places—like Toronto, for example—more than half of all the people were born in different countries outside of Canada. Many people today speak a language that is not the one that they were first taught in childhood.

As the culture critic Nicos Papastergiadis put it, "cultures, which were once seen to be meaningful because they were presumed to be discrete, coherent, stable and unique, are now increasingly seen as interconnected, dynamic, fragmented and amorphous." There is no nation and no ethnic group in the world today that has not been influenced by other nations or groups. The powerful media delivers messages from other cultures or about other cultures almost to every corner of the world and by this infuses new ideas, beliefs and esthetics into all cultures. But, if cultures change and loose stability, how does this affect identity? Can individuals feel to be themselves in the global ecumene without having the stability of any one cultural tradition?

Perhaps we tend to assume uncritically that stable identity derives from one "authentic" cultural tradition and that those who have come to live in-between different cultural traditions or combine elements of several cultural traditions have problematic or pathological identities. The opposite may be nearer the truth. People may feel to be more themselves if they construct their own identity.

While minority ethnic groups may be caught between different cultures, it should be kept in mind that they also inculturate (assimilate) into a broader culture that is dominant in the society in which they live. Chapter 7 shows that such inculturation is ubiquitous and relatively fast from one generation to another. The question that has not been adequately answered is what is it exactly that they inculturate or assimilate into?

In an article entitled "Olga in Wonderland: Ethnicity in Technological Society," Wsevolod Isajiw points out that today the culture of a modern society such as Canada or the United States is made up of at least six, and possibly eight, layers. They include the culture of the majority ethnic group, the minority ethnic groups, regional groups and others, but among these a significant layer is made up of the technological-commercial culture. Central to this layer is the value placed on access to, and use of, the products of technology, and on contact with people who have such access and use. It appears that communities and individuals in modern societies share this layer of culture more widely than any other. It is this layer of culture that brings together different ethnic groups and into which their members inculturate most readily. As Isajiw put it, referring to "Olga" as representing immigrants of diverse ethnicities and their children: "The fact is that, in the New World … . Olga has thrown herself desirously into the technological wonderland, picking up toy after toy as she has been moving up the wonderland's social status escalator."

In our modern society, educational institutions inculcate value patterns that are useful to technologically based economy. Paradoxically perhaps, in the rapidly developing global society, this technological culture seems to be bringing peoples of diverse identities together. Persons with different ethnic identities establish working relationships, in part at least, because they already share certain common technological-commercial values.

However, technological culture, rather than articulate with strong feelings of identity, tends to foster anonymity and impersonal social relationships. As Peter Berger in his book *The Homeless Mind* has pointed out, the technological process, at the very least, introduces a dichotomy of others into the individual's consciousness: individuals become both unique persons and anonymous substitutable functionaries. This consciousness of others carries over into the experience of oneself. A process of self-anonymization occurs, by which it becomes easier for individuals to think of themselves in terms of their external roles—as a worker, professor, manager—rather than in terms of the unique qualities of their personality.

Hence, this technological culture heightens the need for and may well create a search for unique identity. Maintaining selected features from one's ethnic culture may well help to satisfy this need.

As the global society develops a more uniform common culture, it seems likely that specific, diverse ethnic cultures will continue to exist in some form and even flourish. In the end, ethnic cultures may not be so incompatible with the technological-commercial culture after all. Perhaps this is the deeper meaning of the phrase "post-modernity"?

culture in modern society. As was pointed out in the previous chapter, technological culture is the level of culture into which members of diverse ethnic groups inculturate most readily. Social economists and sociologists have long pointed out that it is the marketplace (Furnivall, 1939) and the industrial place of work (Hughes and Hughes, 1952) that brings people of diverse ethnicities together. In modern times, both the marketplace and the place of work are continuously informed and shaped by the technological culture, and the technological culture is something that provides a common ground for people of all or any ethnic background. The heart of the technological culture is the standardization of ways of doing things and of the products of work. The technological culture develops procedures for work that become skills. These can be learned by persons of any ethnic background. The products of technological culture are items of everyday use and enjoyment that can be accepted by persons regardless of their ethnic background.

Standardization of culture, however, tends to foster impersonal social relationships and anonymity. As Peter Berger (1973: 31-33) pointed out, the technological process fosters the consciousness of others as anonymous, substitutable functionaries and makes one think of oneself more in terms of external roles, such as workers, professionals, managers and so on, and less in terms of character traits and qualities of personality. Furthermore, technological culture is oriented towards the present and the future. It establishes no particular links with the past. Rather, it quickly discards all former models as soon as technologically more efficient ones are invented.

Identity, however, focuses on uniqueness and on links with the past. Ethnic symbols, even if they are completely removed from their original, traditional context, become symbols of both uniqueness and a link with the past. They become symbols of one's "roots." Indirectly, technological culture heightens the need for identity and generates a search for it. Ethnic rediscovery is one significant way of fulfilling this need. Thus, on the one hand, technological culture brings people of diverse ethnicities together in the marketplace and in places of work by the inculturation of practical, pragmatic values. On the other hand, it indirectly stimulates the retention of their ethnic identity.

The last factor of ethnic identity retention discussed here is the presence of ethnic diversity in society itself, the awareness of ethnicity that it produces and the need it creates to negotiate one's identity. A society made up of large percentages of persons of diverse ethnic and racial backgrounds, one in which a continuous immigration flow brings new immigrant generations of diverse ethnicities and races, is one in which at least some degree of awareness of one's ethnic background is inevitable. This awareness increases the chance that, even if the other factors are absent, in the population of persons of third or consecutive generation, there will be a constant number who will develop an interest in and seek to rediscover their ethnic identity.

Furthermore, in ethnically diverse and immigrant-receiving societies like Canada and the United States, there is an ever-increasing number of persons of ethnically and racially mixed backgrounds. While in 1871, when the first Canadian census was taken, only 9.9 percent of all husbands in Canada were married to persons outside of their ethnic group, in 1971, this percentage went up to 37.3 (Richard, 1991: 114-119). In the Toronto study (Isajiw, 1990: 76-82), the average outmarriage percentages for the three generations of the five ethnic groups studied were 25 percent for the first generation, 52 percent for the second generation, and 68 percent for the third generation. Thus, with the third generation, the propensity for multiethnic marriages is quite strong with the result that, by 1991, about 29 percent of all Canadians reported themselves to be of multiple ethnic origin (McVey and Kalbach, 1995: 351). In the United States, the statistics on multiracial births over the past three decades are also quite revealing. From the early 1970s to the 1990s, the number of mono-racial babies has grown by 15 percent, whereas the number of multiracial babies has increased by more than 260 percent (Root, 1996: xiv-xv).

Multiethnic and multiracial backgrounds present special problems of identity construction and identity retention. Persons with such a background often have to "negotiate" their identity in relation to the mainstream and in relation to the ethnic groups they come from. This means that in certain situations they may emphasize one side of their background, in other situations, the other side, or they may negate one or the other side or both. K. A. Rockquemore (1997) developed a typology of four different identities that can be constructed as a result of biracial background. According to her, the self can understand his or her identity as a border identity, protean identity, transcendent identity or traditional identity. Border identity is one in which biracial persons see themselves as being on the margin of each race but part of neither one nor the other. In protean identity, biracial persons see themselves as having the ability to move freely from one race to the other, so that they can identify at will with either race. Transcendent identity involves negation of the reality of race and identifying oneself in non-racial or supra-racial terms. Finally, in traditional identity, persons acknowledge their diverse background, but identify themselves with only one race.

This typology is somewhat analogous to the strategies of reaction to one's double socialization, discussed above. The important thing here is that these various ways of identity construction are responses to the demands of outsiders to categorize oneself in relation to one's background. In order to simplify their interaction process, "others" in society often exert strong pressures on individuals to "pigeonhole" themselves one way or another. This simplification, however, often means interaction deriving from biases and prejudices.

A study (King, 1997) documenting variations in the construction of ethno-racial identities has focused on how the demands of the structure of certain social activities influences the emphasis placed on one's ethnicity vis-à-vis one's race. The study used interviews and participant observation to assess the ethno-racial behaviour of Japanese American beauty pageant candidates. The candidates were second or consecutive generations of Japanese-White marriages. Since the pageants took place in the Japanese community context, the candidates were not only to be assessed on the basis of their physical characteristics, but also on the basis of their knowledge of Japanese culture, history, art and the like. The audiences were both Japanese and other Americans. The problem that the candidates faced was the inconsistent expectations of the audience and the judges. The judges and the audience expected that the candidates would represent a Japanese American who had an impressive knowledge of Japanese tradition and, at the same time one, who racially looked Japanese. Thus when the candidate, coming from biracial background, looked very "white," she had to prove her "genuine" Japanese identity by emphasizing her ethnicity, i.e., her knowledge of the tradition. Those, however, who did not have a good knowledge of the tradition would emphasize their race to prove that they were genuine. In other words, they were placed in a position in which they had to negotiate their identity between their race and their ethnicity. The study presented a clearly visible case of how the structure of the institutionalized activity that was derived from the multiracial and multicultural nature of the population created the need to be aware of and articulate both racial and ethnic identities. In everyday life such identity negotiation may not be as apparent as in the case of the beauty pageant, but it is common and no less real.

ETHNIC IDENTITY AND SOCIAL CHANGE

The search for one's identity has often been a driving force in history and society. It has been an underlying factor in two of the most important social processes of the nineteenth and twentieth centuries, social mobility and nationalism. These past two centuries saw the West transformed from a mainly agricultural to a mainly urban and industrial society. The same process of change has taken place more recently in several societies of the East, and is continuing to take place in other societies of the world. This has meant a process of social mobility for large sectors of populations. Social mobility, i.e., the changing of types of occupational positions, either in one's lifetime or from one generation to another, has meant, not only a change in the access to economic resources, but also an increase in prestige and a change in identity to one involving a higher self-esteem.

The process of social mobility involving the transformation of rural societies has been accompanied by nationalisms, i.e., movements for the creation and establishment of independent nation-states. As in social mobility, nationalism has meant not only an access to power, but also a development, on the collective and individual level, of new identity and of new self-esteem. Establishment of nation-states has usually involved a conflict with either a previously dominant class in society, as in the case of the French Revolution, or a conflict with an existing imperial power, as in the case of many Eastern European nations, many African nations, India and so on.

Creation of a new or transformed identity has been a central aspect of nationalism. In their passion to establish this identity and establish themselves as the societal majority, nationalist movements have often moved to extremes and directed their efforts not only against the previous majority groups, but also against other minority groups in society. This has meant conflict over identities and, in the case of emerging nations, establishing one ethnic identity over other identities as the majority identity in a new society. In the case of already established or long-established nation-states, conflict with minorities has often meant that the majority group has felt a threat to its identity, usually unjustified, from the minority ethnic groups.

In all these processes, the search for a new, or rediscovered, transformed identity, one that would enhance self-esteem or would maintain self-esteem, has been a central force. In many established societies, collective efforts by minority groups to retain their identity have led to changes in legislation and to changes in the structure and styles of intergroup relations. Those who organized and worked for social change in interethnic and interracial relations were persons who themselves were conscious of their ethnic identity and turned to social activism to insure justice for those who shared this identity. One such area of change was human rights. In the United States, the National Association for the Advancement of Colored People (NAACP), the most influential organization aimed at changing the discriminatory laws of the country, was established in 1909-1910 by highly educated Black professionals with the support of white educated people. By the 1950s, with the help of the Black clergy, the Black consciousness increased and the Black civil rights movement gained mass support from the Black community (Morris, 1984). This is not the place to document the changes that the Black civil rights movement brought about in the United States; they were substantial. The Jim Crow laws, such as those requiring Blacks to sit only in the back of public buses, or preventing them from making use of all-white restaurants, lavatories, and so on and various other discriminatory laws were abolished, voting rights were restored to the Blacks, segregation in schools, in the military, and other institutions was declared illegal, various programs were established to compensate for the long years of disadvantage that the Blacks had suffered as a result of discrimination, public opinion was turned to respect the identity of the Black Americans. While prejudice and discrimination against the Blacks still remains in the white community, its extent is much less than what it was before the 1950s before the changes in the legal structure and in important social institutions.

In Canada, as was pointed out in Chapter 2, the retention of French identity was legally protected after the conquest and treaties gave the Native peoples some territorial identity. Still, since the 1950s, with the increased education of all ethnic populations and with increased social mobility, ethnic identities have acquired a new form, to a large extent, of the "rediscovery" type. The effect of this has been movements for change of the status of the respective groups. Thus, the nationalism among the French Québecers has moved Canada to introduce various changes, including bilingualism. The heightened identity among the Native peoples has made it possible for them to lay claim to the land that was unjustly taken away from them by false treaties and otherwise, to introduce changes into the Indian Act and to gain recognition internationally.

The "Other" ethnic groups likewise have contributed to changes related to their identity. Notable is the human rights legislation introduced since the 1950s, such as the Ontario Human Rights Code of 1962, the human rights legislation in all Canadian provinces by 1977, the Canadian Human Rights Act of 1977, provincial and federal human rights commissions, and the Charter of Rights built into the Canadian constitution in 1981 (Kallen, 1982; Tarnopolsky, 1979; Hill, 1977).

Another important change introduced in Canada in 1971 was the establishment of the policy of multiculturalism. The movement for the policy was pioneered by third-generation leaders of the "Other" ethnic groups. The purpose was to gain recognition of the identity of these groups alongside the English and the French (Isajiw, 1983). By the 1990s, the changes brought about by the policy included the establishment of new institutions, such as ethnic chairs at different Canadian universities, a large series of publications dealing with ethnic diversity in Canada, such as a set of histories of ethnic groups in Canada, journals dealing with Canadian ethnic diversity, associations bringing together persons of different ethnic backgrounds, such as the Canadian Ethnic Studies Association, and various activities expressing the recognition of ethnic diversity in Canada (Fleras and Elliott, 1992: 68-91).

The social changes that have taken place in relation to the retention of distinct ethnic identities were brought about by the collective action of organizations, associations, agencies and the efforts of their leaders; in short, as a result of the process of interethnic relations. The next chapter will look at the meaning and the factors involved in interethnic relations. We will approach interethnic relations as a process of negotiation between different collectivities.

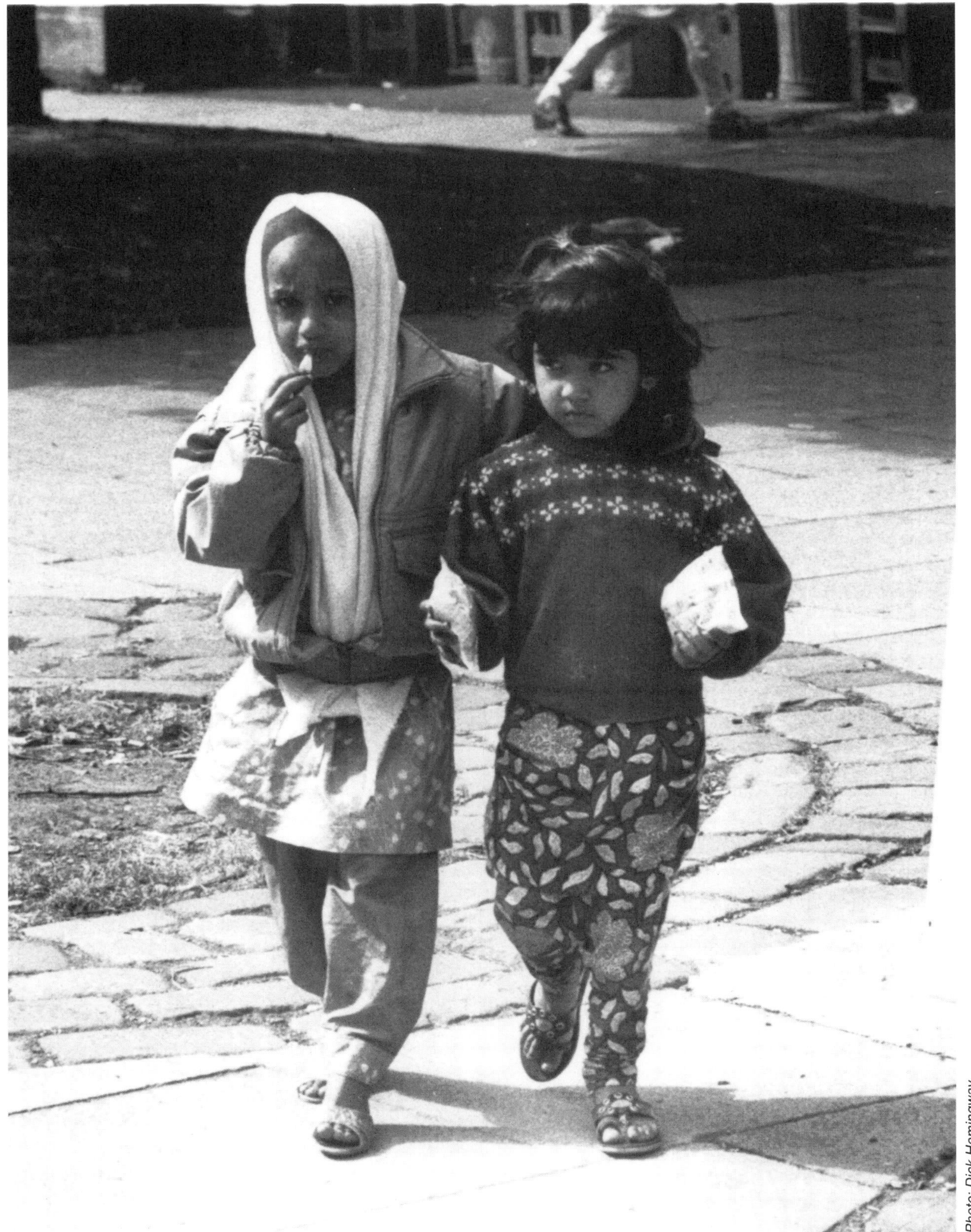

Photo: Dick Hemingway

Young Canadians.

CHAPTER 9

INTERETHNIC RELATIONS

Conflict or Negotiation

How do ethnic groups, as groups, move up our society's status ladder? Does the retention of ethnic identity slow down the social mobility of members of these ethnic groups? What is the role of ethnic elites and mainstream elites in the process of social mobility? What are the politics of interethnic relations? This chapter tries to answer these questions and focuses on two important cases: the politics of Canadian government vis-à-vis Quebec and vis-à-vis the Aboriginal peoples.

In the first chapter of the book, we stated that intergroup relations can be studied from two points of view, from the point of view of society as a whole within which various groups interact and from the point of view of the groups themselves as subjects of the relations. From the point of view of the society, intergroup relations are a process through which integration of society is effected. From the point of view of the specific groups, it is a process through which the groups and their members endeavour to fulfil their values, goals and interests. In consequence, two main problems for society arise: that of access to and allocation of opportunities among the different groups in society in a way that is perceived as just and equitable by all the concerned groups, and that of developing and maintaining solidarity of all the groups with the society as a whole and at least indirectly with one another. In this chapter, we will look at interethnic relations from the point of view of the interacting ethnic groups. In the next chapter, we will look at interethnic relations from the point of view of the society as a whole.

From the point of view of the interacting ethnic groups, the question of opportunities involves improving the status of the group in relations to the other groups in society, or of maintaining the group's status if it is already satisfactory or high. This means changing the group's place in the ethnic stratification system or holding on to it if it is already high, as in the case of the majority group. As in the case of interethnic relations, shifts within the ethnic stratification system can also be looked at from two perspectives: that of the individuals and that of the ethnic group as a collectivity. From the perspective of the individuals, changes of ethnic status mean their own social mobility in the status system of the broader society. From the collective perspective, however, changes of ethnic status mean more options (or fewer, if the mobility is downwards) for collective action of an ethnic group in relation to other groups and to the broader society. Social mobility of an ethnic group changes the relationship of the group to the larger society.

The social mobility of individuals and the collective action of a group are closely interrelated, and it is a combination of both of these that accounts for changes in the ethnic stratification system of a society. That is, the social mobility of individuals by itself works to change the ethnic status of the group, but, at the same time, the social mobility of individuals with collective consciousness increases the potential for more effective collective action of the group, and effective action of the group can potentially influence the change of the group's ethnic status. In turn, the group itself may be a resource for the social mobility of individuals.

We will first look at social mobility and ask: How does ethnic identity relate to social mobility? Is ethnic identity retention a drawback or a resource for social mobility? Then we will examine the agents of interethnic relations. In particular, we will look at the role that ethnic organizations play in interethnic relations. We will consider interethnic relations to be a process of "negotiation" between ethnic groups, particularly between the minority ethnic groups and the majority ethnic groups. We will study the issues over which ethnic groups "negotiate" and the importance of group elites in this process.

ETHNIC GROUPS AND SOCIAL MOBILITY

In broad terms, the concept of social mobility refers to any shift in the social status or social status location of individuals or groups. In the chapter dealing with ethnic stratification, we discussed the determinants of ethnic status. These are also determinants of any social status. The shift in the status can be either upwards or downwards. This is known as *vertical social mobility.* That is, persons or a group may increase or improve their status, as, for example, moving from a position of assistant manager to that of chief manager, from that of a labourer to that of a foreman, from skilled worker to professional worker and so on. Inversely, persons' status may shift downwards, as in the example of many immigrants who held professional positions in their home countries but, because of different professional requirements in their country of immigration, were able to obtain only skilled or semi-skilled kinds of jobs.

There can also be *horizontal social mobility.* This is not so much a shift in the status itself as a shift in status location. That is, persons may move from a skilled or semi-skilled job in one industry to a skilled or semi-skilled job in another industry, or from being a professor at one university to being a professor at another university. There may be benefits or disadvantages in these shifts, but they do not substantially change the basic social status of these persons. Thus, horizontal mobility can be positive when there are some benefits in these shifts, as, for example, somewhat better pay or shorter hours or the like. Similarly, it may be negative when there are some disadvantages in making status location shifts, as, for example, when persons have to change jobs or have to accept lower pay, higher work loads or the like.

Both vertical and horizontal social mobility are sociologically significant. The concepts are particularly useful when comparing the social mobility of different groups. For example, some ethnic groups may have high upward vertical mobility among its members, while other may have little of such mobility. Some may experience a lot of horizontal mobility but little upward vertical mobility. Still others, such as new ethnic groups, may experience a considerable degree of downward social mobility.

Furthermore, sociologists distinguish between *career mobility* and *generational mobility* (also called intergenerational mobility). Career mobility refers to changes in social status during a person's lifetime. It refers to the social status trajectory of one's life. For example, a person may begin his or her adult life as a labourer, but then be promoted to a foreman, later to a manager, and end up as a co-owner or owner of an enterprise. Generational mobility, on the other hand, refers to the shifts in the social status from one generation to another, from parents to children. Thus, a person's father might have been a small farmer, the person himself or herself may become an owner or manager of a manufacturing enterprise, and the person's son or daughter may be a university professor or an elected member of parliament. Career and generational mobility can be either upwards or downwards or a combination of both, or it can be a shift only in status location or a combination of both vertical and horizontal mobility.

• Ethnic Identity Retention: A Drawback to Social Mobility?

In Chapter 5 we discussed the ethnic stratification of society and, in Chapter 8, ethnic identity retention. A question that has been much debated in Canadian sociology has been whether ethnic identity retention is a drawback to individuals' social mobility and change of a group's ethnic status. In Canadian sociological literature, the question was raised first by John Porter. Porter (1965, 1975) proposed the argument that, since statistics showed that in Canada minority ethnic groups, i.e., those other than the British, were over-represented in the lower status occupations and under-represented in the higher status occupations, retention of ethnic identity is a drawback for social mobility as it keeps members of minority ethnic groups from moving up on the status ladder. This came to be known as the "Porter Thesis." In the United States a similar argument, though one theoretically more elaborate, was proposed by Norbert Wiley (1967). Wiley argued that members of minority ethnic groups are socialized to anticipate opportunities in the context of the ethnic community. But ethnic community structures, while offering some mobility possibilities for their members, have a smaller chain of opportunities than does the structure of the mainstream society. They are like links that, instead of connecting with higher levels of the mainstream, lead away from it to a dead end. The career expectations inculcated by minority ethnic groups are therefore lower than those predominant in the mainstream. Hence, psychological commitment to an ethnic group becomes a "mobility trap" for the group's members.

Some ten years later, Porter's thesis was put to critical empirical tests. Analysis of census statistics showed that the thesis was incorrect. Gordon Darroch (1979) re-examined the census data on the occupational status of ethnic groups originally analyzed by Porter and calculated indices of dissimilarity from the national average for each ethnic group. He found that dissimilarity was substantial in the 1931 census for all non-British groups, but showed a sharp decline thereafter, except for Canadian Aboriginal peoples. By 1961, seven of the eleven groups studied had reduced their dissimilarity from the national average to 10 percent or less. Since 1971, with some exceptions, Darroch observed a growing convergence of the social statuses among ethnic groups in Canada. This came to be known in contrast to the Porter Thesis as the "convergence hypothesis." The hypothesis implied that there was a growing vertical mobility among all ethnic groups in Canada, except for the Canadian Aboriginals. Darroch concluded that "for some members of a given ethnic population, there exist serious 'mobility traps'; while for others ethnic identity may be of no consequence to mobility whatsoever. Still others may be able to translate their heritage into distinct occupational opportunities" (Darroch, 1979: 20).

The 1986 Canadian census statistics support Darroch's conclusion. Porter showed that in the mid-sixties the stratification hierarchy consisted of the British and the French at the top, followed by North Europeans, South Europeans and the racial group categories at the bottom. The census statistics on educational achievement, income, and occupation as presented in Chapter 5 show that by the 1990s this order has changed. A number of Middle Eastern, South Asian, East Asian and other groups had higher educational, occupational and income levels than did the British or the French groups. The data thus support the convergence hypothesis, indirectly indicating that there has been a significant degree of social mobility among Canadian ethnic groups. Porter (1985) himself modified his position at the end.

While showing changes in the ethnic stratification system and indicating social mobility in general terms, the census statistics do not give a direct assessment of generational mobility. To do so, one has to compare the educational, occupational and income statistics of parents, their children and their grandchildren. The Toronto study included information about the occupational and educational background of three generations. Analysis of these data also gave support to the convergence hypothesis. It showed (Isajiw, Sev'er, Driedger, 1993) that all four groups studied (German, Italian, Jewish, Ukrainian) enjoyed significant upward occupational and educational mobility across three generations. The study also found that there was no significant relationship between ethnic identity in any of its forms and occupational mobility. That is, retention of ethnic identity was not a drawback for occupational mobility. There was, however, some correlation between retention of some forms of ethnic identity, especially the form connected with high retention of ethnic external cultural patterns, and educational mobility. That is, for some, but not all, ethnic groups, high retention of ethnic external patterns may be a drawback for their higher educational attainment. However, the reverse may also be true, i.e., in some ethnic groups lower educational attainment may influence a higher retention of external ethnic patterns of behaviour. In either case, this relates mainly to the first generation and less so to the consecutive ones. Over the second and the third generations, the groups become more alike, and ethnic identity retention does not affect social mobility. Another analysis of the same data has also arrived at the same conclusion (Reitz and Sklar, 1997).

• Ethnicity and the Societal Elites

An important aspect of the question of social mobility of ethnic minority groups is the question as to what extent ethnic minorities are represented in the elite positions in society and to what extent the elite positions in society are opened to them. Studies of ethnic origins of Canadian elites by Wallace Clement (1975; 1985) and Dennis Olsen (1980) established another line in John Porter's legacy. As was pointed out in Chapter 2, Porter (1965) showed that Canadian power elites are closely intermeshed, and they include very few persons or families of other than British or French origin. Clement (1975) studied this issue in terms of the persons who sit on the boards of directors of the largest Canadian business corporations, and his studies have indicated that the non-British and non-French groups have not significantly entered into these positions. Even the French were found in rather small numbers in these positions, as compared with the British. In other words, members of ethnic minority groups have not been mobile, in any significant numbers, in gaining the elite positions in society.

Similar to the general mobility-trap debate, however, this school of thought became an object of criticism in the 1990s. A number of sociologists (Ogmundson, 1990; Rich, 1991) produced data that showed that Canadian elites may not be as exclusive as the Porter and Clement school has thought.

The Canadian Establishment

by Peter C. Newman

HOW AN ESTABLISHMENT ORGANIZES ITSELF DETERMINES HOW A NATION WILL PURSUE ITS OBJECTIVES. Canada's Establishment consists of a surprisingly compact self-perpetuating group of perhaps a thousand men who act as a kind of informal *junta*, linked much more closely to each other than to their country.

Although their power is waning, they still possess the ability to compel obedience, to shape events and trends—political and cultural as well as economic—in their favour. Their exercise of authority is subtle, not always successful, but constantly aimed at fulfilling Bertrand Russell's definition of power as "the production of intended effects." Operating, outside the constitutional forms, the Establishment's adherents exercise a self-imposed mandate unburdened by public accountability.

Without being a social compact, the confederacy of Canadian Establishments (loosely knit yet interlocking) forms a psychological entity. Its members share habits of thought and action, common sets of values, beliefs, and enemies. They consider themselves an untitled aristocracy whose virtue has been certified by their elevation to one of the dominant elites.

They are, therefore they rule.

Although the Canadian Establishment is coming increasingly under American control, it remains dominated by old Canada Wasps,* holding proud and together through the right career histories and, most emphatically, the right connections. Power tends to connect; absolute power connects absolutely.

There exists no single monolithic Establishment in this country, but *rings* of establishments, and the most important of them all—because it is so concentrated, so powerful, and influences so many others—is that formed by the businessmen who control the Canadian economy's private sector.

Canada's Establishment is dominated by the corporate elite, partly because its members move freely from function to function, sliding in and out of Liberal cabinets, filling the seats on the boards of the main cultural institutions, making themselves felt within the governing bodies of the universities, running most of the institutions that count. "Corporate power is not tangential to Canadian society," James Eayres, the University of Toronto political scientist, has concluded. "Corporate Power *is* Canadian society."

Like the members of any other elite, the Canadian business Establishment's adherents disavow the possession of power, even if they value its exercise. They are too busy to hold political office but like to think they determine who does. They are accustomed to running things—promoting those men (and groups of men) they regard as reliable, blocking the interlopers and all too frequently the innovative, deciding what is good and desirable for the society in which they operate. Much of their influence operates in the form of negative sanctions: invisible barriers unaccountably raised against people and policies they don't accept.

Despite their remarkably similar habits, theirs is a paradoxical kinship, for they belong to an elite that maintains its dynamism through incessant jousting for position within its own careful confines.

Even when the occasional bitter feud erupts into public view these games of power are played to a particular set of rules that are not laid down, even if they are well understood.

Members of this business Establishment touch and greet each other on a wide spectrum of intimacy depending on the commonalty of their objectives at any given moment. But no matter how much their goals may temporarily conflict, they always take one another into account. They accept, understand, and protect each other. ("Make certain you see him before noon," runs the gentle admonition about one of the Establishment's most distinguished power-holders who has a drinking problem.)

Yet it is an Establishment in a state of unprecedented transition. The great business dynasties—except for some Molsons and Eatons—which so recently dominated Canada's economy have all but vanished from contention. Power shifts according to the ways money is made. Leaving behind the railway and banking barons, the mining and oil fortunes, wealth is now flowing out of very different fashions and life styles. There are many more millionaires ("people one hardly knows"); the influence of money grows much more diffuse. Education, breeding, and manners have become deflated currencies among the business elite.

Part of this phenomenon—whose implications for the Canadian social structure have yet to be realized—is that the wealth and authority once organized around families (as they still are in some regional pockets, mainly in the Maritimes) have been replaced by the national power grips of the huge corporations. The most influential men in most Canadian cities and towns no longer belong to local power clusters. Instead, they are the smooth ambassadors of large multinational or transnational corporations. Careers are made in companies, not communities. The equations of power are changing.

---

* More precisely, as Don McGillivray of the *Financial Times* has pointed out, the Canadian equivalent of this form for "White Anglo-Saxon Protestants" should probably be "White Anglo-Celt Protestants" or Wacps.

Source: Peter C. Newman, *The Canadian Establishment*, Toronto: McClelland & Stewart Inc., 1975. Used by permission of the publisher.

From the point of view of the interrelations of minority ethnic groups, membership in the mainstream elite community is significant inasmuch as these members can serve as a resource for the concerns of the ethnic community. This presumes at least some degree of identity with a specific ethnic group on the part of the elite members. The resources that such elites provide can be monetary donations or grants in support of ethnic institutions or causes, or can be influence on behalf of the ethnic group or any of its activities on those who have decision-making power or direct decision making on behalf of the group if the elite members hold relevant decision-making positions. Many of the persons or families who become part of the mainstream elite also become elites in their ethnic community and may serve as leaders of ethnic organizations.

Examples of such elite members are such persons as Samuel, Charles and Edgar Bronfman and the Bronfman family, owners of the Seagrams company whose voice and financial support have been of importance to both the Canadian society and the Canadian Jewish community. Likewise, the Bronfman family members have provided leadership for the top Jewish organizations, such as the Canadian Jewish Congress and the World Jewish Congress (Marrus, 1991; Bronfman, 1996; Gittins, 1995). Other examples of mainstream elites who come from ethnic minority groups and who have also served to provide economic and political resource for their ethnic groups are Paul Desmarais of Sudbury and Montreal, founder of the Bombardier Co., in relation to the French, Thomas Bata of Ontario, owner of Bata Shoe Co., in relation to the Czech community, Stephen Roman, founder of Denison Mines Ltd., in relation to the Slovak community, Peter Jacyk of Toronto, founder of The Jacyk Group, a land development firm, in relation to the Ukrainian community.

There has always been a question as to whether all of these persons and families, or even any of them, have been fully accepted by the mainstream elite community. In any case, even if the Canadian elite structure has been less exclusive since the 1970s than previously, the presence of persons of diverse ethnic backgrounds in the Canadian elite structure has remained small as compared with the persons and families of the majority group background.

The elite we have been talking about up to now represent the economic elite of society. A number of ethnic minority groups have moved into the society's political elite. This mobility has taken place through the electoral process and involved such positions as mayor, member of provincial or national parliament, nominee to cabinet, appointment to royal commissions and so on. In a democratic society, however, in which elected service is always for a limited period of time, political elites do not form stable communities. While political elites are very important in terms of introducing new policies regarding immigration and ethnic diversity and integration of society, they themselves often rely on the economic elites for support in their election and their policies. Analysts of the nature of the Canadian establishment (Porter, 1965; Newman, 1975, 1979, 1998) have pointed out that there is a close interdependence between the top politicians in the country and the economic elite. The economic elite tends to exercise, as it were, negative power on the political sphere. As Newman (1975: 388) pointed out, "much of their influence operates in the form of negative sanctions: invisible barriers unaccountably raised against people and policies they don't accept."

• The Role of Strategic Occupations

Social mobility of minority groups, especially social mobility in the middle class, is an important structural context of contemporary interethnic relations. In this context, a significant role is played by those groups whose members have the opportunity to move into *strategic occupations*. By this concept is meant occupations that involve a degree of influence on the wider circles of the structure of society. Many middle-class occupations carry with them some influence on the position-holders' immediate circle of people, i.e., those for whom they are immediately responsible or those whom they may be in charge of, as, for example, managers who influence their employees, teachers who influence their students, consultants or counsellors who influence their clients and the like. Strategic occupations, however, offer their holders the capacity to influence those who are beyond their direct jurisdiction. For example, a corporation executive may not only have power over the employees of his corporation, but, by serving on the boards of directors of other corporations or by serving on some governmental commissions, may have an influence on the policies of other corporations and on the policies of the government. In other words, while general middle-class occupations have only linear influence, strategic occupations, in addition to the linear, also have lateral influence.

In the modern context, the most important strategic occupations are in business, politics and the media. In the field of business, as indicated above, these are occupations at the top of corporations that allow those who hold them to sit on boards of directors of other corporations and on governmental commissions. The authors referred to above (Porter, 1965; Clement, 1975; Newman, 1979) give ample examples of such interconnectedness between top corporate positions in Canada. In the global context, international interconnectedness between financial corporations has additional significance.

In the political sphere in general, all elected positions are in some degree strategic positions. However, particularly important influence is wielded by those members of parliaments who become appointed to cabinets. The main policy decisions for the entire constituency, be it on the all-societal, federal, provincial or municipal levels, are made mainly by the cabinet bodies and then approved by the elected assemblies. However, within a more limited scope, those members of the government bureaucracy who are on the top levels of civil service also occupy strategic positions. Many elected members of parliaments depend to a large extent on the civil servants for the continuity of their activity from one administration to another and the top civil servants are those who provide it. Since they have to work with many governments their influence can be wide. There are also other positions with the government that are of a strategic nature. We have already mentioned governmental commissions that include persons from business and other professions. There are also numerous committees that decide on the distribution of public grants among different bodies of citizens. Often persons from outside of the government from various professions are on such committees, and they can have an important influence on who gets the funds.

Last, but not least, is the media. This includes occupations that offer decision-making power as to what information is to be widely transmitted. These are the editorial positions with newspapers, journals, magazines, television and radio programs and the positions of the producers of such programs. It also includes the decision-making positions in the cultural media, such as impresarios, drama producers, literature publishers and the like. In the context of the rapid ascendance of an information-based economy and information-based global interdependence, the role of the media is of central strategic importance.

While the direct role of the media is to distribute information, an important indirect function that the mainstream media performs for society is to make specific issues, which may be issues of a few or one group or of a few or one individual, of concern to the entire society. In other words, the media institutionalizes issues and institutionalizes perspectives on them. For example, in the 1990s, crimes of one person, serial killer Clifford Olson, became of concern to Canadian society as a whole through media publicity. This publicity stimulated groups of citizens to propose legislation for Canada that would protect communities from paroled serial killers. Further below we will look at the importance that this function of the media–and in general access to the mainstream media–has for ethnic minority groups.

In regard to the social mobility of ethnic minority groups, the question raised here is: to what extent are members of ethnic minority groups able to move into the strategic occupations of society? The studies of Canadian business elites cited above have indicated that only a few members of some ethnic minority groups have become part of the Canadian corporate business elite. More systematic studies of this and of minority mobility into the other strategic occupations are still to be undertaken. Traditionally, strategic occupations have been held mainly by members of the majority group. Some minority groups, however, have made inroads into some of these occupations more than others. Those ethnic minority groups that make such inroads in significant numbers become what we defined in Chapter 1 as *middle-man minorities.* We explained the concept of middle-man minority there. Here we will indicate in a theoretical way a few aspects of the middle-man minority position that are of significance from the point of view of interethnic relations.

Members of middle-man minorities in strategic occupations are expected by those members of the majority group who are also in strategic occupations to excel at their work. This often serves as a test of the respective minority group and places extra pressure on the middle-man minority members to oblige. A consequence of this can be a strong emphasis on education among the middle-man minority members. Furthermore, middle-man minority members may be expected by the majority group to, as it were, act as spokespersons for other minorities. Their opinions on minority issues may appear more often in the mainstream media and hence may be taken more seriously than the opinion of members of other minorities. They may also act as gatekeepers for some important strategic occupations. Members of the majority group may thus come to depend on the middle-man minority for their relations with other minority groups. All this may make the middle-man minority more visible in the eyes of both the majority group and other minority groups. On the one hand, such groups may serve as models for social mobility of other minority groups. On the other hand, prejudice and racism may result from this, as the majority group may come to see the middle-man minority as a potential threat to their own position and the other minority groups may perceive them as presenting a blockage to their own social mobility. As was pointed out in Chapter 1, middle-man minority groups often come to be, as it were, caught between the groups in the higher and the lower levels of the ethnic stratification system.

We will now look at the nature of the relationship of minority groups to the broader society as represented by the different stages of social mobility.

• Stages of Group Social Mobility and Ethnic Groups' Relationship to Society

When we study the changes in the occupational structure of ethnic groups over a number of decades, certain trends can be observed. These trends are indicators of patterns or stages of social mobility of ethnic groups as groups. The data provided by the Canadian censuses makes it possible to compare the over- and under-representation in various occupational categories of a number of ethnic groups from 1931 to 1971. The data on ethnic groups from the 1981 census to the 1996 census is unfortunately not comparable with the previous censuses, because, since 1981, the ethnic origin question has been substantially modified. The trends from 1931 to 1971 may be indicative only of that period and the specific type of persons that were immigrating to Canada at that time. Nevertheless, these data provide a valuable picture of the historical development of the ethnic aspect of the Canadian social structure. We will use as the starting point of our theoretical analysis John Porter's (1965: 87) notion of entrance status.

The data suggest that historically there have been three stages of occupational mobility of ethnic groups. The first stage was a shift out of the primary and agricultural occupations of the groups that had originally been heavily over-represented in these occupations, for example, the Germans, Dutch, Scandinavians, Eastern Europeans, French and Irish. The second stage consisted of substantially increased participation in the labouring, manufacturing, service, clerical, sales, managerial and professional occupations, with the largest increases in the manufacturing category, but without reaching over-representation in the "white collar" occupations. The third stage appeared when the participation in labouring occupations decreased to the point of under-representation, participation in manufacturing remained constant or began to decrease, but significant increases in the sales, managerial and professional categories reached the point of over-representation and have continued in that direction.

The sociological significance of these stages of ethnic group mobility is that they represent shifts in the groups' relationship to the broader society. The first stage can be said to represent primarily the process of adaptation and cultural incorporation of an immigrant group. Historically, it meant taking over of the urban values of the rapidly urbanizing Canadian society. The second stage can be said to represent the process of greater structural incorporation. It represents a move for better paying, better status jobs, or, in different words, a reach for equality of opportunities, for ensuring one's "rightful" place in the broader society. The third stage means that the minority groups are developing the capability of gaining a measure of influence or power that goes beyond the groups' own boundaries into the broader society as a whole. This can be said to mean a reach for the rights of the establishment, without yet becoming part of it.

In this process of group social mobility, ethnic groups come to establish and rely on voluntary organizations and develop leadership or ethnic elite structures that claim the right to act on behalf of the ethnic group. We will now turn to an analysis of these.

ETHNIC ORGANIZATIONS AND LEADERSHIP

In the first chapter we stated that one important mechanism or means through which interethnic relations take place are ethnic voluntary organizations. Such organizations can be said to "negotiate" with organizations from outside the group, particularly with various societal agencies and institutions. In this section, we will examine the nature of ethnic organizations and their leadership and then we will look at what the "negotiation" process involves.

All ethnic groups establish some organizations. First, however, it is important to distinguish between ethnic organizations and ethnic institutions. Ethnic institutions refer to those institutions within the boundaries of an ethnic group that parallel the basic mainstream institutions of the broader society. The concept of the basic social institution refers to organized complexes of behaviour patterns centring around the fulfilment of social needs recognized by the members of society to be essential to its existence. Since such needs are seen to be so important, these complexes of behaviour patterns include jobs for which persons are remunerated. Examples are economic, political, family, educational, religious, cultural, recreational and health institutions. Minority ethnic groups usually depend on the basic social institutions of the broader, mainstream society, but they also develop at least some institutions of their own that are parallel to those of the mainstream in order to fulfil their members' basic needs according to the groups' cultural identity requirements. Thus, as we pointed out previously, members of many ethnic minority groups set up ethnic businesses, ethnic schools (often only weekend schools) and churches or form minority enclaves in the institutions of the broader society, such as different industries, political parties and the like.

Voluntary organizations are made up of persons who devote their time to the collective work "after hours." They may employ some persons to help them in this work, but their main membership is not remunerated for their time. While basic social institutions have a direct reference to the basic needs of society, voluntary organizations deal indirectly with the basic needs. But while not working primarily to fulfil the basic social needs, voluntary organizations usually dedicate themselves to causes that derive from the basic institutions. In this manner they can provide significant help to the work of the institutions. Thus for example, a voluntary organization dedicated to the study of an ethnic culture can "feed" the results of its work into the respective educational system existing in the ethnic community. Likewise, a minority group's human rights or anti-racism organization can exert lobbying pressure or help to form public opinion on issues of prejudice and discrimination that can have significant effects on the broader society's political institutions and legislation.

Minority ethnic groups' voluntary organizations are of special significance in cases where ethnic groups have few effective institutions of their own. In such cases, voluntary organizations may become "surrogate institutions," performing the work of what in the mainstream society would be done by established institutions. This is particularly the case with ethnic organizations that are involved in political activities, such as lobbying the mainstream government and influencing public opinion. The reason for this is that any political activity by a minority group within a broader society that is not related to the mainstream political institutions cannot perform the function of fulfilling the basic political needs of the ethnic community. Many political parties transplanted by immigrants from their society of origin were relevant to that society, but become irrelevant in the immigrants' host society. Hence, in the minority community itself such political parties, rather than maintaining themselves as institutions, become voluntary organizations.

The exact numbers of ethnic organizations, even within one ethnic community, is not easy to ascertain. Some groups have many organizations, others, only a few. Some ethnic organizations are national, others, local. Many national ethnic organizations have chapters provincially and municipally. New organizations are established and some of the old ones become diminished or defunct. No accurate lists of all ethnic organizations are readily available. In 1974, Statistics Canada published the only official list of ethnic groups and a count of their organizations, but they admitted that this was not a complete list or a complete count. According to Statistic Canada (1974: 282), among the 56 ethnic groups listed, there were 727 organizations. The 10 groups with the largest numbers of organizations were: Italian (66 organizations), Polish (45), German (43), Ukrainian (42), Chinese (36), Greek (31), Jewish (26), Estonian (24), Lithuanian (21), Dutch (20). The 10 groups with the smallest numbers of organizations were: Malaysian, Turkish, Haitian, Latin American, Maltese, West Indian, Pakistani, Philippine, Lebanese-Syrian and Bulgarian, with only 1 to 5 organizations each. Of course, since that time many changes have taken place. Likewise, the under-count in these official statistics was probably substantial. For example, a more careful count of organizations in the Ukrainian Canadian group (Isajiw and Makuch, 1994: 346-349) showed over 100 organizations. A selected count of Black organizations, including African and Afro-Caribbean ethnic groups, in Toronto alone produced 57 organizations (Kasher, 1997: 7-14).

• Expressive and Instrumental Organizations

These numbers, incomplete as they may be, indicate that organizations play an important role in the life of ethnic communities. The roles which they play can be characterized under two types: *expressive* and *instrumental.* According to these two types of roles we can distinguish two types of ethnic organizations: expressive ethnic organizations and instrumental ethnic organizations. Expressive organizations are those whose activities are aimed at expression and cultivation of a group's identity. This includes support of cultural and educational activities, such as concerts, theatre presentations, exhibits, seminars and festivals, and also support of cultural creativity and research and publications on the group's culture and history. Expressive organizations also include recreational activities that reinforce ethnic friendship and familistic ties, such as the activities of various clubs, community houses and organizations that sponsor get-togethers, holiday and anniversary celebrations, banquets, dances, sports activities and the like. In short, expressive organizations are oriented internally towards the ethnic community.

Instrumental organizations are those that are oriented externally, towards the larger society. Their activities are aimed at either adapting members of the group to the larger society or at gaining for the minority group some increased benefits or certain rights and recognition from the larger society. Activities of such organizations as credit unions, which are sometimes attached to ethnic institutions (parishes, schools), aim at betterment of the economic adaptation of their members. They may lend their members money for mortgages or as initial help for a business start, often with more favourable interest rates than those obtained in the mainstream banks or trust companies. The other kind of instrumental organizations undertake political activities. They may exert pressure on the government for legislation favourable to their causes or may try to influence the mainstream public opinion in favour of their causes. These causes may be concerned with human or civil rights, with the goal of eliminating discrimination and prejudice against a group or with bringing about new policies and legislation or with attempts to influence the authorities on behalf of the minority group's country of origin. In short, the effect of the activities of instrumental organizations is to better the ethnic status of the groups they represent. Examples of instrumentally oriented organizations are ethnic professional and businessmen's organizations, human rights or anti-defamation organizations, immigrant service organizations, ethnic national umbrella organizations, ethnic diaspora world congresses and the like.

Most ethnic groups have both expressive and instrumental types of organizations (Kasher, 1997). Instrumental associations may from time to time sponsor some expressive activities for the community, and expressive organizations may from time to time, especially in an ethnic community's critical periods, engage in instrumental activities. However, some ethnic groups place a stronger emphasis on the expressive activities of their organizations than on the instrumental ones, and some groups are usually more effective in their instrumental activities than others. It is the instrumental organizations that most directly enter into interethnic relations on behalf of their ethnic groups.

Interviews with a sample of South Asian women from Atlantic Canada, British Columbia and Alberta and other observational data have shown that, while organizations among South Asian women focused on instrumental issues, such as language training, employment, strategies against violence, discrimination at work, oppression in the household and other instrumental issues, they also developed expressive programs aimed at transmission of the groups' religion and culture to their younger generations (Ralston, 1994).

In the histories of ethnic minority groups, in the early periods after immigration of the first waves of immigrants to North America, most ethnic organizations would be formed around the immigrants' church or temple. These included choirs, laypersons' auxiliary groups, youth groups, cultural groups and various laypersons' committees. With greater social mobility and greater occupational differentiation, more secular organizations, independent from the religious institutions, formed and, with time, would predominate in the ethnic community. As the process of organizational differentiation progressed, many ethnic groups formed umbrella organizations to coordinate the activities of the diverse organizations and to "represent" the group to the outside society. These examples (Kasher, 1997) will illustrate the diversity of such coordinating organizations:

Assembly of First Nations, Federation of Trinidad and Tobago Organizations of Canada, National Council of Barbadian Associations in Canada, Canadian Arab Federation, Clans and Scottish Societies of Canada, Chinese Canadian National Council, Federation des Clubs Sociaux Franco-Ontariens, German-Canadian Congress, Hellenic Canadian Congress, Federation of Pakistani Canadians, Canadian Council of Hindus, Federation of Sikh Societies of Canada, National Congress of Italian Canadians, National Association of Japanese Canadians, National Congress of Filipino Canadian Organizations in Canada, Canadian Jewish Congress, Conselho das Communidades Portuguesas Do Ontario e Manitoba, Federation of Russian Canadians, Canadian Polish Congress, Ukrainian Canadian Congress, Latvian National Federation in Canada, Finnish Canadian Cultural Federation, Maltese-Canadian Federation.

Eventually a number of ethnic groups established world congresses to coordinate the work of their organizations in various countries of the group's settlement, i.e., the group's diaspora. The word *diaspora* refers to members of the same ethnic group dispersed in different areas of the world, i.e., their settlements in different countries.

• Ethnic Leadership and Organizational Effectiveness

As mentioned above, it is the instrumental organizations who engage in interethnic relations, but not all ethnic instrumental organizations are equally efficient in these activities. The effectiveness of organizations depends on a number of factors, such as the educational and occupational backgrounds of their members, the resources that they are able to muster, but, above all, the type and quality of the groups' leadership. Several questions arise in this respect. First, who becomes a leader in ethnic organizations? Second, what kinds of constraints do ethnic leaders typically face and which leaders become the most effective in interethnic relations? Third, what is the typical process or conduct of interethnic relations? We will try to answer these questions one by one.

As in all social phenomena, who becomes a leader in ethnic organizations depends upon a number of factors. Among these is the prestige or status of persons in the community. That is, those who become leaders tend to be persons who for other reasons already have some prestige in the ethnic community. These may be economically or professionally successful people or persons who have previously held leadership positions in other organizations. Often, persons who emerge as leaders in youth organizations when they are young also become leaders later on in their life, in other organizations.

The most important factor of leadership is the perceived ability of persons to solve different group problems. In his study of ethnic leadership, Raymond Breton (1990, 1991: 61-73) asked his respondents to indicate what qualities they thought were most important in a potential leader of their group. Although there were variations between the members of different ethnic groups of whom the question was asked, the largest percentages answered that the most important qualification was education, followed by the persons' organizational ability, by ability to have good relations with people who are already leaders, and then by having wealth and money. What is interesting is that while education was the most important quality mentioned, it is obvious that the respondents saw education as a resource that would enable those who become leaders to have organizational ability and the ability to get along with other leaders. Similarly, the emphasis on possession of wealth and money must have been seen by the respondents as a means of having contacts with already established leaders and a means of using them and the prestige acquired through them as a resource in community functions. Breton (1991: 64) concludes that the wealth of individuals was seen as a set of moral obligations vis-à-vis the community and its members and that the wealthy individuals who refused to identify with the community could be respected and envied, but would also be considered as outcasts or even renegades.

A study of organizational leadership among Arab businessmen in Toronto supports Breton's conclusion. The hypothesis that the investigator, Fayiz Suyyagh (1995) wanted to test was that businessmen become leaders in the community in the early part of the development of their business because their exposure to the community will be useful for their business, but when their business becomes well established, they lose interest in the group's organizational life. Suyyagh's interviews, however, revealed that this was not the case. His findings showed that the prestige gained in business was useful for acquiring organizational leadership, but many successful businessmen kept their leadership positions well after their business was well established. They did so because they felt that they had something to contribute to the community and were successful in doing so.

As we pointed out above, there are two types of ethnic organizations, those which work primarily with the ethnic community's expressive goals and those that work primarily with the community's instrumental goals. The two types of organizations require different types of leadership. Those with expressive goals are organizations that focus on the community internally. While the managerial skills of the leaders are important, what is even more important is knowledge and understanding of the group's culture, at least some knowledge of the ethnic language, sensitivity to the group's internal differences, such as the ethnic community's class structure and its political and religious segmentation, ability to work according to the group's organizational style, which may be completely different from that of the larger society, ability to participate in the group's style of community functions and the like. Persons who are second or third generation may have difficulties participating in the organizational life if it is dominated by persons who are mainly first generation and vice-versa, persons who are first generation may be completely ineffective leaders in organizations dominated by the second or third generation. Likewise, personalities who are more instrumentally oriented may not make good leaders in organizations that are primarily oriented towards expressive goals, and vise-versa.

Leaders in organizations with instrumental type of goals must have a different set of qualities. The organization is oriented towards the larger society and hence a knowledge of the organizational style of the larger society is required. This makes mandatory a good acquaintance with the prevalent laws and regulations, with the current issues of general concern, with the differences in perspectives of the societal political parties and other sectors of society, with the specific issues and demands of other ethnic groups in society and the like. It also necessitates skills in establishing contacts and networking with other leaders, politicians, government officials and leaders of organizations of other ethnic groups in order to improve the ethnic status of the group or to achieve the group's interests. An instrumental leader, as Breton (1991: 67) has indicated, is a "broker" between the ethnic community and the larger society, and he or she must have the ability to function in two cultures and to mediate new ideas and effectively respond to the pressures of both.

Many community members and even the leaders themselves often have serious doubts about the leaders' efficacy in relation to the larger society. Breton's study showed that, on the average, about 34 percent of ethnic community members and 42 percent of ethnic community leaders felt that society's politicians do not take ethnic leaders seriously. It also showed that, on the average, 35 percent of the community members and 57 percent of the ethnic leaders felt that the leaders do not have enough important connections in the larger society (Breton, 1991: 68). What is interesting is that the perceptions of ineffectiveness of the ethnic organizational leaders was highest among the ethnic groups of non-white racial categories and lowest among the middle-man minority groups. Among the West Indians, 54 percent of community members and 79 percent of the community leaders felt that the society's politicians were not taking them seriously, and 65 percent of the community members and 71 percent of the West Indian community leaders felt that they did not have enough connections in the larger society. Implicitly, these data may indicate the prejudice or racism against non-white groups in the predominantly white society.

Prejudice coming from the society's mainstream and a tendency to exclusion by the majority elites is thus one of the major constraints faced by ethnic minority leaders engaged in interethnic relations. Other constraints external to the ethnic group may be a vested interest of outside agencies in having only certain types of persons as leaders of minority organizations. They can achieve this by either exerting pressure, informally or formally, on an ethnic community to appoint only certain kinds of persons as their leaders or acting to increase the prestige of certain persons in the ethnic community whom they would like to see as leaders. This they can do by appointing these persons to prestigious bodies in the mainstream society–committees, positions, or otherwise (Breton, 1991: 74-79)

In addition to these external constraints, there are also many internal constraints that derive from the minority community itself. For one thing, there is the problem of misplaced leadership in ethnic organizations, i.e., persons with qualities that make them expressive leaders placed in leadership positions in organizations with instrumental goals. One reason for this is that expressive leaders acquire prestige within the community, and all organizations like to bring on board persons with established prestige. The preconception is often that if a leader has proven himself or herself in one organization, he or she will be a good leader in another organization. The distinction between expressively and instrumentally oriented organizations is often little understood by members of ethnic communities.

Furthermore, ethnic minority communities are often segmented by regional, political, religious and ideological solidarities, each with their own leadership. This, on the one hand, creates leadership competition for any unified, externally oriented organization, and, on the other hand, may tie down the scope and limit the duration of activities of any leader who receives the support of the majority of organizations. For example, certain courses of action by such a leader may alienate those organizations whose ideology would not permit such action and they may withdraw their support for the leader. There are no enforceable rules that would bind any ethnic organization to necessarily follow any decision made by even the majority of other organizations within the community. Hence, for the outsiders it is often difficult to know if even ethnic umbrella organizations represent the views or wishes of the entire ethnic community. Leaders of umbrella organizations may often suffer from the lack of unified support from the rest of the ethnic community leadership and this takes away from their effectiveness in interethnic relations. The problems in achieving unified leadership, however, should not be seen as something typical only of ethnic minority groups. The leadership of the mainstream society has the same problem. The main difference is that the mainstream society has institutional structures with legal imperatives in accord with which conflicting leadership problems can be resolved. Ethnic minority groups have no such institutional structures, and their leadership conflict is not covered by the mainstream structures. Thus, for example, leadership conflict among political parties of the mainstream society is resolved by popular elections. As a rule, there are no popular elections for leadership that involve all the members of an ethnic community.

Another type of constraint on the organizational effectiveness of minority groups is the problem of slow circulation of leadership. There is a tendency in ethnic organizations to re-elect or re-appoint the same persons time and again, either for the same positions in an organization or for other executive positions in the same organization or for analogous positions in other organizations. It is not uncommon for the same person to be on the executive boards of several organizations at the same time. There are several reasons for this. Since ethnic organizations bring together volunteers, this limits the number of leadership candidates to those who are able or willing to donate their time. This fact may limit the candidates to those persons most dedicated to the organizational cause or to those who are retired and may limit the interest of younger people in active organizational involvement. Furthermore, being a leader or being on the executive of an organization is a status that carries at least some prestige. For many minority group members, such prestige may be very important to their identity. This is particularly true of first-generation persons whose occupations accord them little prestige, or who have been occupationally declassed after immigrating to their host society. It is also true of retired persons. Holding a leadership role in an ethnic organization may socially and psychologically compensate such persons for their lesser or lessened occupational status. This is the phenomenon that "popular wisdom" captures in the saying, "It is better to be a big fish in a small pond than a little fish in a big pond." As a result, persons who hold positions in ethnic organizations may try to hold on to them for as long as possible to the exclusion or alienation of younger generations.

Still another reason for the slow circulation of ethnic organizational elites is that, in some cases, ideological or political groups in the ethnic community try to widen their hegemony in the community and manipulate appointments to organizational leadership of those persons who are committed to them. Once they succeed in this, they try to maintain these appointments as long as possible. As indicated above, groups in the mainstream society may also have an interest in maintaining certain types of leadership in the ethnic minority communities.

A general constraint of most ethnic minority organizations is the lack of a solid financial base. Generally, ethnic organizations depend on the funds acquired from membership dues and from donations from the community members or from grants from outside agencies for special projects. Few ethnic organizations have permanent endowments that ensure long-range operation. Ethnic institutions, such as schools, museums and so on, may fare better in this regard. Lack of a solid economic base forces the work of the organizations to be selective and restrictive in scope. Perhaps the most serious constraint deriving from this is the difficulty of employing professional help that goes beyond the secretarial, on a permanent basis. A consequence of this is that the work of ethnic organizations is often sporadic and lacking in sustained continuity. When there are sufficient member volunteers who are motivated enough to work on projects, an organization may flourish and accomplish much. But when such motivated volunteers are absent, the organization may enter periods of inactivity.

Lack of professionalism in ethnic organizations may be one of its most severe constraints. The problem may be complicated by the fact that the leaders of an organization may themselves have no professional or post-secondary education and may come to perceive professionals as a threat to their own decision-making power.

It should be kept in mind that there are substantial differences among ethnic groups in regard to economic resources, level of education and professionalization among the members of the group and experience in interethnic relations. Some groups have many more resources and much more experience than do others. That is, minority ethnic groups relate to other groups and the larger society from different places on the ethnic stratification ladder. This creates a situation of uneven power among ethnic groups and substantially affects the politics of interethnic relations. Yet, the groups even at the lowest levels of ethnic stratification may be effective in their politics vis-à-vis the larger society. The effectiveness tends to be at its highest when organizational leaders are able to motivate and engage their members in special projects on behalf of the ethnic community in which concrete results of benefit to the community are readily perceivable, and when they are able to effectively use the techniques of intergroup politics. We will discuss such politics next.

THE POLITICS OF INTERETHNIC RELATIONS

Indirect relations. Most ethnic groups in North America do not relate directly to other ethnic groups. Rather, they aim their political activities at the governmental authorities or at the society at large. Likewise, most ethnic groups do not unite with other ethnic groups on the basis of common interests. Instead, as a rule, they seek separate accommodations for themselves via the public authorities. There is a number of reasons for this. Wilbur Rich (1996: 1-9) has tried to provide an explanation and we will explore some of his ideas.

Minority ethnic groups have a certain degree of ethnocentrism by which each group tends to perceive itself as being unique, different from other groups. Hence, they assume that other groups, as groups, would work only for their own benefit. If they occasionally form a coalition with other groups, it would be exclusively for their own self-interest. This creates a certain insularity of ethnic groups from one another. There is a prevalent preconception that, "when the chips are down," each group is on its own and has to work for its own interests by itself.

More often than not, when ethnic groups are directly involved politically with other ethnic groups, they compete or conflict with them. As a result, minority ethnic groups tend to mistrust each other and power differences between groups make coalitions between them unstable and at best temporary. Theodore Caplow (1959, in Rich, 1996), a theorist of coalitions, had pointed out that members of coalitions usually differ in strength and the stronger members seek to control the weaker members regardless of any previous agreements between them.

Even if no coalitions are made, the stronger minority groups have a tendency to act vis-à-vis the majority group as if they were spokespersons for the weaker minority groups. They feel that they well understand the position of the weaker groups and that, by voicing their opinions on the issues of the weaker minority groups, they are providing a service to them. In fact, this is often resented by members of the weaker minority groups and is perceived as an attempt by the stronger minority groups to prevent the weaker groups from speaking for themselves and, in that manner, making them less effective in the competition process. Yet the majority group often prefers to deal with the stronger minority groups.

This, however, does not mean that minority groups do not form coalitions with other minority groups. Such coalitions are usually made on the basis of specific issues, often a single issue, and last as long as there is a chance to resolve these issues together. The most successful coalitions among minority groups are those in which the groups face a common adversary and when they are on more or less the same power level, i.e., no one group has more capacity than the others to prevail over the common adversary by itself.

Issue legitimacy. The central aspect of all intergroup relations are the issues raised by the interacting groups. The issues represent the values and interests that the groups are striving to fulfil for themselves in the context of the possibilities offered in the larger society. The issues, however, may be defined by society as concerns only of the particular group and of no concern to the mainstream. For example, the question of what an ethnic group can do to maintain its identity over a long period of time may be seen as something for which the mainstream of society has no responsibility. Alternatively, the issue can be defined as important for all in society, and therefore the society, as a collectivity, would have some responsibility to help the specific group or set of groups in regard to this issue. The retention of cultural identity by the French of Quebec, for example, has been an issue on the mainstream agenda in Canada. Similarly, the issue of land rights as it relates to the identity of the First Nations has been an issue for all Canadians.

The issues that are defined as being of importance to society as a whole are given legitimacy as being "Canadian" or "American," and it is up to the leadership of the society to find answers to them. Issues that do not obtain such legitimacy tend to be seen as "foreign," "imported," "recondite," "passé" or potentially divisive. For example, by the 1990s, the claim to possession of land by the Canadian Aboriginal peoples has been legitimized on the basis of Aboriginal rights, but it took about one hundred years to achieve this (Berger, 1982: 219-254). The claim of redress for internment of the Japanese Canadians during World War II became legitimate in the 1980s, close to 50 years after the internment (Adachi, 1976). Yet a similar claim for restitution for the internment of Ukrainian Canadians in World War I has not been legitimized as yet, in spite of the efforts of the community leaders (Luciuk, 1988).

Likewise, such issues as helping with the problems in the home countries of the various Canadian ethnic groups, for example, support of political prisoners in the former Soviet Union or in Chile or other countries, have not been usually seen as a "Canadian" issue or problem.

Some issues, however, acquire mixed legitimation. The teaching of various heritage languages as part of the regular high school curricula during regular school hours has been legitimized in some Canadian provinces, such as Manitoba, Alberta and Saskatchewan, but not in others, such as Ontario.

In sum, ethnic groups who want their issues to be successfully received in society must exert efforts to get them on the national agenda as legitimate issues for the society as a whole, i.e., they must turn their own groups' issues into issues for the broader society. The necessary means to achieving this is the minority groups' access to the mainstream media. In modern democratic societies, the media is the main mechanism of legitimizing or de-legitimizing any issue. As was pointed out before, the media is the main agency through which public opinion is formed, and in democratic societies public opinion is a necessary means of exerting pressure on politicians and on those in power. Hence, to be successful with their demands on political authorities, ethnic minority groups have to compete for access to, or the attention of, the mainstream media.

Issue legitimation and the media. We have discussed the media in the context of its role in directly or indirectly disseminating ethnic stereotypes. Positive stereotypes of an ethnic group work to legitimize any cause propounded by that group, and negative stereotypes work to de-legitimize their causes and discourage ethnic communities from pursuing their issues and demands in the larger society. In the context of interethnic relations, the special significance of the mainstream media lies in at least two of its functions. First is the willingness of the mainstream media to provide systematic information on the events taking place in the various ethnic communities. The typical pattern practiced by the mainstream media has been to provide some more or less regular information on events taking place in some ethnic minority communities, but to ignore the events in other ethnic minority communities, except for occasional mention of some larger, controversial or sensational events. Usually those groups who receive more attention in the mainstream media are the majority groups and those ethnic groups that possess more power and influence in the larger society. Many minority groups are dismayed at how the events in their communities, which they consider to be important to Canadian society, are ignored by the mainstream media.

Second, the mainstream media's particularly important function in regard to interethnic relations lies in its editorial reports or articles in which the authors attempt to provide rational discussion of the issues connected with one or another or all ethnic groups. The difference in legitimizing or non-legitimizing any ethnic issues depends on the positive or negative orientation of these discussions and on an attitude of positive concern. That is, even if the conclusions of the discussions of the ethnic issues in the editorials or newspaper columns are not always favourable towards one or another ethnic issue, if they nevertheless project attitudes of positive concern towards them and the groups behind them, the effect can be one of legitimizing the public concern over these issues.

There have been some efforts on the part of the government in Canada to involve the media in ethnic minority issues. In 1986, the federal government created a Task Force on Broadcasting Policy to come up with recommendations as to the greater inclusion of minority groups in the media. The Task Force recommended that Aboriginal peoples and the racial minorities be given more inclusion in the media. In 1988, the Broadcasting Act was passed in which provisions were made for "cultural expression" by enlarging the time devoted by the media for ethnic and racial minorities. Likewise, the Multiculturalism Act of 1988 charged all government agencies, including the mainstream Canadian Broadcasting Corporation, to expand their representation and services to minorities, particularly the delivery of "culturally-sensitive" services.

Yet, the mainstream media coverage of minority issues has remained limited (Fleras, 1994). There are several ways in which the limitation of coverage of ethnic minority issues comes about. One way has been to channel the attempts to expand the media coverage of minority issues into the expansion of the ethnic minority media, sometimes called the "third media," after the English and the French. This has often been welcomed by the third media itself since it reinforces their, often economically limited, work. However, it diverts the efforts towards the legitimization of minority issues in the mainstream society.

Another way in which the issues of many minority groups come to be sidetracked by the mainstream media is by singling out a few minority groups or category of groups and focusing attention on them as those whose issues are the most urgent or most relevant to the total society. In the 1970s, for example, the issues of such groups as Italians, Eastern Europeans and other Southern Europeans gained some consideration in the mainstream media in connection with the newly established multiculturalism policy. From the mid-1980s, when the ethnic composition of immigration to Canada changed to predominantly Asian, the public attention has shifted to race and issues of prejudice and discrimination against different races. The issues of identity raised previously by the other groups have come to be downplayed as not so important, or according to some statements in the media, as "divisive," with the conscious or unconscious effect of moving towards de-legitimizing them. The mainstream media has publicized popularly written works that criticize multiculturalism in Canada (Bibby, 1990; Bissoondath, 1994) and ignored attempts by the concerned groups to answer this criticism (Ewins, 1996). We will discuss this phenomenon further in the next chapter.

Another method used to bring group issues to the attention of the mainstream public, a method used by minority groups themselves in cooperation with the media, is for the group to become more visible through highly visible spokespersons. Such persons are usually erudite enough to capture the public interest and imagination and come to be identified with the case for which they fight. For example, in the United States, persons like Martin Luther King and Jesse Jackson have played decisive roles in legitimizing the issues and the demands of the African American community. In Canada, Ovide Mercredi has performed a similar role for the Canadian First Nations. Similarly, though from a different structural position, both Pierre Trudeau and René Lévesque were highly visible spokesmen for the French issues. Other groups have not had such highly visible personalities. However, there has been a practice of placing individuals into visible symbolic positions as token representatives of minorities. These individuals themselves may not be promoters of any minority issues, but are placed in visible symbolic positions by the mainstream political powers to indicate to the public that the minority groups they originally came from are acceptable in society. Thus, Canada has had French governor generals, a German and a Ukrainian governor general, a Black lieutenant-governor and the like. This practice provides some satisfaction to members of minority groups, but it can also function as a way of deflecting the legitimizing of the groups' real issues.

Lobbying and coalitions. Not all ethnic minority groups rely on high public visibility in pushing towards the fulfilment of their interests and the resolution of their issues. Many prefer to do this with little visibility, by lobbying the political powers (Rich, 1996: 3). Lobbying refers to those activities aimed at influencing one or more public officials to take a certain action or make a decision that would be in the interest of a larger group or community on whose behalf the activity is undertaken. Lobbying activities that are successful involve a combination of measures aimed at public officials. For one, the lobbyist or the lobbyists have to convince the persons holding a public office, a member of parliament for example, that the action that they want them to undertake will be to the advantage of their government or their party. In other words, they have to be able to join their interests with the interests of the group the public officials work for, be it their constituency, the party in power or the public in general.

Furthermore, there has to be some negotiation between the public officials and the lobbyists. That is, the lobbyists must be able to offer something in return to the official for his or her compliance with their requests. Usually, this is the electoral support for the official in the next election of the community that the lobbyists represent. This promise of support, however, has to be validated in some way and the most effective way of achieving it is the exposure of the official's views in the ethnic minority media. This often becomes part of the role that the ethnic minority media play in the interethnic relations process. Politicians in the mainstream system, while intervening or making legislative decisions on behalf of ethnic minority issues, are given exposure and support in the minority media that leads to the support of their election or re-election.

The success of lobbying politicians or public officials, however, is limited if the ethnic lobbyists approach only one person in the mainstream political arena. Politicians and officials know that they open themselves to potentially damaging criticism if they are the only ones who champion an ethnic group's cause. The politician or the official may suffer isolation from his or her colleagues because of the lack of wider support for the issues. Hence, successful lobbyists never work on only one person of power. The marshalling of support for their cause from two or more persons who have actual or potential power is necessary. Successful lobbying by ethnic community leaders necessitates a network of contacts between themselves and a number of persons in power positions. As was pointed out above, Breton's (1991: 61-73) study showed that the

Behind the Veil: Religion, Ethnicity or Politics?

By Paul Eid

Western representations of the Muslim and Arabic world often revolve around the status of women. The practice of veil wearing (the *hijab*) has become for Westerners a strong symbol of women's oppression and submission in Muslim countries and Muslim communities outside of them. Such ideas are seldom the result of objective and well-informed analysis. Often drawn from preconceived notions, and largely reinforced by the media, they increase the chances of "cultural misunderstandings" between Westerners, Muslims and Arabs. This renders any attempt at objectively analyzing veil wearing a difficult undertaking, regardless of the researcher's ethnic or ideological background. The subtle political entailments of the hijab for Arab women may be pinpointed through the study of veiled womens' narratives and feminist literature without, however, reproducing the traditional Western stereotypes about Arabo-Islamic culture.

For most of the newly "free" Arabic countries, the post-colonial era has not marked the end of the struggle against the West. After the departure of colonial powers, during the 1960s-70s, the pervasive influence of Western cultural models remained untouched, thus exacerbating an identity crisis permeating Arab societies. One of the most important catalysts of this identity crisis is the disruptive impact of post-war modernization. The movement toward modernization initiated by ruling elites to emulate the West in achieving technological and economic development has been coupled with the importation of nonindigenous behavioral norms and values. This process of "cultural colonization" was particularly acute within limited circles of elite groups, who often indulged blindly in the mimicry of Western modes of dress and social behaviour considered contrary to traditional Islamo-Arabic values and practices. This situation resulted in a sharp gap between the rulers and the ruled, a gap exacerbated by pronounced class differences related to the maldistribution of economic wealth, and by the generalized corruption prevailing in state institutions. Consequently, this form of Arab identity unquestioningly modeled on Western culture by power elites became unappealing to the increasingly pauperized and uneducated masses.

The only ideology which, from 1952 to the 1970s, almost succeeded in occupying a dominant position within the realm of discourses competing to provide a post-colonial Arab identity is Nasser's Pan-Arabism. Secularized and socialist, it was oriented toward the construction of a collective Arab identity resolutely independent from Western influences and rested on the pillar of Nasser's personal charisma. Because of this latter fact, its tremendous impact throughout the Arab world has not outlived its founding father who died in 1970. There is also a consensus among scholars that the 1967 Arab military defeat over Israel precipitated a sharp decline in Pan-Arabist sentiments. Experienced by Arab masses and intellectuals as an humiliating event, it therefore largely discredited the ruling elites of the time - including Nasser himself—whose "political capital" was, at this point, seriously eroded.

Pan-Arabism and Western-type liberalism's failure to provide the principles needed to shape a post-colonial identity triggered a search for new normative grounds that would give meaning to the idea of "Arabness." Within this ideological vacuum, a new Arabo-Islamic nationalism emerged. It asserted a collective identity freed from remnants of the former "colonized" identity imposed by the West. Islamist discourses and movements grew to become increasingly politicized and militant, thus advocating the Islamization of social structures both in public and private domains. Furthermore, over the past three decades, and despite certain national variations, this religious nationalism has led to the embodiment of orthodox Islamic values in state institutions and in the family. Thus, one can safely contend that religion has tended to become inextricably intertwined with ethnicity in the post-1970s Arab world.

This return to native traditions and customs in the name of Islam was seen by many as a means of resistance against Western cultural hegemony. Although this movement of national assertiveness was to be found in several post-colonial Third-World nations, what was particular to Muslim countries was the strong emphasis given to the issue of women within the context of cultural resistance. Traditional gender relationships became the symbol and the epitomization of a genuine Arab and Islamic identity. This close connection between gender and nationalist issues in newly independent Arabic countries was expressed by Lama Abu Odeh (1993) in the telling image of a woman's body as *"a battlefield where the cultural struggles of postcolonial societies were waged."* Shukrallah (1994) is even more explicit: *"women, as a category, are central to the process of the re-creation of the* [Arabo-Islamic] *community due to their role as 'symbolic cultural bearers' of national traditions."*

The emergence and rapid spread of the hijab has to be understood as one of the chief manifestations of the Islamist discourse's emphasis on the necessity of re-drawing sex roles in order to forge the Arab identity along the lines of religious principles. In this sense, the hijab is more than a simple item of clothing prescribed by religion; it is a strong symbol of the rise of a religious nationalism setting up Islamic values and behaviours as a protective screen against the depraved and "imperialistic" Western culture. Therefore, one can contend that the hijab provides Arabo-Muslims with what Barth (1969), and also Isajiw (1974) would call "ethnic boundaries" separating the "Us" from the "Other," for it provides the community with signs of its cultural distinctness.

This new form of veiling has emerged in Arabic and Muslim countries in general since the end of the 1970s. The new veiled women tend to belong essentially to urban lower and middle classes. They are generally young—in their twenties and early thirties—and can be either students, housewives, or professionals. The latter category generally includes positions such as servant, school teacher, secretary, bank employee, or nurse. "*What the Islamic revival has introduced is the Islamic headdress, the hijab, which covers the hair and neck like a wimple. It is worn with a long loose gown.*" This form of veiling stands in contrast to the traditional scarf, a "folkloric" garment that lower and middle class women wrapped loosely around their head in such a way that allowed unruly locks to be visible.

But the difference between the traditional scarf and the Islamic veil is not only one of form; it is also one of content. The hijab is considered a religious obligation by its wearers and its proponents in general. This claim has led to an important theological debate within the Muslim world. However, from a sociological point of view, even more relevant than analyzing the theological controversy over the hijab is to examine the social significations attached to it. That the hijab is an expression of the refocusing of the collective Arabic identity on traditional Islamic values is an assumption shared by most authors. What seems to be a more controversial issue is whether or not the hijab (and the broader restructuring of sex roles according to this new politicized Islam) perpetuates gender-based power relationships *detrimental* to Arabic women. Such a question has generated a heated debate in both the Western and the Arab world. It has been especially addressed, in the most stimulating and diversified manner, by feminist authors who question the implications of the merging of religion and ethnicity for Arab women.

The critical approach toward the hijab considers the sudden spread of "new veiling" to be a manifestation of the social and political influence of fundamentalist groups. Authors Mimouni (1992), Geadah (1996), Dekmejian, (1995), Messaoudi (1995), Bessis and Belhassen (1992), Hijab (1988), Taarji (1990), Shukrallah (1994), amongst others, argue that these groups have largely engineered the production of the new religion-based Arabic identity. Within two decades, fundamentalist groups achieved a take-over of the process of production of the legitimate religious discourse prevailing in society. This critical approach to the hijab reveals that extremely well-organized Islamist movements have capitalized efficiently on the State's loss of credibility in the eyes of a frustrated urban population pauperized by unprecedented unemployment. Moreover, the pervasive influence of fundamentalism in Arabic countries is seen as a direct consequence of numerous concessions made by Arabic regimes to the most radical factions of the Islamist movement. Accordingly, *"the dominant discourse has convinced a large part of the population that veil wearing is, if not a compulsory Islamic obligation, at least the expression of an identity assertion necessary to check the harmful westernization."* According to this rhetoric, veil wearing aims at hiding a woman's body in order to limit its excessive sexual power. This power is associated with a woman's "perverted nature," which, if not controlled, will lead to "social chaos" *(fitna)*. For Yolande Geadah, such an argument marks a significant yet subtle shift in meanings when compared with the original spirit of the Suras invoked by fundamentalists to justify veil wearing. As the author puts it, *"the contemporary veil is not meant any-more to protect women's dignity and security against men's sexual harassment. It is now meant to protect men and the whole society against the "perversity" of women whose sexual power, in this perspective, ought to be, if not suppressed, at least confiscated."*

Post-colonial feminists contend that the fundamentalist ideology does not hold a monopoly over the symbolism of the veil. They call for the acknowledgement of the plurality of meanings which can epitomize the hijab depending on the different motives invoked by its wearers. Post-colonial feminist authors reject the (structuralist) postulate which considers actors as socially predetermined by external factors. In this perspective, the subject has full control over his or her conscience, and therefore, cannot make a decision contrary to his or her own interest. These theoretical assumptions are adopted to de-victimize women. According to this perspective, the hijab, which should be worn only in the presence of non-kin adults, operates as an *"off-limits sign"* that tells the public, particularly the male public, that although a woman has left the house to study and work, she is respectable and does not expect to be harassed. This has led Lama Abu Odeh (1993), and El Guindi (1981) to argue that the hijab re-empowers its wearer insofar as it legitimates her presence outside the house while neutralizing the tendency of men to associate "public women" with the image of a shameful sexual being.

The argument that the hijab is empowering because it enables women to gain access to the public arena seems to be largely confirmed by the statements of several veiled women. For instance, one university-educated veiled woman from Egypt declared: *"Before* [I started to wear the veil], *it was awful: the cars were always stopping, men bothering me... Now I am really in peace"* (Taarji, 1990). Another veiled woman from Tunis explains her decision this way: *"No one can insult a woman wearing the hijab. No man can undress her with his eyes. They don't dare flirt with her. They respect her"* (Bessis, 1992). An Algerian woman remarked: "*I came to the conclusion that the hijab was for me the best way to gain my freedom. Since men are unable to see in me something other than a sexual being, nor to talk to me in a natural and respectful manner, I decided to eliminate what could arouse their sexual desires. By covering my body, I present myself to them in such a way that they will have no choice but to be interested in my spirit, my behavior. In short* [by veiling myself], *I force him to consider me as a human being"* (Taarji, 1990).

The post-colonial feminist's analysis of the veil is correct when it pinpoints the fact that veiled women's discourses often denote a *"demand for a renewed dignity"* (Macleod, 1992). It is also true that, when it does not lead to pure seclusion, the hijab can indeed be used, as El Guindi (1981) argued, as an indirect way for women to force men to release some of the *"control which they once jealously held"* over them. However, this *"renewed dignity"* entails the tacit acceptance, both by the veil wearer and the public, that a woman who leaves the house, especially when her husband or any male relatives do not accompany her, is of questionable virtue. This discourse delineates a sharp frontier between two representations of women, the mother and wife on the one hand, and the "public woman" on the other. According to the dominant symbolism of the veil, if the mother and wife are highly respectable, the public woman attracts an *a priori* suspicion. Thus, it seems that the dignity and respectability which the hijab provides to its wearers rests to a large extent on a representation of the female body portrayed as a permanent threat to society.

From what the interviews have disclosed, the veiled woman tends to *indirectly* legitimize this (fundamentalist) "demonized" representation of women's nature rather than to overtly embrace it. For instance, one Egyptian working mother of three small children justifies her decision to wear the veil by saying: *"... Before we dressed differently, I don't know why. But this dress is better, when I wear these clothes I feel secure, I know I am a good mother and a good wife. And men know not to flirt with me. So it is not a problem to go out to work, or to shop, or anything"* (Macleod, 1992). Another woman from Egypt declared: *"Now, I feel in peace with myself. Before, people were looking at me as if I was any other girl. Now,* [that I started to wear the hijab] *it's almost as if I was reflecting the image of Islam"* (Taarji, 1990). Another who is married to a local Imam, says that wearing the veil will *"protect her from the suffering endured in hell."* Finally, this Egyptian mother argued that *"this dress says to everyone that I am a Muslim woman, and that I am here working because my family needs me to. Not for myself! I am here because I love my family"* (Macleod, 1992).

Although such examples reveal that one's decision to wear the veil can rest on diverse motives, they disclose a common denominator. They reveal a tendency to set up the hijab as a precondition to attain the status of "good wife and mother" or that of "good Muslim." The implicit corollary of such assumptions is that, on the contrary, unveiled women do not deserve these epithets. Such attitudes help to bring non-veiled women into "social disrepute." Thus, one Egyptian and non-veiled woman declared: *"The veiled woman covers herself and is guaranteed to be perceived as morally good. This creates a problem for me, because I have to prove that I am not a bad girl, that I don't go around with men, and that I can be interested in serious things"* [sic] (Davis, 1992).

Samia, a Lebanese woman, explained that her mother warned her: *"If your husband wants you to put it on* [the hijab], *you'll put it on."* She then added: *"That's what happened"* (Taarji, 1990). Her friend Fatima declared: *"After the Israelian occupation, the proportion of religious meetings increased. Fear of death and suffering became really palpable among people (...). I started to listen to religious tapes. I put on the hijab and my fear of death disappeared ... "* (Taarji, 1990). Nora, 22, from Algeria, explained how she started to wear the veil after she had repeated nightmares in the course of which a *"spirit"* was tormenting and threatening her. The spirit was enjoining Nora to wear the veil. After one month of resistance, Nora yielded to the pressure and adopted the veil. The spirit finally stopped haunting her. According to the interviewer, it seemed that the spirit tormenting Nora was directly associated with her sisters-in-law, who all wore the chador. *"It's been a long time now since my sisters-in-law urged my husband to force me to wear the chador,"* Nora later confessed (Taarji, 1990).

These narratives are telling in that they disclose the influence of a woman's social environment on her decision to wear the hijab. Whether these pressures originate from the husband, the relatives, the community, the mosques, or any other social agency, they all come to the same thing: they reinforce the fundamentalist ideology, which has been largely internalized by a wide range of social actors in today's Arabic countries.

Several post-colonial feminists, as proof of the voluntary character of veil wearing, describe numerous cases where young girls decide to wear the hijab despite the strong opposition of their parents. Such examples are not very surprising when one remembers that since the 1980s, the new Islamist discourse found fertile grounds for its large-scale growth in public schools and universities. Thus, it is not uncommon to encounter inter-generational "chocs" where the children's religious attitude is much more orthodox and conservative than that of their parents. This in itself is a good indicator that the hijab, contrary to the fundamentalist claim, is not a "deeply-rooted" or "ancestral" tradition. It is rather a new tradition which the Islamist movement has recently "constructed" as an essential component of the Arabo-Muslim identity (Geadah, 1996).

Is it possible for a feminist to challenge the sexist significations attached to the hijab without furthering some gender relationships mechanically modelled on Western ones? Inversely, is it possible to fight colonial forms of feminism without ending up legitimizing the hijab as a political symbol representing the inferiority and moral degeneracy of women?

Perhaps one possibility for non-Western feminists to heuristically synthesize both concerns is to pursue reforms in a "native idiom," rather than unquestioningly appropriating Western rhetoric. Thus, the critical deconstruction of the hijab as a sacred religious obligation would have much more appeal to Muslim populations if it was grounded on religious arguments rather than on a Western-type feminism that always refers to the *"sexual exploitation"* of women by *"patriarchal"* institutions. In other words, it would be more appropriate to set against the fundamentalist reading of the Koran and other sacred texts (Sunna, Chaaria, and hadith) a more liberal one fostering egalitarian gender relationships. The Muslim feminist and sociologist Fatima Mernissi recently undertook this approach in her book *The Veil and the Male Elite (1991).* Ironically, Mernissi has attempted to desacralize the compulsory character of the hijab—and all the sexist prescriptions that come with it—by resorting to sacred texts. Such an approach offers a twofold advantage. Given the pervasive social legitimacy that fundamentalism has accumulated over the years, any attempt to change this discourse is doomed to failure as long as its ideological foundations remain unchallenged on religious grounds. Second, as previously mentioned, Memissi's "strategy" is in keeping with a feminism aiming to preserve a native cultural background and, accordingly, to keep a certain distance from a strictly Western feminist agenda.

Source: Unpublished Paper, Collaborative Program in Ethnic and Pluralism Studies, University of Toronto, 1998. Reprinted with permission of the author.

majority of leaders of ethnic communities feel that they have insufficient contacts with mainstream political leaders. The critical number of such contacts that make a difference in lobbying, however, differs from one group to another. This number depends on the group's prestige or the group's general position in the society's ethnic stratification system. That is, in the political order, ethnic groups also form a pecking order, with some groups having a greater chance than others in getting response to their demands (Rich, 1996: 5).

Furthermore, a significant pass-key to success in lobbying is support from wealthy individuals in either or preferably both the ethnic and the mainstream community. Wealthy persons, in addition to their real potentiality of financial support, also have a symbolic value for the community. It is often believed that, the wealthier the persons, the greater the stake they have in their community. Hence, wealthy persons are often taken more seriously by political leaders than those who are not, and their backing or endorsement of ethnic issues carries weight. Analogously, ethnic minority instrumental organizations that involve businessmen and professionals carry more weight with political leaders than do expressive cultural organizations.

Finally, forming coalitions with other groups in negotiating and exerting pressure on the mainstream politicians and leaders is another key to effective lobbying. As was pointed out before, ethnic minority groups tend not to form stable, permanent coalitions with other minority groups. However, on specific issues that equally affect the groups concerned, coalitions are realistic and can be effective. The Assembly of First Nations in Canada is actually a coalition of a number of different Native groups representing mainly the status Indians who live on reserves, organized together in view of the situation that is common to all of them, that of the relationship to the federal government, the Indian Act, land claims issue, potential sovereignty issue of the different groups and other issues. Advisory councils or committees appointed to study the policy of multiculturalism in Canada on both the federal and the provincial levels have been coalitions of minority groups concerned with the issues of their identity in relation to the larger society. The Canadian Arab Federation and, in the United States, the National Association of Arab Americans have been coalitions of Arabs of Lebanese, Syrian, Jordanian, Iranian and other ethnicities concerned with biases and prejudices against the Arabs in North America that derive from the conflictual situations in their home countries. A coalition in Canada that lasted for over 10 years was the Canadian Committee for Captive European Nations, organized in the early 1980s and disbanded in the early 1990s. This was a coalition of leaders of Czechoslovak, Estonian, Hungarian, Latvian, Lithuanian, Polish and Ukrainian ethnic groups concerned with the violation of human rights by the Soviet regime in their home countries. They successfully exerted pressure on the federal government to form an all-party parliamentary committee to monitor human rights violations in the Soviet Union and urged the latter to live up to its commitment to the 1975 Helsinki Accords on observance of human rights (Malarek, 1985).

A special type of coalition is formed between members of the dominant majority group and a minority group. Such coalitions express the benevolent concern of members of the mainstream with the plight of one or another minority group. An example is the National Association for the Advancement of Colored People (NAACP) in the United States, which, in its early period, brought together both the Black community leaders and white professionals to act against racial discrimination and work for the economic and political betterment of Black Americans. Its influence in stimulating the movement for change of the status of the American Blacks was substantial (Morris, 1984). Such coalitions, however, are few. Potentially, they can be more influential than coalitions of only minority groups. Their work tends to follow more conservative lines of action, with an emphasis on gradual change.

In order to understand the specific issues raised by different ethnic groups in relation to the total society, we will try, in the remainder of this chapter, to give a concise review of the issues raised by the two Canadian cases, that of Quebec and the Aboriginal peoples.

QUEBEC IN QUESTION

The aftermath of the conquest of Quebec in 1759 left a structural void for the future generations of Quebec, an economic and political domination by another ethnicity and a historical legacy. These three factors have influenced the relations of the people of Quebec to the British and to the rest of Canada until today. As was pointed out in Chapter 2, the structural void derives from the fact that, after the conquest, the French elite who had formed and maintained the social, economic and political system of New France returned to France and those who stayed had to give a completely new direction to the French community in Canada. While the old elite of New France had been concerned with economic expansion based on the fur trade, those who filled their place focused their attention on preserving their cultural identity for as long a period as possible. This new direction of the elite was taken over by the Catholic Church. The role of the Church in this respect was to an extent conditioned by the terms of the early British Governors' pluralist policy in regard to the retention of French language, religion and culture. The British merchants, however, continuously exerted pressure for assimilation of the French, not only into the British legal system, but also into English culture. The Church was traditionally in charge of education and hence could effectively assume an enlarged role of identity maintenance. It thus fulfilled the role of the new French elite while the economic and political matters were taken over by an elite of British merchants. This created a structure of division of labour in which the financial and business matters were the domain of the British, and agriculture, mostly subsistence farming, a domain of the French. This structure remained unchanged well into the twentieth century.

The real structural changes began to take place in about the middle of the twentieth century. By the 1950s, as a result of a continuous process of industrialization, the majority of the Quebec population was urbanized. Yet, business and the economy still remained dominated by the British. In the 1940s and the 1950s, however, during the period of Maurice Duplessis' leadership of Quebec, and later in a six-year period beginning with 1960, during the provincial regime of Jean Lesage, a number of changes took place that had a significant influence on Quebec's future relations with the rest of Canada. For the first time in more than 150 years, the state of Quebec asserted its authority over the Church. With this, the primacy of the Church in Quebec society withered away. A new, lay, elite began to emerge. One important base for the emergence of this elite were civil service jobs created by the Quebec's expansion of provincial government bureaucracy and the many, often ambitious, public projects sponsored by the provincial government.

Another base for the new elite was the result of the so-called Quiet Revolution, which took place at the end of the 1950s and throughout the 1960s. These were the changes brought about by a rapidly expanding educational and economic system that produced new professionals and new intellectuals. Combined with the expanding ranks of the provincial government bureaucracy, the new middle-class strata of people in Quebec was forming a formidable new elite in the province. This new elite gave rise to a new self-consciousness with a consequent development of a new, Quebec-directed cultural orientation, a new self-conscious intellectual level, and a challenge to the dominance of the English economic class of Quebec. An important aspect of this new consciousness was the territorial factor. While previously the concern with French identity maintenance had extended to all French Canadians, the new elite focused its concern on Quebec whose legal boundaries gave it a solid ground from which to make demands on Canadian society. An important evolvement, highly symbolic, but of practical consequence, was the legislation in 1977 of Bill 101, which declared the Quebec society to be intrinsically Francophone. It required French language to be used, not only in all official transactions, but also in commerce and business; it required commercial signs to be in French and restricted the right of many parents to send their children to English schools. Language thus became an early instrument of reversing the English dominance in Quebec. All this presented a new set of issues to be resolved by Canada, i.e., by the federal government.

The self-consciousness of the new elite included their consciousness of the legacy of the conquest. That is, they saw no legitimacy in the dominance of the Quebec society by the English. In the context of the human rights awareness that emerged in Canada in the 1960s and the spirit of human rights propounded by such international bodies as the United Nations, any argument that insisted on the right of the conqueror made no sense. If historical events resulted in the dominance of one group over another, such dominance could be undone or reversed. While the new elite was in agreement on this, there was no agreement as to what the measures to achieve this were to be.

Photo: Dick Hemingway

Jacques Parizeau, premier of Quebec during the 1995 referendum on sovereignty, blamed the defeat on big business and the "ethnic" vote. Soon after, Parizeau resigned. Part of a rally by East Indians in support of Canadian unity.

Two opposite approaches to this emerged in the 1960s that were to result in two opposing political camps. One approach promoted the argument that the way out of the English dominance for Quebec should be via its own sovereignty. The sovereignist idea had been tried once before in Quebec history, in the unsuccessful 1837 rebellion led by Louis-Joseph Papineau and his associates. Now, however, in the 1960s, the sovereignists' idea had a completely new base with a more popular appeal. The sovereignist movement was made up of a number of different groups, ranging from a radical group (Front liberation du Québec) that advocated independence by violent means, to a moderate sovereignty-association movement (MSA) that advocated Quebec's sovereignty, but in association with Canada. Eventually, in 1968, the different groups were joined in a new political party, the Parti Québécois (PQ), under the leadership of René Lévesque (1978). This party came to power in the province in 1976 and maintained it until 1985. It rose to power again in the 1990s. The most significant moves of the PQ were two referenda on the sovereignty of Quebec, in 1980 and in 1995. Both referenda were lost, even though the question to be voted on was worded differently in each. In both cases, however, sovereignty foresaw some tie with Canada. In the 1995 referendum, the vote was extremely close, 51 to 49 percent, indicating a deep ambiguity on the issue in the Quebec populace.

The other approach, that of the Quebec federalists, argued that the power imbalances between the Quebec French and the English in Canada could best be equalized, not outside of the Canadian federal system, but within it. The leading champion of this approach was Pierre Trudeau, the prime minister of Canada from 1968 and throughout the 1970s into the 1980s. Trudeau represented Quebec's activist intellectual elite of the 1960s, a group of individuals who in the early part of the decade publicized their ideas in the new journal *Cité libre* and who were committed to raising the status of Quebec in the Canadian federation to an equal level with that of the English. As in the case of the sovereignists, the original instrument was to be the French language. But whereas the sovereignists were interested in having French as the official and the

My Quebec

by René Lévesque

Imagine that the entire continent of North America ought to have been French instead of ... Neo-Roman. For indeed our beginnings were incredible. From Hudson's Bay and Labrador in the north to the Gulf of Mexico in the south, from the Gaspé near the Atlantic to the Rockies, from which one can almost see the Pacific, there we were—and there you were—as the discoverers and the first European settlers. When Champlain built his home in Quebec and Nouvelle France was born, the Mayflower pilgrims had not even raised anchor on their journey to found New England.

And so, for a hundred and fifty years soldiers and missionaries and colonists and coureurs des bois wrote a good number of the most extraordinary, if not the most famous, pages of the history of the seventeenth and eighteenth centuries.

However, this history, for a century and a half, was ours—and also yours. And I remember that when we arrived at the last chapter, the one which ended with defeat and conquest, we lost the desire to know what followed, and instead returned indefatigably to the beginning; because what followed, with due respect to our British compatriots, seemed in some way to have become the history of another people.

This is not a nostalgic idealization of a tiny society of some tens of thousands of poor people who, in 1760 in the Saint Lawrence Valley, had to submit to a foreign domination which was destined to remain for a long time. As with all the other colonies of the time, this was as yet nothing more than a modest outgrowth of a metropolis which was both natural and distant, and whose power, once its job was done, should have ended with us as it did elsewhere had its continuity not been broken. Already in fact, distance, the climate, contact with the Indian population, the continental experience had fashioned a mentality and a way of life which were becoming more and more different from that of the mother country. This was a nation, and a French nation certainly, but a nation which was just as able to live its own life and to be a presence in the world as any other.

This is what defeat broke up, but it did not manage to dispel the dream. It was a dream which, though normally unacknowledged, was strong enough to nourish, even today, a national identity and a national idea that only numerical weakness and total isolation prevented us from realizing.

This rapid awakening, which we were ourselves the first to find astonishing, we have given the name the "quiet revolution," which was not ill-founded. Revolutionary it certainly was, if one accepts that a fundamental change can happen without killings and ruins. Quiet, and in consequence marked by a continuity in change, even in the most radical change, which is one of the characteristics of our people. Quietly therefore, but on all levels we saw a liberation which was as sudden as is the breaking of the icepacks on our rivers in the spring. And the ground began to flower and to produce like never before: reform as profound as it was late in the field of education; the initiation of a modern administration, so well organized that it shows signs of a bureaucratic fat which is not exclusively French — but also a jump in social awareness which, on several major points moved rapidly from the back to the foreground; and an increasingly keen consciousness of responsibilities such as the essentials of economic life.

O.K. EVERYBODY TAKE A VALIUM!

Photo: TEP archives

And as is usual, all this was announced by and accompanied by artists, an unprecedented plethora of writers, painters, film-makers, architects, and in particular some superb popular poets, several of whom are well-known in France, who have created for us a repertory of songs which are reminiscent of your old provincial airs that rocked us in our cradles, and in which we now find our own countenance and our accents of today, and a precise echo of our successes, our failures, and our plans. It is this new, renewed Quebec which de Gaulle took the trouble to see. Contrary to what some people have thought, he did not have to "invent" it.

Inevitably this metamorphosis owed it to itself to create an instrument for its political expression and to try to conduct it to its logical conclusion. This instrument is the Parti Québécois. We were just a few hundred, then a few thousand, to bring it into being in 1967-68, with two objectives which have remained coupled since then: sovereignty and association. This means a sovereign State of Quebec which will accept, or rather offer in advance, new links of interdependence with Canada, but links which will this time be negotiated between equal peoples, as a function of their geographic and other unquestionable common interests.

This, briefly, is the national option, inscribed from the beginning in the heart of a political program in which each paragraph, each word, has been rigorously exposed to the attention of every Québecer. But like anyone else, certainly, over and above these existential but not very day-to-day questions which we are resolving—for a while—in the Constitution, our people are also experiencing all the problems, the frustrations and the hopes of the men and women of their time. This is why, on the way, we must also try to respond the best we can, with the power the federal regime deigns to give us, to these requirements of our citizens.

Source: René Lévesque, *My Quebec*. Toronto: Methuen, 1979.

predominant language in Quebec, Trudeau's federalists were legislating it in 1968 as one of the two official languages of Canada. The aim was both symbolic and real. Symbolically, raising the language to the status of the English language would indicate equal partnership between the two groups in Canada. Realistically, the need to use the French language in the state's everyday business would create new opportunities for many French Canadians in the civil service of the federal government and thus raise their social status in the mainstream Canadian society. In turn, non-Francophone civil servants, as well as politicians who wanted to move up in the political hierarchy, would have to learn French and become bilingual and thus move closer in understanding and respect of the French Canadians. A distinguished member of the Trudeau group and one of the initiators of the policy of bilingualism, Gerard Pelletier (1990: 210), made a clear link between language and group identity:

> Added to this [economic inequality] was an even deeper malaise, to which the term "cultural anxiety" applies rather well because it was the product of many years of linguistic bullying and acts of intolerance towards the cultural characteristics of the French-Canadian community. While the economic inferiority of French Canadians had many causes, of which a number had nothing to do with the political structure of the country, this cultural anxiety can be blamed above all on the attitudes of the federal government and the provincial governments of English-speaking provinces.

The legislation of the Official Languages Act of 1969 was preceded by a report of the Royal Commission on Bilingualism and Biculturalism that had begun its work in 1963. The Commission pointed to the inequalities between the French and the English in Canada, indicated that language and culture were inseparable and acknowledged that Canada was made up of two cultures and two societies. It recommended measures to bring about a greater equality between the French and the English, among them bilingual policies.

While the Trudeau government was eager to support the idea of bilingualism, it was not so sanguine about the idea of two cultures or two societies. The latter were notions promoted by the Quebec separatists. Trudeau was a political centralist and a determined enemy of separatism to the point of invoking the War Measures Act in October of 1970 in response to the kidnapping by members of the militant separatist FLQ group of two highly visible political figures.

Trudeau's ambition was to repatriate the constitution to Canada, i.e., to redefine the existing British North America Act that had served as the Canadian constitution since 1867 into being the constitution of Canada according to the proper Canadian procedure. To do so, however, a Charter of Rights and Freedoms was added as an intrinsic part of the constitution. The problem was that the newly repatriated constitution did not include provisions that would give more powers to Quebec than it had had as only a province in the confederation. Thus, when in 1981 all other premiers of the Canadian provinces signed the new constitution, Quebec refused to do so. Since then the federalists have attempted time and again to find, by consensus or by popular vote, a way to give Quebec more power within the Canadian constitutional framework, each time without success. In 1987, in the Meech Lake Accord, the premiers of all provinces, including Quebec, reached an agreement on recognizing Quebec as a "distinct society" and giving it a set of additional powers. The Accord, however, provided that it be ratified by all provincial parliaments and, as it turned out, several provincial parliaments refused to do so, to the Accord's detriment. Similar agreement among the provincial first ministers was reached in the Charlottetown Accord of 1992, but it provided for a national referendum on the concessions to be made to Quebec. The 1992 referendum failed to approve the Accord (McRoberts, 1993a, 1995).

The issues that have continuously frustrated the efforts at complete consensus or full public support for the federalists' attempts to keep Quebec in the confederation have included, first of all, a demand to inscribe in the constitution a statement explicitly recognizing Quebec as a "distinct society." In addition to the right of having French as its official language and the right to protect its culture, the recognition of distinctiveness would mean a number of additional powers for Quebec. At issue has been a Quebec veto on constitutional amendments, its own immigration policy, the right to make provincial nominations of Senators and Supreme Court Justices, limitations on transferring money to other provinces from the taxes collected in Quebec, autonomy in many community services, complete jurisdiction over tourism, forestry, housing, mines, recreation and municipal affairs, Quebec's own "notwithstanding clause" by which its own provincial parliament would have the power to reject decisions of Canada's Supreme Court, a power that only the Canadian national parliament has, and others. All these have been items on the negotiating table between the Canadian government, provincial premiers and the Quebec federalists (Cook, 1995; Johnson, 1994; Waddell, 1986; Trent, Young and Lachapelle, 1996).

What is interesting is the pattern of conservative outcomes, both in the case of the separatist attempts to move Quebec towards sovereignty and Canada's and the federalists' attempts to keep it in the confederation. In the case of the separatists, for all their efforts to convince the people of Quebec that sovereignty is to their advantage, the people of Quebec, while electing the separatist party to power, would not allow them to remove Quebec from Canada. Similarly, in the case of the federal government, for all its efforts to accord Quebec a distinct identity and to allow it special powers in order to keep it in the confederation, the people of Canada would not give the government their full support to make it possible to do so. This pattern may persist in the future.

• "Interculturalism" in Quebec

Quebec itself is an ethnically diverse society. In 1991, of the total Quebec population of 6,810,300 persons, about 25 percent was of ethnic origin other than French (Statistics Canada, 1993: 12-26). Of these, only 4.2 percent (286,080) of the total Quebec population were of British origin. The other five largest groups were made up of 3.0 percent of other European origins (202,075), 3 percent of Asian and African origins (203,055), 1.2 percent of East and South Asian origins (84,710), 1 percent of Aboriginal origins (65,405) and 0.6 percent of Black origins other than African (41,165).

A number of ethnic groups have large percentages of their population concentrated in Quebec. As Table 6 shows, in 1991, 43.8 percent of the Arab population in Canada resided in Quebec, as did 33 percent of the population of Central and South American ethnic groups, 31.2 percent of "Other" European groups, 28.6 percent of West Asian groups, 28.3 percent of the Caribbean, 21 percent of Southern European groups, including Italians and Portuguese, 18.3 of the Black and 13.9 percent of the Aboriginal groups.

The processes of interethnic relations in Quebec have been different from those in the rest of Canada. Two significant processes can account for much of the difference. One is the minoritization of the English, and the other, the Quebec government's policies regarding ethnic diversity. We will briefly discuss each one in turn.

Since the 1960s, as Quebec has legislated various language laws and has asserted itself more and more in relation to English Canada, the English group in Quebec has lost its dominant role. Until the 1970s the Quebec economy was dominated by enterprises owned by English Canadians and Americans. English Canadians were also dominant in the financial and public utility sectors of the economy. The only way that it was possible to decrease or eliminate this dominance was, not through development or strengthening of the existing French-owned enterprises, but through mobility of the French within the English-owned corporations to the managerial level. To this effect the government undertook legislation of a set of language laws that would require that French be the working language of all business, commerce and most education. The government assumed that the conversion of the language practice in the economy would favour the French in business employment policies, which would result in a large scale mobility of the French into managerial positions in all corporations in Quebec (McRoberts, 1993b). Bill 85 in 1968, Bill 63 in 1969, Bill 22 in 1974 and Bill 101 in 1977, all had as their goal the establishment of French language, not only as the official language in Quebec, but also as the language of everyday social use. As mentioned above, Bill 101 in particular is considered as the Charter of the French Language. It provided, not only that the French language be the language in all public transactions, but required that all immigrants to Quebec attend French schools. The English already living in Quebec, however, were allowed to continue sending their children to English schools. French language was seen by the Bill as a unifying device, joining all ethnic groups and their descendants, including the English, into a unified civil society.

Although Quebec's language legislation remained controversial, it did have the effect of bringing significant numbers of the French to the top of the business world in the province and placing the English in the minority position. From then on the English were to be like any other ethnic minority group, participating in the Quebec society run by the French. This minoritization process placed the English group on the defensive in relation to the sovereignist movement in Quebec, prompted formation of English organizations oriented at preventing separation from the rest of Canada or, if separation were to take place, arrangements to retain the areas with large English concentrations, such as Montreal, within the Canadian federation. Research is needed to assess all the consequences of this type of minoritization.

Approach to ethnic diversity in Quebec had gone through several stages. When the Canadian federal government was introducing the policy of multiculturalism at the end of the 1960s and in the early 1970s, the Quebec authorities and much of the public were negatively predisposed to such a policy. Their basic

KEY ISSUES IN CANADIAN ETHNIC RELATIONS

Quebec's Future: Distinct Society or Sovereign State?

The question of what is or what should be the place of Quebec in Canada has been asked since the time of the conquest of New France. The Quebec Act of 1774 and later the British North America Act of 1867 guaranteed that the French in Quebec could keep their culture, language, religion, way of life, and a legal system somewhat different from that of the British. In practice, this has meant that, notwithstanding similarities, Quebec has developed as a society different from that of the rest of Canada. In fact, in many respects, two societies have coexisted side by side in Canada.

Since the 1950's Quebec has developed its own distinct business class of people and its own educated class of people—the intelligentsia. The latter in particular, have heightened the awareness of French Quebec culture, Quebec's history and Quebec's own economic and political interests. The question thus remains: should not the Quebec people take the further step and establish its own full political hegemony over the province? That is, should it not separate from the rest of Canada and become a sovereign state?

As was pointed out in the first chapter, the typical progression among ethnic or cultural groups living on a distinct territory has been from a folk-community to nationality community, to nation, to nation-state. Since the middle of the nineteenth century, Quebec has gone through all these stages, except the last one. Since the middle of the 1970's, each time it came to power, the Parti Québécois (PQ) has worked to bring about sovereignty. It has tried to accomplish this in a democratic manner, by means of a referendum. Two such referenda were held, in 1980 and in 1995, and each time the people of Quebec voted not to separate from Canada, though not by a large margin. In November 1998, in the re-election of the PQ, the popular vote for this separatist party was again almost the same as that for the Liberal party, which is opposed to separation.

This raises the question as to how can one explain this ambiguity among the people of Quebec toward staying in Canada or separating. Is it, as the Premier of Quebec said after the loss of referendum in 1995, that the "other" ethnic groups who settled in Quebec vote against separation and this sways the vote? He argued that the other ethnic groups immigrate to Canada not to Quebec and hence they want to remain with the rest of Canada. Is it that the federal government spends a lot of money to keep Quebec in the Confederation? Or, is it that the Québecois themselves feel more economic security as being part of Canada rather than being independent? Is it that the Quebec business and industry have become so interdependent with the rest of Canadian business and industry that separation may mean a serious disruption of their activities?

The Quebec Flag.

Whatever the cause or set of causal factors for this ambiguity, a question can be raised as to how much difference would it make if Quebec were to separate from the rest of Canada. If it stays in Canada, the federal government will have to make more concessions to Quebec, give Quebec more powers, such as taxation, health and welfare, immigration policy, the "notwithstanding" clause and the amending formula in the constitution, and other powers—things that were envisioned in the failed Meech Lake Accord. In other words, Quebec will most probably be given a status in Canada different from that of the other provinces and one that would make it less dependent on the federal government. On the other hand, if Quebec were to separate what it would have to do immediately afterwards is to negotiate and sign many treaties with Canada in order to maintain normal economic and political relations. This would tie Quebec back with Canada, perhaps even more than it is now, or would be with all the concessions granted.

Yet, how much difference would separation of Quebec make to the rest of Canada? Would Canada be able to maintain a strong economy? Would there not be strong pressures to join the United States? Would Canada be able to maintain its sophisticated social and health policies? Could Canada continue to be a model multicultural country, as it has been for many other nations of the world facing increasing ethnic diversity within their own societies? Would not the world lose a country that presents a unique historical, social and cultural experience?

response was that such a policy was aimed at taking attention away from and undermining the nation-building process of Quebec. The question of giving recognition to diverse ethnic minority groups was seen as permitting them to maintain their preference for the English rather than French language and thus strengthening their link with English Canada. Most immigrants to Quebec preferred sending their children to English schools and felt that they had immigrated to Canada and not just to Quebec.

The effect of Bill 101 on the Allophones, i.e., groups whose mother tongue is other than English and French, was also significant. By 1990, at least three-quarters of all the children of immigrants were schooled in the French primary and secondary schools. Surveys have shown that, whereas in 1971 less than half of the Allophones declared a knowledge of French, by the end of the 1980s the proportion rose to two-thirds. However, knowledge of English among the Allophones also increased substantially in this period of time, showing that English has retained its attraction among them. At the same time, since 1971 the Allophones in Quebec have retained their mother tongues in a higher degree than their counterparts outside Quebec. Being trilingual, the Allophones in Quebec have also been more bilingual in terms of French and English than either the French or the English themselves (Bourhis, 1994).

In regard to Quebec politics, the Allophones have maintained a preference for the federalists. In the provincial elections only a minority of the Allophones would vote for the Parti Québécois and only a minority would support the cause of Quebec's separation from the rest of Canada (Blais and Nadeau, 1995; Bauer, 1994).

The Quebec government had long striven to have its own immigration policy and its own immigration administration that would be, as much as possible, independent from those of the federal government. In 1968, it created the Quebec Ministry of Immigration. In 1978, it signed an agreement with the federal government giving it power in the selection of immigrants. In 1991, as a consequence of the failed Meech Lake agreement, Quebec reached an agreement with the federal government that gave it further substantial powers in regard to immigration. According to it, while the federal government would keep its basic power of admitting immigrants into the country and giving them Canadian citizenship, the Quebec government would take over all other responsibilities pertaining to their reception and integration. For this, it would receive financial compensation (Balthazar, 1996).

Furthermore, in 1975 Quebec adopted a Charter of Human Rights that affirmed the basic human rights and outlawed "exclusion and preference based on race, colour, sex, pregnancy, sexual orientation, civil status, age except as provided by law, religion, political conviction, language, ethnic or national origin, social condition, a handicap or the use of any means to palliate a handicap" (Lachapelle et al., 1993). In the 1980s, when the language laws were in place, Quebec reversed its policy regarding cultural diversity. It accepted a policy called *interculturalism.* This was a pluralist policy that emphasized the inclusiveness of ethnic minority groups. In 1981, the Ministry of Cultural Communities and Immigration (MCCI) was created with the mandate of administering the interculturalism policy. In 1984, the government created the Council of Cultural Communities and Immigration, an advisory body made up of independent persons representative of Quebec's cultural communities. In 1994, however, the MCCI was merged with the Ministry of International Affairs on the grounds that the two departments had somewhat overlapping functions. The effect of this was to reduce the public profile of immigration and the diverse ethnic communities.

In some respects, the policy of interculturalism had been similar to the policy of multiculturalism in Canada (discussed in the next chapter). Its protagonists, however, have claimed that it is basically different. They critique multiculturalism as a "weak" ideology that isolates cultural groups from one another and particularly as overlooking the majority group and overemphasizing minority groups. They argue that, unlike multiculturalism, interculturalism fosters a dynamic interaction between the minorities and the majority that allows the minority groups to achieve a higher level of adaptation to the broader society as individuals (Juteau, 1992).

The distinctive character of interculturalism is that, while it fosters the value of pluralism, its basic cornerstone is acceptance of the French language as the main cementing force of diverse ethnic minority groups. Throughout the history of French-English relations in Canada, language has played a central role as the bulwark of French identity. It also figures centrally in this policy. Furthermore, the ideology places a strong emphasis or encouragement of ethnic minority groups to take an active part in making a contribution to the Quebec society and its emerging identity. It is not clear, however, whether the diverse identities of the minority groups themselves are seen as contributions. Nevertheless, French Quebec culture is seen by the ideology to be dynamic, allowing for the creative development that would result from ethnic diversity.

ABORIGINAL PEOPLES IN CHANGE

The early history of the Aboriginal peoples, or as they call themselves today, the First Nations, has been a movement from what originally appeared to be a trading and treaty relationship to what became an increasing control by, and dependence on, the Canadian government to what is an evolving process of self-control and self-governance. Most of the issues in the relationship between the Aboriginal peoples and the non-Aboriginal society are related to one or the other of these three stages. The initial contact between the two established a trading relationship that appeared to be beneficial to both the Aboriginal communities and the European settlers. The European desire and market for fur pushed the early settlers ever further into the Canadian forested and open landscape, but it also made the non-Aboriginal settler rely on the Aboriginals' knowledge of this landscape and their collective efficiency in animal trapping. The Native trappers, however, developed an interest in the efficiency of the settlers' firearms, their metal implements, clothing material, alcohol, decorative objects and other goods (Innis, 1930; Trigger, 1985).

If it appeared that such a trading relationship would serve as a basis for a balanced social order between the two peoples, it should be remembered that the early numbers of non-Native settlers were small and the contacts between them were often indirect, through the contacts of the *courier du bois* or other intermediaries. As the European population increased and developed a strong demand for land, this kind of social order changed completely. Throughout the eighteenth, the nineteenth and into the twentieth century, the Native peoples were gradually displaced from their lands by the non-Aboriginal settlers. In the period of New France, the French Crown assumed that all the land that was not owned by the settlers was in its jurisdiction, and it could make land grants to French missionary orders so that they in turn would grant sections of it to the Indians for their life and subsistence. This was the origin of the idea of reserves. The idea remained after the conquest of New France. The British, however, created most, though not all, reserves by means of treaties with the Native peoples.

In signing the treaties, the Aboriginal tribes ceded most of their land to the British or later the Canadian government. The British Royal Proclamation of 1763, in regard to land ownership, accepted the principle of the Aboriginal right to land as long as it was not formally ceded by the Native tribes through treaties (Royal Commission on Aboriginal Peoples, 1996: 1: 111-119). Britain established a negotiating relationship with the Aboriginal peoples as the cultivation of friendly relations with them was already a policy of the French, and it was important for Britain to gain that friendship after the conquest of New France in order to maintain the lucrative fur trade and because a military alliance with a number of Indian tribes could be helpful to the Crown in its emerging conflict with the American rebels.

Treaties were made as European settlements expanded. A number of treaties were made by the early governors of Canada. After 1867, 11 major treaties were made as the settlers moved west and north, the last one made in 1929-1930. No treaties, however, were made in British Columbia. The consequence of this can be seen today, when virtually the entire province is under some form of land claims dispute. Each treaty established reserves for the Aboriginal people but surrendered the rest of the territory to the Crown and its government. In return, the tribes would receive cash payments, annual payments, schools and teachers, economic assistance (often in the form of agricultural implements), hunting rights and rifles and ammunition for hunting and the like. Many Indian chiefs were willing to negotiate such treaties for the benefits they brought. Many of them, however, understood the basic terms of negotiation differently from the government negotiators. Today's research has shown that many chiefs did not think that they were surrendering their land for good. Rather, for them, the treaty meant that they were sharing their land with the white settlers. The traditional worldview of the Native peoples did not see land as something nicely divisible into parcels of private property. Rather, land was something that was owned in common and everyone was entitled to be on it. The real issues were the areas for hunting and subsistence (Royal Commission on Aboriginal Peoples, 1996: 1:155-176).

In all these treaties, the Crown and the Canadian government's purpose was to secure as much land from the Aboriginal peoples as possible for the purpose of settlement and development. As the nineteenth century progressed, the goal pursued by the government became more definite and determined. It was the goal of assimilating the Aboriginal peoples into Canadian society completely. This aim became the centrepiece of the legislation that for years to come would be, as it were, a Sisyphean stone for the Aboriginal people, who tried to change it yet found behind it a protection of their basic right to land, i.e., the Indian Act of 1876. The Act reinforced the right to land principle set out in the Royal Proclamation of 1763, but it defined a formal land-surrender process, according to which the Aboriginal land cannot be simply appropriated but must be purchased on a tribe to tribe basis. Further, the Act regulated almost every important aspect of Indian people's daily life. Finally, it defined who was not an Indian. It created the category of "status Indians," referring to male persons of Indian blood who belong to one or another Indian band, children of such persons and women who were lawfully married to such persons. A highly controversial part of the Act was the regulation of marriage outside of the reserve. According to it, a woman who married a non-Indian man would be completely deprived of her Indian status, could not inherit any property left to her by her parents, was barred from any formal participation in the affairs of her band, was prevented from returning to live with her family on the reserve and could not even be buried on the reserve. The same applied to all her children (Royal Commission on Aboriginal Peoples, 1966: 1:281-319). There were many attempts to modify or change the Indian Act and a number of changes have been made. Among them was an amendment in 1985, known as Bill C-31, which reinstated women who married outside the reserve to their Indian status.

• A Painful Legacy

The process through which Aboriginal peoples were dispossessed of their land and livelihood and through which their culture and institutions were being lost and the fact of discrimination and racism against them left, as a consequence, a legacy that is only now being confronted. The policies towards the Aboriginal peoples were based on the assumption that Aboriginal ways of life were at a primitive level of evolutionary development and that cultural and social development could be achieved only by adopting the culture of the European societies (Royal Commission on Aboriginal Peoples, 1996: 3:2). The purpose of the Indian Act and of all the measures used for its implementation was to inculturate and incorporate the Aboriginal peoples into Canadian culture and society. However, the effect of all these efforts was far from incorporation. The Aboriginal people were effectively trapped between their Native community and Canadian society. Economically, while the rest of Canada was rapidly industrializing and generally changing its occupational structure to secondary and tertiary levels, the reserves remained essentially at the level of primary subsistence. Although a percentage of people from various tribes came to be engaged in industrial work, mostly as labourers, fishing, hunting, trapping and agriculture remained the main type of economic activity. Dependence on the government became part of the Aboriginal economy of both the Indians and the Inuit and both on and off the reserves. While there have been variations in the economic level and living conditions among the reserves, in the 1980s, for around 30 percent of the Aboriginal persons and families, government transfer payments were the major source of income. Employment was the major source of income, on the average, for only 30 percent of individuals and families, and about 25 percent received no income at all (Frideres, 1993: 160-62; Satzewich and Wotherspoon, 1993: 95).

The justice system also involves Aboriginal people proportionally more than it involves the general population. Aboriginal people, both Indian and Inuit, make up about 10 percent of the inmate population in federal penitentiaries, while they are only about 2 percent of the total Canadian population. In the Western provinces of Canada, where Aboriginal people make up about 10 percent of the total population, the Aboriginal inmate population of federal penitentiaries reaches 40 percent, while the Aboriginal population of provincial jails exceeds 50 percent. Aboriginal people are more likely to be involved with the justice system at a younger age than non-Aboriginal people. They are apprehended in much higher rates than are non-Aboriginal people by both the child welfare authorities and by the youth justice system (Royal Commission on Aboriginal Peoples, 1993: 86).

The Royal Commission on Aboriginal Peoples (1993: 86-87) concludes that the justice system discriminates against the Aboriginal people. The people feel discriminated against by the police, lawyers, Crown attorneys, judges and probation officers because of their different culture, their different languages and because of their low social standing, low educational levels and high unemployment. As a result, justice officials too often choose apprehension and punishment instead of discretion and alternatives to incarceration. Comparative research on Aboriginal

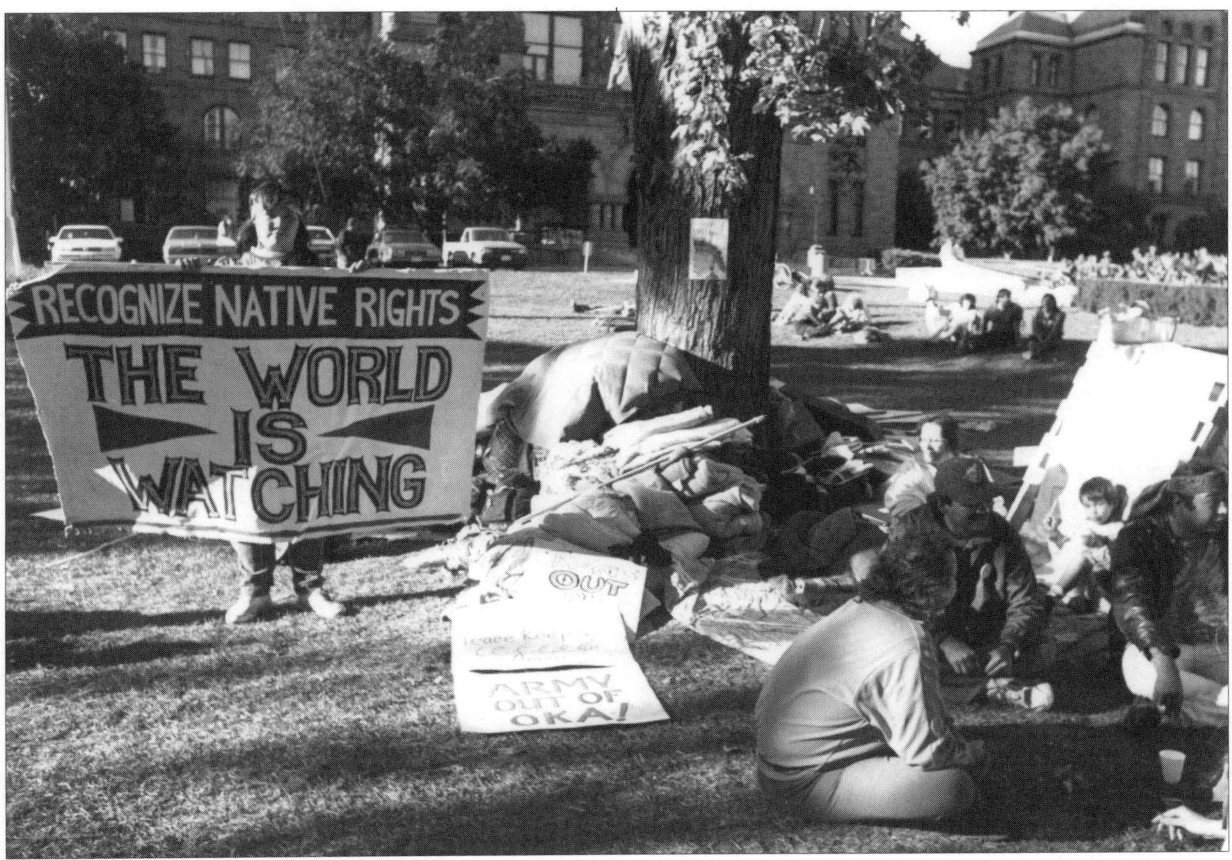

Part of a protest in favour of Native rights in Canada.

peoples in other countries confirms a number of these conclusions (Smandych, Lincoln and Wilson, 1993).

Yet, the process of movement of younger people out of the reserves into urban centres has begun and is changing the character of the Aboriginal community. By 1990, 40 percent of all Aboriginal population lived off reserves (Satzewich and Wotherspoon, 1993: 95). The move off reserves has had an ambiguous consequence on the Aboriginal identity. On the one hand, it has added to the many social problems already emerging on the reserves. One such problem has been child welfare. In all Canadian provinces and territories, Native children are over-represented in the proportion of children in foster homes, adoptions or in care of agencies. Studies have shown that Native children are in the care of provincial and federal child welfare agencies more than three times the rate of all Canadian children. In some provinces, like British Columbia, Alberta, Saskatchewan and Manitoba, they make up 40 to 60 percent of all children in care, and their rate of discharge is below that of non-Aboriginal children (Satzewich and Wotherspoon, 1993: 89).

Child problems often derive from problems in the family. Many families in the Aboriginal community are dysfunctional, due to poverty, high unemployment, alcoholism, poor housing and community turmoil. A survey by Statistics Canada (1991) indicated that over 39 percent of all the Aboriginal respondents surveyed (including on- and off-reserve Indians, Métis and Inuit, but over 44 percent of the on-reserve Indian and over 43 percent of the Inuit respondents) saw family violence as one of the most important issues in their communities. Along with unemployment, alcohol and drug abuse, other burning issues related to family life were: suicide (indicated by over 25 percent of all the respondents, but by over 34 percent of the on-reserve Indian, and over 41 percent of the Inuit respondents), sexual abuse (over 24 percent of all respondents, 29 percent of the on-reserve Indian, and over 35 percent of the Inuit respondents) and rape (15 percent of all respondents,

Looking Forward, Looking Back

Royal Commission on Aboriginal Peoples

Displacement and Assimilation

In this third stage [of the relationship between the non-Aboriginal and Aboriginal peoples], which we have called displacement and assimilation, we have noted how non-Aboriginal western society has become predominant in population and in power terms. Thus it has had the capacity to impose its will on Aboriginal societies—and it has also been motivated to do so.

The motivation was in part economic, as the commercial economy based on the fur trade and other natural resources was pushed from centre stage and replaced by the drive for expansionary settlement of the continent and for agricultural and, later, industrial production. In this context, from a western perspective, Aboriginal peoples were seen to stand in the way, for they inhabited and claimed title to vast stretches of land.

The transition in the relationship was also pushed by the western belief in "progress" and in the evolutionary development of human beings from lesser to greater states of civilization. Long-standing western beliefs in racial and cultural superiority were given a scientific veneer during this stage, as theories such as those linking intelligence to the size of the brain came into play and theories of evolution were used to justify racist assumptions. This was accompanied by a belief in the destiny of European cultures to expand across North America and eventually to take over the whole land base.

In this perspective, western society was seen to be at the forefront of evolutionary development, with Aboriginal peoples lagging far behind. As a result, Aboriginal peoples needed to be protected in part, but also guided - even required—to catch up, in a process of accelerated evolution. Relegated in this way to a secondary position, they were not regarded as appropriate participants in discussions of changed relationship (such as Confederation and the subsequent admission of new provinces to the federation). Rather, decisions were made unilaterally, and a centralized administrative system was established to bring about directed change.

These ideas of how the relationship should be changed were profoundly at odds with Aboriginal conceptions of how relations in human societies and with the natural world should be conducted. In this period, Aboriginal peoples sought to continue the terms of the original relationship—a relationship of equality among nations, where each retained its autonomy and distinctiveness, where each had a separate as well as a shared land base, and where the natural world was respected.

Resistance was particularly strong with respect to efforts to assimilate Aboriginal people or to merge Aboriginal and western societies into one—based, of course, on the western model. If successful, this attempt to eliminate the distinctive features of Aboriginal societies would, from an Aboriginal perspective, have destroyed the balance of life, which requires that each of the societies originally created be maintained in order to sustain the overall functioning of the universe.

This is not to say that, from an Aboriginal perspective, the relationship needed to remain unchanged. Adjustments could be made in the shared land and resource base, for example, as western settlers increased in number. If changes were required, from an Aboriginal perspective they should be made through a process of continuing dialogue and mutual agreement, a process of creating a harmonious environment in which a middle ground could be achieved. This was more likely to happen if concepts such as sharing (lands, resources, or powers) were adopted, instead of concepts such as win-lose or extinguishment.

In contrast to western society's linear conception of progress and evolution, Aboriginal conceptions continued to be based on the concept of the circle. For example, western conceptions spoke of the evolution of different forms of production from simple to more complex, with the latter replacing the former over time (and never to return to them again). By contrast, Aboriginal perspectives continued to emphasize diversity and local autonomy. In this view, different groups have adopted ways of life best suited to their local needs and circumstances; each is equally valid and should not be expected to change unless the group believes that a different model would meet their needs better.

In discussing the previous stage, early contact and co-operation, we suggested that even if Aboriginal and non-Aboriginal societies did not have a shared perspective on the relationship, it was still possible for the fundamental elements of the Aboriginal perspective to be realized in practice. In the period of displacement, there was no ambiguity. The two perspectives were clearly different, and the non-Aboriginal society had the capacity to impose its will. In Mark Dockstator's view, the result was a dysfunctional relationship:

> From one perspective, Aboriginal society was subjected to the external forces of Western society which were designed to displace Aboriginal society.... At the same time and in contrast to this external pressure, Aboriginal society was attempting to maintain the nation-to-nation relationship ...
>
> The dysfunctional nature of the societal relationship caused by the action of two opposite forces on Aboriginal society was further exacerbated by the imposition of a Western-based administrative system. One of the purposes of the system is to place boundaries, or parameters of acceptable behaviour and actions, around Aboriginal society. By restricting and thereby controlling the lifestyle of Aboriginal people, the administrative system acted to isolate Aboriginal society from both mainstream society and the larger physical environment. Consequently, the social ills resulting from the imbalance of Aboriginal society were "turned inward"; the natural release mechanisms

employed by Aboriginal society to vent "negative forces" were foreclosed by the operation of the Western administrative system.

As we have seen from the accounts of key events and issues during this stage, the period of displacement did great damage to Aboriginal societies. They were not defeated, however. Resistance at times took the form of passive non-cooperation (for example, with respect to the enfranchisement initiative), at times defiant continuation of proscribed activities (with respect to the potlatch and the sundance, for instance), and in more recent decades it has taken the form of vocal and organized opposition.

From the perspective of non-Aboriginal society, especially those charged with the conduct of the relationship, it became evident over time that the isolation/assimilation strategy was not working. As early as the first decade of the 1900s, some missionaries and civil servants recognized the lack of success of the industrial and residential schools. By the end of the second decade, efforts were being made to modify the strategy, although initially the direction of change was to tighten the screws of the system rather than to consider alternatives. Thus, the *Indian Act* of 1927 contained stronger measures to intervene in and control the affairs of Aboriginal societies, including further efforts to develop an agricultural economy in the expectation that social and cultural change would follow in its wake. The act was also notable for its response to Aboriginal political organizations pursuing land issues, especially in British Columbia. An amendment was added making "raising a fund or providing money for the prosecution of any claim" a crime unless permission was obtained.

After the Second World War, the search for new approaches to policy continued, especially through the hearings of a joint committee of the Senate and the House of Commons sitting between 1946 and 1948. This provided an occasion for Aboriginal interveners and others to state in strong terms the problems with the existing relationship, but the committee's report was a major disappointment. The recommendations suggested the removal of many of the more coercive elements of the *Indian Act* (and this was accomplished with the amendments of 1951), but the changes fell far short of challenging the prevailing assimilationist framework.

Twenty years later, there was another opportunity to hear Aboriginal voices, as the Federal government worked towards a new policy, but again there was major disappointment with the result. The "Statement of the Government of Canada on Indian Policy, 1969" ignored the consultations that accompanied the policy review and proceeded to recommend measures designed to achieve integration and equality: Indian people were to be allowed to retain their cultures, much as other Canadians do in multicultural society, but they were to give up the other features that make them distinct—elements such as treaties, Aboriginal rights, exclusive federal responsibility and the department of Indian affairs. The overwhelmingly hostile response to this policy initiative on the part of Aboriginal people and subsequent court decisions that recognize the validity of Aboriginal and treaty rights, marked an important turning point in the relationship.

Restoring the Spirit of the Treaties

If seen with broad vision, the story of Crown treaty making with First Nations is one of the richest repositories of meaning and identity for Canadians. It is a story that begins long before the *Royal Proclamation of 1763* and connects the earliest forays of European fishermen to the shores of Newfoundland with the establishment of Nunavut at the end of the twentieth century. Aboriginal nations' contributions to Canada in sharing their wealth with the newcomers should be acknowledged and enshrined forever in Canadian history. Those contributions are unique and incomparable in their historical depth and in their practical significance to Canada today.

Treaties recognized the separate existence of nations but also connected peoples by establishing links of partnership, common interests and shared ceremonies. The practice of dividing and connecting was extended to Europeans at an early stage, as reflected in the Two Row Wampum, a symbolic reminder of the separate but connected paths followed by the British and the Six Nations in the conduct of their relations.

The Aboriginal world view of a universal sacred order, made up of compacts and kinship relations among human beings, other living beings and the Creator, was initially reinforced by the Crown's willingness to enter into treaties under Indian protocols. But subsequent denials of the validity and importance of the treaties have denigrated Aboriginal peoples' stature as nations and their substantial contribution to Canada. Unfortunately, non-Aboriginal people valued treaties as long as they continued to be useful, which often meant until land changed hands, settlements grew, and resources were extracted and converted into money. For their part, First Nations expected that treaties would grow more valuable with time, as the parties came to know each other better, trusted one another, and made the most of their treaty relationships.

In the past, governments and courts in Canada have often considered these treaties instruments of surrender rather than compacts of co-existence and mutual benefit. This is the spirit of colonialism, the agenda of a society that believes it has no more need for friends because of its apparent wealth, power and superiority. The spirit of the treaties, by contrast, is the spirit of a time when the ancestors of today's Canadians needed friends and found them.

It is time to return to the spirit of the treaties and to set a new course to correct the legalistic and adversarial attitudes and actions that have contributed to the badly deteriorated treaty relationships that exist between Aboriginal nations and Canada today.

Source: Looking Forward, Looking Back. Report of the Royal Commission on Aboriginal Peoples. Ottawa: Canada Communication Group Publishing, 1996.

Photo: Courtesy of the Canadian Tourism Commission

In the 1990s, the focus of Aboriginal concerns became the entrenchment of their rights in the Canadian constitution and self-government for their communities. The premise is that a lasting solution to the pressing social, family, educational and cultural problems can be achieved only through full recognition of Aboriginal rights and through Aboriginal self-control over their communities. Above photo: Rankin Inlet, Nunavut (Canada's newest territory).

over 16 percent of the on-reserve Indian, and 25 percent of the Inuit respondents) (Royal Commission on Aboriginal Peoples, 1996: 3:58).

A factor in the Aboriginal family dysfunctionality is the generational effect of the former residential schools. Many children in care of welfare agencies are children of parents who were raised in residential schools when they were young or were themselves children of parents who were raised in residential schools. The intent of the residential school policy was to erase Aboriginal identity by separating generations of children from their families and socializing them, not in the culture of their ancestors, but in the culture of the Canadian mainstream. This process, however, was often done virtually by force with damaging effects to the personality of students. The Royal Commission on Aboriginal Peoples (1996: 3:34-36) has collected a number of testimonials from persons who were raised in residential schools. Among them are such statements as the following, from three different persons:

> I stayed in that residential school for ten years. I hurt there. There was no love there. There was no caring there, nobody to hug you when you cried; all they did was slap you over: "Don't you cry! You are not supposed to cry." Whipped me when I talked to my younger brother. That's my brother, for God's sake. We were not supposed to talk to these people.
>
> I was one of the fortunate ones in the residential school, but the boy who slept next to me wasn't very fortunate. I saw him being sexually abused. As a result, he died violently. He couldn't handle it when he became of age.
>
> I have heard people who have said, "I left that residential school, and I have been like a ship without a rudder." I

> have heard people say, "I have left that place, and I left there just like a robot, with no feelings, with no emotions."

For Aboriginal persons, leaving the reserve for residential schools or to move into urban areas has often meant a loss of self-esteem and a loss of identity. In urban areas, often living in a condition of poverty and barred by prejudice and discrimination from acceptance into the society around them, young Aboriginal persons have tended to feel trapped between their Native identity and the identity of the larger society, neither of which they fully possess. Unlike a number of other minority groups, the Aboriginal groups in urban areas generally have not formed effective social service agencies of their own that could extend assistance and counselling to their own people, particularly to their own young people. The publicly available services have rarely included appropriately trained personnel who understood the background and the identity problems of persons caught between two cultures. The work of public service agencies has been based on a non-Aboriginal value system and worldview. All the initiatives undertaken to remedy this are rather recent (Royal Commission on Aboriginal Peoples, 1996: 3:34, 668-669).

The new initiatives among the Aboriginal peoples have been coming from those sectors of the Aboriginal urban community who have acquired higher educational levels. This has been the positive result of the move off the reserves. The educated sector has made it possible for a new elite to emerge among the Aboriginal groups, an elite cognizant of the ways of Canada and its laws and aware of their groups' position within it. As in the case of other ethnic groups, the main instrument of the new elite's activity for change has been its own organizations, particularly instrumental organizations. However, the base for the elite's activities has remained in the chiefs on the reserves.

Although there have been some Aboriginal politically oriented organizations since the turn of the century, the big quantum jump in Aboriginal organizing came at the end of the 1960s. A precipitating factor was the federal government's White Paper of 1969, which recommended that the Indian special citizenship rights be terminated and that Indians should be given the same citizenship rights and obligations as all non-Indians. It further recommended that the Indian Act be repealed, that the Indian Affairs Branch of the Department of Indian and Northern Affairs be phased out and that the responsibility for all matters concerning the Indians be shifted to the provincial governments. The reaction of the Aboriginal leaders to the White Paper was quick and negative. It stimulated an emergence of new organizations and politicization of the old ones (Satzewich and Wotherspoon, 1993: 228-232). According to a study by James Frideres (1993: 288), while prior to 1970 there had been a total of 119 Aboriginal organizations on national, provincial and regional levels, by 1991 there were 239 such organizations. The focus of their work became the question of citizenship, in particular the elimination of certain restrictions on their citizenship rights, but at the same time retention of other rights that would recognize their status as First Nations (Satzewich and Wotherspoon, 1993: 220).

By the 1990s, the focus of the Aboriginal demands has become entrenchment of Aboriginal rights in the Canadian constitution and eventual Aboriginal self-government and sovereignty. The thrust of the demands has been the premise that a satisfactory solution to social, family, welfare, educational and cultural Aboriginal problems can be achieved only through the attainment of self-control over these issues. All recommendations of the 1996 Royal Commission on Aboriginal Peoples advise that this should be the case.

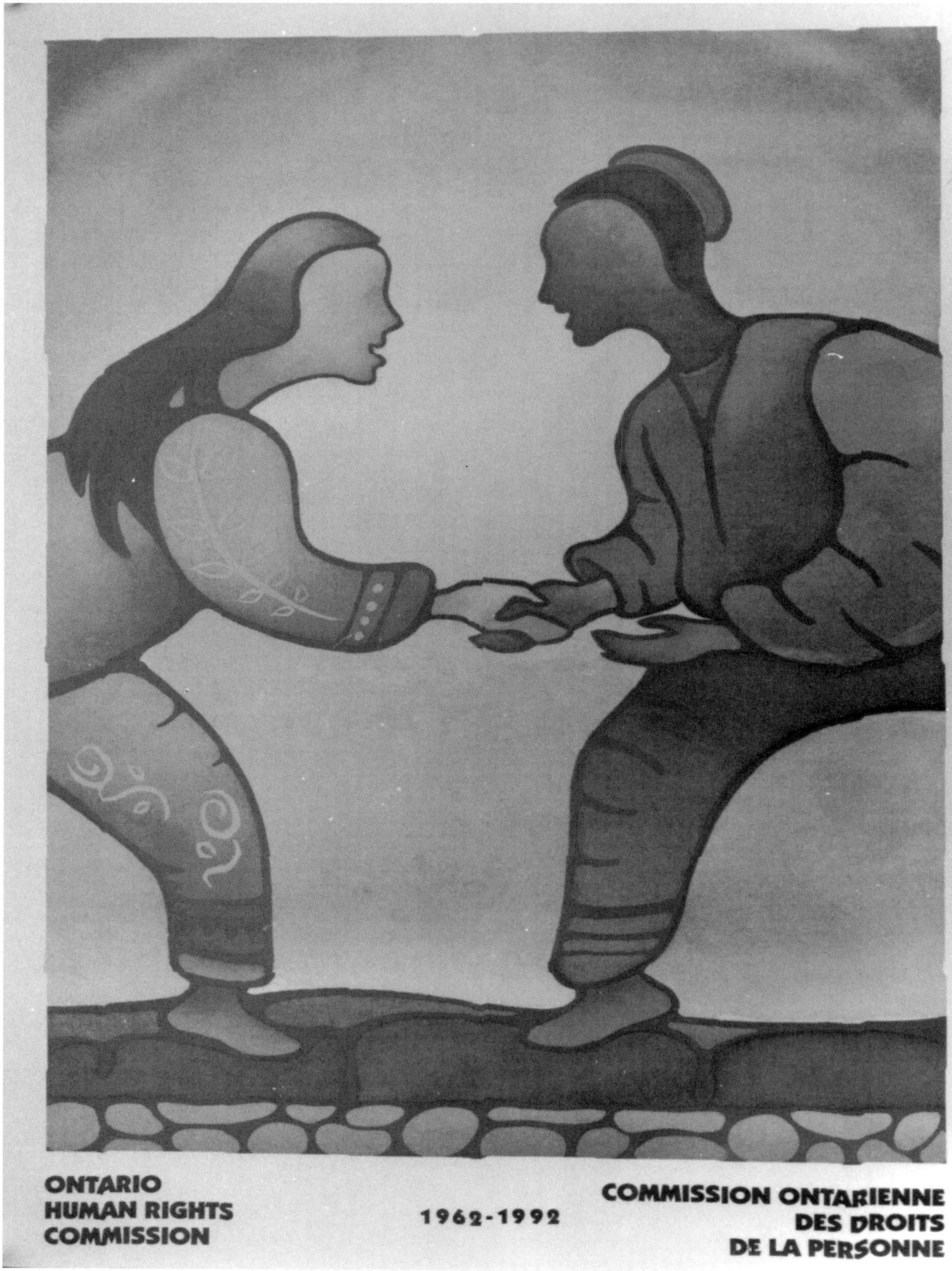

ONTARIO
HUMAN RIGHTS
COMMISSION
1962-1992
COMMISSION ONTARIENNE
DES DROITS
DE LA PERSONNE

Ontario Human Rights Commission

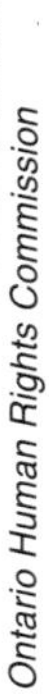

Ontario Human Rights Commission poster.

CHAPTER 10

ETHNIC DIVERSITY AND SOCIETAL INTEGRATION

Meeting the Challenge

This chapter discusses the role that the state plays in interethnic relations and in the process of integrating society into a unity in which all diverse ethnic groups can be a part. It focuses on the importance of human rights legislation and public policies. As a case in point, it discusses the Canadian policy of multiculturalism, its basic principles, it history, reactions and critiques of the policy and the policy's sociological implications. It also points out how national and other symbols influence the process of integration of diverse groups into a unified society. Finally, it tries to spell out the basic principles of interethnic cooperation and conflict resolution.

In Chapter 1, in the definition of interethnic relations, we pointed out that intergroup relations are inherently tied to the problem of the integration of society. That is, from the point of view of society, intergroup relations are a process of interaction by which community-type groups either adjust to each other, so as to effect a degree of social integration, or, by failing to adjust to each other, effect divisiveness in society as a whole.

Whether the one or the other effect takes place depends to a large extent on the responses that are given to the needs, interests and demands of the groups. Since ethnic groups' demands are usually directed at the government, it is the government's response to them that is of importance. The government, however, has to deal with the demands of a variety of groups and often has to weigh the potential consequences of meeting the interests of one group in relation to other groups. In particular, at issue are the interests of ethnic minority groups in relation to the interests of the ethnic majority group. As was explained before, the major institutions of society are shaped and controlled largely by members of the majority group and hence accommodation of minority interests within these institutions may potentially or actually compete or conflict with the interests of the majority group. The predicament that the majority group faces is that, on the one hand, while accommodation of ethnically diverse interests within the institutional mainstream may bring about a greater integration, it may also alienate sectors of the majority group or may be even perceived as threatening to the identity of the majority group. On the other hand, while giving no recognition or not altering the mainstream institutions to accommodate the interests of ethnically diverse groups may be more reassuring to the majority group, it may also, by that fact alone, generate or promote divisiveness in the larger society.

ETHNIC DIVERSITY AND THE STATE

Integration of society means the inclusion of all diverse units in one common social entity and a commitment of all units to this entity. It entails all the processes of social incorporation that have been discussed in the previous chapters. These are the processes of inculturation, structural incorporation of the type that allows upward social mobility of minority group members and the process of identity formation with the society as a whole and with its major institutions. These processes, however, are not automatic. For many members of minority groups, they can be frustrated, interrupted, countervailed or blocked by members of the majority group or by more powerful or influential groups. Integration of society, thus, is not accomplished automatically. It requires conscious action by those in society who are vested with the responsibility for overseeing its order and development, i.e., the state and its government. There seems to be an agreement in society that it is the government's responsibility to see to it that the interests pursued by some do not effect damage to others in society and that diverse interests in society are channeled towards the common good.

The function of the state in regard to interethnic relations is to ensure (1) that all groups, minority and majority, have an opportunity to pursue their needs and interests; (2) that the pursuit of needs and interests of one group, including the state itself, does not infringe on the rights of other groups to pursue their needs and interests; and (3) that there is a social-psychological milieu in society that communicates to all groups the message that they are included in society as full members with the cultural identities they wish to maintain.

Usually a government responds to the needs and interests of various groups in society by means of public policies. *Public policy* can be defined as "a course of action or inaction chosen by public authorities to address a given problem or interrelated set of problems" (Pal, 1987: 4). In this sense, even if a government does nothing to address a problem, as long as this inaction is deliberate, it is a public policy (Pal, 1987: 9). We will discuss concrete examples and the issues connected with public policies later on in this chapter. A policy, however, can be formed by a government either in an *ad hoc* manner or in a systematic manner or by a deliberate lack of forming a policy on an issue.

When formed in an *ad hoc* manner, a policy is usually a response to a specific crisis. For example, in World War I and World War II, the Canadian government instituted a policy of internment of members of ethnic minority groups whom it defined as "enemy aliens." In the first case, the minority group, mostly Ukrainians, were the immigrants from the Austro-Hungarian Empire with whom the Allies, including Canada, were at war. In the second case, the minority group was the Japanese in Canada. In both cases, the policy was a reaction to war and motivated by the fear of a potential enemy, and in both cases the basic human rights of the people of the respective minorities were violated. Until the 1960s, there were no policies in Canada aimed at protecting minority groups against discrimination or other violations of their rights, though, in terms of our definition, the lack of a positive policy can be seen as being a policy.

Systematically established policies are applications of basic principles to which both the interest groups and the government could refer as criteria of policy creation and policy application. Usually such principles are found in state constitutions. In democratic societies, the basic principles governing majority-minority relations have been spelled out as declarations of *human rights.* As diversity within societies increases and as societies themselves come to be more and more linked in the global structure with other societies, human rights become a principle of constancy in group relations involving often radically different cultures and values. Since the end of World War II, the principle of respect for basic human rights has become more widely accepted throughout the world. This does not mean that all nations of the world or even the nations of the Western world fully apply it in their societies (Donnelly, 1989: 49-65). Still, internationally it has become a principle to which individuals and groups, particularly minority groups, can appeal.

HUMAN RIGHTS LEGISLATION IN CANADA

The first clear statement of human rights to be incorporated into the constitution of a state was the American Bill of Rights of 1791. Binding human rights legislation in other countries came much later. In Canada, the national human rights legislation began in 1960 with the passage of the Canadian Bill of Rights during the prime ministership of John G. Diefenbaker. Before that, in the 1950s, various Canadian provinces enacted fair-employment practices and similar legislation, and the province of Saskatchewan had had its own Bill of Rights since 1947. In the 1960s other provinces enacted similar legislation, and by 1975, all provinces in Canada had some human rights codes (Tarnopolsky, 1988: 1024-1025; Kallen, 1982: 42-56).

In 1982, the Canadian Bill of Rights was superceded by the Charter of Rights and Freedoms (Canada, 1982) that was built into the patriated Canadian constitution. The Charter guaranteed the fundamental freedoms of conscience and religion, of thought, of belief, of opinion and expression, including freedom of the press and other media of communication, of peaceful assembly and of association. It guaranteed democratic rights, geographical mobility rights, legal rights, including the right to life, liberty and security of persons, and equality rights giving protection against "discrimination based on race, national or ethnic origin, colour,

Photo: Courtesy of the Toronto Star Syndicate

A new vision of Canada—the repatriation of the Canadian constitution and signing of the Charter of Rights and Freedoms in 1982.

religion, sex, age or mental or physical disability." But the Charter went even further by indicating that this protection "does not preclude any law, program or activity that has as its object the amelioration of conditions of disadvantaged individuals or groups including those who are disadvantaged because of race, national or ethnic origin, colour, religion, sex, age or mental or physical disability." The Charter also reinforced the official bilingualism in Canada by affirming the equality of the English and French languages and by affirming the rights of children to be educated in either language. It also affirmed the multicultural character of Canada and recognized the rights of the Aboriginal peoples of Canada. Finally, the Charter emphasized that all the rights and freedoms referred to in it are guaranteed equally to male and female persons.

In relation to its minority groups, Canada is also bound by the international covenants on human rights to which it is a signatory (United Nations, 1978). These include the United Nations Charter of 1945, the Universal Declaration of Human Rights adopted by the United Nations in 1948, the International Convention on the Prevention and Punishment of the Crime of Genocide of 1948, the International Convention Concerning Discrimination in Respect of Employment and Occupation of 1958, the International Convention on All Forms of Racial Discrimination of 1965 (ratified in 1969), the International Covenant on Economic, Social and Cultural Rights of 1966 (ratified in 1976), the International Covenant on Civil and Political Rights (ratified in 1976) and various other resolutions of United Nations assemblies and international conferences. All these instruments of intergroup relations emphasize both the importance of eliminating obstacles to their equal participation in society for minority groups and ensuring that no country will undertake social incorporation by force, i.e., by denying the minority groups basic rights to identity maintenance. Notable are the resolutions of the Conference on Security and Cooperation in Europe (CSCE) to which Canada is a signatory. Among the resolutions of the Conference's 1990 Copenhagen meetings were the following:

> The participating states will adopt, where necessary, special measures for the purpose of ensuring to persons belonging to national minorities full equality with other citizens in the exercise and enjoyment of human rights and fundamental freedoms (resolution 31).
>
> The participating states will respect the right of persons belonging to national minorities to effective participation in public affairs, including participation in the affairs relating to the protection and promotion of the identity of such minorities (resolution 35).
>
> Persons belonging to national minorities have the right freely to express, preserve and develop their ethnic, cultural, linguistic or religious identity ... free of any attempts at assimilation against their will (resolution 32).

To achieve this they have the right

> to seek voluntary financial and other contributions as well as public assistance, in conformity with national legislation (resolution 32.2).

Similar conclusions were expressed in the Helsinki Summit Declaration of 1992. The Declaration, however, made reference to the social instability that has developed in the world, particularly economic decline, social tensions, aggressive nationalism, intolerance, xenophobia and ethnic conflicts and reaffirmed the intention of the participating states to abide by their resolutions.

Application of human rights legislation to elimination of discrimination or any other injustice, however, requires accepted procedures and special agencies to carry them out. As was explained in Chapter 6, among such agencies in Canada are human rights commissions. While the work of these commissions has shown success, it has often been hampered by under-funding and case backlogs. The human rights approach is a complaints-driven process, and many people and ethnic organizations do not bother, or do not have the resources, to report incidents of discrimination or initiate the process of lodging complaints.

PUBLIC POLICIES AND SOCIETAL INTEGRATION

In modern democratic societies, statements or declarations of human rights are the principles to be followed or taken into account when public policies are developed. The direct means of bringing about societal integration are public policies themselves. However, the process of policy legislation and the process of policy interpretation for the sake of application is rather complex, and the existence of a policy does not mean that the desired effect will be brought about even with the best intentions. Legislation of public policy is often a compromise of various conflicting interests, and the ensuing policy statement is often subject to several possible interpretations. The ministries who are given the responsibility of putting a policy into practice are themselves often not clear as to how a policy statement is to be applied to concrete circumstances (Pal, 1987: 128-132).

In democratic societies, the execution of public policies is usually delegated to agencies, often created for the purpose of carrying out a specific policy, and it is these agencies that, at the end of the day, interpret what a policy is to mean in practice. The real content of a policy is derived thus from a delegated agency (Pal, 1987: 5). Thus, in 1977, the federal Canadian Human Rights Act was legislated, which established that the federal Human Rights Commission would administer the human rights code. It was shown that special bodies, such as the human rights commissions, were more efficient in promoting human rights than were the courts. Even before this, many provinces had established their own human rights commissions to administer the codes. Many provinces also created offices of the Ombudsman, to whom people could complain against practices that violated their rights.

The procedure that a human rights commission would follow was described in detail by the Commissioner of the Ontario Human Rights Commission Dan Hill (1977: 26-27). The procedure would begin with a complaint received from persons who felt they had been discriminated against. The commission would then investigate the complaint to determine the evidence. Once the complaint had been verified, the commission gave those accused a chance to redress their discriminatory practices. This would be done by persuasion, advice or cajoling. If these efforts failed, a public inquiry might be ordered or the case might proceed to the court. Upon conviction, the guilty party would usually be fined a sum of money as determined by the court.

A case dealt with by the Ontario Human Rights Commission in the late 1960s illustrates this procedure. A tavern in a small town had continuously discriminated against Black customers, asking them to leave the tavern if they entered it. White students from a nearby university whose Black friends were asked to leave the tavern lodged a complaint with the commission. The commission investigated and confirmed the tavern owner's discriminatory practice. Thereupon, the commission requested that the tavern owner reverse the practice and open its doors to Black customers. Alternatively, the owner would face charges under the human rights code. The owner complied, and the commission advised the students from the nearby university to keep bringing as many of their Black friends to the tavern as possible to ensure that a non-discriminatory pattern would be established.

In another case, four senior managerial workers filed a complaint in 1989 with the Ontario Human Rights Commission, alleging that they were required to carry out sexist and racist policies. They claimed that their company's president had ordered them to fire women of non-white race whom they had hired (Kallen, 1995:262). The commission investigated and found that this was the case. It reached a settlement with the president of the company by which he would pay close to $300,000 in compensation, apologize to each complainant by letter and pay each employee $8,000 in damages. In addition, to reverse the pattern of discrimination, the commission required the company to establish a program of affirmative action by which women and persons of non-white racial categories would be hired until employment equity was reached.

These two cases illustrate how the agencies who carry out public policies interpret them in practice. Other cases in other provinces would be solved by a quicker move to the courts (Kallen, 1995: 261-263). The work of an agency, however, and the public policy it administers may come under the scrutiny of different interest groups who may exert pressure on the government to interpret the policy in terms of their own perspective. In consequence, the government may modify its own interpretation of the policy in question from one period to another. The case I would like to discuss in this regard is the Canadian policy of multiculturalism. It will illustrate both the process of interethnic politics and the process of development and change of a public policy. This policy is singled out here for special consideration because it has been the only explicit state policy in Canada dealing with the question of societal integration of diverse ethnic identities. It is this policy that has gained the attention of other countries in the world, almost as a distinct Canadian signature. A number of countries, such as Australia, the Netherlands and Germany, have studied Canadian multicultural policy as a possible model for their own policies responding to the issues of increasing ethnic diversity in their countries.

THE POLICY OF MULTICULTURALISM

• Policy Principles and Programs

The policy of multiculturalism was established by the federal government in 1971. As expressed in the original statement, the policy was aimed at a greater integration of Canadian society by providing the diverse ethnic minority groups with a sense of belonging to Canada. Its original aim was identity incorporation, giving ethnic minority groups a public recognition of their identity. The policy gave them a chance to reinforce their identity, but within the Canadian context, and with the mainstream recognizing that ethnic diversity is part of Canadian identity.

The basic principles of the policy are expressed in the statement by Prime Minister Pierre Elliott Trudeau in his introduction of the policy in the Canadian Parliament on October 8, 1971 (Minister of State, Multiculturalism, 1978). It states:

> A policy of multiculturalism within a bilingual framework commends itself to the government as the most suitable means of assuring the cultural freedom of Canadians. Such a policy should help to break down discriminatory attitudes and cultural jealousies. National unity if it is to mean anything in the deeply personal sense must be founded on confidence in one's own individual identity; out of this can grow respect for that of others and a willingness to share ideas, attitudes and assumptions. A vigorous policy of multiculturalism will help to create this initial confidence. It can form the base of a society which is based on fair play for all.

The policy states four objectives: (1) assistance to cultural groups to support and promote cultural retention; (2) the overcoming of barriers to full participation in Canadian society for members of cultural groups; (3) enhancement of national unity through the promotion of cultural exchange and interaction among Canadian cultural groups; (4) assistance to members of cultural groups, particularly immigrants, in learning at least one official language (Minister of State, Multiculturalism, 1978). In short, the policy is based on the premise that the support of the cultural identities of diverse ethnic groups within society, accompanied by exchange and interaction among them, will facilitate the integration of society as a whole. This came to be known as the idea of unity in diversity.

To implement the policy, the government created a special agency, the Multicultural Directorate, originally attached to the Department of the Secretary of State. The Directorate developed a range of programs aimed at fulfilling the policy's objectives. They can be classified under four main headings: (1) programs aimed at assisting the cultural preservation, cultural education and growth of various ethnic groups, including their languages; (2) programs aimed at exhibiting cultural differences to the general public; (3) programs aimed directly at the mainstream community in order to develop a greater tolerance or acceptance of ethnic differences, and thus to reduce prejudices and ethnic and racial discrimination; (4) programs aimed at involving ethnic groups and selected ethnic institutions in the mainstream institutions of society.

The first type of program included grants given to various ethnic institutions, such as schools and cultural centres, to develop their own museums, libraries and archives, to develop courses in language training, the creation of ethnic art and the like. It also included grants to ethnic organizations, such as youth associations and umbrella organizations, for leadership training and organizational activities. The second type of program included grants given to sponsor ethnic dances, festivals, art exhibits and the like. These have been perhaps the most visible aspects of the multicultural programs that have given multiculturalism, at least initially, a high profile. Caravan and Caribana in Toronto, and the Dauphin Festival in Manitoba, are examples of popular annual festivals of this nature, celebrating cultural and racial diversity. Many other major Canadian cities have established similar festivals. In the beginning phases of the policy, activities such as these took up the lion's share of the agency's budget. With time, however, other programs were sponsored, such as ethnic and interethnic conferences, the establishment of multicultural centres in a number of cities, assistance to ethnic language teaching, immigration orientation and citizenship preparation programs. The third type of program has included anti-racism advertising in the media, subways, billboards and films with the aim of projecting positive ideas of different racial groups. Several of these programs have tried to emphasize the economic value of cultural diversity to the general public. A number of these advertising campaigns have also been undertaken by provincial governments who have their own multicultural programs. The fourth type of program has included the establishment of multi-thematic ethnic national institutions and the incorporation of selected ethnic institutions into the mainstream structures. Examples are the Canadian Ethnic Studies Association and the Canadian Heritage Languages Institute. By 1996, to promote the study of Canadian diversity, 30 ethnic chairs had been established at various universities across Canada. A series of histories of various ethnic groups in Canada has been sponsored by the multiculturalism program and published by a major publishing company in Canada. This has stimulated the development of ethnic history as a subdiscipline of Canadian history and has given an impetus to a wealth of sociological and other studies of ethnicity in Canada of which there were previously only a few.

Directly or indirectly the federal multicultural program stimulated the development of other programs and the establishment of agencies and institutions. A Multicultural Television (MTV) channel has been set up in Toronto, and many ethnic programs regularly appear on the Public Access Network across the country. In addition, the publication of books and the production of ethnic films has been supported by the multicultural program. In several Canadian provinces, particularly Alberta, Saskatchewan and Manitoba, the idea of multiculturalism has been instrumental in the inclusion of a number of ethnic languages into regular secondary school teaching programs. In 1996, by a special act of the federal parliament, the Canadian Race Relations Foundation was established to deal more directly with issues of race.

• Historical Background

The origins of multiculturalism policy lie in an attempt to deal with the French-English problem in Canada, a task with which the Royal Commission on Bilingualism and Biculturalism was charged in 1963. Before the Commission could complete its work, it became evident that the problem of Canadian cultures could not be adequately approached without also considering the presence of the "Other" ethnic groups in Canada and the issue of cultural diversity, rather than only the issue of the cultural duality of Canadian society. Volume 4 of the Commission's report, much different in character from the previous volumes, represented a change of the approach in the Commission's work (Canada, 1969). It was no longer possible to emphasize language or cultural autonomy for the French while ignoring or insisting on assimilation of the other groups. By the end of the 1960s, the demographic effects of the constant stream of immigration to Canada had become quite evident. According to the Canadian census, by 1971, the year the multicultural policy was inaugurated, 15.4 percent of the total Canadian population was first generation, that is foreign-born, and 18.5 percent was second generation. In other words, 33.9 percent, or one-third of the total Canadian population, were immigrants or immediate children of immigrants (Kalbach and Richard, 1988). Sociologically, this meant that at least one-third of the total population had been either fully or partially socialized in cultures other than what, in the past, was considered "Canadian." It was thus inevitable that this category of people would begin to make some political demands of their own.

The groups exerting pressure for the enactment of the multicultural policy were the established minority groups, such as Ukrainians, Polish, Italians and others. The original priorities of the policy reflect the needs and interests of these groups. These groups had at least three, and some four, generations in Canada. Their demands were activated by the implementation of the federal government's bilingual policy and its strong commitment to support the French in Canada. Many of the leaders of this movement for the policy were third generation from the Prairie provinces of Canada, such as Senator Paul Yuzyk, Manoly Lupul, Walter Tarnopolski, all three with third-generation Ukrainian background (Bociurkiw, 1978). They were backed by organizations that included second- and first-generation members. Student organizations were particularly vociferous in their support of multiculturalism and comprised many second-generation members.

At the base of the demands of this movement for the policy of multiculturalism was the claim that the identity and contribution to Canadian society of the people who settled the Prairies, and the identity and contribution to Canadian society of all other immigrants and their descendants, had not been adequately acknowledged by Canadians. As a result, at its introduction, the priorities of the multiculturalism policy focused on recognition of the different ethnic Canadian cultures, on support of ethnic language learning for younger generations of those who wanted their children to retain some knowledge of it, on ethnic arts, on support of activities that centred on identity retention and programs that exhibited ethnic cultures to the general public with the aim of increasing their recognition by the mainstream society

• Changes in Priorities

Towards the end of the 1970s, a new sector of society had begun to make demands on the multicultural program. By this time, the ethnic composition of immigration to Canada had changed substantially and, unlike any other period in Canadian history, the single largest category of immigrants were coming from Asian countries. A concern developed among some sectors of the public as to how quickly these new immigrants could be integrated into society, if at all (*Toronto Star*, 1978). As was pointed out in Chapter 2, in the early seventies, a national survey on immigration was commissioned by the government of Canada and published in 1974 as the Green Paper on Immigration. It presented a number of policy options for the government regarding immigration. This prompted considerable public discussion of the subject. The federal government directed the Multiculturalism Directorate to deal with this issue. They did their own study of attitudes towards immigrants as part of a larger study of Canadian attitudes towards multiculturalism (Canada, 1974 and Berry et al., 1977). The study concluded that, although there was a general tolerance among Canadians towards continued immigration, there were indications of concern over it. Unemployment was seen as being related to immigration and any future decline in economic conditions could change the attitude of tolerance. The study, above all, identified a sector of society for whom race was an important concern. It stated that an increased number of non-white immigrants may evoke a racist movement among the whites. As a result, the government concluded that the same general principle of multiculturalism, of giving recognition to ethnic identities, was to be applied to the new groups of immigrants (Berry et al., 1977: 65-88, 248). Multiculturalism thus aimed its efforts at programs to help immigrants adjust to their new society.

It quickly became clear that many problems of immigrant adjustment stemmed from prejudices in Canada against non-white races. The issue came to be defined as the problem of "visible minorities," and in the 1980s the administering body of the multiculturalism policy directed its goals towards this group. By this time, the ethnic groups of non-white categories had become better organized and began to exert more direct pressure on and voice greater critique of the government. This critique included a certain hostility towards the established ethnic groups, the original beneficiaries of multicultural grants. The critique argued that because of racism it was the people of non-white race rather than the established minorities who had the real problems in Canadian society, such as poverty and unemployment, and that money spent on the receding cultures of the established white ethnic groups was a waste. Some of the critique was directed at the idea of multiculturalism itself, arguing that underscoring cultural differences produces greater inequality. As a result, multiculturalism began to re-direct its goals towards the reduction of racism, the equality of opportunities and the equality of treatment (Canada, 1984, 1987: 22-24; Reitz, 1988).

In 1988, the Multiculturalism Act was passed by the parliament. It restated and reinforced the 1971 policy objectives and, in addition, it brought up the issue of equality. It mandated all federal government departments to ensure equal opportunities for employment and advancement for all ethnic and racial groups and required all federal bodies to actively promote the objectives of the multiculturalism policy within their jurisdictions. The Minister for Multiculturalism was assigned the task of coordinating the efforts of the other ministries towards this end. Thus, the federal government had moved somewhat towards the Australian model by broadening the scope of its multiculturalism policy, but without decentralizing its administration.

In the late 1980s and into the 1990s a new critique of the multiculturalism policy emerged, now coming from the majority ethnic groups of society. It presented a new challenge to the goals of the policy. The critique is reviewed below. In addition to this critique, the mid-1990s was a period in which governments were downsizing their budgets.

In the early 1980s, the total annual budget for the administration of the policy was around 30 million dollars. By 1996, it had been reduced to around 17 million. The administrators of the policy were pressed to undertake a re-evaluation of the policy's goals (Canadian Heritage, 1996). Suggestions were made to curtail all the grants to ethnic community organizations. Such grants had been the backbone of the policy in the past and their elimination would reduce the policy to insignificance. Multiculturalism Canada did not follow all such suggestions. However, in the spring of 1997 it issued a new statement of priorities. The statement and the program guidelines (Canadian Heritage, 1997) reaffirmed the government's commitment to the multiculturalism policy, but it focused on three main goals: identity, civic participation and social justice. The goal of identity supports the recognition given to the diverse cultures in Canada with the idea of developing a "sense of belonging and attachment to Canada." Civic participation, however, places a stronger emphasis than previous on the development of a common community, involving a variety of ethnic minority and majority groups in joint cooperative ventures. The goal of social justice emphasizes equity among all groups and the elimination of racism for that purpose. The program, however, for the first time excludes from support the "regular annual general meetings of an organization or association ... festivals, camps, religious activities, celebrations of foreign national days, ongoing production of regular newsletters, newspapers, magazines, journals, and radio and television broadcasts" and a few other activities (Canadian Heritage, 1997: 6).

• Reactions to the Policy

The reactions to and the interpretations of the multiculturalism policy right after it was announced varied substantially. The French in Quebec assumed a fairly negative attitude towards it. Many Quebec leaders saw it as an attempt by the federal government to deflect attention from more important Quebec issues. Some interpreted it as a threat to the future of bilingualism and even the survival of the Francophone community in Quebec (Rocher, 1976; Burnet, 1975; Lambert and Curtis, 1983). Similarly, many of the Canadian Aboriginal peoples were of the opinion that multiculturalism as a policy detracted attention from their unique issues which, having longer historical roots, should take precedence over the concerns of the other ethnic groups. Aboriginal leadership has maintained that gains are to be made by negotiating with the government for special Aboriginal legislation, such as the changes to the Indian Act and the various treaties, and by demanding new policies of direct benefit to them. Such attitudes towards multiculturalism revealed the competition and tensions among the various minority groups as they pursued their interests in relation to the majority group and the society at large.

It is unclear what multiculturalism meant to the dominant majority sector of society when the policy was established, to those of British background in general and to the establishment elites in particular. Sociological surveys indicated that Canadians, including those of British ancestry, favoured the idea of multiculturalism and perceived Canada as a multicultural society (O'Bryan et al., 1976; Berry et al., 1977). However, the establishment elite has maintained that the process of assimilation for all minority ethnic groups should be accelerated in the interest of economic gains, thus rendering the policy unnecessary. Some intellectuals have claimed that the policy is a means for politicians to gain votes at election time. Leftist intellectuals have claimed that the policy has been a method used by the establishment to contain, rather than integrate, minority ethnic groups by offering alternative channels that prevent them from moving into the mainstream positions in society. Still others have looked at it as a method for "cooling off" the "problem groups" in society and allowing the policy to be changed or abandoned once the minority groups' demands have

KEY ISSUES IN CANADIAN ETHNIC RELATIONS

The Nisga'a of B.C.: To Whom Does the Land Belong?

In October 1998, the government of British Columbia signed a treaty with the Nisga'a People that ceded to them 1,992 square kilometres of the territory of British Columbia in the lower Nass Valley northeast of the city of Prince Rupert and gave them virtually sovereign rights over it. The Nisga'a, however, remain under the Canadian Constitution, the general Canadian criminal law and the Canadian Charter of Rights and Freedoms. The Nisga'a themselves have overwhelmingly ratified the treaty, but it still had to be ratified by the B. C. legislature and the federal parliament.

The Nisga'a treaty ended about one hundred years of struggle to bring the issue of their land claims to the point of negotiation and a 20-year long negotiation between the Nisga'a and the provincial government. During this period, the courts had ruled that the Native people's rights to ownership of their land had been extinguished. This had been appealed until finally the courts recognized that such rights still exist. The treaty thus became an important precedent for other Native peoples.

There are those, however, who argue that it is not enough to have the treaty approved only by the B.C. Legislature, that all the people in the province should approve the treaty by means of a referendum. Others argue that such treaty alters the Canadian Constitution and this requires amendment to the constitution which in turn necessitate the approval of all the provinces. Yet, the defenders of the treaty have insisted that once the courts recognized the Native peoples' right to their land, no referenda are necessary and the provincial government can make such treaties by itself.

This raises the question as to whether the right to dispose of large areas of land to a jurisdiction not under the province's rule belongs to all the people of the province. It could be said, for example, that since the Native people's right to land was never extinguished, the non-Native people have no right to make any decisions as to this land.

This raises broader questions. What gives a people or a nation the right to the land it occupies? Is the right given simply by the fact of settlement on land previously not settled by anybody? Or, if the land was settled, does the conquest of a people that took place long ago confer on the victor the right to the land of the conquered? These are big questions, as many current ethnic and nationalistic rivalries around the world boil down to this very question.

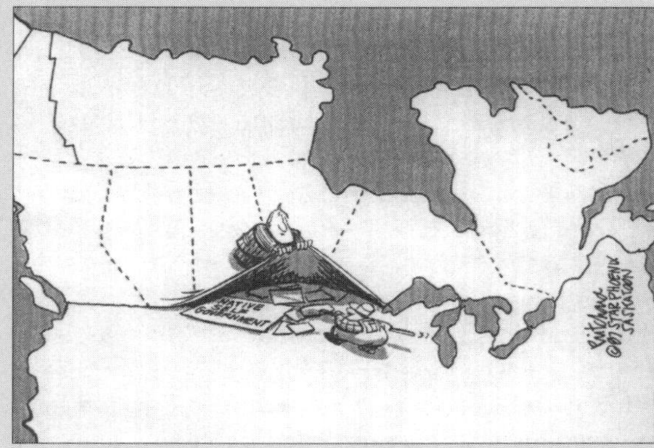

Courtesy of Denis Pritchard

Has "Native self-government" been swept under the carpet for too long?

Those who argue for the right of settlement or the right of conquest often consider themselves to be the "charter groups." Implicitly, this means that such groups have special rights that other "non-charter" groups do not have. Some political figures argue that, by the same token, if immigrant groups settle uninhabited lands after immigration to Canada (as for example did the Ukrainians who at the end of the nineteenth and in the beginning of the twentieth century settled the homestead lands in the Canadian prairies), they too can be called "charter groups." Others, however, argue that any resort to the concept of charter groups has prejudicial or even racist overtones, since it assumes that some ethnic groups have more rights than do other ethnic groups.

In our complex international society, where ethnic conflict seems to sometimes have dreadful consequences, just to raise the "who owns the land" question is enough to underline the difficulties in resolving ethnic rivalries.

Can you have small sovereign states coexisting within a larger sovereign state? Is this "new" idea of a nation-state, a nation that contains a number of areas where sovereign powers are held by the groups who live in these areas, compatible with the traditional concept of nation-statehood? It is possible that in many parts of the world, perhaps even in Canada itself, a lasting co-existence between ethnic groups may depend on whether this question has an answer.

diminished (Peter, 1981; Stasiulis, 1980; Porter, 1972; Brotz, 1980: 41; Moodley, 1983; Zolf, 1980; 1982).

Towards the end of the 1980s the multicultural policy came under new pressures. This time the pressures came from a large sector of the mainstream society, the majority group (Abu-Laban and Stasiulis, 1991). This sector challenged the *raison-d'etre* of the policy itself. In 1991, the government of Canada issued a report of the Citizens' Forum on Canada's Future, known as the Spicer Commission Report (Canada, 1991a). The report was allegedly based on interviews and received briefs from over 400,000 individuals and groups in Canada. On the basis of these, the Commission stated that Canada's use of two languages is widely seen as a fundamental and distinctive Canadian characteristic. Yet, it warned of the danger that the rising public dissatisfaction with the official languages policy would lead to its rejection and recommended an independent review of the policy with the purpose of making clear to Canadians its costs and benefits. It further asserted that all children should have the opportunity to learn both official languages in school.

In a similar way, the report asserted that Canadians accept and value Canada's cultural diversity and that the Commission enthusiastically agreed with the wish of ethno-cultural groups that their backgrounds be respected. It stated that "citizens spoke to us often of their desire to see a definition of being Canadian which can encompass many different origins of our citizens"(Canada, 1991a: 128). Yet, it went on to recommend that those who wish to preserve and promote their languages and cultures should pay for it themselves and that governments have no business entrenching and funding "remembrance of ethnocultural origins."

The report recommended that federal government funding for multiculturalism activities be eliminated, save for the activities that help immigrant orientation and reduction of racial discrimination and promotion of equality. The key goal for multiculturalism should be to "welcome all Canadians to an evolving mainstream–and thus encourage real respect for diversity" (Canada, 1991a: 129). The nature of this mainstream was implied in the report's discussion of the importance of, and concern over, Canadian national institutions and symbols. The report pointed to the dismay that allegedly many respondents had shown over the weakening of such national institutions as VIA Rail, the Canadian Broadcasting Corporation and the Royal Canadian Mounted Police and because of the permission given to the Sikh policemen to wear their traditional ethnic turbans and the like. It recommended that Canadian national symbols of historical value be given more evident importance so that any impression that Canadians are losing their sense of country be dispelled, and that ignoring this issue will further destabilize and weaken the feelings of Canadian unity, "especially among the English-speaking Canadians."

The unequivocal implication was that the Canadian national symbols are the traditional Anglo symbols taken from the British colonial history, and they include little room for any other ethnic symbols, save, at best, for a few French ones. The other ethnic symbols threatened the stability and unity of the country. As in the case of bilingualism, the report suggested that ethnic heritage is something for the schools to teach rather than for the government to policy-make. It recommended that provincial education departments maintain some heritage courses, but only for elementary school immigrant children and for no more than a year, just to assist the newcomers in their transition to new culture and society.

The Spicer Report can be said to be characteristic of the negative mainstream reaction to the policy of multiculturalism 20 years after its introduction. Other conservative mainstream bodies have expressed similar positions regarding the policy, though without the subtlety of the Spicer Commission. The Reform Party of Canada, formed in 1987, had its roots in the Western Canadian, primarily Anglo, populace. Almost from its beginnings, it aimed its main criticism at the policies of bilingualism, immigration and multiculturalism. In 1989 it called for the elimination of the multicultural policy, for the preservation of cultural backgrounds as a matter of purely personal choice and for preservation and promotion of the "national culture" into which immigrants were to be encouraged to integrate. As an example of one aspect of the national culture, it called for preservation of the traditional RCMP dress, that is, it rejected the idea of accommodating the Sikh officers by introducing turbans alongside the traditional RCMP head gear (Reform Party of Canada, 1990: 23-24; Manning, 1992).

These resolutions by the Reform Party were echoed by the Progressive Conservative Party (PC) of Canada at its convention in 1991. The PC Party represents a much wider social base than the Reform Party. It includes in its ranks a significant proportion of the higher socio-economic strata. Interestingly, some of the most negative resolutions regarding immigration and cultural diversity were introduced by one of the most affluent Toronto constituencies. These included such things as the forced return of refugees when the situation in their homeland changes, restrictions on where immigrants can live and the imposition of stetsons as the only headgear for the RCMP. While these resolutions were not passed by the convention, it did pass a set of resolutions by which the policy of multiculturalism was called to be abandoned, the Department of Multiculturalism abolished and instead a national identity be fostered by which all people would be "loyal to the Canadian ideal" (Progressive Conservative Party, 1991: 54).

In the 1990s the mainstream media commented positively on several books published in criticism of the multicultural policy (Bibby, 1990). Particular attention was given to a book written by N. Bissoondath (1994), a member of the "visible minority," who is also a successful novelist. In the book, the author, in an amateurish manner, criticized the policy of multiculturalism as discouraging full loyalty to Canada by its emphasis on the ancestral homeland and heritage. He claimed that it transformed members of minorities into political tools, and, by highlighting the differences among them, it encourages exoticism and divides Canadians. What is interesting about this publication is not so much what it said, but the fact that the mainstream media, after years of ignoring the policy or offering only critical comments about it, gave it high attention and exposure. This was congruous with all the nine editorial-type articles on multiculturalism published from the end of the 1970s to mid-1996 in the only Canadian national newspaper, *The Globe and Mail*, which were all critical of the policy (Ewins, 1996). The evidence clearly shows that the "mainstream establishment" endorsed the negative view of multiculturalism. Although written by a minority member, the book became an ideological instrument of the majority elite.

• Sociological Implications

The responses or reactions to the policy of multiculturalism and the shifts in the priorities of the agency mandated to implement the policy indicate that there are a number of significant sociological processes taking place, as it were, underneath the implementation of the policy. For one thing, there is competition among the different ethnic minority groups for appropriation of the policy, i.e., attempts to have the policy serve the needs and interests of groups other than those who originally pressed for its enactment. Thus the competition is between the old and the new ethnic groups, between groups of non-white racial categories and those of white category, between new emerging middle-man minority groups and other minority groups. Pressures to modify the policy's priorities is in good measure due to this competition.

Secondly, the reactions of the majority groups, both in English Canada and in Quebec, seems to indicate that the objectives of the policy as they were in the past and the retention of diverse identities that it stimulates presents a symbolic threat to the majority's hegemony in Canada. That is, except for Quebec, this is not seen as a real economic or political threat, but rather a threat to the subjective identity of the majority and the symbolic expression of this identity in the Canadian culture. This can explain the pressures coming from the majority mainstream to either discontinue the policy or to change it so that it serves only the purpose of facilitating immigrant adjustment to mainstream society. This objective, while worthwhile in itself, presents a "definition of situation" of ethnic diversity within the larger society different from the one in the original policy. The two definitions of ethnic diversity can be seen as competing definitions. Each definition gives a different picture of the relationship between minority ethnic groups and the society at large. If the policy of multiculturalism is meant to include an emphasis on identity retention, and thus give recognition to the identity of ethnic groups, then the presence of ethnic group diversity is defined as inherent to the very structure of society itself, and the policy functions to legitimize this. If, however, the emphasis is placed *exclusively* on immigration and the elimination of barriers to societal adjustment, then ethnic group diversity is viewed as extraneous to the social structure. Rather, it is seen as a social problem that is to be solved by means of the multiculturalism policy and, theoretically, it will disappear once it is solved. Rather than legitimize the concept of the diversity of cultural identities in society, this position works to foster the idea of its temporariness and by extension, its undesirability.

The problem is that public recognition of diverse identities legitimizes some inclusion of elements of different cultures into the mainstream culture. The Sikh turbans in the RCMP uniform, ethnic languages in regular school programs and so on are examples of such inclusion. Canada already legitimizes English-French bilingualism in the major institutions of society, including on all products sold in Canada. A further extension of this poses questions about the extent to which Canadian culture is to remain being shaped by the majority group. This is the nature of the symbolic threat that the recognition of diverse ethnic identities presents to the majority group.

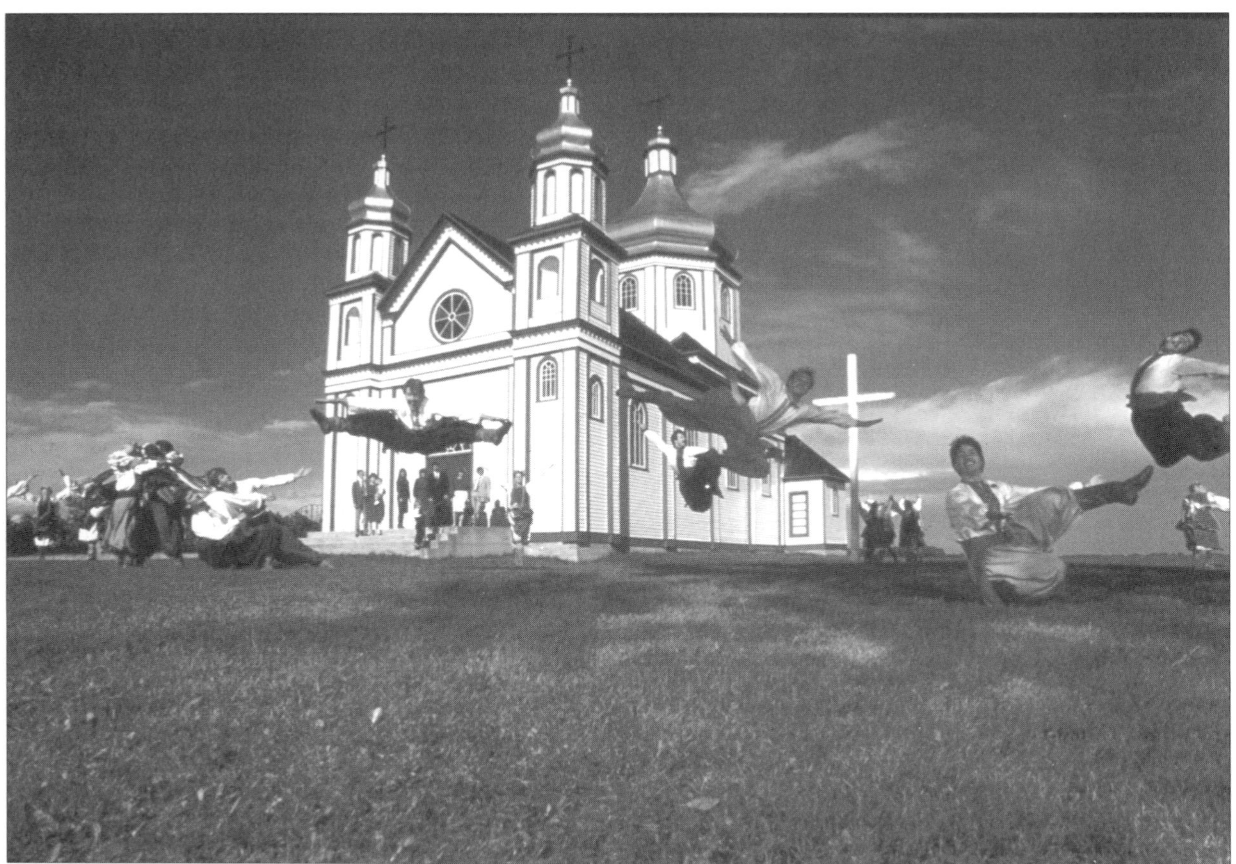

Photo: ISTC

Canada's multiculturalism policy places a value on diversity. Its opponents argue that it goes too far and that what is required is only the enforcement of anti-discrimination and anti-racism principles contained in human rights legislation. Above: Ukrainian Shumka Dancers of Edmonton.

One of the possible responses to the political pressure coming from the majority group could be the abrogation of the policy. This would mean going back to the state of affairs in Canada before 1971 when there was no policy of societal integration. One could argue that the entrenchment of the Charter of Human Rights and Freedoms in the Canadian constitution and the work of the human rights commissions is sufficient to guarantee societal integration. In other words, it is possible in regard to ethnic diversity and societal integration to undertake a policy of having no policy. This option, however, while it may be satisfactory to the majority group, will not be completely satisfactory to the minority groups who in their non-immigrant generations have retained some degree of their ethnic minority identity and would like it to be included as part of their Canadian identity. In most of the twentieth century, Canada had no policies of societal integration other than assimilation. But at the end of the twentieth century, the character of ethnic minority groups is completely different. A major point of difference is that, at the end of this century, most ethnic groups have levels of education much higher than those of the past. This makes them much more self-conscious, including a consciousness of their rights and their position in the structure of society. Hence, to the extent that they choose to retain any aspects of their ethnic identity, to this extent it is bound to have some influence on their participation in society vis-à-vis other identities. Hence, some public articulation of their identities into the mainstream may be called for.

Finally, some advocates feel that the only policy necessary in relation to ethnic minority groups is the policy of anti-discrimination or anti-racism, which is already contained in the human rights principles and in the commissions and courts who implement it. Additional agencies can be established to make its implementation more effective. The implementation of the human rights principles is of basic importance to societal integration, and without it, other policies cannot be effective. However, elimination of discrimination by punitive methods by itself does not place a positive value on diverse identities. It deals with individual rights rather than cultural rights. Hence, indirectly, reliance on punitive measures alone, while aiming at structural integration, may have exclusionary consequences, both social-psychological and structural. Policies of societal integration that place a positive value on diverse cultural identities thus play a significant role in supplementing the anti-racist measures in a society whose population is highly diverse in identity.

In 1991, a report by the Economic Council of Canada (Canada, 1991b:129) was commissioned to evaluate both immigration and multicultural policies. It contrasted the multicultural policy with an option for a policy of assimilation and concluded:

> A change to a more assimilative policy might weaken the positive effects on majority attitudes of the official endorsement of tolerance; it might have a negative impact on those same attitudes because of connotations regarding the unacceptability of the immigrant's culture and identity; and it might weaken positive contact effects on majority attitudes towards immigrants. In addition, a more assimilative policy might have further negative impact on minority-group attitudes by reducing the ability of successful group members to reassure the less successful that the system can work for them too and by weakening the immigrants' sense of cultural security. Thus, a change towards a more assimilative policy could well have a negative overall impact on majority-group attitudes and a very negative impact on minority-group attitudes.

SYMBOLIC CONTENT OF SOCIETAL INTEGRATION

All societies become internally integrated through economic and political interdependence, through the effective leadership of its elites, through the commitment and loyalty of its members and through the symbolic representations contained in its culture. As was pointed out in Chapter 1, culture is a system of encoded community experience. Through the symbols with which members of a community come to readily identify, culture expresses the values, aspirations and norms that derive from the group's historical experience over a number of generations and that give meaning to the lives of the group's members. People who share a culture that is a part of the institutions in which they work and live their daily lives identify with the culture's symbols, and the symbols of this culture stand for the people. Raymond Breton has pointed out the significance of symbols of identity in the lives of society's members. According to him (Breton, 1986:31):

> Individuals expect to recognize themselves in public institutions. They expect a certain degree of consistency between their private identities and the symbolic contents upheld by public authorities, which are embedded in societal institutions and celebrated in public events. Otherwise, individuals feel that they are strangers in society, that the society is not their society.

People recognize themselves in the language predominant in society, in the history, literature and art of their society that they learn in school and in the "great men" of the society who made this history and culture. They recognize themselves in the style of work of people filling positions in publicly visible institutions, such as the government and business. They recognize themselves in such visible, external symbols as the national flag, the national anthem, the country's periodical issues of postal stamps and coins that celebrate persons and objects known to them. Finally, they recognize themselves in the national holidays that publicly commemorate religious or historical events of the past that they consider to be their religion or their past.

The problem for ethnic minority groups is that public symbols usually represent the historical experience and culture of the ethnic majority. This reflects the historical fact that, in the process of formation of modern nation-states, even in highly multiethnic regions of the world, the drive to establish and run the state has been dominated by one ethnic group. Typically, one ethnic group becomes the most active unit in nationality development and nation-state building and becomes the dominant, "majority," group within the territory.

There have been a number of ways in which, historically, one ethnic group emerged as dominant and others as subordinate. This could result from a conquest of peoples by rulers of different ethnicity, a union of territories in which different peoples lived under a powerful ruler, the colonization of new territories by an existing nation-state or even the placement of one ethnic group above others by a colonial administration in running the affairs of a colony. It could take place also in the emergence to dominance of one group from among others in a state that had become de-colonized. Finally, it could also transpire in the migration of different peoples into an existing nation-state in which the hegemony of one ethnic group had been already established, as in the case of North America and an increasing number of economically well-to-do nation-states.

Multicultural Citizenship

By Will Kymlicka

The late twentieth century has been described as 'the age of migration.' Massive numbers of people are moving across borders, making virtually every country more polyethnic in composition. This has also been described as 'the age of nationalism,' as more and more national groups throughout the world mobilize and assert their identity. As a result, the settled rules of political life in many countries are being challenged by a new 'politics of cultural difference.' Indeed, with the end of the Cold War, the demands of ethnic and national groups have taken over centre stage in political life, both domestically and internationally.

Many people see this new 'politics of difference' as a threat to liberal democracy. I have presented a more optimistic view in this book. I have tried to show that many (but not all) of the demands of ethnic and national groups are consistent with liberal principles of individual freedom and social justice. I would not say that these issues can be 'resolved' in any final sense. The issues are too complicated for that. But they can be 'managed,' peacefully and fairly, assuming there is some level of goodwill.

Of course, in many parts of the world, groups are motivated by hatred and intolerance, not justice, and have no interest in treating others with goodwill. Under these circumstances, the potential for ethnic and national groups to abuse their rights and powers is very high. Yugoslavia and Rwanda are only the most recent reminders of the injustices which have been committed in the name of ethnic and national differences, from racial segregation and religious pogroms to ethnic cleansing and genocide.

Given these potential abuses, many people feel a strong temptation to push the issue of minority rights off to the side. Why, they ask, can we not simply 'treat people as individuals,' without regard for their ethnic or national identity? Why can we not focus on the things we share as humans, rather than what distinguishes us? I suspect that most of us have had that reaction at some point when dealing with the new and complicated 'politics of difference.'

However, that response is misguided. The problem is not that it is too 'individualistic.' In many parts of the world, a healthy dose of individualism would provide a welcome respite from group-based conflict. The problem, rather, is that the response is simply incoherent. As I have tried to show throughout this book, political life has an inescapably national dimension, whether it is in the drawing of boundaries and distributing of powers, or in decisions about the language of schooling, courts, and bureaucracies, or in the choice of public holidays. Moreover, these inescapable aspects of political life give a profound advantage to the members of majority nations.

We need to be aware of this, and the way it can alienate and disadvantage others, and take steps to prevent any resulting injustices. These steps might include polyethnic and representation rights to accommodate ethnic and other disadvantaged groups within each national group, and self-government rights to enable autonomy for national minorities alongside the majority nation. Without such measures, talk of 'treating people as individuals' is itself just a cover for ethnic and national injustice.

It is equally important to stress the limits on such rights. In particular, I have argued that they must respect two constraints: minority rights should not allow one group to dominate other groups; and they should not enable a group to oppress its own members. In other words, liberals should seek to ensure that there is equality *between* groups, and freedom and equality *within* groups. Within these limits, minority rights can play a valuable role within a broader theory of liberal justice. Indeed, they must play a role if liberalism is not to be condemned to irrelevance in many parts of the world.

In the traditional birthplace(s) of liberal theory—Britain, France, and the United States—minority rights have been ignored, or treated as mere curiosities or anomalies. This is particularly true of the claims of indigenous peoples. But it has become increasingly clear that minority rights are central to the future of the liberal tradition throughout the world. In many countries of the world—including the emerging democracies in Eastern Europe, Africa, and Asia—the status of national minorities and indigenous peoples is perhaps the most pressing issue.

People in these countries are looking to the works of Western liberals for guidance regarding the principles of liberal constitutionalism in a multination state. But the liberal tradition offers only confused and contradictory advice on this question. Liberal thinking on minority rights has too often been guilty of ethnocentric assumptions, or of over-generalizing particular cases, or of conflating contingent political strategy with enduring moral principle. This is reflected in the wide range of policies liberal states have historically adopted regarding ethnic and national groups, ranging from coercive assimilation to coercive segregation, from conquest and colonization to federalism and self-government.

The result has often been grave injustices against the ethnic and national minorities in many Western democracies. But the failure to develop a consistent and principled approach to minority rights may have even greater costs in the newly emerging democracies. At present, the fate of ethnic and national groups around the world is in the hand of xenophobic nationalists, religious extremists, and military dictators. If liberalism is to have any chance of taking hold in these countries, it must explicitly address the needs and aspirations of ethnic and national minorities.

Source: Will Kymlicka, *Multicultural Citizenship.* Oxford: Oxford University Press, 1995. Reprinted with permission of the publisher.

Whichever the historical route, the result has been a structure of ethnic stratification in which one ethnic group (sometimes two) would be perceived as being superior to others not only politically but also culturally and psychologically. As explained in Chapter 1, the significant fact is that the group on the top, i.e., the majority group, imparts its own cultural characteristics to all major national institutions. It is the elite of this group that forges and becomes the "mainstream" of society and sets the cultural standards for others.

In the past, the idea that a strong nation-state has to have one distinct culture was widely accepted. It was argued that the distinct cultural characteristics equally shared by all members of society, in contrast to all who are not members, act as the links that enable the members to realize that they have interests in common, causing them to draw together with one another when those interests are threatened (Royal Institute of International Affairs, 1963: 253). It was assumed that the presence of other cultural characteristics in society was essentially divisive, because it undermined loyalty to the state and hence made the state ineffective in maintaining a strong position in the world or in pursuing effective social policy at home (ibid., 255-263).

From the perspective of the history of the twentieth century, particularly since World War II, this analysis of ethnic diversity is incorrect. In both world wars the great diversity of ethnic groups in the North American states not only did not undermine the loyalty of the different ethnic groups to the state, but can be said to have been a source of these countries' strength. Even in the European context, such multiethnic states as the United Kingdom, Switzerland and Belgium did not fall apart on account of ethnic diversity.

The symbolic basis for the integration of ethnically diverse societies lies in the inclusion in the public symbolic system of elements that have meaning to the identity of both the majority group and the different minority groups. In this way, on the one hand, the culture of public institutions conveys the idea and feeling that these institutions belong to all groups in society and, on the other hand, members of various ethnic groups, to the extent they retain aspects of their identity, find themselves reflected and recognized in these public institutions. To a greater or lesser extent and in a more or less direct or indirect way, this has been the case in the multiethnic states mentioned above. With increased immigration and retention of ethnic identity across generations, however, innovations in the public symbolic system will be necessary to accompany the process of structural and cultural incorporation.

TOWARDS KEY PRINCIPLES OF INTERETHNIC COOPERATION AND CONFLICT RESOLUTION

• Negotiation

Like social incorporation, societal integration is a two-way process. That is, while policies enacted by the state to achieve integration are of basic importance, in a better educated, self-conscious society, these policies cannot be effective if they derive only from the decisions made by the state officials without the involvement of the groups who would be affected by these policies. The Canadian Indian Act, for example, has been a long-standing source of dissatisfaction among the Aboriginal peoples until, in 1985, they had a chance to influence the federal government to change parts of it. Likewise, the report of the Royal Commission on Aboriginal Peoples of 1996 was prepared with the participation of the members of the Aboriginal communities. Policy decisions on maintaining Quebec within the Canadian federation likewise have continuously been made with the participation of Quebec representatives. In the case of the "Other" ethnic groups, the multicultural policy as it was envisaged in the report of the Royal Commission on Bilingualism and Biculturalism (Canada, 1969) was a result of the proposals of those members of the commission who represented these groups.

What this means is that effective societal integration is a result of intergroup consultation and conflict resolution. In this process, *negotiation* is the main method of intergroup conflict resolution. Negotiation can be understood in a narrower and in a broader sense. In the narrower sense of the word, negotiation involves sets of techniques. Morton Deutsch (1994) has tried to identify a number of such techniques, or in his language, skills, used in constructive solutions to conflicts. He refers to such skills as "active listening," "taking the perspective of the other," distinguishing between "needs" and "positions," "controlling anger," using "I" rather than "you," "reframing issues to find common ground," being alert to misunderstanding deriving from cultural differences and the like. These skills are particularly important when cultural differences are involved.

Keeping in mind the importance of this narrower sense of the word, the emphasis I want to place here is on negotiation in the broader sense of the word. In the broader sense, negotiation refers, not just to settlement of any specific issue, but to the process through which a settlement of a series of specific disputes is achieved over a period of time. There is a basic difference between conflict settlement and conflict resolution. The former is a rational or legal compromise of specific issues at a specific time. The latter involves a transformation of the relationship between the conflicting parties that removes the problems that have caused the conflict (Burton, 1987, 1990).

This type of negotiation involves a modification of attitudes on the part of both the majority group and the minority groups and may involve relinquishing some practices or customs by both. However, as a result of mutual understanding, it may also involve legislation of new policies and laws, acceptance of new public symbols, development of new programs, acts of redress by the government and the like.

• Identity Recognition

Conflict resolutions of this kind, however, can be achieved only if there is a commitment on the part of both the minority and the majority groups to some broader humanistic principles. The most general principle behind a successful negotiation process in interethnic conflicts is that of identity recognition, particularly public recognition given by the government to a minority group. Recognition of the identities of others implies that one can conduct a discourse with them on equal footing. It implies respect for them, not on account of any of their acquired attributes, such as wealth, position and expertise, but simply on account of their being human. It assumes that two human beings can settle any of their problems through a human, rational discourse. The idea of according recognition to other identities is contrary to any racist-type ideology that holds that some people are superior, others inferior. It is also at the basis of the democratic ideology. Refusal to accord recognition can have damaging effects on all concerned. As Charles Taylor (1992: 36) put it:

> Equal recognition is not just the appropriate mode for a healthy democratic society. Its refusal can inflict damage on those who are denied it.... The projection of an inferior or demeaning image on another can actually distort and oppress, to the extent that the image is internalized. Not only contemporary feminism but also race relations and discussions of multiculturalism are undergirded by the premise that withholding of recognition can be a form of oppression.

To be a good citizen in a democratic society one must have a confidence in one's own identity, and to have that confidence, recognition of one's identity by others is necessary. Individual identities, however, derive from group identities. To have a strong individual identity one must feel that the community of which one is *de facto* a member or that the group that is a source of one's identity enjoys acceptance and is not seen as inferior by others, especially by the societal mainstream. Hence, if we are to help solve interethnic conflicts and develop an integrated society in the deeper sense of the word, acceptance of the principle of recognition is a *sine qua non.* In any negotiation, an attitude based on this principle is a prerequisite.

Acceptance of this principle and attitude, however, requires a further knowledge and appreciation of other groups. It requires two types of knowledge as *prerequisite* for a positive solution of ethnic conflicts. First, it requires a specific knowledge of the specific ethnic group or groups in question: knowledge of their history, culture and customs, religion, issues that concern the group and the methods the group uses in approaching these issues. Second, it requires a deeper understanding of the nature of ethnicity and the processes of ethnic development and change. It is this deeper knowledge that will make it possible to understand the issues behind issues, the often inexplicit motives or causes that lie behind the explicit, specific, often changing, day-to-day issues. It is this knowledge of the nature of ethnicity and the processes related to it that this book has tried to provide.

REFERENCES

Abella, Irving and Harold Troper. 1982. *None Is Too Many.* Toronto: Lester and Orpen Dennys.

Aboud, Frances E. 1981. "Ethnic Self-Identity." In *A Canadian Social Psychology of Ethnic Relations.* R. C. Gardner and R. Kalin, eds. Toronto: Methuen Publications, 37-56.

Abu-Laban, Baha. 1980. *An Olive Branch on the Family Tree: The Arabs in Canada.* Toronto: McClelland and Stewart Ltd.

Abu-Laban, Yasmeen and Daiva Stasiulis. 1991. "Ethnic Pluralism Under Siege: Popular and Partisan Opposition to Multiculturalism." Paper presented at the Bi-Annual Meetings of the Canadian Ethnic Studies Association, Winnipeg, October 23-26.

Abu Odeh, Lama. 1993. "Post-Colonial Feminism and the Veil: Thinking the Difference." *Feminist Review,* 43 : 26-37.

Adachi, Ken. 1976. *The Enemy That Never Was: A History of the Japanese Americans.* Toronto: McClelland and Stewart Ltd.

Adolf, Jacek Z. 1977. *Adaptation of East European Refugees and Political Émigrés in Toronto with Special Reference to Immigrants from Poland and Czechoslovakia.* Ph.D. Thesis. Toronto: York University.

AFL (American Federation of Labour). 1949. *Slave Labor in Russia.* Washington, D.C.

Agnew, Vijay. 1986. "Educated Indian Women in Ontario." In *Women and Ethnicity.* J. Burnet, ed. *Polyphony,* 8: 70-72.

Agnew, Vijay. 1990. "Women's Work with Women: The South Asian Context." In *South Asians in Ontario.* M. Israel and N.K. Wagley, eds. *Polyphony,* 12: 64-71.

Agocs, Carol, Catherine Burr and Felicity Somerset. 1992. *Employment Equity: Cooperative Strategies for Organizational Change.* Scarborough, ON: Prentice Hall.

Allport, Gordon. 1954. *The Nature of Prejudice.* Reading, Mass.: Addison-Wesley Publishing Co.

Anderson, Benedict. 1991. *Imagined Communities: Reflections on the Origin and Spread of Nationalism.* Revised Edition. London: Verso Publishers.

Anderson, Elijah. 1990. *Streetwise.* Chicago: University of Chicago Press.

Anderson, Grace M. 1974. *Networks of Contact: The Portuguese and Toronto.* Waterloo, ON: Wilfrid Laurier University Publications.

Anderson, Kay. 1991. *Vancouver's Chinatown: Racial Discourse in Canada, 1875-1980.* Montreal: McGill-Queen's University Press.

Andracki, Stanislaw. 1978. *Immigration of Orientals Into Canada with Special Reference to Chinese.* New York: Arno Press.

Aronson, Elliot. 1988. *The Social Animal.* Fifth Edition. New York: W. H. Freeman and Company.

Ashby, Adele. 1985. *An Inquiry into the Process of Developing a Sense of Canadian Cultural Identity and Canadian Cultural Consciousness.* Ph.D. Thesis. Toronto: University of Toronto.

Atwood, Margaret. 1972. *Survival: A Thematic Guide to Canadian Literature.* Toronto: House of Anansi Press.

Atwood, Margaret. 1993. "Survival." In *A Passion for Identity: An Introduction to Canadian Studies.* Second Edition. D. Taras, B. Rasporich and E. Mandel, eds. Scarborough, ON: Nelson Canada, 258-267.

Avery, Donald H. 1977. "The Immigrant Industrial Worker in Canada 1896-1930: The Verical Mosaic as an Historical Reality." In *Identities: The Impact of Ethnicity on Canadian Society.* W. W. Isajiw, ed. Toronto: Peter Martin Associates Ltd., 15-33.

Avery, Donald H. 1995. *Reluctant Host: Canada's Response to Immigrant Workers, 1896-1994.* Toronto: McClelland and Stewart Ltd.

B&B Report. 1970. *Report of the Royal Commission on Bilingualism and Biculturalism.* Book IV. Ottawa: Queen's Printer.

Babad, Elisha. 1991. "Students as Judges of Teachers' Verbal and Nonverbal Behavior." *American Educational Research Journal,* 28: 211-34.

Badets, Jane. 1989. "Canada's Immigrant Population." *Canadian Social Trends.* Ottawa: Statistics Canada, 14: 2-6.

Badets, Jane. 1993. "Canada's Immigrants: Recent Trends." *Canadian Social Trends.* Ottawa: Statistics Canada, 29: 8-11.

Bagambiire, Davies B. N. 1996. *Canadian Immigration and Refugee Law.* Aurora, ON: Canada Law Book Inc.

Bakan, Abigail B. 1987. "International Market for Female Labour and Individual De-Skilling: West Indian Women Workers in Toronto." *North-South: Canadian Journal of Latin American and Caribbean Studies,* 12:24: 69-85.

Baker, John R. 1974. *Race.* New York: Oxford University Press.

Balakrishnan, T.R. and Zheng Wu. 1992. "Home Ownership Patterns and Ethnicity in Selected Canadian Cities." *Canadian Journal of Sociology,* 17:4: 389-403.

Balthazar, Louis. 1996. "Toward a New Citizenship: The Dynamics of Multi-Ethnicity in French-Speaking Québec." In *Ethnicity and Citizenship: The Canadian Case.* J. Laponce and W. Safran, eds. London: Frank Cass and Co. Ltd., 82-95.

Banton, Michael. 1983. *Racial and Ethnic Competition.* Cambridge, New York: Cambridge University Press.

Barber, Marilyn. 1991. *Immigrant Domestic Servants in Canada.* Ottawa: Canadian Historical Association.

Barer-Stein, Thelma. 1988. "Experiencing the Unfamiliar: Culture Adaptation and Culture Schock as Aspects of a Process of Learning." *Canadian Ethnic Studies,* 20: 71-91.

Barth, Fredrik. 1969. "Introduction" in *Ethnic Groups and Boundaries.* F. Barth, ed. London: George Allen and Unwin, 9-38.

Bauer, Julien. 1994. *Les Minorités au Québec.* Montréal: Boréal.

Beattie, Christopher. 1975. *Minority Men in a Majority Setting: Middle-Level Francophones in the Canadian Public Service.* Toronto: McClelland and Steward Ltd., Carleton Library No. 92.

Beck, E.M., Patrick Horan and Charles Tolbert. 1978. "Stratification in a Dual Economy: A Sectoral Model of Earnings Determination." *American Sociological Review*, 43: 704-720.

Bell, Daniel. 1975. "Ethnicity and Social Change" in *Ethnicity*. N. Glazer and D.P. Moynihan, eds. Cambridge, Mass.: Harvard University Press, 141-174.

Benedict, Ruth. 1983 (1942). *Race and Racism*. London: Routledge and Kegan Paul.

Bennett, John W., ed. 1975. *The New Ethnicity: Perspectives from Ethnology*. St. Paul, Minn.: West Publishing Company.

Berger, Peter. 1973. *The Homeless Mind: Modernization and Consciousness*. New York: Random House.

Berger, Peter L. and Thomas Luckmann. 1966. *The Social Construction of Reality*. New York: Doubleday.

Berger, Thomas R. 1982. *Fragile Freedoms: Human Rights and Dissent in Canada*. Toronto: Clarke, Irwin and Company Ltd.

Berkowitz, L. 1993. *Aggression: Its Causes, Consequences and Control*. New York: McGraw-Hill.

Berry, John W., Rudolf Kalin and Donald M. Taylor. 1977. *Multiculturalism and Ethnic Attitudes in Canada*. Ottawa: Minister of Supply and Services Canada.

Bessis, Sophie and Souhayr Belhassen. 1992. *Femmes du Maghreb: l'enjeu*. J. C. Lattès, ed., 217-235.

Bibby, Reginald W. 1990. *Mosaic Madness: The Poverty and Potential of Life in Canada*. Toronto: Stoddart Publishing Co. Ltd.

Biddiss, Michael D., ed. 1979. *Images of Race*. New York: Holmes and Meier Publishers.

Billingsley, Brenda and Leon Muszynski. 1985. *No Discrimination Here? Toronto Employers and the Multiracial Work Force*. Toronto: The Urban Alliance on Race Relations and the Social Planning Council of Metropolitan Toronto.

Bissoondath, Neil. 1994. *Selling Illusions: The Cult of Multiculturalism in Canada*. Toronto: Penguin Books.

Blais, André and Richard Nadeau. 1995. "Attentes économiques et linguistiques et appui à la souveraineté du Québec: une analyse prospective et comparative." *Canadian Journal of Political Science*, 28: 4:637-657.

Blakemore, Ken and Robert F. Drake. 1996. *Understanding Equal Opportunity Policies*. London: Prentice Hall Europe.

Blalock, Hubert M. 1967. *Toward a Theory of Minority-Group Relations*. New York: Wiley.

Blumer, Herbert. 1969. *Symbolic Interactionism: Perspective and Method*. Englewood Cliffs, N.J.: Prentice-Hall, Inc.

Bociurkiw, Bohdan. 1978. "The Federal Policy of Multiculturalism and the Ukrainian-Canadian Community." In *Ukrainian Canadians, Multiculturalism, and Separation: An Assessment*. M.R. Lupul, ed. Edmonton: University of Alberta, Canadian Institute of Ukrainian Studies, 98-128.

Bogardus, Emory S. 1928. *Immigration and Race Attitudes*. Boston: Heath.

Bolaria, S. and Peter Li. 1988. *Racial Oppression in Canada*. Second Edition. Toronto: Garamond Press.

Bonacich, Edna. 1972. "A Theory of Ethnic Antagonism: The Split Labor Market." *American Sociological Review*, 37: 547-559.

Bonacich, Edna. 1973. "A Theory of Middleman Minorities." *American Sociological Review*, 38: 583-594.

Bonavia, George. 1977. *Focus on Canadian Immigration*. Ottawa: Manpower and Immigration.

Bong, Nguyen Quy. 1980. "The Vietnamese in Canada: Some Settlement Problems." In *Visible Minorities and Multiculturalism: Asians in Canada*. Ujimoto, K.V. and G. Hirabayashi, eds. Toronto: Butterworths and Co. Ltd., 247-256.

Bourdieu, Pierre. 1977. *Outline of a Theory of Practice*. Cambridge: Cambridge University Press.

Bourhis, Richard Y. 1994. "Ethnic and Language Attitudes in Quebec." In *Ethnicity and Culture in Canada: The Research Landscape*. J.W. Berry and J.A. Laponce, eds. Toronto: University of Toronto Press, 322-360.

Bourhis, R.Y. and H. Giles. 1977. "The Language of Intergroup Distinctiveness." In *Language, Ethnicity and Intergroup Relations*, H. Giles, ed. London: Academic Press, 119-135.

Boyd, Monica. 1992. "Gender, Visible Minority, and Immigrant Earnings Inequality: Reassessing an Employment Equity Premise." In *Deconstructing a Nation: Immigration, Multiculturalism and Racism in 90's Canada*. V. Satzewich, ed. Halifax and Saskatoon: Fernwood Publishing and Department of Sociology, University of Saskatchewan, 279-321.

Boyd, Monica. 1994. "Canada's Refugee Flows: Gender Inequality." *Canadian Social Trends*. Ottawa: Statistics Canada, 32: 7-10.

Boyd, Monica, Chris Taylor and Paul Delaney. 1986. "Temporary Workers in Canada: A Multifaceted Problem." *International Migration Review*, 20: 929-950.

Braroe, Niels W. 1980. "Reciprocal Exploitation in an Indian-White Community." *In Ethnicity and Ethnic Relations in Canada: A Book of Readings*. J.E. Goldstein and R.M. Bienvenue, eds. Toronto: Butterworth and Co., 247-258.

Bradwin, Edmund W. 1972 (1928). *The Bunkhouse Man*. Toronto: University of Toronto Press.

Brake, Michael. 1985. *Comparative Youth Culture: The Sociology of Youth Cultures and Youth Subcultures in America, Britain and Canada*. London: Routledge and Kegan Paul.

Breton, Raymond. 1964. "Institutional Completeness of Ethnic Communities and the Personal Relations of Immigrants." *The American Journal of Sociology*, 70: 193-205.

Breton, Raymond. 1986. "Multiculturalism and Canadian Nation-Building." In *The Politics of Gender, Ethnicity and Language in Canada*. A. Cairns and C. Williams, eds. Toronto: University of Toronto Press, 27-66.

Breton, Raymond. 1990. "The Ethnic Group as a Political Resource in Relation to Problems of Incorporation: Perceptions and Attitudes." In R. Breton, W.W. Isajiw, W.E. Kalbach and J.G. Reitz, *Ethnic Identity and Equality: Varieties of Experience in a Canadian City*. Toronto: University of Toronto Press, 196-255.

Breton, Raymond. 1991. *The Governance of Ethnic Communities: Political Structures and Processes in Canada*. New York: Greenwood Press.

Breton, Raymond and Howard Roseborough. 1968. "Ethnic Differences in Status." In *Canadian Society: Sociological Perspectives*. Third Edition. Toronto: Macmillan of Canada, 683-701.

Breton, Raymond, W.W. Isajiw, W.E. Kalbach and J.G. Reitz. 1990. *Ethnic Identity and Equality: Varieties of Experience in a Canadian City*. Toronto: University of Toronto Press.

Bronfman, Edgar M. 1996. *The Making of a Jew*. New York: G.P. Putnam's Sons.

Brotz, Howard. 1980. "Multiculturalism in Canada: A Muddle." *Canadian Public Policy*. VI. Ottawa: Government of Canada, 41-46.

Brown, Rupert. 1995. *Prejudice: Its Social Psychology*. Oxford: Blackwell Publishers.

Buchignani, Norman and D.M. Indra with R. Srivastiva. 1985. *Continuous Journey: A Social History of South Asians in Canada*. Toronto: McClelland and Stewart.

Burnet, Jean. 1975. "Multiculturalism, Immigration, and Racism." *Canadian Ethnic Studies*, 7: 35-39.

Burnet, Jean, ed. 1986. *Women and Ethnicity*. Volume 8, *Polyphony*.

Burnet, Jean with Howard Palmer. 1988. *"Coming Canadians": An Introduction to a History of Canada's Peoples*. Toronto: McClelland and Stewart Ltd.

Burton, J. W. 1987. *Resolving Deep-Rooted Conflict: A Handbook*. Lanham, Md: University Press of America.

Burton, J.W. 1990. *Conflict: Resolution and Prevention*. New York: St. Martin's Press.

Calliste, Agnes. 1987. "Sleeping Car Porters in Canada: An Ethnically Submerged Split Labour Market." *Canadian Ethnic Studies*, 19: 1-20.

Calliste, Agnes. 1988. "Blacks on Canadian Railways." *Canadian Ethnic Studies*, 20:2: 36-52.

Canada. 1969. *Report of the Royal Commission on Bilingualism and Biculturalism*, Book IV: "The Cultural Contribution of the Other Ethnic Groups." Ottawa: Queen's Printer for Canada.

Canada, 1982. *The Charter of Rights and Freedoms: A Guide for Canadians*. Ottawa: Minister of Supply and Services.

Canada. 1984. *Report of the Special Committee on Visible Minorities in Canadian Society: Equality Now!* Ottawa: Supply and Services Canada.

Canada. 1987. *Multiculturalism: Building the Canadian Mosaic*. Ottawa: Report of the Standing Committee of the House of Commons on Multiculturalism.

Canada. 1991a. *Report to the People and Government of Canada*, June 27, from the Citizens' Forum on Canada's Future (Spicer Commission). Ottawa: Minister of Supply and Services.

Canada. 1991b. *Economic and Social Impacts of Immigration*. A research report prepared for the Economic Council of Canada. Ottawa: Canada Communication Group Publishing.

Canada Gazette, 1967. Part II, Vol. 101, No. 17 (September 13). SOR, 1967, 67-434.

Canada Year Book. 1943-1994. Official Statistical Annual of the Resources, History, Institutions and Social and Economic Conditions of Canada. Ottawa: Statistics Canada.

Canadian Heritage. 1996. *Strategic Evaluation of Multiculturalism Programs: Final Report*. Ottawa: Corporate Review Branch.

Canadian Heritage. 1997. *Multiculturalism: Respect, Equality, Diversity; Program Guidelines*. Ottawa: Multiculturalism Canada.

Caplow, Theodore. 1959. "Further Development of a Theory of Coalitions in the Triad." *American Journal of Sociology*, 64: 488-493.

Careless, J.M.S. 1963. *Canada: A History of Challenge*. Toronto: The Macmillan Company of Canada.

Chen, Anita Beltran. 1998. *From Sunbelt to Snowbelt: Filipinos in Canada*. Calgary: Canadian Ethnic Studies Association, University of Calgary, 165-184.

Christensen, Carole P. and Morton Weinfeld. 1993. "The Black Family in Canada: A Preliminary Exploration of Family Patterns and Inequality." *Canadian Ethnic Studies*, 25:3: 26-44.

Chui, Tina. 1996. "International Students in Canada." *Canadian Social Trends*. Ottawa: Statistics Canada, 41: 18-21.

CIC (Citizenship and Immigration Canada). 1992. *Immigration Statistics, 1992*. Ottawa: Publication IM-087-12-93.

CIC (Citizenship and Immigration Canada). 1996. *Profiles, Canadian Population: Selected Statistics*. Immigration Research Series. Ottawa: Government of Canada.

CIC (Citizenship and Immigration Canada). 1997a. *Citizenship and Information Canada Legislation: Immigration Manual*. Ottawa: Integrated Information Management Services.

CIC (Citizenship and Immigration Canada). 1997b. *Immigration Statistics 1994*. Ottawa: CIC Publication 157-03-97.

CIC (Citizenship and Immigration Canada). 1998. *Canada's Immigration Law*. Ottawa: CIC internet publication: <http://cicnet.ci.gc.ca/english/pub/immlaw_e.html>.

Cirtautas, K.C. 1963. *The Refugee*. New York: The Citadel Press.

Clark, S.D. 1962. *The Developing Canadian Community*. Toronto: University of Toronto Press.

Clark, S.D. 1976. *Canadian Society in Historical Perspective*. Toronto: McGraw-Hill Ryerson Ltd.

Clement, Wallace. 1975. *The Canadian Corporate Elite: An Analysis of Economic Power*. Toronto: McClelland and Stewart Ltd.

Clement, Wallace. 1985. "The Canadian Corporate Elite: Ethnicity and Inequality of Access." In *Ethnicity and Ethnic Relations in Canada*, Second Edition. R.M. Bienvenue and J.E. Goldstein, eds. Toronto: Butterworths and Co. Ltd., 143-151.

Cohen, Rina. 1991. "Women of Color in White Households: Coping Strategies of Live-in Domestic Workers." *Qualitative Sociology*, 14:2: 197-215.

Cohon, J. Donald Jr. 1981. "Psychological Adaptation to Dysfunction Among Refugees." *International Migration Review*, 15: 255-275.

Collins, Randall. 1975. *Conflict Sociology: Toward an Explanatory Science*. New York: Academic Press.

Collins, Richard. 1990. *Culture, Communication and National Identity: The Case of Canadian Television*. Toronto: University of Toronto Press.

Con, Harry, R.J. Con, G. Johnson, E. Wickberg, W.E. Willmott. 1982. *From China to Canada: A History of the Chinese Communities in Canada*. Toronto: McClelland and Stewart Ltd.

Cook, Ramsey. 1995. *Canada, Quebec, and the Uses of Nationalism*, Second Edition. Toronto: McClelland and Stewart Ltd.

Cook, Ramsay with J. Saywell and J. Ricker. 1963. *Canada: A Modern Study*. Toronto: Clarke, Irwin and Co. Ltd.

Coon, Carleton. 1962. *The Origin of Races*. New York: Alfred A. Knopf.

Coser, Lewis A. 1956. *The Functions of Social Conflict*. Glencoe: The Free Press.

Cox, Oliver C. 1948. *Caste, Class and Race: A Study in Social Dynamics*. New York: Doubleday and Co., Inc.

Cross, Elsie Y. and Margaret B. White, eds. 1996. *The Diversity Factor: Capturing the Competitive Advantage of a Changing Workforce*. Chicago: Irwin Professional Publishing.

Crowder, Michael. 1978. *Colonial West Africa: Collected Essays*. London: F. Cross.

Curtin, Philip D. 1969. *The Atlantic Slave Trade: A Census*. Madison, Wisc.: University of Wisconsin Press.

Dahrendorf, Ralf. 1959. *Class and Class Conflict in Industrial Society*. Stanford, Calif.: Stanford University Press.

Danziger, K. 1971. *The Socialization of Immigrant Children*. Toronto: York University, Institute for Behaviourial Research.

Danziger, K. 1975. "Differences in Acculturation and Patterns of Socialization Among Italian Immigrant Families." In *Socialization and Values in Canadian Society,* Vol. II. R.M. Pike and E. Zureik, eds. Toronto: McClelland and Stewart Ltd., Carleton Library No. 85: 129-157.

Darley, J.M. and P.H. Gross. 1983. "A Hypothesis-Confirming Bias in Labelling Effects." *Journal of Personality and Social Psychology,* 44: 20-33.

Darroch, Gordon A. 1979. "Another Look at Ethnicity, Stratification and Social Mobility in Canada." *Canadian Journal of Sociology,* 4: 1-25.

Das Gupta, Tania. 1986. "Looking Under the Mosaic: South Asian Immigrant Women." In *Women and Ethnicity.* J. Burnet, ed., *Polyphony,* 8: 67-69.

Dasko, Donna. 1974. "Attitudes Toward Ukrainians in Canada Between 1896 and 1914: A Content Analysis of Three Canadian Newspapers." Unpublished Paper. Toronto: Department of Sociology, University of Toronto.

Davis, Angela Y. 1989. *Women, Culture and Politics.* New York: Random House, 116-155.

Dawson, Carl Addington. 1936. *Group Settlement: Ethnic Communities in Western Canada.* Toronto: Macmillan Publishing company.

Dekmejian, R. Hrair. 1995. *Islam in Revolution: Fundamentalism in the Arab World,* Second Edition. Syracuse: Syracuse University Press.

Denevan, William M., ed. 1976. *The Native Population of the Americas in 1942.* Madison, Wisc.: The University of Wisconsin Press.

De Silva, K.E.A., D.L. Palmer and Jeffrey Reitz. 1994. "An Exchange of Views." *Policy Options,* 15:2: 3-9.

Deutsch, Morton. 1994. "Constructive Conflict Resolution: Principles, Training and Research." *Journal of Social Issues,* 50: 13-32.

Dion, Kenneth L., Brian M. Earn and Paul H.N. Yee. 1978. "The Experience of Being a Victim of Prejudice: An Experimental Approach." *International Journal of Psychology,* 13:3: 197-214.

Dirks, Gerald E. 1995. *Controversy and Complexity: Canadian Immigration Policy during the 1980s.* Montreal & Kingston: McGill-Queen's University Press.

Dirks, Gerald E. 1997. *Intensifying Global Migration Pressures: Causes and Responses.* Toronto: University of Toronto, R.F. Harney Professorship Publications, Lectures and Papers in Ethnicity, Number 25.

Donnelly, Jack. 1989. *Universal Human Rights in Theory and Practice.* Ithaca: Cornell University Press.

Driedger, Leo. 1975. "In Search of Cultural Identity Factors: A Comparison of Ethnic Minority Students in Manitoba," *Canadian Review of Sociology and Anthropology,* 12: 150-62.

Economic Council of Canada. 1991. *Economic and Social Impacts of Immigration.* Ottawa: Minister of Supply and Services.

Edwards, John. 1989. *Language and Disadvantage.* London: Cole and Whurr.

Edwards, John. 1995. *Multilingualism.* London: Penguin Books Ltd.

Ehrlich, Howard J. 1973. *The Social Psychology of Prejudice.* New York: Wiley.

El Guindi, Fadwa. 1981. "Veiling Infitah with Muslim Ethic." *Social Problems,* 28: 465-485.

Elliott, Bruce S. 1988. *Irish Migrants in the Canadas: A New Approach.* Kingston: McGill Queen's University Press.

English-Currie, Vicki. 1993. "The Need for Re-Evaluation in Native Education." In *A Passion for Identity: An Introduction to Canadian Studies.* Second Edition. D. Taras, B. Rasporich and E. Mandel, eds. Scarborough, ON: Nelson Canada, 111-119.

Erikson, Erik H. 1968. *Identity: Youth and Crisis.* New York: W.W. Norton and Company Inc.

Erikson, Erik H. 1974. *Dimensions of a New Identity.* New York: W.W. Norton and Company Inc.

Ewins, Johanna. 1996. *Multiculturalism and the Media: A Content Analysis of Canadian Newspaper Coverage 1977-1995.* Research report submitted to W.W. Isajiw. Toronto: University of Toronto, Department of Sociology.

Ferguson, Ted. 1975. *A White Man's Country: An Exercise in Canadian Prejudice.* Toronto: Doubleday Canada Ltd.

Firestone, O.J. 1969. *Industry and Education: A Century of Canadian Development.* Ottawa: University of Ottawa Press.

Fleras, Augie. 1994. "Walking Away From the Camera." In *Ethnicity and Culture in Canada: The Research Landscape.* J.W. Berry and J. Laponce, eds. Toronto: University of Toronto Press, 340-384.

Fleras, Augie. 1995. "Please Adjust Your Set: Media and Minorities in a Post-Multicultural Society." In *Communications in Canadian Society,* Fourth Edition. B. Singer, ed., 281-307.

Fleras, Augie and Jean L. Elliott. 1992. *Multiculturalism in Canada: The Challenge of Diversity.* Scarborough, ON: Nelson Canada.

Fleras, Augie and Jean L. Elliott. 1996. *Unequal Relations: An Introduction to Race, Ethnic and Aboriginal Dynamics in Canada.* Scarborough, ON: Prentice Hall Canada Inc.

Foster, Cecil. 1996. *A Place Called Heaven: The Meaning of Being Black in Canada.* Toronto: Harper Collins Publishers Ltd.

Foucault, Michel. 1967. *Madness and Civilization.* London: Tavistock.

Fraser, Angus. 1992. *The Gypsies.* Oxford, UK and Cambridge, USA: Blackwell Publishers.

Frideres, James S. 1973. "Discrimination in Western Canada." *Race,* 15:2: 213-222.

Frideres, James S. 1993. *Native Peoples in Canada: Contemporary Conflicts.* Scarborough, ON: Prentice Hall Canada Inc.

Frideres, James S. and William J. Reeves. 1989. "The Ability to Implement Human Rights Legislation in Canada." *Canadian Review of Sociology and Anthropology,* 26:2: 311-332.

Friedland, William H. and D. Nelkin. 1971. *Migrant: Agricultural Workers in America's Northeast.* New York: Holt and Reinhart.

Fuchs, Linda. 1991. "Factors Affecting Level of Happiness among Southeast Asian Refugee Women in Saskatoon." In *Immigrants and Refugees in Canada: A National Perspective on Ethnicity, Multiculturalism and Cross-Cultural Adjustment.* S.P. Sharma, A.M. Ervin and D. Meintel, eds. Saskatoon: University of Saskatchewan, Department of Anthropology and Archaeology, 147-158.

Furnivall, John S. 1939. *Netherlands India: A Study of Plural Economy.* Cambridge: Cambridge University Press.

Furnivall, John S. 1956 (1948). *Colonial Policy and Practice: A Comparative Study of Burma and Nethrlands India.* New York: New York University Press.

Gabbacia, D. 1994. *From the Other Side: Women, Gender and Immigrant Life in the U.S. 1820-1990.* Bloomington: Indiana University Press.

Gans, Herbert. 1979. "Symbolic Ethnicity: The Future of Ethnic Groups and Cultures in America." *Ethnic and Racial Studies*, 2: 1-20.

Garfinkel, Harold. 1967. *Studies in Ethnomethodology*. Englewood Cliffs, N.J.: Prentice-Hall, Inc.

Garn, Stanley. 1971. *Human Races*. Third Edition. Springfield, Ill.: Charles C. Thomas.

Geadah, Yolande. 1996. *Femmes voilées: intégrismes dé masqués*. Montreal: VLB éditeur.

Geertz, Clifford. 1963. "The Integrative Revolution: Primordial Sentiments and Civil Politics in the New States." In *Old Societies and New States*. C. Geertz, ed. New York: Free Press, 105-157.

Geertz, Clifford. 1973. *The Interpretation of Cultures: Selected Essays*. New York: Basic Books.

Geschwender, James A. and Neil Guppy. 1995. "Ethnicity, Educational Attainment, and Earned Income among Canadian-Born Men and Women." *Canadian Ethnic Studies*, 27:1: 67-83.

Ghosh, Ratna. 1984. "Education, Gender, and the Immigrant Experience." In *Multiculturalism in Canada: Social and Educational Perspectives,* R. J. Samuda, J.W. Berry and M. Laferriére, eds. Toronto: Allyn and Bacon, Inc., 327-333.

Gittins, Susan. 1995. *Behind Closed Doors: The Rise and Fall of Canada's Edper Bronfman and Reichmann Empires*. Scarborough, ON: Prentice Hall Canada Inc.

Gobin, Denise. 1998. *Differential Incorporation of Indo-Afro-Caribbean and Punjabi Sikh Youths in Toronto*. Ph.D. Thesis. Toronto: Department of Sociology, University of Toronto.

Goffman, Erving. 1959. *The Presentation of Self in Everyday Life*. Garden City, N.Y.: Doubleday Anchor.

Goldstein, Jay and Alexander Segall. 1985. "Ethnic Intermarriage and Ethnic Identity." *Canadian Ethnic Studies*, 17:3: 60-71.

Golembiewski, Robert T. and Arthur Blumberg. 1970. *Sensitivity Training and the Laboratory Approach: Readings about Concepts and Applications*. Itasca, Ill.: F. E. Peacock Publishers, Inc.

Goode, William J. and P.K. Hatt. 1952. *Methods in Social Research*. New York: McGraw-Hill Book Co., Inc.

Gordon, Milton M. 1964. *Assimilation in American Life: The Role of Race, Religion, and National Origins*. New York: Oxford University Press.

Green, Alan G. 1976. *Immigration and the Postwar Canadian Economy*. Toronto: Macmillan of Canada.

Greenhill, Pauline. 1994. *Ethnicity in the Mainstream: Three Studies of English Canadian Culture in Ontario*. Montreal and Kingston: McGill-Queen's University Press.

Greider, William. 1997. *One World, Ready or Not: The Manic Logic of Global Capitalism*. New York: Simon and Schuster.

Grygier, Tadeusz. 1975. "Integration of Four Ethnic Groups in Canadian Society: English, German, Hungarian, Italian." In *Sounds Canadian: Languages and Cultures in Multi-Ethnic Society*. P. Migus, ed. Toronto: Peter Martin Associates, 158-186.

Guindon, Hubert. 1988. *Quebec Society: Tradition, Modernity, and Nationhood*. Toronto: University of Toronto Press.

Gurr, Ted Robert. 1993. *Minorities at Risk: A Global View of Ethnopolitical Conflicts*. Washington, D.C.: United States Institute of Peace Press.

Handlin, Oscar. 1951. *The Uprooted*. Boston: Little, Brown and Company.

Hansen, David T. 1993. "The Moral Importance of the Teacher's Style." *Journal of Curriculum Studies*, 25: 397-421.

Hansen, Marcus Lee. 1970. *The Mingling of the Canadian and American Peoples*. New York: Russell and Russell.

Hansen, Marcus Lee. 1990 [1938]. "The Problem of Third Generation Immigrant." In *American Immigrants and Their Generations: Studies and Commentaries on Hansen Thesis after Fifty Years*. P. Kivisto and D. Blanck, eds. Urbana and Chicago: University of Illinois Press, 191-203.

Harney, Robert F. 1991a. "A Case Study of Padronism: Montreal's King of Italian Labour." In *If One Were to Write a History: Selected Writings by Robert F. Harney*. P. Anctil and B. Ramirez, eds. Toronto: Multicultural History Society of Ontario, 143-172.

Harney, Robert F. 1991b. "If One Were to Write a History of Postwar Toronto Italia." In *If One Were to Write a History: Selected Writings by Robert F. Harney*. P. Anctil and B. Ramirez, eds. Toronto: Multicultural History Society of Ontario, 63-89.

Hawkins, Freda. 1972. *Canada and Immigration: Public Policy and Public Concern*. Montreal: McGill-Queen's University Press.

Head, Wilson A. 1975. *The Black Presence in the Canadian Mosaic: A Study of Perception and the Practice of Discrimination against Blacks in Metropolitan Toronto*. Toronto: Ontario Human Rights Commission.

Hechter, Michael. 1978. "Group Formation and the Cultural Division of Labour." *American Journal of Sociology*, 84: 293-318.

Hein, Jeremy. 1995. *From Vietnam, Laos and Cambodia: A Refugee Experience in the United States*. New York: Twayne Publishers.

Helling, Rudolph A. 1965. *The Position of Negroes, Chinese and Italians in the Social Structure of Windsor, Ontario*. Toronto: Ontario Human Rights Commission.

Henry, Frances. 1994. *The Caribbean Diaspora in Toronto: Learning to Live with Racism*. Toronto: University of Toronto Press.

Henry, Frances and Effie Ginzberg. 1985. *Who Gets the Work?: A Test of Racial Discrimination in Employment*. Toronto: The Urban Alliance on Race Relations and The Social Planning Council of Metropolitan Toronto.

Henry, Frances, Carol Tator, Winston Mattis and Tim Rees. 1995. *The Colour of Democracy: Racism in Canadian Society*. Toronto: Harcourt Brace and Co., Canada.

Henwood, Karen and Ann Phoenix. 1996. "'Race' in Psychology: Teaching the Subject." *Ethnic and Racial Studies*, 19: 841-863.

Herberg, Edward N. 1990. "The Ethno-Racial Socioeconomic Hierarchy in Canada: Theory and Analysis of the New Vertical Mosaic." *International Journal of Comparative Sociology*, 31:3-4: 206-221.

Herman, Edward S. and Noam Comsky. 1988. *Manufacturing Consent: The Political Economy of the Mass Media*. New York: Pantheon Books.

Herrnstein, Richard J. and Charles Murray. 1994. *The Bell Curve: Intelligence and Class Structure in American Life*. New York: The Free Press.

Herzog, Hanna. 1984. "Ethnicity as a Product of Political Negotiation: the Case of Israel." *Ethnic and Racial Studies*, 7: 517-533.

Hijab, Nadia. 1988. *Womanpower: The Arab Debate on Women at Work*. New York: Cambridge University Press, 51-56.

Hill, Daniel G. 1977. *Human Rights in Canada: A Focus on Racism*. Toronto: Canadian Labour Congress.

Hinkle, S. and J. Schopler. 1986. "Bias in the Evaluation of In-Group and Out-Group Performance." In *Psychology of Inter-*

group Relations. Second Edition. S. Worchel and W.G. Austin, eds. Chicago: Nelson-Hall, 196-212.

Hohn, R.L. 1973. "Perceptual Training and Its Effects on Racial Preferences of Kindergarten Children." *Psychological Reports*, 32: 435-441.

Hooten E.A. 1946. *Up From the Ape.* New York: Macmillan.

Horowitz, E.L. and R.E. Horowitz. 1938. "Development of Social Attitudes in Children." *Sociometry*, 1: 301-338.

Huber, Richard M. 1971. *The American Idea of Success.* New York: McGraw-Hill Book Company.

Hughes, Everett C. and Helen M. Hughes. 1952. *Where People Meet: Racial and Ethnic Frontiers.* Glencoe Ill.: Free Press.

Iacovetta, Franca. 1992. *Such Hard Working People: Italian Immigrants in Postwar Toronto.* Montreal and Kingston: McGill-Queen's University Press.

ICFTU (International Confederation of Free Trade Unions). 1951. *Stalin's Slave Camps.* Brussels.

Ijaz, M. Ahmed. 1984. "Ethnic Attitude Change: A Multidimensional Approach." In *Multiculturalism in Canada: Social and Educational Perspectives.* R.J. Samuda, J.W. Berry and M. Laferriére, eds. Toronto: Allyn and Bacon Inc., 128-138.

Ijaz, M. Ahmed and I.H. Ijaz. 1981. "A Cultural Program for Changing Racial Attitudes." *History and Social Science Teacher*, 17: 17-20.

Innis, Harold A. 1930. *The Fur Trade in Canada: An Introduction to Canadian Economic History.* New Haven: Yale University Press.

Isaacs, Harold. 1975. "Basic Group Identity: the Idols of the Tribe." In *Ethnicity: Theory and Experience*, N. Glazer and D.P. Moynihan, eds. Cambridge, Mass.: Harvard University Press, 29-52.

Isaacs, Harold. 1989. *Idols of the Tribe: Group Identity and Political Change.* Cambridge, Mass.: Harvard University Press.

Isajiw, Wsevolod W. 1974. "Definitions of Ethnicity." *Ethnicity*, 1: 2:111-124.

Isajiw, Wsevolod W. 1975. "The Process of Maintenance of Ethnic Identity: The Canadian Context." In *Sounds Canadian: Languages and Cultures in Multi-Ethnic Society.* P. Migus, ed. Toronto: Peter Martin Associates, 129-138.

Isajiw, Wsevolod W. 1977. "Olga in Wonderland: Ethnicity in Technological Society. *Canadian Ethnic Studies*, 9: 77-85.

Isajiw, Wsevolod W. 1980. *Ethnic Identity Retention.* Unpublished Tables. Toronto: University of Toronto, Department of Sociology.

Isajiw, Wsevolod W. 1983. "Multiculturalism and the Integration of the Canadian Community." *Canadian Ethnic Studies*, 15: 107-117.

Isajiw, Wsevolod W. 1985a. "Toward a Theory of Ideological Movements: Nationalism and Community Change in Quebec and Flanders." *Canadian Review of Studies in Nationalism*, 12: 141-160.

Isajiw, Wsevolod W. 1985b. "Learning and Use of Ethnic Language at Home and School: Sociological Issues and Findings." In *Osvita: Ukrainian Bilingual Education.* M.R. Lupul, ed. Edmonton: Canadian Institute of Ukrainian Studies, University of Alberta, 225-230.

Isajiw, Wsevolod W. 1990. "Ethnic-Identity Retention." In R. Breton, W. Isajiw, W. Kalbach and J. Reitz, *Ethnic Identity and Equality: Varieties of Experience in a Canadian City.* Toronto: University of Toronto Press, 34-91.

Isajiw, Wsevolod W. 1997. "The Policy of Multiculturalism in Canada: Its Social and Educational Functions and the Challenges Posed." In *Methodische Probleme der empirischen Erziehungswissenschaft* (Methodological Problems in the Science of Education). F. Schmidt, ed. Baltmannsweiler: Schneider-Varlag Hohengehren, 187-202.

Isajiw, Wsevolod W. and Tomoko Makabe. 1982. *Socialization as a Factor in Ethnic Identity Retention.* Toronto: University of Toronto, Centre for Urban and Community Studies, Research Paper, No. 134.

Isajiw, Wsevolod W. and Andrij Makuch. 1994. "Ukrainians in Canada." In *Ukraine and Ukrainians Throughout the World: A Demographic and Sociological Guide to the Homeland and Its Diaspora.* A.L. Pawliczko, ed. Toronto: University of Toronto Press, 327-357.

Isajiw, Wsevolod W., Aysan Sev'er and Leo Driedger. 1993. "Ethnic Identity and Social Mobility: A Test of the "Drawback Model." *Canadian Journal of Sociology*, 18: 177-196.

Israel, Milton. 1994. *In the Further Soil: A Social History of Indo-Canadians in Ontario.* Toronto: The Organization for the Promotion of Indian Culture.

Jaenen, Cornelius. 1973. *Friend and Foe.* Toronto: McClelland and Stewart Ltd.

Jasso, Guillermina and Mark R. Rosenzweig. 1995. "Do Immigrants Screened for Skills Do Better than Family Reunification Immigrants?" *International Migration Review*, 29: 85-111.

Johnson, William. 1994. *A Canadian Myth: Quebec, Between Canada and the Illusion of Utopia.* Montreal: Robert Davies Publishing.

Johnston, Hugh. 1989. *The Voyage of the Komagata Maru: The Sikh Challenge to Canada's Colour Bar.* Vancouver: University of British Columbia Press.

Joos, Martin. 1967. *The Five Clocks.* New York: Harcourt, Brace and World.

Judd, Charles M., Carey S. Ryan and Bernadette Park. 1991. "Accuracy in the Judgement of In-Group and Out-Group Variability." *Journal of Personality and Social Psychology*, 61: 366-379.

Juteau, Danielle. 1992. "The Sociology of Ethno-National Relations in Quebec." In *Deconstructing a Nation: Immigration, Multiculturalism and Racism in 90's Canada.* V. Satzewich, ed. Halifax and Saskatoon: Fernwood Publishing and Department of Sociology, University of Saskatchewan, 323-341.

Kalbach, Warren E. 1970. *The Impact of Immigration on Canada's Population.* Ottawa: Dominion Bureau of Statistics.

Kalbach, Warren E. and Madeline A. Richard. 1988. "Ethnic-Religious Identity, Acculturation and Social and Economic Achievement of Canada's Post-War Minority Population." Report prepared for *Review of Demography and Its Implications for Economic and Social Policy, Phase II*, Health and Welfare Canada. Toronto: Population Research Laboratory, Erindale College, University of Toronto.

Kallen, Evelyn. 1982. *Ethnicity and Human Rights in Canada.* Toronto: Gage Publishing Ltd.

Kallen, Evelyn. 1995. *Ethnicity and Human Rights in Canada*, Second Edition. Toronto: Oxford University Press.

Kane, Paula M. 1993. "Irish Catholics." *In Encyclopedia of American Social History.* M.K. Cayton et al., eds. New York: Charles Scribner's Sons, 743-755.

Kasher, Robert J. 1997. *Ethnic Toronto: A Complete Guide to the Many Faces and Cultures of Toronto.* Lincolnwood, Ill.: Passport Books.

Katz, Daniel and Kenneth W. Braly. 1933. "Racial Stereotypes of 100 College Students." *Journal of Abnormal and Social Psychology*, 33: 280-290.

Khong, Jennifer. 1995. "The Pham Family." In *Safe Haven: The Refugee Experience of Five Families*. E. McLuhan, ed. Toronto: Multicultural History Society of Ontario, 117-121.

King, MacKenzie. 1947. House of Commons Debates, May 2, 1947: 2644-47.

King, Rebecca Chiyoko. 1997. "Negotiating Hybridity: Co-Constructing Race and Ethnicity in Japanese American Beauty Pageants." Paper presented at the 92nd Annual Meeting of the American Sociological Association, Toronto, August 9-13.

Kostash, Myrna. 1977. *All of Baba's Children*. Edmonton: Hurtig Publishers.

Krahn, Harvey and John Gartrell. 1983. "Labour Market Segmentation and Social Mobility in a Canadian Single Industry Community." *Canadian Review of Sociology and Anthropology*, 20: 322-345.

Kubat, Daniel, ed. 1984. *The Politics of Return: International Return Migration in Europe*. Staten Island, N.Y.: Center for Migration Studies.

Kurian, George. 1991. "Socialization of South Asian Immigrant Youth." In *Immigrants and Refugees in Canada: A National Perspective on Ethnicity, Multiculturalism and Cross-Cultural Adjustment*. S.P. Sharma, A.M. Ervin and D. Meintel, eds. Saskatoon: University of Saskatchewan, Department of Anthropology and Archaeology, 47-57.

Kymlicka, Will. 1995. *Multicultural Citizenship: A Liberal Theory of Minority Rights*. Oxford: Oxford University Press.

Lachapelle, Guy, et al. 1993. *The Quebec Democracy: Structures, Processes and Policies*. Toronto: McGraw-Hill Ryerson. Appendix I: 410.

Lam, Lawrence and Anthony H. Richmond. 1995. "Migration to Canada in the Post-War Period." In *The Cambridge Survey of World Migration*. R. Cohen, ed. Cambridge: Cambridge University Press, 263-270.

Lambert, Ronald D. and James E. Curtis. 1983. "Opposition to Multiculturalism among Québécois and English-Canadians." *Canadian Review of Sociology and Anthropology*, 20: 193-207.

Lambert, Wallace E., R. Hodgson, R. Gardner and S. Fillenbaum. 1972. "Evaluational Reactions to Spoken Languages." In *Attitudes and Motivation in Second Language Learning*. R. Gardner and W.E. Lambert, eds. Rowley, Mass.: Newbury House, 293-305.

Lan, Kim Sheung-King. 1993. "The Chinese in Calgary: Schooling for Cultural Identity." In *When Cultures Clash: Case Studies in Multiculturalism*. Second Edition. J.W. Friesen, ed. Calgary: Detselig Enterprises Ltd., 167-188.

Lautard, Hugh and Neil Guppy. 1990. "The Vertical Mosaic Revisited: Occupational Differentials among Canadian Ethnic Groups." In P.S. Li, ed., *Race and Ethnic Relations in Canada*. Toronto: Oxford University Press, 189-208.

Lévesque, René. 1978. *My Quebec*. Toronto: Methuen Publications.

Lewin, Kurt. 1948. *Resolving Social Conflicts: Selected Papers on Group Dynamics*. New York: Harper and Row Publishers.

Li, Peter S. 1990a. "The Emergence of the New Middle Class Among the Chinese in Canada." *Asian Culture*, 14: 187-194.

Li, Peter S. 1990b. "Race and Ethnicity." In *Race and Ethnic Relations in Canada*. P.S. Li, ed. Toronto: Oxford University Press, 3-17.

Li, Peter S. 1993. *Chinese Immigrants and Ethnic Enterprise: Transplanted Cultural Thesis and Blocked Mobility Thesis Reconsidered*. Toronto: University of Toronto, R.F. Harney Professorship and Program in Ethnic, Immigration and Pluralism Studies, Lectures and papers in Ethnicity, No. 10.

Lieberson, Stanley. 1961. "A Societal Theory of Race and Ethnic Relations." *American Sociological Review*, 26: 902-910.

Lieberson, Stanley. 1970. "Stratification and Ethnic Groups." *Sociological Inquiry*, 40: 172-181.

Liebert, R.M., J.N. Sprafkin and E.S. Davidson. 1989. *The Early Window: Effects of Television on Children and Youth*. Third Edition. New York: Pergamon Press.

Lim, Lin L. and Nana Oishi. 1966. "International Labor Migration of Asian Women: Distinctive Characteristics and Policy Concerns." *Asian and Pacific Migration Journal*, 5:1: 85-116.

Linville, Patricia W. and Edward E. Jones. 1980. "Polarized Appraisals of Out-Group Members." *Journal of Personality and Social Psychology*, 38: 689-703.

Lippman, Walter. 1936. *Public Opinion*. New York: Macmillan.

Lipset, Seymour Martin and Reinhard Bendix. 1959. *Social Mobility in Industrial Society*. Los Angeles: University of California Press.

Lower, Arthur R.M. 1946. *Colony to Nation: A History of Canada*. Toronto: Longmans, Green.

Lucas, Rex A. 1971. *Minetown, Milltown, Railtown: Life in Canadian Communities of Single Industry*. Toronto: University of Toronto Press.

Luciuk, Lubomyr. 1988. *A Time for Atonement: Canada's First National Internment Operations and the Ukrainian Canadians 1914-1920*. Kingston, ON: The Limestone Press.

Luong, T.M. and C.M. Luong. 1972. *The Great Image Sellers: The Study of the Causes of Difficulties among Immigrants in Canada*. Brooklyn, N.Y.: Pageant-Poseidon.

Lupul, Manoly R. ed., 1982. *A Heritage in Transition: Essays in the History of Ukrainians in Canada*. Toronto: McClelland and Stewart Ltd.

MacCannell, Dean. 1976. *The Tourist: A New Theory of the Leisure Class*. New York: Schoken Books.

Macdonald, Norman. 1966. *Canada, Immigration and Colonization: 1841-1903*. Toronto: Macmillan of Canada.

Mackie, Marlene, 1980. "Ethnic Stereotypes and Prejudice: Alberta Indians, Hutterites and Ukrainians." In *Ethnicity and Ethnic Relations in Canada: A Book of Readings*. J.E. Goldstein and R.M. Bienvenue, eds. Toronto: Butterworths and Co., 233-246.

Macklem, Patrick. 1993. *First Nations and the Law: Cases and Materials*. Toronto: Faculty of Law, University of Toronto.

Macleod, Arlene Elowe. 1992. "Hegemonic Relations and Gender Resistance: The New Veiling as Accommodating Protest in Cairo." *Signs*, 17: 533-557.

Makabe, Tomoko. 1976. *Ethnic Group Identity: Canadian-Born Japanese in Metropolitan Toronto*. Ph.D. Thesis. Toronto: University of Toronto.

Malarek, Victor. 1985. "Clark Considers Human-Rights Monitor." *The Globe and Mail*, February 8: 9.

Malarek, Victor. 1987. *Haven's Gate: Canada's Immigration Fiasco*. Toronto: Macmillan of Canada.

Mallet, Gina. 1977. "Multiculturalism: Has Diversity Gone Too Far?" *The Globe and Mail, March* 15: D.

Mandel, Eli. 1977. "Ethnic Voice in Canadian Writing." In *Identities: The Impact of Ethnicity on Canadian Society*. W. Isajiw, ed. Toronto: Peter Martin Associates Ltd., 57-68.

Manning, Preston. 1992. *The New Canada*. Toronto: Macmillan Canada.

Manpower and Immigration. 1974a. *Immigration Policy Perspectives*. Ottawa: A Report of the Canadian Immigration and Population Study, Vol. 1.

Manpower and Immigration. 1974b. *The Immigration Program*. Ottawa: A Report of the Canadian Immigration and Population Study, No.2.

Manpower and Immigration. 1974c. *Three Years in Canada: First Report of the Longitudinal Survey on the Economic and Social Adaptation of Immigrants*. Ottawa: Canadian Immigration and Population Study.

Manzer, Ronald A. 1974. *Canada: A Socio-Political Report*. Toronto: McGraw-Hill Ryerson.

Marrus, Michael R. 1991. *Mr Sam: The Life and Times of Samuel Bronfman*. New York: Viking Penguin.

Martin, Philip L. 1988. *Harvest of Confusion: Migrant Workers in U.S. Agriculture*. Boulder: Westview Press.

Matas, David with I. Simon. 1989. *Closing the Doors: The Future of Refugee Protection*. Toronto: Summerhill Press.

Mayhew, Leon. 1968. "Ascription in Modern Societies." *Sociological Inquiry*, 38: 112-116.

Maykovich, Minako K. 1975. "Ethnic Variation in Success Value." In *Socialization and Values in Canadian Society*, Vol. II. R.M. Pike and E. Zureik, eds. Toronto: McClelland and Stewart Ltd., Carleton Library No. 85: 158-179.

McDade, K. 1988. *Barriers to the Recognition of the Credentials of Immigrants in Canada*. Ottawa: Institute for Research on Public Policy.

McDiarmid, Garnet and David Pratt. 1971. *Teaching Prejudice: A Content Analysis of Social Studies Textbooks Authorized for Use in Ontario*. A Report to the Ontario Human Rights Commission. Toronto: The Ontario Institute for Studies in Education, Curriculum Series 12.

McGregor, Gaile. 1985. *The Wacousta Syndrome: Explorations in the Canadian Landscape*. Toronto: University of Toronto Press.

McKie, Craig. 1994. "Temporary Residents of Canada." *Canadian Social Trends*. Ottawa: Statistics Canada, 32: 12-15.

McRae, Kenneth Douglas. 1969. *The Federal Capital: Government Institutions*. Ottawa: Queen's Printer.

McRae, Kenneth Douglas, ed. 1974. *Consociational Democracy: Political Accommodation in Segmented Societies*. Toronto: McClelland and Stewart Ltd.

McRoberts, Kenneth, ed. 1993a. *The Charlottetown Accord, the Referendum, and the Future of Canada*. Toronto: University of Toronto Press.

McRoberts, Kenneth, ed. 1993b. *Quebec: Social Change and Political Crisis*. Third Edition (with a Postscript). Toronto: McClelland and Stewart Ltd.

McRoberts, Kenneth, ed. 1995. *Beyond Quebec: Taking Stock of Canada*. Montreal: McGill-Queen's University Press.

McVey, Jr., Wayne W. and Warren E. Kalbach. 1995. *Canadian Population*. Toronto: Nelson Canada.

Mead, George Herbert. 1934. *Mind, Self and Society*. Chicago: University of Chicago Press.

Memmi, Albert. 1965. *The Colonizer and the Colonized*. New York: The Orion Press, 1965.

Mernissi, Fatima. 1991. *The Veil and the Male Elite: A Feminist Interpretation of Women's Rights in Islam*. New York: Addison-Wesley Publishing Company.

Merton, Robert K. 1949. "Discrimination and the American Creed." In *Discrimination and National Welfare*. R.M. MacIver, ed. New York: Harper and Brothers, 99-126.

Merton, Robert K. 1968. *Social Theory and Social Structure*. New York: Free Press.

Messaoudi, Khalida. 1995. *Une algérienne de bout*. Paris: Flammarion.

Michalowski, Margaret. 1996. "Visitors and Visa Workers: Old Wine in New Bottles?" In *International Migration, Refugee Flows and Human Rights in North America: The Impact of Free Trade and Restructuring*. A.B. Simmons, ed. New York: Center for Migration Studies, 104-122.

Miles, Robert. 1982. *Racism and Migrant Labour*. London: Routledge and Kegan Paul.

Mills, David. 1988. *The Idea of Loyalty in Upper Canada, 1784-1850*. Kingston: McGill Queen's University Press.

Mimouni, Rashid. 1992. *De la barbarie en général et de l'intégrisme en particulier*. Paris: Belfond-Le Pré aux Clercs.

Minister of State, Multiculturalism. 1978. "Statement by the Prime Minister, House of Commons, October 8, 1971." In *Multiculturalism and the Government of Canada*. Ottawa: Minister of Supply and Services Canada, 45-46.

Minority Rights Group. 1990. *World Directory of Minorities*. Chicago: St. James Press.

Montero, Gloria. 1977. *The Immigrants*. Toronto: James Lorimer.

Montgomery, J. Randall. 1996. "Components of Refugee Adaptation." *International Migration Review*, 30: 679-702.

Moodley, Kogila. 1983. "Canadian Multiculturalism as Ideology." *Ethnic and Racial Studies*, VI: 320.

Morris, Aldon D. 1984. *The Origins of the Civil Rights Movement: Black Communities Organizing for Change*. New York: The Free Press.

Morrison, Samuel E. 1965. *The Oxford History of the American People*. New York: Oxford University Press.

Morse, Stan and K.J. Gergen. 1970. "Social Comparison, Self-Consistency and Concept of Self." *Journal of Personality and Social Psychology*, 16: 148-156.

Morton, W.L. 1961. *The Canadian Identity*. Toronto: University of Toronto Press.

Mukherjee, Bharati. 1985. *Darkness*. Toronto: Penguin Books.

Myrdal, Gunnar. 1944. *An American Dilemma: The Negro Problem and Modern Democracy*. New York: Harper and Row.

Nagata, Judy, J. Rayfield, and M. Ferraris. 1970. *English Language Classes for Immigrant Women with Pre-School Children*. Toronto: York University, Institute for Behaviourial Research.

Nagel, Joane. 1994. "Constructing Ethnicity: Creating and Recreating Ethnic Identity and Culture." *Social Problems*, 41: 152-176.

Nahirny, Vladimir C. and Joshua A. Fishman. 1966. "Ukrainian Language Maintenance Efforts in the United States." In *Language Loyalty in the United States: The Maintenance and Perpetuation of Non-English Mother Tongues by American Ethnic and Religious Groups*. J.A. Fishman, V.C. Nahirny, J.E. Hofman and R.G. Hayden, eds. The Hague: Mouton and Co., 318-357.

Naidoo, Josephine C. 1987. "Women of South Asian Origins: Status of Research, Problems, Future Issues." In *South Asian Diaspora in Canada: Six Essays*. M. Israel, ed. Toronto: The Multicultural History Society of Ontario, 37-58.

Nash, Manning. 1989. *The Cauldron of Ethnicity in the Modern World*. Chicago: University of Chicago Press.

Neatby, Hilda. 1972. *The Quebec Act: Protest and Policy.* Scarborough, ON: Prentice-Hall of Canada Ltd.

Neuwirth, Gertrude and Lynn Clark. 1981. "Indochinese Refugees in Canada: Sponsorship and Adjustment." *International Migration Review,* 15: 131-140.

Newman, Peter C. 1975. *The Canadian Establishment.* Vol 1. Toronto: McClelland and Stewart Ltd.

Newman, Peter C. 1979. *The Canadian Establishment.* Revised and Updated. Toronto: McClelland and Stewart Ltd.

Newman, Peter C. 1998. *Titans: How the New Canadian Establishment Seized Power.* Toronto: Viking.

Nielsson, Gunnar P. 1985. "States and Nation-Groups: A Global Taxonomy." In Edward A. Tiryakian and Ronald Rogowski, eds., *New Nationalisms of the Developed West: Towards Explanation.* Boston: Allen and Unwin, 27-56.

Nietschmann, Bernard. 1987. "The Third World War." *Cultural Survival Quarterly,* 11:3: 1-16.

O'Bryan, K.G., J.G. Reitz and O.M. Kuplowska. 1976. *Non-Official Languages: A Study in Canadian Multiculturalism.* Ottawa: Minister of Supply and Services Canada.

Ogmundson, Rick. 1990. "Perspectives on the Class and Ethnic Origins of Canadian Elites: A Methodological Critique of the Porter/Clement/Olsen Tradition." *Canadian Journal of Sociology,* 15: 165-177.

Okamura, Jonathan. 1981. "Situational Ethnicity." *Ethnic and Racial Studies,* 4: 452-465.

Olsen, Dennis. 1980. *The State Elite.* Toronto: McClelland and Stewart Ltd.

Olsson, Lars. 1996. "Labor Migration as a Prelude to World War I." *International Migration Review,* 30: 875-900.

Omi, Michael and Howard Winant. 1986. *Racial Formation in the United States: From the 1960s to the 1980s.* New York and London: Routledge and Kegan Paul.

Ossenberg, Richard J. 1967. "The Conquest Revisited: Another Look at Canadian Dualism." *Canadian Review of Sociology and Anthropology,* IV: 4:201-218.

Pal, Leslie A. 1987. *Public Policy Analysis: An Introduction.* Toronto: Methuen Publications.

Palmer, Howard, ed. 1975. "Roundtable on the Green Pater on Immigration." Special issue of *Canadian Ethnic Studies,* 7: 1.

Park, Julian, ed. 1957. *The Culture of Contemporary Canada.* Ithaca: Cornell University Press.

Parsons, Talcott. 1951. *The Social System.* Glencoe, Ill.: Free Press.

Patterson, E. Palmer. 1972. *The Canadian Indian: A History Since 1500.* Don Mills, ON: Collier-Macmillan Canada Ltd.

Pelletier, Gerard. 1990. "1968: Language Policy and the Mood in Quebec." In *Towards a Just Society: The Trudeau Years,* T.S. Axworthy and P.E. Trudeau, eds. Markham, ON: Penguin Books Canada Ltd. (Viking), 207-225.

Penninx, Rinus. 1997. "Immigration and Minority Policies, Public Discourse and Multiculturalism in Dutch Society." In *Multiculturalism in North America and Europe: Comparative Perspectives on Interethnic Relations and Social Incorporation.* W.W. Isajiw, ed. Toronto: Canadian Scholars Press, 221-243.

Percival, John. 1995. *The Great Famine: Ireland's Potato Famine, 1841-51.* London: BBC Books.

Peter, Karl. 1981. "The Myth of Multiculturalism and Other Fables." In *Ethnicity, Power and Politics in Canada.* J. Dahlie and T. Fernando, eds. Toronto: Methuen Publications, 56-67.

Peter, Karl A. 1987. *The Dynamics of Hutterite Society: An Analytical Approach.* Edmonton: University of Alberta Press.

Pineo, Peter C. 1977. "The Social Standing of Ethnic and Racial Groupings," *Canadian Review of Sociology and Anthropology,* 14: 147-157.

Porter, John. 1965. *The Vertical Mosaic.* Toronto: University of Toronto Press.

Porter, John. 1972. "Dilemmas and Contradictions of a Multiethnic Society." *Transactions of the Royal Society of Canada,* 19:4: 193-205.

Porter, John. 1975. "Ethnic Pluralism in Canadian Perspective." In *Ethnicity, Theory and Experience.* N. Glazer and D.P. Moynihan, eds. Cambridge, Mass.: Harvard University Press, 267-304.

Porter, John. 1985. "Canada: The Societal Content of Occupational Allocation." In *Ascription and Achievement: Studies in Mobility and Status Attainment in Canada.* M. Boyd et al., eds. Ottawa: Carleton University Press, 29-65.

Posgate, Dale and Kenneth McRoberts. 1979. *Quebec: Social Change and Political Crisis.* Toronto: McClelland and Stewart Ltd.

Pratt, David. 1984. "Bias in Textbooks: Progress and Problems." In *Multiculturalism in Canada: Social and Educational Perspectives.* R.J. Samuda, J.W. Berry and M. Laferriére, eds. Toronto: Allyn and Bacon Inc., 154-166.

Progressive Conservative Party. 1991. *Resolution Guide from the 1991 General Meeting and National Policy Conference* (August 6-10). Ottawa.

Proudfoot, Malcolm J. 1957. *European Refugees 1939-52: A Study in Forced Population Movement.* London: Faber and Faber Ltd.

Ptolemy, Kathleen. 1989. "First International Consultation on Refugee Women: Geneva, November 1988." *Canadian Woman Studies,* 10: 21-24.

Purbhao, Mary and Stan Shapson. 1974, 1975. *Transition From Italian.* Toronto: Toronto Board of Education Research Department, Study No. 126, 133.

Quimby, George I. 1960. *Indian Life in the Upper Great Lakes: 11,000 B.C. to A.D. 1800.* Chicago: University of Chicago Press.

Radecki, Henry and B. Heydenkorn. 1976. *A Member of a Distinguished Family: The Polish Group In Canada.* Toronto: McClelland and Stewart Ltd.

Ralston, Helen. 1994. "Community Organization among South Asian Immigrant Women in Canada." Halifax: Saint Mary's University, Department of Sociology, Unpublished Paper.

Redfield, Robert. 1956. *The Little Community and Peasant Society and Culture.* Chicago: University of Chicago Press.

Reform Party of Canada. 1990. *Principles and Policies.* Ottawa.

Reid, Angus. 1996. *Shakedown: How the New Economy is Changing Our Lives.* Toronto: Doubleday Canada Ltd.

Reid, Stanford W., ed. 1976. *The Scottish Tradition in Canada.* Toronto: McClelland and Stewart Ltd.

Reitz, Jeffrey G. 1988. "Less Racial Discrimination in Canada, or Simply Less Racial Conflict?: Implications of Comparisons with Britain." *Canadian Public Policy,* 424:14: 436.

Reitz, Jeffrey G. 1990. "Ethnic Concentrations in Labour Markets and Their Implications for Ethnic Inequality." In Breton, R., W.W. Isajiw, W.E. Kalbach and J.G. Reitz, *Ethnic Identity and Equality: Varieties of Experience in a Canadian City.* Toronto: University of Toronto Press, 135-195.

Reitz, Jeffrey G. 1993. "Statistics on Racial Discrimination in Canada." *Policy Options,* 14:2: 32-36.

Reitz, Jeffrey G. and Raymond Breton. 1994. *The Illusion of Difference: Realities of Ethnicity in Canada and the United States.* Toronto: C.D. Howe Institute.

Reitz, Jeffrey G. and Sherrilyn M. Sklar. 1997. "Culture, Race, and the Economic Assimilation of Immigrants." *Sociological Forum,* 12:2: 233-277.

Ruemper, Wendy. 1996. "Models for Change: Antiracist Education for Universities and Colleges." *Canadian Review of Sociology and Anthropology,* 33: 317-335.

Rex, John. 1970. *Race Relations in Sociological Theory.* New York: Schoken Books.

Rich, Harvey. 1991. "Observations on 'Class and Ethnic Origins of Canadian Elites' by Richard Ogmundson." *Canadian Journal of Sociology,* 16: 419-423.

Rich, Wilbur C., ed. 1996. *The Politics of Minority Coalitions: Race, Ethnicity, and Shared Uncertainties.* Westport, Conn.: Praeger.

Richard, Madeline A. 1991. *Ethnic Groups and Marital Choices: Ethnic History and Marital Assimilation in Canada, 1871 and 1971.* Vancouver: UBC Press.

Richmond, Anthony H. 1967. *Post-War Immigrants in Canada.* Toronto: University of Toronto Press.

Richmond, Anthony H. 1969. "Sociology of Migration in Industrial and Postindustrial Societies." In *Sociological Studies 2: Migration.* J. Jackson, ed. Cambridge: Cambridge University Press, 238-281.

Richmond, Anthony H. 1974a. *Aspects of the Absorption and Adaptation of Immigrants.* Ottawa: Manpower and Immigration, Canadian Immigration and Population Study.

Richmond, Anthony H. 1974b. "Language, Ethnicity and the Problem of Identity in a Canadian Metropolis." *Ethnicity,* 1: 175-206.

Richmond, Anthony H. 1994. *Global Apartheid: Refugees, Racism, and the New World Order.* Toronto: Oxford University Press.

Richmond, Anthony H. and Warren E. Kalbach. 1980. *Factors in the Adjustment of Immigrants and Their Descendants.* Ottawa: Statistics Canada.

Ringer, Benjamin B. 1983. *We the People and Others: Duality and America's Treatment of Its Racial Minorities.* New York: Routledge.

Rockquemore, Kerry. 1997. "Doing (Mixed) Race: Biracial Identity as an Interactional Accomplishment." Paper presented at the 92nd Annual Meeting of the American Sociological Association, Toronto, August 9-13.

Roosens, Eugene E. 1989. *Creating Ethnicity: The Process of Ethnogenesis.* London: SAGE Publications.

Root, Maria P.P., ed. 1996. *The Multiracial Experience: Racial Borders as the New Frontier.* Thousand Oaks: Sage Publications.

Rosen, Bernard. 1959. "Race, Ethnicity and the Achievement Syndrome." *American Sociological Review,* 24: 47-60.

Ross, Jeffrey A. 1982. "Urban Development and the Politics of Ethnicity: A Conceptual Approach." *Ethnic and Racial Studies,* 5: 440-456.

Royal Commission on Aboriginal Peoples. 1993a. *Aboriginal Peoples in Urban Centres.* Report of the National Round Table on Aboriginal Urban Issues. Ottawa: Canada Communication Group Publishing.

Royal Commission on Aboriginal Peoples. 1993b. *Path to Healing.* Report of the National Round Table on Aboriginal Health and Social Issues. Vancouver: Canada Communication Group Publishing.

Royal Commission on Aboriginal Peoples. 1995. *Aboriginal Self-Government: Legal and Constitutional Issues.* Papers Prepared as Part of the Research Program of the Royal Commission on Aboriginal Peoples. Ottawa: Canada Communication Group Publishing.

Royal Commission on Aboriginal Peoples. 1996:1. *Looking Forward, Looking Back.* Report of the Royal Commission on Aboriginal Peoples. Volume 1. Ottawa: Canada Communication Group Publishing.

Royal Commission on Aboriginal Peoples. 1996:2. *Restructuring the Relationship.* Report of the Royal Commission on Aboriginal Peoples. Volume 2. Ottawa: Canada Communication Group Publishing.

Royal Commission on Aboriginal Peoples. 1996:3. *Gathering Strength.* Report of the Royal Commission on Aboriginal Peoples. Volume 3. Ottawa: Canada Communication Group Publishing.

Royal Commission on Aboriginal Peoples. 1996:4. *Perspectives and Realities.* Report of the Royal Commission on Aboriginal Peoples. Volume 4. Ottawa: Canada Communication Group Publishing.

Royal Institute of International Affairs, Study Group of Members. 1963 (1939). *Nationalism.* London: Frank Cass and Co. Ltd.

Rublee, Cindy B. and Susan M. Shaw. 1991. "Constraints on the Leisure and Community Participation of Immigrant Women: Implications for Social Integration." *Loisir et Société/Society and Leisure,* 14:1: 133-150.

Salo, Matt T. and S.M.G. Salo. 1977. *The Kalderas in Eastern Canada.* Ottawa: National Museum of Man, Mercury Series; Canadian Centre for Folk Culture Studies, Paper No. 21.

Satzewich, Vic. 1991. *Racism and the Incorporation of Foreign Labour: Farm Labour Migration to Canada Since 1945.* London: Routledge.

Satzewich, Vic and Terry Wotherspoon. 1993. *First Nations: Race, Class, and Gender Relations.* Scarborough, ON: Nelson Canada.

Schafer, D. Paul. 1990. *The Character of Canadian Culture.* Markham, ON: World Culture Project.

Schmid, Carol. 1996. "New Immigrant Communities in the United States and the Ideology of Exclusion." *Research in Community Sociology,* 6: 39-67.

Seidman, Steven, ed. 1994. *The Postmodern Turn: New Perspectives On Social Theory.* Cambridge: Cambridge University Press.

Selzer, Michael, ed. 1972. *"Kike!": A Documentary History of Anti-Semitism in America.* New York: World Publishing Co., Meridian Books.

Sherif, Muzafer, O. J. Harvey, B. J. White, W. E. Hood and C. W. Sherif. 1961. *Intergroup Conflict and Cooperation: The Robber's Cave Experiment.* Norman, Okla.: Institute of Group Relations.

Shukrallah, Halla. 1994. "The Impact of the Islamic Movement in Egypt." *Feminist Review,* 47: 15-32.

Shibutani, Tamotsu and Kian M. Kwan. 1965. *Ethnic Stratification: A Comparative Approach.* New York: Macmillan Co.

Sigler, Jay A., ed. 1987. *International Handbook on Race and Race Relations.* New York: Greenwood Press.

Simon, Julian. 1989. *The Economic Consequences of Immigration.* London: Blackwell.

Simpson, George E. and J. Milton Yinger, eds. 1985. *Racial and Cultural Minorities: An Analysis of Prejudice and Discrimination.* Fifth Edition. New York: Plenum Press.

Singh, Simboonath. 1997. *The Social Construction of Collective "Indian" Ethno-Religious Identity in a Context of Ethnic Diversity: A Case Study of an Indo-Caribbean Hindu Temple in Toronto.* Ph.D. Thesis. Toronto: Department of Sociology, University of Toronto.

Slinger, John. 1971. "Dreams of Eldorado Fade for Portuguese." *The Globe and Mail,* August 26: 35.

Smandych, Russell, Robyn Lincoln and Paul Wilson. 1993. "Toward a Cross-Cultural Theory of Aboriginal Crime: A Comparative Study of the Problem of Aboriginal Overrepresentation in the Criminal Justice System of Canada and Australia." *International Criminal Justice Review,* 3: 1-24.

Smith, Allan. 1990. *Canadian Culture, the Canadian State, and the New Continentalism.* Orono, Maine: The University of Maine, The Canadian-American Center.

Smith, Allan. 1994. *Canada—An American Nation? Essays on Continentalism, Identity, and the Canadian Frame of Mind.* Montreal and Kingston: McGill-Queen's University Press.

Smith, M.G. (Michael Garfield). 1965. *Stratification in Grenada.* Berkeley: University of California Press.

Smith, M.G. (Michael Garfield). 1984. *Culture, Race and Class in the Commonwealth Caribbean.* Mona, Jamaica: Department of Extramural Studies, University of the West Indies.

Smith, Susan. 1984. "Negotiating Ethnicity in an Uncertain Environment." *Ethnic and Racial Studies,* 7: 360-373.

Solomon, R.P. 1992. *Black Resistance in High School: Forging a Separatist Culture.* Albany: State University of New York Press.

Sorensen, Marianne. 1995. "The Match between Education and Occupation for Immigrant Women in Canada." *Canadian Ethnic Studies,* 27:1: 48-66.

Stack, John F., ed. 1986. *The Primordial Challenge.* Westport, Conn.: Greenwood Press.

Stasiulis, Daiva K. 1980. "The Political Structuring of Ethnic Community Action: A Reformulation." *Canadian Ethnic Studies,* 12: 19-44.

Stasiulis, Daiva and Nira Yuval-Davis, eds. 1995. *Unsettling Settler Societies: Articulations of Gender, Race, Ethnicity and Class.* London: Sage Publications.

Statesman's Year-Book, 1993-94. 1993. Hunter, Brian, ed. London: Macmillan Press, Ltd.

Statistics Canada. 1974. *Perspective Canada: A Compendium of Social Statistics.* Ottawa: Ministry of Industry, Trade and Commerce.

Statistics Canada. 1992a. *1991 Census of Canada: Home Language and Mother Tongue.* Catalogue 93-317, Tables 4 and 6. Ottawa: Minister of Industry, Science and Technology.

Statistics Canada. 1992b. *1991 Census of Canada,* Catalogue Cat. 93-328. Ottawa: Minister of Industry, Science and Technology.

Statistics Canada. 1993. *1991 Aboriginal Peoples Survey.* Catalogue 89-533. Ottawa: Ministry of Industry, Science and Technology.

Statistics Canada. 1993. *1991 Census: Ethnic Origin, the Nation.* Catalogue 93-315. Ottawa: Ministry of Industry, Science and Technology.

Statistics Canada. 1996. *Touriscope: International Travel, Travel Between Canada and Other Countries 1995.* Ottawa: Minister of Industry.

Statistics Canada. 1998a. *1996 Census: Education, Mobility and Migration.* Internet: http://WWW.StatCan.CA/Daily/English/980414 (April 16).

Statistics Canada. 1998b. *1996 Census.* Internet Catalogue No. 93F0026XDB96002.

Statistisches Bundesamt. 1994. *Statistisches Jahrbuch 1994 für die Bundesrepublik Deutschland.* Wiesbaden.

Sturino, Franc. 1990. *Forging the Chain: A Case Study of Italian Migration to North America, 1880-1930.* Toronto: Multicultural History Society of Ontario.

Stymeist, David H. 1975. *Ethnics and Indians: Social Relations in a Northwestern Ontario Town.* Toronto: Peter Martin Associates.

Suyyagh, Fayiz. 1995. *Ethnic Enterprise and the Community Dimension: The Case of Arab Business Leaders in Metropolitan Toronto, Ontario.* Ph.D. Thesis. Toronto: Department of Sociology, University of Toronto.

Swyripa, Frances. 1993. *Wedded to the Cause: Ukrainian-Canadian Women and Ethnic Identity, 1981-1991.* Toronto: University of Toronto Press.

Taarji, Hinde. 1990. *Les Voilées de l'Islam.* Paris: Baland Ed.

Tarnopolsky, Walter S. 1979. "The Control of Racial Discrimination." In *The Practice of Freedom.* Macdonald, R.St.J. and J.P. Humphrey, eds. Toronto: Butterworths, 289-307.

Tarnopolsky, Walter S. 1988. "Human Rights." In *The Canadian Encyclopedia.* Second Edition. Edmonton: Hurtig Publishers, 1024-25.

Tastsoglou, Evangelia. 1997. "Immigrant Women and Social Construction of Ethnicity: Three Generations of Greek Immigrant Women in Ontario." In *Advances in Gender Research,* Volume 2. Greenwich, Conn.: JAI Press Inc., 227-254.

Taylor, Charles. 1992. *Multiculturalism and "The Politics of Recognition."* Princeton, N.J.: Princeton University Press.

Teixeira, Carlos and Robert A. Murdie. 1997. "The Role of Ethnic Real Estate Agents in the Residential Relocation Process: A Case Study of the Portuguese Homebuyers in Suburban Toronto." *Urban Geography,* 18:6: 497-520.

Theobald, William F. 1994a. "The Context, Meaning and Scope of Tourism." In *Global Tourism: The Next Decade.* W. Theobald, ed. Oxford: Butterworth-Heinemann Ltd., 3-19.

Theobald, William F., ed. 1994b. *Global Tourism: The Next Decade.* Oxford: Butterworth-Heinemann Ltd.

Thomas, William I. and Florian Znaniecki. 1927. *The Polish Peasant in Europe and America,* 2 vols. New York: Alfred A. Knopf.

Three Years in Canada. Green Paper on Immigration. 1974. Ottawa: Manpower and Immigration.

Toronto Star. 1972. "'Emphasis on Comfort and Convenience is Surprising.'" June 10: 20.

Toronto Star. 1977. "Immigrant Marking Time in Job Quest." March 2: B3.

Toronto Star, 1978. "'Put Immigrants in Their Place.'" February 4: C3

Toronto Star, 1978. "'Quotes Racist' Quit or be Fired Educator Told." May 15: 1.

Trent, John E., Robert Young and Guy Lachapelle, eds. 1996. *Québec—Canada: What Is the Path Ahead? / Noveaux Sentiers Vers L'avenir.* Ottawa: University of Ottawa Press.

Triandis, Harry. 1973. "Interpersonal Attitudes and Behaviour in Race Relations." In *Psychology and Race*. P. Watson, ed. Chicago: Aldine Publishing Co., 241-255.

Trigger, B. 1985. *Natives and Newcomers: Canada's Heroic Age Reconsidered.* Montreal: McGill-Queen's University Press.

Trudeau, Pierre Elliott. 1968. *Federalism and the French Canadians.* Toronto: Macmillan of Canada.

Turner, Jonathan H. and Edna Bonacich. 1980. "Toward a Composite Theory of Middleman Minorities." *Ethnicity,* 7: 144-158.

Ujimoto, K. Victor. 1979. "Postwar Japanese Immigrants in British Columbia: Japanese Culture and Job Transferability." In *Two Nations, Many Cultures: Ethnic Groups in Canada.* J.L. Elliott, ed. Scarborough, ON: Prentice-Hall of Canada Ltd., 338-357.

Underhill, Frank H. 1964. *The Image of Confederation.* Toronto: Massey Lectures, Canadian Broadcasting Corporation.

UNESCO. 1995. *Statistical Yearbook 1995.* Paris and Lanham, Md.

Ungerleider, Charles. 1992. *Issues in Police Intercultural and Race Relations Training in Canada.* Ottawa: Solicitor General of Canada.

UNHCR. 1993. *The State of the World's Refugees: The Challenge of Protection.* New York: Penguin Books.

United Nations. 1953. *Report of the Ad Hoc Committee on Forced Labor.* Geneva: International Labour Office.

United Nations. 1978. *Human Rights: A Compilation of International Instruments.* New York: United Nations Publications. Reprinted in 1980 by Ottawa: Secretary of State, Human Rights Program.

United Nations. 1985. *UN Chronicle.* New York, NY: United Nations Office of Public Information, 1975-1996.

United Nations. 1994a. *1992 Demographic Yearbook.* New York: U.N. Department for Economic Information and Policy Analysis.

United Nations. 1994b. *Statistical Yearbook, Thirty-Ninth Issue.* New York: Department of Economic and Social Information and Policy Analysis, Statistical Division.

Valentine, Victor assisted by I.P. Taylor. 1980a. "Native Peoples and Canadian Society: A Profile of Issues and Trends." In *Cultural Boundaries and the Cohesion of Canada*, R. Breton, J.G. Reitz and V. Valentine, eds. Montreal: The Institute for Research and Public Policy, 47-121.

Valentine, Victor assisted by I.P. Taylor. 1980b. "Native Peoples in Aboriginal Canada." In *Cultural Boundaries and the Cohesion of Canada.* R. Breton, J.G. Reitz and V. Valentine, eds. Montreal: The Institute for Research and Public Policy, 55-69.

Vernant, Jacques. 1953.*The Refugee in the Post-War World.* New Haven: Yale University Press.

Waddell, Eric. 1986. "State, Language and Society: The Vicissitudes of French in Quebec and Canada." In *The Politics of Gender, Ethnicity and Language in Canada.* A Cairns and C. Williams, eds. Toronto: University of Toronto Press, 67-110.

Wade, Peter. 1993. "'Race,' Nature and Culture." *Man*, 28: 17-34.

Walker, James W.St.G. 1997. *"Race," Rights and the Law in the Supreme Court of Canada: Historical Case Studies.* Toronto and Kitchener, ON: The Osgoode Society for Canadian Legal History and Wilfrid University Press.

Wallman, Sandra. 1986. "Ethnicity and the Boundary Process in Context." In *Theories of Race and Ethnic Relations.* J. Rex and D. Mason, eds. Cambridge: Cambridge University Press, 226-245.

Walmsley, N. E. 1954.*Canada's Response to the International Problem of Displaced Persons, 1947-51.* Unpublished Ph.D. Thesis, McGill University.

Weber, Max. 1958. *The Protestant Ethic and the Spirit of Capitalism.* New York: Charles Scribner's Sons.

Weiner, Myron. 1995. *The Global Migration Crisis: Challenges to States and Human Rights.* New York: HarperCollins Publishers.

Weiner, M.J. and F.E. Wright. 1973. "Effects of Undergoing Arbitrary Discrimination upon Subsequent Attitudes toward a Minority Group." *Journal of Applied Social Psychology,* 3: 94-102.

Weinfeld, Morton. 1994. "Ethnic Assimilation and the Retention of Ethnic Cultures." *In Ethnicity and Culture in Canada: The Research Landscape.* J.W. Berry and J.H. Laponce, eds. Toronto: University of Toronto Press, 238-266.

Weinstein, Allen and F.O. Gatell. 1968. *American Negro Slavery.* New York: Oxford University Press.

White, Pamela M. 1990. "The Indo-Chinese in Canada." *Canadian Social Trends.* Ottawa: Statistics Canada, 18: 7-10.

White, Pamela M. and Atul Nanda. 1989. "South Asians in Canada." *Canadian Social Trends.* Ottawa: Statistics Canada, 14: 7-9.

Wiley, Norbert. 1967. "The Ethnic Mobility Trap and Stratification Theory." *Social Problems*, 15: 147-59.

Williams, Robin M. 1964. *Strangers Next Door.* Englewood Cliff, N.J.: Prentice Hall.

Wilson, Kenneth L. and A. Portes. 1980. "Immigrant Enclaves, and Analysis of the Labor Market Experience of Cubans in Miami." *American Journal of Sociology,* 86: 295-319.

Winks, Robin W. 1971. *Blacks in Canada: A History.* New Haven, Mass.: Yale University Press.

Winks, Robin W. 1988. "Slavery." In *The Canadian Encyclopedia*, Second Edition. Edmonton: Hurtig Publishers, 3: 2010-2011.

Woodcock, George and Ivan Avakumovic. 1977. *The Doukhobors.* Toronto: McClelland and Stewart Ltd.

Word, Carl O., M.P. Zanna and J. Cooper. 1974. "The Nonverbal Mediation of Self-Fulfilling Prophecies in Interracial Interaction." *Journal of Experimental Social Psychology,* 10: 109-120.

World Factbook. 1993. Washington, D.C.: U.S. Central Intelligence Agency.

Wu, Cheng-Tsu, ed. 1972. *"Chink!": A Documentary History of Anti-Chinese Prejudice in America.* New York: World Publishing Co., Meridian Books.

Yancey, William L., E.P. Erickson and R.N. Juliani. 1976. "Emergent Ethnicity: A Review and Reformulation." *American Sociological Review,* 41: 391-403.

Yuzyk, Paul. 1953. *The Ukrainians in Manitoba: A Social History.* Toronto: University of Toronto Press.

Zielyk, Ihor V. 1975. "Two Types of Ethnic Communities." In *Sounds Canadian: Languages and Cultures in Multi-Ethnic Society.* P. Migus, ed. Toronto: Peter Martin Associates, 147-157.

Zolf, Larry. 1980. "Mullings over Multiculturalism." *Maclean's*, Vol. 93, April 14: 6.

Zolf, Larry. 1982. "How Multiculturalism Corrupts." *Maclean's*, Vol. 95, November 15: 21.

INDEX